Social Science

Social Science

An Introduction to the Study of Society

TWELFTH EDITION

Elgin F. Hunt
Late Chairman of Social Science Department
Wilson Junior College

David C. Colander
Department of Economics
Middlebury College

PEARSON

Boston • New York • San Francisco
Mexico City • Montreal • Toronto • London • Madrid • Munich • Paris
Hong Kong • Singapore • Tokyo • Cape Town • Sydney

Senior Editor: Jeff Lasser
Editorial Assistant: Sara Owen
Marketing Manager: Krista Groshong
Editorial-Production Service: Omegatype Typography, Inc.
Manufacturing Buyer: JoAnne Sweeney
Composition Buyer: Linda Cox
Cover Administrator: Joel Gendron
Electronic Composition: Omegatype Typography, Inc.

For related titles and support materials, visit our online catalog at www.ablongman.com.

Between the time Website information is gathered and then published, it is not unusual for
some sites to have closed. Also, the transcription of URLs can result in typographical errors.
The publisher would appreciate notification where these errors occur so that they may be
corrected in subsequent editions.

Library of Congress Cataloging-in-Publication Data

Hunt, Elgin F.
    Social science : an introduction to the study of society / Elgin F. Hunt, David C.
Colander.—12th ed.
        p.   cm.
    Includes bibliographical references and index.
    ISBN 0-205-40847-8
    1. Social sciences.   I. Colander, David C.   II. Title.

H85 .H86   2005
300—dc22

                                                                          2003070682

Printed in the United States of America

10 9 8 7 6 5 4 3   09   08   07   06   05

To Wendy

Contents

Preface   *xix*

Chapter 1   Social Science and Its Methods   1

Social Science   3
Social Science as a System of Rules   6
The Scientific Method and Its Application   9
Methodology and the Social Sciences   11

The Methods of Social Science   14
Social Science Approaches to Problems   17
Common Sense in the Social Sciences   20
The Use of Statistics   20
The Interdisciplinary Approach   21

Social Science and Society   23
Continuing Problems   23
Values, Terminology, and Rhetoric   24

Conclusion   24

Appendix   Historical Roots of Social Science   27

The Enlightenment   28
From Philosophy to Social Science   30

Chapter 2   Human Origins   31

The Origin of the Human Species   32
Darwin and the Theory of Evolution   32

Recent Developments in Genetics   35
Some Implications of Recent Developments   36
Sociobiology   37
Punctuated Equilibrium versus Gradual Change   38

The Evolution of Human Beings   40
Science, Faith, and Controversy   40
Predecessors of Modern Humans   42

Conclusion   49

Chapter 3   Origins of Western Society   53

From the Stone Age to the Agricultural Age   53
Early Civilizations   54
The Cradle of Modern Civilization: Mesopotamia and Egypt   54
Development of the Greek Civilization   58
The Persian Empire   58
Roman Civilization   61

The Middle Ages (A.D. 476–1453)   63
The Renaissance   66

The Development of Modern Economic and Political Institutions   68
From Serfdom to Mercantilism   69
The Emergence of Nation-States   71
The Industrial and Political Revolutions of the 1750s to the 1850s   71

Conclusion   74

Chapter 4   Society, Culture, and Cultural Change   77

Culture and the Nature of Society   79
Culture and Its Role in Human Societies   79
The Elements of Culture   80

Cultural Integration   83

Culture, Society, and Social Change   84
Popular Theories of Social Change   85
Factors Causing Cultural Change   86
Language and Cultural Change   89
Factors Stabilizing Culture   89
Social Change versus Social Stability   91

Social Change and Social Problems   92

Cultural Lag and Social Problems   92
Limitations of the Cultural Lag Theory   94

Contrasts among Cultures   95

The Interaction of Humans and Society   95
Cultural Relativism   95
Approach to the Study of Society   96

Chapter 5   Geography, Demography, Ecology, and Society   100

Geography   100
Demography   102

Population Estimates   103
Determinants of Population Growth   103
The Growth of Population over Time   105
The Problem of Counting   107
The Malthusian Theory   107
Population and Means of Subsistence   108
The Concept of Optimal Population   109
The Question of Population Quality   110

Ecology: The Interaction of Geography, Demography, and Environment   111

The Ecological Balance   111
Pollution and Conservation   113

Conclusion   115

Chapter 6   Technology and Society   118

The Industrial Revolution   120

The Development of Industrialism in the United States   121
Standardization, Interchangeability, and Mass Production   122
Technology and Globalization   124
Machines and Unemployment   126

Technology and Social Change   126

Problems Created by Technology   127
Technology, Hierarchy, and Class Systems   127
Natural Resources, Economics, and Technology   129
Natural Resources and the Limits of Economic Growth   130
Global Warming   131

Technology of the Past   131

Technology of the Future   132

The Social Basis for Technological Progress   134

Future Shock?   135

Chapter 7   Psychology, Society, and Culture   138

Socialization of the Individual   139

Significance of the Early Years of Childhood   139

Significance of Differences in Individual Environment   140

Effects of Extreme Isolation on Children   141

Personality and Its Development   142

The Nature/Nurture Debate   143

Explanations of Behavior   145

The Well-Adjusted Individual   146

Adjustment and Normality   147

The Freudian Concept of Personality   147

Pop Psychologies   150

Intelligence, Personal Adjustment, and Normality   150

Testing for Intelligence   150

Intelligence and Personal Adjustment   155

Deviance   156

Major Theories on Deviance   156

Sociological Explanations of Deviance   158

Economic Explanations of Deviant Behavior   159

Summary of Various Perspectives on Deviance   160

Conclusion   160

Chapter 8   The Family   163

Variations in the Family Pattern   163

Number of Mates   164

Selection of Mates   164

Family Control   166

Reckoning of Descent   166

Functions of the Family in Society   **167**

Social Change and Family Functions: An Example   *168*

Variations of Family Patterns and the Functions of the Family   *168*

The Family in the United States Today   **172**

Dating   *174*

Sex and Singles   *175*

Children   *176*

Senior Citizens   *177*

Family Disorganization and Divorce   *178*

Singles   *181*

Living Together   *182*

Homosexual and Lesbian Households   *182*

The Family in Transition   **182**

Technology's Effect on the Family   *183*

The Future of the Family   *183*

Chapter 9   Religion   187

The Nature of Religion   **188**

The Great Religions of Today   **190**

Hinduism   *191*

Buddhism   *192*

Judaism   *193*

Islam   *197*

Christianity   *200*

The Role of Religion in Society   **203**

Religion as a Source of Moral Values   *204*

Impact of Religion on Education, the Arts, and Literature   *204*

The Potential Conflict between Religion and Government   *205*

Chapter 10   Education   208

Schools as Agencies of Social Control   **209**

The Dual Thrust of U.S. Education   *209*

Education and U.S. Democracy   *209*

The Development of U.S. Education   210

Democratic Structure of the U.S. School System   213
Formalization of the School System   214

Examining the School System   217

Technological Change and Teaching   217
Private Schools and Home Schooling   217
Charter Schools, Privatization, and the Problem of School Finance   218
Textbooks   220
School Dropouts   220
Multiculturalism, Collaborative Learning, and Institutional Fairness   221
How Good Are U.S. Schools?   222
The Search for Excellence   224
Changes in the College Curriculum   225
Is the U.S. Educational System Equal?   227
How Much Education Should the Average Citizen Receive?   228

Interaction of Economics, Politics, and Social Institutions   229

Chapter 11   Social and Economic Stratification   233

Types of Social Stratification   234

Estates   234
Castes   234
Social Classes   235

Social Mobility   239

Economic and Social Inequality   241

Causes of Income Inequality   241
Measuring Poverty   242

Reducing Social and Economic Inequality   243

Who Are the Upwardly Mobile?   245
Rising Incomes and Class Distinctions   246
Class Consciousness in the United States   247
Class Consciousness and the Labor Movement   248
Some Conclusions about the U.S. Class System   249

Chapter 12   Stratification, Minorities, and Discrimination   251

Race and Ethnicity   251
Questions of Ethnic and Racial Superiority   252
Racial and Ethnic Prejudice and Discrimination   255
The Melting Pot   255

Minorities   256
Native Americans   256
African Americans   257
Hispanics   266
Asians   268
Immigrants and Minorities   270
Religious Minorities   273
Sexual Minorities   274
Senior Citizens   279

Conclusion   282

Chapter 13   The Functions and Forms of Government   285

The Primary Functions of Government   286
Maintaining Internal Order and External Security   286
Ensuring Justice   286
Safeguarding Individual Freedoms   288
Regulating Individuals' Actions   288
Promoting the General Welfare   289

Debates about the Nature of Government   290
Political Theory and Government   290
Three Views of the Nature of Government   291
Elements of Truth in Each of the Views   294

Forms of Government   294
Democracies   294
Autocracy   299

Governments Are Far from Simple   306

Chapter 14   Democratic Government in the United States   309

Historical Development of U.S. Government   309
The Structure of U.S. Government   311
Structure of the National Government   311
The Nature of Our National Government   314
The Political Process   325
Political Parties   326
Elections   327
The Fourth Estate   330
The Political Elite   331
The Military-Industrial Complex and Pressure Groups   331
Evaluation of the Democratic Political Process   333

Chapter 15   Governments of the World   337

French Government   337
The French Parliamentary System   338
The French Executive Branch   339
Mexican Government   342
Japanese Government   346
Russian Government   349
Saudi Arabian Government   352
Some Lessons about Governments   355
Future Changes in Governments   356

Chapter 16   The Organization of Economic Activities   359

The Nature of an Economy   359
Functions of an Economy   360
Economics and the Social Sciences   360
Economic Wants and Economic Goods   360
The Economic Aspects of Culture   361

The Great Economic Problem   361
Planned and Unplanned Economies   362

The Evolution of Economic Systems   363

From Feudalism to Mercantilism   363
From Mercantilism to a Market Economy   364
From a Market Economy to a Mixed Economy   365

Market Economies   365

How a Market Economy Works   366
The Role of Government in Market Economies   369

The Changing Nature of the U.S. Economy   370

The Upheaval in the Formerly Socialist Economies   371

Historical Development of Socialist Thought   371
Socialism and Communism   371
How Planned and Unplanned Economies Work   373
Problems with Central Planning   374
Why Central Planning Did Not Meet Its Goals   374
Transition Problems from a Planned to an Unplanned Economy   376

The Continuing Evolution of Economies   377

Chapter 17   Government and the Economy   381

Government's Direct Role in the Economy   381

Government-Supplied Goods   383
The U.S. Social Security System   384
Other Government Spending Programs   385
Government's Macroeconomic Role   387

Government's Indirect Role in the Economy   391

The Problem of Regulating the Economy   391
Government Inefficiency and Waste   393

Conclusion   393

Chapter 18   International Political Relations   397

The State in International Relations   397

The Nation-State   399
The Establishment and Disappearance of Nation-States   400

Power in the World Community   401

The Nature and Sources of National Power   401
Other Sources of Power   407
Maintaining Security   408

Foreign Policies   410

Geography and Foreign Policy   410
Values, Ideologies, and Foreign Policy   411

The United States in the World Community   413

The President and Foreign Policy   414
U.S. Foreign Policies   416

Chapter 19   International Economic Relations   420

The Terminology of Trade   421

The Balance of Trade and the Balance of Payments   421
Visible and Invisible Trade   422

Advantages and Disadvantages of International Trade   423

Three Advantages of Trade   423
Disadvantages of Trade   424
Why You Can't Get the Advantages without the Disadvantages   425

Restrictions on International Trade   426

Tariffs on Imports   427
Import Quotas   429
Removing Trade Restrictions   430
Globalization and Trade Restrictions   431

Foreign Exchange   431

The Meaning of Foreign Exchange   431
Fixed and Flexible Exchange Rate Systems   433

Conclusion   435

Chapter 20   The Political Economies of Developing Countries   438

Problems of Developing Countries   441

The Political Consensus Problem   441
The Corruption Problem   442

The Economic Problem   443
The Debt Problem   445
The Population Problem   446
The Brain Drain Problem   446
Mission Impossible: Advice to a Potential Leader   447

Options of Developing Countries   **448**
Political Options   448
Economic Options   448
Foreign Policy Options   448
Population Options   448
The Brain Drain Option   449
Who Will Be the Next Leader?   449

Case Studies   **449**
China   449
Mexico   453
Uganda   456

Conclusion   **458**

𝒞hapter 21   International Institutions and the Search for Peace   461

The Problem of War   **462**
The Causes of War   462
Approaches to the Problem of War   464

The United Nations   **467**
Is the UN Worth It?   468
The UN's Role in Keeping the Peace   470
Other UN Approaches   473

The Outlook for Peace   **474**
Trouble Spots of the World   476
The War on Global Terrorism   482

Index   485

# $\mathscr{P}$reface

Social science is taught in diverse ways. Some courses take a global perspective, some an anthropological perspective, some a psychological perspective, some a sociological perspective, and some a historical perspective—to name just a few. In my view, although each individual social science perspective has something to offer, what distinguishes the social science course is that it looks at problems from as many different perspectives as possible, relying on the scholar's common sense to choose the perspective that is most useful for a particular problem. The commonsense perspective is the social science perspective.

Social science is an important course. All too often our educational system rushes students into specializations before the students have an overall picture—before they know where they want to go. Once they have an overall picture, specialization is necessary, but to specialize before having an overall picture is unfair to students. Students who specialize too early don't develop a commonsense perspective; they aren't sensitive to the interrelationships and resonances among disciplines. At worst, they become slaves of their discipline's approach. At best, they have the wisdom to recognize that there are many approaches to a problem, but their lack of training forces them to recreate the wheel. Knowledge of the other disciplines would have saved them the trouble and been far more efficient.

That's why I am a strong advocate of the social science course. It is one of the most important courses students take in college, and in my view it is a necessary prerequisite to taking courses in specific disciplines. It puts those other courses in perspective.

The changes in this edition have been made to strengthen the presentation and to keep the book current. I have reworked sections that reviewers thought needed work and updated all chapters. In the anthropology chapter, I expanded the discussions of genetic and DNA evidence about origins of humans because this is more definitive than physical evidence, and numerous new findings are being reported. In the geography chapter I dropped the discussion of communities to save space and to eliminate distinctions that some readers thought were almost obvious. I relabeled the psychology chapter to include psychology in the title so that its content is easier to discern in the table of contents. I also expanded the discussion of defense mechanisms and theories of deviance. The religion chapter required major revisions; I expanded the discussion of Islam and presented Rousseau's discussion about the contrasting roles of religion in society in order to form a foundation for discussions of the problems religion is presenting in creating effective governments in Islamic countries. What is interesting about this is that Rousseau foresaw many of the problems that religion could cause for states if it was not appropriately integrated into the state system.

The largest changes were to the political science and economics chapters, which were changed substantially to reflect the new political and economic realities after 9/11. In revising I have also kept in mind the Internet information revolution and the broader technology revolution of which it is a part. I have added more Internet-based questions to the Questions for Review and Discussion material at the end of the chapters, and in the For Further Study sections I have replaced books with more Internet references. To make it easier for students to find Internet references, I have placed links to Internet citations in the book on the book website, www.ablongman.com.

As always, the book benefits from the suggestions of reviewers, colleagues, and students who have e-mailed me. I'd especially like to thank Kevin Roberts and the social science class at Henry Ford Community College, who pointed out an error in the last edition that somehow slipped through the reviewing and editorial process. I'd like to thank them all.

For this edition, I'd like to thank Dr. William M. Downs, Georgia State University; Don Griffin, University of Oklahoma; Lynnel Kiely, Truman College; Errol Magidson, Richard J. Daley Community College; Catherine Montsinger, Johnson C. Smith University; Larry R. Stucki, Reading Area Community College; and Elizabeth Trentanelli, Miami Dade College. Over the last few editions the reviewers have included: Emmanuel Agbolosoo, Navajo Community College; Verl Beebe, Daytona Beach Community College; John Beineke, Kennesaw State College; Thomas J. Bellows, The University of Texas at San Antonio; Dallas A. Blanchard, University of West Florida; Ducarmel Bocage, Howard University; William K. Callam, Daytona Beach Community College; Pam Crabtree, New York University; Bruce Donlan, Brevard Community College; Anthony Douglas, Lornan, Mississippi; Phil A. Drimmel, Daytona Beach Community College; J. Ross Eshleman, Wayne State University; Dana Fenton, City University of New York, Borough of Manhattan Community College; Cyril Francis, Miami–Dade North Community College; Richard Frye, Neuro-Diagnostic Lab, Winchester Memorial Hospital, Winchester, Virginia; Judy Gentry, Columbus State Community College; Paul George, Miami–Dade Community College; Charles F. Gruber, Marshall University; Ghulam M. Haniff, St. Cloud State University (Minnesota); Roberto Hernandez, Miami–Dade New World Center; Charles E. Hurst, The College of Wooster; Sharon B. Johnson, Miami–Dade Community College; Kenneth C. W. Kammeyer, University of Maryland; Rona J. Karasik, St. Cloud State University; H. D. Kirkland, Lake City Community College; Patricia E. Kixmiller, Miami–Dade Community College; D. R. Klee, Kansas City, Missouri; Casimir Kotowski, Harry S. Truman City College; James T. Markley, Lord Fairfax Community College; Stephen McDougal, University of Wisconsin–La Crosse; Karen Mitchell, University of Missouri; Lynn Mulkey, Hofstra University; Roy Mumme, University of South Florida, Fort Myers; Eleanor J. Myatt, Palm Beach Junior College; Quentin Newhouse Jr., Howard University; Annette Palmer, Howard University; Robin Perrin, Pepperdine University; Joseph Pilkington-Duddle, Highland Beach, Florida; William Primus, Miami–Dade North Community College; Roger Rolison, Palm Beach Community College; William H. Rosberg, Kirkwood Community College; Dan Selakovich, Oklahoma State University; Henry A. Shockley, Boston University; Ruth Smith, Miami–Dade Community College; Scharlene Snowden, City University of New York, Medgar Evers College; Barry Thompson, University of Rio Grande; Judy Thompson, University of Rio Grande; Edward Uliassi, Northeastern University; David Wells, Glendale Community College; W. M. Wright, Lake City Community College; Norman R. Yetman, The University of Kansas; and George Zgourides.

At the end of an earlier edition, I included a sheet for students to grade the book and to send me suggestions for improvement. A number of students did this, and their suggestions have played an important role in shaping the book. Most, I'm happy to say, were highly positive, but a few attacked the book and the course. One particularly memorable student flunked me on just about every chapter and wrote the following:

> Until you and this so called science become legitimized I'd rather spend time gorging myself and then vomiting. Guesses, hypotheses, maybes, might be's don't belong in college; they belong in elementary school.

That student obviously read the book, because he is correct: The book doesn't tell the student what is right or wrong, and it does report guesses, hypotheses, and maybes. But that student is wrong about what does and what doesn't belong in college. Guesses, hypotheses, and maybes are precisely what belong in college, because by the time students are in college they can be expected to have the maturity to understand that knowledge is nothing but good guesses, reasonable hypotheses, and logical maybes.

Natural science, which I suspect appeals to my critics more than social science, generally takes the position that students mature even later than at the undergraduate college level, and so the natural sciences don't reveal until senior- or graduate-level courses the maybes and the reasonable guesses on which all science is based.

Social science is different. It presents reality and theory as they are at the undergraduate college level. It doesn't tell you what's right. It presents the observations and the theories as fairly as it can and lets you decide.

I would like to acknowledge the contributions of editorial assistant Sara Owen, who played a valuable role in helping me prepare this twelfth edition. I also thank Helen Reiff, who helped with research and did the index, and especially Pam Bodenhorn, who did research, updated questions, and helped with proofreading.

I also want to mention the unsung heroes—the sales reps who came to me with names of reviewers and suggestions for changes. These sales reps are the backbone of any college publishing company, and I thank them. One rep in particular deserves special recognition. After the death of Elgin Hunt, who was the initial author of this book, she recruited me for *Social Science;* she convinced me and Macmillan to do the book, and she continued to provide unending support and encouragement. This book was always known at Macmillan as "Wendy's book," and it remains Wendy's book, even though it is now published by Allyn and Bacon.

Finally, I want to thank my family for helping me find the time to work on the book.

D. C. C.
January 2004

Social Science

Social Science and Its Methods

chapter 1

After reading this chapter, you should be able to:

- Define social science and explain why it is important
- List the various social sciences
- State the nine steps that make up the scientific method
- Discuss some reasonable approaches to problems in social science
- Differentiate the historical method from the case method and the comparative method
- Distinguish educated common sense from common sense
- Explain why a good scientist is always open to new ways of looking at issues

Theories should be as simple as possible, but not more so.

—**Albert Einstein**

On September 11, 2001, eighteen men boarded airplanes with the intent of crashing them into the World Trade Center, the Pentagon, and the White House or Capitol. They succeeded with three of the planes, causing enormous destruction. The fourth plane crashed, but thanks to passengers who discovered the highjackers' plans and attacked the highjackers, the destruction of the White House or Capitol was prevented. What forces drove these highjackers to undertake such action? What forces led the passengers to organize together to thwart them? What might have prevented the highjackings? Such questions fall under the purview of **social science**—the scientific study of social, cultural, psychological, economic, and political forces that guide individuals in their actions.

Formal social science is relatively new. Nevertheless, a vast amount of information has been accumulated concerning the social life of human beings. This information has been used in building a system of knowledge about the nature, growth, and functioning of human societies. Social science is the name given that system of knowledge.

All knowledge is (1) knowledge of human beings, including their culture and products, and (2) knowledge of natural environment. Human culture has been changing, and knowledge about it has been gradually accumulating ever since the far distant time when humans first assumed their distinctively human character. But until rather recent times, this knowledge was not scientific in the modern sense. **Scientific knowledge** is knowledge that has been systematically gathered, classified, related, and interpreted. It is concerned with learning the concepts and applying those concepts to particulars, rather than just learning a vast amount of information.

Social Science versus the Soaps

Faced with the events that affect our lives, we have two options: We can lose ourselves in a parody of reality, such as becoming experts on the soaps (is Laura really sleeping with John's wife's brother?), or we can try to understand those events—what actually happens. Some educators, following the philosophy of Plato, try to argue the moral superiority of the latter: Better to be an unhappy learned person than a happy fool. Others find that unconvincing. Following Jeremy Bentham, the social philosopher, they prefer happiness. The problem they have with the soaps is that soaps don't make you happy; soaps quickly become boring. You soon play out the options in your head and, often, create far better scenarios than the television writer. It's a bit like tic tac toe: one move (if you know what you are doing) and the game is done. Pinochle is somewhat more interesting, and the good TV shows approach the complexity of pinochle. But here again, after seven or eight cards have been played, the possibilities soon become evident. Chess is a step above this, with its infinite number of possibilities. But still, after thirty or so moves (and often fewer), good chess players can anticipate the outcome and choose to call a draw, resign, or declare victory.

Quite frankly, soaps, tic tac toe, pinochle, and chess are not for this author. I prefer a far more complicated game—one in which I'm both a player and a pawn. That game could be called the game of life, or it could be called the game of society. It is played by some six billion people, each having a wide variety of possible moves that range from shooting up a playground full of schoolchildren to trying to travel farther into outer space, construct faster computers, or improve humans by modifying their genes. The players in the game of society are divided into two types: male and female. These two types have certain drives and desires, and certain rules that are passed on to them, either through their genes or through society's mores.

The ultimate goal of the game is often unclear, although its day-to-day objects can be said to consist of continuing to play the game and to keep the game itself alive. What winning or losing the game might be is clouded. Probably, if we commit suicide we are losers. If we make a million dollars, are admired by our acquaintances for it, and are happy, we are probably winners. Many people even question whether we are playing the game of our own free will, or whether we are merely the pawns of a god who has predetermined all our actions.

This game is far more diverse and interesting than other games. The possibilities are endless and the challenge immediate. It has elements of danger, like Russian roulette (if we really *do* goof, we *will* blow ourselves up). And it has its peaceful moments. But what makes it the most interesting game of all is that we are both the players and the played, at times moving ourselves as we make stupid or foolish choices and contrive sophisticated or imaginative solutions, and at other times watching other players as they make their choices and contrive their solutions. *Trying to understand this game is what social science is all about.* And the reason I am a social scientist instead of a TV fan is that I watch society and try to understand what makes society work. It's a whole lot more challenging and fun than watching the soaps. Moreover, unlike the soaps, watching society has a purpose—if we can understand society, we might be able to make it better.

Social science has fascinated enormous numbers of people, and a whole set of ponderings about the game has already developed. These ponderings concern the nature, growth, and functioning of human societies. This book introduces you to the past ponderings of social scientists.

Primitive peoples acquired much of their knowledge unconsciously, just as we today still begin the use of our native language and acquire many of the basic elements in our culture unconsciously. For the most part, they accepted the world as they found it, and if any explanations seemed called for, they invented supernatural ones. Some primitive peoples believed that every stream, tree, and rock contained a spirit that controlled its behavior.

In modern times our emphasis is on the search for scientific knowledge. We have divided human knowledge into a number of areas and fields, and every science represents the systematic collection and study of data in some one of these areas, which can be grouped roughly into two major fields—social science and natural science. Each of these fields is subdivided into a number of specialized sciences or disciplines to facilitate more intensive study and deeper understanding. Social science is the field of human knowledge that deals with all aspects of the group life of human beings. **Natural science** is concerned with the natural environment in which human beings exist. It includes such sciences as physics and chemistry, which deal with the laws of matter, motion, space, mass, and energy; it also includes the **biological sciences,** which deal with living things. The third field of study is the **humanities,** which deals with literature, music, art, and philosophy. The humanities are closely related to social science in that both deal with humans and their culture. Social science, however, is most concerned with those basic elements of culture that determine the general patterns of human behavior. The humanities deal with special aspects of human culture and are primarily concerned with our attempts to express spiritual and esthetic values and to discover the meaning of life. Whereas the social sciences study issues in a systematic, scientific way, the focus of the humanities is more on the emotions and feelings themselves than on the system employed to sharpen that focus.

Social Science

No field of study is more important to human beings than the social sciences. To understand society is to learn not only the conditions that limit our lives but also the opportunities open to us for improving the human condition. Increasing our knowledge of human society is as important as learning more about mathematics, physics, chemistry, or engineering, for unless we can develop societies in which human beings can live happy, meaningful, and satisfying lives, we cannot reap the benefits from learning how to make better automobiles and skyscrapers, traveling in space, or constructing faster computers. Albert Einstein summed it up: "Politics is more difficult than physics and the world is more likely to die from bad politics than from bad physics."

Because all expressions of human culture are related and interdependent, to gain a real understanding of human society we must have some knowledge of all its major aspects. If we concentrate on some phases and neglect others, we will have a distorted picture. But social science today is such a vast complex that no one student can hope to master all of it. Thus, social science itself has been broken up into anthropology, sociology, history, geography, economics, political science, and psychology. (The boxes in this chapter provide a brief introduction to each of these disciplines.)

This list of social science disciplines is both too broad and too narrow. It is too broad because parts of the fields of history, geography, and psychology should not be included as social sciences. For instance, parts of history and geography belong in the humanities, and parts of psychology belong in the natural sciences. The list is too narrow because new social sciences are emerging, such as cognitive science and sociobiology, that incorporate new findings and new ways of looking at reality. (See box on The Evolving Social Sciences.)

Because all knowledge is interrelated, there are inevitable problems in defining and cataloging the social sciences. Often it is difficult to know where one social science ends and another begins. Not only are the individual social sciences interrelated, but the social

The Evolving Social Sciences

The themes of this book are evolution and change. Thus, it would be surprising if the divisions among the social sciences that currently exist still remain ten years from now. Indeed, with the development of new technology and technological advances in the physical sciences, the distinction among the various sciences is blurring and new sciences are developing. As these fields develop, the boundaries of the various social sciences change.

Interaction among the various social sciences is creating new fields, such as economic psychology, psychological economics, and sociopolitical anthropology. In economics and political science, too, a group of economists is calling for the reintegration of these two fields into political economy, and some schools do have departments of political economy.

Change is also occurring in the natural sciences, and there is interaction between the natural and social sciences. New developments in genetic theory, which will be discussed in Chapter 2, have caused many to believe it is time for a new social science, called cognitive science, which combines psychology, linguistics, philosophy, social anthropology, and molecular biology. Although it is still in the process of formation, a tentative definition of **cognitive science** is the study of how the mind identifies problems and how it solves those problems. For instance, there are more ways to write the letter *s* than there are people who know how to write that letter (all people who write plus the printing press and innumerable typefaces designed for it). Let us identify the problem as how to recognize the letter *s* when we see it. We know the result of the exercise: Everyone who knows how to read can instantly recognize most renditions of the letter *s* (the handwriting of a few college students and some physicians excepted). But we do not currently know *how* we do it. Or, how do you know the face of your roommate from the face of your mother, from the face of the letter carrier, from the face of Brad Pitt? There has been speculation about how the mind works for almost as long as there have been minds, theories, and even experiments, but few specific riddles have been conclusively solved.

Whether these upstart disciplines take hold remains to be seen, but that some change will take place is certain.

sciences as a whole body are also related to the natural sciences and the humanities. The strains of the old song, "The hip bone's connected to the thigh bone . . . ," are appropriate to the social sciences. To understand history, it is helpful, even necessary, to understand geography, and in order to understand economics, it is necessary to understand psychology. Similar arguments can be made for all of the social sciences.

One of the difficulties in presenting definitions and descriptions of the various social sciences is that social scientists themselves don't agree on what it is they do, or should be doing. In preparing this chapter, we met with groups of social scientists specializing in specific fields and asked them to explain what it was that distinguished their field from others. There was little agreement among specialists in a particular social science, let alone among all social scientists. A cynic once said, "Economics is what economists do." If we replaced "economics" and "economists" with any of the other social sciences and its practitioners, we would have as good a definition as possible. Unfortunately, it would not be very helpful to those who do not know what social scientists do.

One important difference among the individual social scientists did come out of these discussions: Even when two social scientists are considering the same issue, because their training is different they focus on different aspects of that problem. Geographers fixate on spaces and spatial relativities, economists on market incentives, and political scientists on group decision making. Thus, although we might not be able to define, unambiguously, the domains of the various social sciences, you will get a sense of the various approaches as we consider issues from various perspectives throughout the book.

The study of social science is more than the study of the individual social sciences. Although it is true that to be a good social scientist you must know each of those components, you must also know how they interrelate. By specializing too early, many social scientists can lose sight of the interrelationships that are so essential to understanding modern problems. That's why it's necessary to have a course covering all the social sciences. In fact, it wouldn't surprise me if one day a news story such as the one in the box below appeared.

To understand how and when social science broke up, you must study the past. Imagine for a moment that you're a student in 1062, in the Italian city of Bologna, site of one of the first major universities in the Western world. The university has no buildings; it consists merely of a few professors and students. There is no tuition fee. At the end of a professor's lecture, if you like it, you pay. And if you don't like it, the professor finds himself without students and without money. If we go back still earlier, say to Greece in the sixth century B.C., we can see the philosopher Socrates walking around the streets of Athens, arguing with his companions. He asks them questions, and then other questions, leading these people to reason the way he wants them to reason (this became known as the *Socratic method*).

Times have changed since then; universities sprang up throughout the world and created colleges within the universities. Oxford, one of the first universities, now has thirty colleges associated with it, and the development and formalization of educational institutions has changed the roles of both students and faculty. As knowledge accumulated, it became

Unified Social Systems Theory Derived

Dateline 2050. Researchers today announced the development of a unified theory of the social sciences. The new theory, which had its early foundations in the work of Ludwig von Bertalanffy, is the equivalent in social science of the unified field theory in physics, which tied together the various forces of nature into a general theory. The formulation of the unified field theory in 2020 solved the problem that stymied earlier physicists such as Albert Einstein. It intensified the efforts of social scientists to develop their own unified theory. The theory, which is also called a unified social systems theory, ties together the various social sciences that, in the nineteenth and twentieth centuries, diverged into anthropology, sociology, history, geography, economics, political science, and psychology. The theory combines the work on complex systems begun by John von Neumann in the late 1940s and early 1950s with game theory, also begun by von Neumann, to form a coherent whole, and captures many of the interrelationships that were previously lost in the fragmentation or divisions of social science. That work was extended in the complexity revolution in science that came into its own in the early 2000s. By combining these theories with recent advances in the separate social sciences, the resulting new unified social science theory provides new insights into how society works.

When she was asked what set her on her path, the social scientist who developed this theory responded that it was the experience in her first social science class, in which she used the classic Hunt and Colander text, *Social Science.* In that class, with the aid of the insights her teacher provided, the scientist grasped the first inklings of how these various theories might be put together, setting the stage for her later achievement.

more and more difficult for one person to learn, let alone retain, it all. In the sixteenth century, one could still aspire to know all there was to know, and the definition of the Renaissance man (people were even more sexist then than they are now) was one who was expected to know about everything.

Unfortunately, at least for someone who wants to know everything, the amount of information continues to grow exponentially while the size of the brain has grown only slightly. The way to deal with the problem is not to try to know everything about everything. Today we must specialize. That is why social science separated from the natural sciences and why social science, in turn, has been broken down into various subfields, such as anthropology and sociology.

There are advantages and disadvantages to specialization, and many social problems today are dealt with by teams of various social scientists. Each brings his or her specialty to the table. For example, I am an economist, but I work on projects with geographers, sociologists, anthropologists, political scientists, and psychologists. More and more interdisciplinary majors are being created; one of the authors of this book teaches in both the economics department and the international politics and economics department at his school. Interdisciplinary graduate schools of public policy have grown enormously. In these programs students study all the social sciences while specializing in one. Figure 1.1 provides a graphic overview of the evolution of knowledge and the present social sciences. (The appendix at the end of this chapter expands on the ideas in this diagram.)

Anthropology

Anthropology is the study of the relationship between biological traits and socially acquired characteristics. Sometimes called the study of humans, it consists of two broad fields:

- Physical anthropology
- Cultural anthropology

Some of the concerns of physical anthropology are:

- Influence of evolution of natural environment on the physical characteristics of humans
- Human evolution: how modern *homo sapiens* evolved from earlier species

Some of the concerns of cultural anthropology are:

- Archaeology, or the remains of extinct civilizations that left no written records
- Organization of preliterate societies
- Characteristics of subgroups or subcultures within contemporary society

Among the topics that interest anthropologists are excavation of formerly inhabited sites, fossils, the gene pool, technology and artifacts, linguistics, values, and kinship.

Social Science as a System of Rules

Today the amount of knowledge is increasing faster than ever. How, then, can a unified social science theory ever be formulated? The answer is found in abstraction and the ability to discover rules or relationships (rather than simply facts) and rules relating rules to other rules.

To understand the importance of knowing rules, think back to grade school when you learned addition. You didn't memorize the sum of 127 and 1,448. Instead you learned an algorithm (a fancy name for a rule) about adding ($7 + 8 = 15$; write down the 5 and carry the 1...). Then you had to memorize only a few relationships. By changing the number system from a base ten system to a binary system (0 and 1 are the only numbers), you cut substantially the amount of memorization (all you need to know is $0 + 0 = 0$; $0 + 1 = 1$; and $1 + 1 = 10$) and you could apply the same rule again and again, adding all possible numbers (an insight that played

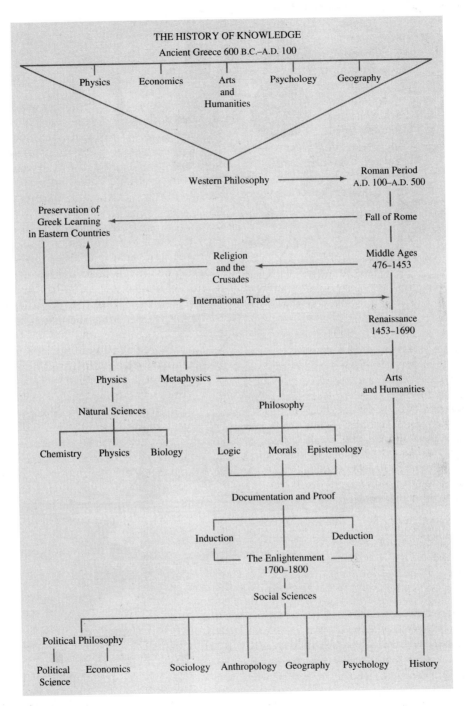

Figure 1.1

Knowledge at a glance. The development of knowledge is messy, but assuming that a picture is worth a thousand words, we offer this sketch of the development of knowledge. Maybe it's worth five hundred words.

an important role in the development of the computer). Knowing the rules saved you from enormous amounts of memorization, but nonetheless gave you access to a large amount of information.

Another way to look at the problem is to think of the library. If you have a small library, you can know nearly everything in it, but once your library gets larger, you will quickly find that having more books makes it harder to know what's in there. However, if you put in place a filing system, such as the Dewey decimal system or the Library of Congress system, you can access the books through a filing system. The rules of the filing system give you the key to great amounts of information, just as the rules of addition, subtraction, or algebra do. General rules, once learned, can be applied to large numbers of particulars. The higher you go (rules about rules about rules), the more you can know with less memorization.[1]

All this is relevant to social science and the 2050 dateline because social science, too, is held together by rules or relationships. If there is to be a unified social science theory, it will be because some student started thinking about rules and how the rules of the various social sciences can fit together. If you understand the general concepts, you can apply them in a variety of circumstances. Thus the future "unified social scientists" will not necessarily know all the facts of a particular social science. Each of the specialties will retain its identity and will likely become even more specialized. But as that specialization occurs, it creates the need for a new specialization that concentrates on tying together the various component parts of social science. The new unified social scientists will know the general rules of the individual social sciences, and the rules of how one social science interacts with another, but they will not know all the specific facts of any one of them.

The preceding argument is a heavy one to throw at you in the first pages of a textbook because it asks you not only to know the lessons of the individual social sciences, but also to go beyond and strive for an understanding of their synthesis. Going beyond is ultimately what learning is all about and what makes it so challenging. We would like to be able to say that we can guide you to a unified social science theory, but the truth is that all we can do is give you a boost and encouragement. After surveying the social sciences, you can decide in which one, if any, you want to specialize; whether you should work toward tying them all together; or whether you should bag the whole approach and go into a premed program.

Sociology

Sociology is the systematic study of relationships among people. Sociologists assume that behavior is influenced by people's social, political, occupational, and intellectual groupings and by the particular settings in which they find themselves at one time or another. Sociologists differ in their approach. Their three major choices are:

- Functionalism
- Conflict
- Interactionism

Sociology's vast subject matter can be identified as a study of people:

- Where they collect
- How they socialize and organize
- Whom they include in and exclude from their groups
- What they do to their environment
- When they confront formulas for control, such as politics, law, finance, religion, education, and social pressures
- Why they change

---

[1]It was an architect, Ludwig Mies van der Rohe, who compressed such exposition into a famous statement, "Less is more."

Geography

Geography is the study of the natural environment and how it influences social and cultural development. Some of the concerns of geography are:

- Ecology
- Climate
- Resources
- Accessibility
- Demography

Geography has practical applications that are manifest in:

- Maps
- Trade patterns
- Industrial and agricultural decisions
- Settlement of population
- Aggression and acquisition

History

History is the study of past events. It is a social science in the sense that it is a systematic attempt to learn about and verify past events and to relate them to one another and to the present. Every event has a historical context within which we commonly say the event must be studied. The subject matter of history is everything that has already happened. The study of history involves:

- Identifying
- Classifying
- Arranging
- Patterning

The fruits of the study of history are:

- Imposition of order
- Appreciation of variety
- Possibilities of prediction
- Realization of limitation

The Scientific Method and Its Application

The **scientific method** is a set of rules about how to establish rules. The use of the scientific method is perhaps the most important tool you can have in studying social science because it enables you not only to learn the lessons of the individual social sciences, but also to go beyond and strive for an understanding of their synthesis.

Conditions Favorable to Scientific Inquiry. Scientific inquiry is possible only in a society in which certain attitudes are developed or tolerated. Successful scientific investigation requires from the investigator not only intelligence but certain mental attitudes as well. One of these is curiosity, which makes people ask two questions: Why? and How? Another is skepticism, which makes people reexamine past explanations and reevaluate past evidence. To reexamine and reevaluate, investigators need objectivity, which enables them to seek impartially for the truth, to make every effort not to allow personal preconceptions, prejudices, or desires to color the observed facts or influence the interpretation of those facts. When these three attitudes—curiosity, skepticism, and objectivity—come together, scientific inquiry can flourish.

In preliterate tribal societies, the obstacles to the development of scientific methods of inquiry are very great. Such societies are much more bound by custom and tradition than are modern societies. The traditional way of doing things is regarded as the only right way. Moreover, any serious deviation from established procedures is likely to be regarded as a danger to the group.

We cannot classify Europe in the Middle Ages as either preliterate or tribal. Nevertheless, respect for tradition, for ancient authorities, and for religious dictates was so strong then that the growth of a scientific spirit was stunted. The free development of modern science had to wait until such movements as the Crusades, the Renaissance, the great voyages of discovery, and the Reformation had loosened the hold of tradition.

The Saga of Hans, the Thinking Horse

The scientific method can be seen in the saga of Hans, the Thinking Horse. Around 1900, according to reports published in a Berlin, Germany, newspaper, there was a horse that was good at math, and when his owner asked him math questions, the horse could answer by tapping out the correct number with one of his front hooves. People who witnessed the horse's ability were puzzled, and they called in a number of social scientists to investigate the phenomenon. To their amazement they found that not only could Clever Hans, as he was known, add and subtract when his owner asked him—he could also calculate square roots. The social scientists were convinced that, against all odds, they had indeed been shown a thinking horse.

Another social scientist, though, a skeptical young psychologist by the name of Oskar Pfungst, had a different idea. He retested Hans, asking a set of questions to which Pfungst himself did not know the answers. He discovered that although Hans succeeded on nearly every question if the questioner knew the answer, the horse failed nearly every question when the questioner did not know the answer. A social scientist's skepticism had shown that Hans could not really reason, even though it seemed as if he could. This true story demonstrates the important trait of skepticism. The scientific community declared that Hans was just a horse.

But a quality those scientists did not show was imagination. Even though Hans could not think and reason, he had an amazing ability: He could almost read minds. When it came to people who knew the answers to the questions they were asking, he could monitor changes in his questioners' posture, their breathing, their facial expressions, and their inflections and speech patterns. He could interpret the signals they were sending and then provide the responses they wanted. This is an ability that some human beings have—although generally to a lesser degree than Hans—and it is an ability that can supplement thinking. Yet it is only at the end of the twentieth century that comparative psychologists showed the imagination to start analyzing this kind of ability in detail.

The lack of imagination exhibited by some scientists in the past limited the scope of the scientific programs they followed. A good scientist must have both skepticism and imagination.

Nature of the Scientific Method.   Modern science is based on the assumption that this is an orderly universe, ruled by the law of cause and effect. Any given set of circumstances always produces the same result. If seemingly identical situations have different results, they were not really alike; some significant difference existed and was overlooked. Further investigation should disclose what this difference was.

Science offers no final explanations of the universe and its phenomena. Time, space, matter, energy—existence itself—are mysteries the ultimate nature of which are probably forever beyond the grasp of the human search. But an accepted scientific theory may be regarded as an explanation, up to a certain point, of a scientific law.

Scientific investigation is seldom simple. Each field of knowledge has its special problems, and investigators must always adjust their methods to the peculiarities of the situation they are dealing with. A method of investigation that is of great importance in some fields is the setting up and carrying out of controlled experiments.

The Experimental Method and Its Limitations.   The **experimental method** is a method of separating out causal factors. It consists of running an experiment many times with only one variant. If the results of the experiments are different, that one variant is most likely the cause.[2] In chemistry, physics, and biology, such controlled experiments play an important role in discovering facts and testing hypotheses. In these sciences an investigator can create a situation in which all the significant factors that bear on a problem can be controlled.

But there are limits to the use of the experimental method when the scientist cannot control the situations that are significant for the solution of problems. In the social sciences, very little use can be made of the method of controlled experiment except in dealing with certain relationships that involve rather small groups, because the investigator cannot control the situations. For example, one way to prove or disprove the proposition that high tariffs bring prosperity would be to apply very heavy duties to all goods entering the United States for a considerable period of time, while holding constant all other factors affecting business activity. If a sustained increase in prosperity followed, we would then have substantial evidence to support the thesis that high tariffs are a cause of prosperity. No investigator, let us say an economist, can control the country's tariff policy, and even if she could, while the high tariff was in effect many other social changes would be taking place, such as strikes, the establishment of new industries, and perhaps even wars. Some of these other changes would doubtless have much more influence on the state of national prosperity than would the high tariff and would make it impossible to separate out the effects of the high tariff from the effects of all these other events.

Most problems of interest to social scientists involve very large groups of people, often society as a whole. Controlled experiments cannot be used in solving such problems. When, however, social scientists can solve a problem by working with small groups, they may be able to make a limited use of the experimental method if the people involved will cooperate. Also, they can study **natural experiments,** which occur when two similar areas or entities choose different policies, and the effects of the different policies can be systematically studied. With natural experiments, researchers do not get perfect control, but they get some.

In the future, with further advances in computer technology, social scientists will study policy issues using virtual social systems, in which a computer replica of numerous interacting individuals creates a virtual system, which can analogue what occurs in the real world. Because of the complexity of social systems, such virtual systems remain a hope for the future, not a reality.

Social experiments are sometimes called experiments, but, unless they have a "control" that followed a different path and hence can be studied as a natural experiment, they are not what we mean by experiment. A social experiment is simply the introduction and "trying out" of new social policies. For example, Oregon's change in the financing of health insurance or Florida's experiments with vouchers for financing education might be called social experiments. The distinction involves the ability to have a control and to be able to replicate the experiment. The less the control, and the less the ability to repeat the experiment, the less sure we are of the results.

Methodology and the Social Sciences

Because it is so difficult to experiment in social science, some people have insisted that it is not science. Except for the prestige carried by the word, whether we call the study of

---

[2]But it is always possible that some other factor was not "held constant." If you remember chemistry experiments in high school, you know how hard it is to keep all other things constant.

Economics

Economics is the study of the ways in which men and women make a living, the most pressing problem most human beings face. It considers the social organization through which people satisfy their wants for scarce goods and services. Its subject matter is often summarized as:

- Production
- Distribution
- Consumption

Some of the topics it includes are:

- Supply and demand
- Monetary and fiscal policy
- Costs
- Inflation
- Unemployment

Economics seeks to explain, guide, and predict social arrangements by which we satisfy economic wants.

Political Science

Political science is the study of social arrangements to maintain peace and order within a given society. It deals with government, and its interests are:

- Politics
- Laws
- Administration
- Theory of the nature and functions of the state
- International relations

It has both a philosophical and a practical base. It examines the theory of systems of government, but it also studies actual practices by which government:

- Taxes
- Prohibits
- Regulates
- Protects
- Provides services

society a science is not important. It is merely a question of definition. If we mean by *science* the natural sciences only, then social science is not true science. If we mean by science only the so-called exact sciences, then again social science is not included. If, however, we use the term *science* broadly, to include all systematic attempts to expand knowledge by applying the scientific method, then social science must definitely be included in the scientific family. What is really important is that social scientists have discovered many significant relationships that are sufficiently dependable to add greatly to our understanding of social behavior and to serve as useful guides in dealing with some social problems.

There has been much debate about the correct methodology to be used in social science. Thomas Kuhn, a famous philosopher of science, defined a **paradigm** as a scientific theory and the core of beliefs that surround it. He argued that scientific progression occurs by paradigm shifts in which, for a long time, scientists will resist change and hold on to an old theory even as evidence mounts up against it, and even when another theory better fits the data. Eventually, however, the evidence in favor of the new theory is so great that suddenly scientists shift their thinking. The process can be likened to the way a drop of water forms on a faucet. It grows larger and larger until it falls. A good example in the sciences is Einstein's relativity theory in physics, which was initially scoffed at but was later adopted because it was consistent with a wider range of physical phenomena than was the earlier gravitational theory of Sir Isaac Newton.

Social scientists have discussed at great length whether Kuhn's theory of paradigm shift is appropriate for the social sciences. If it is, it gives legitimacy to competing theories. If it is not, then the generally accepted theory can be considered the best. The issue has never been resolved, but our understanding of the relevance of theories has advanced.

Imre Lakatos, another famous philosopher of science, has extended Kuhn's arguments by saying that in social science there are generally many competing theories, each being extended through competing **research programs,** or groups of scientists working on a particular problem. For example, in psychology there are the behaviorists and the Freudians. In sociology there are functionalists, conflict theorists, and interactionists. We could cite different theories within each social science. Advocates of each of the paradigms compete for researchers. The group of researchers most successful in competing for followers is the one most likely to grow.

Other philosophers of science go further. Some, like Paul Feurabend, argue that all methodology is limiting and that the correct methodology is no methodology. Still others argue that sociological issues, such as what is likely to advance a scientist's career, rather than the truth of a theory determine what the scientist believes.

In this book, we emphasize the competition among various theories. By doing so, we hope to show how, in social science, controversy plays an important role in the development of our knowledge.

Probably the best way to understand the scientific method is to consider a couple of examples that do *not* follow the scientific method. For instance, consider astrology or numerology. These pseudostudies hold that by analyzing the alignment of the stars or the position of certain numbers, individuals can discover or predict events that will affect them. However, the accuracy of the discoveries or the reliability of the predictions has never been satisfactorily demonstrated to most social scientists. Even though we might turn to our horoscopes and say, "Aha! That seems to fit my character or my experience," if we critically consider these predictions, often we see that the statements are so broad that they can be applied more or less appropriately to a wide range of happenings or possibilities. This is not to say that the social sciences always avoid that. Economics, for instance,

often comes up with predictions from large, highly sophisticated mathematical models (called *econometric models*), and some of these predictions are no better for steering a course than are back-of-the-envelope estimates.

A good social scientist generally takes an agnostic (not believing, but also not disbelieving) position about claims until they can be tested and retested. Consider, for example, parapsychology, which argues that people can transmit certain information independently of all conventional forms of communication. Shirley MacLaine's best-selling book, *Out on a Limb,* convinced many people that the claim of parapsychology is true. Most social scientists remain unconvinced. They hold that, to date, the theories have not been sufficiently demonstrated. In stating that these theories have not been tested, a good social scientist is not dogmatic. It is possible that we social scientists become so tied to our way of looking at the world that we are unable to consider the possibilities of other ways. Who is to say that the tests we accept as conclusive are the "right" tests? Or that our training hasn't biased the tests?

*P*sychology

Psychology deals with the mind and personality of the individual. It is a social science because humans are social creatures. It focuses on the individual and physical processes, such as:

- Biological structure
- Development and maturation

There are various branches of psychology; the most relevant to social science is social psychology. Social psychology is the study of the individual's behavior as it influences and is influenced by the behavior of others. Some specific topics that interest psychologists and social psychologists are:

- Socialization
- Environment and heredity
- Adjustment and maladjustment

These social scientists deal with natural phenomena such as emotion, memory, perception, and intelligence.

Ultimately, however, we must make a working judgment about what is and what isn't an acceptable test, and social scientists' methodology is an expression of that working judgment. It should, however, be presented as a working judgment, not as a set of definitive criteria of what is true and what is false. That's why, generally, good social scientists remain agnostic over a wide range of issues that they just don't have time to investigate. Thus, in many ways, what you will get out of a study of social science and an understanding of its methods is a healthy understanding of the limitations of your powers to know.

The Methods of Social Science

The basic procedures of the scientific method are as important in social science as in physical science. Social scientists must observe carefully, classify and analyze their facts, make generalizations, and attempt to develop and test hypotheses to explain their generalizations. Their problem, however, is often more difficult than that of physical scientists. The facts gathered by the social scientist—for example, those concerning the cultures of different peoples—have similarities, but each fact may also be unique in significant respects. Facts of this kind are difficult to classify and interpret. Further, as we have already noted, the generalizations or laws that the social scientist can make are likely to be less definite and certain than those of the physical scientist.

The difficulty of discovering relatively exact laws that govern social life results from several circumstances. First, the things of greatest importance in our social life—satisfactions, social progress, democracy—are not really measurable. Second, society is extremely complex. It is difficult and usually impossible to find and evaluate all the many causes of a given situation, though often we can discover the factors that were most important in bringing it about. Third, in every social situation there is the human element. Frequently the course of social events depends on the reaction of a few individuals who are leaders, and, except in routine situations, we can seldom predict individual behavior with complete certainty.

If the social scientist finally does succeed in finding uniformities or "laws" of social behavior and in setting up hypotheses to explain them, there is still another difficulty—namely, that investigators can seldom employ controlled experiments to test their hypotheses. To a considerable extent, the social scientist must substitute careful observation and the mental process of abstraction for experiments. The investigator abstracts from a given situation some one factor in order to consider what effect it would have if acting alone. In

"I'm a social scientist, Michael. That means I can't explain electricity or anything like that, but if you ever want to know about people, I'm your man."

order to do this, the investigator imagines that any other factors present remain constant or inert and asks, for example, a question such as: If other factors affecting economic life remained constant, what would be the economic effect of raising tariff rates on imports?

A social scientist who has a thorough knowledge of a situation may correctly calculate the effect of a given causal factor by assuming that all other things remain equal. However, to reach correct conclusions by this method, the investigator must be both competent and painstaking. Even then the dangers of error are great. If anything, there is more need for competence in the social scientist than in the physical scientist. The theories of a physical scientist can often be proved right or wrong by experiments, but this is seldom true of those of the social scientist. An unfortunate result is that it is easier in social science than in physical science to be needlessly vague, to perpetuate errors, and to cover up incompetence.

Social scientists also have more difficulty than physical scientists in being objective. Because they deal with human beings and are human themselves, social scientists find it hard to put aside their own likes and dislikes, their sympathies, prejudices, and frustrations. As a result, they sometimes fall into the trap of trying to justify their own hopes, beliefs, or biases instead of seeking to discover the truth. We should always be on guard against those who pose as social scientists but who, in fact, substitute propaganda and charisma for objectivity and competence.

This does not mean that social science is any less scientific than the natural sciences, or that it is less objective. It simply means that social scientists must be continually on guard against such traps and must be as clear and objective as possible.

The differences between physical science and social science lead to slightly different structures of research. Although there is no ideal structure, a reasonable approach to a problem in social science is the following:

1. Observe.
2. Define the problem.
3. Review the literature. (Become familiar with what others have observed.)
4. Observe some more.
5. Develop a theoretical framework and formulate a hypothesis.
6. Choose the research design.
7. Collect the necessary data.
8. Analyze the results.
9. Draw conclusions.

Using this outline as a rough guide, and recognizing that the specific project and each specific social science determine the exact nature of the methodology to be used, you have a reasonably good method of attack.

Observing.   Notice that social science begins with observation. Social science is about the real world, and the best way to know about the real world is to observe it.

Defining the problem.   Of the various research steps listed, this one is probably the most important. If you've carefully defined your terms, you can save an enormous amount of energy. Put simply, if you don't know what you're doing, no matter how well you do it, you're not going to end up with much. The topic might be chosen for a variety of reasons, perhaps because it raises issues of fundamental social science importance, perhaps because it has suddenly become a focus of controversy, or perhaps because research funds have become available to investigate it.

Reviewing the literature. Knowledge of the relevant literature is essential because it provides background, suggests approaches, indicates what has already been covered and what hasn't, and saves you from redoing what has already been done. It is a way of using other people's observations.

Observing some more. After you have defined your problem and reviewed the literature, your observation will be sharper. You will know more precisely what you are looking for and how to look for it.

Developing a theoretical framework and formulating a hypothesis. Make a statement predicting your results and then clarify what each of the terms in the statement means within the framework of your research. Suppose your hypothesis is: "High price increases sales of fashionable magazines." You should specify how high is high, and compared to what specific price is the price stated to be high; how much of an increase is significant over the circulation the magazine enjoyed at the lower price; what sales are included (newsstand, subscription, or both); and what is "fashionable." Different researchers may define the same term differently, which is one of the reasons why the same research subject can produce different results.

Choosing a research design. Pick a means of gathering data—a survey, an experiment, an observational study, use of existing sources, or a combination. Weigh this choice carefully because your plan is the crux of the research process.

Collecting the necessary data. Data are what one collects from careful observation. Your conclusions will be only as good as your data, so take great care in collecting and, especially, in recording your data. If you can't document what you've done, you might as well not have done it.

Analyzing the results. When all the data are in, classify facts, identify trends, recognize relationships, and tabulate the information so that it can be accurately analyzed and interpreted. A given set of facts may be interpreted two different ways by two different analysts, so give your analysis careful, objective attention. After this step has been taken, your hypothesis can then be confirmed, rejected, or modified.

Drawing conclusions. Now you can prepare a report, summarizing the steps you've followed and discussing what you've found. A good report will relate your conclusions to the existing body of research, suggest where current assumptions may be modified because of new evidence, and possibly identify unanswered questions for further study.

These steps differ slightly from those used by a natural scientist, but only slightly—the primary difference comes in testing a hypothesis. In some natural sciences, it is possible to conduct controlled experiments, where the same experiment can be repeated again and again under highly regulated conditions. In the social sciences, such controlled experiments are more difficult to construct.

The line between social science and natural science is not fixed. In some natural sciences, perfectly controlled experiments are impossible. In cosmological physics, for example, one can't create the universe again and again. Thus, one must speculate about a hypothesis, draw conclusions from that hypothesis, and see whether the conclusions match what one observes in the universe. Alternatively, in the social science of psychology certain controlled experiments are possible—for example, individuals can be given specific stimuli under specific conditions again and again. Thus the difference between the way one deals with the natural sciences and the way one deals with the social sciences can be blurry.

Let's take an example of the use of the social science method—Joseph Holz's study of the implications of teen pregnancy. First, he studied all the writing on teen pregnancy. Then he set up the following hypothesis: Teen pregnancy causes the mothers to be economically and socially worse off than they otherwise would have been. To test this hypothesis, he used data that had been collected over many years tracking the lives of teenage women. From that he extracted two groups—one was a set of teenage women who had become pregnant and borne the child, and the second was a set of teenage women who had become pregnant but had had a miscarriage. He then compared their economic and social positions when they were in their midthirties. If teen pregnancy caused the mother to be worse off, then the teens who had borne their babies should have been in a worse position than those who had had miscarriages. They weren't. He found no significant difference between the two groups: Both were low income, significantly dependent on welfare benefits, and had completed the same number of years of school. The initial hypothesis was false. Teen pregnancy did not make mothers worse off; it was simply a symptom of a larger set of problems. This larger set of problems was so severe that whether mothers had borne a child in their teens made little difference to their economic and social positions.

Holz's findings were published as the government was conducting a costly campaign against teen pregnancy, and his conclusions were unpopular with both liberals and conservatives. Liberals did not like them because his study suggests that much of the family planning advice and sex education developed by liberals was of little help in improving these women's lives. Conservatives didn't like them because his study implies that more substantive changes than simply eliminating teen pregnancy are needed if one is to improve these women's lives and break the cycle of poverty. But good social science methodology is not about pleasing anybody; it is about understanding social issues and social problems.

Notice that although Holz's experiment was not fully controlled, it was as close as one could come to a controlled experiment in the social sciences. It selected similar groups to compare in such a way that there was no obvious reason why these two groups should differ.

Social Science Approaches to Problems

As you review the literature about various social science studies, you will see that social scientists can use many different approaches and methods as they study problems. We first consider alternative approaches; then we consider alternative methods.

Alternative Approaches.   The approach one takes when analyzing a problem reflects one's worldview—the lens through which one sees the world. Four approaches that social scientists use are the functionalist theory approach, the exchange theory approach, the conflict theory approach, and the symbolic interaction theory approach.

The functionalist theory approach. This approach emphasizes the interconnectedness of social life and the difficulty of affecting only one part of society with a policy. Followers of the **functionalist theory approach** are hesitant to make social judgments because all aspects of society have certain functions. Closely related to the functionalist approach is the exchange theory approach.

The exchange theory approach. This approach emphasizes the voluntary exchanges of individuals as reflecting individuals' choices. Thus the structure of society reflects individuals' desires. The **exchange theory approach** lens is one of relative harmony in society, sometimes upset by dysfunctional elements.

The conflict theory approach. The **conflict theory approach** sees far less harmony. Followers of this approach see social behavior in terms of conflict and tension among competing groups or classes. Whereas the exchange theory approach sees individuals' voluntary choices, the conflict theory approach sees force and power directing individual actions.

The symbolic interaction theory approach. The **symbolic interaction theory approach** sees individuals as deriving meaning from the symbols they learn from. Followers of this approach see reality as reflecting less what people do and more what they think and feel. Their motives and perceptions, rather than actions, are emphasized.

These approaches are not necessarily independent of one another. Some social scientists use a combination of approaches to study problems, while some use one at one time and another at another time.

Alternative Methods. In addition to using different approaches, social scientists also use different methods. These include the historical method, the case method, and the comparative and cross-cultural methods.

The historical method. Because most social developments—such as the government of the United States—have unique characteristics, in order to understand them as fully as possible the social scientist must rely heavily on a study of their historical background. We can never understand completely how any historical situation came to exist, because there are limits to our historical knowledge and causes become increasingly complex and uncertain as we trace them further into the past. We can, however, make both historical events and present social situations much more intelligibly by using the **historical method**—tracing the principal past developments that seem to have been directly significant in bringing about a social situation. To trace these past developments, a historian will use many of the same methods as other social scientists such as collecting birth and marriage certificates and classifying those data.

It has been noted that history never really repeats itself. Nevertheless, present and past situations often have such striking similarities that a knowledge of the past can give us insights into present situations and sometimes into future trends.

The case method. Writers on the methodology of social research have devoted a great deal of attention to the case method—its characteristics, its variations, the uses it can serve, its advantages, and its limitations. Here we only describe its basic nature. The **case method** involves making a detailed examination and analysis of a particular issue or problem situation. This can involve a case study of a single person such as that by a psychologist of his client, a single area or town such as a sociologist's study of why a town changes, or even a study of whole countries such as an economist's when comparing various countries.

A case study can be intended to discover how to bring about desirable changes in a particular problem situation: for example, to find the most effective ways of upgrading or rehabilitating a given slum area. But more often the chief purpose of a case study is to throw light on many similar situations that exist in a society. The hope is that an understanding of one or a few cases will illuminate the others and thus aid in solving the social problems they present. The case or cases selected should be typical of the group they purport to represent.

The preceding requirement can be a limiting factor in the usefulness of the case method. Suppose we wanted to make a study of the class structure of U.S. society as a whole. Obviously, it would be easier to select as cases for study several relatively small and isolated cities in various sections of the country. But it is questionable whether these would give us a true picture of the country as a whole, because today a great proportion of our people live in large metropolitan areas where the class structure is likely to be much more complex than in smaller and more isolated communities. However, to study and describe in detail the class structure of such an area may be prohibitively difficult and expensive, and therefore impractical.

The comparative and cross-cultural methods. The **comparative method** was formerly often employed in the hope of discovering evolutionary sequences in the development of human institutions—that is, patterns of social development or progress that would be universal. For example, it was sometimes assumed that there were definite stages in the development of governmental institutions, and it was thought that these stages could be discovered by comparing a society at one level of development with some other society at a different level. Today this attempt to find patterns of social evolution that can be applied to all societies has been largely abandoned.

However, comparison of different societies still plays an important role in anthropological studies through what is called the **cross-cultural method.** This method consists of making detailed studies of the culture patterns of a number of societies for the purpose of comparing the different ways in which their people meet similar needs. These studies sometimes show surprising similarities in the cultural traits of widely separated peoples who appear to have had no direct or indirect contacts with one another.

Comparison of the characteristics of different societies involves problems. At times it is difficult to decide whether two or more societies are independent or should be treated as one. Or consider definitions: If we are comparing the family institution in different societies, we must define *family* broadly enough to cover cultural variations yet specifically enough to make comparisons meaningful. Sociologists do not always agree on just what a family is. Again, if we are comparing unemployment in urban-industrial societies we must agree on what we mean by *unemployment.* For example, in the early 1980s the unemployment rate in Mexico, computed by U.S. standards, was approximately 30 percent. Mexican economists, however, argued that this figure was meaningless because Mexican work habits and culture were different from those in the United States. Much of what was measured as unemployment, they said, was actually individuals who were working at home and not earning money in the marketplace. Thus, although they had nonmarket jobs, they had still been counted as unemployed.

Common Sense in the Social Sciences

Probably the most important lesson to remember when conducting any research is that you should use what might be called an educated common sense. You can understand the analytic argument for common sense by considering the mind as a supercomputer storing enormous amounts of information, not all of which may lie at the surface of recall. This holds true even with the vast increase in computer power. Processing speeds of computers double every eighteen months, according to Moore's Law. That increase has made it possible to do enormous things even with home computers. However, compared with the capabilities of the human mind, even the most powerful computer counts by using its fingers and toes. The mind processes trillions of pieces of information in millinanoseconds (we don't know what they are either, but we do know they are very small). When the results of the models and the minds diverge, it seems reasonable to rely on the more powerful computer—the mind. It makes sense to do so, however, only if the best information has been input into the mind. Common sense is not sufficient; we must use educated common sense.

To see the difference between common sense and *educated* common sense, consider the problem: Does the earth circle the sun or does the sun circle the earth? Uneducated common sense tells us that the sun circles the earth, and that commonsense conclusion became built into society and society's view of itself throughout the Middle Ages. To believe otherwise was heresy. In 1540, Copernicus tried to fit that commonsense view with observations that classical Greeks had made of the heavens. As he went about this task, he discovered that he could get a good fit of the data with the theory only if he assumed the earth moved around the sun. His was an **educated common sense**—rational thought based on observation and the best information available. It was that kind of educated common sense that ultimately led to the scientific method. As specialization makes us focus on narrower and narrower issues, it is important to keep in the back of our minds that scientific analysis has made us look at only part of the problem, and that we must also use our educated common sense to interpret the results reasonably.

The Use of Statistics

Statistics—information in numerical form that has been assembled and classified—provide the social scientist with one of the kinds of information needed to understand social relationships and processes. Statistics do not enable us to measure directly such basic social values as good citizenship, happiness, or welfare, but they are useful in measuring other factors that underlie social life, such as the size of the population of a country, or the number of families whose incomes fall below some level that we set as the minimum for decent and healthful living. Statistical relationships also give us insights into social problems. If we find that the proportion of males in juvenile detention centers who come from broken homes is substantially greater than the proportion of males in the population at large who come from such homes, this suggests that broken homes may be an important factor contributing to juvenile delinquency. But statistics must always be interpreted with care, for it can be easy to read into them conclusions they do not justify. Also, it is sometimes possible to manipulate them so that they appear to show what we want them to show.

Although statistics measure the results of social activity and highlight trends, they have other useful functions: testing theories and discovering relationships. For example, *correlation* is the relationship between two sets of data. A high correlation between sets of data means that if an element in one set rises, its corresponding element in the other set is also likely to rise. Other statistics determine how sure we are of a relationship. We do not discuss these statistics because an introductory social science course is not the place to learn them, but it *is* the place to learn that such techniques of testing relationships exist, and they may be worth your while to study at some point in the future.

If we are going to use statistics, we must have data. Data are the raw numbers describing an event, occurrence, or situation. Social scientists' data come from measuring and counting all occurrences of a particular happening. For example, we might find, "In 1991, there were x number of murders and y number of suicides." One way to get data is to conduct a **survey,** a method whereby data are collected from individuals or institutions by means of questionnaires or interviews. For instance, we might conduct a survey in which selected people are questioned or polled on such matters as their incomes, their beliefs on certain issues, or the political candidate for whom they intend to vote. Figure 1.2 gives an example of such a survey. Statistics can tell us how large a portion of a group must be surveyed before we can be reasonably sure that the results will reflect the views of the entire group. Such techniques are used extensively in surveys such as the Gallup or Harris public opinion polls.

The use of statistics has been greatly facilitated, and therefore greatly expanded, by the computer. The computer has made it possible to record, arrange, and rearrange voluminous information quickly and analytically. Today, enormous amounts of data and other resources are available to anyone with a computer or other access to the Internet.

With the expansion of social data and the enormous increase in computing power, it is more and more possible for social scientists to look for relationships in the data alone, rather than to be guided in that search by theories. Using highly sophisticated statistical techniques, social scientists analyze data, looking for patterns. After they find a pattern, they fit that pattern to a theory. For example, social scientists Stephen Levitt and John Donohue searched the data and found a relationship between the passage of the abortion rights law in the United States and a decrease in crime in later periods. Based on this evidence, they argued that because abortion reduced the number of unwanted children, those children who were born had more guidance, and that it was the law making abortion legal, not any change in law enforcement or increase in the number of inmates jailed, that was mostly responsible for the decrease in crime rates that the United States experienced in the 1990s.

The Interdisciplinary Approach

Modern industrial societies and their problems are becoming increasingly complex, and because no one person today can master all the social sciences, increasing emphasis is being placed on the interdisciplinary approach to many social problems. The **interdisciplinary approach** means that a group of social scientists with different specialties will work together on a certain problem, not all of whose aspects any one of the group fully understands. For some problems, such as those surrounding pollution, it may be necessary to call in, say, a physical scientist, a geologist, and an engineer. But in facing all of these problems, the need for educated people who have a broad sense of problems and interrelationships—who understand the need for a unified social science—is also becoming more and more evident.

Though few social relationships can be reduced to exact and invariable laws, human beings in large groups everywhere show great likenesses of behavior when conditions are

1. Do you worry very much about the AIDS problem?

   __50.4__ No

   __49.6__ Yes ────────┐

   > If yes, what are your specific worries?
   >
   > *1.8 Past-oriented (did past partners tell truth)*
   >
   > *26.6 Present-oriented (e.g., general fear, casual relationships uncertain, others apathetic)*
   >
   > *20.5 Future-oriented (e.g., rapid spread, new means of spreading may be found)*

Directions: For the following items, indicate the degree of your agreement or disagreement by placing an "X" in the appropriate column.

	Strongly Agree	Agree	Disagree	Strongly Disagree
2. Fraternities are the center of social life on campus.	32.5%	47.9%	18.8%	0.9%
3. Fraternities encourage too much illegal drinking.	9.4%	28.2%	53.0%	9.4%
4. Fraternities encourage too much vandalism.	6.9%	15.5%	59.5%	18.1%
5. The fraternity system encourages the development of positive female–male relationships.	3.5%	33.9%	47.8%	14.8%
6. I worry about contracting AIDS.	4.3%	41.9%	39.3%	14.5%
7. There is too much fear of AIDS today.	5.2%	19.0%	50.0%	25.9%
8. There should be much more mandatory testing for AIDS.	13.8%	46.6%	33.6%	6.0%
9. Regarding AIDS, the best statement to describe my concern is, "It won't happen to me."	1.7%	25.6%	45.3%	27.4%

Figure 1.2

One of the best ways by which social scientists collect information is through a survey. This is one page of a fourteen-page survey conducted by college students for their sociology class. Because of time pressures in that particular survey, they were unable to perform an extensive analysis of their data. For this reason, they urged caution in the use and interpretation of the information.

really similar. Thus, there is reason to believe that we can, through systematic study and research, greatly increase our understanding of the nature and development of human societies, and to hope that the attitudes fostered by the interdisciplinary approach itself and the knowledge to which it leads us can ultimately result in greater tolerance and co-operation among diverse groups and among nations.

Social Science and Society

Some people believe that the social sciences are lagging behind the natural sciences. They maintain that not only does social science have no exact laws, but that it has also failed to eliminate great social evils such as racial discrimination, crime, poverty, and war. They imply that social scientists have failed to accomplish what might reasonably have been expected of them. However, such critics are usually unaware of the real nature of social science and of its special problems and basic limitations. For example, they forget that the solution to a social problem requires not only knowledge but also the ability to influence people. Even if social scientists discover the procedures that should be followed to achieve social improvement, they are seldom in a position to control social action. For that matter, even dictators find that there are limits to their power to change society.

Continuing Problems

In modern times, three elements compound the stubborn problems we continue to face:

1. the population explosion
2. the rapidity of technological change
3. instant communication

Today the sheer number of people creates almost insuperable problems, and these are increased by the desire of people for all the comforts and luxuries that modern technology offers and by the rapidity with which developments in one part of the world become known in others through radio, television, films, and the Internet. People in the poorer countries, who formerly knew little about life in the richer ones, become envious and frustrated. At the same time, we in the more fortunate countries learn quickly of the misery in other parts of the world, as well as the misery of some people in our own countries, and we feel guilty and conscience-stricken. All this presents a great challenge to social scientists because the only hope of solving social problems is through study, competent research, and effective communication of findings to the public, especially to the people who have the greatest influence on public opinion and public policy.

One of the great problems in a democracy is getting the majority of people to reach substantial agreement on the major policies that should be followed to create a better society. Social scientists can aid in bringing about this agreement by helping people to understand the issues, the difficulties involved, and the possible steps to a solution. If we express social objectives in sufficiently general terms, agreement is not so hard to obtain. Most people would like to have a heaven on earth characterized by peace and goodwill, with freedom, justice, security, health, and happiness for all. But when it comes to drawing up a blueprint for reaching these objectives, disagreements and obstacles become apparent. Social scientists themselves are not always in complete agreement on what our specific social goals should be or on how we can best work toward them.

In any case, the function of social science and of those who practice it is not primarily to determine social objectives. Its major function is to discover how our objectives can be achieved. The determination of the goals themselves—our social values—is not a scientific problem but one having to do with our likes and dislikes, our esthetic concepts, our moral standards, and our philosophical and religious beliefs. (We have more to say about social values in the following chapter.)

Values, Terminology, and Rhetoric

This chapter began with a quotation from Albert Einstein, who said that "theories should be as simple as possible, but not more so." The same thing could be said about ideas and the expression of those ideas. Unfortunately, specialists have an incentive to develop a terminology that is anything but simple and that often obscures rather than clarifies. One of the many social science teachers who has written us about this book (and in doing so, these teachers have played an important role in its development) described a history conference she attended where "we were treated to such goodies" as

> The sociopolitical internecine amortizations of agronomous proletarization, if solely counterproductive of Jurassic multi-dimensional interstitial extrapolated Augustinian and Aristotelian epistemological diagrammetric middle-sector dichotomies, as measured in the context of paradigmatic vestigiae (though challenged none too effectively, if I am not remiss in saying so, by Freylinghausen's hypothesis delivered at the University of Bordeaux in April 1896) are existentially and polaristically categorized by Nordlinger's Metternichian thermodynamics as tangentially interrelated with studies promulgated by Darffenstangenovich on a scale of one to twenty factored to the 24th power.

Although she may have used a bit of literary license in transcribing the conference proceedings, her point is well taken. She was attending a conference on her specialty, yet she didn't understand what was being said. It happens all the time, not only to students, but to teachers as well. Although there may be valuable ideas in what many specialists have to say, we can't profit from them if we can't understand them, or if we must spend hours translating them.

In a wonderful book, *The Sociological Imagination,* C. W. Mills made precisely this point. He argued that in many social sciences "high theory" is top-heavy with jargon. As an example, he interpreted the sociologist Talcott Parsons's terminology: He reduced it by 80 to 90 percent and at the same time made it more intelligible. Mills wasn't making the point that Parsons's insights weren't good ones; to the contrary, Mills believed that Parsons was a brilliant sociologist. But Parsons's language obscured his brilliant ideas.

Another characteristic of language is that it embodies value judgments and preserves ways of looking at problems. A good social scientist recognizes this and is always open to dealing with reality by alternative modes of expression and new ways of looking at issues.

Conclusion

If this chapter has succeeded in its intended purpose, it should have given you a sense of what it means to be a social scientist. As you saw, the social sciences are evolving: They interact and they move among the humanities, the natural sciences, and the individual social sciences depending on who is working with them. They are fluid, not static, and that fluidity will present problems to anyone who attempts too fixed a definition of any of them.

The ability to handle the fluid definitions, to recognize the shadows as well as the objects without flinching, is an important characteristic that good social scientists exhibit—one which, if learned, will serve you well as you study this book and play the game of life.

Key Points

- Social science is the name given to our knowledge about the nature, growth, and functioning of human society.
- The scientific method is a set of rules about how to establish rules.
- A good social scientist generally takes a wait-and-see position about claims until they are tested and retested.
- A reasonable approach to a problem in social science is to observe, define the problem, review the literature, observe some more, develop a theoretical framework and formulate a hypothesis, choose the research design, collect the necessary data, analyze the results, and draw conclusions.
- Three typical methods in social science are the historical method, the case method, and the comparative method.
- It is important to use educated common sense in the social sciences.
- A good social scientist is always open to new ways of looking at issues.

Some Important Terms

anthropology (6)
biological science (3)
case method (18)
cognitive science (4)
comparative method (19)
conflict theory approach (18)
cross-cultural method (19)
economics (12)
educated common sense (20)
exchange theory approach (18)
experimental method (10)

functionalist theory
   approach (18)
geography (9)
historical method (18)
history (9)
humanities (3)
interdisciplinary approach (21)
natural experiments (11)
natural science (3)
paradigm (12)
political science (12)

psychology (13)
research program (13)
scientific knowledge (1)
scientific method (9)
social science (1)
sociology (8)
statistics (20)
survey (21)
symbolic interaction theory
   approach (18)

Questions for Review and Discussion

1. What is scientific knowledge? How does it differ from knowledge acquired "unconsciously"?
2. Distinguish among the three major fields of human knowledge. What is the emphasis of each?
3. Name the principal social sciences and define the field with which each deals.
4. Why would it have been difficult to carry on scientific investigation in primitive societies or even in the Middle Ages?
5. What is the scientific method?
6. What basic assumption underlies the use of the scientific method?
7. What is the experimental method?

8. Why is it difficult to formulate precise laws in the field of social science?

9. Are there any advantages to having competing research programs?

10. In what sense is social science scientific?

11. Why is it often impossible to study social problems by means of the experimental method?

12. Explain the ways in which the problems of social science differ from those of the exact natural sciences.

13. What are the advantages of the interdisciplinary approach to the study of many social problems?

14. Social science has been broken down into specialties. Why is it a problem to put them back together through a unified theory?

15. What new social science fields do you think will be important ten years from now? Why do you think so?

Internet Questions

1. Using an Internet search engine (for example, Yahoo.com or Google.com), look at the lists of topics included in the guide/directory under Social Science or Society. How many fields are listed? What fields would you add (or delete) in a list of your own?

2. On the website www.howe.k12.ok.us/~jim askew/hsimeth.htm, students have used an abbreviated version of the scientific method to solve the social problem of dating. Use this process to "solve" another everyday problem.

3. Go to www.wikipedia.org and choose one of the fields under the topic heading Social Science. What are the subdisciplines or branches listed?

4. Take the survey about alcohol use at http:// iea.fau.edu/colalc/colalc.asp. After taking the survey, look at the feedback you are given based on your answers. What can the results for this survey be used for?

5. Go to www.ncpa.org/pi/crime/pd08599g.html and read the discussion about Donohue and Levitt's study of abortion and crime rates mentioned in the text. What are some of the alternative arguments that critics use to explain why the crime rate has decreased?

For Further Study

Benton, Ted, and Ian Craib, *Philosophy of Social Science: The Philosophical Foundations of Social Thought,* New York: Palgrave, 2001.

Berlinski, David, *Newton's Gift: How Sir Isaac Newton Unlocked the System of the World,* New York: Free Press, 2000.

Boorstin, Daniel J., *The Seekers: The Story of Man's Continuing Quest to Understand His World,* New York: Random House, 1999.

Fromkin, David, *The Way of the World: From the Dawn of Civilization to the Eve of the Twenty-First Century,* New York: Knopf, 1999.

Greene, Brian, *The Elegant Universe: Superstrings, Hidden Dimensions, and the Quest for the Ultimate Theory,* New York, Norton, 1999.

Herron, Nancy, *The Social Sciences: A Cross-Disciplinary Guide to Selected Sources,* 3rd ed., Englewood, CO: Libraries Unlimited, 2002.

Mills, C. Wright, *The Sociological Imagination,* New York: Oxford University Press, 1959.

Simon, Julian, and Paul Burstein, *Basic Research Methods in Social Science,* New York: Random House, 1985.

Wilson, Edward O., *Consilience: The Unity of Knowledge,* New York: Knopf, 1998.

WWW   Anthropology Resources on the Internet   www.anthropologie.net

WWW   Economic History Resources   www.eh.net/ehresources

WWW   Internet Psychology Resources   www.thepsych.com

WWW   Political Resources on the Net   www.politicalresources.net

WWW   Social Science Research Council   www.ssrc.org

WWW   Sociological Resources on the Internet   www.sonic.net/~markbl/socioweb

WWW   Virtual Library in Economics   www.helsinki.fi/WebEc

WWW   Virtual Library in Sociology   www.mcmaster ca/socscidocs/w3virtsoclib

*H*istorical Roots of Social Science

Natural scientists tell us that the world has been around for some 6 billion years and that living things have been around for at least 3 billion. We will go back, however, only about 2,600 years, when Western philosophy began on the fringes of ancient Greece (some theorists hold that the Greeks responded to ideas from Eastern civilizations, but there are limits to even our broad sweep). The Greeks came to realize that their ancient account of how the world was created and administered—by an enormous collection of gods, or pantheon—was not the only possible explanation. They are credited with being the first to establish rational theory, independent of theological creed; to grasp rational concepts and use them as a way of looking at reality and seeing logical connections; and to be empirical and antimystical. Two great Greek thinkers of the third and fourth centuries B.C., Plato and Aristotle, are responsible for establishing a basis for knowledge as we know it and deal with it today.

The philosophical debates of the Greek period were in many ways the same ones that go on today, explaining how, when all things change, things must also be simultaneously unchanging; otherwise, something would have to be created out of nothing—a logical impossibility. These ideas would later develop into modern physics, including the laws of thermodynamics and the proposition that matter can neither be created nor destroyed—merely transformed. The Greeks also considered many of the issues that later became the social sciences; for example, they considered the role of the state (political science), the way minds interacted with society (psychology), and individuals' interaction within the market (economics). Thus, the history of the social sciences begins with the Greeks. The history, however, is not continuous.

Much of the Greek contribution to knowledge would have been lost (who knows what other contributions actually have been lost?) were it not for its preservation by Eastern civilizations. On their forays into the East during the Crusades (the religious wars from 1095 to 1272 in which Christians in Europe attempted to capture Christianity's traditional territory in the Middle East), Europeans became reacquainted with the learning of the ancient Greeks, and they brought back the body of ancient Greek learning to Europe, where it was generally available by the twelfth century. These ideas spread slowly throughout Europe over the next three hundred years, and by the middle of the fifteenth century, rediscovery of Greek civilization in Europe was widespread. Because the period from about 1453 (the fall of Constantinople) to the end of the seventeenth century was characterized by the rebirth and proliferation of ancient knowledge, it became known as the **Renaissance** (a French word meaning "rebirth"). The Renaissance is a period from about 1453 to the end of the seventeenth century characterized by the rebirth and proliferation of ancient knowledge.

The Renaissance must have been a wonderful time for scholars. The totality of knowledge was still comprehensible by the human mind. An ideal in the Renaissance was that an educated person could know everything and exercise all skills and social graces. A true Renaissance man was willing to take on all comers on any issue.

As the store of knowledge grew, it became harder and harder to know everything, and so people began to specialize. A natural division opened, one between the humanities (the study of literature, music, and art) and physics. The physics part of this division was not refined enough, and soon physics was broken up into empirical studies (which developed into the various natural sciences) and metaphysics (nonempirical studies that developed into philosophy).

The Renaissance was preceded by the **Middle Ages** (a period from roughly A.D. 476, and the end of the Roman Empire, to A.D. 1453, the defeat of Christian religious armies in Constantinople by the Islamic Turks). In the Middle Ages, religion was so central to life that the study of religion was taken for granted, and it tied together all the other fields of study. For example, painters painted religious pictures, musicians wrote religious music, and the study of literature was the study of the Bible and its commentators. Questions that today seem the obvious ones, such as, Why are people divided into classes? and Why are the poor poor? were simply not asked. Things were the way they were because that was God's will. Once one knew God's will, the issue was how to carry it out. For example, medieval scholars believed in a "just" price and that collecting interest on savings was immoral. They taught those principles and condemned those who did not follow their teachings.

As the Renaissance dawned and continued, that religious tie provoked tension as scholars in the various fields of study came to conclusions different from the church's doctrines, beginning a long conflict between religious learning and beliefs and so-called rationalist learning and beliefs.

The tension between religious explanations and rationalist explanations was (and still is) inevitable. The rationalist approach places human reason above faith. In a rationalist approach, one looks for logical connections and is continually asking the question, Can you prove it? This meant that somehow the rationalists had to figure out what it meant to prove something. A religious approach places faith above reason. A religious explanation had no need to prove anything: Explanations were accepted on faith.

Throughout the Renaissance, rationalism more and more replaced religion as the organiz-

ing principle of knowledge, and as it did, the various fields of knowledge became divided along rationalist lines. The humanities still reflected religious issues; the rationalist revolution came much later to the humanities. To the degree that they were considered, most of the issues we now classify under social science were studied as part of history. History was part of literature and the humanities. It was simply a documentation of what had happened—it never asked *why* something happened. To ask why meant failure to accept God's will. Thus it was primarily from philosophy, not history, that most of the social sciences emerged.

The natural sciences and philosophy divided along modes of inquiry and answers to the question, Can you prove it? The study of philosophy itself evolved into a variety of fields, such as logic, morals, and epistemology (the study of knowledge).

Происхождение

The Enlightenment

The **Enlightenment** is the period in which rationalism definitely replaced religion as the organizing principle of knowledge. The Enlightenment began between A.D. 1650 and A.D. 1700 and continued for about one hundred years. It is in this period that the development of the social sciences took hold and flourished.

By the time of the Enlightenment, it had become evident that to know everything—to be a Renaissance scholar—was impossible. Not only was it impossible to know everything, but it was also impossible to know everything about just one subject—say, all of physics or all of philosophy. Individuals began to specialize their study. For instance, chemistry and astronomy were separated out from physics.

In the case of philosophy, as philosophers delved into their subject they further divided philosophy into parts. One part was metaphilosophy, the study of issues that most scholars agreed were not empirically testable. One such issue was: Since God is all-powerful, can he create a rock so heavy he cannot move it? The other division of philosophy dealt with issues that could, in principle at least, be empirically tested. For instance:

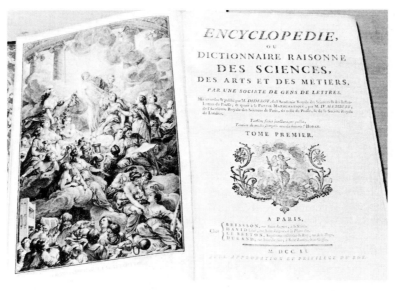

Frontispiece from Diderot's Encyclopédie, *written during the Enlightenment.*

What type of political organization of society is preferable? It is from the second division that the social sciences evolved. (They were called sciences because they were in principle meant to be empirically testable.)

The Enlightenment spawned social science because the Enlightenment rejected the assumption that the classical world of the Greeks and the Romans was perfect. In the Enlightenment (roughly the whole of the eighteenth century), there was a general belief that civilization had improved and so too should the thinking about civilization. Moreover, in the seventeenth century, just preceding the Enlightenment, there was continual turmoil—a long drawn-out war between France and England and a religious conflict between Catholics and Protestants about how to interpret God's will. That fight broke down the religious explanations and made people very much aware of social problems. Which of the two explanations, Catholic or Protestant, was right? Why were they fighting? What could be done about it? The social sciences developed as individuals attempted to explain those social problems and suggest what could be done to solve them.

Although the existence of social problems that require solutions may seem obvious to you, it was not always so obvious. This view is the product of the Enlightenment, which established the "three humiliations" of human beings. These are:

1. The earth is not the center of the universe.
2. We are creatures of nature like other animals.
3. Our reasoning ability is subject to passions and subconscious desires.

Before we experienced these humiliations, thinkers could rely on an order that they believed was established by God. Social problems were set up by God and were to be accepted or endured. Only after the beginning of the Enlightenment did people begin to believe that society and culture are themselves products of history and the evolution of culture—that they had changed and would continue to change.

As is often the case, the change in viewpoint had a paradoxical counterpoint, and human beings' "humiliation" was accompanied by a belief in human beings' power. If society could change, then the change could be, at least to some extent, guided and directed by human beings.

Since its conception, social science has entwined these two aspects. Sometimes it is simply trying to understand, and it accepts our limited powers and our place in the cosmos, and at other times it is trying to change society.

From Philosophy to Social Science

The evolution of philosophy into the social sciences can be seen in France, where philosophers joined to produce an encyclopedia, edited by Denis Diderot and Jean d'Alembert, which appeared over a span of several years in the mid-1700s. The full title of this encyclopedia proclaimed it to be a rational dictionary of science, art, and industry. Unlike earlier compilations, it contained systematic articles on man, society, and method, and a number of the first definitions of the social sciences can be traced to this mammoth work.

There are many ways to look at social problems, and as scholars began considering human beings in reference to their social environment, the diversity soon became apparent. The history of each of the social sciences becomes hopelessly tangled with that of each of the others at this point. In the Enlightenment, scholars were debating one another and ideas were quickly evolving. To capture even a flavor of the interaction and debate leads to a formidable morass, hardly conducive to a social science course. So we will stop our consideration here.

Some Important Terms

Enlightenment (28)
Middle Ages (28)
Renaissance (27)

𝓗uman Origins

chapter 2

After reading this chapter, you should be able to:

- Summarize Darwin's theory of evolution
- Explain the role of mutation in the theory of evolution
- Relate DNA to genes and genetic engineering
- Distinguish between the theory of punctuated equilibrium and the theory of continuous equilibrium
- Summarize briefly the evolution of human beings over the last 30 million years

If a single cell, under appropriate conditions, becomes a man in the space of a few years, there can surely be no difficulty in understanding how, under appropriate conditions, a cell may, in the course of untold millions of years, give origin to the human race.

—Herbert Spencer

Our ancestors in the not-so-distant past believed that the globe we live on was the major focus of the universe and that all the heavenly bodies revolved around it. Today we know that it is only an infinitesimal part of the cosmic universe of space and matter. To human beings, however, this tiny part is more important than all the rest, for the greatest concerns of human beings are themselves, the planet on which they live, their origin, their destiny, and their relationships with each other. Even if they hope for a future life in some far-off heaven, they still long to make their earthly life meaningful and satisfying.

Human beings are first of all social creatures. They normally spend their entire lives in association with other human beings and as members of various organized social groups. The quality of association and membership varies according to the nature of the social group. For members of a family, association is normally constant and close, but as residents of a town or city, human beings' association with the majority of the other residents is only occasional and often impersonal. Modern technology, especially the Internet, is both increasing and developing that association. As people spend more time on-line, they spend less time with their families and geographic neighbors, but they often establish associations with people all over the world.

Physical geography is still important and most people still define themselves as members of a larger society, all bound together to some degree by a common language, common interests, geographic areas, ways of living, common loyalties, and reliance on a common national government for their defense and for much of their general welfare. To a great extent, the ability of people to live happy and satisfying lives depends on the nature of the society they live in.

The Origin of the Human Species

Where and when the human species originated is not known with absolute certainty, but the conventional view is that it was in Africa some five to seven million years ago. Modern scientists believe that sometime millions of years ago the process of evolution produced our first human ancestors when a humanlike creature branched off from the apes. They believe that then a long series of changes created a group of hominids who displayed, over time, more and more of the basic physical characteristics that distinguish modern human beings from all other forms of life. Fossils of humanlike species have been found that date back about five million years, and research in this field is progressing so rapidly that it is possible that by the time you read this even older evidence will have been found. After splitting off from apes, humanlike species are believed to have continued to gradually change to other types of humanlike species in the evolutionary process.

Darwin and the Theory of Evolution

Evolution in its broadest sense refers to any process of progressive change. Thus one may speak of the evolution of the novel, of art, or of religion. But when used without qualification, **evolution** ordinarily means organic evolution, or the theory that all the complex life forms of today have descended from earlier ones that existed long ago. The theory of evolution was popularized by the English biologist Charles Darwin, who devoted his life to systematically finding evidence to support the concept of evolution and to explaining natural selection, which he believed was the mechanism by which evolution was accomplished.

Darwin, in the capacity of a naturalist, made a five-year voyage with a British surveying expedition on the ship *Beagle* (1831–1836). During this time he had unusual opportunities to study a great variety of plant and animal life. He was puzzled by the similarities and differences he found and by the progressive steps that often seemed evident in going from the simpler to the more complex forms of life. Ultimately, he developed his theory of natural selection to explain these relationships. The first major work in which he presented his conclusions was *The Origin of Species* (1859). Later, in another famous book, *The Descent of Man,* he dealt specifically with the evolution of the human race.

Though Darwin was largely responsible for the widespread acceptance by scientists of the concept of evolution, he was neither the first to suggest the idea nor the first to be impressed by the remarkable physical similarity of human beings to certain animals. As far back as the fourth century B.C., Aristotle believed in the gradual development of complex organisms from simpler ones, and a generation before Darwin, the French zoologist J. B. Lamarck had published a theory of evolution. Although flawed, it had many insights. Also, a hundred years before Darwin, the great Swedish naturalist Carolus Linnaeus organized the various species by similarity of their physical attributes. In doing so, he invented the term **primates,** a group of animals including human beings, apes, and monkeys whose outstanding characteristics are their larger, complex brains, high intelligence, and hands and feet adapted for grasping. In his studies, Linnaeus could not overlook the resemblances among these three kinds of creatures.

Natural Selection.   Darwin's concept of evolution was based, in part, on **natural selection,** the proposition that individual members of the various species that have characteristics more favorable for meeting the conditions of life are more likely to survive and pass on their characteristics to future generations. Darwin believed that every species is characterized by the appearance of such individuals; thus the direction that evolution takes is largely determined by "the survival of the fittest."

Genetics studies how the hereditary characteristics of species and individuals are transmitted biologically to their offspring. The precise process of how evolution occurs is still unsettled, but it is generally believed that genetics plays an important role.

The foundation work in genetics was done by Gregor Mendel in the late nineteenth century.[1] He discovered that plants and animals have what he called inheritance factors, now known as **genes,** which he defined as discrete units within cells that retain their original character for generation after generation. Because of this retention, these genes determine the characteristics of future generations. Thus the study of evolution is closely connected to the study of genetics.

Mutation.   Genetics explains the way we are, but it does not explain why and how we change. That occurs through a process called **mutation:** random genetic changes that create new characteristics. In mutation, an offspring has quite different characteristics from those of its parents.

Although we do not completely understand why these mutations occur, we do know that if the resulting offspring survive, their new characteristics can be passed on to future generations. Mutations are random. They seem to be accidents, partial failures of the process by which a species is able to reproduce its kind. We also know that the incidence of mutations is increased by exposure to certain chemicals or types of radiation. Most mutations are neutral, but some are fatal and some are beneficial to the offspring. Beneficial mutations make evolution possible. Over long periods of time, evolution can bring about great changes in the character of a plant or animal species, and in the process the structure and biological functioning of the species often become much more complex.

Examples of changes in a species that seem to be the result of gene mutations and the operation of natural selection (survival of the fittest) are not difficult to find. The peppered moth in Great Britain is a case that has been studied in detail. This moth spends much of its time clinging to trees and is a favorite food of some birds. Until the middle of the nineteenth century, all peppered moths found by naturalists who collected specimens seem to have been light in color. Because the bark of the trees was usually light and often lichen-covered, this served as protection by making it difficult for the birds to see them. But after the Industrial Revolution had been under way for some time, so much soot fell in some areas of central Britain that the tree trunks and branches became darker. This made dark moths harder to see than light ones, and therefore the dark moths lived longer on average and produced more progeny. Because moths go through a great many generations in a relatively short period of time, in some of the more highly industrialized areas of Britain natural selection almost completely replaced the light peppered moths with the dark ones.

Genes contain two **alleles,** one from each parent, that affect particular characteristics. In sexually reproducing organisms, the alleles transmit characteristics from the parents to the

---

[1]As is the case with many major scientific breakthroughs, the significance of Mendel's work was not immediately understood. Although he published his results in 1866, their importance was not recognized until 1900.

Theories, Proofs, and the Darwinian Story

The peppered moth example has been cited in this text and in most other textbooks about evolution for at least the last twenty years. Why do textbook authors all choose this example? We do so in large part because it fits the Darwinian story of evolution so well. Recently, social scientist Michael Majerus pointed out that the moth photos, on which much of the story was based, were staged and that there were serious design flaws with the original peppered moth experiments.

Despite the problems he found in the experiment, Dr. Majerus, and most moth experts, believe that the basic story about the peppered moths holds up and that the story they tell is "qualitatively right." But the recent discussion of the problems with the original experiment provides good insight into the scientific method. The scientific method directs scientists to question everything because there is always a chance that a "proof" will slip through the cracks, leading to false beliefs, especially when a theory comes to be strongly believed by most scientists. The problem is that when reports of observations fit the way we already think, we tend to be less questioning than we otherwise would be. After reviewing the broader evidence, almost all scientists continue to believe that some version of the Darwinian story of evolution holds, but they are continually testing it in order to refine and improve it so that it better fits the empirical data.

offspring. A **dominant allele** is an allele that controls the characteristic that is transmitted to offspring. A **recessive allele** is an allele that will not transmit its characteristics unless both alleles in the pair are recessive. However, if two recessive alleles are paired, they will determine the characteristic affected. The peppered moth presents a relatively simple example of the operation of natural selection. The color of these moths is known to result from a dominant allele, a pair of dominant alleles for dark color, or a pair of recessive alleles for light color.

Human characteristics result from this same combination of dominant and recessive alleles. In the case of eye color, brown eyes are dominant and blue eyes are recessive. A person must have two recessive alleles to have the recessive characteristics; otherwise, the dominant characteristics prevail.

The first human beings or their humanlike precursors probably evolved in tropical regions where survival was possible without clothing. It is likely that they had very dark skin because light skin would have given little protection against the burning rays of the sun. There is debate about whether these people spread into other parts of the world or, instead, whether people developed independently in various parts of the world. Whichever the case, it is believed that in time they became capable of spreading out from Africa, eventually to most of the world. This was probably because their physical characteristics changed. For instance, early hominids probably did not walk upright, but when they developed that ability, they could travel more efficiently. More important, perhaps, was their development of tool making. With tools they could hunt or scavenge other animals, so they could consume more protein and fat than their low-energy vegetarian diet would have provided. Not only their bodies but also their brains would have been charged with more energy. The brain needs lots of energy to grow. As their diet expanded, hominids could physically and intellectually expand their territory.

All early hominids were probably dark-skinned. As they moved, that changed. In the most northern of the territories into which they expanded, the sun was very weak, especially in the long winters, and was often hidden by clouds or fog. Dark skin, which had been an advantage in warm, sunny climates, became a disadvantage because the sun's rays, by penetrating human skin, help produce vitamin D, which is an essential element in nutrition. Populations that remained in these colder regions for very long periods of time—perhaps 100,000 years or more—seem gradually, through gene mutations and the process of natural selection, to have developed much lighter shades of skin.

Limitations of Natural Selection.   Natural selection does not completely account for all evolutionary changes. In small groups, some such changes may result from gene mutations that are harmless but do not create characteristics that contribute to survival. But other characteristics developed by such groups may increase their chances of survival, and so they grow in number and spread over wider areas. Natural selection may explain the dark skins of black Africans and the lighter skins of northern Europeans, but it is not an obvious explanation of some other racial characteristics, such as the different construction of the eyes in Asian and Occidental people, nor does it account for as much similarity as exists. Therefore work in this area will likely continue.

Recent Developments in Genetics

In recent years scientists have significantly extended our knowledge of genetics. Whereas once it was thought that genes were the building blocks of life, today scientists have unraveled the gene and discovered a small building block, **DNA**, or deoxyribonucleic acid, the basic chemical building block of genes. Scientists had known for a long time that DNA existed, but it was only in 1953 that James Watson and Francis Crick unraveled its double helix structure, discovering that DNA resembled a spiral staircase. They found that each of the steps serves as a code word and determines how amino acids are linked into the proteins of which all living things are made. It was like discovering the blueprint for life (but not how life was originally created or what force had drawn the blueprint).

In the 1970s a further advance was made. Professor Paul Berg altered, or spliced, a gene. Rather than merely reading the blueprint, he had changed it. This opened up a whole new field. If scientists could change a gene, they could exercise some control over living organisms by cloning—that is, duplicating—existing forms and, possibly, building new ones. This process is called **genetic engineering**, rearranging genetic material to create new, man-made life forms or change existing ones. In response—demonstrating one of the interconnections between science and other fields that we see throughout this text—the price of genetic engineering stocks on Wall Street went wild as everyone tried to get in on the action.

In 1973 an international project, the Human Genome Project, was begun. Its purpose was to map, or identify, all the human genes. By 2001 the project was completed, with the mapping of a human being's entire set of genes. It's like having a set of directions to what makes us biologically what we are. This achievement was reached through the competitive efforts of government—the National Human Genome Research Institute directed by James Watson and his successor, Francis S. Collins—and a private enterprise, Celera Genomics, headed by J. Craig Ventner. They found that humans had only about 30,000 genes, about 11,000 more than a worm, and that humans share many genes with a wide variety of animals.

This genetic map has given us a much better understanding of the genetic causes of differences among people and what can cause changes in people. Scientific research using

Analyzing DNA.

this enormous amount of raw information has taken off in many directions, and will likely have to be complemented by a study of the many proteins that are the building blocks of cells. Thus a new applied science, protomics, is building on the genome project. This study is still in its early stages, although some scientists believe that soon they will be able to combine the nonliving chemicals that make up DNA, and by combining them in the right proportions, be able to turn those chemicals into something living. The major breakthroughs from genetic engineering for medicine are, however, probably decades away.

Having our genetic codes presents many social and ethical dilemmas. Can we extend life spans by one hundred years? If we can, should we? Can we create new life forms? If so, what rights would they have?

Back in 1988, cloning got a lot of publicity when white mice that had been genetically altered were patented by the U.S. Patent Office so that the laboratory that had developed these mice could sell them to other laboratories for various scientific procedures. Before that, there had already been genetic engineering of plants to improve basic grains such as rice, leading to India's "green revolution" and more food at less cost for its people. In 1997, Scottish scientists succeeded in cloning sheep.

Since that time, many more species of animals have been cloned. Some people even believe that it may be possible to clone extinct species, a fantasy explored in the book and movie *Jurassic Park*. In the near future, it is likely that scientists somewhere will clone humans, raising many ethical questions that society has not yet dealt with. The American Medical Association has endorsed limited human embryo cloning for medical purposes, but there are major debates about where medical research should draw the line.

Some Implications of Recent Developments

Changes in technology present society with extraordinarily difficult questions. If, for instance, parents could choose characteristics for their children, what characteristics would they choose and how would their decisions affect the overall population? Will a line be drawn forbidding cloning of human beings but permitting genetic alteration and possibly control of existing human beings? Who would draw such a line and how would its boundaries be enforced? The information gathered by researchers may be used in unforeseen and possibly undesirable ways. For instance, a government might collect knowledge about its citizens and use it to manipulate them. Or pension systems might use it to identify potentially long-lived people and charge them more for pensions. Or insurance companies might use the information to deny medical coverage to individuals who are predisposed to certain diseases. We can expect significant social repercussions from this scientific enterprise throughout the twenty-first century.

Moral, political, religious, scientific, and governmental forces will undoubtedly mobilize on an international scale for debates on these issues. Thinking about them gives you a sense of how new discoveries can have profound effects on the social system

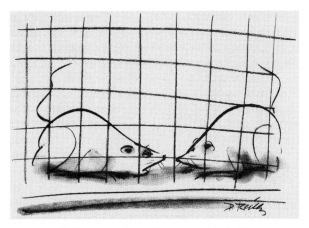

"It'll never work out. She's patented, he isn't."

in which we live. In short, our future social evolution will likely be substantially influenced by the information we have about our human evolution. What we know will change what we are.

Should the Species Be Regrouped?   As our knowledge of biology has progressed and we have developed far more information about the genetic makeup of life-forms, our abilities to differentiate species and to place them in orders of progression have changed enormously. The divisions of the species that we currently use were created by Carolus Linnaeus (1707–1778). His divisions were determined primarily by physical traits. As our knowledge of genetic makeup has improved, we have come to realize that physical similarities do not necessarily imply genetic similarity, and vice versa. Given the importance of genetic makeup, it would seem logical to organize the species by genetic components. However, division by physical characteristics is still the dominant division used. This is an example of the inertia in any system of knowledge and terminology. They evolve slowly.

Sociobiology

The study of genetics is not the only evolution-related field to experience progress; the study of evolution itself has progressed, and on one front it has been extended.

A group of scientists called *sociobiologists* has argued that human behavior evolves in the same direction that anatomy and body chemistry do: to increase the chances of survival of the species. Behavior that does not increase chances of survival will eventually lead to destruction. **Sociobiology** is a combination of sociological and biological reflections that theorize a genetic basis for human behavior.

In a 1975 book, *Sociobiology, the New Synthesis,* Harvard entomologist (one who studies insects) Edward O. Wilson advanced the thesis of sociobiology and expanded it in a 1978 book, *On Human Nature,* and a 1982 book, *Genes, Mind and Culture.* The arguments supporting sociobiology are complicated, but an example may help clarify the reasoning sociobiologists use. People are born with an inherent fear of strangers. This fear is a necessary genetic trait; it is a form of "prepared learning" that can be seen in infants less than a year old. If infants did not have this fear, they would be more susceptible to attack and thus less likely to survive. Over generations, more individuals who exhibit this trait generally will survive than individuals who do not, and eventually the genetic trait will become inherent in the species.

The argument may seem simple and of little consequence, but if we replace "strangers" with "persons of another race" the argument becomes more problematic and conflicts with our society's views on equity. People can justify or at least rationalize any behavior as being "in their genes." Therefore sociobiology has provoked strong attacks that it "justifies racism." In response, sociobiologists point out that their argument is not that genes directly control behavior, but rather that genes play a role. Wilson states, "We're suggesting that there is a mechanism which one sees during evolution continuously around the circuit: genetic change, cultural change, genetic change, and so on." The issues raised are highly controversial and are reminiscent of the free will–determinism issue early Christian philosophers debated. Do we do what we do because we are programmed to do it, or do we do it by choice? We suspect the debate will continue for some time.

The concerns about the almost singular focus of sociobiology on genetic natural selection has led to the development of a new field of psychology—evolutionary social psychology. This field accepts that biological and genetic factors play a role in explaining behavior but argues that other factors are also important.

Punctuated Equilibrium versus Gradual Change

Evolution theory is also being challenged on another front. Darwin saw evolution as a gradual process of natural selection and survival of the fittest as the most likely phenomenon. Now evolutionists such as paleoanthropologist Niles Eldredge and polymath Stephen Jay Gould[2] argue that evolution is characterized by long periods of relative stability that are punctuated by sudden changes, followed by more stability, followed by more changes, and so on. One hypothesis why this occurs is that changes in environment cause species to diversify and specialize into several new niches, creating new lineages. In Gould's theory, a species will be unchanged for thousands or hundreds of thousands of years and then suddenly something will happen that will change it (perhaps gene splicing?) or even wipe it out. The authors think of Gould's theory as macroevolution—periodic sudden large changes—and of the concept of gradual evolution as microevolution, a continuous, almost unnoticeable succession of small changes.

Archaeologists examine a fossil.

The debate centers on fossil evidence from millions of years ago that paleoanthropologists find in their digs. In the study of evolution, archaeologists have found fossils that demonstrate the changes various species such as humans have undergone. However, large gaps that scientists expected to fill eventually somehow remain. It is here that Gould's theory enters. Gould's **punctuated equilibrium** theory holds that evolution is a stop/go process of sudden change, with long intervening periods of no change.

The difference between punctuated equilibrium and gradual evolution can be seen in Figure 2.1. The straight upward-sloping line represents the traditional view, and the new view, punctuated equilibrium, is depicted by the horizontal lines with sudden upward jumps or stages every million

---

[2]A *polymath* is a person of encyclopedic learning, and the term has been applied to Gould because he was a biologist, geologist, and historian; he was also a leading theorist on large-scale patterns in evolution and an informative writer.

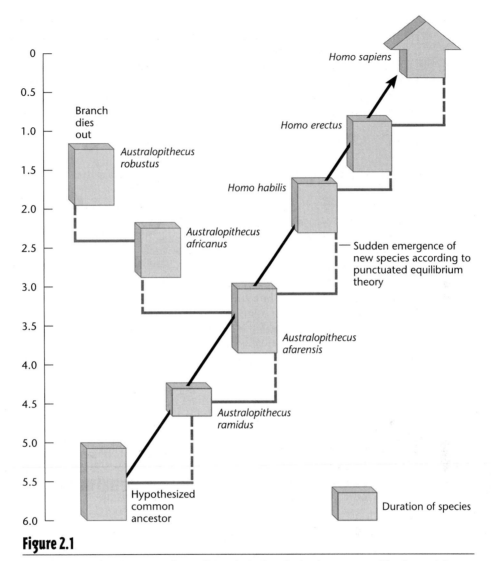

Figure 2.1

A new theory of evolution. In the traditional view, evolution is represented by the straight, upward-sloping line. In the new view, equilibrium is represented by the horizontal lines with sudden upward jumps at intervals of thousands or hundreds of thousands of years. Note that the lengths of the time periods on the vertical axis are the estimates of some authorities. Other authorities give other lengths of time, but all authorities agree that the time periods are very, very long. In the interest of simplicity, the graph does not show all the species that are now extinct but are thought to have existed at various periods along the way to Homo sapiens.

or so years. An example of sudden jumps has been found by Peter Williamson, a Harvard archaeologist, in snail fossils at Lake Turkana in Kenya. He discovered that over a two-million-year period there were two sudden changes in which major evolutionary changes

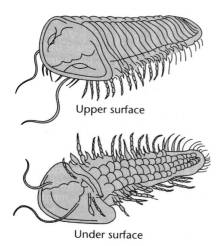

Upper surface

Under surface

Trilobytes resembled modern wood lice. The discovery of their fossils challenged Gould's theory of punctuated equilibrium.

occurred, and in between almost no change occurred. Thus, in Gould's view, evolution is merely a series of revolutions interspersed with long periods of calm. The punctuated equilibrium theory of evolution has attracted interest because it explains parts of the phenomenon that the old theory could not explain. For example, his theory could explain the sudden disappearance of dinosaurs millions of years ago. If evolution were a continual process, they would have died off slowly.

Gould's punctuated equilibrium theory was challenged in 1988 in the work of Peter Sheldon. Researchers before Gould had noted a significant gap in a set of crab-related creatures called trilobites. In the evolution of these trilobites, it appeared that there was a sudden stop, and then the set picked up again but with some different characteristics, especially in the number of ribs they had. The absence of trilobites that would have filled the gap with a steadily changing number of ribs had been cited as supporting Gould's theory. However, through painstaking work, Sheldon found specimens that filled in the gaps, showing that the average number of ribs the trilobites contained changed slowly over time.

Sheldon's findings generated much debate, and the general feeling was that both sides were in some way correct and that some changes may be punctuated and others may be gradual. But these views are evolving as more evidence is likely to be found in years to come.

The Evolution of Human Beings

Much of what happens in abstract scientific theory does not make news, except for articles in such periodicals as *National Geographic* or *Scientific American*. However, because it has seemed to some people to go against the Bible's version of creation, evolution has stirred popular press controversy from Darwin's time to ours, especially on the part of fundamentalists who believe in literal interpretations of the Bible.

Science, Faith, and Controversy

Just how much controversy it has caused can be seen in some famous court trials that have dealt with the issue. In 1925, for example, in the state of Tennessee a high school biology teacher, John Scopes, was prosecuted for, and found guilty of, breaking a state law forbidding the teaching of evolution in the public schools. The law and others like it in several neighboring states were not repealed until the late 1960s. In recent years, evolution has again made headlines, this time over attacks by a group called scientific creationists. **Scientific creationism** is not a science, but rather the belief that all present life-forms were spontaneously created at one point in time. Proponents have helped pass statutes in a number of states requiring the teaching of what are actually religious objections to evolution wherever the latter is presented in public school classes and textbooks. In response, publishers have suggested to their authors that they tone down the discussion of evolution in textbooks so that it is acceptable to the scientific creationists. The result has been that some textbooks have devoted only minimal discussion to evolution. Many educators have complained, and in 1985 California did something about those complaints. It informed publishers that unless their books dealt with the issue head on, their books would be dropped from public school purchases in California.

To put the matter bluntly, no organization of U.S. professional scientists has given any scientific support to creationism. In fact, almost all recognized scientific authorities strongly reject such assaults on academic freedom, the traditional scientific method, and the American principle of separation of church and state. A 1982 federal court decision endorsed the scientists' view by throwing out an Arkansas law mandating the study of scientific creationism in the state's public schools on grounds that creationism is not a science but religion, as it rests on a spiritual, not objective, premise and thus violates the separation of church and state principle that is part of the U.S. Constitution.

At the close of the twentieth century, the Kansas State Board of Education decided that individual school boards could choose whether to teach evolution. This step evoked spirited discussion throughout the country and does not represent a major trend in U.S. education. One of the objections to the provision was that its implementation would place graduates of Kansas school systems outside the mainstream of U.S. scientific theory and thus at a disadvantage in many future careers. Few Kansas school boards chose to discontinue the teaching of evolution, and in the state elections of 2000, several proponents of discontinuance who were running for reelection to the state board were defeated. The controversy has continued and in the early 2000s, local school boards of various states have had occasional clashes over textbook choices because of the evolution issue.

These debates are relevant here because scientific creationists have used Gould's new evolutionary theory of sudden rather than gradual evolutionary changes as scientific evidence to support their position. They say that the physical evidence of earth's multibillion-year existence can be explained by a series of creations, each one replacing the one before it. But as Gould explained in the court case, his theory is not antievolutionary; it merely challenges the *process* whereby evolution occurs.

The actual issues of what should be taught in classrooms are too complex to be addressed here. However, it must be stressed that although there have been sound professional scientific criticisms from time to time of the specifics of evolution, responsible scientists have not denied its basic point. The phrase *scientific creationism* is in many ways a contradiction in terms. Creationism begins and ends with a belief that life sprang from a sudden act of divine power and has not appreciably changed. This is an essentially religious version of natural origins. Science studies cause and effect and thus looks for continuity. This is not to say that religious faith cannot coexist with science. Ultimately "existence" or "being" must be explained, and no scientific theory can yet explain how something was created out of nothing.[3]

In the mid-1990s, a more acceptable but still controversial method of integrating religion into science developed. It was called **intelligent design** and it was the center of a fight about a textbook entitled *Of Pandas and People*. The central thesis of intelligent design is that the world is too complex to have developed on its own and that it can only

---

[3]Most religions solve this problem by postulating a god who created all, but as many Sunday school students have pondered, that still leaves open the question of who created God. At some point, faith must still play a role, and when an explanation relies on faith rather than reason, it becomes a religious explanation. Even the "big bang" cosmological theory has no explanation of what "banged."

be explained with some concept of initial intelligence. This is different from scientific creationism in that it does not challenge evolutionary evidence. It simply adds to it a theory of what is behind evolution. Critics see it as a sneaky way to introduce creationism into schools, while supporters see it as an acceptable hypothesis because it discusses issues that science and empirical evidence do not contradict.

Predecessors of Modern Humans

Some of the most interesting finds have concerned the evolution of humans. Though humans are closely related to the other primates, we are not certain how they evolved. However, with allowance for oversimplification, a basic outline can be drawn up.

The origin of life is thought to have occurred billions of years ago as one-celled organisms arose from the primordial ooze. Over the millennia, the organisms evolved into a wide variety of life-forms. Primates, from which humans developed, evolved some 65 to 70 million years ago, and a monkey–apelike creature from which the human species evolved is thought to have appeared somewhere between 22 and 38 million years ago. This apelike species is considered the common ancestor of modern apes and humans. Figure 2.2 gives you a general sense of that evolution. Each box in it represents a different species.

First let us explain that a **species** is a broad category of individuals who look alike and can mate with each other to produce fertile offspring. Today's humans are the only members of the species *Homo sapiens* (reasoning man).[4] They are also the only surviving human species. At least two other human species, *Homo habilis* (man with tool-making ability) and *Homo erectus* (man who stands up straight), have long since become extinct. All three of these types of human belong to the same umbrella category, or genus.

A human type more distantly related to us than any of the species just mentioned belongs to a separate genus, *Australopithecus,* creatures who have been extinct for millions of years. Humans and *Australopithecines* belong to the family *Hominidae,* along with several kinds of apes, both living and extinct. And the whole family belongs to the larger group of primates.

From Apelike Creature to Hominid. The date when these apelike creatures began to change to **hominids,** humanlike creatures who stood on two feet, is unclear, but it is believed to be somewhere between 6 and 10 million years ago in Africa, and several million years later in Europe and Asia. The fossil record for these time spans is poor or nonexistent, so the estimate is based on genetic differences between living humans and living primates combined with estimates of how long it has taken for the differences among these creatures to occur.

There is much debate about the lines of descent of humans and other primates. In trying to resolve this debate, researchers are turning more and more to the realm of molecular biology and chemical analysis of DNA done in the laboratory. According to fossil evidence, the evolutionary split between human beings and apes might have occurred as early as 25 million years ago and continued for a long time. This view was strengthened by a fossil said to be of a 15-million-year-old prehuman jawbone found in 1991 in southern

---

[4]To distinguish early modern humans from contemporary modern humans, some authorities use the term *homo sapiens sapiens* for the latest humans. In simplifying, we have not made this distinction, but it is useful to know that the term exists and what it means.

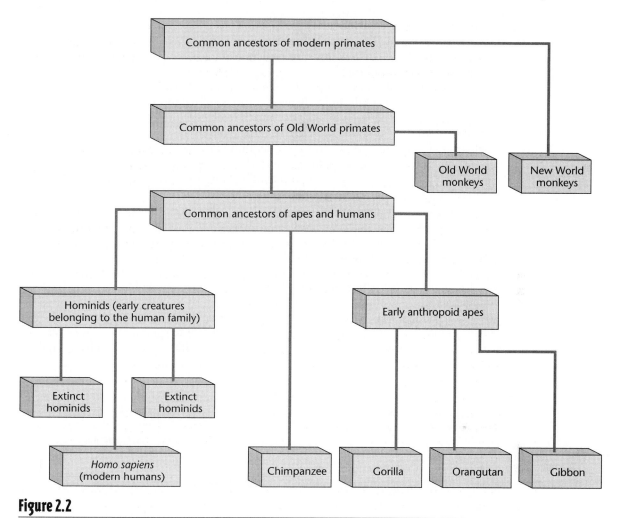

Figure 2.2

Possible lines of descent of humans and other higher primates from their common ancestral type.

Africa. This evidence, however, is contradicted by comparison of blood substances from human beings with those from chimpanzees, indicating the divergence was far more recent—perhaps only 7 million years ago. The DNA analysis has tended to support the later dating.

Although there is a dispute as to when the transition from ape to hominid occurred, anthropologists generally agree that all the primates, including hominids, once lived in trees and that during this period they developed limbs of great strength, with prehensile fingers and toes for grasping branches. Most primates, including the gibbon and the orangutan, still live in trees, but gorillas, like humans, live on the ground. Chimpanzees sleep in tree nests but spend much of the daytime on the ground. Apparently, one reason for this descent to the ground was their increase in size. Gorillas typically weigh from 400 to 600 pounds and are far too heavy for life in the trees. Even chimpanzees are too heavy to swing about through the branches unless they choose them with care. The great apes can, like humans, walk on two legs, but they have not achieved the human's erect posture and normally walk on all fours.

Perhaps the most important physical difference between human beings and apes is in the size and complexity of the brain. Between various animal species there seems as a rule to be some relationship between intelligence and the weight of the brain, especially its weight in relation to the body. But the most important factor is the organization of the brain. The chief advantage of large size seems to be that it provides space for additional cells and for more complex mechanisms. On the average, chimpanzees are smaller than humans, but some weigh as much as 120 or 130 pounds. The brain of a small human being typically weighs about three times that of a chimpanzee of the same body weight, and a normal human cerebral cortex, the part of the brain most concerned with memory and thought, may have ten times as many cells as the cerebral cortex of a typical ape. Today there seems little doubt that this complex brain is an essential basis of the human power to acquire a vast store of memories, to use word symbols, and to carry on abstract thought.

With respect to behavior, there are both striking similarities and striking differences between apes and human beings. Like humans, apes have family life and care for their young. They have emotional responses, can express gratitude and shame, and are often sociable and cooperative. On occasion they compete with one another, and sometimes they engage in play. Certain chimpanzees have responded well to training in various types of behavior such as smoking, riding a bicycle, eating with knife and fork, and drinking from a bottle. They have also shown ability to solve problems requiring reasoned judgment. But

*T*he Search for Eve

The development of genetic research has introduced a new battleground in the debate about our past. The work of molecular biologists has challenged many evolutionists' conviction about the timing of the human family tree and where it first took root. Until the early 1990s, some molecular biologists argued that the evolution from prehistoric to modern *Homo sapiens* occurred in one place, and that humans descended from one woman who lived approximately 200,000 years ago.

These molecular biologists examined the genetic differences between chimpanzees and humans and found that the differences were surprisingly small—so small, in fact, that they believe chimpanzees parted company from humans only about five to seven million years ago. The microbiologists went on to examine mitochondrial DNA, which is inherited only through the mother, from the placentas of 147 pregnant women, choosing women from all over the world. They found that the differences in DNA among people all over the world were amazingly small, which suggests that the differences among peoples of the world are also small. Hypothesizing that about 2 to 4 percent of the DNA components will mutate over the course of a million years, they came to the conclusion that some time around 200,000 years ago a woman must have existed from whom all now-living human beings are descended. Their research caused much debate. In 1992, however, they discovered an error in their calculations and admitted that their results were far less conclusive than they had previously believed, but they still believed it had elements of truth.

This research has continued. Bryan Sykes, an Oxford geneticist, argues that he has found "the seven daughters of Eve," that these women lived 45,000 years ago, and that all existing humans descended from them.

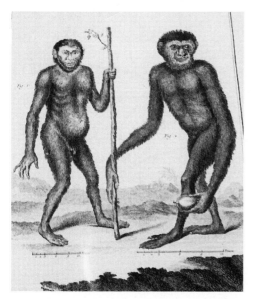

This eighteenth-century drawing from Diderot's Encyclopédie *shows what some people at that time imagined early humanlike creatures to have looked like.*

to all these accomplishments there are limits that argue unmistakably for the superior intellectual qualities of human beings.

The problem for physical anthropologists is to fill in the gaps of precisely how humans evolved, or if the evolutionary theory of punctuated equilibrium discussed earlier is true, to explain why the changes occurred when they did. In the last century, and especially since the 1930s, anthropologists have made tremendous strides in solving the puzzle. Archaeological finds date our ancestors back about 6 million years ago, and a wide variety of early hominid fossils have been given forbidding names such as *Africanus ramidus, Zinjanthropus,* and *Orrorin Tugenessis.*

A key element in determining when to date the start of modern human history is when these early hominids began using tools. Discoveries of tools with skeletons have been dated from 2.5 to 1.6 million years ago. This group of hominids is called *Homo habilis* because *habilis* means "maker."

Remaining Gaps.   Despite advances in fossil discoveries, there are still significant gaps in our knowledge of our ancestors, even among experts with their detailed and technical grasp of the subject. For instance, what happened during the intervening years? Were these apelike beings the predecessors of modern humans or only of apes? Did humans start out in a number of places or in only one, from which they dispersed throughout the world? These questions are still unanswered and probably always will be. However, genetic studies are leading to more specific answers. The latest genetic data suggest that all humans descended from Africa and spread throughout the world along the lines shown in Figure 2.3.

From Hominids to Homo Sapiens.   The earliest known species of *Homo* (human), *Homo habilis,* emerged from these early ancestors. *Homo habilis,* had a larger brain but smaller teeth than these early ancestors, and probably produced stone tools and other stone objects.

As we move closer to our own century, our information increases somewhat, but despite substantial progress, it is still sketchy and incomplete. An important find occurred in 1891 in Java when a Dutch surgeon, Dr. Eugene Dubois, unearthed another piece of the puzzle: *Homo erectus. Homo erectus* lived from about 1.8 million years ago to possibly as recently as 250,000 years ago and was a hunter who knew how to use fire.

It is believed that about 1.8 million years ago in Africa, *Homo erectus* developed from *Homo habilis* and then dispersed to Europe and Asia about a million years ago. *Homo erectus*'s brain was even larger and the teeth even smaller than *Homo habilis*'s. The lessening of tooth size indicates that dependence on hard food such as nuts and seeds, which requires powerful teeth and jaws, was decreasing as human diet veered toward softer foods such as fruit and, increasingly, meat. *Homo erectus* seems to have been very strong—which would have facilitated hunting.

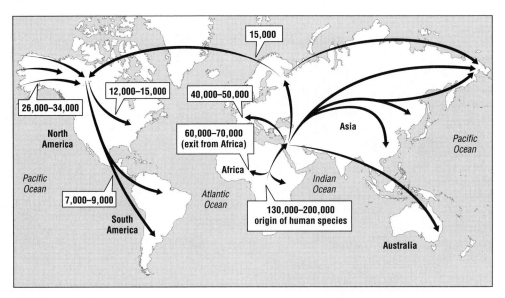

Figure 2.3

Early human migration.

Among *Homo erectus*'s nonbiodegradable waste are found more sophisticated objects than *Homo habilis* made, such as axes, and there is evidence, from ashes and charred material, that toward the end of *Homo erectus*'s existence, *Homo erectus* learned to use fire.

In 1997 two Spanish paleontologists, José Bermudez de Castro and Juan Arsuaga, announced that their study of 800,000-year-old fossils found in Spain leads them to believe that ***Homo antecessor*** (man who goes before) is a separate species who is a possible common ancestor of Neanderthals and *Homo sapiens* (discussed below). They speculated that the fossils they found in northern Spain represent emigrants from Africa.

Homo erectus seems to have become extinct nearly 500,000 years ago. The reasons are not at all clear. Artifacts of *Homo erectus,* while more sophisticated than those of their predecessors, do not show much change over more than a million years. Thus, one theory holds that *Homo erectus* may have been too conservative and inflexible to adapt to changing conditions.

Another theory is that *Homo erectus* did change, separating into two branches. One branch was the Neanderthals and the other was the modern human, *Homo sapiens.* **Homo sapiens** is a group of hominids who began to differ from their predecessors by their larger brains and by the better quality tools they made. European and African sites have yielded some fossils of these human ancestors ranging roughly from 200,000 to 300,000 years old, but according to genetic evidence they may have existed as long ago as 800,000 years—earlier than the fossil record. We call ourselves today members of *Homo sapiens.* A 2003 fossil find of modern man in Ethiopia fits with recent genetic studies of the time and place of the emergence of humankind. These support the replacement theory—"Out of Africa"—that a late migration of humans eventually supplanted all other humanlike species that were around the world at the time, such as Neanderthals.

Homo sapiens (reasoning man) was a species composed of people who were more highly developed than *Homo erectus*. They first appeared in Africa and Europe about the same time that *Homo erectus* was disappearing. Once again we see the new people displaying larger brains than the people they were replacing, and they differed so much from *Homo erectus* that they were assigned to a new species. It is the species to which all modern human beings belong today. However, early *Homo sapiens* shared many characteristics with *Homo erectus*. They seem to have been unable, for instance, to adapt to harsh climates, or to find food more easily than did *Homo erectus*.

Neanderthals.   Remains from periods longer than 100,000 years ago are few. We do know, however, that the evolutionary network produced the **Neanderthals,** who bore a close resemblance to modern human beings, about 100,000 years ago. Despite this close resemblance, the recent fossil evidence and genetic studies strongly suggest that the Neanderthals were not our ancestors. Instead, they probably shared a common ancestor with modern man. If modern features already existed in Africa 160,000 years ago, we could not have descended from a species like the Neanderthals.

Neanderthals get their name from the Neander Valley in Germany, where in 1856 the first evidence of their existence was found. They lived in Europe and spread to Asia, although a few researchers believe they developed independently in Asia. Physically, they differ from all other people, modern or extinct, in the shape of their heads and, strangely, in the length of their thumbs, which were about as long as their other fingers.

It used to be thought that Neanderthals were dim-witted, slouching cavemen completely covered with hair. But this reputation is based on just one fossil, which modern scholarship has proved happened to be that of an old, diseased, and injured man. He was approximately forty or forty-five years old when he died—very old for people at that time. Healthy Neanderthals probably walked erect. Objects found at Neanderthal sites show that Neanderthals could make complex tools, and characteristics of their skulls, and what can be deduced from skulls about their brains, mean that they probably could speak, although perhaps not with the full range of sounds that modern humans make. Sites also show that they did not necessarily live in caves, but if they did they altered the caves to make them more livable. Sometimes, it appears, they built shelters rather than settled in caves. In 1996 scientists digging at a Neanderthal site in Slovenia announced they had found what appeared to be a musical instrument, a flute made from a bear bone.

As we will discuss in later chapters, the development of language capability was a major evolutionary step. (See also accompanying box on the uniqueness of the human species.) It allowed the species much greater interaction and hence social development than could occur in nonspeaking species. In doing so, it made the passing on of learned knowledge about the environment much more efficient. It also allowed the species to create concepts of time, space, and quantity, thereby creating the potential for symbolic interaction.

The Neanderthals were powerfully built but somewhat shorter—about 5 feet 4 inches—than present-day males. They had sloping foreheads, heavy ridges over the eyes, large wide noses, and protruding jaws, and the Neanderthal brain was larger than that of the average modern person. A tribute to their humanity is the fact that among the buried remains are people who were handicapped or aged, which means that Neanderthals cared enough and were organized enough to provide for these economically unproductive members of their communities.

*I*s the Human Species Unique?

There is an ongoing debate among social scientists about whether the human species is unique. The argument that human beings are unique emphasizes that (1) only humans can think and reason, (2) only humans can communicate with others by means of language, and (3) only humans can use tools. Each of these points is debatable. Social scientists who argue that human beings are not unique point out that animals have solved enormously complex problems, some better than humans have.

Certain social scientists argue that language is not limited to humans and have shown that chimpanzees can communicate by sign language and by touching geometric symbols. One chimp has learned over 150 different signs, and a psychologist has taught a gorilla, Koko, more than 500 words. Moreover, Koko can express emotion: When her pet cat was killed in a traffic accident, she mourned its death. After a time, she "asked" to be given another cat to care for and love. Moreover, the gorilla specifically asked that it be replaced with a Manx cat (a highly unusual breed remarkable for having no tail).

The ability to use tools, disputants hold, is another characteristic not unique to human beings. Yes, humans have a greater ability to devise and use tools, and that ability has given them power over other creatures, but power is not necessarily differentiation, and animals use a variety of tools and social structures. For example, the cattle-tending ant gets honeydew by cultivating aphids and other insects who secrete it, and it even constructs shelters, such as underground galleries, in which to herd its aphids.

To counter these arguments, supporters of human uniqueness assert that the power of the human mind to solve complex problems goes far beyond that of animals and that although animals can learn words, they cannot learn syntax, an important aspect of language. As the linguist Noam Chomsky put it, to say that animals can communicate with each other by language is like saying that because people can rise into the air by jumping they can fly like birds, only not as well.

What difference does it make whether human beings are unique? A lot. Consider the following questions: Is it morally wrong to use animals in experiments? Should we eat meat? If you believe that human beings are unique, it is relatively easy to argue that animals can and should be used by human beings. If human beings are not unique, then it is much harder (but not impossible) to argue in favor

Teaching Koko to read.

of using animals in ways that we would not use human beings.

In the space between these two views on the morality of killing living creatures, we find a number of places where we can draw a line. It may, for example, be okay to kill a cockroach, but not a dog, a cow, or a pig. Precisely where to draw that line is the problem, however, and some radical thinkers have even argued that not only is there nothing distinctive about human beings, but that it is moral for society to eliminate individuals whose life is no longer worth living—for instance,

people with brain damage or individuals who have lived out their "useful" lives and are no longer able to care for themselves.

Don't expect any of these debates to be settled any time soon; rather, we ask you to acknowledge here, and throughout this book, that recognizing the arguments of many sides, considering them thoroughly and objectively, and coming to a conclusion that does not stubbornly exclude every other theory are the essential qualities of a good social scientist.

To date, few Neanderthal sites have been found from the period 35,000–60,000 years ago. Because this is also the period in which they seem to have disappeared, there is little or no evidence of why they disappeared. Theories of what happened include the following: (1) they interbred with another group, Cro-Magnons (discussed below), and eventually Neanderthal characteristics were completely absorbed into Cro-Magnons; (2) they battled with Cro-Magnons in a struggle and were annihilated; and (3) they wandered away into regions that were too environmentally inhospitable for survival. Recent genetic testing seems to confirm, at least in Europe, that Neanderthals were replaced rather than absorbed into the Cro-Magnon gene pool.

Cro-Magnons.   There is another group of people whose origins are uncertain but who may have been the immediate precursors of *Homo sapiens*. **Cro-Magnons** were anatomically modern, tall, well-built people with skull capacity comparable to that of present-day humans. They are called Cro-Magnons from the name of the French village near which the first specimens were found in 1868. Cro-Magnons and other early anatomically modern sapiens existed before Neanderthals disappeared. In western Europe, no Cro-Magnon skeletons have been found older than 30,000 years, but 40,000-year-old tools that archaeologists believe must have been made by modern people have been found at a number of western European locations. Cro-Magnons appear to have flourished only beginning about 35,000 years ago. Their remains have been found at various European sites and, in smaller numbers, in the Near East, China, Indonesia, Australia, and Africa.

The remains indicate that they were not as strong as Neanderthals, probably because they didn't need to be. Less strength, for instance, means less food is necessary, so the same total amount of food could support a larger population.

Conclusion

Modern people are distinguished from their ancestors by more than physical characteristics. By about 35,000 years ago, they were exhibiting cultural sophistication, for example in the cave paintings that can still be seen, especially in southern France and northern Spain. The closer we come to our own times, the more evidence we find of such strategies as coping with cold climates by the construction and use of clothing and the building of shelters. There is also evidence of increasingly complex social organization and even some limited trade with groups as much as ninety miles apart.

There is, as is true of much anthropological theory, debate about these findings. For instance, one method of dating used was a controversial technique that relates the age of the human remains to the detection of when the artifacts discovered with the human remains were last heated. There are innumerable unanswered questions about the development of human beings. For example, what is there in the theory of natural selection that explains the various emergences of human behavior? And did most sophisticated behavior appear at roughly the same time, or were there successive advances? Because work continues in this fascinating field, it is likely that the answers to at least some of these questions, and to some of the other questions that you can think of, will one day be discovered, or at least deduced.

The Cro-Magnons, like the Neanderthals, were hunters and gatherers; they roamed from place to place in search of food and survivable weather. As we see in the next chapter, about 11,000 years ago that changed. The change was due to a technological development.

At this point, we stop our consideration of the origins of human beings, leaving the development in what anthropologists call the Stone Age, a period beginning more than 600,000 years ago and lasting to about 10,000 B.C. We make this break not because Stone Age humans were physically different from modern human beings, but because of the technological developments of the Stone Age, which significantly modified the way individuals interrelate.

Key Points

- Darwin's theory of evolution centers on the survival of the fittest or natural selection; beneficial mutation makes evolution possible.
- Genes contain DNA, which is the building block of living organisms. DNA contains the codes that determine an organism's development.
- Sociobiologists argue that behavior that decreases chances of survival will eventually be eliminated from human behavior.

- Whether evolution is punctuated or continuous is still much in debate.
- The evolutionary split between human beings and apes occurred more than 25 million years ago.
- The search for human origins has led to many fossil finds but not to a definitive statement: "This is where human beings began."
- Cro-Magnons may have been the immediate precursors of *Homo sapiens.*

Some Important Terms

alleles (33)
Cro-Magnons (49)
DNA (35)
dominant allele (34)
evolution (32)
genes (33)
genetic engineering (35)
genetics (33)

hominids (42)
Homo antecessor (46)
Homo erectus (45)
Homo habilis (45)
Homo sapiens (46)
intelligent design (41)
mutation (33)
natural selection (33)

Neanderthals (47)
primates (32)
punctuated equilibrium (38)
recessive allele (34)
scientific creationism (40)
sociobiology (37)
species (42)

Questions for Review and Discussion

1. Why do we say that the human being is a social creature?
2. Why are humans, apes, and monkeys all placed in the biological order of primates?
3. Explain Darwin's theory of evolution.
4. How have modern geneticists modified Darwin's theory?
5. Can scientists create life? What possibilities can you see in genetic engineering?
6. How does sociobiology explain the development of human behavior?
7. What is the theory of punctuated equilibrium, and why is it important?
8. Should scientific creationism be taught in schools? Why or why not?
9. How long ago do you think humanlike creatures appeared on earth? Why is it so hard to determine the date, and why do you think we keep trying?
10. Who are some of the earliest precursors of human beings? What makes them like us? What makes them unlike us?
11. What three abilities gave humans advantages over all other creatures? Are humans unique?

Internet Questions

1. Read the short essay at www.cs.colorado.edu/~lindsay/creation/punk_eek.html, Specialization of Punctuation. What are some of the examples given as evidence for punctuated equilibrium? Is one mechanism of evolution singled out for these cases?
2. Pick one of the articles about a recent discovery in paleoanthropology listed on www.talkorigins.org/faqs/homs/recent.html. What was found? Where was it found?
3. Go to www.pbs.org/wgbh/evolution/library/11/1/real/e_m_sc_1.html. What are vestigial organs?
4. According to the information at www.ananova.com/news/story/sm_564642.html?menu=, even though humans and chimps share 98.7 percent of their genes, what makes them so different?
5. What does this business—www.savingsandclone.com—do, and what are the four areas?

For Further Study

Croswell, Ken, *Planet Quest: The Epic Discovery of Alien Solar Systems,* New York: Free Press, 1997.

Darwin, Charles, *The Origin of Species,* Irvin, Charlotte, and William Irving, eds., New York: Ungar, 1959 (first published in 1859).

Dawkins, Richard, *Climbing Mount Improbable,* New York: Norton, 1996.

Dennett, Daniel C., *Darwin's Dangerous Idea: Evolution and the Meaning of Life,* New York: Simon & Schuster, 1995.

Dunbar, Robin, *Grooming, Gossip, and the Evolution of Language,* Cambridge, MA: Harvard University Press, 1997.

Jolly, Alison, *Lucy's Legacy: Sex and Intelligence in Human Evolution,* Cambridge, MA: Harvard University Press, 1999.

Maddox, John, *What Remains to Be Discovered: Mapping the Secrets of the Universe, the Origins of Life, and the Future of the Human Race,* New York: Free Press, 1999.

Marks, Jonathan, *What It Means to Be 98% Chimpanzee: Apes, People, and Their Genes,* Berkeley: University of California Press, 2002.

Morris, Desmond, *Bodytalk: The Meaning of Human Gestures,* New York: Crown, 1995.

Norell, Mark A., et al., *Discovering Dinosaurs: Evolution, Extinction, and the Lessons of Prehistory,* Berkeley: University of California Press, 2000.

Nuland, Sherwin B., *The Wisdom of the Body,* New York: Knopf, 1997.

Olson, Steve, *Mapping Human History: Discovering the Past through Our Genes,* Boston: Houghton Mifflin, 2002.

Oppenheimer, Stephen, *Out of Eden: The Peopling of the World,* Essex: Constable and Robinson, 2003.

Sykes, Bryan, *The Seven Daughters of Eve,* New York: Norton, 2001.

Williams, George C., *The Pony Fish's Glory: And Other Clues to Plan and Purpose in Nature,* New York: Basic Books, 1997.

Wilson, Frank R., *The Hand: How Its Use Shapes the Brain, Language, and Human Culture,* New York: Pantheon, 1998.

WWW   Action Bioscience   www.actionbioscience.org

WWW   Creation/Evolution Newsgroup Archive   www.talkorigins.org

WWW   Genetic Engineering News   www.genengnews.com

WWW   Human Genome Project   www.doegenomes.org

WWW   National Center for Genetic Engineering and Biotechnology   www.biotec.or.th

WWW   A Science Odyssey: Human Evolution, Interactive   www.pbs.org/wgbh/aso/tryit/evolution/shockwave-nojs.html

WWW   Sociobiology   www.ship.edu/~cgboeree/sociobiology.html

Zimmer, Carl, *At the Water's Edge: Macroevolution and the Transformation of Life,* New York: Free Press, 1998.

Origins of Western Society

chapter 3

After reading this chapter, you should be able to:

- Explain why the domestication of animals and control of land were central developments that created society as we know it today
- Trace the development of modern civilization from Mesopotamia and Egypt to today
- Explain the Greek and Roman origins of modern civilization
- Distinguish three periods of the Middle Ages
- Explain the importance of the Renaissance to modern civilization
- Define the Age of Revolutions

Time is a river of passing events, and its current is strong. No sooner is a thing brought to sight than it is swept by and another takes its place—and this too will be swept away.

—Marcus Aurelius

Throughout most of the remainder of this book, we look at and contrast the origins, development, and operation of societies' cultures so that we can better understand modern problems. However, at this point it seems advantageous to take a whirlwind tour of history and the development of Western culture. On this tour, we see some of the influences that have led to the formation of the types of societies we have, and although what we can cover in a chapter is severely limited, we can at least introduce you to some of the terminology we use when we describe historical periods. The chief purpose of our tour, though, is to gain some historical perspective and use it to find continuity and similarities among periods and developments that, if we glance at them casually and individually, seem different from one another.

In the next section, we take you on that whirlwind tour, covering millennia in half pages. In doing so, we consider the origins of Western culture as embodied in the social, political, and economic institutions that shape our modern society.

From the Stone Age to the Agricultural Age

We ended the last chapter with a cliffhanger, saying some technological development significantly changed the nature of humankind and society. If you guessed that this development was the bow and arrow, you were right in guessing that Stone Age humans developed these, but wrong in thinking that was what caused the change. The bow and arrow improved Stone Age humans' ability to hunt but did not change the basics of their daily lives. Another technological development *did* fundamentally change society. Central developments that created society as we know it today occurred when human beings learned that they could exercise control over the land (through cultivation by hoe) and animals (through domestication for carrying, riding, pulling, and the systematic practice of egg gathering and milking). These developments moved human beings from the Stone Age to what we call the **Age of Agriculture,** a period beginning about 11,000 years ago and characterized at first by the storing of wild crops and then by the cultivation of land, domestication of animals, and creation of permanent communities. The Age of Agriculture changed the habits of most human beings from those of roving hunters to those of people living in a more or less fixed community.

The importance of these developments for society cannot be overemphasized. People could live in one place; they could accumulate more physical items and pass those on to their children. Moreover, once they could be assured of food, they could devote time to other aspects of life. During the Age of Agriculture, pottery was invented, making it easier to store surplus liquids; it was discovered how to make cloth from both flax (linen) and wool. Moreover, because agriculture and domesticated animals required constant care, people built permanent buildings, usually in clusters. Thus began villages.

The agricultural revolution produced significant population growth in what is now the Middle East and Europe, although village living fostered disease because there was little or no understanding of the need for sanitation. Moreover, the same technological developments that made farming possible also made warfare more effective. Horses provided better transportation, and bows and arrows provided better attack mechanisms. Archaeological excavation has revealed various weapons from this period. Although many could be used in hunting, they are also suitable for attacking and for holding off attackers. Conflict and the lack of sanitation kept the level of population from exploding.

Early Civilizations

Slowly over this period people addressed two issues that are crucial to the preservation and extension of the human life span: They learned about the need for sanitation, and they began to try to solve the problem of constant fighting. These developments were most pronounced in the Middle East. Approximately 4000 B.C., large numbers of people began moving into the lowlands of Mesopotamia (modern-day Iraq) and Egypt. During this time, writing developed (about 3000 B.C.) and with it began what we call recorded history. Because of that development we have a much better knowledge of this period than of prerecorded history.

The Cradle of Modern Civilization: Mesopotamia and Egypt

Although we do not know the reason for the development of cities in the Middle East, we can deduce that it was made possible by improved methods of cultivation, which created a surplus of food and improved sanitation conditions. Once in existence, cities took on the purposes of administration, commerce, and entertainment. It seems likely that in order to protect themselves from constant warfare, individuals submitted to a powerful leader, and for that protection they had to pay a certain percentage of their farm output.

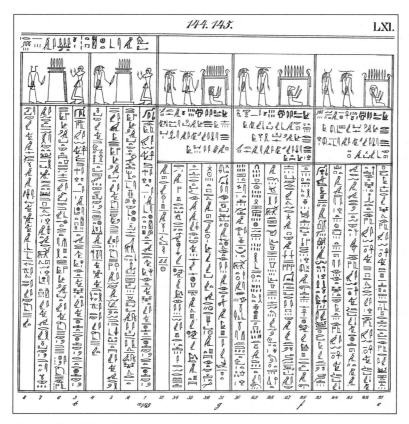

Early writing: hieroglyphics.

Thus began our basic political institution, which is the gathering of people into a spatially and ethnically defined unit organized and run by a small group whose efforts provide the stability within which individuals in the unit can work, play, buy, sell, and plan because they have been willing to recognize and pay administrators who will enforce accommodation among the members of the unit and defend the peace against outsiders.

Agricultural surpluses also created questions about the division of the surplus and the opportunity for other groups to take it away. Because of constant fighting among various localities, it probably became obvious to people that some method of stopping the fighting would make everyone better off, either because one group had won over all others or because they could come to an agreement. To further these ends, small localities coalesced into more or less unified kingdoms.

As the size of a kingdom increased, the leader of the kingdom likely became more and more removed from the ordinary inhabitants. As this happened, the leader became closely identified with divinity, either as a god or as a delegate of a god, and a feature of these early Middle Eastern countries was the king-god. The king-gods, in turn, appointed priests, and thus began pagan religious institutions.

As the kings gained power, they also gained control of the ownership of land, which was in the process of being transferred from individuals who farmed the land to the

Looting and Reporting History

The Iraq War of 2003 was won by the United States in short order, presenting the United States with the much harder problem of keeping the peace. Although few Americans knew it, the Iraq War took place in what was formerly Mesopotamia, which meant that an enormous amount of artifacts of world history was to be found in the museums of Iraq. After the fall of the Iraqi government, anarchy broke out in Iraq, and widespread looting took place. One of the buildings that was looted was the National Museum of Iraq. Newspapers reported that it was almost totally stripped of its treasures.

Liberal newspapers that had opposed the war made this big news (i.e., they reported it on the front page) and attacked the U.S. government for failing to protect the treasures of the world's history. Then suddenly the major attacks stopped,

as news filtered through that most of the precious items had not been stolen, but instead had been put into hiding by the museum staff. Now it was the conservative newspapers, which had supported the war, that were writing page one stories of the initial overreaction of the liberal press, while the liberal press reported the new information on back pages where few people read it.

What should one make of all this? First, that museum curators are quite resourceful in protecting their museums. Second, that antiquities are important, and the world community should do all it can to protect them, even in war. Third, don't completely trust what you read in the newspapers, especially what is written during periods when feelings are running strong on opposing sides. And finally, to get the best sense of what is really going on, it makes sense to read both liberal and conservative newspapers.

The stele of Hammurabi. The ancient legislator is shown on the left. He is discussing his laws (carved below) with the Sun God.

nobility who protected the land. We see in this process the organization of society into a military aristocracy, a priesthood, and, finally, a laboring class of landless peasants. Wars created the lowest class; the captured losers in a war became slaves. By about 3000 B.C., this organization had become stable and within it people, freed from the basic struggle merely to live another day, could begin to trust, to create, and to provide for the future. If we name the result *civilization*, we may say that by about 3800 B.C. a group called the Sumerians had civilized the Mesopotamian area, which is in modern-day Iraq.

To have an organization requires codifying its rules. To do that, one must recognize that what has been going on has in fact been going on and that there is a certain order in those activities. For example, when a child was murdered, the parents probably became angry and attempted some type of revenge, which brought on revenge for revenge in a cycle of individual retribution. If rules that incorporated the revenge could somehow be established, impulsive killing could be avoided. To do that, someone had to record those rules so that they could be known and followed, by both the leaders and the subjects.

The **Code of Hammurabi** is an early collection of rules, or laws, set up by King Hammurabi of Mesopotamia about 4,000 years ago. The code set up an "eye for an eye" system of retribution, combined with humanitarian rules such as prohibitions against defrauding the helpless.

The Mesopotamian political organization did not last; another group of individuals, less civilized and more warlike, soon overran the Sumerians. This group was the Semites. Even though the Semites won

𝓜ilestones of Civilization

Stone Age	2,500,000–10,000 B.C.*
Humans appear in China	25,000 B.C.
Age of Agriculture	11,000 B.C.
Copper Age	6500 B.C.
Egyptian civilization	5000 B.C.
Near Eastern (Mesopotamian) civilization	4000 B.C.
Bronze Age	3800 B.C.
Indian civilization	3000 B.C.
Chinese civilization	1800 B.C.
Iron Age	1000 B.C.
Greek civilization (at its height)	700 B.C.–500 B.C.
Roman civilization	753 B.C.–A.D. 476
Japanese civilization	A.D. 57
Middle Ages	A.D. 476–A.D. 1453
Crusades	A.D. 1095–A.D. 1291
Renaissance	A.D. 1400–A.D. 1600
Reformation	A.D. 1517–A.D. 1690
Voyages of discovery	A.D. 1450–A.D. 1600
Age of Revolutions	A.D. 1750–A.D. 1850
Victorian era	A.D. 1837–A.D. 1901
Edwardian era	A.D. 1901–A.D. 1914
World War I	A.D. 1914–A.D. 1918
World War II	A.D. 1939–A.D. 1945
Postwar nuclear era	A.D. 1945[†]

*Many of these dates are estimates or are subject to debate, or both.

[†]Many wars have occurred since 1945 and are still occurring, but the end of World War II began an era conventionally called "Postwar."

their war, they did not win the cultural competition, and their culture was soon absorbed into the Sumerian culture.

As the Semites were absorbed into the Mesopotamian culture, another culture, similar to the Mesopotamian, was flourishing in Egypt. Like Mesopotamian society, Egyptian society was ruled by a king-god. Because of the geography of the area, Egypt was free of hostile invasions (the sea and the desert made it difficult for attackers to menace Egypt). Combined with the warm, predictable climate and the fertile farmland of the Nile, this led to an extremely productive society that generated significant agricultural surpluses. The pyramids, great funerary temples, and rock-cut tombs in which the kings and queens of Egypt were laid to an uneasy rest are evidence both of the power of the king-gods and of the enormous surpluses generated by that culture.[1]

---

[1]Every known burial site has been shorn of its contents, whether by ancient marauders or modern archaeologists.

Development of the Greek Civilization

Throughout southern Europe, parallel developments like those in Mesopotamia were taking place, although they did not reach into most of those regions until much later. In Crete, part of ancient Greece, pictographic writing was known as early as 3000 B.C., but what we have defined as the civilizing process did not flourish until later—its heyday there was from about 2000 B.C. to about 1200 B.C., at which latter time physical Cretan civilization was suddenly destroyed, probably by an earthquake, tidal wave, volcanic eruption, some combination of these disasters, or even an invasion by the Doric tribes of the north. What exactly happened cannot be determined, simply because of the sheer finality of whatever it was that destroyed human constructs.

From about 700 B.C. to 500 B.C., a new Greek civilization emerged, and many of the roots of Western civilization and institutions are to be found here. For example, Western political organizations have their foundations in the Greek **polis,** or political community. The Greek polis was originally an agricultural village. These villages or cities were also independent political units. The two most famous are Sparta and Athens (today Sparta is a town of about 5,000 inhabitants, whereas Athens bustles with more than a million people and is the capital of modern Greece). The citizens of such a unit were seen as relatives of each other, theoretically descended from a common ancestor. The Greek philosopher Aristotle argued that the polis was a natural outgrowth of the human being's nature. He felt that without law and justice the human being was the worst of animals; with law and justice, the best.

The concept of the polis and its increasingly skillful and sophisticated implementation resulted in the growth of such cities and in the growth of their contacts with each other and with other civilizations. With the development of trade, industry, and colonization, a new class of people, the merchants, became wealthy and important. This change caused trouble for the polis: division within the ruling aristocracy and the establishment of tyranny, or rule by a tyrant, a monarch or leader who had gained power in an unregulated but not necessarily wicked way and who governed through one-man rule. This is one example among many in the history of economic changes and changes in the distribution of wealth leading to changes in both politics and the social relations among people. Although the concept of "tyrant" was antithetical to the polis, and the custom of rule by tyrant lasted only about a hundred years, tyrants played a role in reducing civil wars among the polis and in encouraging economic and social change necessary for the development of technology, the arts, and literature; reducing the grip of the aristocracy; and, paradoxically, giving more people the potential for roles in government.

The Persian Empire

In the fifth century B.C., the Persian Empire arose in lower Mesopotamia, and in the fourth century B.C. the Macedonians conquered the various city-states that made up the world of Greece. The Macedonians had no polis and were ruled loosely by a king. A council of aristocracy served as a check on the king's power, and by 338 B.C. one of these kings, King Philip II, had conquered Athens and other Greek city-states, a plan that he conceived and carried out over a period of thirty years. Philip was assassinated in 336 B.C., and his rule was assumed by his son, Alexander the Great, who was not yet twenty years old. By the time Alexander died, overcome by a sudden and unidentified disease when he was only

The Eastern Connection

In this chapter and throughout this book, we have concentrated on Western culture, institutions, and history. We have done so because we have to stop somewhere; to include the East we would have to make the book twice as long. However, it would be inappropriate not to mention some of the multitudinous ideas in Western culture that first developed in the East.

In terms of beginnings of civilizations, the East developed slightly later than the West, but once developed, it quickly surpassed the West in political and economic organization, in technology, and in sophisticated philosophy.

Language—India, five or six thousand years ago. The language is Indo-European, and today half the world's population speaks languages derived from it. These include Hindi, Lithuanian, Russian, Greek, Gaelic, Latin, German, all the Scandinavian languages, English, Italian, French, Spanish, Portuguese, Romanian.

History—India dates the beginning of the modern era at 3102 B.C.

Bronze casting—China, 1600 B.C.

Monotheism (only one god, not multiple gods)— Iran, sixth century B.C.

Kite—China, 400 B.C.

Sanskrit grammar, with 3,873 rules—India, 500 B.C.

Great Wall of China—begun in 209 B.C.

Cable suspension bridge—China, 100 B.C.

Sophisticated eye surgery, including cataract removal—India, before A.D. 33

Wheelbarrow—China, A.D. 231

A centralized nation-state—as early as the sixth century A.D., Japan had a system of centralized government (borrowed from China)

Arabic numerals (0, 1, 2, 3, 4, etc.)—India, ninth century A.D.

Trade—by the second century A.D., China was trading with Rome

Movable type (made of clay)—China, A.D. 1045

Movable type (made of metal)—Korea, A.D. 1302

Paper money—China, A.D. 811 (it was called flying cash because it could be transported so much more easily than silver or copper coins)

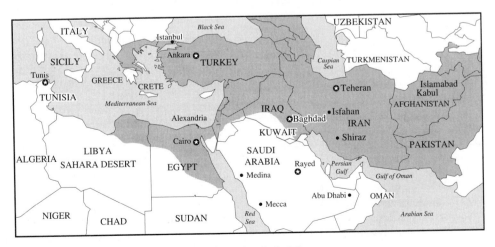

The Persian Empire (shown in the shaded area) at its height.

thirty-three years old, he had solidified his father's conquest of Greece and then gone on to conquer Egypt, almost all of what we now call the Middle East, and the greater part of India. To Alexander is attributed the demand, "Bring me more worlds to conquer."

Greek Civilization in the Persian Empire.   Notice that in contrast to the previous sections, we titled the last section "The Persian Empire," not "The Development of the Persian Civilization." The reason is that the Persian legacy was not cultural; its legacy was primarily the creation of an empire. Alexander's empire did not end the cultures and civilizations that made up the Persian Empire and, although conquered militarily, Greek culture won out over the Persian culture. Even the Persian Empire did not last long. After Alexander's sudden death in 323 B.C., the empire quickly collapsed. It is the Greek, not the Persian, cultural legacy that most strongly influenced modern society.

Many Greek ideas and institutions were revived almost eighteen hundred years later in what became known as the Renaissance. (*Renaissance* may be translated "rebirth," and Greek ideas were some of the concepts that were reborn.) Because of their predominance in the Renaissance, the ideas of Greek society played a central role in the subsequent history of Western civilization.

How the Greeks Tried Laughing All the Way to the Peace Talks

In the year 413 B.C., Athens suffered a terrifying defeat: Its navy was destroyed. The opposing army, the Spartans, was nearby and well equipped. Allies not only deserted Athens but also joined the enemy. Aristophanes, a famous comic writer, chose to face this despair by writing a play.

Lysistrata is about a unique way to enforce peace. The plot is simple: The heroine, Lysistrata, organizes the women of both sides to refuse sex with their husbands and lovers until the men agree to end the war.

Initially most of the women are unwilling to give up sex themselves. Lysistrata convinces them by rational arguments that her plan will work. She persuades the older women to join, giving them a vital task—guarding the public treasury so that no money can be disbursed for the war. She holds them together when they waver after suffering without men for a long period (well, five days—but it's clear Aristophanes thought that was a long time). She knows, and she makes them realize, that if they stick together, and if they can endure longer than the men can endure, they will win.

When the men debate with her, she wins every point.

The men give in first. And their reward is even more than they hoped, because the women remind them that both sides worship the same gods, both sides have in the past done noble deeds in aid of the other, and in this quarrel surely they can compromise. After a little bickering, the opposing armies do come to an agreement, after which both sides join in a satisfying feast of all domestic joys (including, but not limited to, eating and drinking).

As you can see, the play is far more complex than it may have seemed at first. It is about sex, money, reason, greed, graft, war, politics, organization, cunning, religion, prejudice, psychology, folly, resolve, accommodation, denial, and triumph. It is even about love. In short, it is about the issues of social science.

P.S. *Lysistrata* is a play. In real life, the Spartans did not attack Athens immediately, and while they hesitated, the Athenians were able to build a whole new navy, defend their city, and win an honorable peace. What part the women of Athens played in the real peace must be left to your imagination.

Roman Civilization

As we mentioned earlier, individuals were organizing into social groups throughout southern and middle Europe in a period beginning about 4000 B.C. If we had thousands of pages to explain and you had hundreds of years to study, we could recount the history and interaction of these groups. We are forced to be selective, however, and the next civilization that we have time and room for is the Roman, which developed in what is now Italy. It developed later than many of the others, and as late as 1000 B.C. it remained a collection of unorganized tribes.

About 1000 B.C., Italy was invaded by its warlike neighbors who imposed their language and social organization on almost all of Italy. In the eighth century B.C., small villages were amalgamated into the city-state of Rome, and by the sixth century B.C. it had overthrown its foreign conquerors and become the center of Italy and Italian culture. Rome's dominance constituted what we call the Roman Empire, and it was to last almost a thousand years.

The Roman state was one in which the king, or caesar, was elected, although the office appears to have tended to remain in the same family. The ruler had extraordinary powers and could make arrests and even order capital punishment, but what was called the senate had veto power, and it was ultimately from the senate that the ruler derived his authority.

Individuals in Rome fell into two categories: the patricians and the plebeians. The patricians had all the power and privilege; the plebeians could hold no public or religious office. However, the need for the plebeians to fight in the constant wars that Rome undertook gave them power, and by 450 B.C. they were strong enough to enforce their demand for a major codification of Roman law. As the patrician–plebeian distinction broke down, another class distinction, based on wealth, contacts, and birth, developed, and most of the Roman leaders came only from the few families in this new aristocracy.

Roman civilization endured until the fifth century A.D., but it did not remain static. The Roman republic was transformed into the Roman Empire, and pagan religion gave way to Christianity; by the fourth century A.D., Christianity was the state religion.

Ruins of the Roman Forum.

The Romans exercised their power for centuries, and their influence pervades Western civilization today. They overran Greek civilization and incorporated it into their own, so that when Roman influence is transmitted to us, Greek influence is transmitted to us. Here are some of the things that make us live as Romans today:

The dominance of the family

The custom of women to rule in household matters and to have certain legal property rights

Political patronage

The "network" system of contacts for social and professional advancement

Ingenuity in solving technical problems

Reliance on and practice of all manner of engineering and inventive art

The concept of empire

Existence of a military-industrial complex

Second homes and resorts

Large agricultural holdings

The lure of city life

A flexible legal system that is constantly changing to suit circumstances, relying on a body of precedents to interpret and modify statutes

The names of all of our months and the organization of our calendar

From the four phenomena that are the most striking in Roman history—military undertakings, engineering, law, and political administration—we pick out the last as basic to all the rest. Roman political administration was efficient, reasonable, flexible, realistic, and humane. Because the government was so well organized, Rome was able to devote its ample excess energies to building, manufacture, agriculture, literature, trade, moral philosophy, and world conquest. Rome also had the leisure and Latin language to develop, refine, and express its thoughts, principles, discoveries, speculations, and decrees. Today, Latin forms the basis of hundreds of thousands of words in the English language, although semantically English is a Germanic language. However, Rome's success also had its negative side: Along with the benefits came complacency, ambition, greed, arrogance, and tyranny. Because these traits are more dramatic than the steady march of its well-ordered society, today we often think of ancient Rome in terms of the religious conflict, savage combat, extravagant public carnivals, graft, brutal suppression of opposition, and dissolution that eventually weakened control over enormous territory[2] and caused popular uprisings, financial collapse, and military defeat—in short, the fall of the **Roman Empire,** the enormous territory encompassing Great Britain, most of Europe, northern Africa, and the Middle East administered by the Romans.

Rome was attacked by other groups from both the north and the south, and by about A.D. 500 the population of the empire had declined from an estimated 1.5 million to about 300,000, and Rome, as a civilization, ended. Why did it end? It is hard to say, and maybe that is not even the right question. Edward Gibbon argues in *The Decline and Fall of the*

---

[2]The empire was constantly conquering, annexing, and losing pieces of territory, but at its largest, about A.D. 200, it included what we call today the Middle East, North Africa, Spain, Great Britain, and most of present-day Europe.

Roman Empire that perhaps the question should not be, Why did Rome fall? but, Why did it last so long?

The Middle Ages (A.D. 476–1453)

With the fall of Rome came the advent of a period we now call the **Middle Ages,** from about A.D. 476 to A.D. 1453, between Roman civilization and modern civilization.

The Middle Ages began in 476 with the defeat of the Roman Empire by wandering tribes that roamed over much of what is now northern and central Europe.[3] Even though the northern tribes had conquered Rome, Roman culture at least partially conquered the northern tribal culture. The tribes began to adopt some of the technological, social, religious, and political structures that the Roman Empire had developed.

As Roman culture spread north, Muslim culture spread across North Africa and into all of Spain and Portugal. Because Muslims controlled the Mediterranean Sea and Europe's contacts with the Orient were curtailed, Europe was forced into a kind of isolation. The coastal cities became less prosperous, and workers were displaced from seagoing occupations to agriculture. Wandering decreased, agricultural activity increased, and life became centered on a manor, or **feudal estate**—an area ruled by a lord. The land on the feudal estate was worked by **serfs,** peasants who were bound to a particular manor (feudal estate) and subject to their feudal lord's will. Christianity, which had been flourishing in the Roman Empire, retained and strengthened its influence, partly because it had modeled its administrative structure on the efficient civil Roman organization.

The church consolidated its political and military power by asserting its independence from civilian rulers and by fending off attempts by the Muslims to encroach further on Europe. It also had the time and energy to fight bitter quarrels within its own ranks on matters of religious doctrine. Meanwhile the holders of large manors quarreled, reconciled, and rearranged their allegiances among themselves and the various kings and civil administrators. The local lords, the kings, and the church constantly jockeyed for power, wealth, and land as they all struggled to control these available resources and seize them from one another.

Manor life in the early Middle Ages was relatively straightforward: You were born, you lived a life similar to that of your parents in the same place that they lived, and you died, leaving your children to continue the process. The manor estate was owned by the feudal lord, although ownership was not defined in the way we define it today. Land was not thought of as something that could be bought and sold, but rather as something that belonged to the lord because it belonged to the lord. The peasants, or serfs, did the work on the farm and in return received protection from the lord and enough food to live. The lord provided some security from attack.

What is simple has a tendency to become complex. As the lords became accustomed to managing the land, they began to feel like real owners and to act like owners. Toward the end of the tenth century, the concept of land ownership gained acceptance. This was logically followed by preoccupation with acquiring more and more land while concern for preserving the old feudal way of life faded.

---

[3]The Eastern Empire, which had been officially divided from the western Roman Empire in A.D. 395, survived until 1453, when the Turks conquered its capital, Constantinople. Today Constantinople is the Turkish city of Istanbul.

Origins of Pakistani Society

Although there isn't space here to discuss the origins of Eastern society, it is so important that you have some sense of Eastern culture that we offer brief insights into other countries' social, cultural, political, and economic institutions throughout the book. Here, Pakistan will be our example.

As a nation-state, Pakistan has been around for about fifty-five years, but it has origins that predate the birth of Islam (A.D. 622), the religion today of the majority of its inhabitants. By 5000 B.C., a civilization was already flourishing in the Indus Valley, then still a part of India. Excavations of its two greatest cities, Mohenjo Daro and Harappa, show that it had an extensive system of civic administration as well as sewage, drainage, and irrigation systems.

About 1500 B.C., this civilization was supplanted by a group of Indo-European tribes from central Asia who established their own rule over India and instituted a caste system to maintain a permanent hold over the conquered people, from whom, however, they assimilated many things. In the fourth century B.C., when Alexander the Great advanced up the Indus River, a group called Mauryas was already laying the foundations of the first Indian Empire, which saw the growth of economics, learning, and Sanskrit (Sanskrit is one of the earliest of languages, the mother of dozens of the world's modern languages). The Mauryas's

religion was Buddhism, different from the Hinduism of the conquered people. Then in the eighth century A.D. the Arabs invaded north India and fostered the religion of Islam there.

The Indian Empire was united by a Turkish dynasty, the Mughals, the greatest of whom was Akbar (1542–1605). He gave administrative unity to the country; advanced the notion of secular as opposed to religious rule; promoted the concept of Indian indivisibility; encouraged tolerance among all races and religions; raised splendid monuments and cities; married Hindu princesses to solidify alliances; and patronized poets, painters, and scholars. Akbar was a Muslim and under his rule much of India converted to Islam.

In 1757 India was conquered by the British, who originally came as traders but who exploited internal dissensions to take over the country. In 1947 British rule ended. At that time Pakistan was created, but the new country was physically divided by a portion of north India that lay between Pakistan's eastern and western sections. This situation proved unworkable, and in 1971 the eastern section broke away to become the independent state of Bangladesh.

Thus today Pakistan is an independent, unitary country, located on the northwest border of India. Its other bordering neighbors are Afghanistan, Iran, and China.

At the end of the tenth century, a series of strong rulers in what are now the countries of France and Germany succeeded in imposing centralized government on parts of Europe. Administrative systems developed in which the interests of the various classes—the lords, the church, the peasants, and the townspeople—were represented. The decline of the feudal manor meant that many of the workers who had been attached to those manors went back into the towns looking for other kinds of jobs. Because of technological improvements having to do with methods of plowing and rotating crops, it took fewer agricultural workers to provide more food. As the towns grew, their economies grew, too. People bought and sold within the town, towns traded with each other, regions had an interest in keeping the peace in order to protect trade, and Europe became strong enough even to venture into the Mediterranean Sea.

Two motives interacted to begin the end of Europe's isolation: religion and commerce. In the Middle Ages, religion played a central role in all individuals' lives. In fact, the Catholic Church was the primary institution for people outside of the manor. It controlled education, it controlled knowledge, and it told people how they should live their lives. Moreover, the church owned enormous amounts of land and had significant economic and political power. That power was demonstrated by the **Crusades,** a series of religious wars between the eleventh and thirteenth centuries that, the church said, were necessary to recover Jerusalem (modern-day Israel) from the infidels.

The contacts the Crusaders made with Arab culture introduced new products to Europe, taught the Europeans what Arabs had learned about science and mathematics, and revived interest in Greek culture. The Crusades stimulated trade and made the merchants of Venice, Pisa, and Genoa rich. This new merchant class changed the internal structure of the society of the Middle Ages because most merchants had been formerly landless adventurers. Its growth and the growth of the cities in which trade prospered changed the nature of the social system.

Whereas life on the manor was structured and individuals' roles were well defined, in the cities there was ambiguity about roles, and individuals had the freedom to choose what they could be. Although by modern standards the cities were merely small towns, they offered the opportunity for wealth and the amusements and intellectual variety that we associate with cities. The freedom of the cities had attracted many serfs and peasants, especially those whom new agricultural technology had dispossessed from manor lands. When this occurred, the landed nobility lost power and in their weakened state were taken advantage of by the merchants, who sided with the kings. The loose associations that had previously existed were solidified into modern **nation-states,** separate countries with defined borders and populations with the same language and more or less the same interests, administered by rulers who sought to foster the particular nation-state's economic, political, social, and cultural growth.

As Europe grew richer, the nation-states and the church had more to fight about. All were rich and wished to be richer, were powerful and wished to be more powerful. The worst fight was between the English and the French and was called The Hundred Years' War. It raged from 1337 until 1453, more than a hundred years, but there were periods of peace, or at least periods of exhaustion when both sides rested. What was it about? It was about whether the French should rule in England or the English should rule in France. It was about prestige, about who was smarter and stronger, about boundaries and national identity. It was about what all wars are about.

Worse even than The Hundred Years' War was the **Black Death,** or bubonic plague, a disease transmitted by rats. In the 1290s, bubonic plague arrived in Sicily, carried there by sick rats from ships in the Middle East trade. The plague was carried from country to country by commercial routes, attacking all of Europe as far as Norway, where it died out about 1350. It had probably just run out of victims. There are all kinds of estimates of how many people died, but a generally accepted figure is 40 percent of Europe. Population levels did not recover for two hundred years.

This population change had enormous social and economic consequences. For example, so many people were killed by the plague that the surviving workers were able to command much higher wages. Cities grew wealthier. Even the Catholic Church profited because it received so many inheritances and religious fees. Landholders, on the other hand, suffered because their workers died off, the demand for food dropped (fewer people to eat it), and they had to pay higher prices for the things they bought.

Struggles within the church went on all during this period. One of the questions was, Shall it be the pope or shall it be the individual churches who set policy? The papacy was weakened by these quarrels, and monarchs moved into the power vacuum. Religious life

*I*s a Modern Plague Possible?

It was trade that made the West rich, but it was also trade that brought the bubonic plague to Europe. Can such a calamity happen again? The answer is yes. One indication that it can happen again was seen in 2003 when the SARS illness, which killed approximately 10 percent of its victims, spread from China to around the world. SARS had no cure, and it spread like the common cold.

With the increased interconnections among countries that occur with globalization, it is becoming harder and harder to keep an illness geographically constrained. In 2003 it looked as if SARS was being contained through draconian measures of quarantines, limitations on travel, and careful tracking, although there were fears that it might reoccur. But even if it does not reoccur, SARS is a warning that another disease with a longer incubation period, so that it is difficult to detect, could spread worldwide and become a modern-day plague. And as the world becomes more globalized, the chances of that happening increase.

An engraving depicting victims of the plague.

became subject to civil control. Although the papacy still had a stronghold in Rome, its power base shrank and it lost much of its unquestioned authority over the rest of Europe. Religious debates had fostered new ways of looking at the world, and intellectual Europe was ready for new ideas.

New ideas were about to arrive. In 1453, Constantinople, which was under Christian control, fell to the Turks, who were Muslims. Among the refugees who escaped to Europe were Greek scholars, who brought with them learning and traditions that fueled the Renaissance.

*T*he Renaissance

The Middle Ages ended sometime in the fifteenth century, when scholars of the time decided that they were embarking on a "new beginning." They called the new beginning the Renaissance. **Renaissance** means "rebirth," and it occurred after the Middle Ages when the knowledge of the ancient Greeks and Romans was reestablished and reason, critical thinking, and the arts flourished. Architecture, sculpture, painting, and even engineering and critical investigation were created by artists such as Leonardo da Vinci, Raphael,

Marco Polo's Travels

One of the ways in which the West learned about the culture of the East was through the tales of explorers. One of the most famous was Marco Polo, who traveled throughout the East. The map traces Marco Polo's travels. His description of where he went isn't always easy to identify on modern maps, but he followed this plan more or less. He was one of the earliest travelers from West to East. He reached Beijing on a trading mission in 1275 and remained in China for seventeen years. As late as the nineteenth century, the book he wrote about his travels continued to be almost the only source of information the West had about the remote areas of central Asia. Some of the things the West learned about from Marco Polo were tattooing, coal, condensed milk, paper money, and fuel oil.

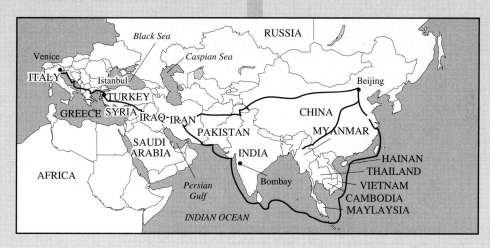

Michelangelo, and Donatello. The Renaissance encouraged critical thinking, and people no longer necessarily accepted the dictates of the church elders on all topics under the sun.

In 1517 such critical thinking put in motion a set of events that came to be known as the Protestant Reformation, when a German Augustinian friar by the name of Martin Luther posted ninety-five theses against indulgences on the door of the castle church of Wittenberg. Indulgences are reductions in, or even elimination of, the time a sinner would otherwise have to spend being punished in the next world. They are granted by the Catholic Church to sinners in return for actions such as saying certain prayers or visiting certain holy shrines. In Luther's day, the practice had been corrupted because the church sold indulgences for profit. Luther was outraged by this practice. He believed that human beings must be saved not by indulgences but by faith alone. Luther's posting of the theses was a direct challenge to the pope's absolute authority. With this challenge, Luther and other Protestant theologians began a forced retrenchment of church power and created a complex of hostilities between groups that can still be seen today, for example, in the antagonisms between Protestants and Catholics in Northern Ireland.

The importance of free thinking and rationality to the events that shaped our world can be seen in the popular saying to the effect that the philosopher Erasmus (1466–1536), who was one of the strongest advocates of rationality, "laid the egg that Luther hatched."

Artist's impression of fifteenth-century Florence.

Throughout the Renaissance, the influence of religion remained strong. The Protestant Reformation challenged only those aspects of the Renaissance that paid obeisance to traditional religion. The Reformation replaced it with a religion that gave a stronger role to the individual. Other Renaissance values, such as the importance of education, religion, and obedience to God, were maintained.

As we discussed earlier, until the latter part of the Middle Ages the individual feudal lords had strong powers, and although they were tied together into loose confederations with a king or monarch, often the individual lords had more power than the monarch. The expansion of trade, the development of cities, and the creation of a new merchant class led to a new set of alliances that made possible the development of the modern state. The Renaissance solidified that development. The states continued to develop throughout the 1700s, and by the end of that century, most of the states of Europe that we are now familiar with had been formed as monarchies.

Throughout this period, the middle class, consisting of merchants and wealthier peasants, continued to grow, but the focus on traditional life remained. Change was considered bad, and tradition remained the important focal point, governing the direction of society.

The Development of Modern Economic and Political Institutions

Throughout the Middle Ages and the feudal system, markets existed, but they were not the chief ways by which individuals acquired the goods they needed for existence. Markets and trade did, however, provide luxuries and a variety of goods, and throughout the Middle Ages a set of fairs developed during which individuals bartered these goods. Merchants acquired more and more income from the trade at these fairs and gradually became strong enough to join with the king in reducing the rights of the lords. These changes occurred simultaneously with the Renaissance. In the Middle Ages, people looked

Of You Hated Inquisition I, Wait until You See Inquisition II

The phenomenon known as the Inquisition was not exclusively medieval and did not occur just once.

Inquisition I: The Medieval Inquisition

The medieval Inquisition began in 1233 when the Roman Catholic pope replaced local bishops with his own appointees. Their duty was to inquire into heresy (theories of religion that differed from the official Roman Catholic version). The inquisitors would give notice that they were coming to a locality and why. People would have a month to come forward voluntarily and swear they were not heretics. Usually the inquisitors believed them and that was that. But some people did not come forward.

In every age and country there are a bunch of nosy neighbors, and nosy neighbors would denounce this or that person to the inquisitors. Then the inquisitors would hold a trial. The accused could have legal counsel and could appeal to the pope if the decision was adverse. However, the accused could not find out who had accused him or her (on the other hand, the accused could give the inquisitors a list of his or her enemies, and if an enemy's name was the same as an accuser's name, the accusation of that enemy was thrown out). The pope's appointees were generally willing to believe heretics who swore that they would give up their heresy and be good.

But if people were found guilty, they were turned over to the local ruler for punishment. The most common punishment was imprisonment, although once in a while one of these unfortunate people was burned alive at the stake. It was not until the 1800s that the custom was abolished. Until then it was a fact of life in France, Italy, and Germany.

Inquisition II: The Spanish Inquisition

This is properly known as "The Spanish Inquisition," and it was much worse than Inquisition I. It was established by the Spanish rulers Ferdinand and Isabella, the same folks who brought you Christopher Columbus, the New World, and America. (No one is all bad, but no one is all good, either.) Inquisition II was harsher and tried many more people than the medieval Inquisition. It is the so-called Spanish Inquisition that is famous for torturing both the accused and the unlucky witnesses, for handing out guilty verdicts right and left, and for using the preferred punishment of burning at the stake. Because Inquisition II was run by the Spanish kings and queens, the Roman Catholic pope did not really approve of it, but papal authority did not succeed in abolishing it until 1820.

P.S. People were usually heavily drugged before they were burned at the stake. Sometimes, though, the authorities were mean and nasty, and if they thought the accused was especially wicked, the drugs were omitted.

---

at the economy quite differently than we do today. Economic activity was not seen as necessarily good in itself; tradition, rather than the profit motive, guided people's actions. Everyone knew one's place and roles were well defined. There were a few free individuals, such as the merchants, and as a by-product of their traveling from place to place, a variety of cities or marketplaces sprang up where individuals from the manors could go to trade with the merchants. But all of these events would not have brought much change were it not for the Crusades, which sped up and significantly increased the breakdown of the manorial system.

From Serfdom to Mercantilism

During this time there was a gradual transition from the system of **serfdom,** feudal obligations owed by vassals to their lords based on a percentage of their agricultural output or days of labor, into payments of money due for rent owed. Thus the central economy shifted from a system of traditional obligations to a system based on the exchange of products and services for money. The lords were in favor of this movement because the expanding trade required them to have money in order to deal with the merchants. The expanded wants generated by this trade left many lords impoverished, and the merchants had incomes significantly exceeding those of the richest lords. At that point, the landed aristocracy began to view their ancestral manors not just as something that belonged to them but as possible sources of cash, and when sheep became profitable they began to enclose the land that had been previously held in common, so that the sheep could graze on it. This made it more and more difficult for the tenants to support themselves. Enclosure dispossessed many tenants and created a new type of labor force—individuals without land who moved into the cities and led a marginal existence or wandered from place to place.

Although serfdom was not formally abolished in France until 1789, and in Germany not until the 1850s, by the 1700s the market economy was definitely emerging, although it had yet to receive full legal and political status. The new economic order was **mercantilism,** an early phase of capitalism in which private ownership and profits were important, but in which there was significant state control. In a mercantilist system, the king granted rights for individuals to conduct a variety of trades, the state was intricately involved in all aspects of commerce and business, and countries all tried to export more goods than they imported and to build up their gold reserves. Technological developments continued throughout this time, but in the 1700s technological changes themselves fundamentally altered the methods of, and needs for, labor.

A Ripple from the Third Crusade

When returning to England from the Third Crusade at the end of the twelfth century, King Richard the Lion-Hearted was taken captive by Henry VI of France, and the English were forced to pay a large ransom for him. In order to pay that ransom, Richard's younger brother, John, who was ruling England in Richard's absence, had to establish high taxes, which did not decline after Richard's release. The high taxes, together with John's military and administrative failures, caused a revolt against the English monarchy. The English nobles, backed by the church and by solid citizens of the towns, forced John, who had come to the throne after Richard's death, to accept the Magna Carta. The **Magna Carta,** "the great charter," forced the king to agree that free men had rights and liberties that could not be trampled on. We quote from the Magna Carta to show how bad the conditions must have been that forced the revolt, and to show you why the Magna Carta is said to be the basis of some of the rights we ourselves take for granted today.

No constable . . . shall take anyone's . . . chattels without . . . paying for them in money.

No sheriff . . . shall take horses or wagons . . . except on permission.

We . . . will not take the wood of another man . . . except by permission of him to whom the wood belongs.

No free man shall be taken, or imprisoned, or dispossessed, or outlawed, or banished . . . except by the legal judgment of his peers, or by the law of the land.

To no one will we sell, to no one will we deny or delay, right or justice.

Various coins. The shell could have been spent in Africa as recently as a hundred years ago. The next two are ancient Chinese, and then we progress through time and space: North India, the Middle East, Rome, and Arabia—until we reach our own penny and quarter.

The Emergence of Nation-States

As the individual states grew and trade picked up, the monarchs attempted to consolidate and broaden their power by supporting the merchants in voyages to Africa (in search of gold) and India (in search of spices). Such voyages avoided the Arab land routes by which gold had been making its way to Europe and the long, arduous overland route between western Europe and India through which pepper, cloves, and other spices came. Thus we have a variety of voyages of discovery such as Columbus's that tremendously broadened possibilities for society. It was through these voyages in search of still better routes to India that what became the United States enters the picture of Western development.

The emergence of nation-states led to numerous wars both within and among nations. These included the French Wars of Religion (1562–1598), the Thirty Years' War (1618–1648), the Glorious Revolution in England (1688), the Great Northern War between Sweden and Russia (1700), the War of the Spanish Succession (1702–1714), and many others. Such wars continue through much of history, and the threat of conflict is the most important problem still facing the modern world.

The Industrial and Political Revolutions of the 1750s to the 1850s

The period of time from 1750 to 1850 is often called the **Age of Revolutions** because of the enormous economic and political changes that occurred during that time.

In the 1750s, once again technological changes had enormous influence on all parts of society. These technological changes were so important that the next significant period is called the **Industrial Revolution,** a period from 1750 to about 1900 characterized by the invention of machines that had the effect of greatly increasing total output and reorganizing work patterns and social relationships. Although the Industrial Revolution began in

Drawing of early Industrial Revolution factory, from Diderot's Encyclopédie.

England, its influence soon spread throughout the world. The revolution was spurred by technological developments such as John Kay's flying shuttle[4] (1733), James Hargreaves's spinning jenny (1765), James Watt's steam engine (1769), and Richard Arkwright's power loom (1769). These inventions made it possible to produce much more output than had hitherto been possible, and in doing so created the need to reorganize the types of work that individuals did.

In order to produce these machines and use the technology, individuals were needed in cities to work in factories. Thus people leaving the rural manors had an alternative. Because pay was often initially higher in factories than on the farm, a migration began into the cities where people hoped to get jobs. The Industrial Revolution further strengthened the power of the merchants, who had allied themselves with the monarchy.

On the political front, this period witnessed both the American and French Revolutions. In 1776 the American Revolution began, weakening the English empire and establishing the rights of individuals relative to the state and ruler. The pressures that had erupted in the American Revolution were founded in the same conditions as those that later caused the French Revolution. Because of the wars that had marked much of the 1700s, governments had significant debts on which they continually had to pay high interest. On the eve of the French Revolution (1789), the interest paid on the French debt was more than half of France's total budget. As the merchants grew tired of paying this

---

[4]This was a technological advance but not, like the U.S. shuttle, a space vehicle. The invention of the flying shuttle frustrated the textile industry because it enabled workers to weave so much cloth that the spinners of thread from which it was woven could not keep up; it was a challenge to the textile industry that was met by offering a prize to anyone who could invent something to increase the threadspinners' productivity. The prize was won when the spinning jenny was invented.

debt, the middle class aligned itself with some members of the aristocracy, leading to a revolution in the way societies were organized. The power of the king was eliminated, and there was a declaration of the rights of man and citizenship. The French Revolution, embodying the ideas of the emerging social sciences, changed the political and economic organization of society.

The Industrial Revolution took hold in the 1800s. The middle class grew enormously and, with its newfound political power, pursued an increasingly important role in running the economy. During this time there was significant social experimentation as the state and the organization of society went through the process of reform and of throwing off tradition. Throughout this period, societies and individual countries became more clearly defined, and by 1850 in western Europe the concept of a nation-state with parliamentary government ruled the day.

But these nation-states had to learn to live together, and their failure to do so and to discover a way to negotiate settlements of disputes among them led to continued warfare and significantly changed the boundaries separating nation-states. As a result of wars, many new nation-states have sprung into being, whereas from time to time old ones have died out. During the nineteenth century, Turkish authority was expelled from most of Europe, and new states took its place on the Balkan Peninsula: Greece, Bulgaria, Serbia, Romania, Albania, and Montenegro (later included with Serbia in Yugoslavia). Approximately twenty new states were formed from the old holdings of Spain and Portugal in the New World. About the middle of the nineteenth century, China and Japan opened their doors to Western trade. They, too, entered the community of nation-states, in 1842 and 1854, respectively.

World War I was a war between Germany, Austria-Hungary, and Turkey on one side and Britain, France, Belgium, Italy, Luxembourg, Bulgaria, parts of Yugoslavia, Russia, Japan, and the United States on the other side, that lasted from 1914 to late in 1918. It tore down the old multinational states of Austria-Hungary and Estonia, and redrew other parts of the European map. Lasting from 1939 to 1945, **World War II** was a much more international war and was fought between Germany, Japan, and Italy on one side, and the United States, Canada, the British Empire, most of Europe, much of Asia including China, many of the Western Pacific countries, and the Union of Soviet Socialist Republics (USSR) on the other side. It led directly to the establishment of Israel. Korea and Germany were each divided into two new political units. After World War II, a surge of nationalism took place in the colonial areas of Africa and Asia, and in the 1960s a number of African and Asian states emerged from the British and French empires.

Beginning in the late 1980s, additional dramatic changes have taken place. The USSR broke up, and political subdivisions within the USSR, such as Russia, Georgia, Uzbekistan, and the Ukraine, all became independent countries. The wall between East and West Germany was torn down and those two countries reunited to become one Germany. Poland, Czechoslovakia, Hungary, Romania, and other communist-dominated countries of eastern Europe changed their political systems, orienting themselves more toward the West than to the USSR.

These changes have made the United States the world's sole superpower, giving it the power to exert its will throughout the world. Whether it had the right and moral authority, and whether it made sense to do so, was much in debate, and these are questions we will consider in more depth in later chapters.

Conclusion

That's it: the history of Western civilization in a chapter—not the most thorough or complete history, but one that will give you some sense of the origins of our society and the institutions that we consider throughout much of the rest of the book.

Key Points

- The development of agriculture and the domestication of animals played key roles in the establishment of fixed communities, which were essential to modern civilization.
- Egypt and Mesopotamia formed the cradle of modern civilization.
- The Greek civilization that significantly influenced our own emerged from about 700 to 500 B.C.
- In the fifth century B.C., Roman civilization emerged and remained dominant until the fifth century A.D.

- In the Middle Ages the church dominated life.
- The Renaissance was a period when the arts flourished and people were encouraged to question some church dictates.
- The Age of Revolutions, from about 1750 to 1850, led to the emergence of our modern economic and governmental systems.

Some Important Terms

Age of Agriculture (54)
Age of Revolutions (71)
Black Death (65)
Code of Hammurabi (56)
Crusades (65)
feudal estate (63)

Industrial Revolution (71)
Magna Carta (70)
mercantilism (70)
Middle Ages (63)
nation-states (65)
polis (58)

Renaissance (66)
Roman Empire (62)
serfdom (69)
serfs (63)
World War I (73)
World War II (73)

Questions for Review and Discussion

1. What are some of the developments that changed human beings from roving hunters to people living in fixed communities? What responsibilities and functions did the towns grow to provide?
2. What are some of the legal systems that have existed in Western society? Do you think any of their provisions have relevance today?
3. What conditions enabled certain classes of society to grow wealthy? Do you think concentrations of wealth were a positive or a negative factor for the nature of society?

4. Name some human characteristics that persist over time in the development of Western society.
5. In thinking about your life today, can you identify any ideas that may have come from the Greeks? From the Romans? From the Middle Ages? If so, what are they? (If you prefer, choose some of the other periods discussed, such as the Reformation and the Industrial Revolution.)
6. How did the Arab world influence the development of Western society in the Middle Ages? Do you see any parallels with the situation in the Middle East today?

7. What did the peasant get from the feudal lord, and what did the feudal lord get in return? Do you think it was a fair exchange?
8. How did the church affect life in the Middle Ages? Did its influence change in the Renaissance?
9. How did trade and commerce develop? What do you think your life would be like today if the only things you could buy were those that were grown or manufactured within ten miles of your house?
10. What was revolutionized by the Industrial Revolution?
11. Name some of the wars that altered the course of Western society. Why do you think they led to change?
12. Identify some of the institutions that have grown up in Western society. How are they changing society today?
13. What is the most important problem facing Western society today? What solutions can you think of?
14. With the breakup of the USSR into independent countries, what are some of the consequences you see for the United States?

Internet Questions

1. Using http://library.thinkquest.org/3588/Renaissance/GeneralFiles/Transporter.html, pick a character(s) (for example, Bartholomew the Physician or Arabella and Elizabeth at the clothing store). Read about their lives during the Renaissance. Now go to www.learner.org/exhibits/middleages/resources.html, and compare aspects of everyday life in the Middle Ages to that of the Renaissance. Name two differences.
2. Go to www.asis.com/sfhs/women/Chelsea.html. How did the Industrial Revolution affect the role of women?
3. Read about the Black Plague at http://nhnh.essortment.com/historyofblac_rrow.htm. What were the symptoms? How did people try to avoid the disease?
4. What are the five major groupings in the Age of Revolutions (1750–1850)? Pick one and list the important events. You can use http://campus.northpark.edu/history/WebChron/WestEurope/AgeRevs.Chron.html.
5. Go to www.mnsu.edu/emuseum/prehistory/aegean. Read about the ancient Greek civilization of the Mycenea. How did this civilization fall?

For Further Study

Anglo, Sydney, *The Martial Arts of Renaissance Europe*, New Haven, CT: Yale University Press, 2000.

Bartlett, Robert C., *The Idea of Enlightenment: A Postmortem Study*, Toronto, Canada: University of Toronto Press, 2000.

Burrow, J. W., *The Crisis of Reason: European Thought 1848–1914*, New Haven, CT: Yale University Press, 2000.

Diop, Cheikh Anta, *The African Origin of Civilization: Myth or Reality?*, Chicago: Lawrence Hill Books, 1994.

Fletcher, Joann, *Chronicle of a Pharaoh*, New York: Oxford University Press, 2000.

Heilbroner, R., *The Worldly Philosophers*, rev. ed., New York: Simon & Schuster, 1980.

In Arab Lands, Bonfils Collection, University of Pennsylvania Museum, intro. by Douglas M. Haller, Cairo, Egypt: University of Cairo Press, 2000.

Larner, John, *Marco Polo and the Discovery of the World*, New Haven, CT: Yale University Press, 2000.

Lobo, Tatiana, *Assault on Paradise*, trans. Asa Zatz, Willimantic, CT: Curbstone Press, 1999.

Margolis, Howard, *Copernicus: How Turning the World inside out Led to the Scientific Revolution*, New York: McGraw-Hill, 2002.

Maurice, Charles S., and Charles W. Smithson, *The Doomsday Myth: 10,000 Years of Economic Crises*, Stanford, CA: Hoover Institution Press, 1984.

Newman, Paul B., *Daily Life in the Middle Ages*, Jefferson, NC: McFarland, 2001.

Reventlow, Henning, *The Authority of the Bible and the Rise of the Modern World,* Philadelphia: Fortress, 1985.

Schiavone, Aldo, *The End of the Past: Ancient Rome and the Modern West,* trans. Margery J. Schneider, Cambridge, MA: Harvard University Press, 2000.

Staloff, Darren, et al., *Great Minds of the Western Intellectual Tradition,* audio/videotapes, Springfield, VA: The Teaching Company, 2000.

Tritle, Lawrence, *From Melos to My Lai: War and Survival (Down the Centuries),* Cambridge, MA: Harvard University Press, 2000.

WWW   Ancient World Database   http://eawc.evansville.edu/eawcindex.htm

WWW   The Fertile Crescent Interactive   www.mnsu.edu/emuseum/prehistory/middle_east/index.shtml

WWW   The Industrial Revolution, a Trip to the Past   http://hometown.aol.com/mhirotsu/kevin/trip2.html

WWW   Internet Modern History Sourcebook   www.fordham.edu/halsall/mod/modsbook.html

WWW   Medieval Crusades   www.medievalcrusades.com

WWW   Timeline of Ancient Greece   www.wikipedia.org/wiki/Timeline_of_Ancient_Greece

WWW   Timeline of Ancient Rome   www.exovedate.com/ancient_timeline_one.html

Society, Culture, and Cultural Change

After reading this chapter, you should be able to:

- Explain why culture is necessary to hold society together
- List some important elements of culture
- Summarize briefly three popular theories of cultural change
- List five factors that cause culture to change
- List three factors stabilizing culture
- Discuss the cultural lag theory and its limitations
- Explain the doctrine of cultural relativism

Culture is the sum of all the forms of art, of love, and of thought, which, in the course of centuries, have enabled man to be less enslaved.

—André Malraux

Human beings are social beings. We cannot understand their nature independently of their social environment. That is why we call our discipline social science.

To understand human beings' role as social beings, we must understand culture. To understand culture and its key role in social science, it is helpful to consider an analogy to physics. When we studied physics in high school, we were taught that there are electrons, protons, and neutrons. Together, these made up atoms, atoms made up elements, and elements made up matter. Since that time, learning physics has become much more difficult. Physicists have discovered smaller and smaller particles, which they tell us are the building blocks of all matter. These building blocks include quarks, leptons, and ghostly particles called gluons, whose existence is assumed by physicists because something has to hold matter together. Quarks and leptons make up matter; gluons hold matter together.

Why are quarks, leptons, and gluons relevant to social science? Because just as physicists need to assume the existence of gluons to hold matter together, social scientists must assume a force that holds society together. Without gluons, quarks and leptons would fall apart and the world as we know it would not exist. Society has a similar force holding it together. Why don't you just haul off and clobber your neighbor when he or she does something wrong? Why don't countries always enter into war to get what they want? What sensibility makes it possible for society to continue to exist and to coordinate the individual wills of some six billion individuals? The answer is culture, and the social science equivalent to the gluon is culture, embodied in social institutions, mores, conventions, and laws.

Culture is the total pattern of human behavior and its products, embodied in thought, speech, action, and artifacts. It is the way of thinking and doing that is passed on from adults to children in their upbringing and can be thought of as the shared language, norms, and values of a society. Culture is dependent on the capacity for learning through the use of tools, language, and systems of abstract thought. It includes not only patterns of behavior as such but also the attitudes and beliefs that motivate behavior. Culture creates human beings and human societies. Reciprocally, by slow accumulation over many generations, culture is the product of human societies and of the individuals who compose them.

Cultures as we know them have evolved through a long process of change. **Cultural evolution** is the name given to this gradual, accumulative process. Any modern culture is largely the product of the originality and initiative of great numbers of individuals in times past, though in most cases the contribution of any one person has been so small that it cannot even be identified.

Because culture is learned by association with other human beings, the character and personality of all human beings are in large part reflections of the society in which they live. Individuals acquire their knowledge, skills, customs, ideals, religion, and morals from their social environment. This is made possible through socialization. **Socialization** is the process that shapes the personality of individuals so that they can adjust to and become members of society. In the United States, most of us feel, think, and act like U.S. citizens because we have spent all our lives in a mainstream U.S. social environment. If, from earliest childhood, we had associated only with a group of Inuits who had never had any contacts with the mainstream U.S. culture, we probably would not understand nor feel comfortable with that culture.

This does not mean that all people in a culture are alike in their personalities. There are significant differences in our family backgrounds and in many other aspects of our personal social environment. To develop human nature, we must be human beings and inherit human potentialities; no two people will ever react to the same environment in exactly the same way. Biologically inherited differences affect the intelligence and temperament of every person and therefore affect thinking and behavior. In any given individual, social inheritance and biological inheritance are so closely bound together that we can never be sure of the relative influence of each. However, for nearly all of us the general pattern of life is largely determined by our social environment. Almost everything we believe or know or do we learn from observing other people, from listening to other people, or from reading and thinking about what other people have written.

Culture is an enormously vague concept that is difficult to grasp. Perhaps the easiest way to understand culture is to answer a few questions:

1. Should children, age eleven to fifteen, sleep in the same beds as their parents?
2. Should women be allowed to drive?
3. Should females be circumcised?
4. Should people wear swimming suits on public beaches?

Most of you from the United States, I suspect, answered the questions (1) no, (2) yes, (3) no, and (4) yes. Why do I suspect that? Because you come from a shared culture. But if you were from another country, or a part of the United States that is not affected by mainstream U.S. culture, your answers would likely be different. For example, according to Richard Shweder in his book *Why Do Men Barbecue? Recipes for Cultural Diversity*, in Mali and Somalia women are repulsed by the idea of not circumcising women. Similarly, in Saudi Arabia some women (although it is a decreasing number) see it as simply inappropriate for a woman to drive. Many more examples could be provided, but these should be sufficient to give you a sense of how culture is the shared beliefs of a society.

Culture and the Nature of Society

Even though the personality of each individual is in great part molded by society, it is clear that society can have no existence apart from the people who constitute it. **Society** is a body of individuals living as members of a community. The characteristics of every society are gradually shaped and changed over succeeding generations by innovations introduced by the people who belong to it. The influence of any one individual may be small, but the contributions of many individuals over long periods of time can be great.

It is important to pay close attention to our definition of society. A group of people does not necessarily constitute a society. A number of people who come together temporarily, and perhaps accidentally, are merely a crowd, or an unorganized aggregate. To constitute a society, a group must be bound together by established relationships. It must, in other words, be organized.

Though the basis of any society is a group of individuals, equally important to its establishment is the continued existence of the group over a period of time. A crowd brought together for a football game is an aggregate, but it is not a society. Its members are physically close together, and for the moment are united by a common interest. However, any sense of unity they may have is superficial and temporary. When the game is over, they disperse. They are not together long enough to organize into a society. But if the same people were marooned for a year on an uninhabited island, they would be forced to organize themselves into a society.[1] They would develop common ideas, interests, and techniques for living and working together. It is the sense of living together as a community that makes up a society.

Culture and Its Role in Human Societies

There is a problem in precisely defining culture because it has a variety of aspects. But our earlier definition of it is probably the best. Culture is the way of life that the people of a society follow. It includes all knowledge, beliefs, art, morals, law, customs, and any other capabilities acquired by a human being as a member of society.

In short, culture is the total pattern of human behavior and its products embodied in thought, speech, action, and artifacts. Culture is also dependent on the capacity for learning through the use of tools, language, and systems of abstract thought.

As you can see, the culture of a society includes everything in the lives of its members that is of human origin—that is, everything they learn through their direct or indirect

---

[1]In 2000 the television program *Survivor* assembled a small group of people on an uninhabited island. The basic purpose was to allow viewers to watch the difficulties this group would have in making decisions. Had there truly been no hope of rescue, and no need to "eliminate" individuals periodically, the group would probably have organized and cooperated in a much more socially beneficial manner.

contacts with other people. It includes the customary ways of behaving in everyday life, religious beliefs, moral standards, the way family life is organized, the methods used to provide food and shelter, language, government, and forms of artistic expression.

The Elements of Culture

Culture develops only through the association of human beings and thus presupposes society; at the same time, culture is what makes a human society possible. Only when people develop in some degree a common culture can they function as an organized group, for only then do they know what to expect of one another and how to behave to meet the requirements of the group. A society can exist because human beings have the capacity for creating culture and, what is equally important, for sharing it with their contemporaries and transmitting it to succeeding generations. Culture creates societies and societies depend on culture. In short, culture is a social mechanism influencing all aspects of society including social norms (its conventions, mores, and laws), institutions, and the concepts that motivate them, together with a society's technology, its material products, and its values. Let us consider briefly some of these elements of culture.

Social Norms: Conventions, Mores, and Laws. **Conventions** are the simple, everyday customs of a group that represent the usual ways of behaving. Conventions change slowly, and many of them are very persistent. In our society, it is customary or conventional to sleep on a bed; to eat at a table; to handle our food with knives, forks, and spoons; and to greet an acquaintance on the street. All these are conventions. Conventions are established customs to which we attach little moral significance. We may think that people whose conventions are different from ours are themselves different, but we try to understand those differences, not ostracize people because of their differences. For example, we will probably wonder about a woman who shaves her head, but our social practice will be to try to act as if we notice nothing unusual.

Punk dressers challenge social norms in Great Britain.

Mores (pronounced mor-rays) are conventions that would have serious consequences if they were violated. They include those customs that must generally be observed by all members of a society for the culture to survive. People who disregard mores are usually seen as more than slightly odd or eccentric—their character definitions are beyond weird. Although a violation of a society's mores would not necessarily land a person in jail, it would incur social punishment in the form of peer disapproval. For example, a claims adjuster who showed up at the insurance office and completely disrobed would have violated one of society's mores and, even if not arrested for indecent exposure, would nevertheless face informal punishment. On the other hand, a person who wears informal clothing to a wedding reception is merely violating a convention.

In contrast to mores and conventions, which are merely customs taken as understood in governing the conduct of the group, laws are more exact, and are generally recorded, codified, and enforced as a means of securing public obedience. **Laws** are the principles and regulations established in a community by some authority and applicable to its people, whether in the form of legislation or of policies recognized and enforced by judicial decision. Violations of laws may carry severe punishments and/or ramifications for the offender. Being caught speeding results in a small fine, whereas premeditated murder may be punishable, at least in some states, by death. What is against the law and the punishment for violation of laws vary in different societies. For example, in some Islamic societies it may be against the law for a woman to appear in public with her face uncovered, and stealing may be punished by the loss of one's hand. In the United States, there are no laws about covering one's face, and stealing results in a jail sentence, at most.

Social Institutions.   A **social institution** is an established complex pattern of behavior in which a number of persons participate in order to further important group interests. Institutions are usually organized around some central interest or need. Government, for example, provides the necessary order and coordination among individuals. The church, temple, mosque, and synagogue are the institutions that enable people to express their religious beliefs by joining others in worshipping a deity or deities in established rituals. The school provides for formal education of the young while the family, one of the most basic of all social institutions, helps meet many of the needs of daily life, such as those for shelter, food, close companionship, and affection.

It is possible to analyze the structure of social institutions as four closely related elements, as sociologist William Graham Sumner has done. These elements are personnel, equipment, organization, and ritual. By personnel Sumner meant the members of the group especially qualified and duly selected to perform certain services. Teachers in educational institutions and the officers of business corporations are two examples. By equipment he meant the material and nonmaterial possessions of the group, with the aid of which the purposes of the institution are carried out. Taking a high school as an example, the material equipment includes the buildings, playing fields, parking lot, school buses, desks, chairs, computers, screens, tapes, swimming pool, library books, chalkboards, and other tangible items. The nonmaterial possessions include educational philosophy, faculty morale, school spirit, the dress code, and the support of the students' parents. The organization of an institution consists of the various special relationships of the members to one another and of the ways in which they arrange and use the equipment. Organization usually requires some concentration of authority. Certain individuals hold positions of authority, others of subordination, and the positions people hold greatly influence their relations with one another and with the group. The ritual of an institution consists of the customs and regulations that determine the behavior of members when they perform their various prescribed roles.

Material Products.   Strictly speaking, culture is never material. It is in the minds and personalities of people. It is what they have learned from their social environment—attitudes, beliefs, knowledge, and ways of behaving. However, important in every culture is knowledge of how to produce and use a variety of material products, including food, clothing, houses, tools, machines, and works of art. **Cultural objects (artifacts)** are products of human skill and effort that are essential to the functioning of a society. Cultural objects are more than mere expressions of the culture that produces them; they become essential to its functioning because without them people could not carry on the necessary activities of daily life. This is strikingly true in a modern industrial society. Such a society would be paralyzed if it could not use computers, airplanes, cars and trucks, telephones, power plants, factories and their machines, supermarkets, and fast-food outlets, to name a few.

Language. **Language** is a body of words and the system for their use common to a people who are of the same community or nation, the same geographical area, or the same cultural tradition. Language is intrinsic in the societies and cultures of humans. Benjamin Lee Whorf argued that each particular language embodies and propagates a worldview. Groups of people speaking the same language, therefore, communicate in the same cultural tone. Cultural assumptions and observations are locked into a society's language. For instance, communication between multilingual people transmits cultural differences between societies.

Language plays a central role in the development and transmission of culture. It allows communication, which is essential for the coordination of activities. It allows cultures to save and transmit a knowledge of their history. Writing allows many further uses of language, widening its ability to store and accumulate knowledge. Writing allows cultures to be preserved and passed on in expanded ways. But language also creates limitations. The structure of the language influences the way individuals look at issues and can therefore incorporate many hidden biases.

Social Values. **Social values** are the motivating power that makes institutions function effectively. They are the things that a given society considers desirable because they are believed to contribute to the good life and the general welfare. In our cultural environment, honesty, courage, justice, and respect for law and for the rights of others are highly regarded social values. So also, on a somewhat different level, are financial success, health, and education.

Fast-food restaurants have been integrated into U.S. culture. They are as American as Old Glory.

Individuals' desires tend to reflect the values stressed in the societies to which they belong. U.S. society is often said to be materialistic. This may not be a wholly correct characterization, yet it contains an element of truth. In our modern United States, we have great respect for success in business, entertainment, and sports, and we also lay great stress on the importance of raising standards of living and abolishing poverty. Because we put such a high value on material welfare, many of our people have come to regard the earning of more and more money as their major life objective. Others, of course, look on money merely as a means to achieve more important objectives. These more important objectives may involve such "higher" social values as the education of one's children; charity; the appreciation and encouragement of art, science, and religion; and the rendering of public service.

Social values make institutions function effectively. The church, temple, mosque, or synagogue, for instance, will be a dynamic force in society only as long as a large portion of their members firmly believe in a supreme being or spiritual guide and have faith that their religious organization is an essential instrument for the growth of the soul and the creation of a good society. Where religion has a strong hold on a society, it is usually a conservative force tending to preserve established moral values.

Social values are relative rather than absolute. They often vary widely from one culture to another, and each individual acquires from his or her own culture ideas of what is desirable or undesirable, good or bad, right or wrong. In some societies, sexual relations before marriage are regarded as a cardinal sin; in others they are permitted or even expected. In some societies, women must be very plump to be regarded as beautiful; in others they must be rather slim. In most if not in all modern societies, the killing of infants is regarded with horror, but some nonliterate tribal societies see it as commendable under certain circumstances—for instance, if the infants have physical disabilities.

*C*ultural Integration

Alphabets of different cultures, from Diderot's Encyclopédie.

Cultures or societies contain certain aspects that are similar among all cultures. These aspects or traits are called universals. A **cultural universal** is an aspect of culture that is found in all cultures. Religion, for example, is a cultural universal, as is the existence of some form of government, family life, and national ideals. **Cultural alternatives** are those cultural characteristics that are not necessarily shared by other cultures. For example, some cultures might place the elderly in a subordinate role, whereas others might place them in an exalted role. Therefore, exalting old age is a cultural alternative; not all societies do it.

Traits differ not only among cultures; they also differ within cultures. **Cultural integration** is the degree to which a culture is internally consistent and homogeneous. In large, complex modern cultures such as that of the United States there tends to be more diversity. In small, preliterate cultures such as the Amazon Indian culture of the Yahma tribe today there tends to be less diversity. Thus these cultures are more unified.

In U.S. culture, which greatly values freedom of choice with respect to both ideas and things, life is more complex and stressful. Many social problems such as crime, teenage rebellion, alcohol and drug abuse, and emotional disorders result from our greater ability to choose options. For example, if culture determined what job you would have when you graduate, your life would probably be less stressful. Even cultures that place a high value on freedom must achieve some measure of balance between shared cultural traits and the potentially disintegrative forces of nonshared traits. Since about 1960 we have seen in the United States a decline in the social behavioral consensus that was more typical of the earlier years of the twentieth century. Some social scientists believe that this flexible value system could cause serious trouble for our society. Whether they are right, and whether our society will move toward more shared cultural traits, remains to be seen.

As you can see, culture is the glue that holds society together, but like glue it can also cause difficulties for society. The reason is that societies are in constant transition, and to be successful a society must adjust to new technologies and relations with other societies. The glue that really held society together in one time period may be the sticky mess that in another time period entraps some members of society. Therefore, to understand the role of culture in society, we must consider the process of social change, the factors that contribute to that change, and the effect that change has on culture.

Culture, Society, and Social Change

The culture of a society is constantly evolving to fit new situations. For instance, wars can create almost instantaneous change and can focus a society's interest, money, and energy on a single goal—winning. Total emphasis is placed on war-related activities rather than on more diverse activities. Whether a country wins or loses, the postwar society will substantively differ from the prewar society. Some of these changes will be the result of an opponent's war effort, and others will be the result of interaction with members of other societies.

The rate of social change has gradually gained momentum through the course of human social development. In early times it started slowly. Many thousands of years ago all human beings belonged to small, preliterate groups. Though the groups varied greatly in the nature and complexity of their cultures, as a rule the customs and traditions of each were so firmly established that its members tended to follow much the same way of life over a great many generations. Then the rate of social change increased. In effect, social change has behaved much like a snowball rolling down a hill. First it starts out small and moves slowly; then as it picks up more snow and gets larger, it gains momentum.

Certain factors have been especially important in contributing to an increased rate of change. Outstanding among these is the development of agriculture. The growing of crops forced people to live in permanent dwellings. Increasing the food supply through storage brought about an increase in population and, gradually, the growth of towns and cities. Another important factor is the invention of writing, which made it possible to record human knowledge and to transmit it to future generations more adequately than ever before. As the sum total of human knowledge increased, the rate of its accumulation accelerated.

Later developments that did much to speed up the rate of social change include the invention of printing, the rise of modern science, and the Industrial Revolution, which began in England in the mid-1700s. The Industrial Revolution represented a shift in the methods of production; it entailed the replacement of hand tools by machines and power tools, and initiated the movement away from small-scale agriculture to the development of large-scale industry. This necessitated enormous numbers of workers for the factories, fewer workers in the fields, and therefore enhanced urbanization, the movement of people from rural to urban areas. A more recent factor of great importance in accelerating change has been the annihilation of distance through the development of rapid transportation and communication. Today we can use satellite transmission to simulcast events and ideas all around the world while they are actually happening or being formulated.

Not only is the rate of technological change increasing, but so is the interaction among cultures. This is especially true in developing countries. Western science and technology are now spreading throughout the world at an accelerating pace, and further westernization is a likely prospect for many developing countries. The **Internet**—an interconnected set of computers through which people can communicate and transfer information—has transformed the communication of individuals with one another and is in the process of making our world one enormous community.

One result of increasingly close contacts with distant lands is that the peoples of the world are becoming more and more alike in their customs, the products they use, and the ways they earn a living. Wide cultural differences among peoples can still be found and may never completely disappear. Today bitter enmities seem ineradicable within countries such as Bosnia and between countries such as India and Pakistan. However, cultural differences are, on the whole, diminishing, and at a more rapid rate than ever before.

We would be wrong, however, to see the diffusion of cultural traits as a one-way street. Styles of dress, food specialties, art forms, and modes of thought in other continents and societies are bringing changes to our own culture. Change in itself is not necessarily good or bad. It only means that old situations are being replaced by new ones. Evolution has more definite implications than change. Evolution implies a gradual development from simpler forms of life, art, technology, or social organization to more complex forms. **Social evolution** is the long and complex process of change and interaction by which cultures gradually develop. Whether this change is desirable is debatable. From a Western, ethnocentric perspective, we often think of change as progress, but from a broader perspective, change is not necessarily progress—it may be regressive change. Change cannot be seen as progress unless we know what the life goals are and how those changes help us meet those goals. Views of what life goals should be differ; hence, views of whether social evolution is progressive differ.

Popular Theories of Social Change

Human beings have a tendency to glorify the past. Some become firmly convinced that the good old days of their youth and childhood were far superior to the present. One of the earliest theories of social change was that held by certain Greek philosophers who believed that humankind once lived in an ideal golden age. From this we gradually descended to a silver, then a bronze, and finally an iron age.

A quite opposite theory of social change has been popular in Europe and the United States in the last century or two. This is the doctrine of inevitable progress, the belief that the world is getting better and better. Not even two world wars and a multitude of smaller wars have been able to shake the faith of those who firmly hold this doctrine.

Another theory of social change, popularized by Oswald Spengler and Arnold Toynbee, is that such change runs in cycles. According to their theory, institutions, societies, and civilizations pass through cycles of growth, climax, and decline. Modern civilization is no exception and is bound ultimately to disintegrate. This cycle theory of social change is based on the idea that history repeats itself. Some cycle theorists maintain that modern civilization is now on the verge of a decline, and to support this contention they point to the fate of certain past civilizations, including ancient Greece and the Roman Empire. Cycle theories vary considerably, but they all tend to support the thesis that civilizations first advance, ultimately reach a peak, and finally decline.

Other attempts to explain social change have relied on the supernatural, racial characteristics, economic conditions, cultural diffusion, or invention. Any given culture, however, is the result of too many factors to be explained adequately by any simple formula. Yet one thing is sure: Change is inevitable. Humans' relationship to their environment is dynamic, no matter where they live, and this dynamic relationship produces change.

Factors Causing Cultural Change

We now look at some of the most important social forces that cause cultural change, together with the problems that change has brought about. We begin with a discussion of technological development; then we examine the role of religion, ideologies, cultural diffusion, wars, planned group action, geography, and climate.

Technological Development.   Technological development begins with discovery and invention. A **discovery** is learning something about the physical or social environment that was not known before. In the past, explorers have discovered new islands and continents, astronomers have discovered laws that regulate the motions of the heavenly bodies, and anthropologists have discovered many interesting differences between the cultures of preliterate peoples. Discoveries about the natural world often furnish the basis for inventions. For example, the discoveries of some of the great scientists about electricity made it possible for Thomas Edison to invent the incandescent electric lightbulb and other useful devices.

An **invention** is a new way of doing something or a new object or mechanical device developed to serve some specific purpose. It is a cultural innovation devised by one or several individual members of a social group. Inventions may be either material or nonmaterial. Familiar machines such as the lawn tractor and the airplane are material inventions. Old-age insurance and crop rotation are examples of nonmaterial inventions. One of the greatest of all nonmaterial inventions was the alphabet, which made possible our present system of writing and printing.

An invention is really a special kind of discovery, and hence no sharp line can be drawn between the two. We can call the making of fire by striking together flint stones either a discovery or an invention. All mechanical inventions involve the discovery that materials combined and used in certain ways will produce certain desired results. Inventions bring about changes in technology, and in modern societies technological change has been a powerful force behind social change.

A good example is the computer, which is changing our lifestyle and culture in many ways. Computerized robots are replacing workers in many jobs, tiny robots are being considered for medical uses, and the Internet is changing the way we shop and communicate with others. Similarly, developments

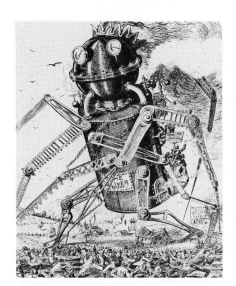

Robot replacing workers. This 1882 cartoon was called "Demon destroying the People."

in biotechnology are changing our lives and soon may make it possible for us to choose characteristics for our children and to influence medical treatment.

Technological change has become so important to understanding society that we devote an entire chapter, Chapter 6, to a deeper consideration of the issues.

Cultural Diffusion.   Once a new cultural element is well established in one society, it may spread to others. **Cultural diffusion** is the name given to the spread of cultural traits from one social group to another. In other words, not all the elements found in the culture of a given group were invented or developed within that group. In most cases, the greater part of the content of any culture has been borrowed from other cultures. In most societies, cultural diffusion is an extremely important factor in social change. Societies that are isolated from outside contacts tend to be static, whereas those that can readily communicate with other groups constantly acquire new cultural elements. However, contact does not always lead to cultural diffusion. For example, the Amish society in the United States has significant contact with mainstream U.S. culture. Despite this contact, Amish society has maintained its separate cultural identity through careful nurturing and has shunned many modern technological developments.

Cultural diffusion, more than any other factor, has been responsible for the development of Western civilization. Western civilization was nurtured in Europe, and its center is still there. Yet most of the basic elements of this civilization did not originate in Europe but were borrowed from other peoples in other parts of the world. Our modern number system, so much more flexible than that of the Romans, was borrowed from the Arabs, who in turn borrowed it from the Hindus in India. Without this number system or a good substitute, it would be almost impossible for us to carry on the mathematical calculations now required by both business and science. Again, our alphabet, which with modifications is used for writing and printing all European languages, was borrowed originally from the Phoenicians of Africa. It seems probable that they, or a neighboring people speaking a similar Semitic language, were the original inventors.[2]

Ideas and Ideologies.   Social change may also be initiated by new ideas. Relatively simple, practical ideas may result in inventions that soon are accepted and become a recognized part of the cultural pattern—a new type of dance, a new kind of business corporation, or a new mechanical gadget. However, not all new ideas are of this type. Some represent important changes in social attitudes and basic social values. Such ideas may in time gain a powerful hold on minds, as did the concepts of "liberty, equality, and fraternity" of the French Revolution, or the civil rights movement in the United States in the 1960s. Often they come to represent hopes and aspirations that, though they can never be fully realized, can be approached in a variety of ways. Once ideas of this kind become well established in any society, they become a powerful force for continuing social change in directions that are thought to lead toward their realization.

Even in the modern world it usually takes considerable time for major new ideas to gain a firm foothold. Various writers have maintained that social change is always motivated by the discoveries or theories of great thinkers of a past generation. Karl Marx, for example, had little effect on society during his lifetime; British economist John Maynard

---

[2]The Phoenician alphabet contained only consonants. The Greeks, who were the first Europeans to appropriate this alphabet, added vowels.

Keynes's economic ideas of the 1930s did not have any great impact on the public and on government policies until the 1960s.

An **ideology** is an organized system of ideas for remodeling society so as to bring it "nearer to the heart's desire." We may regard it as a composite of ideas, values, and emotions. Those who believe in an ideology often support it with religious fervor. Fascism, communism, socialism, and democracy are all ideologies. Each has its system of values, and each would organize society—supposedly to further the common good—according to a somewhat different pattern. No ideology ever achieves the ideal society that its adherents envision. We regard our U.S. society as democratic, but we are often keenly aware that we fall short of the democratic ideal in many ways.

Collective Action.   Most social changes take place gradually and are not planned and carried out by a central agency. At times, however, social changes of importance are brought about more or less rapidly by planned group action. Group action by an entire society, such as a modern nation, usually means government action, because the government is the only agency that can make and enforce rules that in theory apply to the whole social group. Japan is a nation that has experienced a great social transformation within the past 150 years. It has changed from a feudal society to a modern, highly industrialized democracy. Much of this change has been brought about by government policies that were specifically designed to bring Japan into the modern world.

The outstanding twentieth-century examples of drastic and far-reaching social changes carried out by governments on a vast scale are found in the former Soviet Union and in China. There, in two of the largest and most populous countries of the world, when the communist leaders came into power they completely changed in a relatively short time many basic aspects of the political, social, and economic structure. In an attempt to create societies based on the communist ideology of Karl Marx, the state seized vast amounts of property from the middle- and upper-class owners, uprooted millions of peasants from their holdings and put them to work on collective farms or communes, and took over the operation and expansion of practically all productive enterprises. But the achievement of such broad and rapid changes was possible only through the establishment of powerful dictatorships that had small regard for the rights and freedoms of individuals.

In the 1990s, many of these communist dictatorships ended. Eastern Europe went through dramatic upheavals: Several communist systems were overthrown; the Soviet Union broke up into various countries; and all of these countries experienced enormous political, social, and economic change. What the end result will be won't be known for many years. It may be an adoption of a Western-style market economy, or it may be the establishment of some new system.

Important social changes can also be brought about in democratic countries through planned government action, but only if the action has popular support. However, such changes are implemented more slowly and are much less drastic than those that can be made by a communist society or a dictatorship. In democracies, social changes planned by government are usually embodied in legislation that is designed to meet certain social problems. For example, in the United States acts of Congress and of state legislatures have almost eliminated the employment of child labor; at the same time, they have helped increase school attendance, both by providing free public schools and by making school attendance compulsory. Legislation under the New Deal, from about 1932 to 1937, established in their original forms our farm income–support program and our Social Security system. It also stimulated the growth of labor unions by strengthening their legal position and their bargaining power. Now, in the 2000s, those structures are being questioned.

Legislation, however, has its limitations. To be effective in promoting social change in a democracy, it must either reflect the established beliefs of the people or it must change those beliefs relatively quickly. If legislation violates what the majority of citizens believe to be their just rights and privileges, it has little chance of success. For instance, the Prohibition amendment to the U.S. Constitution, legally in force from 1919 to 1932, failed and was finally repealed because the majority of Americans felt that outlawing the sale of liquor was an unreasonable violation of their personal liberties.

Geography and Climate.   When people live in a given region over a long period of time, they become adjusted to local conditions of geography and climate. A society, for example, set on the edge of an ocean would be more prone to utilize marine resources—fish for food, shells as jewelry, and perhaps greater trade owing to the oceanic access—than would a landlocked society. Changes in the natural environment can and do occur. In extreme cases, droughts, earthquakes, the exhaustion of important natural resources, changes in climate, and the like may require radical cultural adjustments.

Geography and climate are also important factors in social change when people migrate from one region to another. The European settlers who emigrated to the Americas, Africa, Australia, and New Zealand found many differences of climate, topography, and natural changes, especially in food, clothing, houses, and ways of earning a living. We consider these issues in more detail in Chapter 5.

Language and Cultural Change

Social change takes place over long periods of time and is often difficult to discern. Because our perceptions of the past are imperfect, our knowledge of the past is also limited and imperfect. We don't know what was; we only know what is. One way to get an idea of the change that takes place is to consider the evolution of languages. Some social scientists believe that all modern languages sprang from a single root—a tiny population that probably lived in Africa or Asia about twenty thousand years ago. A sense of this evolution is shown in Figure 4.1. According to this theory, all differences in modern-day languages are the result of independent evolution of varying branches of this root language.

How much a language can evolve can be seen by comparing the Old English phrase for "How are you?" in a book like *Beowulf* (eighth century A.D.): "Hal! Geard weallas!" (it reads like a foreign language) to that same phrase in Shakespeare (16th–17th century A.D.): "How art thou?" to a modern variant: "How ya doin'?" Given how much languages can change without our noticing, we should not be surprised by how much cultures can change and how different cultures can be.

Factors Stabilizing Culture

The various factors of social change lead to a dynamic, continually altering society. Change and culture will often conflict, with culture providing strong resistance to social change. In present-day United States, underlying the many changes constantly taking place in our culture is a great body of stabilizing elements that give continuity to our way of life.

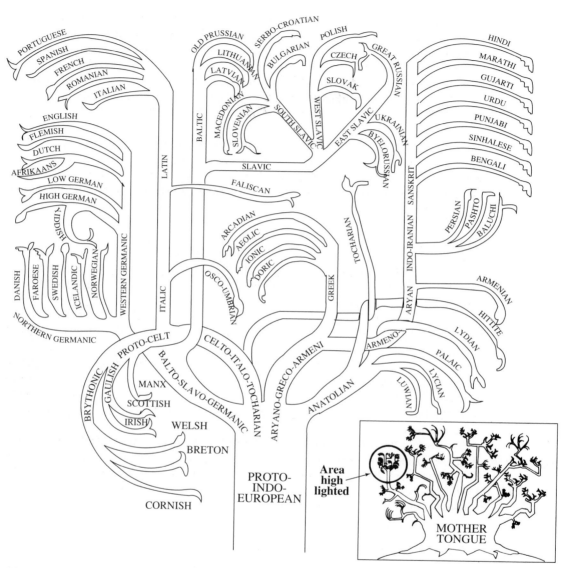

Figure 4.1

According to some linguists, all of our languages sprang from a single root of a mother language. The diagram shows the hypothesized language tree.

Stability of Social Norms.   In spite of the high value that some industrial societies place on so-called progress, human beings appear to be basically conservative. The human mind and personality are so constituted that once people acquire certain beliefs, attitudes, and patterns of behavior, they have difficulty changing them. This is especially true of the basic elements in our culture, which we acquire unconsciously in the impressionable years of early childhood. Our beliefs and attitudes may include some approval of change—for example, changes in fashions—but only within limits. The mores, the principal institutions of our society, and even many of its conventions are so firmly impressed on us that they become an essential part of our own personalities. For example, the tradition that women need to be protected from the harsh realities of commercial competition, the rough and tumble of military life, and the demands of heavy physical labor played a role in the failure of the passage of the Equal Rights Amendment to the U.S. Constitution.

Habit.   A chief reason for the persistence of conventions, mores, and social institutions is that they become largely habitual for all members of the social group. **Habits** are ways of behaving that have been learned so well that they can be carried on without conscious attention. Once acquired, however, they are difficult to change because they become a part of the individual's personality.

Value Attachment.   Another reason for the persistence of conventions, mores, and institutions is that we and our group attach values to them. In the case of conventions, these values may be small, but in the case of the mores and certain basic institutions they are great. When we believe that established patterns of behavior have high moral value and when, in addition, they arouse in us strong emotions, these patterns become resistant to change.

Social changes of any importance, even though favored by the majority, are likely to meet opposition from many individuals and groups who have vested interests. A **vested interest** is a privilege or advantage that an individual enjoys because of the status quo, which is the existing state of affairs. A worker who is a skilled plasterer has a vested interest in the plastering trade, and is not likely to favor substituting wallboard for plaster. Various unions in the building industry, in order to protect the jobs of their members, have fought against prefabricated housing and have insisted on retention of slower, more expensive, on-the-spot building methods.

Industry and labor are not alone in opposing, for selfish reasons, the introduction of new elements into our culture. Many people stand to lose by changes in the status quo, not only materially but in power or prestige. Theologians, philosophers, and scientists have again and again opposed new ideas and new knowledge for fear that their own established beliefs and theories would be discredited.

Social Change versus Social Stability

Many of the things we value in our modern society—for example, our relatively high standards of living—could not have been brought about without a receptive attitude toward social change, because all change produces new situations. However, if change occurs very rapidly it may create new problems for which we are unprepared. Instead of introducing a better world, it can bring on periodic crises and give people a constant sense of uncertainty and insecurity. Every social group feels the need for some degree of stability. If this stability is to be maintained, change in our basic institutions must be gradual. It must take place by evolution rather than by revolution.

For any large modern society to meet the needs of its people requires a remarkably complex organization; the organization can be challenged, it can be adapted, it can be changed, but any belief that it can be destroyed and quickly replaced with something better is unrealistic. Social revolutions are never complete, and they bring few of the results that were envisioned. The communist revolution in Russia, after years of struggle and confusion, produced Stalin; and the National Socialist revolution in Germany produced Hitler.

Social Change and Social Problems

Although not all social scientists would agree on the exact nature of a social problem, for our purposes the following definition suffices. For a social problem to exist, two conditions must be fulfilled. First, there must be wide recognition of some condition that adversely affects the welfare of a significant number of people. Second, there must be a belief that this condition can and should be changed. In other words, a **social problem** is a situation that has been recognized as adversely affecting the welfare of large numbers of people and for which it is believed a solution exists. To admit the existence of a social problem clearly implies the possibility of change, for no matter how undesirable a situation may be, it is not a problem unless we believe there is a way to change it. In primitive societies, drought, famine, and pestilence may not have been regarded as problems because nothing could be done about them. They were simply accepted. However, they became problems if it was believed there were ways to avert them—for instance, by making adequate sacrifices to the gods.

In a sense, social problems are always individual problems, for it is individuals who experience their adverse effects. We call them social problems for two reasons: first, because they affect such a significant proportion of people as to constitute a threat to the welfare or safety of the whole group; and second, because they cannot be adequately met by individuals. If they are to be solved at all, it must be by some kind of group action. This becomes clear when we consider such major social problems as widespread poverty, disease, recurrent periods of mass unemployment, crime, family disorganization, and war.

As would be expected, a large modern society is much more likely to possess complex social problems than a smaller society. Larger societies often contain important subgroups with differing cultural patterns, and these subgroups are likely to be subject to inconsistencies, strains, and conflicts that speed up social change and often are intensified by it.

When we attempt to define and study any particular social problem, we encounter certain difficulties. For one thing, every social problem is closely related to a number of other social problems and is therefore highly complex. To fully understand one problem we must know something about the others. Thus, to understand fully the problem of family disorganization and divorce, we may, for example, need to know something about poor housing, unemployment, and social classes.

There is seldom any simple or complete solution for a major social problem. The causes are always complex, and practical remedies are difficult to find or implement. Moreover, the action necessary to solve or mitigate a social problem may be effectively blocked by public indifference and ignorance and by the opposition of vested interests. This does not mean that all attempts at social improvement are useless. It does mean, however, that a number of our major social problems are likely to remain with us in some form or degree for the indefinite future.

Cultural Lag and Social Problems

Though some elements in culture may change while others remain relatively constant, the various aspects of a given culture are by no means entirely independent of one another.

*A*re You P.C.?

Social change affects our everyday life. A recent example of this is the P.C. phenomenon, which has been much in debate on college campuses and elsewhere since the early 1990s. P.C. stands for politically correct. To be P.C. is to be attuned to some unstated but nonetheless strong and reasonably well-defined set of social norms that emphasizes minority rights, women's rights, social justice, and environmentalism. It is a derogatory term that was created in response to the social pressure on individuals to meet those norms.

In the early 1980s, the pressures on many college campuses for individuals to be P.C. were rather strong, but the phrase did not exist. New courses, course requirements, and departments were instituted at many schools in women's studies, ethnic studies, and the environment.

The underlying philosophy of some of these pressures went against the grain of some individuals, as did the sometimes strong-arm tactics (such as sit-ins and taking over buildings) supporters used to implement and demand change. Supporters justified these strong-arm tactics on the grounds that ours is a repressive society and given that repression, the ends justify the means.

This justification went against the grain of another Western social norm—toleration and respect for others' rights—leading a number of people, including some who support the social norms that the strong-arm tactics were meant to achieve, to repudiate the movement. It also led to the creation of the term *P.C.,* a term that had been used by Nazis to describe individuals who held the belief that the white Aryan race was superior to all others. The Nazi association of the term brought out the dissonance between the strong-arm tactics used by some P.C. supporters and the norms of toleration and respect for individual rights.

The debate between P.C. supporters and opponents concerns conflicting social norms—toleration versus social justice. P.C. supporters argue that one should not be tolerant of injustice, and that if our society were truly tolerant and maintained respect for all others, the movement wouldn't be needed. But because our society isn't, it is necessary to be intolerant of injustice and intolerance. Social science doesn't tell us whether the P.C. movement is right or wrong, but it does help us put it in perspective and have a better appreciation for the inevitable tensions that social change brings about.

To illustrate, religion may have a substantial influence on technological change. On the one hand, it may encourage technological change by teaching that material progress is in accord with the divine will; on the other hand, it may discourage such change by teaching that mechanical innovations are works of the devil.

The late eminent sociologist William F. Ogburn assigned great importance to what he called *cultural lag* as a source of social disorganization. According to his theory, the culture of any society constitutes a pattern of interrelated elements. Once integration and stability have been achieved, a change in any one part of the pattern may create strains and disturbances in the closely related parts. Eventually, adjustments will be made to restore harmony, but meanwhile there may be a considerable time lag during which tension persists. In modern industrial societies, it is technological change that sets the pace. According to Ogburn's theory, technological progress produces rapid changes in the material aspects of our culture, but the nonmaterial aspects fail to adjust, or they do so only after an excessive time lag. As a result, many troublesome social problems are created.

Cultural lag is the slowness in the rate of change on one part of a culture in relation to another, resulting in a maladjustment within society. A frequently cited cultural lag is the failure of political organizations to adjust to advances in transportation. To illustrate, the present system of counties and county governments in the United States was established when the only way to travel to the county seat was by horse and buggy. Because twenty miles or so was the practical limit of a day's travel, larger units of local government would have been difficult to administer. Today there is no such restriction on travel, for by automobile we can travel more than 100 miles in two hours or less. Business can be conducted by fax or by the Internet instantaneously. For example, I worked on this book while teaching university professors in Bulgaria and communicating with my U.S. publisher by phone, fax, and e-mail. Students of government now maintain that most of our rural counties are far too small to be efficient units of local government. However, our governmental institutions are so resistant to change that any substantial modification of existing county lines is almost impossible.

Limitations of the Cultural Lag Theory

The cultural lag theory is useful, provided we clearly understand its meaning and its limitations. In the first place, we must not assume that changes in the material aspects of culture always precede changes in the nonmaterial aspects. There is a constant interaction between the two, and in the long run technological progress itself is largely dependent on certain nonmaterial factors such as social attitudes and forms of social organization. Most, if not all, of the material products of culture originate in the human mind, and new material devices will not be invented and put to use unless the nonmaterial cultural atmosphere is favorable. The rapid material progress characteristic of present-day society is itself the result of earlier changes in our nonmaterial culture, changes that made possible the development of modern machine technology. We have already called attention to some of these earlier developments. One was the increased receptivity to change that was brought about by historical movements such as the Renaissance, the Reformation, and the great voyages of discovery. Another closely related factor was the development of mental attitudes that made it possible to apply the scientific method to the search for truth.

In the second place, when changes occur in the material culture we may sometimes have difficulty in agreeing on the kinds of adjustments needed in the nonmaterial culture. Consider, for example, the invention of the automobile and its widespread adoption as a means of transportation. The automobile brought about many social changes, including changes in the customs of courtship and dating. One of its effects was to enable dating couples to escape, to some degree, the close supervision of their elders. Did this represent an unsatisfactory adjustment of our nonmaterial culture to the automobile? Some observers maintained that it did. They considered it an example of cultural lag and argued that new ways of supervising dating couples had to be devised to maintain moral standards. Others, however, regarded greater freedom in the relations between the sexes not as a problem but as a development that represented social progress.

But even if there is general agreement that the nonmaterial culture has not satisfactorily adjusted to changes in the material culture, making the desired adjustments may be difficult or, conceivably, impossible. The word *lag* implies optimistically that the satisfactory solution of social problems resulting from technological change is merely a matter of time, but in some cases this time may never come. Our society's increased medical knowledge of fetal abortive processes has only added to the social conflict surrounding that issue, for instance.

Contrasts among Cultures

The interaction between culture and social change leads not only to social problems within a society but also to problems among various societies. The reason is that different cultures often evolve along quite different paths. For example, in our culture women and men are considered equal. In certain other cultures, a woman's role is fundamentally different from a man's role. (For example, in some Islamic societies a woman is not allowed to drive a car.)

Archaic tribal societies often differ from one another greatly, but unless they are brought into contact with powerful outside influences, they tend to be relatively stable. Industrial societies are much more subject to change. In them people's wants tend to multiply rapidly, as do the products with which to satisfy them. From one culture to another, family relations, economic activities, government, religion, and art take on an endless variety of forms.

The Interaction of Humans and Society

Though we are all, in part, products of our cultural environment, no two persons will have exactly the same personal experiences. Furthermore, they will not inherit biologically the same physical and nervous constitutions, and these inherited differences will cause them to react differently to many of the elements in their cultural environment.

Thus the study of humankind is a complicated one that moves from unique traits of individuals to general aspects of society and back again to unique aspects of individuals. Therefore, such a study must encompass a wide range of issues.

Cultural Relativism

The doctrine of **cultural relativism** asserts that all cultures are for the most part equally valid. That is, cultures develop in a way that best suits the population's needs, and the cultural traits within a culture have a specific purpose.

Today few students of society would question the proposition that any culture that has enabled a group to meet its basic needs, and to survive over a long period of time, is worthy of respect, as are the individuals who practice its customs and follow its moral precepts. Cultures are not as a whole good, bad, right, or wrong; they simply exist and must be judged relative to their own value system. Therefore, to understand other cultures, we must try to look at them through the eyes of those who have been brought up under their influence rather than through our own eyes. If we do this, we may find that these cultures meet needs we have failed to recognize. For example, nineteenth-century missionaries to certain South Sea islands were shocked to find that the native women wore no clothing above the waist. Part of their mission was to convert the women to wearing Mother Hubbards, shapeless dresses that kept their bodies well covered. To the missionaries, this seemed a great gain. But from a health standpoint, it may have been unfortunate. In the tropical rainy climate of the islands, the Mother Hubbards were wet much of the time, and they may have contributed to poor health.

Ethnocentrism is the tendency to judge other cultures by a person's own culture and its standards, the belief of a group that its people and its way of life are superior to

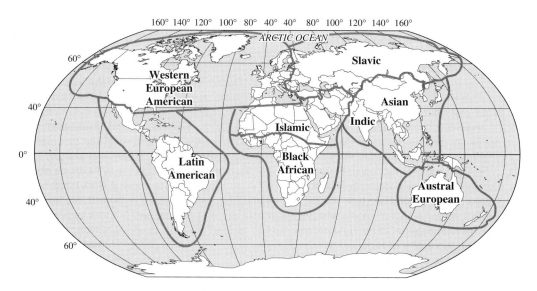

Cultural regions of the world.

all others. An extreme example in the twentieth century was the Nazi doctrine that the Germans were a superrace. In modern societies, feelings of ethnocentrism and chauvinism increase during times of insecurity or economic depression. Pre-Nazi Germany was in a severe depression, which many believe enabled Adolf Hitler to rise to power. In the late twentieth century, we saw, or were forced to recognize, the power of religion as a divisive force. In countries such as Northern Ireland, India, Pakistan, and the former Yugoslavia, opposing religious groups have fought bitterly with each other within their own borders, and their internal differences can affect their relations with foreign countries as they sometimes attempt to influence beliefs in other nations. Frequently these religious convictions are mixed with political problems, making the cultural issues complex and recalcitrant.

At one time, ethnocentrism may have had a survival value for some nonliterate tribal societies by giving them confidence in the superiority of their own people and own way of life. But nowadays, although ethnocentrism still contributes to the cohesion of a society, survival is likely to depend on achieving understanding and cooperation among races, peoples, and nations. Although some ethnocentrism is necessary to hold a society together, the conscious cultivation of ethnocentrism generally results in misunderstanding, prejudice, ill feeling, and conflict.

Approach to the Study of Society

In this book we are primarily concerned with the nature of modern U.S. society. Most of the discussion is therefore centered on our own culture and its basic values and on the problems that arise in connection with efforts to achieve these values. However, we can understand our own society better if we see it in perspective. Hence, throughout the book we call attention to other societies and cultures, to the characteristics common to all cultures, and to the differences that distinguish them.

Because it is not the function of science to determine social values, we simply assume for the most part the validity of the basic ideals of our own democratic society, and occasionally we attempt to clarify these ideals. But our principal efforts are concerned with giving a picture of the general character of U.S. society. We explain its values and its social institutions. We also discuss its failures to achieve its goals and the frustration and conflict that are sometimes the result, and we consider the nature of its major problems and explore the possibilities of solving them through social action.

Key Points

- Culture holds society together.
- Important elements of culture include social norms, social institutions, material products, language, and social values.
- Three popular theories of cultural change include the "good old days" theory, "the world is getting better" theory, and the "change runs in cycles" theory.
- Five factors that cause culture to change are technology, cultural diffusion, ideas and ideologies, collective action, and geography and climate.
- Three factors stabilizing culture are stability of social norms, habit, and value attachment.
- The cultural lag theory states that a change in any one part of culture may create strains and disturbances in the closely related parts.
- The doctrine of cultural relativism states that all cultures are for the most part equally valid.

Some Important Terms

conventions (80)
cultural alternatives (83)
cultural diffusion (87)
cultural evolution (78)
cultural integration (83)
cultural lag (93)
cultural objects (artifacts) (81)
cultural relativism (95)
cultural universal (83)

culture (78)
discovery (86)
ethnocentrism (95)
habits (91)
ideology (88)
Internet (85)
invention (86)
language (82)
laws (80)

mores (80)
social evolution (85)
social institution (81)
socialization (78)
social problem (92)
social values (82)
society (79)
vested interest (91)

Questions for Review and Discussion

1. What is the definition of culture given in the text?
2. What is cultural evolution?
3. What are some examples of conventions, mores, and laws found in U.S. society?
4. What are social institutions? What are the four elements of a social institution as stated by William Graham Sumner?
5. What are social values? Give some examples. Do you think Americans could ever accept infanticide as a positive social value? Why or why not?
6. Why are the cultures of primitive societies more integrated than the cultures of modern industrial societies?
7. Explain the relationship between culture and society.

8. What developments of the last five or six centuries do you think have been of greatest importance in speeding up the rate of social change? Explain why in each case.

9. Distinguish between the concepts of social evolution and social change.

10. Explain the relation to social change of the following: discovery and invention, cultural diffusion, ideas and ideologies.

11. Why does social change usually encounter strong resistance? Is this fortunate or unfortunate? Explain.

12. What is a social problem? Why is a particular social problem often difficult to define or isolate?

13. State the theory of cultural lag and discuss its limitations.

14. What is cultural relativism? How does this concept relate to ethnocentrism?

15. Of today's major social problems, which three seem to you most critical? Defend your choices.

16. Sometimes we are dissatisfied with aspects of our social system. Should we therefore dismantle it completely and start over? Why or why not?

*I*nternet Questions

1. The site www.toolpack.com/culture.html discusses cultural change at the organizational (business) level. What is organizational culture? Name the four companies used as examples of successful cultures.

2. Look through the website for the United States Golf Association, www.usga.org. Is the USGA a social institution? Do golfers form a society?

3. The Navajo Nation is the largest Native American tribe in the Southwest; see www.Navajo.org. What are their stated objectives?

4. Go to www.unesco.org/courier/2001_7/UK/doss.htm. What were the Native American languages used for coded messages in World War I and II, and why were they so effective?

5. According to www.engl.virginia.edu/courses/enwr1013/public_html/Karen/krr3p2.html, does body piercing challenge the social norms or is it convention?

*F*or Further Study

Coveney, Peter, and Roger Highfield, *Frontiers of Complexity: The Search for Order in a Chaotic World*, New York: Fawcett Columbine, 1995.

Ehrlich, Paul R., *Human Natures: Genes, Cultures, and the Human*, Covelo, CA: Island Press Shearwater Books, 2000.

FLASH! The Associated Press Covers the World, New York: Abrams, 1998.

Fukuyama, Francis, *The Great Disruption: Human Nature and the Reconstitution of Social Order*, New York: Free Press, 1999.

Glover, Jonathan, *Humanity: A Moral History of the Twentieth Century*, New Haven, CT: Yale University Press, 2000.

Harrison, Lawrence E., and Samuel P. Huntington, eds., *Culture Matters: How Values Shape Human Progress*, New York: Basic Books, 2000.

Jenness, Valerie, and Ryken Grattet, *Making Hate a Crime: From Social Movement to Law Enforcement*, New York: Russell Sage, 2001.

Kammen, Michael, *American Culture, American Tastes: Social Change and the 20th Century*, New York: Knopf, 1999.

Mead, Margaret, *Continuities in Cultural Evolution*, New Haven, CT: Yale University Press, 1964.

Shweder, Richard, *Why Do Men Barbecue? Recipes for Cultural Diversity*, Cambridge, MA: Harvard University Press, 2003.

Skoepol, Theda, *The Missing Middle: Working Families and the Future of American Social Policy*, New York: Norton, 2000.

Wolfe, Alan, *One Nation, After All: What Middle-Class Americans Really Think About—God, Country, Family, Racism, Welfare, Immigration, Homosexuality, Work, the Right, the Left, and Each Other,* New York: Viking Press, 1998.

WWW   Adherents of Cultural Relativism   www.quantonics.com/Famous_Crites.html

WWW   Business Culture Guide   www.executiveplanet.com

WWW   Center of Applied Linguistics   www.cal.org

WWW   Cultural Studies Central   www.culturalstudies.net

WWW   Internet Society   www.isoc.org

WWW   Social Change Links   gsociology.icaap.org

WWW   Urban Legends and Folklore   http://urbanlegends.about.com/library/glossary/bldef-folklore.htm

Zeigler, Alexis, *Conscious Cultural Evolution: Understanding Our Past, Choosing Our Future,* Charlottesville, VA: Ecodem Press, 2000.

Geography, Demography, Ecology, and Society

chapter 5

After reading this chapter, you should be able to:

- Identify the major countries on a map of the world
- Explain why many people believe population growth is a problem
- State the Malthusian theory and explain how technology can affect its predictions
- Explain how culture and the environment interact
- Explain how geography, population, culture, and the natural environment interact—and affect the ecological balance

Why do people do what they do where they do it?

—J. Rowland Illick

In the last chapter, we discussed culture, the glue that holds society together. In this chapter, we look at society from three slightly different perspectives—a geographic perspective, a demographic perspective, and an ecological perspective—discussing each in terms of its interrelationships with culture. Each of these perspectives highlights certain problems that societies face and provides a foundation for a better understanding of those problems.

Geography

In 1988 the National Geographic Society commissioned a study called "Geography: An International Gallup Survey." It tested 10,820 people in nine countries on their ability to identify sixteen spots on a map of the world. U.S. citizens could identify about half the places, but citizens aged eighteen to twenty-four could identify fewer than seven. People in Sweden, by the way, did the best. As a follow up, in 2002 there was a new National Geographic-Roper study on geographic literacy among young adults, and the United States came in second to last. Less than half of the U.S. citizens could identify France or Japan on a map, and just one-half could find the state of New York. The survey also looked at the world's cultural, economic, and natural resources. U.S. citizens were least likely to know that the Taliban was based in Afghanistan, and over one-third estimated the population of the United States to be ten times the actual number. The Swedes, again, were top scorers, though even they did not earn a mark of excellent.

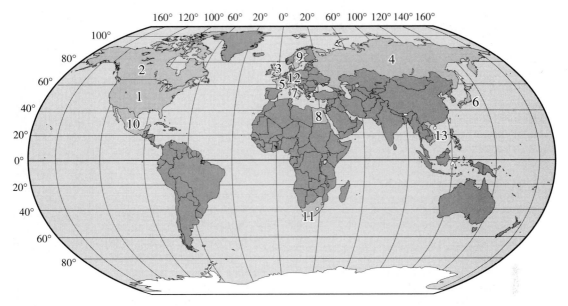

A geography quiz. Can you name the countries that are numbered on this map? Be careful; countries sometimes change their names suddenly. Within the past twenty years, Burma renamed itself Myanmar, Kampuchea changed its name back to Cambodia, and Zaire changed its name to Republic of Congo (its name before it was called "Zaire" was "The Congo"). The answers to our quiz follow (they're printed upside down).

1. United States, 2. Canada, 3. England, 4. Russia, 5. France, 6. Japan, 7. Italy, 8. Egypt, 9. Sweden, 10. Mexico, 11. South Africa, 12. Germany, 13. Vietnam

On this page you'll find a map of the world. To keep our quiz easy, we are asking you to identify only thirteen countries (leaving out the other three spots the National Geographic asked about). The countries we ask you to name are numbered. Let's hope you're as smart as the Swedes (who scored about 75 percent).

Even if you scored 100 percent, you do not necessarily know geography.[1] Geography is far more than the knowledge of where places are. **Geography** is a social science that focuses on the spatial interaction of human beings with each other and with their physical environment. Geography considers questions such as why cities are located where they are, how the environment shapes society's culture, and why some areas develop while others don't. For example, one explanation why central Africa was little touched by Western culture before twentieth-century technological advances in transportation is that all

---

[1]If you think you did well on our little quiz, remember that the places we chose were some of the most obvious. If we had asked you for cities, rivers, and oceans, the quiz would have been more difficult.

Do You Understand Space?

Geographical facts are concerned with space. Where is New York City, and how far is it from Wichita, Kansas? If you had the time and money, could you drive from Singapore to Paris?

Here is a short quiz on such geographical facts. The answers are below, but they are printed upside down (a manipulation of space).

1. What is the capital of California?
2. In what country is the mouth of the river Nile?
3. What is the largest city in the United States?
4. What is the difference between the Arctic and the Antarctic?
5. Japan is an archipelago. What is an archipelago?
6. If you superimposed Indonesia on a map of the United States, it would be as wide as the continental United States. Where is Indonesia?
7. Popocateptl is a volcano that had not erupted since 1802, but in late 2000 it began to spew flames and ashes that were considered so dangerous the government evacuated more than 40,000 people from their homes along the base of the mountain. Where is Popocateptl? Vesuvius is another famous volcano. It erupted in A.D. 79, burying an entire city in cinders and ashes. Where is Vesuvius?

8. What is the largest city in Canada?
9. What country or countries border the Black Sea?
10. Venice is famous because so many of its "streets" are really canals. Can you name another city that is laced with waterways that serve as streets?

Answers: 1. Sacramento. 2. Egypt. 3. New York City. 4. There are a lot of differences, but the most dramatic is that the Arctic is at the northern top of the world and the Antarctic is at the southern bottom of the world. Others: The Arctic has people and polar bears; the Antarctic has penguins but not native people. 5. A string of islands. 6. Northwest of Australia. 7. Popocateptl is in Mexico and Vesuvius is in Italy. Both are still active. 8. Toronto. 9. Georgia, Ukraine, Turkey, Bulgaria, and Romania. 10. There are many. Stockholm, Amsterdam, Bangkok, Jakarta, and Vancouver are some. Where are those cities, by the way? (Sweden, Netherlands, Thailand, Indonesia, Canada.) You probably can think of some others.

of its rivers flow toward the sea—it was just too difficult, too expensive, or both, for explorers and entrepreneurs to struggle against the current.

Where does such knowledge fit into the social sciences? As we emphasized in Chapter 1, there is enormous overlap among the social sciences. Therefore it is not only geographers who have considered the location of cities, the effect of environment on culture, and why some areas develop rather than others. Sociologists have considered these points, too. In fact, sociologists and some social scientists other than geographers were the first to raise many of the issues we discuss in this chapter. When geographers are asked about this, they say that sociologists are actually geographers. That claim seems to be a bit of social science equivocation, but it is less important to know which social science has had a particular idea than it is to know the idea itself.

Demography

Societies are made up of people. Whereas geography approaches the study of society by means of a spatial dimension, demography approaches it through a people dimension.

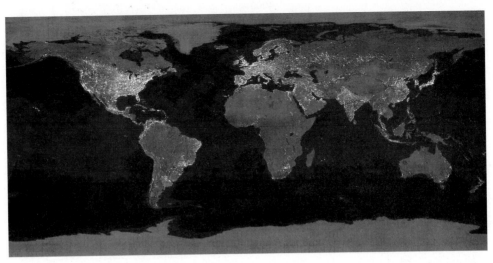

A global inventory of human settlements (taken by satellite). The lighted areas show dense settlements.

Demography is the study of the number and characteristics of a population. It is concerned not only with the number of people in an area but also with the factors that may be causing their number to increase or decrease. These include matters such as the state of health care and sanitation, the extent to which birth control is practiced, and the availability of food and other resources. Further, demography concerns the distribution of people among countries and regions and the different kinds of people who make up any given population and their physical, mental, and cultural characteristics. In this connection, demographers classify and count people on the basis of characteristics such as age, gender, marital status, occupation, income, nationality, and race.

Population Estimates

When we add up the population statistics for all countries, we conclude that there were approximately 6.3 billion people in 2003. Population is divided up unevenly among countries and regions (see Figure 5.1). China has the largest population of any country, with about 1.3 billion people; and Asia, with about 3.74 billion people, has the largest population of any region.

Determinants of Population Growth

Because two key determinants of the population of any country are its death rate and its birthrate, these deserve special consideration. Figure 5.2 shows the U.S. birthrates and death rates since 1960.

The current world death rate is considerably lower than in the distant past. How much further the death rate will drop in coming years will depend both on changes in the age composition of the world population and on the rate of advance in medical science. Although some further reduction in the death rate can be predicted, unless we make great advances in controlling degenerative diseases and the aging process itself, the

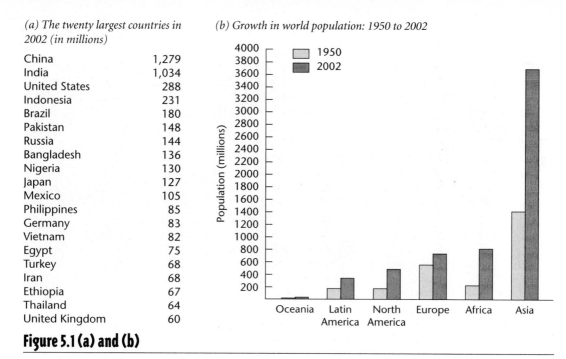

(a) The twenty largest countries in 2002 (in millions)

China	1,279
India	1,034
United States	288
Indonesia	231
Brazil	180
Pakistan	148
Russia	144
Bangladesh	136
Nigeria	130
Japan	127
Mexico	105
Philippines	85
Germany	83
Vietnam	82
Egypt	75
Turkey	68
Iran	68
Ethiopia	67
Thailand	64
United Kingdom	60

(b) Growth in world population: 1950 to 2002

Figure 5.1 (a) and (b)

The populations of the twenty largest countries are listed in (a). In (b) distribution of the world's population by regions is given for 1950 and 2002. (Some of the changes are due to changes as to which region countries are included.) Note that Oceania includes Australia. (Source: United Nations.)

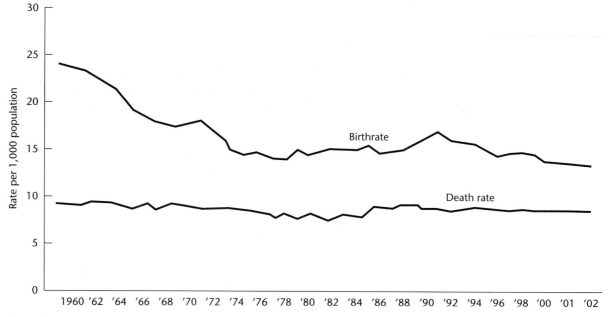

Figure 5.2

U.S. birthrates and death rates, 1960 to 2002. (Sources: U.S. Bureau of the Census; U.S. Department of Health and Human Services, *National Vital Statistics Report.*)

future of population growth will depend largely on the trend of the birthrate. As death rates decline, the world population will increase unless birthrates also fall. Developing countries have already seen their populations increase because of their declining death rates, despite the efforts of some of them to decrease their birthrates.

In Europe and the United States, the birthrate has been declining since the nineteenth century, although upswings have occurred periodically in one country or another. In the United States, for example, although the birthrate rose slightly in the beginning of the 1990s, most demographers believed this was a temporary phenomenon. In 2003, the U.S. birthrate saw its lowest level since data collection started in 1909. Most experts agree that the long-run decline of the birthrate will likely continue due to social and economic forces that make people less willing to accept the trouble, expense, and responsibility involved in raising large families.

Birth control has been so effective in the United States and western Europe that their population growth has slowed to a crawl. In less developed countries where children play an important economic as well as social role in the family, the population growth has continued at a high rate despite governmental attempts to slow it down. In India a program to force sterilization was a factor in the fall of the government of Indira Gandhi in 1977. She was later reelected and the program was significantly modified.

In China strong social and economic pressures to have only one child are applied to families. These include peer pressure (families deciding to have more than one child are often socially ostracized), economic pressure (families deciding to have more than one child are deprived of certain rights to housing, whereas those agreeing to have only one child are financially rewarded), and counseling (the party leaders visit and explain the reasons and need for birth control). The one-child program has not halted the rise in the birthrate because, despite official pressures and even fines of as much as $1,000 for families having more than one child, many couples are choosing to have more children.

Probably the most original approach to reducing the birthrate exists in Thailand, where the head of the family planning services uses a condom as his calling card. There, rather than university names or slogans on T-shirts, many wear T-shirts with the message, "A Condom a Day Keeps the Doctor Away." Contraceptive information is printed on things such as bottle caps, towels, and ice cream sticks.

The Growth of Population over Time

The past history of population has been one of significant but not continual growth. Instead, it has been marked by periods of expansion and contraction. Since 1800, however, the world population has grown rapidly.

Why Population Has Grown Rapidly since the 1800s. The great increase in world population since 1800 has resulted directly from a continuing decline of the death rate. Two factors are responsible for this: first, great advances in sanitation and health care, and second, a relatively rapid increase in the per capita output of both food and manufactured goods, so that for large numbers of people standards of living rose substantially above a subsistence level. In part, the increase in per capita output was made possible by the opening up for trade and settlement of some of the undeveloped areas of the world. Principally, however, the increase was a result of the Industrial Revolution. The great advances of science and technology in the nineteenth and twentieth centuries made it possible for the world to support a rapidly rising population. Furthermore, in Western industrial countries not only has it been feasible to support larger populations, but it has been possible to support them at higher standards of living than were known in the past.

Unequal Population Growth since the Late 1800s.   In the latter part of the nineteenth century, certain of the less developed parts of the world began to experience some of the benefits of modern science, industry, and transportation. Sanitation and improved health care began to reduce the death rate and to increase the rate of population growth. Some of the less developed regions of the world, such as Asia and Latin America, made substantially greater gains in population than Europe, the United States, and Canada.

However, increases in population in the developing areas of the world often occurred at the expense of standards of living. Birthrates remained high and production expanded slowly. If an increase in the food supply temporarily put off famine or relieved malnutrition, it was soon matched by a further increase in population. Since 1900 the population of Asia has increased fourfold; today nearly 60 percent of the people of the world are found there, but a large portion are still living at a bare subsistence level, despite economic growth.

Population Growth in the Future.   As you can see in Figure 5.3, demographers believe that world population will grow more and more slowly. They see the net gains in population decreasing at the beginning of the twenty-first century and almost ending by the beginning of the twenty-second century.

Net gains in world population

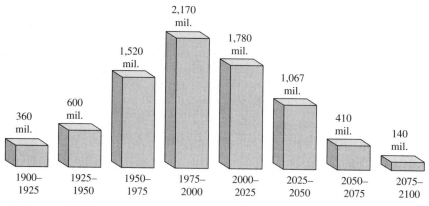

Figure 5.3

Population growth's peak period. Current trends suggest that additions to world population will come more slowly in the future. (Source: Population Division of the United Nations.)

That decrease will not help equalize the population among areas; the rate of population growth is, and will probably continue to be, much higher in some areas than in others. For instance, in western Europe and the United States the growth is expected to be much lower than in Africa or Latin America.

The Problem of Counting

This section discusses population estimates. It is important to remember that they are *estimates* and that some of them are not very good estimates. In fact, we have practically no population figures that are based on an actual census except for those of relatively recent years. A **census** is an official, systematic count of the number of people who live in a given area. Usually when people are counted, other kinds of information about them, such as age and gender, are also gathered. Lacking any census figures, we can make only rough guesses about populations and population changes that occurred before the latter part of the eighteenth century.

The first reliable census of a European country was taken by Sweden in 1749. In the United States, the first census was taken in 1790. About that time, or not long after, several other European countries began to take censuses, and by 1850 reasonably accurate figures were available for western Europe, the United States, and some countries in other parts of the world. Today we have fairly dependable population statistics for most countries, yet even the simplest numbers, such as how many people there are in a country, are often subject to debate. Although U.S. census figures are about the best in the world, after all the counting of our full 1990 census was done, there were still disputes about how many people were missed. The Census Bureau accepted that it actually missed about 12 million people in its count and that it double counted about 7 million people, making its count about 5 million (12 million minus 7 million) too low. Final compilation of the U.S. census of 2000 shows the total U.S. population at 281,421,906. This means that 33 million people were added to the total population from 1990 to 2000, representing the largest increase ever in population from census to census. The U.S. Census Bureau believes that this may be because this time there was better than expected counting of undocumented immigrants.

Why are the statistics not better? Ask yourself how you would work out a system to count about 280 million people who are constantly on the move, including homeless people and illegal aliens, and you'll quickly see why. Planners of the U.S. census of 2000 discussed using sampling techniques to "fill in" for the numbers of people who are missed when they are not individually counted, but the issue was politically charged. The moral of this story is that social scientists use census data but they use them carefully. They use their own estimates of the future even more carefully.

The Malthusian Theory

For more than a century, most discussions of the population problem have started from the theory of Thomas Robert Malthus concerning the relationship of population to the means of human subsistence. Malthus was a Church of England clergyman and an early English economist. In 1798 he published a short treatise called "An Essay on the Principle of Population as It Affects the Future Improvement of Society." During the next thirty years or more, he revised this treatise six times. The seventh and final edition was not published until 1834, after the author's death. Throughout all these editions, the basic argument remained the same, but in the second and later editions Malthus brought together a considerable amount of data to support his population doctrines.

Population and Means of Subsistence

Reduced to its simplest terms, the **Malthusian theory** is the belief that a population tends to outrun the means of subsistence. This was not a new idea, but Malthus developed it with such clarity and force that his treatise attracted wide attention. He contended that people are impelled to increase their numbers by a powerful natural urge, the attraction between male and female. As a result, if there are no obstacles population will increase rapidly and without limit. Furthermore, it will increase in geometric ratio—that is, by multiplication. By this Malthus meant that if a population could double in, say, twenty-five years, it would double again in the next twenty-five years, and so on indefinitely. He believed, however, that the means of subsistence could be increased only in arithmetic ratio—in other words, slowly and to a limited extent. Consequently, population would always tend to press against the food supply. When the food supply became inadequate to support more people, any further increase in population would be prevented by the "positive" checks of malnutrition, famine, disease, and war.

Malthus's belief that population growth would necessarily tend to outrun means of subsistence was based on the law of diminishing returns. In terms of the relationships between land, labor, and food output, the **law of diminishing returns** means that if more and more people are employed on a given area of land, even though total output may continue to expand, beyond a certain point average output per worker will shrink.

Crowded street in New Delhi.

The amount of good farmland in the world is limited. Once all the undeveloped regions of the earth have been settled and cultivated more or less intensively, further attempts to increase food production will become less and less effective because they will bring into operation the law of diminishing returns. It will still be possible to increase output by employing more workers on the land already cultivated or by cultivating land that is less fertile. However, assuming no advances in agricultural technology, this will bring about a decrease in the average output per worker, a decrease that will become greater and greater as attempts are made to raise production to higher and higher levels. It is possible that advances in agricultural technology might, for a long time, more than offset this tendency toward diminishing returns, but they could not do so indefinitely if population continued to grow. Sooner or later the amount of land per person would become impossibly small.

Malthus recognized that certain preventive checks might conceivably slow population growth by reducing the birthrate. These preventive checks he summarized under the general heading of "moral restraint." By this term he apparently referred to premarital chastity and late marriage. However, he did not believe that these preventive checks were likely to be practiced sufficiently to have much effect in keeping down births. Malthus apparently opposed both postmarital abstinence and contraception. He thought that marriage and its sexual satisfaction should carry with them the risks of bringing children into the world along with the responsibility to support them. Otherwise, people would get something for nothing and be deprived of their main incentive for economic improvement.

Because Malthus had little hope that the preventive checks would be effective in keeping population from exerting pressure on the means of subsistence, he was pessimistic about the chances of greatly improving the economic condition of most people. However, in the final edition of his essay he recognized that conditions in Europe were slowly improving in spite of the growth of population, and he expressed the hope that some way might yet be found to make possible the "gradual and progressive improvement" of human society.

The Concept of Optimal Population

Given the level of technological development, in any country growth of population beyond a certain point would mean lower standards of living. Relative shortages of farmlands, fuels, timber, metals, and other resources would develop. On the other hand, a very small population would also have disadvantages. In very thinly populated areas, it is often difficult to maintain law and order, to provide medical and hospital services, or to provide schools. Also, there are not enough people to build adequate roads or to make it worthwhile to operate public transportation services. The **optimal population** is the population that would maximize welfare for its members. What, then, is the optimum, or best, size of population from the standpoint of maximizing welfare?

Actually, there is no way of determining with even approximate accuracy what the optimal population of a country would be at any given stage in its development. Yet for any country there is likely a point beyond which an increase in population would strain its resources and reduce average output per worker, and hence reduce standards of living.

This view, however, is disputed by Julian Simon, author of *The Ultimate Resource,* who argued that people are the ultimate resource and that there can be no such thing as too many people. People create ideas, and as they do they create the technology by which the world can support an ever-larger population.

Most demographers do not share Simon's optimism. They believe that India, Pakistan, and China have already exceeded their optimal quantity and that the United States and western Europe are approaching theirs. But such views are primarily held by demographers from the United States and western Europe who have a Western cultural bias, and any statements about optimal population are inevitably culturally determined.

Poor have-not nations, for example, lay the blame for shortages of resources and other goods on the excessively wasteful policies of developed countries, with their emphasis on consumption rather than conservation. Some critics claim that Western nations are using the population issue and the need for reduced birthrates in countries with high birthrates as another form of imperialist control over these areas, which were so recently freed from colonialism.

The Question of Population Quality

In the past, some students of human society have been concerned about the possibility that social forces would bring about a serious deterioration of the biological quality of human populations. They feared that the danger would be greatest in the countries that have made the most social and economic progress. This deterioration, they felt, might take two forms: (1) a decline of the physical quality and stamina of individuals, with an increasing incidence of physical defects, and (2) a decline of native intelligence—that is, the capacity for mental development.

Their arguments as to why this might happen were varied. One was that the advances we have made in medicine and science have meant, among other results, that it is easier for children who are weak or have physical disabilites to survive, grow to maturity, and have children of their own. Modern medicine makes the principle of the survival of the fittest inoperative, or greatly weakened. In short, humanitarianism and science, instead of saving the human race, will ultimately destroy it, they argue in a worst-case scenario.

A second argument being made today is a socioeconomic one. It goes as follows: With the development of the two-income family, intelligent individuals will choose careers over marriage and family and will have few children, leaving the less advantaged and less educated to bear the majority of the children. To support this view, they usually point to the difference in the birthrate between the upper and middle classes on the one hand and the less advantaged classes on the other.

No one can be certain to what extent economic and social success result from inborn qualities that the upper classes possess in greater measure than the other classes. We know that individual success depends on both social environment and biological inheritance. There is always an interplay between the two. But to move from this obvious fact to a belief that we can determine whether society will be better or worse off when one socioeconomic group has children while another does not is a difficult step that few are willing to take. Moreover, most people are unwilling even to consider the social measures required to ensure that only certain groups have reproductive rights.

Given modern developments in genetic engineering, these issues are likely to become more and more important. For example, it is now possible with amniocentesis to check a fetus for gender and for some birth defects long before it is born. Eggs from one woman can be transplanted into another, and sperm can be frozen to be used for artificial insemination. Some time in this century it may be possible to change the genetic characteristics of sperm and eggs so that children's characteristics can be controlled. In principle, couples might go to a genetic engineering company and order the type of child they want ("girl who will grow up to be 5 feet 7 inches tall and weigh 128 pounds,

"Frankly, I think we'll regret introducing these organisms into the environment."

with an IQ of 217," and so forth). The questions society faces are, Should such technologi-cal advances be allowed to continue? And if they do, who should do the specifying?

Some societies have taken an active role in trying to control the genetic qualities of their population. For instance, Singapore, whose government has successfully adminis-tered severe laws against drug dealing, pornography, and littering, attempted in the 1980s to institute a program whereby extra privileges were promised to women university graduates who married and had children. At the same time, it was proposed that bo-nuses of $5,000 be awarded to less educated mothers who submitted to sterilization. The government's stated reasons for these proposals were that uneducated women were having twice the number of children as college graduates were, and the prime minister claimed that this would "deplete the talent pool" and that the "level of competence would decline." However, women and others perceived the program as unfair; scientists questioned the assumptions on which it was based; less educated women did not want to be sterilized, even for $5,000; women did not want to be treated as breeding stock; and the experiment was withdrawn after about a year and a half.

Ecology: The Interaction of Geography, Demography, and Environment

Geography and demography come together in a consideration of environmental issues and ecology. The **environment** is the sum of all the external influences that impinge on the human organism. These influences exert their effects through physical stimuli that produce sights, sounds, tastes, smells, and other bodily sensations. These sensations make us aware of our environment, and through them we are able to interpret this environment and react to it.

The **social environment** is composed of the elements in our surroundings that are human or of human origin. The **natural environment** is composed of the nonhuman elements in our surroundings. The general character of our social environment depends chiefly on the culture of the group to which we belong. The character of our natural envi-ronment depends primarily on the climate, water resources, soil, topography, plant and animal life, and mineral resources of the part of the world we live in. However, once human beings have lived in an area for a long time, they are certain to have made changes, for better or worse, in their environment. It then becomes difficult to draw a sharp line between the constructed physical environment and some aspects of the natural environment.

The Ecological Balance

Ecology is the science concerned with the interactions between living things and their en-vironment. The environment of each species of organism includes not only the inanimate world but also all other living species that affect it directly or indirectly. It includes the population density of its own members and the character of their behavior.

Human ecology is the part of ecology that deals with the way in which human socie-ties adjust to their environments. It considers the processes by which populations adapt to their surroundings, taking into account the technology and the types of social organi-zation by which adjustment is achieved. Human ecology applies some of the findings of

A forest of skyscrapers and signs in New York City.

the biological sciences to problems dealt with by the social sciences.

In the world of nature, there is normally a movement toward ecological balance. **Ecological balance** is the term applied to the state achieved when each plant or animal species, with its own characteristics and needs, has adjusted to its environment and survived, and when other species, which have likewise adjusted to the environment, prevent it from expanding indefinitely and from crowding them out. Most species depend on other species for food or for meeting other needs. Though the natural ecological balance is not absolutely static, normally it changes slowly over long periods of time. New species that can make superior adjustments evolve and may destroy or crowd out old species and render the latter extinct, or changes in climate may occur such that some species cannot survive.

Modern times have brought rapid changes in the ecological balance in many parts of the world. Sometimes the results have been good from the human point of view, but sometimes they have been almost disastrous. When rabbits were introduced into Australia where they had no natural enemies and multiplied by the millions, they became a national problem. By building the St. Lawrence Seaway, engineers allowed lampreys to enter the Great Lakes, where they almost completely destroyed the whitefish. People have caused the introduction of insect pests from one part of the world to another, often with disastrous results. After World War II, the nearly worldwide use of an insecticide called DDT did indeed control or eliminate undesirable insects, but it also destroyed or damaged other forms of animal life and even human health.

Examples of threats to the ecological balance are many: industrial pollution, smokestack emissions, acid rain, depletion of water tables, and paving over of fertile soil and plant and animal habitats. These by no means exhaust the list, and we have not even attempted to describe ecological catastrophes on whole continents, such as Africa. Since the 1970s, the United States has had to face the fact that many industrial, military, and agricultural chemicals are not only lethally affecting animal life but also exercising long-term effects on human health, and that the cost of eliminating these chemicals and repairing their ravages (where possible) is astronomical. The costs are incalculable of policing hazardous waste disposal, discovering and salvaging previously used sites, finding alternative chemicals to those that have caused trouble, and devising safe methods for disposal of wastes from indispensable activities such as radioactive medical technology. Today, given snowballing technological growth, the possibility of irreversible change is enormous. For example, the explosion in worldwide commerce

Hometown, USA.

and travel has already meant that plants, animals, and insects have traveled outside their natural habitats and are crowding out or eliminating plants and animals in the localities to which they emigrate. In the same way, the migration of viruses is predicted by some scientists to spread nearly untreatable disease far from the sites to which such viruses were formerly confined.

Pollution and Conservation

A major concern of ecologists is **pollution**—the destruction of our natural resource base by the productive process. Over the past fifty years there has been extensive pollution of rivers, lakes, and forests by sewage and industrial wastes. As early as the 1950s, even in such a large body of water as Lake Erie, pollution reached a level that destroyed commercial fishing and made most beaches unusable. Pure air also has become scarce in many of our urban centers, where the inhabitants often must breathe a mixture of air combined with auto fumes, dust, and various waste products from trash fires, incinerators, and the smokestacks and flares of industrial plants. Improperly disposed toxic chemicals and various noxious waste products have invaded the soil in some areas, and sometimes whole communities must be moved while their former homesites are cleaned up. In other communities, people suspect that various illnesses are caused by this kind of problem, but no cleanup seems immediately practical. In the United States, a federal law enacted near the end of the twentieth century mandated that by 2000 nuclear waste must be safely disposed of in sites where no leakage will occur for "thousands of years." This mandate has proved impossible to implement, partly because it is seemingly beyond current technology, but principally because people do not want such a site anywhere near where they live, and we are seeing much vigorous disagreement as localities all strive to avoid being chosen. NIMBY (Not In My Back Yard) has become a watchword of modern times.

*I*s Skin Cancer in Your Future?

One of the worrisome changes that has occurred in the past thirty years is the depletion of the ozone layer by synthetic chemicals, specifically chlorofluorocarbons (CFCs). That's of concern because the ozone layer in the atmosphere shields the earth from the sun's ultraviolet rays. For years scientists predicted that this would happen if we persisted in using CFCs, which are cheap and useful and appear, for instance, in the Styrofoam cups that enable you to carry hot coffee around your dormitory or in your car. But proof that the scientists were right came only in the late 1980s when an international team documented the depletion.

In response, the U.S. Senate voted to ratify an international treaty that would cut the use of CFCs in half by 1999.* Environmentalists argued that even if the treaty is ratified by all countries, it would be too little, too late. They forecast a number of horrors that the depletion will cause, including increased incidence of skin cancer, suppression of immune systems, decreased crop yields, and disruption of the aquatic food chain. The year 1999 has come and gone, and reaching the goal of the treaty at a future date is still uncertain. Efforts to control pollution and mitigate the horrors do continue on a global scale, but we will not know for many decades what the positive results might be.

*A number of colleges and restaurants are doing their part by no longer using Styrofoam cups. So when you burn your hand on your next cup of coffee, remember, it's for a good cause.

Some pollution is an inevitable consequence of production, presenting society with a trade-off: Do we want more material things, or do we want a more pristine environment? In making that decision, both the costs and benefits must be considered.

Although people can agree on the need for conservation and strong antipollution efforts when costs are not considered, when costs are considered there is significantly less agreement. Let's consider some of these costs. They involve restrictions on individual actions, relocation of industry and jobs, new bureaucracy, and the development of expensive new technology. In assessing the issue of pollution, the costs as well as the benefits must be considered. Therefore it is unlikely that we will decide to institute a "no pollution" policy; that would be impossible. And even approaching a standard of "little" pollution would be too expensive. Instead we are likely to choose an "optimal level" of pollution.

Since the 1960s, the United States has made considerable gains in fighting pollution, but it has not been easy. The central problem is what is called the "tragedy of the commons." Because the environment belongs to society and not to specific individuals, no individual has the incentive to care for it. A number of governmental antipollution agencies have been established. The **Environmental Protection Agency (EPA)** is the most important government antipollution agency; it directs antipollution efforts and monitors environmental problems. Some of its gains have been impressive. In the early 1950s, Lake Erie was so polluted by untreated sewage from surrounding areas that many forms of animal life could not inhabit it. Today it is well on the way to recovery. Sewage treatment plants were mandated, and firms were prevented from dumping industrial waste into the lake.

Laws also were passed dealing with oil spills so that companies responsible for the spillage are responsible for cleaning them up. Similar laws have been passed concerning other types of pollution.

Many environmental issues have international dimensions. An example is our recent effort to control global warming. Many scientists believe that the emission of industrial waste gases is causing global warming and that this global warming could have dire consequences in the future. In 1997, delegates from 160 countries attended a ten-day conference on this subject in Kyoto, Japan. This conference resulted in the issuance of a document called the **Kyoto Protocol,** which provided that industrialized countries must cut emissions of these gases, especially carbon dioxide.

Many in the United States were upset that only industrial countries would be required to reduce emissions and that developing countries such as China and India would not have to comply. The exception of developing countries was justified by the argument that they began emitting later than industrial countries, and they need to "catch up" economically. The Kyoto Protocol set 2000 as the date for its accomplishment. No industrial nation met that deadline, and in fact by 2000, U.S. emissions were about 13 percent above 1990 levels. The problems of the protocol, which has no enforcement mechanism, have been dealt with by setting the deadline further and further ahead. The U.S. Senate (in 1998) and President

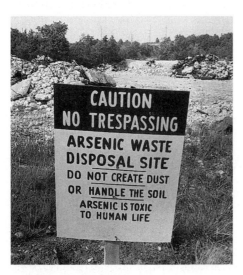

A toxic waste disposal site.

George W. Bush (in 2001) announced that they would not support the protocol because they believe it will be bad for the U.S. economy and, moreover, would not work even if attempted. Nonetheless, it was passed, and by 2003 most countries in the world had signed or ratified it. The United States was the only large industrialized country that did not sign. Instead, President Bush declared the protocol fatally flawed, and he set forth what he called the Clear Skies Initiative, which was a plan to combat global warming through voluntary measures, with a cap-and-trade approach that rewards industries that reduce pollution. In a cap-and-trade approach, a total amount of pollution is determined (the cap) and new sources of pollution must buy the rights to pollute from existing polluters who agree to lower their pollution by an offsetting amount so that total pollution does not increase.

Conclusion

This chapter has reviewed geographic, demographic, and ecological problems that society faces and has shown some of the ways society meets them. Of the three types of problems, the geographic problems are the most constant, but with new technologies even these can change. The Internet, for example, has made it possible for more individuals to work in more rural areas and has increased the range of areas where businesses can operate.

Demographic problems are constantly changing: As societies become richer, their population growth generally decreases on its own. Nonetheless, population problems play central roles in many countries' social problems. Whereas demographic problems generally decline as a country gets richer, ecological problems often become more severe. But the wealth of society also gives it the means to deal with those ecological problems. Whether it actually does deal with them is a political issue; often, even though the means are there, the political will is not.

Social scientists study such problems and work on alternative solutions that circumvent the political problems. Finding an acceptable alternative is seldom easy, but that work generally leads to a better understanding of the problem and of alternative solutions.

Key Points

- Knowing the geography of the world is an important skill.
- The world population has fluctuated over time, but since the 1800s it has grown substantially.
- The Malthusian theory is the belief that population tends to outrun the means of subsistence.
- The law of diminishing marginal returns: If more and more people are employed on a given area of land, beyond a certain point—even though the total output may continue to expand—average output per worker will shrink.
- The birthrate and the death rate interact to determine population growth.
- The ecology of our world is affected by human action, the life and death of species, climate changes, productive changes that result in pollution, and conservation measures.
- There is often a trade-off between economic production goals and environmental goals.

Some Important Terms

census (107)
demography (103)
ecological balance (112)
ecology (111)
environment (111)
Environmental Protection
  Agency (EPA) (114)

geography (101)
human ecology (111)
Kyoto Protocol (114)
law of diminishing returns
  (108)
Malthusian theory (108)
natural environment (111)

optimal population (109)
pollution (113)
social environment (111)

Questions for Review and Discussion

1. What are some of the questions that geography is concerned with?
2. How does geography interact with sociology?
3. How many people are there in the world?
4. What is the world's most populous country? Explain some of the problems that country faces in trying to limit its population growth, including the problems it will have if it is successful.
5. What is the Malthusian doctrine? Have the predictions of Thomas Malthus come true?
6. Identify some of the reasons that the world population has grown in the past two hundred years.
7. What are some possible ways to limit population? Mention natural causes as well as those encouraged by government or other policies.
8. In practice, are all policies for limitation of population growth acceptable? If not, which ones would you argue against?
9. What are some of the costs of pollution? What are some of the gains from pollution? It would be very expensive to clean up areas that have been polluted. What are some ways you can think of to pay for such cleanups?
10. You are a government planner in the country of Growthlandia. You would like to know where to build new schools, where to close schools, and whether it makes sense to embark on an ambitious program to expand the number of job opportunities. What would you like to know about the composition of Growthlandia's population now and how that population is likely to change in the next fifteen years?

Internet Questions

1. Go to an atlas site (for example, www.atlapedia.com) and look at a country or region. Look at its physical and political map. What borders it? Which borders are natural?
2. At www.cptr.ua.edu/kudzu, read about kudzu. What is it? What are its benefits to southeastern United States?
3. Using the United Nations Statistical Division site, http://unstats.un.org/unsd/demographic/default.htm, what are some of the trends found in "The World's Women 2000"?
4. Go to www.geohive.com/global/index.php. Looking at the latest figures for populations of countries by sex, what two countries have the highest percentage of females? Of males?
5. What is the ozone layer according to the EPA, www.epa.gov/docs/ozone/science/q_a.html#q1? What is today's UV index value for your zip code (www.epa.gov/sunwise/uvindex.html)?

For Further Study

Amato, Ivan, *Stuff: The Materials the World Is Made Of,* New York: Basic Books, 1997.

Bryson, Bill, *A Walk in the Woods,* New York: Broadway, 1998.

Bureau of the Census, *Current Population Reports,* Washington, DC: Population estimates for the United States issued monthly; special reports from time to time.

Burnett, Jonathan, *Planning for a New Century,* Covelo, CA: Island Press Shearwater Books, 2000.

Dean, Cornelia, *Against the Tide: The Battle for America's Beaches,* New York: Farrar, Straus & Giroux, 1999.

Diamond, Jared, *The Wealth and Poverty of Nations,* New York: Norton, 1998.

Malthus, Thomas, *An Essay on the Principle of Population, or, A View of its Past and Present Effects on Human Happiness,* New York: Cambridge University Press, 1992 (first published in 1798).

McPhee, John, *Annals of the Former World,* New York: Farrar, Straus & Giroux, 1999.

Mead, Margaret, ed., *Cultural Patterns and Technical Change,* New York: New American Library/Mentor, 1956.

Newbold, K. Bruce, *Six Billion Plus: Population Issues in the Twenty-First Century,* Lanham, U.K.: Rowman & Littlefield, 2002.

Poinar, George Jr., and Roberta Poinar, *The Amber Forest: A Reconstruction of a Vanished World,* Princeton, NJ: Princeton University Press, 2000.

Safina, Carl, *Song of the Blue Ocean: Encounters along the World's Coasts and beneath the Seas,* New York: Henry Holt, 1998.

Simon, Julian, *The Ultimate Resource,* Princeton, NJ: Princeton University Press, 1981.

Smith, Norris, *Changing U.S. Demographics,* New York: H.W. Wilson, 2002.

Statistical Abstract of the United States, Washington, DC: U.S. Bureau of the Census, issued annually.

Sullivan, Robert, *The Meadowlands: Wilderness Adventures at the Edge of a City,* New York: Scribner, 1999.

Whitfield, Peter, *New Found Lands: Maps in the History of Exploration,* New York: Routledge, 1998. Chapter 5.

WWW   Ecology Communications   www.ecology.com

WWW   The Environmental Protection Agency   www.epa.gov

WWW   Foundation for Clean Air Progress   www.cleanairprogress.org/index.asp

WWW   GeoHive—Global Statistics   www.geohive.com/index.php

WWW   Maps and Geography www.nationalgeographic.com/resources/ngo/maps

WWW   The United Nations   www.un.org

WWW   The U.S. Bureau of the Census   www.census.gov

Technology and Society

After reading this chapter, you should be able to:

- Define technology and explain its importance
- Explain how the Industrial Revolution significantly changed all aspects of society
- Discuss the role that technology plays in social change
- Present both sides of the limits-to-growth debate
- List some of the important technological developments of the past
- Speculate on likely important technological developments in the future

Political activity is shadow-play . . . ; technology is the underlying reality. Engineers, not poets, are the secret legislators of the world.

—David Warsh

Technology is the universe of tools, means, and methods through which we interact with our environment. We devote a separate chapter to technology because it is an integral cog in social and cultural change. It both causes social change and is itself influenced by culture. In our brief overview of history, we saw the importance of technology—in the initial establishment of cities, made possible by crop cultivation; in the spread of population to overcome environmental limitation, through the use of fire; and in the evolution of our thinking about society, by means of printing. That evolution is continuing. Computers, robots, gene splicing, nuclear research, interactive information systems—all are currently in the process of changing our society, presenting us with new problems and new horizons. Exactly how that technology will affect society is hard to predict, but that it will change it is certain.

We begin our consideration of technology with a short quiz (p. 119). In the left column we list six technological advances that have helped shape our society. In the middle column is a set of dates and in the right column a list of names. These are, of course, only some of the best-known discoveries; the list could go on and on. Moreover, each of these technological developments has a compelling story accompanying its introduction, and even more interesting effects that it has caused. For example, the process of canning food was developed in 1810 by an enterprising Frenchman, Nicholas Appert. The stimulus for this invention came from Napoleon Bonaparte. As early as 1800, Emperor Napoleon recognized the importance of preserving food after nearly losing the Battle of Marengo because of a lack of provisions. The emperor realized that a reliable method of

*C*an You Match the Date and Name with the Invention?

1. First motorcar	(a) 1876	(aa) Alexander Graham Bell
2. Telephone	(b) 1896	(bb) Thomas Edison
3. Incandescent lightbulb	(c) 1854	(cc) Guglielmo Marconi
4. Radio	(d) 1835	(dd) Elisha Otis
5. Elevators	(e) 1876	(ee) William Henry Fox Talbot
6. Photography	(f) 1885	(ff) Karl Benz

1—f, ff; 2—a or e, aa; 3—a or e, bb; 4—b, cc; 5—c, dd; 6—d, ee.

food preservation would enhance his chances of military success. Therefore Napoleon offered a set of prizes for technological improvements, including food preservation, believing that France lagged behind its rival, Great Britain, in technology.

When Appert, a cook who had worked in a wine cellar as a champagne bottler, heard about the prizes, he began work on a method to preserve food. It was many years before he perfected his process. Drawing on his experience as a cook and a bottler, Appert had an idea that he might be able to preserve food in champagne bottles by filling them with food, sealing them, and boiling the bottles. Although he did not know why the food in the bottles did not spoil (we now know it was because he had sterilized the contents of the bottles), still he was successful, and soon bottled food (and later, canned food) allowed individuals to eat vegetables in winter and to preserve meat over long periods. The desired result—better provisioning of armies—was accomplished, along with the far more widespread benefits that preserved food meant for public health.

Canned food was important in the early 1800s because there were no mechanical refrigerators. At that time, the only way to refrigerate food was by storing ice, which was cut from ponds in the winter and kept till the next winter, insulated by hay in windowless structures known as icehouses. In the United States, some southern states imported ice all year round from these icehouses. (As you can imagine, much of it melted, and one year in Apalachicola, Florida, the price rose to $1.25 a pound—about $50 in today's dollars.)

John Gorrie, a doctor trying to solve the problem of malaria, which was rampant in Florida at the time, discovered that the disease occurred more frequently in hot, humid weather. He felt he could reduce its incidence if he could lower the temperature of his hospital wards. At first he did this by blowing fans over blocks of ice, but when an ice shortage pushed the price to high levels, he decided there must be a better way. He was aware of some recent discoveries in chemistry—specifically, that compressed gases, when expanding rapidly, will absorb heat from their surroundings. He constructed a steam engine that would compress air (a gas) in a cylinder. As the piston withdrew, it would allow the air to escape and expand into another cylinder. Gorrie put a brine solution around this cylinder and found that it would get cold because the air inside the cylinder was cold. By pumping this cold air into his hospital wards, he invented the first air conditioner.

He also discovered that by placing water around the brine solution he could draw heat from the water to such an extent that the water turned to ice. Gorrie realized the enormous possibilities of the ice-making machine and tried to market it, but could not find any financial backing; he died a poor and broken man. For the next twenty years, people tried to perfect the invention, but with only moderate success. By the 1900s, however, the process was sufficiently developed that refrigerators became a commercial reality.

The social effects of refrigerators were enormous. People could buy larger quantities of food at lower prices. They no longer had to make as many trips to the store, which meant that neighborhoods provided fewer social and commercial contacts. Eventually refrigerators played an important role in destroying the basis for neighborhood stores and replacing them with the modern supermarket and modern advertising, both of which created profound changes in urban, suburban, and rural society.

Changes in refrigeration technology are ongoing. Thermal acoustic methods of cooling, in which sound waves are used to do the cooling, and magnetic field cooling are being explored as more efficient and less harmful methods of achieving refrigeration.

We recount these stories of the development of the food canning process and of refrigerators not because these inventions are unique—we could have chosen numerous other examples—but because seeing a particular instance gives us a better sense of the tremendous and far-reaching influence that technological progress can have on society.

The Industrial Revolution

The technological developments chosen for the quiz at the beginning of this chapter date from the 1800s. In part, that is because the discoverers of many earlier inventions are unknown. (Actually, historians often debate the origin of many technological discoveries, including modern ones.) But it is also because in the nineteenth century there was simply an enormous number of technological improvements. We limited the quiz to a few items you are likely to be able to identify. Many eighteenth-century inventions have become so outdated that many people alive today have never seen them, such as the steam locomotive that used to pull railroad cars. After a lull, technological improvement began to expand enormously about 1760. The period after that date is called the Industrial Revolution.

The **Industrial Revolution** is the name given to the sum of all the changes in economic and social organization characterized by the replacement of hand tools with power-driven machines and by the concentration of industry in large establishments. It had its beginnings in England around 1760. There, for the first time people began to employ power machines for industrial production and to build factories to house them. By 1800 this movement had made substantial progress.

The English Industrial Revolution was brought about by a cumulation of inventions. A new invention in one industry was followed by improvements and inventions in related industries. This is well illustrated by the textile inventions of the eighteenth century. These inventions were first employed in the cotton goods industry, which was relatively small and new, and the machinery was operated by water power. When James Watt devised a greatly improved steam engine, the revolution really took off. Machinery for producing cotton textiles was modified and applied to the production of woolen cloth, the output of which expanded by leaps and bounds. Costs and prices were so reduced that a great new demand developed for both wool and cotton products.

The developments just described gave England an advantage over its competitors. Because England was able to mechanize its industries so much sooner than other coun-

The interior of a nineteenth-century cotton factory.

tries, it was for many years the workshop of the world. Its production, trade, and wealth rose to what were then regarded as high levels. But in time industrialism began to spread to other nations.

The Development of Industrialism in the United States

In the early nineteenth century, the machine industry and factory system began to develop in the United States. The Napoleonic Wars (1803–1815) and the War of 1812 gave U.S. industrialization a strong push because they made it difficult for the United States to import English textiles.[1] To make up for the resulting shortage, many new textile factories were established in this country. Employers had to pay higher wages than their counterparts in the English factories, but as long as English textiles were not available, they could operate profitably. When peace came to Europe and normal trade was reestablished, many of these new factories were forced to close down. Others, however, survived, and from that time on the United States gradually became more and more industrialized.

In some respects, conditions in the United States favored industrialization. First, our domestic market was rapidly growing. Second, raw materials were plentiful. Third, labor was relatively scarce and wages were higher than in Europe, partly because workers kept leaving their jobs to settle on free or cheap land along the frontier. Although this raised costs of production, it also put a premium on the introduction of labor-saving machines. To reduce costs, as many operations as possible were shifted to power machines. As a result, production increased much faster than the number of workers, standards of living gradually rose, and wealth began to accumulate.

---

[1]Two of the adversaries in the Napoleonic Wars were France and England; two of the adversaries in the War of 1812 were the United States and England. Both wars disrupted U.S. trade with England.

Standardization, Interchangeability, and Mass Production

Early machines were crude by our standards. Because their parts did not fit together perfectly, they ran with a great deal of noise and clatter and frequently broke down. Often their products were imperfect, so that further work had to be done on them by hand to make them acceptable. One of the greater advances in industrial technology was the gradual development of precision machines that would run smoothly and that could also turn out standardized, accurately made, and hence interchangeable parts for more or less complex finished products such as watches, guns, washing machines, and automobiles. This development made it physically possible for a machine to produce thousands of units of a given part, all so nearly alike that they could be freely substituted for one another. **Standardization**—the production of uniform, substitutable parts—was made possible by a humble but far-reaching development, the improvement of measurement devices. Similar small improvements have played large roles in shaping our society, so it is worth describing this one in detail to give you a sense of the mundane aspect of technological development.

To understand the problem of standardization, think of a car. If you blow a piston, you go out and buy a new one. Getting the new piston is not cheap, but it is a lot cheaper than if you had to have a machinist make a new piston to fit your individual engine. It would probably cost twenty or thirty times as much. Extending this analogy to other areas, much of the machinery—for example, dishwashers, tractors, and photocopiers—we use today relies on **interchangeability,** the ability to substitute one part for another. Without it, there would be far fewer goods than we now have, and those that we do have would be more expensive.

So interchangeability is important; that's obvious. But if it is obvious that interchangeability has so many advantages, why weren't early machines built with interchangeable parts? The reason is a technical one: To achieve interchangeability in machines, tolerances (variations in size and shape) must be less than one-thousandth of an inch. With the tools available in the 1700s and early 1800s, even the best, most skilled machinist could not approach such tolerances, so interchangeability was only a dream until some method of achieving those tolerances could be found.

As has happened with many inventions, the strongest impetus for standardization came from the armed forces. Before and during the American Civil War (1861–1865), each rifle had to be produced separately. If one broke, a skilled machinist or gunsmith was needed to repair it. These craftsmen, using a variety of tools, would fashion a musket or even a rifle. Each musket had to be built precisely; that is, all the parts, such as the stock, barrel, and lock, had to fit together and work as a coordinated whole (hence the phrase, "lock, stock, and barrel"). But precision did not mean interchangeability. A gunsmith would work the individual components until they fitted together, but as he modified each part to fit the others, he made it specific to that weapon; the part worked in no other. To repair rifles, armies had to have their own musket makers who would fix individual muskets that had broken in the field. Armies would also keep armories where they made individual weapons, and armories were an important part of the defense capacity of any country.[2]

About 1820 one of the skilled musket makers, John Hall, argued that this procedure was inefficient, and that armies would have a tremendous advantage if their muskets had

---

[2]Later we discuss the modern military-industrial complex (the interconnection between the military and business) and its implications for society. It is important to remember that the military-industrial complex is not a new phenomenon but has existed for as long as societies themselves have existed.

interchangeable parts. All an army would have to do would be to carry spare parts, which could easily be used to repair a broken weapon. It would not only be cheaper, but it would also be far more efficient. As we stated earlier, technological requirements for interchangeable parts were enormous because if all parts were to be interchangeable, each musket not only had to fit together precisely, but it also had to be identical to every other in a way that two individuals each producing an entire musket could not accomplish.

To meet the problem, Hall developed a method of precision machine production. The movement to precision machine production required a number of small but extremely important technological breakthroughs, which included measuring from a standard pattern rather than from each piece and the development of dies by which individual parts were compared and tested. With these developments, machines could reach a level of precision and consistency necessary for interchangeability, a level much higher than even the most skilled worker could achieve.

Rather than a machinist measuring each part, a machinist could make an initial part, or die, and then a machine employing a micrometer could produce a duplicate, using a process similar to the one hardware stores use today to duplicate keys. The machine traces the original and fashions the new part to conform. By means of this process, each part is sufficiently identical so that interchangeability is possible. There are, of course, some minute variations, but by making each part and measuring it relative to the original with a micrometer, a skilled machinist can keep the variations between the individual pieces at an acceptable level for interchangeability.

Social and Economic Effects of Interchangeability.   Once interchangeability was introduced, the production process quickly changed and the pace of the Industrial Revolution quickened. In the early 1900s, Henry Ford carried through this development with the introduction of the **assembly line,** a production technique in which each worker in a factory performs a single operation on an item as it is passed along. Because of this innovation, the price of a car was lowered in the 1920s from some $1,600 to about $300.

With standardization and machine production, while one machine was making one part other machines could be making other parts, and using an assembly line great quantities of the finished product could be turned out by merely assembling the proper parts. Thus standardization led to **mass production,** the use of standardized parts to construct great quantities of a product on an assembly line.

Naturally, it does not pay to make large amounts of a product if they cannot be sold. But when the market is large enough, the use of standard interchangeable parts makes mass production possible and substantially reduces costs. To construct an expensive machine to make a standardized part would not pay if the machine could be used to produce only a few units of output, because the original cost of the machine would have to be allocated to these few units. But if mass production is possible and a machine can be employed to produce thousands or hundreds of thousands of units, the portion of the cost that must be

A mass-produced robotic doll.

charged to each unit becomes small or even negligible. It then pays to use a machine in place of human labor whenever one can be devised to perform a necessary operation. When standardized parts made by machines are combined into a finished product on a modern assembly line, as in the automobile industry, mass production reaches a high level of efficiency.

The effects on society of interchangeability and mass production were enormous. Individual skilled workers were no longer held in such high esteem; their pay fell, their social position fell, and the skill level necessary to produce goods fell. In response, they led movements against the use of new machines. As the status of skilled workers fell, the status of the owners of machines rose. Fortunes were built by industrialists, and high society had to make room for these newly rich. Business provided a way to move up the social ladder, and as businesspeople moved up, they brought their own values and worldview. Armies and arms became less costly; war and killing increased.

As the interchangeable-parts approach to production spread, these effects were multiplied. With the development of low-priced cars, the limitations geography placed on society changed and the nature of cities changed. Low-priced tractors increased productivity in farming, lowering food prices and forcing more and more people off the farms. None of these changes would have occurred as early as they did if Hall had not figured out a way to machine-tool more exactly.

We could continue describing the myriad effects that flowed from the improved measuring systems, but the previous discussion should be sufficient to start you thinking about these and other technological developments. As you ponder these issues, remember that technological developments are still occurring. The development of gene-splicing techniques, robots, computers, and the Internet has already changed our society and working habits significantly.

For example, in early societies strength and physical ability were important characteristics necessary for the existing level of technology. Because women bore children, were uniquely able to feed them, and on average were physically weaker than men, they generally stayed home caring for the children while males hunted. The Industrial Revolution lessened that division but did not eliminate it. The developments in technology, however, have diminished the importance of an individual's physical strength, making the male–female roles based on them no longer relevant, if they ever were. (Some authorities claim that men's physical advantages over women are minimal.) Thus many of the cultural aspects of society, such as the patriarchal family, have come into question.

The new technological developments can be expected to further this change, but they will also lead to new ways to deal with it. The technology of the Industrial Revolution, for example, required individuals to work in a factory with everyone on hand at the same time. This technology eventually led to an eight-to-five workday with weekends off. With the development of computers, fax machines, and e-mail and the Internet, the need for a workplace separate from one's home has decreased, and more people are working at home or with flexible hours. Such changes have made work and family life easier for two-income families, and the movement toward flexible work schedules can be expected to continue.

Technology and Globalization

The development of technology is generally associated with specialization and increased trade because trade allows individuals and companies experiencing a technological change to become better at what they do (this is called learning by doing). As they become better at it, they can produce products at less cost. Additionally, trade allows companies to take advantage of economies of scale—the bigger a firm's production facilities, the lower its per unit costs of the good. For example, making one car is extremely expensive; making many cars has a much lower per-car cost.

If a company can produce something more cheaply, it can out-compete other firms and hence make enormous profits. With those profits, it can spend more on research and development and can gain more and more of the market, as long as other firms cannot duplicate that technology quickly. When this happens internationally, it falls under the heading **globalization**—*the integration of world economies.* Globalization has been occurring at a fast rate in recent years, and traditional societies are often shaken by change, as less expensive goods come in from more technologically advanced countries.

Technology also affects traditional societies in another way. Firms are always looking for cheaper ways to produce goods. If they can hire workers in a traditional society at a lower rate than they can in their own society, if allowed to do so they will often transfer production facilities. Another aspect of globalization involves the movement of production facilities and technology from one economy to another. In recent years, enormous amounts of manufacturing activity in the United States have been transferred to countries such as India and China, with profound effect on their economies and culture. It has made them better off materially, but has also introduced large income inequalities and westernization of their culture, which many people consider a loss.

The Internet is speeding the process of globalization, making it possible for firms to easily compare prices of goods throughout the world and to communicate cheaply over long distances. Therefore we can expect much discussion of globalization throughout the early 2000s.

Modern Technology and the Need for Skilled Workers.   A belief once widely held is that machines reduce the need for human skills. It was said that before the machine age the individual worker was an artisan who performed by hand all the operations on the product. The worker was a weaver, a shoemaker, a candlemaker, or a tailor. Standards of technique were high, and because one worker made the entire product, a high level of skills was demanded. After the advent of machines, individual skills became almost useless. Machines performed the principal operations required to make a product, and the worker became an automaton whose function was to operate or feed the machine, perhaps doing nothing but moving a lever up and down or placing a piece of metal in a machine, removing it when the machine had operated, and repeating this task all day long. Such work required no skill, and so the typical worker became a common laborer instead of an artisan.

The reasoning presented here is plausible but highly misleading. Before the age of the machine, skilled craftspeople represented a tiny portion of the working population in most countries. The great majority of the people lived and worked on the land. The work was heavy, the hours long, and the returns small. It is true that the introduction of machines put certain skilled artisans out of work or forced them to work in factories as unskilled labor. For example, after the introduction of the power loom in England in the eighteenth century, the price of cloth dropped so sharply that skilled handweavers could no longer make a living at their trade. This does not mean, however, that the introduction of machinery reduced the total demand for workers with special skill or training. Quite the contrary. The skills required became different, but in the long run the machine industry made it necessary for a much larger portion of the population than ever before to acquire specialized skill, training, or knowledge. Furthermore, in modern factories purely routine and mechanical jobs such as feeding materials into a machine are continually disappearing because machines can be devised to perform these operations automatically. An outstanding characteristic of modern automation is the constant shifting of routine activities from people to machines.

To compensate for this loss of routine jobs, modern machine technology has created great numbers of jobs that require specialized skill or knowledge. There are engineers who plan and design machines and factories; skilled construction workers, plumbers, and electricians; and a great variety of machinists and mechanics who aid in making, operating, and repairing machines. There are people who are especially trained in the organization and administration of industrial enterprises, in advertising and selling, and in various phases of transportation. There are accountants who keep records, and a great many skilled clerical workers including stenographers, word processors, and data processors.

The development of robots has reduced the number of routine jobs even more but has increased the need for skilled technicians who assemble and repair them, the systems engineers who devise plans for using them to solve business problems, and the programmers who put these plans into operation.

Machines and Unemployment

In addition to the belief that machines reduce the demand for skilled workers, there is an even more persistent notion that has little foundation in past experience—the idea that advances in machine technology, by replacing labor, progressively decrease total job opportunities and total employment. This belief had a strong appeal in the 1930s when millions were out of work. At that time, many writers argued that our economy had become "mature" and that in order to provide enough jobs in the future, it would be necessary either to spread the work around by progressively shortening the work week or else to have the government keep creating more jobs through an expanding program of public works. In addition to shortening the work week, it was often proposed that young people should be kept in school longer and that older workers should be retired at earlier ages.

No one questions that machines displace individual workers from certain jobs and that in the short run this often creates difficult problems. For example, the use of diesel engines and electric power by railroads has made obsolete the position of "fireman"—the employee who shoveled coal into the locomotive boiler that produced the steam for the train's steam engine—but because of union support, railroads had to fill this position for many years after steam power ceased being used by trains. However, such problems are temporary. Ultimately, advances in machine technology tend to reduce costs and prices (assuming a constant value of the dollar) or to hold them down, and by enabling people to buy more goods, they create new employment opportunities. If some industries employ fewer workers, others employ more. At the same time, new products are introduced and new industries are established.

Technology and Social Change

As you can see from our discussion of the Industrial Revolution, technology plays an important role in determining a society's culture. The patterns of a society's daily activities are greatly influenced by its technology—that is, by the kinds of goods, including services, that it knows how to produce and by the methods it employs to produce them. In primitive societies, for example, production is carried on with the aid of simple hand tools, and people spend most of their time hunting, fishing, tilling the soil, preparing food, making clothing, and constructing crude shelters. On the other hand, in modern industrial societies such as ours, millions of men and women spend most of each week in offices, factories, or laboratories, and often they travel long distances by automobile, bus, or train to reach their places of work. Therefore to understand cultural and social change, we must understand its interaction with technology.

That technology has played a dominant role in shaping our modern world is beyond question. Culture, to be sure, is much more than technology. But modern civilization as we know it could not have developed without its technological base. Technology largely determines the way in which people use their habitat and the extent to which they can benefit from the potential resources it may contain. When Columbus came to America, the territory that is now the United States could probably support, by the methods of production known to the Native Americans, fewer than half a million people. Today the same territory supports more than five hundred times as many and provides them with a much more plentiful and dependable supply of material goods. This difference cannot be explained in terms of the natural environment. It is explained mainly by the fact that our modern industrial technology is vastly superior in productive efficiency to the technology the Native Americans had.

Problems Created by Technology

Although technological progress has conferred great benefits on the human population, it also has created many problems. Work in the first factories took people away from their homes all day and disrupted the established pattern of domestic life. It also forced large numbers of people to live close to their new places of work, which in turn resulted in crowded industrial towns and cities. On the other hand, there is evidence that even the early factories gave the masses more opportunities to earn and a better chance of survival. One indication of this is the fall in the death rate and the increase in the rate of population growth that has occurred over time.

Technology, Hierarchy, and Class Systems

The effects of technology on society are so pervasive that some social scientists claim that technology is the primary determinant of social and cultural relations. Some social scientists argue that mass production and the assembly line, where each individual does one task repeatedly, developed not because they were more technically efficient, inasmuch as you can get more output from a certain amount of work, but because they established and fortified social divisions. For example, suppose there are two kinds of a machine that can produce widgets. One kind requires each individual to work on a part with no one supervising. The other kind requires a supervisor directing individuals to perform specific tasks. Even if the first kind of machine provides a cheaper way to produce a widget, if the decision were left to the supervisor, he or she would be unlikely to choose the one that eliminated the supervisor's job.

Social scientists who use this line of reasoning argue that the social class structure of capitalism is inevitable with the capitalist means of production. They argue that even

Qwerty

When considering the interrelationships between technology and social institutions, it is instructive to think about the keyboard.

You will note that the first six letters on the top of the keyboard spell QWERTY. When you learned keyboarding, you learned to memorize the positions of these keys, and you got to where you could type anywhere from 5 to 150 words per minute. You might wonder how the letters were given those positions, instead of being arranged some other way. They were put there on purpose by an inventor, Christopher L. Sholes. Initially, typewriters were built with letters in serial fashion, but it was found that people could type too fast on such a keyboard, and often the keys would lock together when pressed in succession too quickly. Sholes developed the QWERTY keyboard

to minimize the occurrence of such stickiness. Of course, the problem of keys sticking was relevant only for the earliest typewriters. The "golf ball" typewriters developed in the 1960s and the electronic typewriters of today have no such problem at all, and neither do computer terminal keyboards. Yet QWERTY, the innovation devised for a specific purpose at an earlier time, remains standard for all of these keyboards. Redesigning the keyboard would mean that teachers must retrain and experienced typists must relearn how to move their fingers, so it seems unlikely that such a change will take place.

Precisely the same set of issues is relevant to a variety of existing technologies and social institutions. Although they may have had a purpose at one time, they might be limiting now. The mere fact that they are limiting does not mean they will be changed.

communist countries, which in theory attempted to avoid class divisions, nevertheless maintained the class divisions of capitalist society as long as they used capitalist technology and capitalist modes of production. When a technology is designed for a boss and a worker, unless these divisions are maintained the technology cannot be effective. Communism self-destructed because it did not develop its own technology. Only by developing an alternative technology, one not designed to hold workers down, can any society divest itself of class structure.

This argument is subject to much criticism, but the fact remains that capitalist technologies have inevitably developed a class system. (But so, too, have precapitalist and noncapitalist countries.) Concern about this effect of technology kept China from encouraging Western technology. Through much of Mao Ze-dong's Cultural Revolution of the 1960s and well into the 1970s, China attempted to purge many of those Western technologies. However, under a new leader in the late 1970s and early 1980s, China reversed its position and began the conscious introduction of Western technology into its system, with the intention of pushing economic development. The debate, however, continues, especially because the recent upheavals in formerly socialist societies have been marked by increasing inequality.

Similar debates can be heard in discussions of the future of the class structure in the United States. For example, the economic theorist Michael Piori has argued that technology is pushing society in the opposite direction, and that with the use of computers and robots the very nature of capitalist societies will change. He argues that with the new developing technologies, robots will do the work of blue-collar workers and thus class distinction will no longer be embodied in technology. He believes that in the future there will be far less class distinction in the United States than there now is.

Natural Resources, Economics, and Technology

One of the debates that often surfaces among social scientists concerns whether there are sufficient resources for society to continue to grow and whether we will some day reach a limit to growth. It is relevant to our discussion of technology because technology provides a necessary link between resources and the economy. To see this link, we need to consider the nature of economic activities, natural resources, and technology.

Economic activities are those activities concerned with making a living, and they necessarily play a major role in every culture. Their character is largely determined by three factors. First, all human beings have wants for many kinds of scarce goods. **Scarce goods** are goods that exist in limited quantities and that we can obtain only if we produce them or if we offer something valuable in exchange for them. The desire to satisfy specific wants is the motive behind all economic activity.

The second factor that guides economic activity is available resources. Economic goods such as food, clothing, houses, and weapons cannot be created out of nothing. If people are to have goods, they must find the materials in nature—natural resources—from which the goods can be produced. Unless people can find such materials, their wants will remain unsatisfied no matter how great their efforts. With ingenuity, however, they may discover that they can turn to their advantage materials that at first seemed quite useless. The third factor controlling economic activity is technology, meaning knowledge of how to use resources to produce desirable goods, including services.

Both the technology of a society and the economic activities in which its people engage are greatly influenced, though by no means wholly determined, by the extent to which various natural resources are available. For example, power is an essential in a modern industrial economy, but even a modern economy cannot make extensive use of power unless substantial amounts of power-producing resources are available. Furthermore, the methods used to generate power tend to depend on the relative availability and cost of water power, coal, natural gas, petroleum, sun, wind, and fissionable materials such as uranium. In the future, the methods employed are also likely to be greatly influenced by the success with which we can eliminate the contributions most of them make to polluting or otherwise damaging our environment.

The key element in the process is that natural resources have meaning only in reference to technology. Because technology transforms natural resources into products that can satisfy economic wants, the supply of natural resources depends on the type of technology we have. If a technology develops that can turn sand into a steel-like substance cheaply, then there will be an almost unlimited amount of building material. If we can develop a technology that can turn sunlight into energy cheaply, energy will be almost unlimited. Thus technology holds the key to growth and the solution to shortages.

Natural Resources and the Limits of Economic Growth

With regard to natural resources, the United States is in a relatively fortunate position, for it is probably better supplied with them than any other similar area in the world. This endowment of natural resources has provided the material basis for our phenomenal economic development and our present political and military strength. We have great areas of fertile farmlands and forests. We are relatively well provided with sources of power such as petroleum, natural gas, coal, and sites for hydroelectric plants. We also have large reserves of iron ore and other important minerals. True, we lack certain metals, such as nickel, chromium, and tin, but ordinarily we have no difficulty in importing these from abroad.

But although our position is still strong with respect to most basic resources, the outlook for the future is not clear. Concern about the future availability of resources reached a high point in the 1970s as ecologists argued that we were headed for doom. Their argument was twofold: Either we were going to run out of natural resources or the pollution resulting from production was going to destroy us.

From the perspective of the early 2000s, it seems that much of the ecological concern at that time was overdone. We still have vast reserves of low-grade iron ore; similarly, we have vast reserves of shale oil and sand oil. The problem is one of costs and developing the technology that makes extraction of these natural resources economically feasible. The remaining reserves involve a high cost of extraction and therefore cannot be utilized unless the price to the consumer is raised. At 20 cents per gallon for gas, there would likely be a gasoline shortage; at $5 per gallon, there will likely be enough for many years to come. In fact, this is how the market system is designed to work. As a good becomes scarcer, its price rises. Because of that price rise, we use less of it and individuals devote more resources to designing new technologies to achieve the same result without using that resource. For example, plastics were developed during World War II because of the shortage of natural rubber. Similarly, in response to the higher prices of gasoline in the 1970s, the average size of automobiles decreased significantly. Then, as gasoline prices fell in the 1980s and 1990s, larger and more powerful cars once again came into vogue. In the early 2000s, concern for the supply of gasoline has sparked a tentative move toward the development of hybrid cars that derive at least part of their power from electricity.

Goods can become scarce by other means than by being used up. In the United States, the federal government is pushing to have automobile manufacturers develop vehicles to run on energy that is less polluting than gasoline. Therefore in the early twenty-first century we will see more vehicles designed to run on electricity and natural gas because government policy has made gasoline "scarce" through limiting its use; it has also made gasoline expensive, because people who won't give up gasoline engines will pay more to obtain that scarce good.

Over the long run, changes in the relative availability of natural resources have an even greater effect on our culture. For example, cities developed as an efficient means of bringing people together before the existence of automobiles and low-cost transportation. When gasoline was introduced, it stimulated the development and spread of automobiles, which in turn reduced the relative advantages of cities. In the 1950s, we saw the result: a movement back to the country to the areas around cities that became known as suburbia. In the 1970s, as the price of gasoline rose, the relative advantages of city life increased and many city areas were revitalized. At $5 a gallon, that revitalization would likely become a major boom.

Despite these benefits, we still should be concerned about natural resource shortages. High prices can cause hardships, and the cultural change that accompanies relative price changes is often difficult. To be aware of the need for change and to be careful with resources can lessen the impact of that change or at least reduce the problems associated with it.

Global Warming

One of the ecological effects of modern society that has been much in the news is **global warming,** the gradual warming of the earth's temperature due to the burning of fossil fuels. Most scientists are now convinced that global warming is taking place, and we know that the average surface temperature of the earth is already higher than it was a hundred years ago. The Intergovernmental Panel on Climate Change, established by the United Nations, includes two thousand scientists, and their consensus is that global warming is a significant potential problem. These conclusions were reinforced at the Kyoto, Japan, conference in 1997. If nothing is done about global warming, these authorities say, in the year 2100 the average surface temperature of the earth will be about 4.5 degrees Fahrenheit warmer than it was in 1900. Contrast this projected increase over only one hundred years with the estimate that in the thousands of years from prehistoric times until now the earth has warmed, at most, only 9 percent. However, some scientists disagree with these opinions and believe that such temperature changes are part of a natural fluctuation over thousands of years and may not be related to emissions of gases caused by fossil fuel burning.[3]

Nevertheless, the question remains: What to do about global warming? At the 1992 Earth Summit in Brazil, most of the countries of the world signed treaties to cope with global warming and other environmental problems. Those treaties provided for worldwide reduction of polluting gases followed by periodic assessments of the economic consequences. Despite the 1992 Summit agreement, by 2000 U.S. emissions of waste industrial gases were about 13 percent higher than in 1990 and are continuing to rise. The United States produces more such pollution than any other country. China produces the second-highest amount, even though it has reduced its carbon dioxide emissions by 20 percent since 1992. It has done this by increasing fuel prices enormously—121 percent. The Kyoto treaty addressed global warming, but it exempted developing countries. Moreover, the United States, the largest industrial country in the world, refused to sign it, in part because it exempted developing countries.

Global warming remains a continuous issue, with political, economic, environmental, cultural, and health implications that mean the problem will be near the forefront of global concern for many years to come.

Technology of the Past

At the beginning of this chapter, we gave you an easy quiz on technological developments. To put you in the right frame of mind to consider the technology of the future, for which we need to take a wider view of technological development, we now look further into the past and consider technology over a broader horizon. Remember that humans have become humans only through the developments of technology, some of which occurred within human beings through biological evolution.

---

[3]Carbon dioxide is the principal polluting gas, but environmentalists have also targeted five others: methane, nitrous oxide, hydrofluorocarbons, perfluorocarbons, and sulphur hexachloride.

Looking to that past and taking a broad view of technology, then, we can see that some major "technological" developments occurred thousands of years ago. Some are presented here.

Teeth. The ability to use teeth to crack hard foods such as nuts, seeds, and rind gave *Ramapithecines* access to more foods than other early creatures had. *Ramapithecines* appeared about 15 million years ago and some authorities class them as hominids; others call them common ancestors to hominids and apes. Neanderthal teeth (100,000 to 36,000 years ago) show that they were used to hold objects.

Hands. The ability to use their hands to throw and shake things gave an advantage to primates who stood on two feet. Anthropologists believe that primates began to stand on two feet at least 4 million years ago.

Brains. About 2 million years ago, primate brains began to grow larger. Primates began to use their brains and hands not only to use objects as tools but also to make tools. Some of the earliest made tools were for chopping and digging.

Fire. Cave evidence that may be as old as 700,000 years shows by the charred remains of cooked animals that hominids had learned to make and use fire. It seems that among the animals they cooked were other hominids.

Wooden shelters. As early as 400,000 years ago, hominids had begun to use trees to build shelters.

Spears. Cro-Magnons had spears by at least 35,000 years ago. They could hunt and eat large animals, if the large animals did not eat Cro-Magnons first.

Bows and arrows. By about 20,000 years ago, humans knew how to use bows and arrows to kill small, fleet animals from a distance. Hunters were safer and at the same time had a wider choice of protein.

As you can see from the list, technology (the means by which humans interact with their environment) progressed slowly at first, as humans learned to use their physical attributes in new ways. Then, as the human brain developed further, a new method of technological change occurred—change brought about through thought and reasoning. This change sped up the process of technological change, and by 7,000 years ago it had led to the development of cities, to writing, and to recorded history.

We stopped our list at 20,000 years ago because we compiled it not in any attempt to be comprehensive, but to make you think about what technology is and what it can be used for. What results can you think of that came from controlling fire and the energy it produces? How do combinations of one technology with others extend the range of human habitats? What do hunting and building imply about cooperation and planning? Do you draw any conclusions from the preponderance in the list of actions such as biting, throwing, chopping, burning, and impaling? If you were to continue the list, what lifestyles would you see developing?

Technology of the Future

We considered past developments simply to set you thinking about technologies of the future and the effects that the development of those technologies might have on society.

What we meant you to learn from our consideration of the past is that society fifty years from now is likely to be quite different from society today, and the technologies that we develop will play an important role in shaping that future.

But what technologies will develop? Some seem obvious. Computers will progress and become more and more integrated with household appliances. Refrigerators will keep track of what you need to order from the on-line grocery store and place your order for you. On-demand television over the Internet will free people from having to watch a particular show at a particular time. Interaction with these new devices will be by means of voice recognition, not through keyboards. Likewise, discoveries in biotechnology will change entirely the way we interact with our bodies; cures for cancer and other diseases will be found, our bones and tissues will be programmed to repair themselves, and we will have the ability to choose characteristics of our offspring.

In considering the effects of technology on the future, you will quickly see that predicting the future is one of the most difficult but enjoyable activities of social science; it allows the imagination to roam. Will spaceships like the *Enterprise* develop out of our current space shuttle efforts? Will we find new technologies that totally change our lives, such as instant transportation or intelligence transfers? The possibilities are endless and not always pleasant for specific individuals. For example, if a machine were developed to implant knowledge in students without the use of teachers, many educators would likely be out of a job, and rather than students going to school for sixteen years, they would merely attend school for information updates once a year.

Such fanciful ideas are probably a long way off, but clearly life in the mid-2000s will be significantly different from life in the early 2000s. Early in this century, robot factories may be commonplace and you may have a robot helping you with both your housework and job. Gene-splicing and genetic engineering could bring about even more changes. Numerous created life-forms could be kept in special areas and released for special purposes. For example, if there is an oil spill, oil-eating bacteria would be released. If we need more gasoline, new organisms that improve the process of making gas would be sold to oil firms. Or if you need a new type of plant to decorate a room, you would design it and put in your order.

 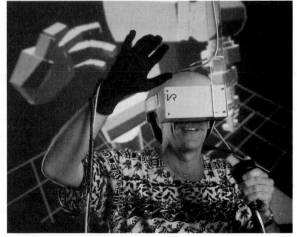

Modern technology: (left) The International Space Station. (right) A virtual reality demonstration.

*T*imeline: The Future

2010 Breakthrough in medicine; method delays aging process and extends average life expectancy by ten years (world population increases; causes Social Security programs to fail).

2012 Developments with Buckeyballs redefine matter; diamonds and metals no longer scarce.

2013 Fusion reactor created that makes energy "too cheap to meter"; oil companies go broke; gas stations are eliminated.

2015 Genetic engineering means fabricated human replacement organs roll off assembly line. Amputated limbs can be regrown.

2020 Human cloning perfected; all parts of body can now regenerate themselves.

2045 Computer chips developed to place in the human head; eliminates the need for teaching.

2110 Temperature rise on earth means snow and ice at the poles melt and oceans flood all low-lying areas. Miami is no more.

2160 Various complicated life-forms reproduced from organic chemicals create significant debate about morality and meaning.

2190 Major viral outbreak from genetic engineering experiment; half the world population dies.

2210 Instant transportation created; old-fashioned means of transportation—cars, legs, and so forth—no longer needed.

2240 Human body shapes modified to eliminate useless appendages.

2270 Life-forms discovered in different galaxies now reachable with instant transportation.

2280 The starship *Enterprise* returns safely to home base.

The technology of the future will probably involve changes that are much more imaginative than those we have just speculated on. Some imaginative technological changes and their potential effects are listed in the accompanying box. Each of these ideas is fanciful, but each has been advanced by futurists at one time or another. They are placed here not because we expect them to materialize, but to make us reflect and think about their implications for society and culture. Each would change society in ways that are difficult to fathom. Each would have social, economic, and cultural consequences that in turn would affect society's ability to use that technology to its advantage and not to its detriment. Seeing that society uses technology for good rather than evil is what social science is all about.

The Social Basis for Technological Progress

Because of the extensive social changes these new technological developments involve, they may never come about. Technological progress occurs only as long as social conditions encourage and make it possible; quite likely, someday conditions could change in such a way as to stop it. There have been times and places in the history of the world when people have lost ground instead of making progress.

Many factors might in the long run greatly retard our technological progress. The costs of the research and equipment necessary for meeting certain problems of pollution are likely to be resisted by many corporations and also, where government is directly involved, by many taxpayers. Technological progress also tends to be slowed by organized pressure groups that have an interest in limiting the output of certain products and in

Oops

United Technologies advertisement.

opposing the introduction of new methods or products in order to maintain the demand and the prices for the things they sell. For example, labor unions often oppose the introduction of methods or materials that might reduce the jobs available to their members, and producers of building materials sometimes seek to discourage the introduction of substitutes for their products, even though these may be better and cheaper and may use materials that are more plentiful. Again, many farmers demand that the government take measures to reduce farm output in order to raise farm prices and incomes.

A more subtle influence that might slow up technological progress would be the growth among our people of a less receptive attitude toward change. This might result not only from a lack of interest in consuming more goods, but also from a feeling of indifference toward improving both the quality of goods and the quality of the environment; or it might result from a gradual dilution of the spirit of adventure and from an increasing emphasis on security. Change and progress often seem dangerous and disturbing. They put some people out of jobs and force them to seek types of employment that are not to their liking. They cause some business enterprises to fail, even though others may be expanding rapidly. A society that puts its whole emphasis on stability and security is not likely to look with favor on radical technological innovations.

Future Shock?

A pioneer in the field of futurology, Alvin Toffler, warned in his 1971 book *Future Shock* of the "shattering stress and disorientation that we induce in individuals by subjecting them to too much change in too short a time." According to Toffler, the accelerating rate of change, particularly in technology, in the last part of the twentieth century had occurred so fast that it overwhelmed the adaptive powers of ordinary persons. He argues that we must learn to understand and control the rate of change at this "turning point in history at which people either vanquish the processes of change or vanish, at which point, from being the unconscious puppets of evolution they become either its victims or its masters." Thus Toffler became a leading advocate of controlled technological change. On the other side are the advocates of stronger reliance on the new technology. This view gained momentum in the early 1990s as the United States and the world economy experienced high rates of unemployment and slow growth. The new technology was seen as a way of escaping these economic problems.

Which of the two forces—the forces for change or the forces for preventing change—will win out is unclear. Regardless of which one wins, their interaction will make the world of the future an exciting one to live in and an exciting one for social scientists to study.

Key Points

- Technology comprises the tools, means, and methods through which we interact with our environment.
- The Industrial Revolution significantly changed all aspects of society through its introduction of interchangeability and mass production of material products.
- Technology influences culture, and culture influences technology.

- The limits-to-growth debate has two sides, and we will find out which side is correct only when it is too late to do anything about it.
- The development of teeth, hands, brains, fire, wooden shelters, spears, and bows and arrows are some of the important technological developments of the past.
- Potential technological developments in the future are limited only by the imagination.

Some Important Terms

assembly line (123)
economic activities (129)
globalization (125)
global warming (131)

Industrial Revolution (120)
interchangeability (122)
mass production (123)
scarce goods (129)

standardization (122)
technology (118)

Questions for Review and Discussion

1. Give an example of a technological advance that has greatly influenced your own life and explain what its effect on you has been.
2. Name some technological change that took place in the past and explain how you think it has changed conditions ever since being introduced.
3. What was the Industrial Revolution? What are some of the reasons it was successful in the United States?
4. Why are standardization and interchangeability so important to mass production?
5. When it became possible for machines to make products that had formerly been made by hand, what effects did this have on the number of people employed? On the level of wages? On the profit of employers? On the quality of the products?
6. Explain how the technology of the assembly line led to other technological and cultural changes.
7. If the use of robots in factories becomes widespread, do you think this will mean a loss of

jobs and a rise in unemployment? Why or why not?
8. The jobs of some individuals are replaced by particular technological changes. What are some of the ways of dealing with this problem?
9. Technology can be very expensive in terms of its effect on the quality of the air, water, soil, and general environment. How can this expense be dealt with?
10. Technology can be very expensive in terms of the amount of money it costs. Where do you think this money comes from?
11. Do you think the advantages of technology are worth the disadvantages? Why or why not?
12. Are there any technological changes you think should not be made? What are they? If you oppose a particular technological change, what alternative solution do you have for the problem that change was meant to address?
13. Try your hand at predicting a technological change that may occur in the future. What effects on society might that change produce?

Internet Questions

1. Using the website www.inventionfactory.com/history/RHAbridg/bb.html, find out what the Brooklyn Bridge is suspended from. How thick are the cables?
2. Go to www.usbr.gov/dataweb/dams/nv10122.htm and read about the Hoover Dam. How large is the structure? Where is it located and when was it built?
3. Visit www.urbanlegends.com/products/beta_vs_vhs.html. What company marketed Betamax for video recording? What is one of the reasons for its failure?
4. What is one of the latest advances in technology listed by the National Institute of Standards and Technology, www.nist.gov, and what is its planned use?
5. According to the Sierra Club, www.sierraclub.org/globalwarming, who are the culprits of global warming? Using the calculator at www.sierraclub.org/iwantmympg/calculator.asp, what does the Sierra Club estimate your savings (in dollars and emissions) would be if the government raises the fuel economy standards?

For Further Study

Appleyard, Brian, *Brave New Worlds: Staying Human in the Genetic Future,* New York: Viking Press, 1998.

Brown, David E., ed., *Inventing Modern America: From the Microwave to the Mouse,* Cambridge, MA: MIT Press, 2002.

Gershenfeld, Neil, *When Things Start to Think,* New York: Henry Holt, 1999.

Gilder, George, *How Infinite Bandwidth Will Revolutionize Our World,* New York: Free Press, 2000.

Gleick, James, *Faster: The Acceleration of Just about Everything,* New York: Pantheon, 1999.

Goldberg, Ken, ed., *Robo in the Garden: Telerobotics and Telepistemology in the Age of the Internet,* Cambridge, MA: MIT Press, 2000.

Hazen, Robert M., with Maxine Singer, *Why Aren't Black Holes Black: The Unanswered Questions of the Frontiers of Science,* foreword by Stephen Jay Gould, New York: Anchor Books/Doubleday, 1997.

Kolata, Gina, *The Road to Dolly, and the Path Ahead,* New York: Morrow, 1998.

Kurzwell, Roy, *The Age of Spiritual Machines: When Computers Exceed Human Intelligence,* New York: Viking Press: 1998.

Mead, Margaret, ed., *Cultural Patterns and Technical Change,* New York: New American Library/Mentor, 1956.

Menzel, Peter, and Faith D'Aluisio, *Robo Sapiens: Evolution of a New Species,* Cambridge, MA: MIT Press, 2000.

Moravec, Hans, *Robot: Mere Machine to Transcend Mind,* New York: Oxford University Press, 1999.

Simon, Leslie David, *NetPolicy.com: Public Agenda for a Digital World,* Baltimore, MD: Johns Hopkins University Press, 2000.

Slater, Lauren, *Prozac Diary,* New York: Random House, 1998.

Toffler, Alvin, *Future Shock,* New York: Bantam, 1971.

Warshcauer, Mark, *Technology and Social Inclusion: Rethinking the Digital Divide,* Cambridge, MA: MIT Press, 2003.

WWW   Arts and Science Collaborations, Inc.   www.asci.org

WWW   The Center for Democracy and Technology www.cdt.org

WWW   EPA, Global Warming Site   http://www.yosemite.epa.gov/oar/globalwarming.nsf/content/index.html

WWW   The Science and Technology Society   www.avs.org

WWW   Technofile, Consumer Technology Information http://twcny.rr.com/technofile

WWW   Time 100, Builders and Titans   www.time.com/time/time100/builder/index.html

WWW   World Peace through Technology   www.peacetour.org

Psychology, Society, and Culture

After reading this chapter, you should be able to:

- Explain how culture and personality are related
- Summarize the nature/nurture debate
- State the importance of positive and negative reinforcement
- Discuss Maslow's hierarchy
- Differentiate the id, ego, and superego
- Explain how IQ is calculated and the problems with its use
- Define *deviance* and name five sociological theories about deviance

If I am not for myself, who will be?
And if I am only for myself, who am I?
And if not now, when?

—Rabbi Hillel

Culture is created by the individuals within that culture, but individuals' personalities are in turn shaped and molded by culture. In this chapter we take a social psychology perspective and consider the relationship between the individual and society. Much of our discussion will center on personality. **Personality** is the total organization of the inherited and acquired characteristics of an individual as evidenced by the individual's behavior. Culture's role in shaping individual personality is major, whereas each individual's influence on culture is usually slight. As individuals, people must accept their culture much as they find it, and if they hope to lead satisfactory lives as human beings, they must adjust to it.

This dependence of the individual on culture sometimes makes culture appear to be an independent entity, something that has an existence and continuity irrespective of the people who are its carriers. This impression is strengthened when we view culture historically and note that many of its basic elements persist generation after generation. Two hundred years ago the English language in its essential characteristics was not very different from what it is today. Yet of all those who spoke English two hundred years ago, not a single person is now alive.

For some purposes it is convenient to think of culture as if it had an independent, objective existence. In the final analysis, however, this is untrue. All cultures have been created by people. When we analyze culture closely, we find only a series of patterned reactions that are characteristic of the individuals who belong to a given group. It is people who hold beliefs, have attitudes, practice customs, and behave in conformity with patterns accepted by the group. Cultures are built up so slowly and gradually that it is seldom possible to isolate the contributions made by particular individuals. In a large society, the individual is only one among millions. Furthermore, most individuals accept the social situation in which they find themselves and make little attempt to change it.

The fact that people as individuals are shaped by their culture does not mean that they are deprived of all freedom to control their behavior, to choose their mode of life, and even to affect the conditions that surround them. Any general cultural pattern is flexible to a degree and permits some variations from the norms. In simple primitive societies, the permissible variations may be rather limited, but in modern complex societies they are great. However, in any society the average individual is seldom aware of the extent to which culture restricts freedom. Culture becomes so internalized—so much a basic part of personality—that most of the time people do not wish to behave in ways other than those that are culturally approved. Only in special situations do they become keenly aware of conflicts between their own desires and the kind of conduct that is socially permissible.

Socialization of the Individual

Socialization plays a major role in the development of human personality. This does not mean that a child's personality may not be greatly influenced by its biological inheritance and by contacts with the physical environment. For the most part, however, a child learns from people the patterns of behavior and the attitudes, beliefs, and expectations that motivate behavior. All of these are largely cultural in origin, and therefore, as a child grows and develops, its behavior reflects to an ever-greater degree the culture of the society into which it has been born.

Significance of the Early Years of Childhood

The experiences of the young child within the family group seem to have the greatest influence on the development of human personality. Very early a normal baby begins to recognize familiar faces, sense approval and disapproval, seek attention, and in other ways react to the social environment.

Our personalities develop in this early childhood. Although there are still tremendous gaps in our knowledge, we have discovered some of the ways in which children learn. One of the leaders in this discovery was Jean Piaget, a noted psychologist, who developed several widely accepted theories on the development of children. His first point is obvious: Very young children think differently from adults. For example, many children think their shadow is a living entity that follows them wherever they go. Similarly, imaginary friends fly around the room at night, and inanimate objects, from marbles to vacuum cleaners, have very human characteristics. Reality for them blends in with imagination. As we grow older, most of us learn to separate reality from imagination. If, however, an individual lacks the right environment, he or she will not be able to do so, and may go through an entire lifetime living in a semifantasy world.

Piaget finds it useful to divide a child's life into four stages. From birth to two years, a child is primarily concerned with learning about physical objects. From two to six or seven years, the youngster learns about symbols in language, dreams, and fantasy. Next he or she begins to learn about abstract concepts such as numbers and the relationships between them. Finally, from ages twelve to fifteen the child masters purely logical thought and learns to understand double messages, such as irony and double entendres.

In order to develop normally both emotionally and mentally, a child must be accepted and receive affection, but overprotection and overaffection are not desirable, for they tend to lead to dependency and immaturity. At the other extreme, parental rejection and lack of affection create feelings of insecurity and inferiority, and often bring on compensatory reactions such as aggressive, rebellious, or domineering behavior.

As young children grow, they come into contact not only with parents, brothers and sisters, and perhaps other members of the household, but also with outsiders such as relatives, neighbors, and playmates. They acquire greater physical competence and greater skill in the use of language and continually make adjustments to new people and new situations. These early experiences leave nearly indelible impressions and influence the "set" of each one's personality.

Significance of Differences in Individual Environment

It is questionable whether any two individuals have precisely the same hereditary characteristics, though in the case of identical twins there is a close approximation to this situation. Certainly, no two individuals have exactly the same social environment. Some of the differences in individual environments are obvious to the most casual observer, but other differences are not so easy to see.

We are all aware that in a country such as the United States people often grow up in social environments that differ widely. To begin with, there are noticeable differences in the language, attitudes, and customs of the people in different regions. Also, even in the same region there are differences between rural life and city life; and in a city of even moderate size there can be found a great variety of more or less distinct social groups. Among the more important of these groups are those set off from one another by differences in income and social prestige, religion, nationality, or race. But differences in individual social environment go further than this. In any given social group, particular families are likely to differ significantly from one another in their modes of life, so that a child brought up in one family may have a quite different environment from that of a child reared in another.

All these differences are fairly obvious. It is not quite so obvious, but nonetheless true, that two children brought up in the same family at the same time may have quite dissimilar environments. This is because social environment depends not only on people, but also on the nature of personal relations with them. One child in a family may be loved by the parents, given every advantage, perhaps be overindulged, whereas another child may be disliked, neglected, even mistreated. Clearly such children do not have at all the same environment, and the differences are sure to have deep and lasting effects on their mental and emotional development, on their personalities, and on their relations with other people in later years.

Effects of Extreme Isolation on Children

The study of children who have been largely isolated from social contacts demonstrates the importance of socialization by showing what happens in its absence. It also considers the possibility of compensating in later years for development that failed to take place earlier at the normal time.

It is impossible to find children who have been completely isolated from other human beings from the time of birth. The reason is simple. The human infant is so helpless that it cannot possibly survive without receiving some care from older people who understand its needs. However, cases have been reported of children who, in early life, have been partially or completely isolated from human contact over considerable periods. These reports are of two types: (1) cases of **feral children**—children who have lived in a wild or untamed state with animals—and (2) cases of children kept isolated in a room, basement, or attic and given little attention except for being provided with food and drink. (Less extreme examples of isolation occur with children who are merely neglected, or who are cared for, more or less impersonally, in institutions.)

Stories of feral children appeal to the imagination. They have been told in all ages about children believed to have been cared for when very young by boars, wolves, bears, or other animals. These stories have nearly always been spread by hearsay, and it is doubtful whether any of them are based on fact. Perhaps the oldest of such tales is about the legendary founders of Rome, the twins Romulus and Remus, who are said to have been abandoned as infants and suckled by a wolf. As you might have noticed, our history of the world skipped these legendary twins.

The one report that has some credibility is of two children found in a wolf den in India. They could not talk, and they are reported to have run on all fours and in other respects to

According to legend, the founders of Rome were human twins, Romulus and Remus, who were nurtured by a wolf.

have exhibited animal-like behavior. Under human care, they responded very little to the attempts made to socialize and educate them, and both died at an early age. Most psychologists believe that they most likely suffered from **infantile autism,** a condition in which a child is unable to respond emotionally to others. Most psychologists believe these children, not very long before they were found, had been abandoned because they were autistic.

Though stories of feral children should be regarded with skepticism, there appear to be well-authenticated cases of children who for considerable periods of time were locked in basements, attics, or upstairs rooms and isolated from almost all normal human contacts. One case involved a girl named Isabelle who, because she was illegitimate, was kept secluded in a dark room with her deaf-mute mother until she was six and a half years old. In another case, a girl named Anna was kept in a room alone until she was about six.

In each of these cases, when the girl was discovered her behavior in many respects resembled that of an infant or a wild animal. But Isabelle, when placed in a normal social environment and given special training, caught up rapidly. In a few years, she was making good progress in school and gave the impression of a bright, cheerful, energetic little girl. However, when Anna was placed in a normal environment, she made much less progress, and she was still considered mentally disabled when she died at the age of ten and a half.

We have no way of knowing why Anna failed to develop as much as Isabelle. Perhaps Isabelle's close contact with her deaf-mute mother gave her a sense of being loved and secure, and thus she enjoyed a great advantage over Anna in her emotional development, or it may be that she received more expert attention after she was removed from isolation. It is also possible that Isabelle's biological inheritance was superior to Anna's.

In 1970 a thirteen-year-old girl, who was given the name Genie, was found. She had been tied up and kept in a room without human contact by her elderly parents, who were psychologically disturbed. She had been fed only milk and baby food and was never spoken to. She was incontinent, could not speak, and weighed only fifty-seven pounds. After she was found and brought into a hospital, she learned to communicate, but, although her mother said that she had been normal at birth, Genie's IQ was only 74 and her language ability never fully developed.

Personality and Its Development

To have a full understanding of the relationship between individuals and society, it is helpful to have a clear concept of the meaning of personality. It has been said that every human being is in some respects like all others, in some respects like some others, and in some respects like no others.

As we mentioned earlier, personality may be defined as the total organization of the inherited and acquired characteristics of an individual as evidenced by the individual's behavior. It is the product of the interaction between an individual's original biological nature and his or her social and natural environment. Therefore it bears the imprint of four things:

1. The inherited potentialities of the individual
2. Natural environment
3. The culture of the individual's society
4. Unique personal experiences

However, once personality has begun to form it becomes an independent force that may play a dominant part in its own future development and in the adjustment of the individual to the total environment.

The Nature/Nurture Debate

The human baby is a helpless creature at birth. It cannot walk; it cannot talk; it cannot even sit up, turn itself over, or grasp an object it is offered. It is not equipped, as are most animals, with a large number of hereditary **instincts,** inherited complex patterns of behavior that do not have to be learned. Instincts enable animals to satisfy needs that arise at various stages of their development. A good example is the nest-building instinct of birds.

Human babies at birth have instincts, but they also have an innate capacity for growth and development. Gradually, a baby learns to adjust to its environment, and in the process it slowly becomes conscious of itself as a person, separate from its environment. As it develops physically, its power to learn keeps increasing, but all the patterns of behavior that will later characterize it as a normal human being must be learned, and the learning process is not always easy.

The drives that a baby inherits are urges to satisfying basic needs such as those for sleep or food. When these are not satisfied, they are felt as tension or discomfort. These drives provide the stimulus for learning. One of the most powerful of human drives is hunger. To satisfy hunger, a baby depends on its mother's breast or a bottle. But when it becomes hungry, nourishment is not always present, and as its discomfort increases, it cries. This may bring the breast or the bottle and with it the pleasure that is felt as hunger is satisfied. Before long the baby associates crying with the appearance of the nourishment, and so it cries as soon as hunger begins in order to bring the satisfaction. This illustrates the beginning of the learning process and perhaps also the beginning of the development of personality.

B. F. Skinner, a psychologist who did extensive research in this area, strongly emphasized the influence of society on the individual. He saw individuals' personalities shaped in large part by conditioning. He believed that individuals' behaviors could be changed by **operant conditioning**—altering individuals' habits by behaviors (operants) that themselves have an observable effect on the environment affecting an individual. Operant conditioning is often discussed in terms of **positive reinforcement, negative reinforcement,** and **punishment.** Procedures that strengthen behavior are called reinforcement; those that suppress behavior are called punishment. There are two types of reinforcement and two types of punishment, as outlined in Table 7.1.

It is important to note that punishment is not the same as negative reinforcement. If you speed and get a speeding ticket, you experience a positive punishment. If, however, the judge offers you the choice of attending a driver education class or losing your license, that's an example of negative reinforcement. You attend the class to avoid a worse alternative—losing your license. To summarize, positive and negative reinforcement are both procedures that strengthen behavior. Positive and negative punishment are both procedures that weaken behavior.

The effects of reinforcement and punishment on personality leave individuals with some hard choices. For example, should parents console or ignore a child who is crying? Consoling can reinforce negative crying behavior; on the other hand, ignoring might make the child feel unloved and have a negative influence on the child's development.

Table 7.1

Types of Punishments and Reinforcements

PROCEDURE	STIMULUS EVENT	EFFECTS	EXAMPLES
Positive reinforcement	Applying a desirable stimulus	Strengthens responses that precede occurrence of stimulus	Praise
Negative reinforcement	Applying an undesirable stimulus	Strengthens responses that allow escape from stimulus	Harsh criticism
Positive punishment	Applying an undesirable stimulus	Weakens responses that precede occurrence of stimulus	Speeding ticket
Negative punishment	Loss of a desirable stimulus	Weakens responses that lead to loss of stimulus	"Time out"

Skinner did extensive work with laboratory animals such as rats and rabbits to test his theories. He and his adherents have shown that animals can be taught to do things such as push on a bar in order to receive food or water. Such laboratory work is, on the whole, noncontroversial (except when the experiments directly harm animals). But when Skinner's theories are extended to humans and to the way humans learn, they can be controversial.

Some researchers have emphasized the influence of punishment and reinforcement so strongly that little room remains in their theories for any other determinants of personality. Moreover, they have derived from these theories a number of proposals for education and rehabilitation programs that are controversial. For example, Skinnerians developed programmed texts that provide fast positive reinforcement for students. Also, some sex criminals may submit themselves to a rehabilitation program in which whenever they are shown sexually arousing pictures, they experience an electric shock (negative reinforcement) that is designed to modify their behavior.

Skinner's emphasis on the environment's role in shaping personality is disputed by many psychologists who emphasize instead the role of **heredity,** the genetic transmission of characteristics from parent to offspring. The debate between the two sides has often been called the nature/nurture debate. The **nature/nurture debate** focuses on whether heredity or environment is more important in determining the personality and the success in life of an individual. It is like asking, Which is more important in making an automobile run—the gasoline or the engine? Quite obviously, if the car is to run at all, both gasoline and an engine must be provided. Likewise, if a baby is to develop normally, it must have both a reasonably adequate biological inheritance and a reasonably adequate social environment.

If we could somehow take two identical individuals and place them in different environments, we could answer the question. However, no two people are physiologically identical (even identical twins have some slight differences), and no two people have the same environmental background. Instead researchers must concentrate on groups of people to determine whether heredity or environment is more important. For example, are people's sexual desires determined by nature or nurture? This is an open question, but in 1991 a respected researcher found distinct differences in the brains of homosexuals and the brains of heterosexuals, which suggests a stronger role for nature. He emphasized, however, that his study was tentative. Many studies have been done since and we still have no definitive answer, but there is a leaning toward nature setting the scene for nurture. Surely, we will hear more about this debate in the future.

Recently, a test of the nature/nurture question was conducted with respect to obesity. The population studied consisted of adopted children, and the question posed was, Would the children resemble their biological (nature) or their adoptive (nurture) parents? In this study, it was found that children of obese biological parents tended to be obese. The obesity of the adopted parents had little effect. In this case, nature seems more important than nurture.

Recent discussions of the nature/nurture debate have tended to emphasize the complex interaction between the two. For example, measures of the inheritability of intelligence rise with age, from 40 percent in childhood to 60 percent in adulthood. James Flynn, a psychologist in New Zealand, suggests the reason is that a slight difference in intelligence at birth leads caregivers to treat children differently, with the seemingly brighter child being more strongly reinforced in learning, while the seemingly less bright child receives negative reinforcement.

Explanations of Behavior

The nature/nurture debate is part of a larger debate in psychology about how best to understand behavior. We will distinguish three general approaches: the cognitive approach (under which we include the psychoanalytic approach), the behavioralist approach, and the humanist approach. The **cognitive approach** focuses on thought as the initiator and determinant of behavior. Although there are many different cognitive approaches to behavior, the most well known is the Freudian approach to psychology, which we discuss below. Freud's approach, sometimes called the psychoanalytic approach, focuses on unconscious thought and its relation to conscious thoughts and actions. This cognitive approach has led to a variety of approaches to therapies besides that of Freud, one of which is Albert Ellis's "rational emotive therapy," also discussed below.

The second approach is the **behavioralist approach,** which focuses on actions, not thoughts. B. F. Skinner was an advocate of this approach. The behavioralist approach has a recent addition—what might be called the biopsychological approach. The biopsychological approach, which flows from biology as much as it does from psychology, sees behavior simply as responses to chemical stimuli in the body (although its basis is not often put so bluntly). In this approach, one's genetic structure is believed to determine the ranges of behavior one will display; the chemical messengers determine specific behaviors within that general range. The mind is seen as just another part of the physical world. The third approach is the **humanist approach,** which emphasizes the entire being and his or her interrelationship with culture. Abraham Maslow's work, discussed below, is an example of this humanist approach.

These approaches are not mutually inconsistent, and recently a group of therapists emphasizing a combination approach—a cognitive behavioralist approach—has been gaining ground. The cognitive behavioralist approach emphasizes that thoughts can be "operants of the mind." Thus cognitive approaches focusing on thought are opened up to behavioralist analyses focusing on behavior.

Before we move on to discuss how these different approaches lead to different treatments of maladjustment, let us briefly consider Abraham Maslow's theory of the well-adjusted individual and Freud's conception of the personality to give you a little better idea of the differences that varying approaches can lead to.

The Well-Adjusted Individual

Probably the most famous theory of the development of a healthy personality is that of Abraham Maslow, known as Maslow's hierarchy. **Maslow's hierarchy** states that there are five levels of human achievement, each of which must be satisfied before the next is attempted. They are shown schematically in Figure 7.1.

Self-actualization, the level of human achievement in which one is well adjusted to one's reality, is the highest level, according to Maslow. A person need not be famous, or the best in the field, in order to be self-actualized. Rather, we are self-actualized when content with life and capable of handling the problems that all of us must face. Because each level of the hierarchy must be satisfied before the next can be attempted, few of us reach self-actualization; even for those few who attain that highest level, it is a constant effort to stay there and not slide back down.

What do we mean by good social adjustment? There are dangers in setting up social adjustment as an ideal to be sought. If an individual were perfectly adjusted to the environment in the sense of having no problems or tensions and not wishing that anything were different, that person would stagnate. On the other hand, if we mean by a well-adjusted person someone who loves life and finds it interesting and stimulating, that person must have dissatisfactions, problems to be dealt with, and goals to be achieved. Good adjustment must be a dynamic concept, and there is no simple formula for it that will apply equally well to everyone.

The truly well-adjusted person has developed a strong and balanced personality that can suffer misfortunes and recover from them. It should be emphasized that disappointment, pain, and grief are common experiences of life that come to all of us from time to time. The well-adjusted person can deal with these without being crushed.

Much research has gone into studying the genetic component of adjustment. In one study, psychologists David Lykken and Auke Tellegen surveyed 732 pairs of identical twins and found that their level of happiness was the same regardless of their surroundings. Another study reinforced this finding and discovered that the actual circumstances a person experiences have little to do with the satisfaction that person experiences. For example, people in China were happier in measures of subjective well-being than people in Japan, even though people in Japan were ten times richer.

In a book that attempted to pull all these ideas together, University of Pennsylvania psychologist Martin Seligman tried to explain what these findings meant for people searching for the "good

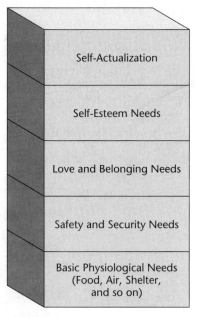

Figure 7.1

Abraham Maslow's hierarchy.

life." Although we don't have time to discuss much of the book here, one of his suggestions will give you a sense of the ideas he raises. Specifically, he suggests: Keep your illusions. For example, he argues that happy couples—the couples who stay together happily—are ones who do not see their spouse objectively, but instead see him or her through rose-colored glasses and think that the spouse is better than he or she actually is. We leave a consideration of Seligman's additional ideas to you as an optional research project, but we're sure you will do it (even though deep down we have our doubts) because we are trying to be optimists, which is another of Seligman's suggestions of how to have the good life.

Adjustment and Normality

Good adjustment and normality do not have precisely the same meaning when applied to personality, but their relationship is close. Conversely, a normal person in any society is necessarily a reasonably well-adjusted person. In cultural terms, a **normal person** is one who has acquired the basic attitudes and behavior patterns of the culture sufficiently well to be accepted and approved by the group. In any society, a well-adjusted person is likely to be recognized as a normal person. This normal person may not in all respects represent the typical person in the group, or the statistical average, but the normal person's behavior must not deviate too far from what is acceptable. The cultural norms are determined by the group. Types of behavior that in one culture would be quite normal might in another culture be regarded as wholly abnormal.

The Freudian Concept of Personality

Probably the best-known name in psychology is Sigmund Freud, who lived from 1856 to 1939 and spent most of his life in Vienna, Austria. He was trained as a physician but specialized in neurology, and in those days this meant that most of his patients were people with emotional problems.

Freud became famous as the originator of the system of psychotherapy known as **psychoanalysis,** a method of analysis based on the exploration of unconscious mental processes as manifested in dreams and disturbed relationships with others. Essentially, the method of psychoanalysis is that of free association. A patient is induced to express anything that comes to mind in the hope of uncovering memories or ideas of which the patient is unaware but that may be causing mental and emotional conflicts. For example, perhaps a terrifying experience in early childhood has been repressed below the level of consciousness. The psychoanalyst believes that if the patient can be helped to recall such an experience, the patient will be able to deal with it realistically, so that the mental disturbances it has been causing will disappear. But to bring unconscious mental processes to the level of consciousness takes time and persistence on the part of both the psychoanalyst and the patient.

In time, Freud became recognized as one of the great original thinkers in the field of psychology, and today most psychologists believe that he made important contributions to our understanding of the human personality. But his theories have been the center of much controversy.

The Id, Ego, and Superego.   To Freud, personality consisted of three major systems or "structures," which he called the id, the ego, and the superego. In the normal person, these

"Well, son, now that you've found yourself, who are you?"

three personality systems cooperate to enable the individual to satisfy basic needs and desires within the environmental setting, but when they are in serious conflict with one another, various mental disorders will result.

According to Freud, the **id** is the part of our personality controlled by the pleasure principle. It is driven by the goals to seek pleasure and avoid pain. It is the immature, selfish side of our personalities. Its counterpart, the **superego,** is our primitive conscience, which develops as we grow older and is guided solely by our morals. The third major structure of the personality is the **ego**—the personality component that most immediately controls behavior and is most in touch with external reality—which plays referee between the other two systems, sometimes allowing us to seek pleasure, at other times allowing the superego to guide us to more restrictive behavior. The id, ego, and superego are, of course, not independent entities. Rather, they are convenient terms to designate different groups of forces that interact within the human personality.

Defense Mechanisms.   Among the many elements of Freud's psychology are **defense mechanisms**—behaviors that individuals use to avoid facing issues. These include:

- Displacement, in which one redirects one's anger away from the real target and toward an innocent target. For example, a frustrated worker kicks his dog.
- Reaction formation, in which an individual connects an anxiety-causing impulse with an overemphasized opposite. For example, people who are unconsciously attracted to the same sex may develop an intense hatred of gays.
- Projection, in which unacceptable urges in oneself are attributed to others. For example, a spouse who is tempted to have an affair becomes unduly suspicious of his or her partner.
- Rationalization, in which one gives excuses for one's shortcomings. For example, after you fail an exam and flunk out of school, you say that it was all boring anyhow, and you prefer doing active, not mental, work.
- Fantasy, in which one avoids one's real worries by living in a fantasy world. For example, you don't study but rather spend all day dreaming of the great job you will never get because you didn't study.
- Sublimation, in which one transforms an unacceptable need into an acceptable ambition. You study hard because you hate the textbook author's stupid jokes.

Defense mechanisms include other behaviors that we all follow to varying degrees, but this list should give you a good idea of what is meant by defense mechanisms.

Perfection Blueprint

If the perfect child will make the perfect adult, the early 1980s produced a recipe to satisfy society's appetite for good adjustment. Judith Martin wrote two no-nonsense books that explained how to perfect the child. Briefly stated, her rules are for parents to nag, to start early, to set a good example, and to keep at it. She based her system on the belief that if the child acts perfect, the child is perfect.

She has no patience with uncertainties such as, "Who is to decide what is right and wrong, what is proper and improper?" and "What difference does it make which spoon you choose for the soup?" If you teach your child to sit up straight and your child learns to do that, then, Martin believes, your child will look nice, will seem to be paying attention in school, will be paying attention in school, will be learning lessons, and will be on the road to success and perfection.

She advocates advancing by increments, or steps. Say please and thank you to the baby; withhold the candy until the toddler says please; give the child a place at the dinner table when she no longer spits spinach around the kitchen; let the kid eat in a restaurant when he has learned not to interrupt adults' conversation; send the eighth grader off to buy her own clothes when she has learned to polish her own shoes and press her shirt before starting out for school.

There are old-fashioned sayings that summarize these ideas, such as "Manners maketh man" and "Handsome is as handsome does" and even "Go along to get along." Social scientists call this process socializing. Or it could be called civilizing. Whatever you may think of her methods, Martin has hold of a basic principle. If individuals can be molded to a standard set by the society in which chance has deposited those individuals, the standards will be preserved, the people will get along with each other, everyone will know what to expect, there will be no surprises, and the world will run smoothly.

The Oedipus Complex.   Probably the best-known aspect of Freud's work is the **Oedipus complex**—a child's sexual attraction to the parent of the opposite sex—so called because of its analogy to the Greek myth about Oedipus, the man who unknowingly killed his father and married his mother. Freud's formulation of the Oedipus complex grew out of the fact that rather early in his career he believed he had uncovered, in the unconscious mental processes of his neurotic patients, fantasies of sexual relations with the parent of the opposite sex, combined with jealous anger against the parent of the same sex. Later he came to believe that a strong sexual attraction to the parent of the opposite sex, along with jealousy of the other parent, is a universal experience of childhood in the years before the age of five. After this period, the Oedipus complex is repressed and disappears from the conscious mind because of recognition of the impossibility of fulfilling the sexual wishes; also, in the case of a boy, because of fear of retaliation from the father. At this stage, the child begins to identify with the parent of the same sex. Freud believed that the Oedipus complex was an essential factor in the development of every child's personality and hence in determining the nature of all human societies.

The Oedipus complex received much publicity and aroused widespread opposition. Many people found it difficult to accept in the form in which Freud presented it. He made it clear that the Oedipus complex referred to a definite desire of the child for sexual relations with the parent of the opposite sex, and to jealousy of the other parent because of the sexual relationship, but in our society it seems doubtful that most very young children have even a vague concept of the existence or nature of sexual relations. Certainly many do not, and in that case it is hard to see how they can desire them or be jealous on account

Motivational speakers such as Tony Robbins abound. They will tell you that you can do anything you want, if only you try their simple methods.

of them. Even among psychoanalysts who subscribe to most of Freud's theories there are those who question or reject the theory of the Oedipus complex.

Pop Psychologies

Modern scientific psychology is supplemented by what might be called pop psychology, in which the more scientific theories are translated and digested, making them available for popular consumption. One such translation is transactional analysis, or TA, which in some respects is similar to Freud's theories. It was made famous by Thomas A. Harris's best-selling book, *I'm O.K., You're O.K.,* and it breaks down the human personality into three "parts"—parent, adult, and child—which roughly coincide with the superego, ego, and id of Freud. According to TA, when two people interact they must be using the same mode of personality (preferably the adult voice). When one's parent mode attempts to address another person's child mode but the receiver is thinking in the adult voice, confusion of the message and frustration result. Other pop theories circulating in the 1990s included ESP (extrasensory perception), scream theory, and channeling. The pop psychology of the early 2000s has a common theme—the quick fix. These theories include psychohypnosis, neuro-linguist programming (NLP), timeline therapy, and emotional freedom techniques (EFT), and while we do not discuss these here, they make interesting research topics.

Intelligence, Personal Adjustment, and Normality

Before we move on to discuss some of the approaches various psychological theories lead to, let us consider the issue of intelligence and its role in determining personal adjustment and normality. Although this subject is not directly related to personal adjustment, it is an important topic that often causes confusion.

In every human society, individuals have varied **intelligence,** which is the ability of a person to understand the situations that confront him or her and to make satisfactory adjustments to them insofar as such adjustments depend on learning and thinking. Low intelligence has prevented some people from making an adequate adjustment to their environment. But only in recent decades have systematic efforts been made to define and measure intelligence or other mental qualities.

Testing for Intelligence

Mental tests are intended to discover or to measure the mental characteristics of an individual. One of the earliest mental tests is described in Greek mythology. During the Trojan War, according to the story, a Greek named Ulysses paid no attention to the government's call to arms. The authorities visited him and found him plowing up the beach and sowing salt. Determined to see whether he was pretending to be insane, they placed Ulysses's only son in the plow's path. Ulysses quickly turned aside, and the test was deemed conclusive proof that he was sane.

Modern mental tests are based on the assumption that we can predict the reactions of an individual in various situations by giving specially designed tests in which similar conditions are involved. Furthermore, we assume that by presenting an individual with a large variety of sample situations, we can estimate how that person's abilities compare with those of other people.

Psychologists employ various types of tests to determine the characteristics of an individual. One type attempts to measure general intellectual ability; this is known as an intelligence test. Another type explores the individual's basic interests by presenting various hypothetical choices and asking the subject to express preferences. A third type is intended to measure aptitudes for certain kinds of work. A fourth is known as a test of achievement and is essentially a test of how well certain skills have been learned or certain kinds of knowledge have been assimilated. A fifth is intended to discover special abilities or disabilities and is generally given to children or adults with disabilities. Finally, a sixth type of test used by psychologists tries to determine the individual's personality structure and basic emotional needs. This type of test is known as a personality, or emotional adjustment, test.

All these tests are used by clinical psychologists to diagnose the power and potentialities of the individual as they exist at any given stage of development. On the basis of such tests, psychologists are able to learn something about the mental difficulties of an individual and judge the possibilities of helping the individual to overcome them.

Mental Age and the IQ.   The best-known psychological test is the IQ, or general intelligence test, which attempts to reduce the many dimensions of intelligence to a single number that estimates a person's mental age. To do this, researchers devised a wide variety of test items, from the simple to the complex, and arranged them in order of difficulty. They then tried these items out on a large number of children at various grade levels. On the basis of this experience, they assigned a mental-age value to each item. Their procedure in assigning questions or problems to various ages was as follows: If a certain item was responded to correctly by as many as 65 to 75 percent of the children whose age was, say, 8 years, but by a smaller percentage of children below that age, it was considered a test of 8-year-old intelligence. They then grouped several items of appropriate difficulty, usually five, to test children of each age. If a child could answer the questions for all levels up through those for 8-year-olds, but none of those for the years above that, mental age was considered to be 8 regardless of actual or chronological age. But the child received proportionate credit for any questions actually answered.

For example, if the child could answer all the questions for 8-year-olds, and three out of five of those for 9-year-olds, mental age was considered 8.6. If the child could also answer two out of five of the questions for age 10, a mental age of 9 was assigned. Later, other psychologists refined the technique so that each mental year consisted of twelve mental months. For example, each test item might represent two mental months, in which case six items would represent a mental year. Each person tested would then receive two months' credit toward a mental age for each item answered correctly.

Once the concept of mental age was developed, it was only a step to the notion of expressing a ratio between the mental age and the chronological age of an individual. This ratio was called the **IQ,** or **intelligence quotient**—an index of an individual's tested mental ability as compared to the rest of the population. IQ is calculated by dividing the mental age by actual age and multiplying the resulting fraction by 100. Multiplying by 100 expresses the ratio or fraction as a percentage, but it is not customary to write "percent" after the number expressing IQ. The formula for finding IQ may be written as follows:

$$IQ = \text{Mental Age/Chronological Age} \times 100.$$

Let us see how this formula works in practice. A child 8 years old having a mental age of 8 is an average child. IQ would be $8/8 \times 100 = 100$. It is apparent, therefore, that an IQ of 100 represents average intelligence. If a child 8 years old had a mental age of 12, as indicated by an intelligence test, that 8-year-old would obviously be very bright. This would be indicated by IQ, which would be $12/8 \times 100 = 150$.

Today it is often the practice to assign an individual a percentile rank rather than an IQ. **Percentile rank** is a ranking of an individual with reference to other individuals in a certain group when all individuals in the group are ranked in order from the most capable to the least capable. The hundredth percentile consists of the 1 percent of the group who have made the highest scores. The first percentile consists of the 1 percent who have made the lowest scores. Similarly, the 50th and 51st percentiles consist of those who have made average scores. Figure 7.2 shows the IQ rankings for society.

Mental tests indicate that there are great differences in intelligence in our population. This fact has long been known, but tests have made our knowledge more definite. Though these and other psychological tests are being used more widely than ever before

IQ Score	Category		Percentage
20		PROFOUND	
30			
40	Retarded	SEVERE	0.4%
50			
60		MODERATE	
70	Mildly Retarded		2%
80	Borderline		7%
90	Dull Normal		17%
100	Normal		25%
110	Normal		25%
120	Bright Normal		17%
130	Superior		7%
140			2%
150			
160			
170	Very Superior		0.4%
180			
185			
200			

Figure 7.2

Percentage of children at different IQ groupings.

in schools, in government, and in business, they are also being subjected to increasing criticism. Nevertheless, mental tests are probably the best means we have for comparing the mental powers of large numbers of individuals.

Limitations of IQ and Other Tests.   Many of the early experimenters believed they had devised tests that did not depend on acquired knowledge but were essentially a measure of innate or inherited mental ability. Hence, they thought, the scores of individuals on such tests could not be affected by any ordinary differences in environment. However, various studies and experiments have demonstrated beyond a reasonable doubt that factors such as differences in family environment and schooling may have a substantial effect on the scores individuals make on standard intelligence tests. For example, when identical twins are separated early and reared in different types of homes, the twin reared by parents of superior social, economic, and educational status almost invariably does better on an intelligence test than the other member of the pair, and sometimes the difference is fairly substantial.

Another example is that people who take the same test thirty years after entering high school will score in direct relation to how much education they have received in that span of time. Yet another chink in the armor of IQ test infallibility comes from Robert Rosenthal of Harvard University and Lenore Jacobsen, an elementary school principal in San Francisco, who successfully convinced a group of teachers that certain students were gifted. According to *Pygmalion in the Classroom*, in which the study is published, the students, who actually were chosen at random, surpassed their classmates and became high-level achievers. These "brighter" students scored an average of 12.22 points higher on achievement tests administered at the beginning and end of the year, compared with only an 8.42 point improvement from their classmates. The only difference between the two groups was in how the teachers responded to their learning needs.

Another indication of the limitation of the IQ test is the fact that scores on the same test have been increasing over time. Because it is almost impossible that intelligence is rising that fast, this suggests that there are sociological aspects to the test and that the test reflects those sociological aspects.

In recent years, some social scientists have argued that standardized intelligence tests are racially biased as well. Again, this relates to the environment in which the child is raised. A black child raised in a low-income area may not know what the capital of Greece is, but the lack of that one bit of information does not indicate less learning ability than a child from a high-income background enjoys. Others disagree, arguing that it is not "white information" that is being tested.

The conclusion we can draw from such studies is that the scores people make on intelligence tests are a result of their previous experiences as well as of their inherited mental aptitudes. Where conditions of environment have been similar, differences in scores may be a rough indication of differences of innate mental aptitude. However, we must be cautious in assuming that any two given individuals have really had the same, or nearly the same, environment.

Some educators say that these intelligence tests are knowledge tests, not necessarily tests of intelligence. Currently there is a trend to use different kinds of tests, such as assessing a portfolio of a student's work or testing on a computer where the computer selects the next question based on how the test-taker has already answered the preceding questions. However, it is expensive to develop new tests, to persuade schools to adopt them, and to train educators to administer and grade them. The standard IQ tests currently employed will probably continue to be widely used for many years.

Your IQ Is 132? So What?

Is the intelligence level of people in the United States falling? If it is, why?

Charles Murray, an author who treats various social and political issues, thinks the intelligence level in the United States is falling and that he has found out why. He explained his theories in a 1994 book called *The Bell Curve* (written with co-author Bruce Herrnstein).

In that book, he concludes that the average level of U.S. intelligence is falling because some large groups of non-white Americans and some large groups of non-white immigrants to the United States have lower IQs than large groups of whites (but East Asians, he says, have higher IQs than whites). He reaches this conclusion because of the results of his research on IQs (the average IQ of some groups is lower than that of others) and because he takes the further step of treating IQ as the measure of intelligence.

Many social scientists consider Murray's arguments wrong and prejudiced. Murray insists they are not. He points out that although large groups may exhibit a particular average test score level, individuals in any of the groups may vary widely in intelligence, and no assumptions should be made about any individual's intelligence based on the overall scores for a particular group. Murray explains that his position is that one group is not inferior to another, just different.

Whether or not Murray's research is prejudiced against or toward any particular group or individual, he is open to criticism just because he equates IQ with intelligence. The book claims that IQ measures intelligence and that IQ/intelligence depends primarily on what you're born with, rather than what you get from living. But although IQ scores are definitely measurable, and one group or another does on average score higher or lower than others, there is a lot of doubt among social scientists as to what an IQ score means. So Murray's work is widely criticized. Still, Murray's controversial books on social policy topics are useful to consider; they make for spirited and challenging discussion, whatever their effect on the real world of politics and social interaction may be.

Intelligence Is Far More Than Mental Manipulation. All tests are useful only if we recognize their limitations. IQ tests tell us something about the probable intelligence of an individual at the time a test is taken, but they do not and cannot measure innate or inherited mental potentialities. A possibly more serious limitation grows out of the difficulty of defining intelligence in such a way that all the elements that enter into it can be correctly rated by a test. It is doubtful whether the concept can be defined with much precision and whether the relative intelligence of different individuals, especially at the higher levels, can be determined with much accuracy. Defining intelligence is problematic, but our earlier definition—that intelligence is the ability of a person to understand the situations that confront him or her and to make satisfactory adjustments to them insofar as such adjustments depend on learning and thinking—is probably the best we can do.

The more intelligent a person is, the better able he or she is to do the following:

1. Perceive a situation as a whole rather than partially or incompletely
2. Learn quickly
3. Concentrate thought and learning in a desired direction
4. Find satisfactory solutions, either with or without help from others

High intelligence probably requires considerable imagination and originality, for to solve a difficult problem we may need to think of and to evaluate a number of novel approaches.

𝒲ho Stands Stress Better: Men or Women?

It used to be thought that women were more emotionally and psychiatrically disabled and had more symptoms of stress than men. However, in 1984 the National Institute of Mental Health (NIMH) completed a six-year study of psychiatric ailments and concluded that although women tend to suffer more than men from phobias and depression, men suffer more than women from alcohol abuse, dependence on drugs, and long-term antisocial behavior. Taking all psychiatric disorders into account, the NIMH study found that both men and women are about equally likely to be affected. Even so, women have often continued to be perceived as more subject to psychiatric problems because the study also showed that women seek professional help twice as often as men do. In fact, though, it could be argued that women have a healthier attitude than men because they do seek help, whereas, according to the study, men tend to mask their depression with alcohol.

You can probably see the tendencies in your own life. Women talk with other women; they discuss their problems and they expose and examine their weaknesses. Men generally hide them and are far less likely to have close male friends with whom they discuss personal problems. Instead, male friends do things together. It is the "macho" thing to do.

When we assume that a so-called mental test measures intelligence, we are assuming that the mental abilities required for correct answers to its questions are the same as those needed for solving the sometimes complex problems encountered in real life. This is not always true, for mental tests have many limitations. For example, they must be completed within a limited period of time on the theory that this makes the scores of individuals more comparable. But some of the world's greatest achievements have been made by people who have acquired the habit of thinking through difficult problems slowly, checking at every step to avoid missing some important consideration. Furthermore, to allow one's mind and imagination to wander with a purpose, to take time to search for the unusual or unlikely aspects of a situation, is one kind of intelligent behavior. It is also an important ingredient in originality or creativity. IQ tests don't measure such abilities. Much research has been done on multiple intelligence models, which assume that there are several different dimensions of intelligence, and that these dimensions cannot be reduced to a single meaningful number such as is attempted with IQ. Researchers have yet, however, to come up with a single alternative.

Intelligence and Personal Adjustment

Intelligence, especially if we mean intelligence measured by IQ tests, has little relation to one's ability to adjust except at the highest IQ levels (above 150) and lowest IQ levels (below 60). Both of these extreme groups often have a harder time adjusting to society than do people in the middle ranges.

The reason that IQ generally is not important is that personal adjustment has more to do with emotional stability and coming to terms with what one is as a person than it does with one's ability to score high on a test.

Even if IQ tests did measure intelligence accurately, it should be pointed out that intelligence and success are not synonymous. Many high-IQ individuals have difficulty coping with life; they might be able to solve a complicated mathematical problem, but they haven't the faintest idea how to interrelate with other people. Business leaders generally fall in the average (normal and bright normal) IQ category, not the superior or very superior categories. They have qualities such as internal fortitude, drive, ambition, ability to work with others, and imagination, which are necessary and probably more important than superior intelligence for business success. We can speak from experience; being at a university we're around people with high IQs all the time and, quite frankly, many of them can be real pains.

Deviance

One of society's tasks is to coordinate the actions of millions of individuals so that they fit together. Society's way of doing this is to develop **norms**—expectations about what constitutes appropriate or acceptable behavior. By definition, most people follow those norms. Individuals' actions are called **deviant** when those actions conflict with society's norms.

There are a number of things to note about the concept of deviance. The first is that it is a relative concept. An act can only be considered deviant relative to some norms, and there is enormous arbitrariness in setting those norms. Thus picking one's nose in public and wiping the result on one's hair would be considered somewhat deviant in the United States. In the Yanomamo tribe in South America, that is the norm; not following that norm is the deviant behavior. To make this relativity clear, some sociologists have emphasized that it is society's reaction to the act, not the act itself, that makes something deviant.

Some societal norms are codified into law. A **crime** is a deviant behavior that violates legal norms. All crime is deviant behavior, but not all deviant behavior is crime. In this chapter, we consider crime and the punishment of crime. We should point out, however, that the study of crime and its punishment is part of a larger social science study of deviance, and that there has been extensive theorizing about deviance. Most of that theorizing quickly gets too complicated for a general social science course, but it is important to recognize how the study of crime fits into social science. Therefore, before we consider crime and punishment, let us briefly introduce you to some of the broadest of these perspectives on deviance.

Major Theories on Deviance

All of us exhibit some deviant behavior. Every so often any well-adjusted person says, "Phooey on the norms!" and lets go, blowing off steam to release tension. Such limited deviant behavior is often condoned and is even admired by society. It gives the person an identity, a personality. However, there is a line and if one crosses it, one's individuality becomes too much for society. Society wants you to be different, but not too different.

There are a variety of perspectives on deviance and explanations of why people step over the line. Psychologists tend to look within individuals—into their upbringing or into their genetic makeup. Sociologists, by contrast, tend to look for factors outside individuals—such as social conditions within society.

As soon as one explores these explanations more carefully, one quickly gets caught up in competing perspectives, each of which has its own terminology and theoretical nuances. We'll leave those issues for a sociology or psychology course and try here to introduce you briefly to some of the major perspectives and theories.

Psychological and Biological Explanations of Deviance.   We do what we do because certain chemicals are released to the brain. These chemicals tell us what actions to perform. The chemicals that are released are themselves determined by a combination of what we eat, our genetic makeup, and the way we are brought up. Psychological and biological explanations of deviance focus on such biological or physiological explanations of criminal behavior.

Some of the psychological explanations of deviance focus on **personality disorders,** abnormalities in individual personalities caused by hereditary factors or by upbringing. These disorders might result, for example, from emotional deprivation—lack of love—in childhood or from being brainwashed by television programs in which crime is glorified. Or, alternatively, these explanations focus more on neurological and biological issues resulting from heredity or psychological causes. Let's consider one of those subissues: the issue of genetic and biological predisposition to deviance and crime.

Genetic and Biological Predisposition to Deviance.   The idea that there is a criminal type has long been a popular belief among laypeople and among some criminologists. For example, in the late nineteenth century a noted Italian criminologist, Cesare Lombroso, claimed that criminals are less sensitive to pain and more subject to epilepsy than normal individuals. He found criminals to have heads higher at the rear than at the forehead, longer lower jaws, flattened noses, scanty beards, long ears, and other physical peculiarities. He explained these peculiarities as atavistic reversions to the characteristics of early savage ancestors. Later studies have totally discredited Lombroso's theory.

Modern approaches have not concentrated on body type but rather on genetic structure. Some studies have argued that there is a causal link between the presence in some males of an extra Y or "male-producing" chromosome (designated the XYY syndrome) and criminal behavior. Much of this work has been discredited, and in 1971 Richard Fox labeled it a modern myth.

The advent of sociobiology has brought another resurgence of biological explanations of criminal behavior. Sophisticated studies, such as one by Sarnoff Mednick and Karl Christiansen in 1977, have suggested some biological predisposition to criminal activity. They found that boys adopted at birth whose biological parents were criminals were more likely to be criminals than those with noncriminal parents, even though neither group knew about their parents.

Yet another attempt to establish a biological basis for crime took place in 1985, when James Q. Wilson of Harvard and Richard Herrnstein of the University of California published *Crime and Human Nature,* in which they argue that crime is a matter of relating costs (getting caught and punished) with the benefits of crime. The authors hold that for certain types of individuals, such as those with athletic builds and slightly lower than average IQ (92), the costs are outweighed by the immediate benefits; that is, punishment for crime occurs with a lag, whereas the benefits of crime are immediate. They hold that this means individuals' time preference (how much they value the present relative to the future) plays an important role in determining whether a person is predisposed to crime. As with most theories that focus on a biological basis for crime, these theories are much in debate.

Sociological Explanations of Deviance

The group that has had the most to say about deviance and crime is composed of sociologists. To introduce you to the sociologists' perspective, we will briefly discuss differential association theory, control theory, labeling theory, strain theory, and illegitimate opportunity theory. These theories are part of two broad sociological perspectives: (1) a symbolic **interactionist perspective,** which sees individuals interpreting social life through symbols that we learn from the groups to which we belong, and (2) a **functionalist perspective,** which sees all activities in society as having a function. Differential association theory, control theory, and labeling theory fall within the symbolic interactionist perspective. Strain theory and illegitimate opportunity theory fall within the functional perspective.

Differential Association Theory. **Differential association theory** argues that deviant behavior is often itself simply behavior that is conforming to norms. The difference is that they are deviant norms. For example, some groups develop a different set of values or norms—such as toughness and the ability to take chances—that are considered deviant from the dominant norms.

This theory, put forward by the sociologist Edwin Sutherland, argues that whether people deviate or conform is most influenced by the groups with whom they associate. Because different groups have different forms of deviant behavior, people who associate with different groups experience an "excess of definition" and in some groups seem deviant. For example, street gangs can require individuals to "stand up" to an insult, and if one is insulted one is expected to respond by defending one's honor with physical violence.

Differential association theory comes more into play when significantly different cultures interact. In the Hmong culture of Southeast Asia, one of the ways one finds a wife is to "capture" her and forcibly have sex with her. In the United States, that is called kidnapping and rape, both of which are serious crimes.

Most people will agree that differential association theory explains some deviant behavior, but most also argue that it should not be used to condone it. Society must have norms, and individuals must learn to conform to those norms and abide by those that have been codified into law.

Labeling Theory. **Labeling theory** focuses on the significance of labels given people (such as names and reputational labels). These labels assigned by society to groups can tend to make the actions of certain groups criminal and the actions of certain other groups noncriminal. A classic study of the effects of labeling was done by the sociologist William Chamblis. He studied two groups of adolescent lawbreakers in a high school. He labeled one group "the Saints" and the other group "the Roughnecks." Both groups were wild, into drinking, truancy, vandalism, and theft, but the Saints were seen by their teachers as headed for success whereas the Roughnecks were seen as headed for trouble. The cause of this distinction was family background and social class. The Saints came from respectable, middle-class families. The Roughnecks came from working-class families. This led to a number of differences: The Saints had cars so their debauchery was spread over the entire town and was less conspicuous; the Roughnecks did not have cars and their actions, taking place in the same area day after day, made them conspicuous and drew the attention of the police. They also had different "styles of interaction" when caught by police. The Saints were seemingly apologetic and penitent; they showed a seeming respect for the police and were generally let go with warnings. The Roughnecks showed contempt for the police and consistently had the book thrown at them. The results were predictable: The Saints became doctors and lawyers while the Roughnecks became criminals.

The issues here are obviously more complicated than captured by this brief discussion of Chamblis's study, but the idea should be clear: Labels make a difference in how people are treated and in many cases can become self-fulfilling.

Control Theory.   **Control theory** argues that the desire to rebel is more akin to our natural desires but that certain forces prevent us from doing so. Control theory argues that the question is not, Why do people deviate from society's norms? Rather, the question is, Why don't we deviate more than we do? To prevent such deviation, society has developed norms and institutions that subtly control us and our actions. Much of the subtle control is instilled by parents during our childhood, and thus the type of family we come from and the type of friends we have in early childhood play major roles in determining how much deviance we will exhibit.

Strain Theory.   Strain theory falls within the functionalist sociological perspective. Functionalists argue that deviance is a necessary part of a society; it clarifies moral boundaries and affirms norms; it promotes social unity and brings about necessary social change.

Successful industrialized societies must arouse discontent in people in order to instill within them the desire to advance and better themselves. Strain theory was developed by the sociologist Robert Merton and other functionalists. **Strain theory** argues that when the social structure does not provide equal access for economic success, but instills in all people a functional striving for economic success, the result is a social strain. This social strain can result in a variety of reactions, one of which is crime. Notice the difference between strain theory and the psychological theories. Strain theory sees deviance as a product of society, not of individuals. Society creates crime and criminals.

Illegitimate Opportunity Theory.   A slightly different take on the functionalist perspective on crime is the illegitimate opportunity theory, put forward by sociologists Richard Clower and Lloyd Ohlin. This theory argues that crime is all around us but that different social classes have distinct styles of crime. All individuals are imbued with the desire to achieve material success, but the lower social classes have significant barriers to achieving that success legally. They are, however, presented with **illegitimate opportunity structures**—opportunities to make larger amounts of money through "hustles" such as drug dealing, pimping, and gambling. Society sees all these as crimes. The more privileged class does not face the barriers and its crimes are "white-collar crimes" such as tax evasion and false advertising, which are not prosecuted as much and are not so widely seen as bad.

Economic Explanations of Deviant Behavior

Economists tend to see all issues through a prism of costs and benefits. Thus, their explanation for crime and deviance is that the costs of crime exceed the benefits and that the way to decrease crime and deviance is to increase its costs. For example, the death penalty increases the cost of a crime to an individual, and economists argue that having the death penalty helps prevent killings. Critics argue that killing is generally an irrational act—a crime of passion in which the penalty plays only a very small role; thus, having the death penalty will not significantly reduce killings. (Both sides are still debating the empirical evidence.)

Similarly, economists argue that lower income individuals are more likely to commit an "equal payoff" crime than are high income individuals because the cost to the higher income individuals of going to jail is higher. Similarly, a rich person is less likely to be deterred by a fine than a poorer person because the same fine has less meaning to the rich person. Finland has an interesting application of this view. It makes all traffic fines income sensitive, so that a rich person pays a much higher fine than a poor person. Thus, a rich person might have to pay $200,000 if caught speeding.

Even economists admit that much is left out of their cost–benefit approach to crime (and to many issues). But they argue that its simplicity and clear statement often shed some light on an issue that is missed by other approaches, especially when the economic approach is combined with a good understanding of the strengths and weaknesses of other social science approaches.

Summary of Various Perspectives on Deviance

Our discussion has only touched on the various theories of deviance. Many, I am sure, led to reactions from you such as "But how about. . . ." To really get into those issues, you'll have to take a psychology or sociology course on deviance. Before we move on, however, let us point out that the theories are not mutually exclusive, and our brief overview of them has not done them justice. Deviance is not a simple issue, and truly understanding that issue requires study beyond that which can be presented in an overview course such as this.

Conclusion

As you can see from the discussion in this chapter, and as you probably know from your own life, adjusting personality to fit society and adjusting society to fit personality are not easy. These adjustments involve a continual effort extending from birth to death. For many of us, it will seem an almost insurmountable effort in which the cards are stacked against us. It is precisely this feeling that leads so many into pop psychology.

This chapter presents a variety of theories and therapies, and almost all of them have some value. Perhaps the most useful lesson here is not so much what the theories are (although this knowledge is necessary) as it is that psychological problems are prevalent among most members of society. It is all too easy to see ourselves as out of step and others as well adjusted (or vice versa).

In terms of the course, the important lesson is to understand the processes by which individuals and societies interrelate. Society is composed of individuals, but society as a whole is much more than the sum of those individuals. Thus individual development and societal development make up a two-way street.

An evolving society will always have its adjustment problems, and each one of us who is a part of society plays a small role in that adjustment. As we adjust, so too does society.

Key Points

- Culture is created by the individuals within that culture, but individuals' personalities are in turn shaped and molded by culture.
- Both nature and nurture affect personality and individual development.
- Positive and negative reinforcement help shape an individual's personality.
- Self-actualization is the highest level of Maslow's hierarchy of needs.
- Freud saw personality as consisting of three major systems: the id, the ego, and the super-ego.

- Defense mechanisms are behaviors that individuals use to avoid facing issues.
- IQ tests can be useful, but only if their limitations are kept in perspective.
- Deviant behavior is not a crime unless there is a law against that behavior.
- Five sociological explanations of crime are differential association theory, control theory, labeling theory, strain theory, and illegitimate opportunity theory.

Some Important Terms

behavioralist approach (145)
cognitive approach (145)
control theory (159)
crime (156)
defense mechanism (148)
deviant (156)
differential association theory (158)
ego (148)
feral children (141)
functionalist perspective (158)
heredity (144)
humanist approach (145)

id (148)
illegitimate opportunity structures (159)
infantile autism (142)
instincts (143)
intelligence (150)
interactionist perspective (158)
IQ (intelligence quotient) (151)
labeling theory (158)
Maslow's hierarchy (146)
nature/nurture debate (144)
negative reinforcement (143)

normal person (147)
norms (156)
Oedipus complex (149)
operant conditioning (143)
percentile rank (152)
personality (138)
personality disorders (157)
positive reinforcement (143)
psychoanalysis(147)
punishment (143)
self-actualization (146)
strain theory (159)
superego (148)

Questions for Review and Discussion

1. Does culture control people or do people control culture? Explain the relationship between the two.
2. Some outstanding individuals have made significant contributions to our culture. Name someone who you think has done this, and discuss that person's contribution.
3. Discuss some of the factors in childhood that influence an individual's personality.
4. Explain how, according to Skinner, operant conditioning shapes personality.
5. Which is more important in the development of personality, environment or heredity? Explain the relationship between the two.
6. Contrast the three approaches to the determination of behavior: cognitive, behavioralist, and humanist.
7. According to Maslow, what are the five levels of human achievement?
8. What are some of the characteristics of a well-adjusted individual?

9. Explain some of the contributions that Sigmund Freud made to the understanding of human personality.
10. Explain the IQ test and what it tries to measure.
11. Why may an act be a crime in one society but not in another?
12. Explain how criminal behavior could be behavior conforming to a group norm.
13. According to the strain theory, is crime necessary for a successful industrial society?
14. In what way is the labeling theory similar to the illegitimate opportunity theory of criminal behavior?

Internet Questions

1. Jung was a psychologist and a peer of Freud. The site www.tearsofllorona.com/jungdefs.html has a glossary of Jungian terms. What is an Electra complex?
2. The site www.indiana.edu/~reading/ieo/digests/d94.html is about home schooling/socialization debates. Go to Stough, 1992. According to Stough's research, does home schooling limit socialization?
3. Go to www.psych.umn.edu/psylabs/mtfs/special.htm to answer the question: As twins grow older, do they become less similar to one another?
4. Take a free IQ test, such as that found at www.intelligencetest.com. What aspect of intelligence do you believe the test is designed to evaluate? What other aspects of knowledge are there?
5. Pick a child from the list on www.feralchildren.com/en/index.php. What or who was the caregiver? Do you believe the story? For all the children listed, what was the most common caregiver? Where would she or he most likely be from?

For Further Study

Come, James P., *Waiting for a Miracle: Why Schools Can't Solve Our Problems—and How We Can*, New York: Dutton, 1998.

Hersch, Patricia, *A Tribe Apart: A Journey into the Heart of American Adolescence*, New York: Fawcett, 1998.

Kennedy, Donald, *Academic Duty*, Cambridge, MA: Harvard University Press, 1998.

Martin, Judith, *Miss Manners' Guide to Rearing Perfect Children*, New York: Atheneum, 1984.

Maslow, A. H., *Psychology of Science: A Reconnaissance*, Chicago: Regnery-Gateway, 1969.

Nabhan, Gary Paul, *Cultures of Habitat: On Nature, Culture, and Story*, Washington, DC: Counterpoint, 1998.

Neisser, Ulric, ed., *The Rising Curve*, Washington, DC: American Psychological Association, 1998.

Nussbaum, Martha C., *Cultivated Humanity*, Cambridge, MA: Harvard University Press, 1998.

O'Brien, George Dennis, *All the Essential Truths about Higher Education*, Chicago: University of Chicago Press, 1998.

Pinker, Steven, *How the Mind Works*, New York: Norton, 1997.

Seligman, Martin, *Authentic Happiness*, New York: Free Press, 2002.

Simmons, Rachel, *Odd Girl Out: The Hidden Culture of Aggression in Girls*, New York: Harcourt, 2002.

Small, Meredith F., *Kids: How Biology and Culture Shape the Way We Raise Our Children*, New York: Doubleday, 2001.

WWW   B. F. Skinner Foundation   www.bfskinner.org

WWW   The Jean Piaget Society   www.piaget.org

WWW   Library of Congress, Freud: Conflict and Culture   http://lcweb.loc.gov/exhibits/freud

WWW   Maslow's Hierarchy of Needs   http://chiron.valdosta.edu/whuitt/col/regsys/maslow.html

WWW   Mental Health.net Personality Disorders   http://personalitydisorders.mentalhelp.net

WWW   Personality Tests   www.2h.com/personality-tests.html

WWW   Social Psychology Network   www.socialpsychology.org

The Family

After reading this chapter, you should be able to:

- List four variations in family patterns and discuss where such variations can be found
- List three functions of the family and explain how variations in family patterns serve those functions
- Discuss the state and problems of the U.S. family today
- Discuss the effects of technology on the family and what effect future changes in technology are likely to have on the family

It is characteristic of man that he alone has any sense of good and evil, or just and unjust, and the like, and the association of living things who have this sense makes a family and a state.

—Aristotle

Of all the institutions that shape our personalities and help us adjust to changing environments, the **family**—a group of persons closely related by marriage, blood, or some other bond who deal as a unit with the outside world—is the most important. It is within the family that we are initially socialized. If our family unit isn't working, we are likely to have personal and social problems.

In the United States, many still tend to think of the family in terms of a mother, father, and one or more dependent children, typically with the father working and the mother staying at home. This vision of the family is still strong, but that kind of family is now in the minority in the United States; in fact, fewer than 10 percent of our households meet this description. Moreover, the concept is by no means accepted in all parts of the world.

Similarly, many of our other ideas about marriage and the family are not universally held. For example, in the United States we have come to assume that everyone should have a free choice in selecting a mate, but this is definitely not a worldwide custom. Some societies have quite different ideas of marriage and family.

One stable point can be claimed, however: Throughout history, among all peoples in the world, the family has been the continuing and basic primary group.

Variations in the Family Pattern

In addition to the **two-parent family**—mother, father, and one or more children—there are also the **single-parent family,** consisting of either a mother or father, but not both, with one or more children; the **extended family,** consisting not only of parents and children, but also of other relatives such as grandparents, aunts, and uncles; and the **gay family,** consisting of two men or two women and their children.

Number of Mates

In the Western world, monogamy is the traditional, and in most places the only, legal form of the marriage relationship. **Monogamy** is a form of marriage relationship in which there is one husband and one wife. This is by far the most widespread form of marriage all over the world, even where other forms are allowed or encouraged. Given the increasing frequency of divorce in the United States, some researchers have suggested that we should develop a new name—**serial monogamy**—to describe our standard formal relationship, which is marriage between one husband and one wife followed by a dissolution of that marriage and a subsequent marriage between that same husband or wife and another opposite-sex partner.

Polygamy is the term used for plural marriage, but this is divided into two types: **polygyny,** meaning one husband and two or more wives, and **polyandry,** meaning one wife and two or more husbands. A polygamous family may be thought of as two or more nuclear families bound together because all the children have one parent in common. Some writers also recognize a form of plural marriage called group marriage, or cenogamy. **Cenogamy** is a form of union in which several men are married to several women, but such relationships are uncommon. **Gay marriage** is a union between adults of the same sex. Around 1970, at least in the United States, this last term began to be used as such relationships were formed more and more openly. These relationships create new social and legal problems with which our society is still struggling.

Where polygyny is sanctioned, it is practiced both for its prestige value and for its economic advantages. Among the Tupis of South America, for instance, as well as in sections of Africa, wealth and distinction are measured in terms of how many wives a man has. Often the wives not only perform domestic services, but they also work in the fields and thus contribute to the support of the entire family group. Sometimes, as in the Trobriand Islands of Micronesia, the income of a chief depends on the annual endowments received from the families of his wives. The first wife usually has the responsibility of administering the affairs of the household, but she is not necessarily the favorite wife. In many cases, each wife keeps a separate household, and the husband rotates his attention among them.

Polyandry is comparatively rare. It is found mainly in some parts of Tibet and also among some aboriginal tribes of India, where a woman may marry two or more brothers. There are also cases of polyandry among a certain few indigenous people of Canada, in the Marquesas Islands, and among the Bahima in Africa, but it is the least common of the main forms of marriage.

Selection of Mates

The rules governing the choice of mates are as diverse as the societies in which they have developed. The rules differ not only from one society to another but also among subgroups, such as social classes, within a society. They usually include various limitations on the persons of the other sex who are eligible to marry any given individual.

Let us first consider some of the rules governing eligibility. For instance, in India a person of one caste finds it difficult to marry an individual from another, and until

An arranged Indian wedding.

recently, in a country such as South Africa a person of one race was not permitted to marry someone from another race. In some societies, one may never marry a blood relative, no matter how distant, and in others one may marry only within the kinship group.[1] The governing factors on the one hand are the fear of incest, or sexual activity among people who are close kin, and the desire for alliances. At the other extreme is the fear of marrying anyone too unlike the social group to which one belongs (in the case of certain small groups, this necessarily means marrying a relative). In the majority of modern societies, both forces operate, and therefore most people find their search for acceptable marriage mates limited to persons not closely related but within the same general social group.

Rules govern the actual choice of a marriage partner. Some societies have **arranged marriages,** marriages that are arranged by one or more persons other than the marriage partners because it is believed that a marriage is as much the concern of the families as of the individuals involved. The arguments in favor of such marriages include alliances of wealth, property, or political power, or the belief that young people are too immature, inexperienced, and impulsive to consider properly all the factors necessary for an enduring and successful marriage.

Many Asian families in the United States still arrange marriages for their children, many of whom are highly educated. In some societies, wives are obtained by kidnapping or by capture, perhaps in a raid on a neighboring tribe. Sometimes the kidnapping is genuine, and sometimes it is a ritual that carries out a previous understanding.

The other principal type of selection we call personal-choice mating. **Personal-choice mating** implies the custom of personal freedom in mating, with relatively little interference from others. This is the type of marriage we are familiar with in mainstream society. However, this freedom of choice is not restricted to our own country, nor indeed to our own time, although we again emphasize that mating activities must always be carried on within the framework of the prevailing local laws and mores.

---

[1]Marriage within the kinship or other social group is known as *endogamy. Exogamy* refers to marriage outside the group.

The techniques involved in personal-choice mating differ from one society to another, as do the moral and legal sanctions governing them. For example, among the polar Eskimos in earlier days there was not only complete freedom of choice by mutual agreement in the making of a permanent marriage, but before marriage there was also a sanctioned period of group living, during which experimental mating took place among the youth of the community. Children resulting from this arrangement were not considered illegitimate but belonged to the mother and the man who eventually became her husband. One of the criteria often used by the man in choosing a wife was her demonstrated ability to bear children, just as one of the criteria for the woman in choosing her husband was his demonstrated ability to provide for her and her children.

Family Control

No one type of family control has ever been universal, but three main patterns have prevailed: patriarchy, matriarchy, and the equalitarian family. A **patriarchy** is a form of social organization in which the father is the supreme authority. A **matriarchy** is a form of social organization in which the mother is the supreme authority. An **equalitarian family** is one with shared control, with neither the father nor the mother as superior.

In a patriarchal culture, the father is not only the head of the family, but society also considers that the children belong to him and that he has authority over their lives, even, in some cases, the right to give or sell them in marriage. The patriarchal family was found among the early civilizations around the Mediterranean and has been carried down through Christian civilizations to modern times. Our colonial fathers maintained the patriarchal system, and there are still many families in the United States, as well as in other parts of the world, in which the father is the recognized authority in the family, although with some modifications.

Societies in which family control actually rests with the mother are exceptional. In most so-called matriarchal cultures, as among the Zuni Indians in the southwestern part of the United States, the mother does not usually have direct control, as one might suppose. More often it is the mother's brother who wields authority and controls the children. But the family takes the mother's name and usually lives with the mother's parents or other relatives. The husband may move in with them, but he is apt to spend more time with his own mother or his sisters' families, helping to control their children. Because he has no control status with his own children, he is actually more of a playmate and friend to them.

Within the last hundred years, family control in the United States has gradually shifted toward the partnership, or equalitarian, form. As women have increasingly gained equal educational, economic, and political rights and privileges, the control of the family has more and more come to be shared by both marriage partners.

Reckoning of Descent

In the Western world, we use the **bilateral method** of reckoning descent, counting our ancestors on both our father's and our mother's side because our biological inheritance comes from both. However, this is not the universal practice. Some societies use the **unilateral method,** in which an individual is deemed to belong to either the father's or the mother's family and ancestors are reckoned only in the male line of descent or in the female line. A **patrilinear system** determines descent through the male line; a **matrilinear system** determines descent through the female line. This may not seem logical to us, but

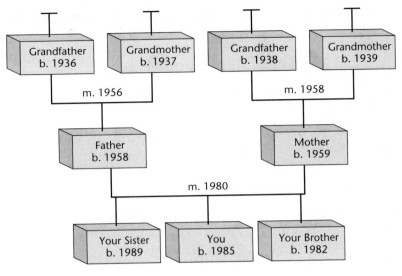

Figure 8.1

How to draw a family tree.

it does simplify matters for those who use it. Imagine being asked to name your ancestors for twenty generations back. The African chief who reckons his ancestry by patrilineal descent would know the twenty names required. In our society, we would have to remember 1,048,576 names. Few carry their family tree back that far, but many families keep a family tree like the one in Figure 8.1.

Names and naming systems are important symbols. In the United States, although we generally acknowledge our descent bilaterally, the name we carry is usually that of our father or husband, emphasizing the patrilineal line of ancestry; however, in recent times more married women have been keeping their birth names.

The preceding examples illustrate the many diverse customs that prevail in families throughout the world. Despite such diversity, are there basic points regarding marriage and the family on which all societies agree? There must be some underlying reasons for the survival of this institution through all the changes that have taken place over centuries. Perhaps the answers can be found in the functions of the family, for although ways of carrying out these functions differ in every society, they remain the force motivating the family as an institution.

Functions of the Family in Society

The family has many functions:

It must reproduce the species; otherwise the species will end.

It must see to it that the young are reasonably well adjusted, so that they don't cause trouble for society and that they grow up to be productive in the biological and physical sense.

It must provide sufficient satisfaction for parents to keep them well adjusted so they don't make trouble for society.

Social Change and Family Functions: An Example

Society relies on families to fulfill these functions, and when they don't succeed, other social institutions must adapt. Let's consider an example: the biological function of families, or the need to reproduce.

Until recently few married couples were voluntarily childless, but in the last twenty years the number of families having no children has been increasing. During this time, many women, both married and unmarried, delayed childbearing and pursued professional education, gaining a foothold in their careers. Often they married other professionals. The incomes of these professional couples tended to be high but so were their expenses and their ambitions. They chose to put off having children, which they were able to do because, among other reasons, of advances in contraceptive techniques and increasing sanction of these techniques.

A number of those couples who put off having children are experiencing what might be called the thirty-seven-year-old syndrome, in which couples approaching the end of the woman's childbearing years are opting to have at least one child before the woman reaches an age at which pregnancy is unwise or impossible. This countervailing trend became apparent in the 1980s and has continued through the early 2000s. A phenomenon surfacing at about the same time was that of unmarried women not only welcoming but actively seeking pregnancy, sometimes with partners selected only for this occasion or through any of a number of other fertilization methods.

Reasons for desiring more or fewer children vary in different societies. In agricultural societies, especially if land is plentiful, people are likely to desire large families because children tend to be an economic asset. In industrial societies, where children are more costly, families tend to have fewer of them. If the trend toward childless couples continues, society will have to find some other way to reproduce itself. For the United States, this may well mean an increase in immigration.

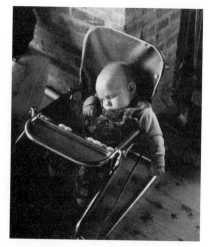

The little darlings (sometimes).

Variations of Family Patterns and the Functions of the Family

What family structure best meets these functions? That's hard to say because it depends on individuals' psychological development and the technology and exigencies of the society. Let's consider some variations of family groups in reference to modern society.

Number of Mates.   Our society is primarily a monogamous one in which a family group includes a male and a female. Why?

One of the reasons is that this family grouping works well for reproduction. Given current technology, that's the way society reproduces itself. If reproductive technology required three (or only one) for reproduction, there would be pressure for a different number of mates.

A traditional family.

Another reason is that children take enormous amounts of time. A one-parent family has a difficult time meeting either the child's or the parent's psychological needs. As a matter of fact, a two-parent family has a difficult time meeting the child's and the parents' psychological needs, especially if both parents are working. This places two types of pressure on social institutions. One pressure is for an extension of the family, either by including a third mate or by extending the family and including grandparents, aunts, or uncles as part of the primary family unit. The second pressure is for society to develop institutions such as day care to remove part of the childrearing burden from the family.

A third important reason the family group consists of a monogamous male and female is for the psychological adjustment of the individuals. According to some social scientists, "three's a crowd" is more than just a pat phrase. Individuals have psychological needs to be accepted and loved, making mates of some type necessary, and the need for security argues for a single mate. Some individuals might prefer more than one mate for themselves, but few would prefer that their mate have more than one mate. The development of strong friendships outside of marriage often results in strong feelings of jealousy. Those feelings are in part genetic; most species have developed instincts that encourage the propagation of the individual's genes, and humankind is no exception.

Recent work in evolutionary psychology emphasizes this psychological aspect. Some experts claim that those traits leading to procreation will be fostered in individuals and that there is a relationship between physiology and human characteristics. Thus, while there is a strong tendency toward one-to-one mating, there is also a strong tendency in both the male and the female to stray and have other mates.

Finally, a fourth reason is that from society's point of view the monogamous relationship provides a mate for most people because males and females are born in nearly equal numbers.

As we stated above, although the majority of relationships are monogamous, there is a frequency of turnover of mates—called serial monogamy—and a certain amount of infidelity within marriage. Thus, while our system is monogamous, it is not so in a strict sense.

Selection of Mates.   Western societies generally allow individuals to select their own mates. Such a selection process is by no means universal; families in Eastern societies generally choose mates for the children. The problem with family selection is the possible incompatibility of mates and a failure to fulfill the psychological function of marriage, although as some of our Eastern friends point out, given the number of divorces and unhappy marriages in the West, self-selection doesn't seem to do such a good job of meeting the psychological functions.

The advantage of family selection is that it is more likely to fulfill economic and social stability goals. When hormones play an important role in mate selection, economic and social considerations are often forgotten.

Living and Loving

A key role of the family is procreation. A society needs children, but not too many. Maintaining the proper balance of numbers of children is a difficult social problem. Take Singapore, for example, a small, rich country in Asia. Singapore's population control incentives were very successful and reduced the birthrate from a 4.7 percent annual increase in 1965 to a 1.5 percent annual increase in the late 1980s. Then the government began worrying that the country would have too few young people to support the elderly, so it switched tactics and strongly encouraged marriage.

The government established a number of programs to encourage the 30 percent of college-educated women who were unmarried to get married. The programs included dating services, "love classes," and advice to men about how to act on a date. One of the program booklets lists "some nutty ideas" for dates, such as "playing Scrabble on the beach armed with a dictionary and a thesaurus."* I leave it to you to decide whether this advice is transferable to the United States. Perhaps we could modify it some: Why not ask your date if he or she wants to go to the beach and discuss the questions at the end of this chapter? How about . . .

. . . The measures didn't work so well in Singapore either. After they were introduced, the birthrate continued to fall. In the early 2000s, Singapore established financial incentives for having children. A second child earns couples about $3,000, and a third child is worth about $6,000. Despite this program, the 2002 birthrate was at an all-time low.

*A thesaurus is a reference book set up like a dictionary, except it provides a list of synonyms.

Of course, as we saw in Chapter 4, social stability is not necessarily a goal of society. Cultural diffusion is also necessary, and one of the reasons Western societies have adapted better than Eastern societies to the changing technologies may be that self-selection of mates creates social instability that allows and generates change.

Family Control and Reckoning of Descent. Western societies are generally patriarchal and use a bilateral method of reckoning descent. These customs do not seem to fulfill significantly any of the functions of the family other than the need for the psychological adjustment of the male. Society does need to fulfill the childrearing function, and it is true that women bear and nurse children and have evolved both genetically and socially so that, on average, a woman is better able to deal with children than a man is, at least until the child reaches the age of about three. Maternal instincts exist. But this patriarchal reality only suggests that the male will most likely maintain the uninterrupted income-earning activities, not that the male will have control of the family.

What maintains the patriarchal system is, in large part, social and genetic inertia. Male dominance is built into the social and genetic structure of society. The fact that it is built in does not mean that it cannot, or will not, be changed. It simply means that it will only be changed through conscious effort and moral commitment to equality.

Other Western Family Characteristics and Functions of the Family. We could go on listing Western family characteristics and discussing their function, but there isn't space, and besides, it is an activity best left to you. Think of other characteristics, such as the age at marriage. Estimate what the average age is (later in the chapter we give you the information), and then try to explain what functions are served by getting married at that

𝒥s an Arranged Marriage in Your or Your Child's Future?

Dating is a pain, love is nonexistent, and romance is for the birds. According to Ramdas Menon, a sociologist at Texas A&M University, more and more Americans, especially those with Asian, African, and Middle Eastern backgrounds, are taking this view and leaving the problem of whom to marry up to their parents. They want their parents to arrange marriages for them, often to people they never meet until the parents of the prospective bride and prospective groom have settled things among themselves. Does this make sense? Maybe it does. It takes pressure off the mates. The custom also preserves culture, brings individuals from similar backgrounds together, often unites and strengthens economic ties, and keeps premarital expectations low.

age. Why not earlier, say at age thirteen or so, as soon as people are sufficiently developed sexually to have children?

Another interesting question in relation to the functions of the family is what is likely to happen to the family as the age structure of society changes. Consider Figure 8.2, which shows the increase in the elderly as a percentage of the total population. What is likely to happen to the family as this occurs? How will the family unit deal with the changes incurred by such a population shift?

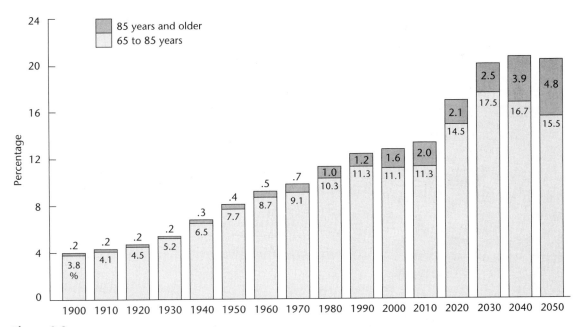

Figure 8.2

The aging of the United States. By the year 2050, over 20 percent of Americans will be over the age of 65 and almost one-fifth of these will be over 85. (Source: U.S. Bureau of the Census.)

In the next section we look at the U.S. family today. As you read, consider the functions of the family and how well the characteristics fulfill those functions.

The Family in the United States Today

One of the causes of the revolutionary changes in twentieth-century life in the United States was our massive transition from an agricultural, rural nation to one that is mainly commercial-industrial and urban. With the mass movement of people to cities throughout the late nineteenth and early twentieth centuries, housing costs increased and both family and home size shrank. People no longer worked mainly at home, although initially most women stayed home to care for the family. However, technological advances in labor-saving household appliances and family planning freed women for leisure and market-oriented activities. Children's help around the house was no longer required as much as it was on the farm; the number of children per family declined, and the city's recreational offerings often drew parents and children in different directions.

Modern transport—the car in particular, which came into widespread use in the 1920s—served to make us an on-the-go nation; home became a place to sleep or to get away from. The car itself and the two-car family helped in large measure to build the post–World War II commuter suburb. Postwar affluence, fed by commercial wealth, advertising, and the credit economy, helped lure us away from the waste not, want not Puritan ethic of the nineteenth century, when debt meant disgrace. Smaller families and the dramatic increase in the number of families in which both parents work—often earning two high incomes—have led to a return from the suburbs to city life, as many seek the distractions and satisfactions of the fast track.

With women playing more vital roles away from home, their dependence on males for survival has lessened. Moreover, many other forces have driven women toward more self-sufficiency and a search for satisfaction both in marriage and outside of it. Today both males and females demand more of marriage and of each other, which adds to the stresses of modern life. The fully liberated man (of whom there are still only a few) shares major decisions, roles, and work with his wife, but many women find that they continue to be allotted the major share of the domestic duties, even while working full time. In other households, the patriarchal male finds great difficulty in accepting the wife's autonomy, but a great many do, nevertheless, make the adjustment.

Even with shared responsibilities, the two-earner family cannot provide full-time care for children. This situation has placed more responsibility on the schools, many of which provide not only lunches but breakfasts and may stay open beyond the normal school day to provide some place for the child to remain until the parents' workday is over. Fortunate families have found good day-care centers, but these are not equitably distributed and tend to be expensive. Moreover, most good centers have waiting lists. Many children come home after school to empty houses or apartments and fend

As more and more women have entered the labor force, fathers have had to become nurture providers, not always with the most finesse.

How to Be a Good Wife

One way to get an idea of the change that has occurred in the nature of the family is to look at old textbooks. For example, a 1960 home economics textbook included a section entitled "How to Be a Good Wife." It included suggestions such as the following :

- Have dinner ready for him when he comes home from work; let him know you have been thinking about him and his needs.
- Touch up your makeup and be refreshed when he arrives.
- Prepare the children; wash their hands and faces. They are little treasures and he would like to see them play the part.
- Clean up the house before he arrives. Make him feel that he has reached a haven of rest and order.
- At the time of his arrival, eliminate all noise. Greet him with a warm smile.
- Let him be the first to talk.
- Never complain. Try to understand his world of strain and pressure and his need to be home and relax.

When I showed the list to my wife, she smiled and reminded me to have dinner ready for her and the kids when she got home from work.

for themselves, sometimes even supervising younger brothers or sisters, until a parent arrives. These children have become known as **latchkey children,** children who have their own house key and immediately lock themselves in once inside their homes.

The sexual revolution of the 1960s and the enhanced sense of independence experienced by both men and women loosened many moral restraints. The mobility and easy anonymity of modern cities have made it possible for husbands and wives to widen their circle of friends. Often this freedom has caused them to become less content with one lifelong mate. A phenomenon described as serial marriage has resulted, in which people have several husbands or wives over the course of their lives, although not more than one at a time. Because each partner may bring to the new marriage one or more children and may be sharing the custody of those children with other former mates, family relationships can become complicated and challenging to emotional and material resources.

Despite these changing roles, the family remains an important element of life in the United States. In many ways, the family has merely adapted to the changing cultural climate in the United States, and, we suspect, most of you see marriage and a family somewhere in your future. Many people who had moved away from family relationships are returning.

Table 8.1 gives you an overview of some U.S. family characteristics. Notice the large percentage of nonfamily households; this category has been growing over the past decades. For a better sense of the changes that are occurring, in the next part of the chapter we consider the issue of dating in the United States. Because much of the material presented about dating is familiar to you, we approach it in a slightly different way—as if it were written by an anthropologist about people from another culture. This allows you to take a more objective look at issues in which you are active.

Table 8.1

U.S. Family Household Characteristics, 2002

TYPE OF FAMILY	NUMBER IN MILLIONS	PERCENTAGE OF TOTAL
Married couple	56.7	52
Male head of household, no spouse present	4.4	4
Female head of household, no spouse present	13.1	12
Nonfamily households	35.0	32

Source: U.S. Bureau of the Census, *Current Population Reports.*

Dating

Because U.S. customs allow self-selection of mates, people who eventually marry must first meet. Some of the ways people meet are through school, work, religious institutions, sports, walking the dog, amateur dramatic societies, and networks of friends. Underlying everything in this list is the assumption of common interests, and this illustrates the principle of **endogamy,** marriage within defined groups. This may not be a conscious goal, but it is a prevailing result. **Exogamy,** in contrast, is marriage outside a similar social unit.

After two people meet, they get to know each other better through formal or informal dating. Dating allows people to get acquainted with each other on an intimate and, hopefully, a mature plane. It also gives them an opportunity to evaluate themselves in an interpersonal situation outside the family and serves as a form of recreation. In the 1950s, dating was often formal, with the boy picking up the girl and escorting her to a social event. Although the boy was no longer required to ask her parents' permission to take the girl out (as he would have been in the 1800s), he was obliged to see the parents and exchange some conversation when he came to the girl's house to pick her up. At these—often awkward—meetings, the parents would "size up the lad" and inform him that they expected their daughter home by a certain hour (say midnight if it were a weekend evening). In the 2000s, arranging a date is more informal. Often one person, male or female, will phone or speak to the other and suggest they get together and possibly do something, such as go to a movie or ride in a sports car. The ritualistic meeting of the parents can come later, or not at all, whatever seems to occur naturally.

Sometimes this relationship moves to formal dating, but often it does not, although both individuals have a sense (often different) of how much freedom the relationship allows them in terms of seeing, talking to, and being with other individuals. A vocabulary often develops to describe how individuals feel about relationships. For example, at my college some students who want a one-to-one relationship are described as "velcro."

Most relationships are not necessarily expected to end in marriage. Usually an individual has relationships with a variety of people before finding one that seems right. In fact, there are likely to be several right ones, or no right one. An eighth-grade girl explains: "Next year we'll be in high school, and then I'll ditch him to date a sophomore. No freshman girl ever dates a freshman!" Older individuals are likely to be less concerned about

Dating in the 1940s.

age or year in school and more concerned with emotional, economic, and social compatibility. The difficulty in finding a satisfactory mate is so great that singles ads in newspapers, in magazines, and on the Internet are booming. Here's one such ad:

> IS THERE A CARING considerate, attractive, ambitious woman out there who seeks companionship, fun, possible marriage? Considerate, attractive, ambitious M.D., 37, 5 ft. 8 in, tired of the singles race, divorced, two children, income in the $150 thousand range, looking for psychologically aware, vibrant, professional, bikiniable woman to share opera, skiing, sailing, art galleries. She's blond, in her 20s, doesn't smoke, and wants me. Send photo/phone.

Some make better reading than the preceding, and many are more interesting than the soaps.

Sex and Singles

There are enormous differences in sexual codes, even within the same town; the sexual revolution of the 1970s spread in a complicated pattern. The sexual revolution also brought with it an increase in sexually transmitted diseases. Depending on the individual's upbringing, sexual relations can begin at any stage of the relationship. In large cities and in suburban communities, sexual relations often begin as early as age twelve, which as we stated earlier is an argument for starting marriage much earlier. In families where religion or other organized moral standards prevail, however, the slogan "good girls don't" still carries some weight, and in such families, girls wait until the serious stage of a relationship, or later, before having intercourse. It should be noted that a dual standard still exists; there is a less strict guideline than "good boys don't."

For black women and an increasing proportion of white women, early sexual activity often leads to teenage girls becoming pregnant while still in school. Over one-third of U.S. births are now to unmarried women, and for black women the proportion is even higher. Approximately 70 percent of all black children are born to unmarried mothers. In the black community as a whole, over 50 percent of all one-parent families are headed by mothers who have never been married. Through the 1980s, the issue of teenage pregnancy was seen as a predominantly black issue, but beginning in the 1990s, with an increasing proportion of white teenage pregnancies, the issue now extends beyond racial lines.

In the early 2000s, teenage birthrates have declined across all race and ethnic lines, although rates for African American and Hispanic teens continue to be higher than those for other groups, with 19.7 percent of African American births being to teenage mothers compared to 10.6 percent for whites. The birthrate is still around 50 per 1,000 teenage women, and although this is a 25 percent decrease over the last ten-year period, it is still the highest rate of all industrialized nations. (Both increased use of contraception and increased abstinence are credited for the decline.)

Another issue that confronts singles—indeed, anyone, married or single, who is not in a monogamous relationship—is sexually transmitted disease. In addition to centuries-old venereal diseases such as gonorrhea and syphilis, there is now herpes, chlamydia, genital warts, and acquired immunodeficiency syndrome (AIDS), a breakdown in the immune system.

Even intense relationships often do not lead to marriage. Individuals often have a number of serious relationships before they finally marry. It is also common for couples to live together for periods of anywhere from a month to many years before making a decision to marry, and some decide never to marry. A Gallup poll taken in the 1980s found that about 50 percent of the responding college students thought it was helpful to live together before marriage; many thought it didn't matter one way or the other, and only about 27 percent thought it was harmful. However, all but 2 percent thought it was extremely important to remain faithful to one's mate after marriage.

In deciding whether (and whom) to marry, romantic love plays a role, but increasingly individuals are considering, in addition to love, other issues, especially in relationships where both members are planning a career. Whose career will come first? What happens if they are assigned jobs in different locations? If one supports the other in order to further his or her education, what obligations are incurred? To meet these complex issues a number of couples are entering into formal marriage contracts (prenuptial agreements) that spell out the obligations and expectations of both so that the love relationship is not shattered.

After a period of decision, most individuals marry. Marriage is a more or less permanent contract between a man and a woman under which they are expected to live together and to provide a home for their children. The contract has legal, and in many cases religious, sanctions.

Entering into this contract creates many new responsibilities involving not only the couple but also the families from which they came and various other social groups. The partners immediately assume new statuses: the husband/wife status, the in-law status, and the family status. Even if the parties have previously lived together, marriage involves a major change.

Such an important shift of roles, even though desirable and pleasurable, involves a good deal of adjustment. This has not been made easier by the swift pace of social change in the United States. In a static society, the role expected of each spouse is well understood, but in a dynamic society such as ours it is easy to be uncertain about just what is expected. This confusion may be increased in cross-marriages between faiths, nationalities, or races. Even if hazards are eliminated, our common heritage of diversity is constantly changing the social pattern for everyone. Hence adaptability has become an important personality characteristic in marital adjustment.

Children

As we stated earlier, for an increasing number of families marriage and having children are not necessarily linked. This is creating what is sometimes called an underclass that has little chance of escaping the poverty it grew up with. This underclass has to deal with a different set of pressures than does the middle class.

Middle-class culture, although it has more or less condoned living together, tends to put pressure on middle-class individuals to get married if they have children or want

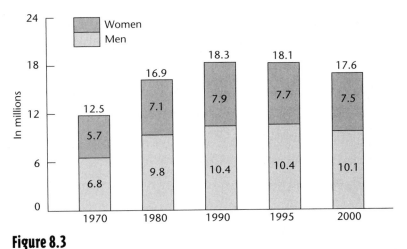

Figure 8.3

Adults ages 18 to 34 living with parents. (Source: *Current Population Reports,* U.S. Bureau of the Census.)

to have children. Thus most middle-class couples choose marriage. Marriage establishes the economic responsibilities for both mother and father, and even if the parents split up, both retain legal responsibility for the children. Thus the spouse who does not have legal custody is responsible for child support and possibly alimony. Later, when we consider divorce, we deal with these issues in more detail.

The decision to have a child is not an easy one. Children involve major responsibilities and hard work. Often it means giving up one spouse's potential income or, if both parents work, worrying about child care, education, and privacy. Moreover, parenting is no longer eighteen years and out. Many adult children are coming home to live with their parents (see Figure 8.3). This trend was strongest in the 1980s when economic times were tough; it decreased somewhat with the booming economy of the late 1990s.

In spite of the responsibility and hard work children bring to a couple, most people feel that the rewards are compensatory. The number of children that couples are willing to have, however, is smaller than two or three generations ago, and following a temporary rise in the 1940s and 1950s, the average has been dropping.

Senior Citizens

As children grow up and leave home for college, for a job, or to establish their own households, the family dwindles in size to the original two.

For the middle-class ideal family, a number of years then follow, perhaps as many as fifteen or twenty, before retirement—years in which there is time for more active participation in social and civic affairs or, for spouses who have not worked outside the home before, for employment. Companionship is now the strong bond between the couple. Shared experiences throughout the childrearing years cement this bond, but a new and satisfactory pattern of life without the children at home must be developed if the couple is to remain happy. Generally, couples are able to make the adjustment. In fact, research studies have shown that a couple's happiness declines with the birth of a child and tends to renew when the children leave. Thus, for the parents no less than for the children, maturing of the children represents a period of weaning or emancipation. When the children return on visits, their relationship is on an adult, companionable basis, and if there are grandchildren, they can provide the grandparents with a new interest in life.

The family ideal is not always reached. In the less-than-ideal family, the couple can't stand each other but stay together because they don't have enough money to live apart, or one leaves or has already left the other in order to take up with someone else or just to live alone. Whether they stay together when they want to be apart or one leaves and sets up another household, often there is a haunting loneliness for one or both members of the couple. Another less-than-ideal family type is the one in which the parents aren't speaking to the children because they have had to take second jobs to pay the kids' college loans, which the kids have defaulted on. There are countless variations of the less-than-ideal family. For the less-than-ideal family, retirement can mean being kicked out of a current job and shunted into a low-paying one that is necessary to make ends meet. As the Russian novelist Leo Tolstoy wrote in the opening sentence of his novel *Anna Karenina*, "Happy families are all alike; every unhappy family is unhappy in its own way."

When the time finally comes for the couple to retire from their regular jobs, many couples, if in good health, still have years of activity ahead. Successful adjustment to retirement also depends on personal temperament. Some individuals welcome the release from routine and responsibility; they are flexible enough to have little trouble in finding interesting ways to spend their time; others feel lost when deprived of their previous work. Health and money are also important factors.

Family Disorganization and Divorce

The preceding section described the development over time of a married couple who remain married. More and more, this is a less typical chronology. Figure 8.4 gives the marriage rate and the divorce rate since 1900. The marriage rate has fluctuated since 1900 but in recent years has remained close to 8.5; in other words, 8.5 people out of every 1,000 get married. The divorce rate increased in the 1970s and has been decreasing since the 1980s. Table 8.2 shows the approximate ratio of divorces to marriages from 1890 to 2000. We must remember several qualifications when considering the divorce rate. For instance, if in a given year there is one divorce for every two marriages, it does not mean that half the marriages in that year ended in divorce; rather, in that year some people got married and others, who had been married for anywhere from one day to fifty years or more, got divorced.

Statisticians have various methods for determining the number of marriages that end in divorce. One study of a group of married couples over time indicates that nearly 40 percent of first marriages end in divorce, about 80 percent of those people enter a second marriage, and almost 45 percent of the second marriages also end in divorce. Though we now have approximately one divorce for every two marriages, only about one in four households is a single-person household, because many divorced people marry again.

Why Do People Get Divorced?   There are almost as many reasons why people get divorced as there are divorces. Most can be combined into some type of incompatibility:

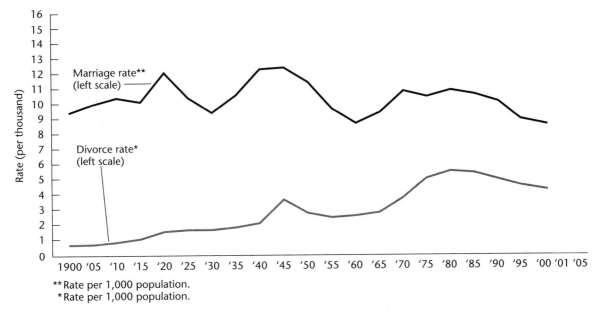

Figure 8.4

Marriages and divorces, 1900 to 2001. (Source: U.S. Bureau of the Census, *Statistical Abstract of the United States,* and monthly *Vital Statistics Report.*)

One or both of the partners are not getting what they want out of the marriage. Sometimes a third party is involved whom one of the partners finds more attractive than his or her mate, but often the marriage would have been in trouble even if there had been no third party.

Table 8.2
Approximate Ratio of Divorces to Marriages, 1890–2001

YEAR	RATIO	YEAR	RATIO
1890	1 to 18.0	1970	1 to 3.1
1910	1 to 12.0	1980	1 to 2.0
1930	1 to 5.8	1990	1 to 2.1
1950	1 to 4.3	2000	1 to 2.1
1960	1 to 3.9	2001	1 to 2.1

Source: U.S. Bureau of the Census, *Statistical Abstract of the United States.*

When we think about the institution of marriage—two individuals deciding that they want to spend the rest of their lives together—the number of divorces is not surprising. Most friendships don't last a lifetime, so why should a marriage? Those marriages that don't have serious problems are often with partners who share a common set of values and who not only love each other but also respect each other's capabilities and integrity. Not many partners fit these characteristics, so there aren't many rock-solid marriages.

People often marry in the hope, belief, or expectation that their partner will change. A maxim of marriage counselors is that people don't change, or if they do change, you can expect it to be in the opposite direction from what the other partner wants. In word processing, most personal computers use WYSIWYG (pronounced wizzywig)—what you see is what you get—presentations. Most courtships involve WYSIBTWYG (pronounced who knows how)—what you see is better than what you get—presentations.

Some Caution about Divorce Statistics.   Divorce statistics are often used as a measure of family disorganization, and the present high divorce rate is cited as proof that the U.S. family is in serious trouble. However, higher divorce rates today than in the past are not entirely the result of more family unhappiness. In earlier generations, many couples avoided divorce even though their married life was unhappy. They avoided it because it meant social ostracism or, in the case of women, poverty because there were few opportunities for them to earn a good living. As the possibilities for divorced people increased and it became easier to get divorces, more unhappy couples have chosen this route.

Legal Grounds for Divorce.   There are many legal grounds for divorce, and they vary with the laws of each state. Among these are incompatibility, adultery, desertion, cruelty, non-support, bigamy, felony conviction, and fraudulent contract. Although the legal grounds for divorce are of some interest and significance, they often have little to do with the real reason behind a couple's desire to end a marriage. Often a husband and wife who wish to divorce cooperate to bring about real or apparent fulfillment of the necessary legal conditions.

Beginning in the 1970s, many states introduced **no-fault divorces,** in which irreconcilable differences serve as sufficient grounds for divorce. Under these laws, a marriage partner need not be declared guilty or at fault as was previously required, making the process of divorce much easier. In the 1990s, the movement shifted back in some circles. Louisiana introduced voluntary **covenant marriages,** in which divorce as an option is harder for people to get. Other states are watching this process develop and if it's successful, the idea may spread. By 2003, legal covenant marriages were available in Arkansas, Arizona, and Louisiana (bills have been put up in many other states but have not passed). In most states, you do not have to be a state resident to get married in the state, or to "upgrade" an existing marriage into a covenant marriage. So, when someone proposes marriage, he or she may now have to specify whether it is a covenant marriage proposal or a regular marriage proposal.

Breaking Up Is Hard to Do.   Even if one is not in a covenant marriage, divorce often presents serious difficulties, especially when a couple has joint property and children. The parties must decide who gets what. Some of the problems are demonstrated by the following examples.

1. A wife has put her husband through school and has not furthered her own education. One year after he becomes a lawyer, they decide to get divorced. They have no property or children.
2. The same as (1), only it is the husband who put the wife through school.
3. A couple decides to break up after six years of marriage. They have two children, a house, a dog, and innumerable items of personal property. Both have careers but the wife's is more successful, and her income is twice that of her husband's.
4. The same as (3), only this time the husband's parents have given them the house.

In these examples as in real life there are no easy answers to what responsibilities two divorcing people have to each other, and couples often end up in court. Generally, however, both parties are encouraged to come to a reasonable pretrial settlement.

Singles

The number of individuals choosing not to marry and the large number of divorces have created the class called singles. These people live alone or as a parent in a single-parent family. As a group, singles have increased substantially in the past twenty years. This group includes divorced people but also an increasing number of people who have never been married. As you can see in Table 8.3, more and more people are postponing marriage. As the number of singles has grown, so too has the number of activities designed for them. Health clubs for singles, singles clubs, singles bars, and video dating services have proliferated.

Not only has there been a significant increase in the number of singles, but there has also been an important increase in the number of single-parent households. Whereas in 1960 there were approximately 2 million single-parent families, in the early 2000s that number had grown to over 12 million, or about 34 percent of all families with children under age eighteen. Most of these are female-headed households. In theory, ex-husbands or fathers are required to help support their children, but in practice many shirk this responsibility.

Table 8.3

Singles Who Have Never Been Married

	1970	1980	1990	2000	2002
Men					
25 to 29 years	19.1%	33.1%	45.2%	49.1%	53.6%
30 to 34 years	9.4%	15.9%	27.0%	29.5%	34.0%
Women					
25 to 29 years	10.5%	20.9%	31.1%	34.5%	40.4%
30 to 34 years	6.2%	9.5%	16.4%	20.6%	23.0%

Source: U.S. Bureau of the Census, *Current Population Reports.*

Gay Marriage and Discrimination

The recent push for legalization of gay marriage in the United States is an interesting example of how cultural norms evolve and interact with legal structures. One of the major arguments put forward for gay marriage is that not to allow gay marriage discriminates against individuals according to sexual preference. This is true, but it is also irrelevant, because laws by their very nature discriminate. A law must draw arbitrary lines somewhere, and the debate about legalizing gay marriage concerns where to draw an arbitrary line, not any deep-seated discrimination about homophobia.

For example, the United States has laws against polygamy in all forms, and those laws are just as discriminatory as laws against gay marriage. In fact, the United States actively prosecutes polygynists, and that prosecution is supported by a large majority of the population. Were there to be no discrimination based on sexual preference, all types of marriages, including cenogamy, would have to be legalized.

The point is not that gay marriage should or should not be given legal standing. The point is simply that laws inevitably include arbitrary lines that discriminate. Whether a law should be changed does not depend on whether the law discriminates, but on whether we, as a society, want that type of discrimination inherent in the law.

Living Together

In the 1970s, statisticians documented a dramatic increase in the number of unmarried people living together. This trend has continued and in 2002, the number of unmarried couples living together was about 4.2 million. Some of the reasons people live together without getting married are unwillingness to commit themselves to long-term relationships of any kind, desire to avoid legal complications when breakups they believe to be inevitable occur, experimentation, and the existence of an undissolved marriage of one or both partners. The practice, although traditionally frowned on, has gained acceptance, and many parents refer as casually to their children's living-together arrangements as they do to marriages.

Homosexual and Lesbian Households

Although acknowledgment of homosexuality is still not the norm, an open attitude toward this orientation, whether of men or women, is becoming more and more common. Members of these groups have fought publicly since the late 1960s for specific legal rights, including the legalization of single-sex marriage. Most such efforts, though, have concentrated on essentials such as employment benefits, the right to adopt or receive custody of children, inheritance rights, and visitation rights when one member is hospitalized. Same-sex marriage is legal in the Netherlands, Belgium, and Canada. In the United States, Massachusetts has been required by its courts to reconsider same-sex marriage. Vermont has allowed civil unions since 2000. A **civil union** is a legally recognized commitment of two individuals; while not marriage, civil unions offer many of the same benefits.

The Family in Transition

The family has been and will continue to be a social institution in transition. A major reason is its interdependence with technology.

Technology's Effect on the Family

Apart from the general effects of technology on society, we can identify some specific technological developments that have affected the family. Although the medical technology of population control has had its failures, such as the intrauterine device, which led to infection and sterility in some women, as well as its social upheavals, such as that caused by the legalization of abortion and subsequent attempts to criminalize it again, many safe and effective means of birth control have been developed. New ones, such as implantation of a capsule under the woman's skin, a day-after pill, and female condoms are coming along as well. A woman's ability to plan her pregnancies has revolutionized family life.

Another aspect of the revolution is technology enabling infertile women to have children. In the mid-1980s, the infertility rate among women in prime childbearing years had almost tripled since 1965, and much of the increase was attributed to smoking, pollution, abuse of recreational drugs and alcohol, and some of the means of contraception themselves. Today medical science can deal effectively with a significant number of infertility cases for both men and women. Treatments for men and women include medication and surgery. There are also various methods of fertilizing a woman's egg outside the womb and returning the fertilized egg to the womb. It is sometimes possible to use frozen sperm to fertilize the egg. Some of the medications, known as "fertility pills," are so successful that they result in multiple fertilized eggs—sometimes so many that one or more fertilized eggs must be removed from the womb so that the remaining ones can survive. A fertilized egg from one woman can be placed in the womb of another woman, usually when a woman cannot, or does not want to, go through a pregnancy herself, and occasionally when the second woman wants to give birth to a child but cannot do so without receiving a fertilized egg. There are several variations of these methods and many reasons that women use them.

Another influence of technology on the family has been the personal computer. It is not unusual for families to own one or more personal computers; some workers run their own businesses by way of the Internet, and some employers supply their workers with home computers. These people can work at home, and this alternative, both lucrative and attractive, has also meant flexible hours and the ability to supervise a home and children while working and earning a living.

Labor-saving devices for the home have remained essentially unchanged for thirty years, but the ingenuity of manufacturers means that we can look forward to refinements in these appliances. Some are liberating and some are not: The convenience of the work that they do is sometimes offset by the difficulty of learning to operate and maintain them. The robot that can do more than simple repetitive tasks and will clean the gutters, do the ironing, water the plants, mow the lawn, complain to the credit card company, rewire the telephone, fix the overhead door, and let the cat in is not in plain sight at this time.

The Future of the Family

The changing role of the family has left society with hard questions. Who will guide future generations? Who will be tomorrow's parents? What can prevent today's family crisis from becoming tomorrow's national disaster? Can adults please themselves as much as they hope to while producing equally happy, well-adjusted offspring who will be the solid citizen mothers and fathers we would wish for the next generation? Can

"The family can't disappear as a social unit soon enough for me."

both wife and husband find the satisfaction they seek at home, at work, and in their leisure hours, combining the goals of personal freedom and success so compatible with "single-blessedness" with the emotional security and commitments of wedlock?

Many individuals and groups have suggested what they believe to be effective ways to reinvigorate the family. Some of their ideas include outlawing abortion, banning busing, allowing school prayer, and prohibiting sex education in the schools. Without taking a stand on any of these issues, we doubt that they will contribute to the stability of families, although they may well be desirable for other reasons. Society changes and so too do the institutions in it. With new technologies, the optimal economic division of labor changes, and as it changes, so too do the functions of families.

Serious challenges to the family's survival are realities. With more women being brought up to regard higher education and careers as their birthright, marriage will be only one of several paths they can choose. Many couples, deterred by high divorce rates, are deliberately opting not to marry or, if they do wed, not to have children, in view of the staggering costs of parenthood. When they do have children, those children are often left much more on their own than in the past. Consequently, rather than deriving their values from the family, these children acquire most of their values from films, television, videocassettes, the mass magazines, the Internet, and peers.

It seems likely that changes to adapt the family to the new realities—such as flexible working hours, more shared jobs, infant care, and familial leaves for both sexes—will help achieve the goal of holding the family together. The family may take new forms as social trends demand; it may bend with the winds of change. But the diagnosis of the family unit's imminent death seems premature.

*K*ey Points

- Four variations in family patterns are determined by the number of mates, selection of mates, family control, and reckoning of descent.
- Three functions of the family are the biological function, the psychological function, and the economic function.
- Family patterns evolve to meet these functions.

- The U.S. family today is quite different from its counterpart of fifty years ago.
- Technological change has significant effects on the family and will continue to have such effects in the future.
- The diagnosis of the family unit's imminent death is premature.

Some Important Terms

arranged marriage (165)
bilateral method (166)
cenogamy (164)
civil union (182)
covenant marriage (180)
endogamy (174)
equalitarian family (166)
exogamy (174)
extended family (164)

family (163)
gay family (164)
gay marriage (164)
latchkey children (173)
matriarchy (166)
matrilinear system (166)
monogamy (164)
no-fault divorce (180)
patriarchy (166)

patrilinear system (166)
personal-choice mating (165)
polyandry (164)
polygamy (164)
polygyny (164)
serial monogamy (164)
single-parent family (163)
two-parent family (163)
unilateral method (166)

Questions for Review and Discussion

1. Why is the family often regarded as the most important of all social units?
2. State some important considerations in choosing a mate.
3. What are some methods of family control?
4. Why is it easier to trace your descent under a unilateral system than a bilateral system?
5. In today's circumstances, is the institution of the family really necessary for the propagation of the species? Defend your answer.
6. Monogamy is the most widespread form of marriage. Give some reasons for this.
7. What changes have the economic functions of the family undergone? Are they less important than formerly? Why or why not?
8. What changes has the physical-care function of the family undergone in the last few generations? Is it still important?
9. Describe the custom of dating as practiced in the United States, and explain the purpose it serves.
10. Describe some types of families other than the husband/wife/children household.
11. Does marrying for love eliminate consideration of compatibility and economic and social factors?
12. Can you think of some major adjustments that a newly married couple must make in their way of life? What further adjustments would be required by the arrival of children?
13. What are some of the problems that a married couple must meet after the children have left home?
14. What are some of the factors that have contributed to high divorce rates?
15. What is no-fault divorce?
16. What implications does the increase in single-parent homes have for society?
17. How can family disorganization be reduced? By better marriage laws? By making divorce more difficult? Or by other methods?
18. Is the family likely to retain its present importance as a social institution? Why or why not? Could a satisfactory substitute be devised?

Internet Questions

1. According to Charlotte Allen, http://adams.patriot.net/~crouch/artj/allen.html, why did old-fashioned manners and family structure give women more freedom and fulfillment?

2. Go to the website, www.mixconnections.org/article_miscegenation.html. What does *miscegenation* mean? When did the first U.S. law appear against miscegenation? When did the Supreme Court strike down *Loving v. Virginia*?

3. Check out the article at www.familytree magazine.com/articles/oct00/dna.html. How can the new DNA research be used by genealogists?
4. Using www.vermontcivilunion.com/union/faq.html, name five of the legal benefits of civil union status in the state of Vermont.

5. From www.census.gov/population/www/soc demo/hh-fam/cps2002.html go to Table C4. How many children live in an extended family with one or both of their parents and at least one of their grandparents? How many live with their grandparent(s) without either of their parents present?

For Further Study

DiFonzo, J. Herbie, *Beneath the Fault Line: The Popular and Legal Culture of Divorce in Twentieth-Century America,* Charlottesville: University of Virginia Press, 1997.

Doyle, Laura, *The Surrendered Wife: A Practical Guide for Finding Intimacy, Passion and Peace with a Man,* New York: Simon & Schuster, 2001.

Duda, Karen, *The American Family,* New York: H. W. Wilson, 2003.

Hackstaff, Karla B., *Marriage in a Culture of Divorce,* Philadelphia: Temple University Press, 1999.

Harrington, Mona, *Care and Equality: Inventing a New Family Politics,* New York: Routledge, 2000.

Howe, Neil, and William Strauss, *Millennials Rising: The Next Great Generation,* New York: Vintage Books, 2000.

Lamb, Michael E., ed., *Parenting and Child Development in "Nontraditional" Families,* Mahwah, NJ: Erlbaum Associates, 1999.

Moynihan, Daniel Patrick, *Family and Nation,* New York: Harcourt Brace Jovanovich, 1985.

Nelson, Margaret, *Working Hard and Making Do: Surviving in Small Towns,* Berkeley: University of California Press, 1999.

Paul, Pamela, *The Starter Marriage and the Future of Matrimony,* New York: Villard Books, 2002.

Tolliver, Susan Diane, *Black Families in Corporate America,* Thousand Oaks, CA: Sage, 1998.

Waite, Linda J., and Maggie Gallagher, *The Case for Marriage: Why Married People Are Happier, Healthier, and Better Off Financially,* New York: Doubleday, 2000.

Wallerstein, Judith, et al., *The Unexpected Legacy of Divorce: A 25 Year Landmark Study,* New York: Hyperion, 2000.

Williams, Joan, *Unbending Gender: Why Family and Work Conflict and What to Do about It,* New York: Oxford University Press, 2000.

WWW Diversity Forum www.diversityforum.com/resources/index.html

WWW Convenant Marriage Links www.divorcereform.org/cov.html

WWW Divorcenet—Divorce Resources www.divorcenet.com

WWW Genealogy Sites www.cyndislist.com

WWW National Council on Family Relations www.ncfr.org

WWW National Family and Parenting Institute www.nfpi.org

WWW Single Scene www.azsinglescene.com/library.htm

WWW Vermonters for Civil Unions www.vtcivilunionpac.org

$\mathcal{R}$eligion

After reading this chapter, you should be able to:

- Explain why religion has existed in all societies
- State the problem that fundamentalist religions pose for the state
- List the five great religions of today and summarize their beliefs
- Discuss the role of religion in society

The more I study science
The more I believe in God.
—Albert Einstein

From A.D. 1095 to 1272, Europeans went to war to recapture territory that had traditionally been controlled by Christians from the Muslims. The Crusades, as those wars were called, changed the nature of society. As evidenced in today's problems of worldwide terrorism and fighting in the Middle East, religion is still leading to wars and still changing the nature of society. The importance of religion to society cannot be overemphasized.

If we think of religion as including all beliefs in supernatural powers, conceived of as controlling people's lives, and including various types of spirits and gods, then religion probably had its beginnings in some of the earliest human societies. The findings of archaeologists and anthropologists suggest that from time immemorial humans have sought explanations of their existence and of natural phenomena that went beyond the range of what they could learn from the ordinary experiences of life or from observation of the natural world.

An aspect of life that from very early on troubled people was the inevitability of death, and religion often promised them a life beyond death. Also, as cultures and civilizations developed, people longed to find purposes and satisfactions in life that would transcend the needs and desires of everyday living and thus give human existence greater dignity and meaning. Religion helps satisfy this longing because of the concepts common to all of its forms: the incorporation of a code of ethics; the use of myths or stories; the organization of intellectual doctrine; the display and comfort of ritual; the fostering of community and regard for others; and the hope of some intense, personal experience such as the answering of prayer.

That religious beliefs, institutions, and rituals have been a major element in the cultural patterns of most societies cannot be doubted. Even in modern industrial societies many of our oldest values and traditions are rooted in religion. In our own country, evidence of religious influence is rich. It includes the millions of people who attend religious services; the thousands of houses of worship; the celebration of holidays (holy days) such as those associated with Christmas, Easter, Passover, Yom Kippur, Ramadan, and Kwanzaa; and those ceremonies that are both private and official, such as weddings and funerals, and rites such as baptisms and bar mitzvahs.

In this chapter, our purpose is not to show the truth or falsehood of the doctrines of any particular faith. Rather, it is:

1. To describe the nature of religion and the general character of certain major religions of the past and present.
2. To give some attention to the role that religion has played in the development of human societies, not only to integrate and stabilize them but also, at times, to create conflicts.
3. To consider the present-day influence of social change on religion and, conversely, the influence of religion on social change.

The Nature of Religion

Today when we say that a person is religious we usually mean he or she believes in the existence of a supreme being and that this belief determines moral precepts and behavior to an important degree. Religious people believe that some things are of great value, or sacred, and they are likely to belong to a religious organization such as a church or synagogue; at the least, they attend religious services, even if on a sporadic or occasional schedule, where they commune with others whose beliefs are similar.

Religions vary greatly. Most include a belief in God or gods, some concept of an afterlife, and some theory of salvation, either by earning the right of entry into heaven or the privilege of reincarnation in a higher form of life or a higher social status. But some religions seem to have no God in any sense in which we ordinarily use that term. One of these is original Buddhism, which, unlike some later forms of this faith, is a religion without a deity, without a personal concept of God, and without any theory of salvation except the bliss of escaping perpetual rounds of reincarnation and suffering by achieving **Nirvana,** a state in which all desire and even all consciousness is lost.

Religions can have both spiritual and civil elements. **Civil religion,** a term that was first used by Rousseau, refers to religious beliefs that lead people to want to live by the laws of the land. It is a means of motivating people, out of fear of the divine power over them, to "subject themselves willingly to the governmental laws." This is in contrast to spiritual religion, which is only concerned with heavenly things and cares little what happens in this world. Neither civil nor spiritual religions are a threat to the state. However, when the two elements of religion combine, and the spiritual aspect of religion becomes interested in happenings of the world and unwilling to accept the laws of the land, the state and religion can come into conflict. Fundamentalist elements of religions, such as fundamentalist Christianity and fundamentalist Islam, often combine the two and hence come into

Left: *Sundial, or "The Hitching Post of the Sun," in the Temple of the Sun at Machu Picchu. It is believed that the temples of the Incas did not have roofs because it was important not to obstruct the entrance of the sun, moon, and other deities.* Right: *The Great Sphinx and the Pyramid of Khafra.*

conflict with the state. No longer does the individual subject himself or herself willingly to government laws, but instead is often in direct conflict with those laws. Sometimes this conflict becomes violent. We can see this in both fundamentalist Christian attacks on abortion centers and fundamentalist Islamic attacks on western targets.

It is not easy to give a formal definition of religion that is wholly satisfactory, but the one suggested by Hans-Joachim Schoeps in the *Religions of Mankind* is useful and is the one we will use. According to him, "**religion** may be defined, in its broadest sense, as the relationship between man and the superhuman power he believes in and feels himself to be dependent upon." Such a relationship is expressed in various ways, including feelings of trust or fear, legends, myths, prayer, rituals, and the application of religious precepts to the conduct of life.

What religions the earliest human beings practiced is a matter for speculation, but there are some tribal groups today, such as African bushmen, whose way of life is, or has been until very recently, so removed from modern technology that it is tempting to liken their beliefs to prehistoric ones. A graphic example can be seen in the classic film *The Gods Must Be Crazy.* In the first fifteen minutes of this film, Kalahari bushmen are seen living a life that we feel must have been unchanged for thousands of years. Suddenly, a Coke bottle is tossed out of a plane passing overhead and lands among them. The bushmen view the bottle as a gift from the gods, but it causes changes, including tests of faith, which themselves celebrate the imagination of primal human spirit. Ultimately, the bushmen decide they want to get rid of this "new technology" in order to preserve their way of life.

The Great Religions of Today

Today there are innumerable religions and sects, including the religions of people who still live in tribal groups. But if we are to list the great religions of the world, each of which is still a vital force in the lives of many millions of human beings, we should include at least five, namely, Hinduism, Buddhism, Judaism, Islam, and Christianity. In the world, about 80 percent of the population identifies itself with some organized religious group. In the United States, Protestant or Catholic Christians are the largest groups, as you can see in Figure 9.1a. The Christian religion is also the largest in the world, as you can see in Figure 9.1b. Unlike in the United States, however, the largest percentage of Christians in the world is Roman Catholic rather than Protestant. Muslims and Hindus are the next two largest religious groups in the world.

Whether Confucianism and Taoism in China and Shintoism in Japan should be included in the great religions of today is questionable. Under the current regime, the status and future of China's ancient religions are uncertain. Furthermore, Confucianism is often said to be more a philosophy than a religion. Shintoism is the ancient religion of Japan but has had strong competition from Buddhism. In 1868 reformed Shintoism was made the official religion, but after World War II religious freedom was declared. However, some calculate that millions of Japanese still retain their faith in Shintoism. It is a mixture of nature, ancestor, and emperor worship and is closely associated with Japanese nationalism, although the concept of the emperor's divinity was officially abolished in 1945. Still, when Emperor Hirohito died in 1989, there was an outpouring of sadness in Japan and the introduction of a new era and a new calendar beginning at year zero.

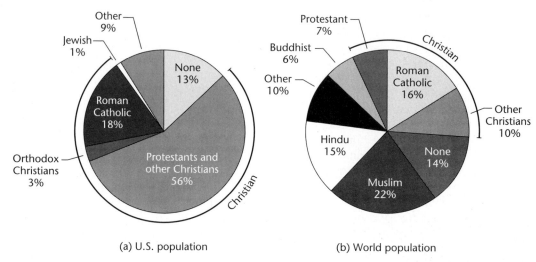

(a) U.S. population   (b) World population

Figure 9.1

(a) Religious identification of U.S. population; (b) Religious identification of world population. (Source: Adherents.com and extrapolations from the *Yearbook of American and Canadian Churches.*)

Hinduism

Hinduism is the religion and social system of the Hindus, the majority of whom live in India. Since ancient times, it has had a strong hold in India, and even today it dominates the lives of the majority of its people. A minority of Indians have been converted to foreign faiths such as Christianity or Islam, or to religions such as Buddhism, Jainism, or Sikhism, all three of which developed out of Hinduism itself.

Unlike many religions, Hinduism has no founder, no distinct set of creeds, and, although it has many clear-cut paths to salvation, no unique path. It holds that the soul inhabits successive bodies in its journey through the universe, and thus all life, including insect and plant life, has a soul. All beings, even the gods, must die and be reborn in an endless cycle. Some believe that this cycle can be escaped through asceticism, in which personality is lost and the believer becomes one with the Absolute. Although Hinduism claims to be monotheistic, its High God has many forms, of which the two best known are Vishnu the creator and preserver and Siva the destroyer. There are thousands of lesser gods. No one attempts to remember all of them, but each has its place in folk affection; the believer will tell you, "They are all the same god."

All life is sacred because all life has a soul. The sacrifice of living creatures, a characteristic of some Hindu ceremonies, is explained by precisely this: Because life is sacred, its sacrifice to the gods is vitally meaningful. Today, however, partly because of the economic value of animals, sacrifices are almost always represented by flowers and food (the gods eat the spiritual portion of the food; the material portion is consumed by the givers). Many animals are sacred: The cow is revered because she represents Mother Earth. She is never to be injured or killed (sick and starving cows roam the countryside and crowded city streets; they have been known to attend the movies in Calcutta). Other especially sacred creations are monkeys, snakes, the banyan tree, the herb known as basil, all mountains and rivers, and rocks of unusual shape.

Hindus are divided into four castes: (1) scholars and priests (Brahmans, a word meaning "source of life," or "expansive force"); (2) administrators of the state; (3) commercial and agricultural entrepreneurs; and (4) workers who perform the tasks the three higher classes shun—for example, sweeping floors, cleaning bathrooms, and repairing shoes. This **caste system,** in which individuals are differentiated in the jobs they can have, is hereditary, and although it has been officially outlawed for decades, it has proved almost impossible to eradicate and to transfer to a higher caste is very difficult.

There are hundreds of kinds of Hindus, of which the Sikhs form one of the most important in the modern world. *Sikh* is derived from a Hindu word meaning "disciple," and **Sikhs** are disciples of a group of gurus whose tenets are most easily expressed by naming principles to which they are opposed: the caste system, the priestly hierarchy and ritual, and idolatry. Sikhs are skilled farmers and shrewd businesspeople, and they are considered among the world's finest soldiers. They subscribe to such Hindu beliefs as birth and rebirth and

Siva, a Hindu god.

the transmigration of the soul. In India intense religious hatred exists between Sikhs and followers of the dominant Hinduism, and this enmity is fortified by political and regional rivalries. In 1984, after the Indian Prime Minister Indira Gandhi had ordered a military attack on the sacred Sikh temple of Amritsar (which resulted in many Sikh deaths and great damage to the edifice), she was assassinated on the grounds of her official residence; Sikhs are widely believed to have been responsible. Since then there has been ongoing tension in the Punjab region of India, where the majority of Sikhs reside.

An outward sign of Hinduism is its concentration on counting and classifying, creating categories into which to fit individual manifestations. This is usually explained as a method of imposing order on a complicated world, but it can also be seen as a means of imposing disorder, or of proving, by the endlessness of the effort, that the world cannot be categorized. This characteristic enables Hinduism to incorporate diverse and even contradictory principles if Hindus find them good.

Hinduism has been gaining popularity in the West under the auspices of movements such as Hare Krishna. Many Americans have become disenchanted with modern-day society and the principle of rationality on which it is based. They argue that rationality has led us into the mess we are in and that it is time to turn to faith and mysticism.

Buddhism

Although Buddhism, for the reasons outlined in this section, is now rare in India, it is probably the most widespread religion of the Eastern world, teaching that by right thinking and self-denial its followers can achieve Nirvana. It developed out of early Hinduism, and one of its chief objectives is to free people from the endless cycle of reincarnations that is part of Hindu doctrine. Buddhism was founded more than five hundred years before Christ by a young Nepalese prince, Shakyamuni Gautama, who later became known as Buddha ("the enlightened one"). He is also sometimes called Siddhartha, "the perfected" or "completed one." After observing the troubles of his father's subjects, the prince became convinced that all life results in suffering and that the only escape is to overcome desire for life and its pleasures. Therefore he left his parents and his princely existence and became a wandering ascetic monk in order to seek a cure for suffering.

He succeeded in entering a trance in which he remembered his former incarnations and perceived himself as having already passed through so many stages that he had been ready to have himself born to his current circumstances in order to preach to others. Gautama had thus reached Enlightenment and could be called Buddha. He emerged from this state of contemplation, or Nirvana, although tempted by evil forces to remain dallying there, and went to Banaras, on the Ganges River in India, to explain how others could attain Nirvana—namely, by realizing that life is suffering, suffering springs from a burning thirst for material and spiritual riches, suffering ceases when the thirst is renounced, and we cease to thirst by passing through eight stages: right views, right aspiration, right speech, right conduct, right livelihood, right effort, right mindfulness, and right contemplation.

All of these concepts can be, and have been, divided into their own subcategories, but the heart of Buddha's teaching is gentleness, compassion, rationality, and moderation. Everyone can become a Buddha, although very few actually do so. More numerous than Buddhas are *bodhisattvas,* people who have given up or delayed entering Nirvana in order that they may stay to help others. The Buddha's preaching did not involve appeals to a higher being, because his experience of widespread suffering rendered him incapable of

Buddha, revered in the Far East.

believing in a beneficent creator. It did involve contemplation and relinquishing; in an advanced state, one realizes "There is nothing."

The Buddha's birthplace (Kapilavastu), the place of his Enlightenment (Bodh Gaya), the place where he gave his first sermon (the deer park in Sarnath), and the place where he died (near Kapilavastu)—all in India or Nepal—are today the main destinations for Buddhist pilgrimages. Nevertheless, Buddhism is not one of the major religions of India today, having declined for many reasons, but principally because Islam overtook it both philosophically and materially, and in the eleventh century A.D. Muslims (also called Moslems) destroyed the Buddhist monasteries and dispersed the monks.

Over the centuries, as Buddhism gained converts and spread to other countries it underwent many changes, some of which greatly increased its popular appeal. Also, a variety of sects developed. It spread to Tibet, China, Korea, Japan, Southeast Asia, and Ceylon, taking on markedly different forms in different areas. In the south of Asia, in countries such as Sri Lanka, Myanmar, and Thailand, Buddhism is firmly established and is said to have retained more of its original character than in other regions.

Although Buddhism is primarily an Asian religion, in the 1970s small Buddhist sects sprang up in the United States. Many of these sects disbanded in the late 1980s, but a few remain. The Buddhist monastic community was founded by the Buddha himself, and its organization and character are said to be the one element in Buddhism that has changed relatively little over the centuries. Even to this day Buddhist monks shave their heads and wear the traditional yellow robes. You are likely to see some sect members in the streets of a big city dressed in this traditional garb. Zen Buddhism, transcendental meditation, and yoga, all Buddhist practices that do not require more than several hours of practice a day, have also spread.

Judaism

Though Judaism has played an important role in world history, the total number of its adherents is relatively small. In 2002 the entire Jewish population of the world was probably only about 14 million, compared with about 2 billion Christians and 1.3 billion Muslims.

Judaism developed out of the religion of the ancient Hebrew tribe. According to the Bible story, a great leader of this tribe, Abraham, put his trust in a single God to guide him and his people in their migrations. During their wanderings, the Hebrews, or Israelites as they came to be called (after Jacob, or Israel, the grandson of Abraham), moved into the fertile Nile delta to escape famine. There they were eventually enslaved by the Egyptians.

During the period of their slavery, probably sometime between 1450 B.C. and 1400 B.C., there arose a great leader, Moses. He led the Israelites to freedom, as God had directed him, and came to be commonly regarded as the real founder of Judaism. After the escape of the Israelites from Egypt, Moses ascended Mount Sinai, where God appeared to him and through him made a sacred covenant with what were by then the twelve tribes of Israel. That covenant required that the Israelites acknowledge "the God of Israel" as ruler of the world and creator of heaven and earth. In return, God recognized the people of Israel as his chosen followers. Moses had been instructed by God to call him *Yahveh,* or as it is sometimes translated, Jehovah. When Moses came down from the mountain, he brought with him two stone tablets on which were inscribed Yahveh's Ten Commandments. These were later amplified into the many commandments and prohibitions set forth in the **Torah**—the Pentateuch, or the Five Books of Moses—which is part of both Jewish scriptures and the Christian Old Testament.

Judaism has several unique characteristics. First, though it makes claims to universality, it was and still is primarily the religion of a group of people who can, with qualifications, regard themselves as descendants of the ancient Israelites. Jews believe that they were chosen by God, but they do not believe that being chosen by God makes them special. They do not understand why they were chosen, and they regard it as a burden as much as a blessing. In fact, in the Book of Exodus, God suggests to Moses that perhaps he should begin again with a less fractious tribe. According to Jewish theologians, God chose the Jews simply because he had to begin somewhere. They do not see it as an honor or as a sign that they are superior, attitudes that are attributed to them by some non-Jews.

Second, Judaism has preserved much of its essential character for more than three thousand years. It has done this in spite of the fact that for more than nineteen hundred years, ever since their last major rebellion against Rome was crushed by the Emperor Hadrian in A.D. 135, Jews have been a widely scattered and often persecuted minority among alien peoples. Finally, and most important, Judaism was the first great religion to develop a clear and unequivocal concept of a single God as the creator and ruler of the universe.

Although some Jews believe in the resurrection of the dead and that people must account beyond the grave for their good and evil deeds, unlike some other religions Judaism is a world-affirming, not a world-denying, faith, and it requires that Jews enjoy this life and use their abilities for the service of humankind. It looks for the coming of the **Messiah**—the expected deliverer of the Jews—and for a messianic age in which the kingdom of eternal peace will prevail and all evil impulses will be removed from the human heart. But it rejects the Christian belief that the Messiah has already come with his message of salvation.

From the Middle Ages to early modern times, the rights of Jews in Europe were greatly restricted, and they were forced to live in special sections of the cities called ghettos. The French Revolution and Napoleon did much to free Jews from the ghettos. But later there was a backlash, and it was not until after the social upheavals of 1848 that in most countries Jews received full rights of citizenship on a more or less permanent basis. But this did not end their troubles, for the very success that many of them soon enjoyed in the professions stirred up new waves of **anti-Semitism**, or feelings of hatred and dislike toward Jews.

The freeing of the Jews in the nineteenth century from their former restrictions brought about great changes in Judaism. Gradually Jews, not only in Europe but also in the United States, became divided into three major groups: the Orthodox, who resist change in beliefs and ritual; the Reform, who reject much of Jewish traditionalism and believe that Judaism should be regarded as a changing and developing religion; and the

Conservatives, who cannot accept the orthodoxy but who object to an extreme break with traditions and therefore seek a middle way.

Jews are sometimes called a race, but anthropologists remind us that this term is inaccurate. Originally they belonged to that branch of the Caucasoid race that inhabited the Arabian peninsula and spread into the fertile crescent to the north of it. They once formed a nationality, the ancient Hebrew nation. But later they were dispersed over almost the entire world, and over the centuries they interbred to some extent with the non-Jews of the countries in which they lived. Also, they converted several non-Jewish peoples to Judaism. The word *Jew* comes from Judaism, which is their religion. After World War II, some of them migrated to the ancient homeland and created the new nation of Israel.

To determine the number of Jews in the United States with any great accuracy is impossible. This is partly because many persons of Jewish ethnic background maintain no affiliation with any temple or other Jewish organization, partly because there has been an appreciable amount of intermarriage between Jews and non-Jews, and partly because Jews disagree on who is a Jew. Tradition says anyone born to a Jewish mother is a Jew. However, in the 1980s the Reform rabbinate, representing about a quarter of U.S. Jews, extended recognition to those whose only Jewish parent is the father.

There is an increasing emphasis on individual choice in Judaism, including rising numbers of conversions. Some Jews see these processes as endangering their traditional view of themselves as chosen by God, but others welcome these trends. At present it is estimated that there are about 6 million people in this country who can be classified as Jews. More than one-third of all U.S. Jews live in metropolitan New York, and considerable numbers are concentrated in other large cities such as Los Angeles, Philadelphia, Chicago, and Miami.

Jews are sometimes considered to be primarily a religious group, but in a poll taken by *Newsweek* only 43 percent of U.S. Jews said they considered themselves religious. According to political scientist Daniel Eleazar of Temple University, only 20 percent of the Jewish

A Jewish family celebrates Passover seder.

population worships regularly. Of the others, 40 percent maintain nominal affiliation with a temple but usually attend services only on the high holy days of Rosh Hashanah and Yom Kippur.

On the average, U.S. Jews have markedly higher incomes than the rest of our population, though over half a million fall below the family poverty level as set by agencies of the federal government. Jews also, on average, have higher levels of education than other groups and, in proportion to their numbers, are much better represented in business and the professions.

Prejudice against the Jews, or anti-Semitism, has existed for centuries and has been strong in certain countries. Sometimes it has been tied to religion; sometimes it has been rationalized by dislike on the part of the majority of the population for certain cultural or "racial" characteristics, largely imaginary, attributed to the Jews as a group. In some parts of eastern Europe, anti-Semitism has at times gone to such extremes that thousands of Jews were killed, as in the **pogroms,** or organized massacres, that occurred in czarist Russia. But it was in Nazi Germany that anti-Semitism reached its height, and the Holocaust, in which 7 million Jews were killed, has affected Jews and everyone else in a variety of ways.

Partially because of feelings of guilt for allowing the Holocaust to occur, the Western nations supported the establishment of the state of Israel after World War II. Israel was established from lands over 50 percent of which were owned by Palestinian Arabs. After the 1948 war for control of this land, a huge number of Palestinian Arabs were displaced and moved to refugee camps in neighboring Arab states where they and their descendants still live. This area of the Middle East became a prime source of international friction.

Former Nazi government women burying Jews at a concentration camp after World War II.

Palestinian children run for cover in front of an Israeli tank.

In 1994, after almost fifty years of conflict, the Jews and the Palestinians officially agreed to become reconciled and to live in peace. That agreement was meant to culminate in a permanent peace treaty between the Palestinians and the Israelis, but disputes about borders prevented any permanent agreement, and in 2004 the two sides were still engaged in fighting and serious disputes, and seemed further away from peace than ever.

Islam

Islam, like Judaism, is a religion based on divine revelation, and its messenger, Mohammed, like Moses, made no claims to divinity for himself. He believed only that he had been chosen by God, or Allah, to receive from the angel Gabriel revelations of Allah's will. These revelations, which became frequent, he repeated in full to those who would listen, and shortly after his death they were assembled by his friend Abū Bakr to form the **Koran,** the holy scriptures of the Muslims. Abu became the first successor, or caliph, to carry on Mohammed's work. The Koran begins as follows:

In the name of Allah, the Beneficent, the Merciful.

[1.1] All praise is due to Allah, the Lord of the Worlds.

[1.2] The Beneficent, the Merciful.

[1.3] Master of the Day of Judgment.

[1.4] Thee do we serve and Thee do we beseech for help.

[1.5] Keep us on the right path.

[1.6] The path of those upon whom Thou hast bestowed favors. Not [the path] of those upon whom Thy wrath is brought down, nor of those who go astray.

The Koran is accessible on the Web in formats that are easily searchable for specific topics, and, given the importance of Islam to modern world affairs, browsing through it is definitely a worthwhile activity.

Mohammed was born about A.D. 570 at Mecca, in the western part of what is now Saudi Arabia. According to tradition, he was orphaned and became a ward of his grandfather and, later, of an uncle, both of whom were prominent members of the Koreish tribe. Later he was a merchant, and at about the age of twenty-five he became the business advisor to a rich widow, fifteen years his senior, whom he eventually married. Meanwhile he had come into contact with the Arabian religion of his time, which was a mixture of animism and polytheism. Mohammed had also learned something about Judaism and Christianity from his acquaintances in Mecca who were followers of both religions. His contacts with Jews and Christians may have contributed to his dissatisfaction with the beliefs and practices of his fellow Arab tribesmen.

Though Mohammed himself initiated the religion of Islam, he was greatly influenced by Christianity and Judaism. He considered that he was completing and perfecting the work of Moses, Jesus, and other heavenly messengers whom he recognized as his forerunners. But Mohammed denied the Christian doctrine of the Trinity and the divinity of Christ. According to the Koran, God is one and God is eternal. He neither begets nor is begotten.

In Arabic, *Islam* means "submission," and Muslims are submitters to the will of God. The devout Muslim's goal is fairly simple: It is to perform one's duties as outlined in the Koran and as exemplified by the acts of Mohammed in his lifetime. The Koran is infallible.

The so-called Five Pillars of Islam state the indispensable religious duties of a believer:

1. Acceptance and frequent repetition of the creed, "There is no God but Allah and Mohammed is his messenger"
2. The performance five times a day of prescribed rituals of prayer and devotion
3. The giving of alms to the needy
4. The fast during Ramadan, the month when the angel Gabriel appeared to Mohammed
5. The pilgrimage to the Kaaba stone at Mecca once in a lifetime by those who can afford it

From the seventh century to the eighteenth century, Islam spread as far west as Spain and as far east as the Philippines. It was able to do this through its access to trade routes from its original home in Arabia and through military conquest. Islam's influence ebbed and flowed, but by the end of World War I in 1918 it had reached a low. By the second half of the twentieth century, however, with political independence and national consciousness, Islam was enjoying a resurgence and again extending its influence. Today its principal distribution is in the Arabian peninsula, North and West Africa, the Middle East, Turkey, Afghanistan and the Indian subcontinent, parts of the former USSR, and Indonesia. In the United States, the number of Muslims is growing, and some authorities predict that there will be more Muslims than Jews in the United States in this century.

The Sects of Islam.   After Mohammed's death, Islam split into two factions: the **Shiites** (the sectarians, followers of Ali, cousin to the Prophet), who believed that Ali was the legitimate successor to Mohammed, and the **Sunni** (the traditionalists), who believed that Abū Bakr, the oldest companion of Mohammed, was the legitimate successor. Today Sunnis constitute about 85 percent of all Muslims and Shiites constitute about 15 percent. There are also smaller sects of Islam, including the Sufis and the Wahhabis, and though they are small in number, they can play important roles in the interaction between the Islamic world and the Western world.

The difference between Sunnis and Shiites concerns who should be seen as the legitimate religious authority in society. Shiites follow a system of Imamah. They believe that the existing Imam is the true leader of Muslims, and that all true Muslims must submit to his rule. Imams are appointed by existing Imams, which means there is a line of succession that always assumes a living Imam as ruler. Because Imams carry enormous power among believers to tell people what to do, Imamah can, and often does, come in conflict with governments, which also claim the right to tell people what to do. An example is Iran, which has a Shiite majority. Iran has both a religious authority—the Imam—and a democratically elected government, and there is often confusion about which authority is in charge.

A Palestinian Islamic family celebrates Eid al-Adha, the feast of sacrifice.

Sunnis do not follow a system of Imamah. This means that Sunnis are generally more content with having a secular ruler as long as that secular ruler does not interfere with the spiritual dimension of religion. In Iraq there are both Sunnis and Shiites, with the Shiites in the majority. However, Iraq had never been a democracy, and, up until 2004 the Sunnis were in charge. It was in part to keep the Shiite majority out of power that the United States had earlier supported Saddam Hussein in his war with Iran.

After the Iraq war of 2003 the United States struggled with setting up a democratic government, which it stated was one of its goals, in a country with a Shiite majority, a majority whose beliefs often put religious rule by an Imam above secular democratic rule. The type of problem the Shiite sect presents today was the kind of problem that led Rousseau early on in his discussion of democracy to despair of the relationship between religion and government, and to call on government to set up a civil religion that avoided the conflict.

Islamic Fundamentalism.   In recent years, there has been much discussion of Islamic fundamentalism and its connection to terrorism and **jihad,** which in Arabic means "striving," but which is commonly used to denote a sacred war against the Western world. As with all fundamentalist religious groups, there is much dispute about what is meant by fundamentalist Islam. According to the dictionary, fundamentalism consists of "strict maintenance of ancient or fundamental doctrines." The problem is that there is generally ambiguity about what those doctrines are, and the issue comes down to who is interpreting them. As interpreted by Osama bin Laden, these ancient doctrines require Muslims to fight against the Western world and to reestablish an Islamic state, regardless of the costs to society and humanity. Other Muslims interpret it quite differently, and many simply want to be left alone to follow their spiritual beliefs, leaving secular matters to government. Their concern is with religion, not government. The difference between the two has sometimes been called the difference between revivalists, who want to be spiritually devout, and fanatics and extremists, who exploit this devotion for political ends.

For many fundamentalists, the empowerment of Islam, which is God's plan for humankind, is a sacred end, and it can be achieved only through the establishment of an Islamic state.

Ayatollah Khomeini, who led the Islamic revolution in Iran, combined fundamentalism with the Shiite belief in the role of the Imam and argued that because Islamic government is a government of law, and because a knowledge of law is necessary for anyone to rule, the person who should rule is the person whose knowledge of the law surpasses all others. Under this interpretation, it is appropriate to revolt against existing secular governments and replace them with rule by Islamic clerics, such as himself. This view fit Shiite views much better than it fit Sunni views, which preferred a separation between religion and secular government. Thus, Shiites tend to be more fundamentalist than Sunnis. Khomeini also claimed that the West was on a crusade to eliminate Islam from the world, that Western ways were bad. In so doing he portrayed the United States in particular as the great Satan, claiming that good Muslims would reject U.S. technology and way of life.

More recent Islamic scholars such as Hasan alt-Turai and Sayyid Muhammad Husayn Fadlallah have argued that the problem is not that the West is on a crusade to eliminate Islam, but instead that the West has dispossessed Muslims. Unlike Khomeini, these scholars argue that Islam could selectively borrow technology and institutions from the West. These debates are still going on in Islamic society, and the outcome will likely play an important role in the peace of the world.

Christianity

Christianity, the principal religion of the Western world, developed from Judaism, and the greater part of the Christian Bible (the Old Testament) still consists of Jewish sacred writings. The ancient Jews believed that at his chosen time God would confound their enemies and set up a new Jewish kingdom under a Messiah (deliverer) descended from King David. Later some came to believe that the Messiah would come down from heaven at the end of the world, at the time of the resurrection of the dead, and would carry out the last judgment.

Jesus of Nazareth, the founder of Christianity, was born in Bethlehem, about A.D. 1. This date in itself is an example of the power of religion. In Western cultures, events that took place before the birth of Christ are dated "B.C.," meaning "Before Christ." For instance, in Chapter 3 we said that humans first appeared in China about 20,000 B.C. The term "A.D." stands for the Latin words *anno domini*, which literally translated mean "in the year of our Lord." This term is used to begin numbering all over again, with A.D. 1 as the year of Christ's birth. The year A.D. 2000 means the two thousandth year after Christ's birth.[1]

At some point in Jesus' life, he became convinced that he was the Messiah, or Christ, and the divine son of God. Often he is called Jesus Christ, which simply means Jesus, the Messiah. Soon after he started his ministry, at about the age of thirty, he converted and

---

[1]Twentieth-century scholarship indicates that Christ was actually born about 4 B.C. There will be no attempt to renumber dates, as that task would be impossible, and the Western world's dating system will continue to use A.D. 1 as a reference point. An alternative way of designating A.D. and B.C. is C.E. (Common Era) and B.C.E. (Before the Common Era).

gathered around him the **Apostles,** the twelve close associates who were to be his chief aides and who were to carry on his ministry after his death.

Our knowledge of Jesus' teachings comes to us indirectly. He did not write them down but depended on his disciples to preach from memory what he had taught. Our chief sources are, first, the Gospels of the New Testament and, second, the Epistles. But these were prepared long after Jesus' death. The four Gospels are thought by historians to have been written between A.D. 65 and about A.D. 100. Presumably they were based on documents in which some of his followers had recorded his sayings as they remembered them and also certain circumstances of his life. But how accurately his sayings and the events of his life were recorded, or how much was changed or added by successive copiers or revisers of the Gospels, historical scholarship cannot tell us with any certainty.

Jesus never doubted the reality of God or of his own special relationship to God. But he knew he had not been sent, as some of his hearers hoped, to deliver the Jews from Rome by reestablishing the earthly kingdom of David. Rather, he had been sent by his Father to show all of humanity, Jews and Gentiles alike, the way to heavenly salvation. Like many Jews of his day, he believed that the long-foretold messianic kingdom of God would come rather soon, but for him it was a kingdom in heaven, which was only for those who would believe in him, who would truly repent of their sins, and who would surrender to the will of God before it was too late.

Jesus taught that the most important things are to believe in God, do His will, and believe in Jesus as the son of God. God is utterly good: supremely righteous and just, but also forgiving and merciful. Therefore, people should trust him completely and regularly seek spiritual aid through prayer. Jesus also taught that God demands we love one another, friend and foe alike, and this has been one of the most difficult teachings for devout Christians to interpret and to apply as a practical guide in daily conduct. Jesus also taught his disciples to obey the Ten Commandments, which God transmitted to Moses on Mount Sinai, and to follow the golden rule. The latter states, "Do unto others as you would have them do unto you."

Jesus' success in drawing crowds in Galilee soon attracted the attention of the leaders of the two principal Jewish sects, or parties, in Jerusalem—the Sadducees and the Pharisees. They had their own differences, but both became enemies of Jesus because his teaching and his actions did not always follow the dictates of either Judaic law or tradition. After he had been preaching for three or four years, Jesus decided to go to Jerusalem at the time of the Passover, when Jews from a wide area would be assembled for the great annual festival. This gave the enemies of Jesus an opportunity to stir up ill feeling against him among the people. Finally they seized him, made accusations against him, and denounced him to the Roman governor, Pilate, on the ground that he claimed to be king of the Jews. Pilate doubted Jesus' guilt but when the crowd demanded death, the governor acquiesced and ordered his crucifixion at Golgotha.

Three events reported in the Gospels and the Epistles are of crucial significance for Christianity: (1) the Last Supper of Jesus with his disciples on the evening before the crucifixion, (2) his crucifixion, and (3) his resurrection on the third day after his death. Even before coming to Jerusalem, Jesus had foretold his death and resurrection to the twelve apostles. The key belief of the Christian religion is that in some sense Jesus died to redeem the sins of humankind and thus opened for them the way to salvation. In the sacrament of Communion, or the Eucharist, which was first celebrated by Jesus with the twelve disciples at the Last Supper, devout communicants believe that they enter into a special relationship with Christ. The wine they drink and the bread they eat symbolize, or in Catholic doctrine actually become, the blood and body of Christ. The communicant is thus strengthened in his or her attempts to achieve salvation by the redemptive power that Christ achieved through his death and resurrection.

The Early Christians. The spread of Christianity after Jesus' death was relatively rapid, but the early Christian groups, or churches, were only loosely linked. By the end of the first century, however, administrative organization had begun to develop in Rome and elsewhere, and bishops began to assume authority not only to appoint priests to oversee local churches but also to settle disputes over doctrine. Gradually the primacy of the bishop of Rome became recognized throughout the empire, and by the end of the third century, he had taken the title of pope.

The Middle Ages and After. Before the final collapse of the Roman Empire in the West in A.D. 476, the Church of Rome had become strong enough to prevent the complete breakdown of order and civilization that might otherwise have resulted from the successive invasions of the empire by Germanic tribes. During the Middle Ages, the church dominated the religious and intellectual life of Europe and to a great extent its politics and economics. Meanwhile the eastern Roman Empire with its capital at Constantinople (now known as Istanbul) still survived, and the Eastern Church, later known as the Orthodox Church, became increasingly independent of Rome. The final break, or schism, between the two parts of the church occurred in 1054 and remains to this day.

The next great defection from the Church of Rome did not occur for several hundred years. In the fifteenth century, perhaps even earlier, many Christians felt that the church was undergoing moral decay. The Renaissance, which brought a renewal of interest in art, literature, and the works of classical antiquity, undoubtedly contributed to a general stir and unrest. Reformers began to urge that religion revert to its sources. The result was the

The Cathedral of Notre Dame in Paris.

Christian worship.

Reformation, the Protestant revolt against traditional Catholicism, which began in 1517 when Martin Luther posted his call for reform on the door of the church in Wittenberg, Germany. Other important leaders of the Reformation included Ulrich Zwingli and John Calvin in Switzerland and John Knox in Scotland.

The Reformation led to a considerable period of religious and political turmoil, including religious wars and repression of dissident groups in various countries, and though it did not win over the majority of Catholics to Protestantism, it did result in substantial defections from the Roman Catholic Church. But the Protestants who succeeded in gaining freedom from control by Rome did not succeed in joining to form a major independent church body. Instead they divided into a considerable number of sects, or denominations. Several of these, including the Puritans and Quakers, played an important role in the settlement of the English colonies in America.

European migration to the Americas and to areas such as South Africa, Australia, and New Zealand carried Christianity with it. In some areas, such as the United States and Canada except Quebec, Protestant settlers from northwestern Europe were in the majority. In other areas, as in practically all of Latin America, settlers came largely from overwhelmingly Catholic countries such as Spain, Portugal, and Italy. Christianity was also carried to other parts of the world by the strong missionary movement that developed in the nineteenth century, but in most non-Christian countries missionaries succeed in converting only a small fraction of the people.

The Role of Religion in Society

There can be little doubt that in primitive societies and in the earliest civilizations religious beliefs and practices were a strong integrative factor in most societies. Because of these beliefs and practices, people knew how they must behave individually and as a group to avoid the ill will of the gods and to win their favor. They knew certain things were sacred and that if the group was to avoid famine or other misfortunes, no one must be allowed to treat the gods with disrespect. Religious beliefs were tied to rules of behavior and usually gave strong support to custom and tradition.

In the early history of civilization, almost every "nation" had its own gods and sometimes, as in ancient Egypt, the king himself was regarded as divine. Even in twentieth-century Japan, up until 1945 Shinto doctrine held that the emperor was a descendant of the sun goddess. As a result, the people were drawn together not only by their common beliefs but also by their participation in common rituals of prayer, praise, and sacrifice.

Not infrequently, however, in the more highly developed civilizations of the world, differences in religious beliefs have been a source of social conflict, especially when groups with different religious beliefs have lived within the same national borders. To get an idea of the potential problem, look, for example, at Northern Ireland, where Protestants and Catholics clash, and at India, where Hindus clash with Muslims.

Religion as a Source of Moral Values

Religion, then, can be a socially disruptive force, but it seems clear that over the years its major influence has been to integrate and stabilize nations and cultures. In the Western world, where Christianity in its various forms is by a wide margin the predominant faith, our ethical and moral values have over the centuries been modified and given greater vitality by the teachings of the Christian religion.

Religion's integrative force derives from the fact that it gives divine authority to ethical and moral principles. Without people's adherence to such principles, it would be difficult to maintain an orderly society with free elections and a wide range of personal freedoms, to produce goods with enough efficiency to hope to eliminate poverty, and in general to maintain the level of civilization we have already achieved.

Through its influence on individuals, religion also has an impact on economic and political institutions. The great German sociologist Max Weber (1864–1920) developed this thesis in his book *The Protestant Ethic and the Spirit of Capitalism.* According to his theory, the new Protestant sects that developed out of the Reformation, especially those that were influenced by the doctrines of Calvin, made a major contribution to the economic prosperity of England and western Europe and to the development of modern industrial capitalism. They did so because they believed in the **Protestant ethic,** the theory that God expects good Christians to work hard, to save, to invest their savings, and to show business initiative. The Protestant ethic also played a major role in the development of the American ideals of rugged individualism, private enterprise, and financial success.

Putting a high value on work and on the kinds of behavior necessary for material progress was never a Puritan or Protestant monopoly. It is a characteristic found everywhere among people who are determined to improve their condition, and it can be found in all societies and cultures.

Impact of Religion on Education, the Arts, and Literature

The influence of religion on education, the arts, music, and literature is pervasive. During the Middle Ages, the church and especially the monasteries preserved ancient literature and kept learning alive. In the United States, from colonial times until well into the nineteenth century, most of our colleges and universities were started and controlled by religious organizations. Many of them are still church controlled, and some religious bodies operate extensive systems of secondary and primary schools. Many of the great works of art of ancient Greece and the European Renaissance are representations of personalities or events with religious significance. In the field of religious music, we find such outstanding composers as Bach and Handel, and in literature we have great poems such as Dante's *Inferno* and Milton's *Paradise Lost*.

Buddhism and Hinduism have inspired temples, paintings, and sculpture of great sophistication, mystery, ferocity, and beauty; particularly in India, these represent unparalleled fecundity and vitality. In some countries such as Indonesia and China, the entire history and development of the religions are carved over acres of temple structures or wrested from vast rock-cut caves and cliffs, constituting some of the greatest artistic and historical monuments in the history of human ingenuity. In Japan, hundreds of great gardens have been created to the quiet glory of Buddhism and Shintoism. An Islamic prohibition of representations of the human figure means that the classics of their art are exhibited in architecture, caligraphy, and intricate floral and geometric patterns. Sanskrit, which means "perfect language," was developed in India to preserve religious traditions. In fulfilling this function, Sanskrit also became a great literary language and one of the Indo-European languages from which have derived most of the major languages spoken today in Europe, Iran, parts of Asia, and the Americas.

In China the poetry of the eighth-century figure Wang Wei is one of the reasons the Tang dynasty is called the golden age. It has some Buddhist undertones, but only sixty years later the poetry of Han Shan is overtly Zen Buddhist. In India the *Ramayana* and the *Mahabharata* embody nearly all of the religious stories and myths on which the country is nurtured. In Japan we might mention the Shingon Buddhist novel of the eleventh century, *Tale of Genji*.

The Potential Conflict between Religion and Government

The previous two sections discussed the positive elements of religion for society. But religion also plays what some consider negative roles. Specifically, it can undermine the state and lead people to fight others, all in the name of religion. The Crusades were an example of Christianity leading to war against Muslims, and recent jihad terrorist attacks are an example of Islam leading to attacks against Western countries.

Christianity and democratic government have made their peace, with religion playing the spiritual role that Rousseau saw for it as a type of civil religion. The pope's decrees do not undermine Western governments, and a Catholic in government is seen as following his or her own judgment rather than the pope's decrees on issues such as gay rights or abortion. The same is true of many other religions.

This is not the case, however, with Islam, and Islamic fundamentalism poses the threat of religion that Rousseau foresaw that it could. How those theological decisions play out will make a significant difference in what happens in the War on Terror.

Key Points

- Humans have always been troubled by the inevitability of death and the meaning of life; their interest in these issues has led them to religion.
- The five great religions of today are Hinduism, Buddhism, Judaism, Islam, and Christianity.
- In current society, religion is a source of moral values, and it significantly influences all aspects of life.
- Modern religions face serious questions. Disputes arise both within religions and among religions.

- Religion has played a central role in society for thousands of years and is likely to do so for thousands of years in the future.

- Religion presents a potential problem for secular government if religion extends its influence beyond the spiritual realm.

Some Important Terms

anti-Semitism (194)
Apostles (201)
caste system (191)
civil religion (188)
jihad (199)
Koran (197)

Messiah (194)
Nirvana (188)
pogroms (196)
Protestant ethic (204)
Reformation (203)
religion (189)

Shiites (198)
Sikhs (191)
Sunni (198)
Torah (194)

Questions for Review and Discussion

1. Why has religion had a strong appeal to human beings from earliest times?
2. To westerners, Hinduism seems a strange faith. Why?
3. How did Prince Shakyamuni Gautama found Buddhism?
4. What are the unique characteristics of Judaism?
5. How did Islam begin? What was the origin of the Koran?
6. State some of the similarities of Islam to Judaism or Christianity; also state some of the more important differences.
7. What are the Five Pillars of Islam?
8. What potential problems does fundamentalist Islam pose?
9. Why is our knowledge of Jesus' teachings indirect?
10. List as many as you can of the more important teachings of Jesus.
11. Explain how Islam spread from Arabia to other parts of the world from the eighteenth century to the present day.
12. Why are religious beliefs likely to strengthen the moral and ethical principles of a society? How are they likely to create dissension and war?
13. On balance, has religion been an integrative or divisive factor in today's society? Defend your answer.
14. Why did Rousseau believe that governments needed to create a civil religion?

Internet Questions

1. Go to www.tibet.com/DL/biography.html. What is a Dalai Lama? Who is the current Dalai Lama?
2. Using information found in www.infoplease.com/ipa/A0193627.html, explain what the Dead Sea Scrolls are. Who wrote them?
3. Who were the Knights Templar, according to www.knightstemplar.org. What was their original purpose?
4. Why do Mormons, members of the Church of Latter Day Saints, invest so much time and energy in genealogy (www.familysearch.org)?
5. Using the list of countries' religious makeup, http://worldfactsandfigures.com/religion.php, what countries have indigenous beliefs as their largest percentage?

For Further Study

Ahmed, Akbar S., *Islam Today: A Short Introduction to the Muslim World*, London: Tauris, 1999.

Blowhansen, Thomas, *The Saffron Wave: Democracy and Hindu Nationalism in Modern India*, Princeton, NJ: Princeton University Press, 1999.

Borowitz, Eugene B., *Judaism after Modernity: Papers from a Decade of Fruition*, Lanham, MD: University Press of America, 1999.

Budde, Michael L., and Robert W. Brimlow, *The Church as Counterculture*, Albany: State University of New York Press, 2000.

Cohen, Rich, *The Avengers*, New York: Knopf, 2000.

Cooper, David Edward, *World Philosophies: An Historical Introduction*, 2nd ed., Boston, MA: Blackwell, 2003.

Forbes, Bruce Davis, and Jeffrey H. Mahan, eds., *Religion and Popular Culture in America*, Berkeley: University of California Press, 2000.

Hexham, Irving, and Karla Poewe, *New Religions as Global Cultures: Making the Human Sacred*, Boulder, CO: Westview, 1997.

Humphries, Jefferson, *Reading Emptiness: Buddhism and Literature*, Albany: State University of New York Press, 1999.

Kessel, Barbara, *Suddenly Jewish: Jews Raised as Gentiles Discover Their Jewishness*, Hanover, NH: University Press of New England, 2000.

Rosen, Jonathan, *The Talmud and the Internet: Journey between Worlds*, New York: Farrar, Straus & Giroux, 2000.

Sharma, Arvind, *The Concept of Universal Religion in Modern Hindu Thought*, New York: St. Martin's Press, 1998.

Viswanathan, Gauri, *Outside the Fold: Conversion, Modernity, and Belief*, Princeton, NJ: Princeton University Press, 1998.

WWW   Academic Info Religion Gateway   www.academicinfo.net/religindex.html

WWW   Adherents.com   www.adherents.com

WWW   American Religion Data Archive   www.arda.tm

WWW   BuddhaNet   www.buddhanet.net

WWW   Christianity Today   www.christianitytoday.com

WWW   Islam Online   www.islamonline.net/english/index.shtml

WWW   Judaism 101   www.jewfaq.org

WWW   World Council of Churches   www.wcc-coe.org

Yusa, Michiko, *Japanese Religions*, London: Routledge, 2002.

Education

After reading this chapter, you should be able to:

- Explain how schools serve as agents of social control
- Give a brief history of the development of U.S. education
- Discuss the main problem facing our school system
- Summarize the evolution of the college curriculum
- Explain why the methods of funding education contribute to unequal education

A human being is not, in any proper sense, a human being till he is educated.

—Horace Mann

Everything you do involves, or should involve, learning or education. Education is a never-ending process that begins with the socialization of the child and continues through all of adult life. In common usage, however, the term education has a more limited meaning. **Education** refers especially to efforts, usually by the more mature members of a society, to teach each new generation the beliefs, the way of life, the values, and some portion of the knowledge and skills of the group; it also refers to efforts to learn on the part of those who are the objects of teaching.

In modern society there is so much to learn that any one person can acquire, at most, only a very small part of the total knowledge. Therefore individuals must special-ize in particular fields. Furthermore, in many fields, such as medicine and engineering, the knowledge and skills required have multiplied until they not only take years to learn but also require highly specialized educational arrangements in colleges, universities, and research institutions. Thus, as our modern industrial society increases in complexity, it becomes more and more dependent on formal education—that is, on a system of school-ing—both for transmitting and for developing its cultural heritage. In the United States, we have created a school system that provides more opportunities for more people than any the world has ever known. In 2003 we spent well over $750 billion to meet the needs of almost 70 million students at all levels of the educational ladder.

In the early 2000s there is enormous concern about what we are getting for that money. Are we simply **credentializing** individuals, which means using school diplomas as a way to limit entry into jobs but not to train people appropriately? Why do U.S. students rate so poorly when compared internationally? Should we be providing "schooling"—the teaching of knowledge and skill—or should we be providing broader educational and social skills—the teaching of critical thinking and multicultural topics? And, finally, how can we get more for less?

Schools as Agencies of Social Control

In her book *Miss Manners' Guide to Rearing Perfect Children,* Judith Martin writes that "every child is born ignorant . . . and is civilized by two things, example and nagging." In many ways, example and nagging are education, and it is education that civilizes us. Put more formally, it is through education that society transmits to individuals the knowledge dealing with the ways of life of the group. Education is a prime agency of social control, and decisions made about how to educate play crucial roles in deciding the direction society will take.

The Dual Thrust of U.S. Education

In the United States, such socialization is deeply embedded in the schooling process, but it is modified by attempts to foster individuality and to maintain individual and **academic freedom**—the freedom of students and teachers to pursue, discuss, and teach knowledge without hindrance or censorship. In other countries, education concentrates more on instilling discipline; individuality is frowned on (see accompanying box on "Real Education in Pakistan"). For example, in Japan and in other Eastern countries students face strict disciplinary codes and, according to international tests, they learn more.

The **dual thrust of U.S. education**—both the development of individuality and the socialization of students—leads to a tension in our attitude toward education. How much freedom should students be given? Should government determine what is taught, or should teachers and parents decide at the local level? Should private schools be subsidized with government money? And if they are, should they be subject to government control? Private schools have pushed for government financial support without control; public education advocates have resisted such moves.

"It's one thing for the National Commission to comment on the quality of teaching in our schools. It's another thing entirely for you to stand up and call Mr. Costello a yo-yo."

Education and U.S. Democracy

The dual thrust in education exists because education not only educates people, but it also prepares them to fit into society. It makes the many disparate parts of our population fit together. For that reason, education serves as a fundamental building block of U.S. democracy. It does so in the following ways:

The Thinker, by Auguste Rodin.

1. *By teaching the masses of our citizens to be literate,* public education makes it possible for them to communicate with one another more effectively beyond the local community and to learn something of politics and public policy by reading newspapers, magazines, and books. This enables people to vote more intelligently and to choose leaders more wisely.

2. *The public schools teach children to get along with different kinds of people.* In many areas, the students who attend these schools come from widely varied social, economic, national, and racial backgrounds. Also, extensive efforts have been made to integrate children who have special learning, physical, or emotional problems into the mainstream classrooms. Though going to school together will not necessarily make all children love one another, it does tend to create better understanding and to give all groups a keener sense of their common U.S. heritage.

3. *Our system of public support for education reduces inequalities of opportunity at all educational levels.* The masses of our people, even at the lower income levels, are now receiving an education up through high school. Large numbers are going on to college or technical and professional schools, in part because they can attend publicly supported schools with low tuition and in part because there are many government loan and grant opportunities.

4. *Finally, and by no means least important, our public school system has enabled us as a nation to make much more effective use of our human resources.* In the public schools, we discover many students who have unusual ability, even those who come from unfavorable social backgrounds. The talents of most such students would never be brought to light if it were not for free public schools. Once discovered, they can often be encouraged and helped to develop their capacities to the maximum. Thus, not only do they themselves lead fuller lives, but as scholars, scientists, or leaders in other fields, they also make a contribution to the welfare of the nation. Our public school system is by no means a perfect instrument, either for achieving complete equality of educational opportunity or for enabling us to make maximum use of our human resources, but it has helped us to take great strides toward both of these objectives.

The Development of U.S. Education

American interest in education goes back to earliest colonial times. Within about fifty years of the first settlement at Plymouth, Massachusetts, in 1620, all the New England colonies except Rhode Island had passed legislation making it mandatory for parents and the masters of apprentices to ensure that their charges learned both a trade and the elements of reading, writing, and religion. Before long, laws were passed making it compulsory for towns to establish elementary schools. These early schools received some public support, but they also charged tuition.

In spite of early beginnings in New England, the idea that all citizens of a democracy should be taught at least reading, writing, and arithmetic was slow to take hold. The

ℛeal Education in Pakistan

Education in Pakistan reflects the country's hierarchically structured society. In Pakistan the concept of individual freedom is subordinated to the demands of self-discipline and obedience to elders. When your father (men are given more respect than women) says to do something, you do it, or you get beaten. (Physical punishment is quite acceptable in Pakistan.)

When you enter school, normally at the age of four, you have already been thoroughly indoctrinated by your parents to give the teacher that same respect and unquestioning obedience. The school day is rigidly organized; it has none of the free-form organizational structure that permeates U.S. schools. School begins with a general assembly in which all students line up in rectangular formations to recite the Holy Koran and sing the national anthem. If you refuse to sing, you're beaten—but nobody refuses.

The dress code is strictly enforced, and improperly attired children are either punished by their teachers or sent back home with a note telling the parents to turn up the next day with their child. Students up to the thirteenth grade (the final year of high school) are required to stand up when a teacher enters the classroom, greet him—the teachers are mostly men, especially in the senior classes—and sit down only when allowed to do so by the teacher. Throughout the lecture, all students are expected to sit in an upright position and preserve utter silence. Troublemakers (i.e., noisy kids) are caned (i.e., beaten). Students are not to question what the teacher says; the teacher's word is supposed to be almost as sacrosanct as the Holy Koran.

After the eighth grade, students normally split up into two streams, the science group and the arts group. The students have little choice in this matter; their grades and parental pressure are the two most important determining factors. Generally the brighter students are channeled into science and the second-raters are channeled into the arts.

Most Americans wouldn't like this system; they would see it as demeaning to the students and inconsistent with U.S. cultural mores. But in Pakistan, it works. It instills in students a work ethic and discipline that serves them well at the university level, both at home and abroad, and most Pakistani university students are glad they went through it, rather than through what they would describe as the namby-pamby U.S. educational system.

founders of our republic were not thoroughly democratic in all senses of the word. Although the Declaration of Independence pronounced that all men are created equal, most of our early leaders had limited faith in the ability of the common citizen either to vote wisely or to profit from education. Everywhere, the right to vote was restricted to the few by property and other qualifications, and except perhaps in New England, only a small minority of the people even learned to read and write.[1]

This situation did not change radically until well into the nineteenth century, when a new spirit of democracy began to be felt. It permeated the entire country but was especially strong in the recently settled regions west of the Alleghenies and along the rapidly advancing western frontier.

This new surge of democratic sentiment brought about the election of Andrew Jackson to the presidency in 1828. Jackson was a product of the frontier, and he represented the new democracy of the expanding West. In the period from Jackson's election to the Civil War, public elementary education became firmly established. In the 1830s, Alexis de Tocqueville, a French author, visited the United States and expressed astonishment at the

[1]Women were not allowed to vote in national elections until 1920.

The Country School, *1871, by Winslow Homer.*

ever-growing belief in and commitment to public education. In Europe, education was still restricted to members of the wealthy class and the clergy.

By 1860 tax-supported elementary schools had been opened in many states. During these years, some publicly supported high schools were also established, but for the most part secondary education continued to be provided by the private academies that had succeeded the early colonial Latin grammar schools. These academies increased rapidly in number, but not until some time after the Civil War did the idea of publicly supported high schools begin to gain wide acceptance.

Since 1865 there has been a phenomenal expansion of education in this country. In 1870, five years after the end of the Civil War, the number of children attending elementary schools was less than 7 million, and enrollment in public high schools was only 80,000. Some children were also attending private grade schools and academies. In 2003, total enrollment in elementary schools, public and private, approached 40 million, and enrollment in secondary schools was more than 15 million. In 1870 less than half the children five to seventeen years old were attending school, and the average number of days attended by each child was only 50. In the early 2000s, almost 100 percent of children from the ages of five to seventeen are in school at least some days every school year, and on the average, children attend school for about 165 days a year.

The most striking expansion of education in the twentieth century was in the colleges and universities. In 1920 there were fewer than 600,000 students enrolled in all of our institutions of higher learning. Enrollment in colleges and universities was less than 25 percent of high school enrollment. In 2003 the number of students in colleges and universities had increased more than twenty times, to more than 15.5 million.

The overall trends since 1960 can be seen in Figure 10.1. Until 1970, school enrollment rose at all levels. Then, in the 1970s, school enrollment began to decline. This trend was in large part caused by the completion of schooling of the children of the World War II baby boom. Enrollment in elementary schools started to rise again in the late 1980s due to the secondary baby boom (baby boomers' children). As the children of this secondary boom are getting older, the enrollment in later grades is also rising. Through all these trends, college education enrollment has risen as higher percentages of students go on to college and as older individuals decide to attend college.

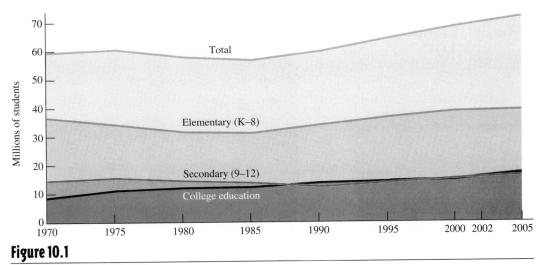

Figure 10.1

School enrollment by level of instruction, 1970 to 2005. (Source: National Center for Education Statistics. 2005 figures are projections.)

Democratic Structure of the U.S. School System

The school structure of the United States is quite different from what is traditional in most countries. Before World War I, nearly all European countries had what is called a dual school system, and in spite of some changes since, European schools still retain much of this dual character. A **dual school system** separates, at an early age, the children who expect to go on to a college or a university from those who do not, and provides a different type of education for each group. In Mexico all children are given an exam at about the age of twelve, after completing six years of primary education. Students who do well are sent to special "secondary" or university preparatory schools; others are sent to vocational, agricultural, or technical schools after completing their elementary education. This holds true in most European countries, too, although the age and grade level at which children are segregated varies from country to country. In Germany the age at which the examination is usually taken is ten; in Great Britain it is twelve.

In the United States, we developed in the late nineteenth century a so-called unitary system. In a **unitary school system,** most children (unless they have dropped out along the way) attend the same type of school and follow a course of study that eventually leads to graduation from high school after twelve years. They are then ready, supposedly, to go on to a college or university. The door to further education is, so far as possible, kept open all along the line.

Of course, not all courses prepare students to enter a college or university. Even so, our school system is fairly successful in keeping open the doors to further educational advancement because the student who has not taken a college preparatory course can often qualify for some type of college training by merely making up a few required admission courses. Also, many colleges are flexible in their entrance requirements for students who give evidence, by test scores or otherwise, that they have the ability to do good work in college.

Education in Some Other Countries

In this chapter we focus on the U.S. educational system. Our system is not the only way to educate. Let's take a brief look at how educational systems work in some other countries.

Germany

Schools are divided into three categories: grammar, technical, and vocational. The system grooms the gifted students and also tests the abilities of those who will become skilled workers. Equal emphasis and status are accorded the sciences and the arts. Adolescents are treated like adults, and students see how success in education is connected to earning a living. Some weaknesses are that the grading system is not as disciplined as it is in some countries and that vocational training is seen by some as being too traditional, without encouraging future entrepreneurs.

Denmark

The general structure is similar to that of Germany. In Denmark, however, if parents are dissatisfied with their public school, they can get together to set up their own school, and the government will pay 90 percent of the cost. At the university level, where students used to be able to take as long as they wanted to get a degree, there are now detailed schedules to discourage students from wasting time.

France

Scientific and technical schools enjoy a high status. Adolescents understand the tradition of spending most of their time working for a rigorous general examination. Vocational training has been weak, but recently the government has mandated employers to spend 1 percent of their sales receipts for training workers. Simultaneously, the government has encouraged vocational schools to expand, setting forth clear, ambitious goals.

Britain

Britain has a national curriculum, tested by national exams. Parents can send their children to the best available school, and the government finances schools on the basis of how many students they are able to attract. Exam results are published and schools are ranked comparatively, so parents can make informed decisions about which school to choose. Schools are encouraged to escape from supervisory bureaucracies and run themselves independently. As in some other European countries, vocational schools need improvement, but Britain is working on this task.

Japan

Japan has what some call "a cult of education." Students attend for long hours. Even after regular school hours, many attend evening, holiday, and weekend "cramming" schools to get extra education. Schools are run economically. Most of the school buildings are shabby and ill-equipped by Western standards. Students are required to help with some tasks, such as serving in the cafeteria. These tasks are believed to improve character, and they help keep school costs low. Competition is intense because students know their adult careers depend on how well they do in school. Also, the importance of education is demonstrated by the parental pressure exerted on children to excel. Parents endure financial and other sacrifices to pay for extra schooling. In recent years, the Japanese Ministry of Education has tried to discourage overly long hours, as they have been embarrassed by the statistics on teenage suicide and nervous breakdowns attributed to overwork at school.

Formalization of the School System

An institution as important as education quickly acquires a formal structure, and by 1880 the structure of schools in the United States had evolved into the familiar 8-4-4 system—a graded eight-year elementary school, a four-year high school, and a four-year college. As

How Much Does It Cost?

Some countries spend more on education than do other countries. The graph below shows the percentage of total spending that selected governments devote to education.

The amount of money spent doesn't necessarily measure the effectiveness of an education system. What does seem to matter is the students' understanding that success in education leads to economic success, parents' determination that the students do well, and government support for choice and innovation combined with insistence on consistent standards.

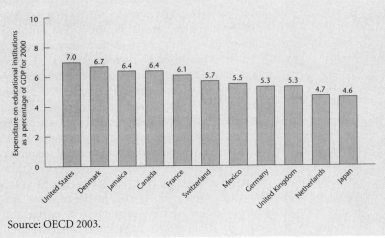

Source: OECD 2003.

inevitably as a formal structure developed, so did the criticism and evolution of that structure. Increasing criticism of the 8-4-4 system after World War I led initially to the establishment of junior high schools in many communities. These schools took over the seventh and eighth years of schooling from the grade schools and the first year from the senior high schools. The junior high school made it possible to begin secondary education earlier and facilitated the introduction of new types of courses. In the 1970s, the evolution continued, and elementary school was reduced to five years, junior high was changed to three years of middle school, and high school was extended to four years, making the 5-3-4-4 system common for most communities by the 1990s.

Education prior to the grade school years also changed. For example, in most U.S. communities a year of kindergarten was added at the bottom of the scale, preceding the first grade. Later still, private nursery schools became common for very young children, and in more recent years, programs have been introduced for young children from disadvantaged backgrounds. For example, **Head Start** is a federal program that seeks to enhance the social and intellectual development of students as young as three years old.

Evolution has also occurred at the college level. A good example is the community college movement, which developed slowly at first. In the early 1920s there were only a few such schools throughout the country. The first public community colleges were usually established by school districts as a kind of extension of high school. Often they were begun in high school buildings and their classes were taught by high school teachers, preferably those with some graduate school training. Just as some educators had

The Decline of Standards

argued earlier that the first two years of college should be moved down to the secondary level, some now regarded the community college as an extension of secondary education. In fact, however, most of the early community colleges followed rather closely the curricula of the first two years of the four-year colleges and universities, and they were chiefly concerned with preparing their students to enter such institutions in their junior year. By the end of the 1930s, the number of community colleges had substantially increased, and because most of them were established in areas where college education had not earlier been available, they gave many young people a better opportunity for getting at least some college training.

After World War II, in response to the increased demand for higher education, the number of two-year colleges, both private and public, rose rapidly. In the early 2000s there are about 1,650 in the United States, with a total enrollment of nearly 6 million students, among whom are 38 percent of all undergraduates. Community college enrollments account for 45 percent of all black students and 52 percent of all Hispanic students.

Gradually, as community colleges multiplied and more and more students crowded into them, their function changed to parallel more closely the initial concept of such colleges as an extension of high school. Now **community colleges** are colleges designed to meet the diverse needs of students who could benefit from some extension of their high school education. Community colleges are no longer regarded primarily as institutions preparing students to enter four-year colleges in the final two years. They still do this, but their design has been expanded to meet the needs of the community in which they are located. Especially for students who want to save money, community colleges, dollar for dollar, are a wonderful bargain. Various types of vocational training have been introduced, some of them technical. Courses are offered to train auto mechanics, beauty shop operators, salespeople, medical and dental assistants, laboratory technicians, and various other types of workers. The community college has become an institution that seeks to provide training that not only will produce better citizens but that also will meet the needs of our economy for a greater number of trained workers and the needs of young people for jobs that will yield both satisfaction and a reasonable level of income.

Exactly what that training should be is subject to debate. Some advocate traditional academic studies and others favor a vocational focus. Vocationalists argue that courses should provide skills needed in business. Traditionalists argue that there is a danger of students becoming narrow job specialists without common interests. They feel that job-specific skills can be learned on the job and that colleges should be designed to teach people to think and understand the world around them. The debate is likely to continue.

Examining the School System

The preceding history of the school system should give you a good sense of the U.S. educational system and how it developed. It is a compulsory system through age eighteen, usually the last year of high school, and it is a broad-based college system. It is also an expensive system costing hundreds of billions of dollars. Given education's significant role in modern society, it should not be surprising that there is a constant examination of the school system: how it delivers its services, how it is paid for, what it teaches, and what its results are. These continuing efforts to understand and improve the system will inevitably introduce changes.

Technological Change and Teaching

As with other institutions, technology changes both the method of teaching and what needs to be taught. With the development of computers, for example, the process of writing is changing. Computer programs are now available that correct grammatical, spelling, and stylistic mistakes. It is predicted that some time in this century these programs will expertly translate onto paper the words and ideas that a person speaks into them, making obsolete much of what is now taught in grammar and composition classes. Such changes would parallel those already accomplished in math by calculators, which have made nearly obsolete the necessity to do arithmetic mentally or on paper. Books will also change, and where full on-line bibliographies have become available through computers, many library skills are no longer necessary; we simply need to know how to use the relevant computer program.

What the long-range future holds is limited only by our imagination. Perhaps with the advance in the analysis of the brain, by 2040 teachers and schools may be obsolete, and students may simply hook up their brains to various data banks that directly translate knowledge from computer memory to student memory. Luckily for teachers, that time is not yet here.

Private Schools and Home Schooling

Private schools have always been a part of the U.S. educational system, and total enrollment in them is about 10 percent of all schoolchildren. Schools defined as private or independent include religious schools, private nonsectarian schools, and home schools. In 2002, there were over 27,000 independent schools. Of the country's 53 million school-age children, over 5 million attended independent schools and nearly 1 million were home-schooled, a figure representing over 11 percent of total school enrollment. Figure 10.2 gives you a sense of how public school enrollment has compared to private school enrollment.

A large number of these private schools have religious affiliations. Instruction in some of the religious schools is based on systematized programs, such as the one published by Accelerated Christian Education, Inc., of Lewisville, Texas. The pool of students in religious schools is estimated to be more than one million, and about half of these use the Accelerated Christian Education method of silent, individual study using workbooks and cassette recorders. There are several thousand different workbooks compiled to be

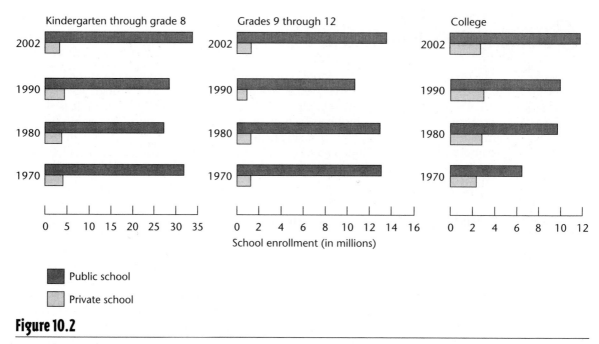

Figure 10.2

School enrollment from 1970 to 2002. (Source: National Center for Education Statistics.)

"distinctively Christian," and each student goes through as many as sixty-five different workbooks in a school year.

These systems are inexpensive and easy to set up. They use church space and incur no additional expenses for heat, utilities, and most equipment. Students from these schools who have taken the California Achievement Test have, on average, scored above the national norms in every subject.

Despite the significant amount of such activity and the fact that the choice of independent schools is growing rapidly, the total number of students in and from these schools is still statistically small. There is speculation that such schooling may lead to isolation, narrow interests, poor socialization, and alienation from the mainstream. These conclusions have not been subjected to testing. The results from the California Achievement Test provide at least some evidence that alternate systems of schooling are providing acceptable academic results. As educators gain more experience from work with these types of schools, we are likely to see many studies, reports, and recommendations on the subject.

An alternative to private schools is home schooling, in which parents teach their own children at home. As concern about public schools has increased, so too has home schooling, but it remains uncommon.

Charter Schools, Privatization, and the Problem of School Finance

Good schooling costs money, so it is not surprising that the taxpayers who pay for it often try to pay less. Historically, education in the United States is paid for largely by

First graders pass through the hallway in a charter school.

local property taxes—taxes on land, houses, and businesses in the school district. Because many property owners do not have children in school, some of them object to increases in school taxes. This leads to periodic community dissension and failure of the voters to pass school budgets. A second effect that local financing of schools has is significant differences in tax burdens among school districts. School districts with large amounts of valuable taxable property find that they can support schools with a much lower tax rate per property owner than can districts with little valuable taxable property. The result is significant differences in availability of funds for schools.

The inequity in this funding method has come under attack in the courts, and a number of states face legal mandates to change school finance methods by instituting some method of equalizing tax burdens and available resources. In Michigan, for example, the school property tax was eliminated a few years ago and replaced with a sales tax. In 1997 Vermont and New Hampshire were both forced to deal with state court decisions mandating major changes in the way property could be assessed for school purposes.

Attempts to change these financing methods have led to more dissension and to pushes for privatizing education so that it is no longer supplied by government, but is instead supplied by private, for-profit businesses. Under the typical privatization plan, students are given a voucher worth, say, $5,000, which they can use to attend whichever school they want. Advocates push for such privatization programs using the phrase "school choice," because students would have a choice of schools. Opponents of such schemes argue that the private schools would "skim the cream," taking the easy to educate students and leaving the difficult and expensive to educate students in public school. They also argue that it would significantly change the socialization function of the public schools and, hence, change the nature of U.S. society. Although a number of privatization initiatives have been put forward, in the early 2000s none had passed.

One initiative that has passed in about thirty states is **charter schools**—decentralized schools based on a charter between an individual or group (usually teachers, parents, and others in a community) and its sponsor (usually the local or state school board). Charter schools are designed as an alternative to private and public schools. Although largely controlled by parents and teachers, their financing is usually provided by the state in which they're located. About 10 percent of charter schools are run by businesses, most of whose hopes to make a profit are fixed on the vague future. Their structure minimizes bureaucracy and promotes innovative approaches to learning by empowering teachers and parents to create the curriculum. Accountability is achieved by performance tests that determine whether the charter is renewed. Over the next few years, these schools will be watched closely so that the quality and breadth of the programs that emerge can be measured.

Textbooks

After systematic testing had been developed as a research tool beginning in the 1920s, educational testers reached the conclusion that the elementary curriculum was too hard, and they targeted the textbook. Since then textbooks for elementary schools have tended to become less and less rigorous. Long words and complex grammatical constructions are frowned on, as are connective words. According to Harriet Bernstein, textbook expert of the Council of Chief State School Officers, the word *because* does not appear in most U.S. schoolbooks before the eighth grade. Some believe that these simple books continue to be used because overworked, undertrained teachers need something easy to teach from.

The situation is complicated by the claims of various ethnic, religious, political, and other pressure groups. For instance, nutritionists who believe that refined sugar is a health hazard have succeeded in some states in having removed from children's textbooks most references to cake and candy. The results can sometimes be unintended; in one case, these omissions resulted in stories about a child having a birthday—with no birthday cake.

Textbooks developed for high schools and colleges have some of the same characteristics. Open several and stand back so that you cannot read the print: You will find that they all tend to look alike. Popular strategies include frequent subheads, charts and pictures, boxed material appearing in the middle of a page to relieve the blocks of print, and glosses in the margins that enable the student to get the gist of the chapter without reading the main text. Publishers demand these devices because that is what sells, and textbook writers comply.

In our view (yes, it is true that textbook authors have views), textbooks coddle students too much. We make learning too easy, so students don't have to think. Nevertheless, we coddle (a word that probably shouldn't be used because it is too unusual), although less than other textbook writers do, because teachers and publishers say that a truly thought-provoking (and therefore painful) textbook wouldn't get published and wouldn't get read.

School Dropouts

When education becomes too painful, students drop out. According to data compiled by the U.S. Bureau of the Census, as many as 50 percent of high school students in some major cities drop out before graduating. Nationwide, the percentage of high school students dropping out is much lower. In the twenty years from 1975 to 1995, the dropout rate for all high school students was about 14 percent. In that same period, however, when we look at the dropout rate for individual groups, the picture is more distressing. In the twenty year period beginning in 1975, the dropout rate for high school students of Hispanic origin was about 35 percent, and the dropout rate for black high school students was about 20 percent.

In the decade from 1985 to 1995, the dropout rate (those age fifteen to twenty-four who dropped out of grades 10–12) remained stable at around 5 percent, but Hispanics continued to drop out at higher rates than other groups. In 1996, 9 percent of Hispanics left school before completing a high school program, compared to 6.7 percent for blacks and 4.1 percent for whites. In 2000 the dropout rate was down to 4.8 percent—4.1 for whites, 6.1 for blacks, and 7.4 for Hispanics. But the percentage of sixteen- to twenty-four-year-olds who were dropouts in 2000 was 10.9: 6.9 white, 13.1 black, and 27.8 Hispanic.

A number of programs have been established to deal with dropouts. In New York City, for example, workers for Operation Far Cry contact dropouts from high school by phone and attempt to persuade them to return to school. Other areas have tried flexible school scheduling, work-study plans, and identification and counseling programs. In a cash-for-class project, one California school paid students to attend school. Another option for high school dropouts is to work for a General Equivalency Diploma (GED), which is equivalent to a high school diploma. In the early 2000s, well over 500,000 GED degrees were being granted each year.

The high dropout rate is a problem not only for the individual student but also for the entire community. Education has a direct relationship to crime, and in the long run the higher the average level of education, the lower the crime rate. Dropping out of high school also affects one's ability to get a job; the unemployment rate among dropouts is roughly twice as high as the unemployment rate for high school graduates.

Multiculturalism, Collaborative Learning, and Institutional Fairness

People learn in different ways, and various groups respond differently to alternative learning environments. Much of our current learning environment is what Peggy McIntosh, an education specialist at the Center for Research on Women at Wellesley College, calls "winner-killer competitive," which she argues is not conducive to some minority cultures' and women's backgrounds. The current system, she argues, is biased toward white males and does not provide a **collaborative learning environment,** in which students learn to work together, helping each other excel rather than competing with others to beat them down.

McIntosh's theories are highly controversial, but aspects of them are making their way into mainstream educational practices in what is called the **multiculturalism movement,** the movement to make social institutions unbiased with respect to all ethnic and cultural groups.

One example of this multicultural movement is Uri Treisman's work with black college math majors. Treisman is a mathematics professor at the University of Texas at Austin who has studied in depth the reasons why black students made up a disproportionately small number of college math majors, whereas Asian students made up a disproportionately large number. Together with a number of social scientists, he conducted research to find out why. He found that the cause had nothing to do with ability. The groups he was looking at (students at the University of California at Berkeley) had equal ability in math in their high schools and on standardized tests. The difference was more in the institutional structure of the program. He found that Asian students tended to work on problems together in informal social groups, so studying math became part of their social interaction. On the other hand, he found that black students' social activities did not include any such interaction, as they were drawn to black cultural centers that did not include other math majors. Thus they did not experience the type of collaborative learning that the Asian students did. He set about to change that and successfully instituted collaborative learning exercises that, together with other institutional reforms, significantly increased the percentage of black math majors at the University of Texas.

There are many more such examples at all levels of the educational system, and over the next ten years we can expect to hear much more about how institutional structure affects learning behavior.

Are Boys Discriminated against in School?

Discrimination takes many forms, and as one type of discrimination is corrected, others are created. Take the discrimination against girls in education alluded to in the text. In the 1970s and 1980s, this topic was much discussed, and a large majority of the population felt that the educational structure discriminated against girls. That view led to the passage of the Gender Equity in Education Act in 1994, which specifically banned discrimination against girls in school. Ten years later it is not girls whom social scientists feel are being discriminated against; it is boys. The signs of discrimination are many. Girls, on average, get higher grades than boys; girls are more likely to be in advanced placement and honors courses; and girls attend college in higher percentages than boys.

The suggested reasons are varied. Some include:

- Teachers tend to choose "feeling" books that appeal to girls rather than "action" books that appeal to boys, so boys don't learn to read.
- Math is being taught with words, with which girls excel, rather than with numerical algorithms, with which boys excel.
- Competition, which boys thrive on, is portrayed as bad, and "cooperative learning," a learning style that girls do better with, is portrayed as good.

Also varied are the suggested solutions. Some want to make boys more like girls, so that they relate to feelings rather than to action. Others want to make school more conducive to masculine ways of learning. Still others say we should simply get rid of the Gender Equity Act, which was too much, too late; it went into effect when women had already achieved equity.

Whatever the answer, we can expect to hear more about the issue in the future.

The ways in which discrimination occurs can be subtle, although sometimes when pointed out they are not so subtle after all. For example, Gary Mitchell, a New Jersey attorney, sent his child to a progressive school and was struck by the awards given out in the child's kindergarten class. The awards given to students of one gender were for best thinker, most eager learner, most imaginative, most enthusiastic, most scientific, best friend, best personality, hardest worker, and best sense of humor. The other gender's awards were for all-around sweetheart, sweetest personality, cutest personality, best sharer, best artist, biggest heart, best manners, best helper, and most creative. I leave it to you to figure out which gender got which list of awards.

How Good Are U.S. Schools?

Probably the most important questions we can ask about our educational system are: Does it deliver? and, Are students receiving a good education? The answers are not a unanimous yes. Many argue that there has been a marked decline in the effectiveness of education over the last few decades; students graduate without knowing the fundamentals of reading, writing, spelling, and arithmetic, especially in depressed inner-city areas. Starting in 1995, SAT scores rose substantially, as you can see in Figure 10.3. This was not because students were doing better, however, but because the test scores were **normed,** that is, adjusted to fit a predetermined scale. Whereas previously 450 had been the median score, after norming 500 was the median score. Thus someone who in 1997 received a verbal score of 505 would have received only a 428 in 1995. In other words, the scores were simply raised, on average, by 45 points. Why do this? Cynics suggest it is the only way to raise scores. The

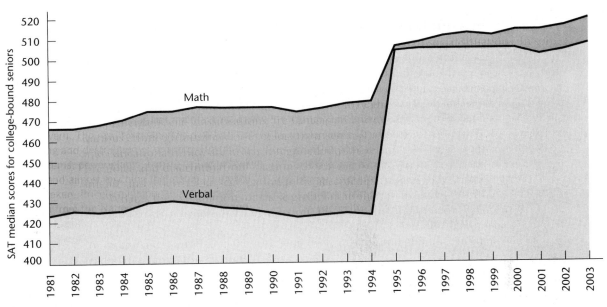

Figure 10.3

SAT scores for college-bound seniors, 1981–2003. In 1995 the scores were normed at a higher level. There was no large, sudden increase in unnormed scores. (1981–1994 scores are median scores; 1995–2003 scores are mean scores. There are only small differences between the mean and the median scores; the jump is caused by the renorming.)
(Source: Based on information from the College Entrance Examination Board.)

SAT administrators say it is to give students a better sense of where they stand in relation to other students. We leave you to decide which answer is the most persuasive. (To be fair to the SAT, in reporting the scores, they also raised recent previous scores.)

Starting in 2004, the SAT tests changed significantly:

- Instead of two sections, there are three, with a two-part writing test being introduced. This means that the highest score will be 2400, rather than 1600.

- The verbal reasoning section was renamed "critical reading," and analogies will be dropped.

- The math section added higher-level math problems.

The hope in making these changes was that the test would better reflect what colleges are looking for and give those students who take harder courses an edge.

Educators justify the shortcomings in our schools in a variety of ways. They argue that many modern-day students do not want to learn and have little ability to master traditional academic subjects. Teachers are then under pressure to lower standards. It seems unreasonable to give failing grades to, say, 50 percent of a class, no matter how poor it is; naturally many principals and parents would blame the teacher. In addition, teenagers with little schooling now have trouble getting jobs. If they leave school, they may just wander the streets and get into trouble. So in many schools most marginal students are promoted regardless of their lack of achievement.

The tendency to pass students from grade to grade on the basis of little or no achievement is strengthened in some schools by the policy of social promotion. This means promoting students along with their classmates regardless of whether they reach a minimum standard of achievement in their studies. The theory is that it is better for social reasons to keep them with their own age group, whether they learn anything or not, and at all costs to avoid stigmatizing them as failures. However, promotion on this basis does not help matters much. Students who have not learned elementary mathematics in the lower grades become completely frustrated or indifferent if they must attend math classes in the upper grades. Thus, so-called education consists only of going through the motions of attending classes. Not only do these students become a problem to the teachers and hinder the other students from learning, but they also often feel their own inadequacy more keenly than if they had been held back. Whether under these conditions students gain anything by remaining with their own age group or by staying in school at all is open to question. If this problem is to be solved, we probably must address it early in a child's life.

The Search for Excellence

In response to many criticisms of the U.S. educational system, measures to stem what critics call a tide of mediocrity have been instituted. The reforms have been mostly on the state and local level and have increased salary scales, lengthened the school day, improved teacher certification standards, given teachers more responsibility, and put in place frequent standardized testing in a variety of grades and subjects so that students' performance will be monitored in a measurable way.

*C*an You Read This?

About 9 percent of adult Americans whose native language is English can't read English. That's what the U.S. Bureau of the Census says. If we're talking about people whose native language is not English, then the Census Bureau says 48 percent can't read English. Put these two groups together and they add up to about 27 million people.

Here are a few of the test questions that many people couldn't answer:

1. Pick another word for *sickness:*
   The patient has the right to ask for information about his sickness.
   benefits/payments/expenses/illness
2. Pick the best fill-in for the blank:
   Don't allow your medical information card to
   _____ by any other person.
   be used/have destroy/go lose/get expired
3. Choose the answer that means the same as the phrase with a line under it:
   We cannot see you today. When can you return?
   When was the last time you came?
   Who should you call when you come?
   On what date can you come again?
   Are those the papers you can return?

Of course, no test is perfect. For instance, all the preceding questions seem to imply that the person taking the test is sick. Some authorities have challenged the Census Bureau study by criticizing the test. But as one of the critics said, "What does it matter if there are 10 million or 20 million? We're not even taking care of a small fraction of them. There are too many."

On July 1, 1994, a federal law about national education standards went into effect. This law, called the Goals 2000: Educate America Act, recommends academic standards for grades 4, 8, and 11 and encourages states to design new ways to measure student performance. The goals, to be achieved by the year 2000, include the following:

1. All students will arrive at school ready to learn.
2. The nation's high school graduation rate will be at least 90 percent.
3. Students will be competent in English, history, geography, foreign languages, and the arts.
4. U.S. students will lead the world in math and science.
5. All adults will be literate.
6. Every school will be free of violence and drugs.

The year 2000 arrived and the goals were not met, although spending on schools increased and there were pockets of improvement. In the presidential election of 2000, education was a central topic, and both candidates said they would increase federal spending on education significantly over the next decade. The winner, George W. Bush, also promised to establish national standards and to make schools accountable. To accomplish this, in 2002 Bush pushed for and eventually signed the No Child Left Behind Act. This law was a sweeping reform that redefines the federal government's role in K–12 education. It is based on four principles: stronger accountability, increased local control, expanded parental options, and emphasis on proven teaching methods. The most expensive and controversial aspect of this program is its emphasis on standardized testing. One side sees high-stakes tests as defining accountability, the other as stifling broader learning and forcing teachers to teach to a test, not to teach for understanding. The debate about this program is continuing, with no definitive results about its effectiveness.

Changes in the College Curriculum

Until the middle of the nineteenth century, higher education consisted chiefly of learning the ancient languages, mathematics, philosophy, and theology. Some attention was also given to modern foreign languages and the social sciences, but these held a place of less importance. After the Civil War, however, the curriculum began to show the effects of new developments in science, technology, and other fields of knowledge. As enrollments increased and the interests of students became more and more diverse, scientific, technical, and vocational training were increasingly introduced at the college level. Subjects and courses of study multiplied until it became impossible for any student to take more than a very small portion of the total offerings.

The Development of the Elective System.   To meet this problem, the elective system was adopted. This permitted students, with some restrictions, to determine their own courses of study. But the results were not always satisfactory, for often students chose a hodgepodge of unrelated subjects, and at the same time they frequently missed entirely any acquaintance with some of the basic fields of human knowledge.

The shortcomings of the elective system led to two developments. First, colleges began to require students to major in one field of knowledge by taking a substantial proportion of their work in this field. At the same time, they began to require students to spread some of their courses in such a way that they became acquainted with at least several of the basic fields of knowledge. The expression *liberal education* came to be associated especially with the attempt to give students breadth of understanding.

This attempt led to the rapid spread in the 1930s of survey courses covering broad fields of knowledge such as physical science, biological science, social science, and the humanities. Sometimes all students were required in their first and sophomore years to take a core curriculum consisting of several of these survey courses. After World War II, courses of this type continued to spread; this book was originally written for such a survey or basic course in the social sciences.

To this period belong terms such as **general education,** college programs that are intended to broaden students' intellectual horizons. Sometimes the term is used merely as a substitute for the older term *liberal education.* Both expressions refer to a type of training designed to go much beyond narrowly practical or vocational objectives. But although liberal education emphasizes the desirability of learning something about a variety of subjects, general education puts more stress on the importance of not missing completely any of the major fields of human knowledge.

Following the Fads.   In the late 1960s and throughout the 1970s, colleges and universities restructured their curricula to be relevant. Students in the 1960s were interested in the social issues of their times. As the 1970s progressed, students became less interested in social issues and more interested in money and how to get it. As a result, institutions of higher learning experienced a demand for courses related to business and the professions such as law, medicine, engineering, and banking. By 1985 the majority of college students were majoring in business or business-related subjects.

From 1950 to the early 2000s, college enrollments quintupled, which contributed to the relaxing of standards, the dropping of course requirements, and the introduction of courses such as family food management and automobile ownership. In the mid-1980s, as many as half the students who entered college as first-year students failed to get degrees.

Almost as soon as colleges began to allow flexible requirements and courses of study, and instituted courses and even whole departments in response to trendy demands, they started thinking about making the curriculum more rigorous. By the late 1970s, some col-

$\mathcal{S}$ocial Science: No Fad

Social science has been around a long time; it is no fad course. It is one of the courses that provides students with an education in their culture and civilization. Various incarnations of this particular book have been a staple of social science courses since the 1930s when nine Chicago professors put their notes together and created a selection of readings for their students. It has since been revised many times to keep it current.

It has been "Hunt and Colander" since the early 1980s.

As the social sciences have split into their various components, it's been harder and harder to find professors with training and inclination to teach the course, but because it provides a necessary and broad overview of social science thinking, it is precisely the type of course that reformers are advocating.

leges and universities were experiencing the equivalent of the back-to-basics movement in elementary and secondary school practice. This took the form of eliminating superficial survey courses, returning to requirements of Greek and Latin, asking students to take more math, and trying to ensure that students had at least some knowledge of fields that are considered part of a broad liberal education but that many students would not study unless they were required to.

These tendencies were at once summed up and endorsed in 1984 when the National Endowment for the Humanities (NEH) made its report, *Excellence in Education*. This report argued that colleges had not made good on "promises to make you better off culturally and morally," and that "colleges have been ripping off students." It attributed this to poor management and ill-conceived curricula, and suggested that the money invested in a college education would serve a more useful purpose if the parents would instead give that sum to a child to buy a small business.

That report reinforced the already existing tendency to make curricula more rigorous. Some colleges have thrown out their entire catalogs and redesigned their curricula from scratch; others have reshaped curricula to deal with both content and structure.

For instance, responding to the report's complaint that colleges fail to give students "an adequate education in the culture and civilization of which they are members," some schools have set up curricula in terms of fields of knowledge, which they variously designate as "perspectives," "ways of looking at the world," or "modes of inquiry"; the specifications for perspectives might include "science, society, and human values." Because employers want employees who can write and think, colleges are placing more emphasis on composition and math. It has now become acceptable to assert that faculty, not students, know more when it comes to deciding on course content.

Is the U.S. Educational System Equal?

Although the U.S. educational system provides greater opportunities for the masses than any other country, it still perpetuates inequalities that are difficult to justify. The most striking of these is found in comparing the situation of blacks with whites, as we already discussed in earlier chapters.

Figure 10.4, which shows the percentage of black adults compared to the total number of adults who have completed four years of high school, demonstrates some of the strides we have made since 1950, but also shows our need to make further gains.

As discussed, a second inequality in education is based on wealth and income. Because most localities finance their education with property taxes, variations of taxable wealth in different regions and localities cause significant variations in educational opportunities. In many poor areas, residents find it impossible to provide adequate school facilities for their children. In the 1970s, a Supreme Court case determined that the use of the local property tax to support education perpetuated inequality, and states were directed to explore alternative ways of financing. In the early 2000s, most states are still in the exploratory stages.

Even if all localities received equal support for education there would still be inequality. There is a close correlation between the amount of schooling received by children and the income status of their families. The higher the family income, the greater the likelihood that a child will finish high school or go to college.

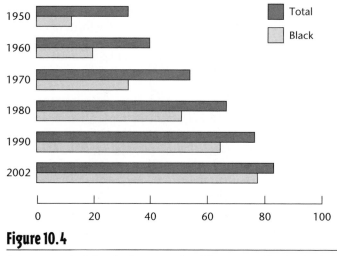

Figure 10.4

Percentage of adults who have completed four years of high school or more, 1950 to 2002. (Source: U.S. Bureau of the Census, *Statistical Abstract of the United States.*)

How Much Education Should the Average Citizen Receive?

How far should the formal education of the average citizen be carried? Grade school? High school? Junior college? This basic question must be answered as our school system changes and develops, but there is no simple response. For every person there is certainly a limit to the time that can be spent in acquiring a formal education. Where this limit is depends on the temperament, abilities, interests, and purposes of the individual, on the kinds of education available to the person, and on the costs that must be met by the student, the parents, and the community.

Today few people would question that a grade school education is worth the cost for almost everyone. Also, there is general agreement in this country that a high school education is desirable and worth the cost for the majority of young people, though perhaps for many of them we are not providing the most helpful kind of curriculum. The situation with respect to higher education is somewhat different, and we may well question whether it is desirable for the great majority of young people to complete four years of college. Many people believe that we should set admission standards that would limit enrollments in four-year colleges and universities. But there seems to be increasing support for the point of view that eventually most young people should have at least the equivalent of a two-year community/junior college degree. As you can see in Figure 10.5, the percentage of our population receiving a high school and college education has increased substantially since 1960.

With junior colleges and community colleges becoming more adaptive to current needs, high school graduates today can more easily find the kind of further education that suits their abilities and needs. For those who have no liking for it, the indefinite extension of formal academic education holds no magic. But it is increasingly difficult for adolescents without training to find jobs. This largely explains the increasing emphasis

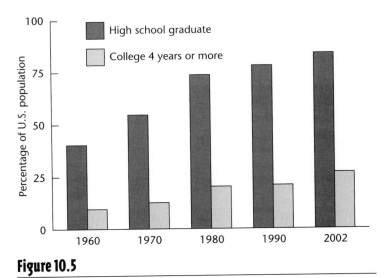

Figure 10.5

Educational attainment (persons age 25 years and over). (Source: U.S. Bureau of the Census.)

on providing more vocational schools and also more vocational courses in community colleges. However, this may also reflect both the recent conservative trend that has swept the country and a return to concern with developing skills that make the U.S. competitive in the world economy.

But what of individuals who are not interested in further schooling and who in some cases may have little ability to benefit from a high level of vocational training? There is still a great deal of relatively unskilled work that needs to be done and for which people would pay if willing workers could be found at reasonable wages. One difficulty is that we have been downgrading the dignity of commonplace work, of jobs that are useful but provide only small or moderate pay and offer no glamorous future. In doing this we have robbed many young people with limited ability of the chance to learn how to work and, by gaining confidence and experience, to find a useful and independent place in life.

Interaction of Economics, Politics, and Social Institutions

Most subjects in social science can be isolated for purposes of study, but in reality they are not isolated. So it is with the educational system. Our educational system includes cultural values and thereby plays an important role in shaping other social, economic, and political institutions, but simultaneously it is shaped by them. The state of education in the early 2000s is a case in point. All agree that school systems could and should do a better job. The question is, how? Some argue that the answer is to spend more and more—for instance, to improve teachers' pay and to provide schools with the latest technological equipment. Others argue that the ideal answer is to become more efficient—for teachers to work harder, for students to study harder, and for administrators to decide that schools do not need so much administration and to eliminate their own jobs. But don't hold your breath waiting. Individuals in educational institutions are likely to opt for the easy path. Students aren't going to be motivated to study harder unless provided with incentives to do so. It's the same with teachers. And there is almost no way administrators are going to eliminate their own jobs.

The response of many parents to the problems in public education is to move their children to private schools, thus circumventing the culturally integrating role of the public school system. Different groups become more inwardly self-sufficient, and political divergences widen. Those differences, in turn, lead to even less money being spent on public schools.

To offset the reduced flow of federal money into the system, some people have advanced ideas such as tuition tax credits to parents of children attending private schools or federal income tax credits for certain education situations. But to the degree that tax credits for private schools work, they further reduce the nation's pool of common experiences; and there is disagreement as to whether targeted income tax credits would reach their targets or would turn out to be economically insignificant.

Another area in which the interaction of economics, politics, and social institutions can be illustrated is that of setting teacher standards. The concepts of setting standards, certifying competence, and mandating the teaching of certain basic subjects are admirable, but all are liable to abuse. Teachers are divided in their view on certification. Teachers who have been teaching for years feel it is unfair for their competency suddenly to be questioned and tested. New teachers feel that their own recent educations qualify them in the latest methods and believe that if the older teachers had nothing to fear, they would not protest competency tests. Both groups can unite in their scorn of agencies that set educational standards when the staffs of the agencies have no professional educational training. Yet taxpayers do not want to leave certification in the hands of the very people who are to be certified.

The point of these discussions is twofold: (1) there are no easy answers to difficult questions, and (2) what we do in one area of society is likely to have significant effects in other areas. Only by considering all those effects and recognizing the pitfalls in implementing the easy solutions can we hope to develop wise social policy.

*K*ey Points

- The U.S. educational system has a dual thrust: It attempts to develop students' individuality and to socialize students.
- U.S. educational institutions are a product of their history.
- The main problem facing our educational system is how to provide excellent, equal education efficiently, inexpensively, and in a manner that appropriately socializes the students.

- The college curriculum has evolved from a rigid system that taught specific subjects to an elective system with significant freedom and varied courses.
- An important reason why our educational system is not equal is the methods used to fund it.

Some Important Terms

academic freedom (209)
charter school (219)
collaborative learning
    environment (221)
community college (216)
credentializing (208)

dual school system (213)
dual thrust of U.S. education
    (209)
education (208)
general education (226)
Head Start (215)

multiculturalism movement
    (221)
normed (222)
unitary school system (213)

Questions for Review and Discussion

1. Explain the difference between education and socialization.
2. How does free public education contribute to the development of U.S. democracy?
3. Discuss the development of U.S. education since colonial times.
4. What factors have contributed to increasing enrollments at the primary and secondary levels?
5. How does the structure of the educational system in the United States differ from that of Europe?
6. Discuss the history of community colleges.
7. Discuss the changes that have taken place in school curricula over the past hundred years.

8. What differences in educational opportunities exist?
9. How can multiculturalism and collaborative learning improve the effectiveness of schools?
10. Discuss some types of schools that are alternatives to public schools.
11. What conclusions can be drawn concerning the progress made in U.S. education over the past hundred years? What still remains to be done?
12. Give an example of a political issue influencing an educational issue.

Internet Questions

1. According to www.ericfacility.net/databases/ERIC_Digests/ed372146.html, what are the three basic types of multicultural education programs and what is the focus of each?
2. Go to www.americanmontessorisociety.org/home.html. What is the Montessori approach to education?
3. The National Center for Policy Analysis, www.ncpa.org/pi/edu/feb98a.html, finds Hispanic dropout rates extraordinarily high; what is blamed?
4. According to the government website for the No Child Left Behind Act, www.ed.gov/nclb/landing/jhtml, which students will be tested and why?
5. Go to http://edreform.com/school_reform_faq/charter_schools.htm. According to the Center for Educational Reform, what are charter schools?

For Further Study

Bloom, Allan D., *The Closing of the American Mind: How Higher Education Has Failed Democracy and Impoverished Souls of Today's Students,* New York: Simon & Schuster, 1987.

Cookson, Peter W., and Kristina Berger, *Expected Miracles: Charter Schools and the Politics of Hope and Despair,* Cambridge, MA: Westview Press, 2002.

Cutler, William H., ed., *Parents and Schools: The 150-Year Struggle for Control in America,* Chicago: University of Chicago Press, 2000.

Delpit, Lisa, *Other People's Children: Cultural Conflict in the Classroom,* New York: New Press, 1995.

Dwyer, James G., *Vouchers within Reason: A Child-Centered Approach to Education Reform,* Ithaca, NY: Cornell University Press, 2002.

Giuliano, Gina, *Education: Reflecting Our Society,* Detroit, MI: Gale Group, 2002.

Howard, Tharon, ed., *The Electric Networks: Crossing Boundaries/Creating Communities,* Portsmouth, NH: Boynton Cook, 1999.

Levinson, Meira, *The Demands of Liberal Education,* New York: Oxford University Press, 1999.

Wagner, Tony, *Making the Grade: Reinventing America's Schools,* New York: Routledge/Falmer, 2002.

WWW   American Association of Community Colleges www.aacc.nche.edu

WWW   Educational Resources Information Center www.eric.ed.gov

WWW   Home Education Research Institute   www.nheri.org

WWW   Institute for Higher Education Policy   www.ihep.com

WWW   National Center for Education Statistics   www.nces.ed.gov

WWW   United States Department of Education   www.ed.gov

WWW   United States Distance Learning Association www.usdla.org

Social and Economic Stratification

After reading this chapter, you should be able to:

- List three types of social stratification
- Discuss the role of social mobility in making some social stratification acceptable to society
- List three sources of income inequality
- State what the poverty threshold is in the United States
- Discuss six issues that any practical program for meeting the problems of economic inequality must take into account
- Explain what is meant by the U.S. class system and how it relates to class consciousness

> . . . all the animals are equal here, but some are more equal than others.
>
> **—George Orwell**

The people of every society can be divided into groups—sometimes along clear-cut lines, sometimes only roughly. **Stratification** is the grouping of people according to differences in income, occupation, power, privilege, manner of living, region where they live, age, gender, or race; you can probably think of other categories. Stratification, in the sense of differentiation, is not necessarily bad. People differ and that difference adds diversity to life. But when there is a **hierarchy**—when one group considers itself better, or maintains privileged access to society's resources—questions of social equity are raised. Many systems of social and economic stratification do create a hierarchy of superior, intermediate, and inferior groups; that hierarchical stratification is our primary concern in this chapter.

Social stratification appears to be unavoidable. Some activities and some kinds of work are more important to a society than others. Some can be carried on only by people of outstanding ability with special training or experience. Political offices must be filled, economic activities must be organized, medical services must be provided, and military forces must be commanded. Those who play important roles in such activities acquire power and prestige. Usually they also acquire larger than average incomes and various special privileges. In addition, because these individuals tend to associate principally with one another, they develop common attitudes and modes of living. Sometimes they entrench themselves in their positions by means of legal and religious sanctions, but even without these safeguards, they can often pass their superior status along to their children.

When firmly established, social stratification contributes to social stability. It means general acceptance of the fact that certain groups perform certain functions, as do their children after them. Competitiveness is reduced because people know their place in society and the paths they are expected to follow. When social stratification is less rigid and there are more opportunities for an individual to change status, dissatisfaction and conflict may be more evident.

Types of Social Stratification

There are three principal types of social stratification: estates, castes, and social classes. We are chiefly interested in the last type because social classes represent the major form of stratification found in modern industrial societies. However, some knowledge of estate and caste systems will contribute to our understanding of the nature of social classes.

Estates

When used in a discussion of stratification, the term **estate** refers not to land but to groups such as the nobility, the clergy, merchants, artisans, and peasants. The estate stratification system developed in Europe under feudalism. The estate to which a person belonged, and its place in the social hierarchy, were determined chiefly by custom, occupation, rights and obligations with respect to land, and other legal sanctions.

In an estate system, the position of an individual in society is nearly always inherited from parents; the lines between groups are clearly drawn, and almost everyone knows just where he or she belongs. They may even be required to dress in a particular way to indicate their station in relation to others. The opportunity for mobility is small, but it is entirely possible within the framework of law and custom. In feudal times, a noble could free a serf from bondage to the land in return for a special service, or a king could bestow a title of nobility (the Queen of England still bestows titles today). Military service and the priesthood are also possible avenues of upward mobility in an estate system.

The medieval estate system, with its relatively rigid social categories, was better suited to a static than to a dynamic society. It gradually disintegrated under the impact of changes such as the decline of feudalism, the Industrial Revolution, and the rise of democratic ideology, with its strong emphasis on freedom and equality.

Castes

Caste is a rigid class distinction based on birth, wealth, or some other distinguishing characteristic. Within a discussion of stratification, the caste system is usually associated with India, where until recently it had prevailed for about three thousand years. In the 1980s, the legal underpinnings of the caste system were removed in India, but the cultural legacy remains and caste still plays an important role in Indian life. Under the caste system, an individual acquires a social position at birth. The great vitality of the caste system seems to arise from the fact that, besides being firmly established by custom, it is an integral part of the Hindu religion. It is based on the doctrines of karma and transmigration. **Karma** is the belief that every person should fulfill in this life the duties associated with membership in a caste. The doctrine of **transmigration** holds that if a person fulfills duties sufficiently

Poor, low caste Indian farmers.

well in this life, that person will in a future life be reborn or reincarnated into a higher caste. A caste system is even more rigid than an estate system because in theory there is no way of moving to a higher status except through death and reincarnation. In practice, a very limited amount of upward shifting does occur.

Social stratification systems having some of the characteristics of the one in India have been found in other societies. In the United States, blacks, especially in the South, have been called a caste by some writers. To support this designation, they point out that blacks belong by birth to a socially underprivileged group and that, at least in the past, it was very difficult for them to enter groups predominantly occupied by whites. Until 2000 it was even technically illegal in some states for blacks and whites to intermarry. Alabama, in 2000, was the last state to repeal its law. (The law had not been enforced since the 1960s.)

Despite these similarities, most observers believe that the position of U.S. blacks differed considerably from that of the members of a low Hindu caste. In the first place, even before recent reforms, blacks were subject to no rigid occupational limitations, and some achieved high positions in government, business, and the professions. Even more important, their inferior social position was not based on religious sanctions; rather, it was and is contrary to most Americans' religious teachings and democratic ideals of freedom and equal opportunity for all human beings.

A closer analogy to the caste system than the U.S. situation would be the **apartheid system**—a separation of the races—in South Africa, where until recently blacks could not hold the same jobs or live in the same places as whites, and their interrelations with whites were severely limited. Apartheid was condemned by most other countries; in the early 1960s, it was overthrown altogether in the southern African country of Zimbabwe, and in the 1990s it was abolished in South Africa.

Social Classes

Although most modern industrial societies do not have formal stratification systems, they do have a type of social stratification called a social class system. Unlike estates and castes, these social classes are not supported by any legal or religious sanctions, and they are not clear-cut, definitely delimited groups into which every person in the community can be placed. The fact that social classes are not perfectly clear-cut entities is proven by the inability of social scientists to come to any general agreement on just how many of them should be recognized as existing. In a democratic industrial society, social status is a continuum, with individuals and families scattered along it from top to bottom. If we divide people on this social scale into two, three, or more social classes, we must do so arbitrarily.

Social scientists also have difficulty deciding just what criteria should be used in determining social status. Some would place an individual (or family) in a given class entirely on the basis of economic considerations. Those who take this point of view

A symbol of apartheid in South Africa.

usually put their chief emphasis on income. Others, probably the majority, would determine the status of an individual by general social standing—that is, by whether the community, on the basis of various criteria, places the individual high or low on the social scale. Income would be only one factor. Some of the common stratification hierarchies are shown in Figure 11.1. In it the classes are shown as a diamond rather than a pyramid to emphasize that in the United States, the middle classes tend to be the largest. The combination of hierarchies—education, occupation, and income—forms an individual's socioeconomic status.[1]

Social Class Defined. A **social class** consists of those people in a community who are somewhat similar in their economic status, their attitudes and beliefs, their educational attainments, their ways of living, the regard in which others hold them, and their power or lack of power to influence community affairs. According to this definition, social class is, in some degree, a subculture. People whose social statuses are similar are not only likely to live in the same neighborhoods, associate largely with one another, and marry one another, but they are also likely to show similarities of speech, manners, and moral standards as compared with people who are higher or lower on the social scale.

Because social classes, like other types of stratification, represent superiority/inferiority relationships, some writers have compared the class structure of society to a layer cake. At

the top of the cake is a thin layer consisting of a small group of people who have the highest economic and social status. At the bottom of the cake is another thin layer representing those whose economic and social status is very low and whom the community regards as of little account. Between these two extremes, at various levels, lie thicker layers, which represent the great majority of the population. The chief objection to this analogy is that the divisions between social classes are not as definite as those between the layers of a cake.

Social classes are not organized groups like families or communities. Rather, they are useful concepts. They are also social realities, but only in the sense that the people of any complex society can be divided roughly into a few large groups in such a way that those in each group have about the

Class structure in the United States. Shoe shines are almost invariably given by blacks. Some argue that this is because society fails to offer better opportunities.

---

[1]There are many ways to classify the population. One imaginative survey undertook to see if "You are what you eat" is a defensible statement. The survey, covering some 13,000 households, identified five strata: (1) meat and potatoes households (30 percent); (2) child-oriented households: hot dogs, peanut butter, and soft drinks (25 percent); (3) seriously concerned over diet (15 percent); (4) natural-food enthusiasts (15 percent); and (5) sophisticates: quiche, raspberry tofu, and instant gourmet dinner (15 percent).

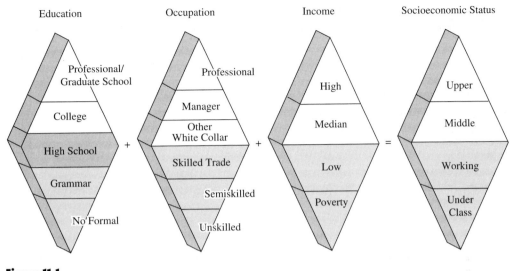

Education		Occupation		Income		Socioeconomic Status
Professional/ Graduate School		Professional		High		Upper
College		Manager		Median		Middle
High School	+	Other White Collar	+		=	
Grammar		Skilled Trade		Low		Working
No Formal		Semiskilled		Poverty		Under Class
		Unskilled				

Figure 11.1

Socioeconomic hierarchies.

same general social standing and other similarities. Because the lines of division among classes are both vague and arbitrary, many individuals are difficult to place. The more class layers there are, the greater the difficulty of distinguishing between them and determining just where individuals fit.

In order to classify individuals into socioeconomic classes, it is generally necessary to average a variety of characteristics. This is normally done by a weighting system; points are allocated for various characteristics, these points are added up, and individuals within certain ranges of points are assigned to certain categories. For example, people with advanced education may get many points, but high income also confers many points, so somebody with high income and low education and somebody with low income and advanced education may fall into the same socioeconomic group after the weighting process. Using the weighting system allows us to organize people into upper class, upper middle class, middle class, lower middle class, and lower class. Some of the characteristics looked at are occupation, sources of income, type of housing, and the area within which the subject lives. Figure 11.2 presents typical class divisions and characteristics.

Most people do have some idea of the social class to which they belong, though they may not give it the same name that a sociologist would. For example, a family may think of themselves as ordinary people; a sociologist might classify them as belonging to the lower middle class. Members of a social class recognize that they have more in common with others at a similar social level than they do with those above or below them. Also, as we have noted, they are likely to live in those areas and do those kinds of work that bring them into especially close association with people like themselves.

The Family Basis of Social Class.   The primary unit of stratification is the family, for except in rare cases all members of a family are regarded as belonging to the same stratum, or layer. Much the same social status is shared by all members of the immediate family

Class levels	Approximate percentage of population	Likely occupation	Likely education	Religious affiliation	Approximate annual income (some overlap between classes)	Residential neighborhood	Leisure activities	Newspaper reading
I. Upper class 	5	Independently wealthy Lawyers Professionals Doctors Accountants	Seventeen or more years of school, college, and beyond	Jewish Episcopalian Congregational A few Roman Catholics	Over 200,000 Some extremely high Much inherited wealth	Very elite neighborhood Expensive houses	Music, cultural Travel "Serious" reading Elite clubs Active sports (tennis, golf, sailing)	*Wall Street Journal New York Times*
II. Upper middle class 	20	Small businesspeople Teachers Lawyers Professors Managers of small firms	Around fifteen years College	Congregational Jewish Some Catholics	Between 70,000 and 250,000 Most earned income by salary	Good neighborhoods Moderately expensive homes	Cultural events Formal parties Travel Racquetball Surf the Internet	*Wall Street Journal New York Times*
III. Middle class 	35	Administrative Clerical Chain store managers Technicians Salespeople	High school and some college	Methodist Baptist Many Catholics	Between 25,000 and 70,000 Salary Some wages	Private homes, medium sized Some tract homes	Visiting friends Television Movies Some "light" reading	Local paper
IV. Lower middle class 	25	Skilled labor Industrial workers	Ten to twelve years	Methodist Many Catholics	20,000 to 35,000 Hourly wages	Apartments Small tract homes Trailers	Visiting relatives Television Detective novels Observer sports (baseball, football) Bowling	*National Enquirer*
V. Lower class 	15	Unskilled labor Unemployed	Elementary school	None Pentecostal Extreme fundamentalist groups	Under 20,000 Poverty and welfare	Blighted areas Poor apartments	Television Visiting relatives Bowling	None

Figure 11.2

Social classes: Sociologists do not completely agree about how many classes there are in the United States because classes overlap considerably and there are not sharp breaks between them. It is generally possible, however, to identify five or six basic social classes. (Source: Authors' modification of U.S. Bureau of the Census, "Money Income and Poverty Status of Families and Persons in the United States.")

group. As a rule, the most important factors in determining social class are the occupation and the wealth and income of the breadwinners in the family.

Such occupations as law and medicine, high government positions, and the management of large business enterprises yield considerable prestige because they require more than average ability and training; other occupations, such as keeping small stores or working at skilled trades, are regarded as respectable; but some occupations, especially those that require only unskilled manual labor, are looked down on by many members of the community. In general, the regard in which an occupation is held is closely correlated with the income it yields, although there are exceptions to this rule. A federal judge, for example, may have more prestige but less income than the owner of a catering service.

Membership in social classes tends to be transmitted in the same family line from generation to generation because children are likely to acquire much the same attitudes and modes of living as their parents, to receive similar educational advantages, to enter similar occupations, and to inherit whatever wealth their parents may possess.

Social Mobility

Any class system is somewhat inconsistent with the democratic ideal of equal opportunities for life, liberty, and the pursuit of happiness. Certainly, lower-class children do not have the same opportunities as those in the upper classes. In the United States, we try to avoid thinking in terms of "low class" and "high class," but there is no escaping the fact that some people are economically and socially better off than some other people. Fortunately, it is also a fact that the United States offers an almost unlimited environment in which people are able to move up—and sometimes down—with respect to how society views them and how they view themselves. Thus, in the United States we have a remarkably **open class system,** a system in which class lines are not definite, and for many people the possibilities of moving upward are excellent.

Mobility in a class system is much greater than in caste or estate systems. It is difficult to measure, however, and it may vary considerably in different societies. There is normally thought to be a great deal of upward social mobility in the United States. The term **social mobility** refers to the comparative ease with which we can improve (or worsen) our social and economic standing in society. In fact, it was a nineteenth-century U.S. novelist who gave his name, Horatio Alger, to stories of ordinary Americans who have improved their social and economic status through commitment, dedication, hard work, education, thrift, moral rectitude, and, very often, help from family, friends, teachers, employers, and scholarships and government programs.[2] Downward mobility is also a possibility, and although there is not much proof, many believe that the spoiled children of the idle rich will eventually land in the gutter.

In a 1960s study, Gerhard Lenski found that 33 percent of all males in the period from 1945 to 1965 were upwardly mobile. Downward mobility at that time was clearly present but its incidence was not well documented. In the 1970s, the U.S. expectation of upward mobility began to erode. A study by Featherman and Hauser in 1978 found that one-fourth of all persons aged 21 to 53 had slid to an occupational level below their first jobs. A study by Greg J. Duncan and colleagues compared mobility between the 1968–1979 and 1980–1987 periods and found that the incidence of upward mobility for those in the lower class declined while upward mobility for those at the upper income levels rose, leading to a shrinking middle class. Just as for those in the Lenski study, upward mobility was not assured in the 1980s.

In the early 1990s there was much concern about an increase in downward mobility. Experts felt that many children would not achieve the social and income levels that their

---

[2]Horatio Alger was born in 1834. He wrote hundreds of stories with titles such as *Ragged Dick* or *Luck and Pluck* in which his young heroes went "from rags to riches." Alger worked hard, saved up a fortune, and gave his money away. He died poor in 1899.

parents before them had achieved. However, Raymond Wong found in 1994 that social mobility has not changed much in most industrialized nations. In 2000 and early 2001, as the U.S. economy was advancing at a fast pace, there was less concern about downward mobility, and there was significant discussion of twenty-year-old dot-com billionaires. When the economy is expanding, concern about one's relative position decreases somewhat. (In mid-2001, the U.S. economy slowed, many of the dot-com billionaires were reduced to millionaires, and there was a bit more concern about relative positions.)

One of the best ways to advance from one class to another is through education (see Table 11.1). Education allows individuals access to job possibilities that otherwise would not be open to them, and in doing so it raises their income.

One method that *doesn't* lead to class advancement is to increase income without attention to other issues. Social scientist Susan Mayer developed a statistical model that predicted what would happen to a child's prospects for success in life if the annual income of the child's family were doubled. She found that if the increased income were the only factor in the life of a child in that family, the child's chances of becoming a successful adult would hardly improve at all. Intelligence, determination, good health, and a willingness to cooperate were far better predictors of advancement.

Table 11.1

Starting Salary Offers to New College Graduates in 2003, by Selected Fields of Study

BUSINESS	
Accounting	$42,005
Economics/Finance	$40,413
Marketing	$35,698
HUMANITIES, SOCIAL SCIENCES	
Communications	$29,586
Psychology	$27,194
English	$35,538
ENGINEERING	
Chemical	$51,301
Computer	$52,722
Electrical	$50,615
HI-TECH	
Computer science	$50,352
Information systems	$41,414

Source: Salary Survey, NACE, Winter 2003.

Economic and Social Inequality

We focus on an individual's money income because that is what we collect figures on. True inequality depends on much more. For example, say you have a choice of poor health and an income of $100,000 per year or good health and $25,000 per year. Which would you choose? Probably the latter, for people's true income includes all aspects of their position. Because we cannot measure true income, most studies focus on monetary income and individuals' standard of living.

Even if we focus on money income, we still have difficulty in determining how much of a problem income inequality is. For example, how much poverty do we have in the United States today? That depends on how the word is defined. In terms of what poverty means in India or China, or even in terms of what it meant in this country or Europe a hundred years ago, we have very little poverty. Almost no one here literally dies of starvation, but tens of thousands do in Africa.

It is true that there are homeless persons who sleep on the streets or in all kinds of makeshift shelters such as large packing cartons in the cities of the United States, but this is most often because of other kinds of social problems (a spirit of independence carried to psychotic extremes, for instance, or policies of releasing marginally competent people from mental facilities). It is not because there are no programs or funds available to shelter this population.

On the other hand, large numbers of people depend on welfare payments to live, and many who do not receive such payments have incomes so small that they must live in depressing or unsafe surroundings, wear shabby clothes, and buy cheap food. They cannot afford to spend money for travel, entertainment, or education, and if they are out of work or if an emergency such as serious illness arises, their only recourse is public aid or charity.

In 1996 Congress passed a welfare reform law designed to drastically reduce the number of people on long-term welfare assistance and to help them improve their economic status through measures such as education, job training, child care facilities, and medical assistance. Two results of this law have been to put millions of low-income people in jobs and to reduce welfare rolls significantly. However, some of the people who have found jobs still do not make enough money to support themselves and their families; many people are somewhat worse off than they were under the previous system; and there is still a large population of low-income people. Advocates of this reform law hope that as the reforms have more time to work, and as government modifies the law when people's unmet needs become severe, there will be a continued reduction in the numbers of people who need welfare assistance. This is a social issue that will continue to be in the news in the twenty-first century.

Causes of Income Inequality

Differences in income arise directly from three sources: variations in earnings from personal services, differences in the amounts of property owned, and variations in transfer payments from government. Differences in the earnings of individuals are the most important. These differences are based partly on occupation and partly on the personal qualities of those engaged in each occupation. The most basic of the factors

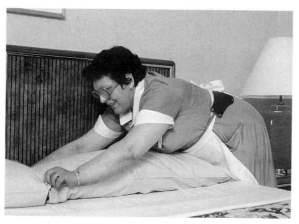

Hotel maids are often poorly paid.

that determine income variations between occupational groups is demand and supply.

In general, occupations that are not easy to enter because they require special aptitudes and long training are highly paid because the supply of workers is small relative to the demand. On the other hand, occupations classified as common labor, which anyone can enter with relatively little ability or training, tend to be poorly paid. But within each occupational group there are often great differences in individual earning power, especially at the higher professional and managerial levels.

For example, in 2003 average hourly earnings of construction workers were about $18.00, whereas the average hourly rate for retail trade workers was only about $10.00. Although in recent years the average annual pay in San Jose, California, was almost $41,000, in Birmingham, Alabama, it was only about $30,000. The differences persist, in part, because of differences in the cost of living. Farmers' average annual income (about $24,000 in 2003) is lower because it is cheaper to live in the country; the average pay in California is higher, but so is the cost of a meal or an apartment.

Tables 11.2a–d show the distribution of income by percentage of families; by regions of the country; by representative states; and by race, gender, and household status. As you can see, income is distributed unequally in the general population and also by place where one lives, by race, by gender, and by occupation.

Measuring Poverty

In order to measure poverty in a country, we must define the term. It isn't easy to do so. In the United States, the Social Security Administration and the Bureau of the Census attempt to do this by determining the **poverty threshold,** that is, the minimum amount of income needed to maintain a living standard above the poverty level. Obviously, the poverty threshold will be lower for an individual than for a family, and it will differ for families of different size. It will also change with fluctuations in the cost of living.

To be above the poverty level, an individual or family must have enough income to obtain food, clothing, and shelter that will maintain health, plus some margin for other necessary expenditures. Just what minimum income is essential at any given time and place cannot be determined with any great precision, and hence any specific poverty threshold is to some degree arbitrary. However, after a careful and objective weighing of the facts, the determined cutoff can have enough meaning to be useful. Each year, the Bureau of the Census publishes poverty thresholds for single ("unrelated") individuals and for families of various sizes. The level at which the poverty level is set is important because that level determines which families receive government assistance.

According to census estimates, the total number of Americans in poverty in 2002 was about 33 million, or 11.7 percent. For a family of four (excluding Alaska and Hawaii), this represented an annual income of about $18,100 in 2002. In 2003 the poverty level for a

Table 11.2a
Money Income of Families by Percentage in the United States, 2001

Under $10,000	5.3%
$10,000–$14,999	4.3%
$15,000–$24,999	11.3%
$25,000–$34,999	11.9%
$35,000–$49,999	15.7%
$50,000–$74,999	20.8%
$75,000 and over	30.7%

Table 11.2c
Median Family Income in Four States, 2001

Hawaii	47,439
New York	42,114
Oklahoma	35,609
West Virginia	29,673

Table 11.2b
Median Family Income by Region, 2001

North	57,000
Midwest	54,096
South	46,688
West	51,966

Table 11.2d
Household Median Money Income by Race, Gender, and Household Status, 2001

White	44,517
Black	29,470
Hispanic	33,565
Male householder	40,715
Female householder	28,142
Married couple	60,471

Source: U.S. Bureau of the Census.

family of four rose to $18,400. As you can see in Figure 11.3, the percentage of people in poverty depends on race and ethnicity. Blacks and Hispanics are much more likely to be in poverty than are whites.

These measures of the number of Americans in poverty should be accepted with some reservations. Undoubtedly, many of those included had incomes that were only temporarily extremely low, or had savings with which to supplement current income, or owned homes and lived in communities where they could get along reasonably well on a small income, or were young people getting help from parents. However, after all such allowances are made, it is clear that a substantial amount of poverty exists in this country.

Reducing Social and Economic Inequality

It would seem that a country as rich as the United States should be able to eliminate poverty, if what we mean by that is just providing everyone with enough income for physical comfort and security.[3] To do so, the United States has instituted a variety of

[3]If we define poverty in relative terms, as many sociologists do, then to some degree the problem will always be with us. No matter how much incomes rise, if we assume the continuance of substantial inequalities, people with relatively low incomes will continue to be deprived of various things that the rest can enjoy.

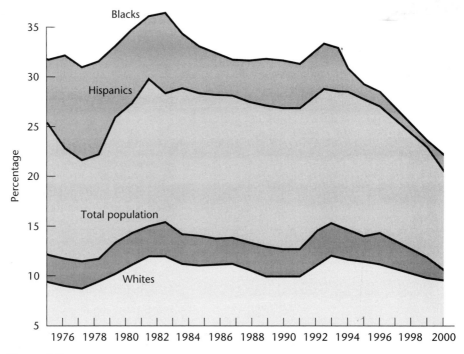

Figure 11.3

Percentage of poverty by race. (Data after 1992 are based on 1990 census controls and are not strictly comparable to earlier data.) (Source: Based on statistics from U.S. Bureau of the Census, *Current Population Reports,* and *Statistical Abstract of the United States.*)

programs including public welfare, unemployment insurance, Medicare, Social Security, and Supplemental Security Income (SSI). In many ways these programs have succeeded, but they have also introduced new problems.

Because few people favor a completely equal distribution of wealth and income, and because neither justice nor expediency would seem to be advanced by such a policy, any practical program for meeting the problems of economic inequality must represent a compromise among several objectives. Such a program should take into account the following:

1. The social importance of raising the standards of living of the people who are at the bottom of the income scale
2. The desirability of an income distribution that the public can accept as more or less just
3. The importance of providing all children with adequate educational and economic opportunities, regardless of their parents' incomes
4. The need to provide adequate health care for all citizens
5. The need for private savings as a source of capital for industry

Homeless women on the streets.

6. The need for adequate incentives to stimulate efficient production and economic progress

If we can eliminate real poverty without creating a class of people who depend permanently on a public welfare benefit, we will have cured one of the worst evils of an unequal income distribution. If we can solve the problem of providing all children with educational and economic opportunities that match their potentials, we will have solved another.

Perhaps we should also seek ways to prevent an excessive concentration of wealth and economic power in the hands of a relatively small number of individuals and families. One of the functions of the progressive income tax is to do just that: People with high incomes pay higher taxes than people with low incomes, and the government uses some of its tax revenue to help pay for low-cost housing, public transportation systems, transfer payments, health care, and other measures that redistribute income. Under some of the programs, such as student loans, wealth is sometimes distributed to people who are far above the poverty line; on the other hand, socially desirable expenses—such as those for higher education—may also be so high that even generous incomes cannot meet these costs.

For many years there has been some question about how effective the income tax is in redistributing income, given that wealthy individuals have often been able to take advantage of many special exemptions and deductions, often called tax loopholes, in the tax laws. Over the years, Congress has changed the tax rates, the loopholes, and the nature of taxation itself. In the 1980s, the progressivity of the income tax was reduced, but at the same time some of the loopholes were eliminated. In the 1990s, income tax progressivity was raised slightly, but it was reduced again in the early 2000s.

Who Are the Upwardly Mobile?

In studies of people who have achieved upward mobility, certain related traits have become evident: race, gender, being an only (or first) child, and a belief in deferred gratification, which is when a person is willing to trade off an immediate pleasure for a future goal. The first and second of these are so important that we treat them in a separate chapter under the subject of discrimination. The third is probably related to income (it has been found that rich people are more likely to have only one child) and is not within an individual's control. The last trait, however, can be and is probably the most important. How much a belief in

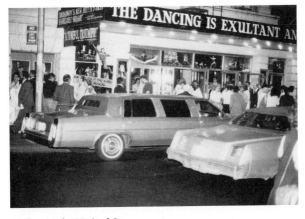

Riches in the United States.

Up, Down, and Out

If you pay $25,000, can you get your name in the *Social Register*? If you drop your subscription, can you get your name out of the *Social Register*? Should you let people know you are in the *Social Register*? Do you use the *Social Register* for a phone book? Do you know anyone who knows what the *Social Register* is?

To some people, these are important questions. The book comes out annually and tries to limit the number of names to around 33,000. Some people get into it without trying; some people have always been there and can't get out; some people are in it by virtue of their office (U.S. presidents, for instance). Marrying up won't get you in and might get your spouse deleted. If you get in and want to be sure to stay in, don't get divorced, start an acting career, or go to jail.

deferred gratification can be fostered is debatable. Your beliefs are, in large part, transmitted from your parents through continually supportive feedback, and by the time you reach college age, these beliefs are probably set.

Thus, for most of you, whether you are or are not to be upwardly mobile may have already been determined and is partially built into your personality. Of course, luck (such as being in the right place at the right time for a job) plays an important role, and many people who have the traits associated with being upwardly mobile may find themselves disappointed. For example, if you had a crisis the night before you took the college boards, you may have done poorly on them, which may have played a role in whether you won a scholarship. Bad luck is not pleasant, but it is a fact of life and should not be considered unusual. No one ever said life is fair.

Discussions of mobility often overlook one simple fact: Room at the top is always limited. When we talk about social mobility, we are apt to think of opportunities to move upward in the social scale, but we must remember that as some people, or their children, move up, others, or their children, are likely to move down. Assuming no increase in the proportionate size of the upper class, a high degree of mobility means only that it is fairly easy for some citizens who have ambition, energy, and intelligence to move up the social ladder and displace those who are less ambitious or less capable.

What are the conditions that contribute to social mobility? Probably most important of all is social change. In a changing society, the old order is always being disturbed, and new ways of achieving wealth or position keep appearing. For the past two hundred years, industrialization, with its ever newer methods of production and types of business organization, has provided opportunities to climb the economic and social ladder. Migration and geographic expansion also have provided opportunities. In the United States in the 1990s, rapid technological progress created new occupations and changed the nature and requirements for old ones, and this process will continue in the future.

Rising Incomes and Class Distinctions

Although the average U.S. standard of living has been high for a century or more compared with that of the rest of the world, in the depressed 1930s it was possible to say that one-third of the nation was ill fed, ill housed, and ill clothed. For that matter, many of those somewhat above the lowest third were living in what would seem today a rather meager fashion. In the relatively prosperous 1920s, the situation had been a little better, but even then the incomes of many were low compared with the present.

Although neither inequality nor social classes have been eliminated, it remains true that in recent years an increasing proportion of the people in the United States have been

Table 11.3

Distribution of Household Income in 2001 CPI-U-RS Adjusted Dollars

Year	Under $10,000	$10,000–$14,999	$15,000–$24,999	$25,000–$49,999	$50,000–$74,999	$75,000 and over
			PERCENT DISTRIBUTION			
1970	13.2	22.4	15.4	21.5	18.0	9.6
1980	11.5	23.4	13.9	18.4	19.4	13.4
1985	11.5	22.3	13.9	17.2	18.7	16.4
1990	10.6	21.2	13.3	17.3	18.9	18.6
1995	10.0	22.3	12.9	16.3	18.4	20.1
2000	8.7	19.9	12.5	15.4	18.6	24.9
2001	9.0	20.2	12.4	15.4	18.4	24.6

Source: U.S. Bureau of the Census.

able to attain what has traditionally been regarded as the middle-class mode of life. To some degree, class distinctions are blurred today because many skilled manual workers have such good incomes that they can no longer be identified as members of the lower classes by the houses they live in, the clothes they wear, or their leisure activities. Table 11.3 gives you an idea of the distribution of U.S. income over time.

The social stratification of European societies of the seventeenth or eighteenth centuries could be reasonably well represented by a pyramid because most people were near the bottom and very few were at the top of the social scale. Changes in the composition of the social scale have gradually but steadily occurred because of technological changes. There are still comparatively few people near the top, but there has been a great expansion of the middle classes, and many have moved from the middle to near the top. The expansion of opportunities in the Internet and computer-related businesses has meant that computer literacy and imagination, not social class, are the central requirements for entry to a higher class. As all these changes continue, there has been a corresponding shrinkage of the lower classes. In the United States today, far more people occupy a position in the middle than near the bottom, and our class structure can no longer be represented as a pyramid.

Class Consciousness in the United States

Most Americans are not highly **class conscious,** that is, overly concerned about their status in society and the standing of other people in relation to them. Ambition usually takes the form of a desire for a more satisfying job, more income, or more personal prestige. Any resulting change in social status is usually secondary or wholly incidental. Relatively few Americans have a strong desire to move into a higher social class except insofar as this may help them to achieve other objectives.

Why are Americans so comparatively free of class consciousness? Partly, the reasons are historical. We never did have a hereditary nobility, and throughout our early history rapid growth and expansion resulted in considerable social mobility. It is more than a coincidence that, although a number of our presidents have come from wealthy or aristocratic families, some have had very humble origins.

In more recent times, other factors have tended to keep class consciousness at a low level. One is the general rise in standards of living. Even though people may not change their position in the social scale, they feel they are making progress when their incomes rise and when they can improve their way of life. Also, in the United States in recent years differences in income between different social classes have somewhat diminished.

Another factor that has tended to reduce class consciousness and discontent is **horizontal mobility,** the opportunities that exist for moving from one job to another, and oftentimes to a better-liked job. This horizontal mobility gives people the feeling of making progress, even though the change has little effect on income or social status. Finally, in our society there are many ways of achieving recognition in special groups such as political parties, churches, and fraternal societies, and to many people this is more important than moving into a higher social class.

Class Consciousness and the Labor Movement

In his criticism of capitalist society, Karl Marx, the nineteenth-century father of communism and one of the founders of the field of sociology, divided the populations of industrial societies into two classes—**capitalists,** or owners of the means of production, and the **proletariat,** or workers, who were exploited by the capitalists. The proletariat's labor was used to further the capitalists' own profits, without consideration of the workers' needs. Marx felt that the increasing exploitation of workers would lead to an increasing class consciousness among the proletariat. Marx's division of the classes is not the only division. Max Weber, an outspoken critic of Marx's views, argued that property is not the sole basis of class. Instead class is determined by the three *p*'s—property, prestige, and power. Weber's more general concept of class is accepted by numerous sociologists, but their views of how to quantify prestige and power often differ substantially.

In the early 1900s, as the labor movement grew there was considerable concern that this growth would increase class consciousness in the United States. There is little evidence, however, that it has done so, and the development of unionism in the United States has not been a class movement. Rather, it has represented attempts on the part of particular groups of workers to improve their own economic position. Working people as a whole have never developed any strong feeling of solidarity. One indication of this is the wide diversity in working-class people's views on social, economic, and political questions. For example, the Teamsters Union has often supported the Republican party, and the United Automobile Workers Union has traditionally supported the Democrats.

Marx believed that under capitalistic exploitation the condition of the workers would become worse and worse. Eventually they would rise up in revolt, seize the means of production, and establish a socialist state under the "dictatorship of the proletariat." Actually, the standard of living of the working people in most industrial countries, quite contrary to Marx's prediction, has been rising for the last hundred years and more. Therefore most sociologists today tend to use a modification of Weber's concept of class rather than Marx's concept.

Some Conclusions about the U.S. Class System

In spite of the statement in the Declaration of Independence that "all men are created equal," everyone knows that in many ways people are not equal. They are not born with equal potentialities for learning and achieving, nor are they born into equally favorable social environments. Nevertheless, equality before the law and equality of opportunity are strongly cherished democratic ideals. Over the years, we have been striving in the United States to come closer to these ideals, and since the Declaration of Independence was written, we have made considerable progress toward them.

Key Points

- Three types of social stratification are estates, castes, and social classes.
- The existence of social mobility allows people to move from one class to another and makes the social and economic stratification more acceptable to society.
- Three sources of income inequality are variations in earnings from personal services, differences in the amounts of property owned, and variations in transfer payments from government.
- The poverty threshold in the United States is that level of income needed to maintain a living standard above the poverty level. In 2002 the poverty level was set at about $18,100 for the average family of four.
- Any practical program for meeting the problems of economic inequality must take into account the poorest people, the need for health care, justice, children's rights, and the need for savings and incentives.
- The U.S. economic class system is not strongly developed, in part due to historical factors and in part due to the market economy, the government, and the underlying U.S. ideology that sees class consciousness as a negative trait.

Some Important Terms

apartheid system (235)
capitalists (248)
caste (234)
class conscious (247)
estate (234)

hierarchy (233)
horizontal mobility (248)
karma (234)
open class system (239)
poverty threshold (242)

proletariat (248)
social class (236)
social mobility (239)
stratification (233)
transmigration (234)

Questions for Review and Discussion

1. Name the three principal types of social stratification and briefly describe the nature of each.
2. How has the position of blacks in our society resembled, and how has it differed from, the position of a low Hindu caste?
3. Societies can be stratified in a variety of ways. What is the major form of stratification in modern industrial societies?
4. What difficulties are encountered when we attempt to divide the people of an industrial society into clear-cut social classes?
5. Why is social class a family matter rather than an individual matter?
6. What are some of the principal factors that may contribute to class mobility?
7. Why is upward social mobility necessarily limited in any society?

8. Why are Americans not highly class conscious?

9. What factors have been operating in the United States in recent years to reduce class distinctions? Can you name any factors that, in your opinion, have had the opposite effect?

10. Why has the kind of class conflict Karl Marx predicted never developed anywhere?

11. Characterize the U.S. class system from the standpoint of (a) the sharpness of class distinctions, (b) the degree of class consciousness, and (c) the amount of social mobility.

12. Is U.S. society becoming more stratified? Defend your point of view.

*I*nternet Questions

1. Using http://hindunet.org/varna, list the four social orders in India's caste system. In ancient India, were people born into their caste?

2. Looking at the U.S. Department of Health and Human Services' poverty guidelines, http://aspe.hhs.gov/poverty/index.shtml, what is the most recent poverty threshold for a family of six? In Alaska? In 2000?

3. Go to www.doi.gov/hrm/pmanager/st3f.html, the site of the Department of the Interior, Upward Mobility Program. What is the purpose of this program?

4. Go to www.jobweb.com/SalaryInfo/default.htm and choose the latest information for salaries. What is the average salary for a liberal arts major in criminal justice? What is the top job for the latest graduates?

5. Using the information found at www.census.gov/hhes/www/saipe/faq.html, what is SAIPE? What statistics does the program produce for all individual counties of the United States?

*F*or Further Study

Brown, Michael K., *Race, Money, and the American Welfare State*, Ithaca, NY: Cornell University Press, 1999.

Chamberlin, J. Gordon, *Upon Whom We Depend: The American Poverty System*, New York: Peter Lang, 1999.

Crompton, Rosemary, ed., *Renewing Class Analysis*, Malden, MA: Blackwell, 2000.

Frug, Gerald E., *City Making: Building Communities without Building Walls*, Princeton, NJ: Princeton University Press, 1999.

Greider, William, *One World, Ready or Not: The Manic Logic of Global Capitalism*, New York: Simon & Schuster, 1997.

Hooks, Bell, *Where We Stand: Class Matters*, New York: Routledge Press, 2000.

Kuttner, Robert, *Everything for Sale: The Virtues and Limits of Markets*, New York: Twentieth Century Fund/Knopf, 1997.

Levine, Rhonda F., ed., *Social Class and Stratification: Classic Statements and Theoretical Debates*, Lanham, MD: Rowman & Littlefield, 1998.

Malhotra, Anshu, *Gender, Caste, and Religious Identities: Restructuring Class in Colonial Punjab*, New York: Oxford University Press, 2002.

Manza, Jeff, *Social Cleavages and Political Change: Voter Alignment and U.S. Party Coalitions*, New York: Oxford University Press, 1999.

Rose, Fred, *Coalitions across the Class Divide: Lessons from the Labor, Peace and Environmental Movements*, Ithaca, NY: Cornell University Press, 2000.

WWW   Bureau of Labor Statistics   www.bls.gov

WWW   National Association of Colleges and Employers   www.naceweb.org

WWW   National Center for Children in Poverty   www.nccp.org

WWW   Occupational Outlook Handbook   www.bls.gov/oco

WWW   U.S. Bureau of the Census, Income   www.census.gov/hhes/www/income.html

WWW   U.S. Bureau of the Census, Poverty   www.census.gov/hhes/www/poverty.html

WWW   U.S. Department of Health and Human Services   www.os.dhhs.gov

Stratification, Minorities, and Discrimination

chapter **12**

After reading this chapter, you should be able to:

- List four reasons for racial prejudice
- Distinguish between minority and dominant groups
- Discuss the race problem in the United States today
- Distinguish Chicanos from Latinos and explain the problem of illegal Mexican immigration
- Discuss briefly the problems of religious minorities
- Discuss briefly the problems of sexual minorities
- Give arguments for and against age discrimination

Wrong never lies in unequal rights, it lies in the pretension of equal rights.

—Friedrich Nietzsche

In Chapter 11, social stratification was considered primarily along economic and social lines. Societies are also stratified along racial, ethnic, and cultural lines. Questions of discrimination based on a person's race, religion, ethnicity, age, gender, or even sexual preferences, and issues of busing, job quotas, and right to jobs—these issues are not of the past, but rather appear daily in the media.

Many of you may feel that you are well aware of the problems, either because you have lived them or because they have been extensively discussed at home or in school. This chapter is necessary, nonetheless, both to provide you with a sense of the history and dimension of the issue and to give you a standard by which to judge your own views. The issues of equality and discrimination are as pertinent today as they were fifty years ago, when social scientists first considered these issues.

Race and Ethnicity

Although all human beings belong to the same species, *Homo sapiens,* they exhibit many physical and cultural variations, including differences in height, weight, skin color, and the shape of the head and face. Any group of people, if isolated from others over a long period of time, will develop differentiating physical characteristics. Thus it is possible to distinguish groups of people by these characteristics and to call those groups a race.

To classify the peoples of the world by race is a problem; there are few national dividing lines and those dividing lines are arbitrary. In addition, a range of gradations within races can be found. One classification has divided most people into three groups based on physical variations—Caucasoids, Mongoloids, and Negroids. The problem with this classification is twofold. First, it reflects social constructions that are loosely based on biological differences. However, the biological differences between so-called races are often far fewer than the biological differences between individuals of the same "race." What do we mean by social construction? Consider hair color: There are redheads, brownheads, and blondheads, yet because our social system doesn't distinguish among them, hair color does not delineate race. But skin color does, not because blacks and whites are inherently different, but because our social system differentiates them.

Second, over time migration has led to a mixing of the races, and ranges of gradation within races can be found. Thus race as a classification system is losing significance. The U.S. Bureau of the Census dealt with this classification problem when it prepared the year 2000 census forms by listing a large number of ethnicities, such as black, white, Hispanic, of Hispanic origin, Pacific Islander, and many others, including "Other," leaving people to classify themselves in any way they pleased. Golf star Tiger Woods, who is of Thai and African American descent, tried to devise a unique term for his heritage, and this may mark a trend. The year 2000 is not the first time the Census Bureau has changed its race classification system, and you should not be surprised to see more changes in the terminology used to describe race. Some even argue that the government should be prevented from collecting information on race because having that information leads the government to be less race-neutral in its policies than many believe it should be. Why should the government care how many people consider themselves black or Hispanic? We are all Americans.

Another way of classifying groups of people is by their ethnicity—whereas race is a biological classification system, ethnicity is a cultural classification. An **ethnic group** is a group of people who identify with each other on the basis of common ancestry and cultural heritage.

In popular usage, ethnic differences are often confused with racial differences. Ethnic differences between groups in matters such as nationality, language, and religion are important, but they do not constitute differences in race. It would be incorrect, for example, to speak of the French race or the German race. France and Germany are adjacent countries, and the people who live on one side of the border are physically little different from those who live on the other side. It is also misleading to call the Jews a race. They have no physical characteristics by which they can be dependably distinguished from non-Jews in our population. What holds them together as a group is primarily religion, history, and social tradition—that is, ethnic ties.

Racial and ethnic differences fall into distinct categories and are largely independent of each other. The frequently made assumption that race determines culture has little scientific or factual basis. Where different racial groups have lived in close association for some time, as in Hawaii, they are likely to have much the same culture; on the other hand, members of the same race living in different parts of the world often exhibit cultural patterns that are radically different. To see the truth of this last statement, we need only compare the culture of black Americans with that of blacks living in the Congo basin of Africa.

Questions of Ethnic and Racial Superiority

Some people believe that one race or one ethnic group is innately superior to others in intelligence and creativity, and that this superiority largely explains the high degree of civilization certain groups have been able to achieve. This may seem superficially plausible because many of the recorded scientific and social advances (or at least the ones familiar to whites of European descent) in the last several hundred years have been made by the Caucasians of Europe.

Such a view would be extremely shortsighted. Over the centuries, the particular groups who have taken the lead in the advances of civilization have changed. First it was the Sumerians and the Egyptians; later the people of India and China, the Jews, the Phoenicians, and the Persians; still later the Greeks and Romans; then for a while the Arabs; and finally the peoples of northern and western Europe. But we need go back only two thousand years or less to find Roman writers who looked on the then-primitive Britons and Germans as not only crude and uncivilized but also stupid. In other parts of the world, well-organized societies developed, but they either disintegrated or were destroyed by invaders, disease, or natural disasters. These include the Maya and Inca civilizations in the Americas, and various kingdoms in black Africa south of the Sahara.

There is no convincing scientific evidence to support the contention that some races biologically inherit a greater capacity for development than others. Which society leads the world development of civilization is the result of a combination of other factors such as favorable climate and soil, migrations that stimulated change by bringing together peoples with different cultural backgrounds, and the fortuitous making of some important discoveries and inventions. Such advances tend to lead to further advances, a gradual accumulation of technical skills, an increase in food output, a slow growth of population, and the development of towns and cities. Every group of people has its bright and dull individuals, its great intellects and its idiots.

It is possible that, on average, there are some inherited mental and psychological differences between racial groups, just as there are physical differences. Statistics collected by Richard Herrnstein and Charles Murray in a controversial book entitled *The Bell Curve* suggest that in the United States, on average, Americans of Asian descent score a few points higher than whites on IQ tests, and blacks score about 15 points lower than whites. These statistics, and the usefulness of IQ tests in measuring mental abilities, have been challenged on a variety of levels. But even if the statistics are correct and IQ tests actually measure mental ability, it is not clear whether the difference in scores is inherent in the races or is socially determined. Moreover, averages say nothing about individuals, so most social scientists say that no policy inference can be drawn from such statistics.

Even if some inborn mental and psychological differences exist, they do not necessarily mean superiority or inferiority any more than do differences in skin color, hair texture, or head shape. In any case, such differences are minor compared with the great differences that exist between individuals in every race.

Discussions of race are often emotionally charged. Some social scientists argue that the entire concept of race is socially determined, that it is reflective of the socially imposed divisions and not of the important, inherent divisions. Therefore discussions of race do not belong in social science. We treat the issue of race not because we believe it important, but simply because it is discussed in our society, and we believe it necessary to address issues that are being discussed. Regardless of whether the concept of race is a meaningful concept in a democracy, the important thing is to treat each person as a human being, to judge on that person's own merits, and to provide every opportunity to develop and use whatever capabilities that person possesses.

Ethnic Cleansing

Ethnic divisions affect every country, and in many ways they are worse abroad than they are in the United States. Let's consider two cases where they are particularly bad: Bosnia and the countries of central Africa.

Bosnia

In Bosnia there is significant hatred among the many different factions that make up the population of the country. The most numerous are Bosnians, Serbs, and Croatians. Bosnians, who are primarily Muslims, make up about two-fifths of the population; Serbs, who are mainly Eastern Orthodox Christians, make up about one-third of the population; and Croats, who are primarily Roman Catholic, make up about one-fifth of the population. This diversity in the area has existed for over a thousand years and has been the cause of continuing dissension. When Yugoslavia collapsed in 1991, that dissent broke into widespread and devastating political, economic, and religious fighting.

The various factions embarked on programs of "ethnic cleansing." As one side or another was temporarily victorious, the temporarily defeated were killed, tortured, or driven from their homes, causing most of the rest of the world to worry about the stability of the country and the fate of its people. Efforts by many countries, including several European powers and the United States, resulted in an international conference held in Dayton, Ohio, in 1995 that ended the worst of the incidents. However, the hatred aroused and intensified by the ethnic cleansing movement has persisted as the factions flare up and violate the Dayton Accords. Bosnia remains a very unstable political, economic, and religious situation.

Central Africa

In the early 1990s, the world became aware of a fierce tribal war in the central African country of Rwanda, where two principal tribes, the Hutu and the Tutsi, tried to exterminate each other. In 1993 the Hutu tribe was defeated, and hundreds of thousands were killed, mutilated, starved, or otherwise destroyed. Hundreds of thousands more managed to escape into the neighboring country of Burundi. Burundi could not support such a huge number of refugees, and worldwide assistance was only partially effective. In Burundi the Hutu were in the majority but the Tutsi controlled the military, and so the warfare continued. This led to hundreds of thousands of refugees escaping to the neighboring countries of Zaire and Uganda.

The influx of refugees into Zaire upset the ethnic and political balance there between Hutus and Tutsis, and hundreds of thousands of members of both tribes were killed. In 1997 there was a radical change of government and even the country's name was changed (from Zaire to Democratic Republic of Congo). While international organizations tried to find solutions, in 1997 the situation in Zaire became so intolerable for the Rwandan Hutu and other Rwandan refugees that those who had survived the warfare made their way back to Rwanda.

Because large numbers of members of these tribes live in all of the countries of central Africa, the Hutu/Tutsi conflict is not confined to any one of these countries. The Congo is mineral rich and the competition for the land and its resources exacerbates the rivalries in this politically unstable area. Political alliances shift often. In 2002 the first Tutsi president of Rwanda signed a peace accord with the Congo, which agreed to a disarming of Hutu militiamen. The conflict is far from resolved and will continue to give rise to international concern into the indefinite future, but in the early 2000s the ethnic ferocity had diminished from the heights it reached in the mid- and late 1990s .

Mass graves of victims of genocide in Bosnia.

Racial and Ethnic Prejudice and Discrimination

Race relations vary greatly in different societies and in different social situations. In some cases there is relatively little friction between members of different races. **Prejudice**—an adverse judgment or opinion formed beforehand or without knowledge or examination of the facts—exists, but ethnic barriers are not sufficient to prevent considerable social contact and frequent intermarriages. This seems to be the situation today in Hawaii, where the principal racial classifications are Caucasian and Asian/Pacific Islander. Though the various ethnic groups have not yet lost their sense of identity, residentially, economically, and educationally they are nearly integrated. But there are other places in the world where prejudice and **discrimination**—actions, behavior, or treatment based on prejudice—are intense and where racial segregation is the accepted pattern.

What is the explanation for these great variations? Many people feel that prejudice is inevitable, that it is an inherited aversion. But the belief that human beings inherit attitudes has long been discredited by psychologists, and racial prejudice cannot be accounted for by any such simple explanation. Moreover, attitude and prejudice need not necessarily lead to discriminatory actions.

Writers have suggested various reasons for racial prejudice. Prominent among these are:

1. Influence of tradition
2. Psychological need of individuals to belong to a particular, identifiable group
3. Building up of the ego by cultivating a feeling of superiority
4. Usefulness of prejudice as an economic and political weapon

Each of these could be expanded on enormously, but we will leave that to sociology courses. Here, we simply want you to consider your own attitudes, to ask yourself whether they reflect prejudice, and if so to consider the reasons behind that prejudice. After you've done that, take the next step and ask yourself whether your prejudices show up in discriminatory actions. If they do, evaluate whether you find those actions justified.

The Melting Pot

Because of its heterogeneous population and the tendency of immigrant groups ultimately to become assimilated, the United States has often been called the melting pot. Although the white colonial population was predominantly British, other nationalities were also represented. During the nineteenth century, this country received 30 million immigrants, and in the early twentieth century more millions arrived. A few came from almost every section of the world, but the great majority were Caucasians from Europe. In the last thirty years, immigration from Asian countries to the United States has been high and will likely continue to be high through the early 2000s.

The groups whose basic patterns of life were not too unlike those of the early British settlers became assimilated in a relatively short time; others were assimilated more slowly. But from the beginning there were non-Caucasian groups whose assimilation seemed impossible because they differed not only culturally but also racially from the majority of the American people. Today there are still unassimilated groups, including Hispanics, who are largely Caucasian but who have come to this country rather recently; Asians, whose physical characteristics set them apart from white Causasians and who

Stratification in the Former Soviet Union

The United States is not the only country that has problems with prejudice and discrimination. These problems are universal. Take the former USSR, for example. It was a country with more than a hundred nationalities. The Russian nationality was the largest (about 50 percent of the population), and it controlled about 90 percent of the top posts in the Soviet Union. Many of the other nationalities were not happy about that Russian dominance.

Until the late 1980s, the Soviet Union dealt with its minority problem by refusing to allow any dissent and by maintaining a secret police force to ensure stability. Joseph Stalin, for example, moved the Crimean Tatars from their native lands when he became displeased with their actions. The communist government kept the nationalist groups under control. When the communist structure collapsed in the late 1980s, so did the communist government's solution to the nationality problem.

The problems surfaced in the late 1980s. Under his policy of glasnost ("openness"), Mikhail Gorbachev reduced the police-imposed limitations on individual action. The result has been unrest among a number of Soviet minority groups, such as that between the Armenians and the Azarbaijani. There was fighting and rioting between the two groups, but the Azarbaijani retained their domination over the Armenians, who, however, continued to grumble. In the 1990s, sufficient minority groups demanded recognition that the entire political structure of the Soviet Union broke apart into a number of different countries. The Soviet Union was no longer a union and a major reason was the nationality problem. Ethnic conflicts persist in the early 2000s in many of the former Soviet republics, especially Chechnya, Armenia, Azerbaijan, and Tajikistan.

sometimes find themselves the subjects of economic and educational discrimination; and individuals of Middle Eastern descent, whose connections with Islam have subjected them to discrimination as the United States struggles to balance the "War on Terror" with individual liberties.

Minorities

If various groups were different but essentially equal, prejudice and discrimination probably would not be a central concern of social scientists. But as was the case with social and economic stratification, racial and ethnic groups are not viewed equally: **minority groups** are groups of people singled out for unequal negative treatment and who regard themselves as objects of collective discrimination, and **dominant groups** are groups of people singled out for positive treatment. The term "dominant group" is used rather than "majority" because the dominant group may be a minority, as was the case with whites in South Africa.

In the remainder of this chapter, we introduce you to the important minority groups in the United States.

Native Americans

The Native Americans were the first settlers of what is now the United States. Although the date is uncertain, anthropologists believe that they came from Asia about 30,000 years ago. After Europeans began to colonize North America, the Native Americans were slowly outnumbered and eventually conquered. Today they are a relatively small minority, and for a long time they were the most isolated of all minority groups and perhaps the most deprived in education. Recently, Native Americans have taken the initiative in efforts to increase ties with the dominant U.S. culture, to improve their educational and employment opportunities, and in some cases to restore lands taken in the eighteenth and early nineteenth centuries by procedures that Native Americans have attacked in the courts.

The policies of the dominant white population toward Native Americans have undergone changes in the past century from (1) enforced isolation and segregation, to (2) forced integration into U.S. society, with almost disastrous results for the Native Americans culturally, economically, and physically, to (3) a policy of much more gradual assimilation. The present government policy toward them is based on the Indian Reorganization Act of 1934, which was designed to encourage Native American tribes to revive their own traditions and to manage their own political and economic affairs. Although many Native Americans choose to live on reservations, they can live where they like; they are U.S. citizens and can vote; they pay certain taxes, and they receive Social Security benefits; they may own private property; and they are free to leave the reservation at will and to seek employment anywhere they wish. But off the reservations they sometimes encounter prejudice and have difficulty in adjusting to the white culture. Also, some of them are handicapped by poor health, a lack of education and skills, and the language barrier. Each of the tribes has its own language or dialect, which is usually very difficult for a person who is not a member of the particular tribe to learn. According to the federal Bureau of Indian Affairs, there were originally about three hundred different languages spoken by Native Americans in what is now the United States, and possibly as many as two hundred still survive. If in addition the tribe is isolated, the processes of education and assimilation are extremely slow. For instance, it is still the case that many Navajos, one of the largest tribes in the United States, do not yet speak English.

African Americans[1]

Blacks constitute approximately 35 million people, or 12 percent of the U.S. population. American blacks are for the most part descendants of slaves brought over to the United States in the seventeenth, eighteenth, and early nineteenth centuries. According to one estimate, at least 14 to 15 million black slaves were landed in the Americas, North and South, from 1600 to the latter part of the nineteenth century.

The African Origins of U.S. Blacks.   The main source of slaves in the seventeenth and eighteenth centuries was the Gulf of Guinea in Africa. This area was more densely populated than most of Africa, and as merchants had already established trade with the outside world in ivory and gold, it was easy to provide slaves also. The trade routes of the Guinea people were evidence of a relatively advanced culture. Although they were a nonliterate people, the inhabitants of this area were among the leaders of black Africa in agriculture, metalwork, pottery, and sculpture.

---

[1]Significant debate continues about whether "African American," "Afro-American," or "people of color" should be substituted for "black."

An illustration shows the cramped quarters on a slave ship.

As early as the fifteenth century, Spain and Portugal imported slaves from Africa, but the first ship of slaves did not arrive in America until 1619, when it landed blacks in Virginia for labor in the English colonies. Plantation owners needed a large force of controllable workers, and black slaves were the answer to this need.

Although importation of slaves into the United States became illegal in 1808, the need for a controllable workforce did not subside, and thousands of slaves were smuggled in despite the laws. These practices continued until the Civil War, when, in 1863, Abraham Lincoln signed the Emancipation Proclamation. Abolitionists were a strong force in the North, but aside from humanitarian concerns, political leaders also saw emancipation as a way to cripple the South further during the war.

The Emancipation Proclamation changed the legal status of slaves but not their social status. The systematic legal segregation of blacks was promoted by what were called Jim Crow laws,[2] and the voting rights of blacks were effectively blocked in the southern states. White supremacy propaganda became intense and was often accompanied by violence.

The Race Problem Today. The problems of present-day blacks in the United States differ from those of any other minority group in this country. To begin with, blacks in the United States are so far removed from their African homeland that much of their cultural heritage is difficult to identify today. Though their cultural patterns may differ somewhat from those of other Americans, they are essentially American by culture, as reflected in their language, customs, education, and religion. But the position of the black minority is still influenced unfavorably by the fact that it is the only minority in this country whose ancestors once served a long period of slavery to whites. No other minority groups have experienced the social and psychological upheavals caused by slavery, followed by sudden emancipation and then by a long period of discrimination and segregation, some of it enforced by law. In addition, blacks tend to differ from whites in skin color, hair, and features more than other minority racial groups, and this has contributed to the strong personal prejudice that sometimes exists between whites and blacks.

Although the status of blacks has advanced in many ways in recent decades, they still suffer from prejudice and discrimination and from handicaps that are the legacy of past discrimination.

---

[2]The name Jim Crow is thought to have come from a character in a popular minstrel song written by Thomas D. Rice in 1832.

I vory and Ebony or Evory and Ibony?

Over the years there has been a considerable amount of mixing of the races. Much of this mixing occurred under slavery when slave owners fathered children by black mothers. The great abolitionist leader Frederick Douglass was the son of a white father by a slave mother. Just how much white ancestry U.S. blacks have cannot be determined with certainty, but some geneticists have attempted to make an estimate.

Most of the ancestors of U.S. blacks came from certain areas in West Africa. By compar-

ing the percentages of the West African natives who carry a certain gene (the rhesus-factor allele R^0) with the percentage of U.S. blacks and U.S. whites who carry it, geneticists estimate that, on the average, the ancestry of U.S. blacks is probably about 30 percent white. Other researchers have estimated that about 75 percent of all U.S. blacks have at least one white ancestor.

Similarly, it is estimated that about 25 percent of whites have at least one black ancestor. As intermarriage continues, these percentages will increase, making blacks and whites more and more physically indistinguishable.

Legal Discrimination and Segregation.   We have already described briefly the rise of legal segregation in the South. The constitutionality of the state laws on which it was based was long a matter of dispute because the Fourteenth Amendment to the Constitution of the United States, adopted in 1868, provides that no state may deny any person equal protection under the laws. The question was whether segregation constituted denial of equal protection. Those who attempted to challenge these laws in the courts had no important success until 1954, when the U.S. Supreme Court, in the case of *Brown v. Board of Education*, outlawed segregation in public schools.

The *Brown* decision reversed a decision made by the Court in 1896, when, in the case of *Plessy v. Ferguson*, it had issued a decision approving segregation of blacks and whites by state legislation. The decision in *Plessy v. Ferguson* was based on the so-called **separate-but-equal doctrine,** that is, the theory that providing separate educational, recreational, and other public facilities for blacks was not denying equal protection under the laws if these facilities were equal to those for whites. In practice, this equality proved to be a myth.

The *Brown* decision outlawing school segregation opened the way for challenging other segregation laws, and within a decade or so it became clear that they were all unconstitutional. However, the breaking down of segregation, especially in the case of schools, has proved to be a slow and difficult process. Some confusion has resulted from disagreement about whether court decisions and civil rights acts passed by Congress merely annul laws or public policies that require or encourage attendance at segregated schools, or whether they also place an obligation on communities and school boards to take positive measures to eliminate **de facto segregation**—segregation that occurs because of social and cultural, not legal, reasons. **De jure segregation** is segregation based on actual segregation laws. Do these decisions and acts make illegal the segregation that results because some residential areas are wholly black and others wholly white, or make illegal the segregation brought about partly because some parents, black as well as white, may prefer to have their children attend segregated schools?

Since 1954 many major pieces of civil rights legislation have been passed. For example, the Civil Rights Acts of the 1950s and 1960s enforced the voting rights of blacks

Martin Luther King, Jr., at the 1963 civil rights march in Washington.

and prohibited discrimination on the basis of race, sex, or national origin in public accommodations, federally assisted programs, and housing.

Causes of Blacks' Frustration.   Despite all of this legislation, for many blacks there has been little progress, and the frustration level has at times led to riots and civil disturbances. Blacks' frustration is grounded in both social and economic conditions. Though the economic condition of blacks has, on the average, improved greatly, it has by no means caught up with that of whites. In 2000 blacks earned a median income that was only about 60 percent of that earned by whites.

The reasons for this lower income are complicated and varied. They include discrimination, family structure, age structure, occupation, and education. We find that blacks make up a higher proportion of the labor force for low-skilled jobs than their numbers would predict, and a lower percentage of managerial jobs. Additionally, their unemployment rates are higher. Table 12.1a shows that black unemployment rates have consistently remained at higher levels than those of the other major groups (whites and Hispanics). The unemployment rate is especially high among young black males, as can be seen in Table 12.1b.

Much of the problem can be attributed to past and present discrimination against blacks. Discrimination has robbed some blacks of the incentive to acquire the necessary education and training to fill jobs that require not only willingness to work but also more than average skill, training, and education. They believe they will not be given such jobs even if they are qualified to fill them. As a result, to them it makes no sense to acquire marketable skills. To make matters worse, especially in the North, a large proportion of blacks live in neighborhoods where crime is rampant and housing substandard.

Progress toward Equality.   Notwithstanding these problems, the average economic condition of blacks has improved. Many blacks have moved into career-level and skilled

Table 12.1a
Unemployment among Races

YEAR	ALL RACES (%)	WHITE (%)	BLACK (%)	HISPANIC (%)
1975	8.5	7.8	14.8	Not available
1980	7.1	6.3	14.3	10.1
1985	7.3	6.5	14.0	10.6
1990	5.5	5.1	12.0	8.7
1995	5.6	4.9	10.4	9.3
2000	4.0	3.9	8.5	7.0
2003	6.0	5.2	10.9	7.5

Source: U.S. Bureau of Labor and Statistics, *Employment and Earnings.*

Table 12.1b
Unemployment by Age Group, 2003

AGE GROUP	WHITE MALES (%)	BLACK MALES (%)
16–19	14.8	39.7
20–24	8.1	18.9
25–34	5.1	9.2
35–44	4.1	11.8
45–54	3.8	6.9
55–64	4.0	5.2
65 and over	2.9	5.0

Source: U.S. Bureau of Labor and Statistics, *Employment and Earnings.*

jobs. The major credit for the job advancement of blacks should probably go to those individuals among them who have had the ambition and the willingness to work and to acquire education and training. But they have been helped by organized efforts to give blacks far greater opportunities than were available to them in the past. These efforts are being made by government agencies, colleges and universities, corporations, and various other private groups including some organized by blacks themselves. They range all the way from trying to train the hard-core unemployed for specific jobs to providing qualified blacks with scholarships or fellowships for advanced study.

In the past, a significant factor in restricting the economic progress of blacks has been discrimination by labor unions, many of which refused to accept them as members. Some still strongly resist admission of blacks, but the number of such unions that discriminate is declining. Building trade unions in large cities have been especially slow in accepting black apprentices except in token numbers, but under pressure they are adopting more liberal policies.

In the past, black business or professional people were generally limited to their own community for a market for their services. Today the situation is changing. Many corporations are actively seeking qualified blacks to fill professional or administrative positions. This is not always easy, because there are still relatively few blacks with good college training and even fewer with degrees from graduate or professional schools, and the competition to hire them is intense. But progress is being made, and black enrollment in college and professional schools has risen significantly in the past decades.

From 1960 to 2002, the percentage of blacks completing four years of college rose from about 3 percent to about 15.5 percent. The percentage of blacks completing high school rose from 20 percent in 1960 to about 77 percent in 2002. In addition, as black political power has grown and the demands for equality have mounted, more and more professional and administrative jobs have been opened to blacks in public institutions such as hospitals, schools, and state and local government agencies.

Part of the reason for this increase was **affirmative action programs,** programs designed to favor minority groups. Such programs have come under attack in the late 1990s and early 2000s. In California and Texas, where these programs were overturned by the courts and replaced by need-based and race-neutral—rather than race-based—programs, the number of blacks in higher education decreased. This decline has led to the development of programs that seek diversity in other ways, such as admitting a certain percentage of the top students from public high schools. Though this has boosted minority enrollments, many college officials remain opposed to ending affirmative action.

In the early 2000s, affirmative action will be much in the news. Much of the debate will concern precisely what is meant by affirmative action and how it translates into policies. Does it justify numerical quotas, and if so, what is the nature of those quotas? Does it require that race be the major factor in decision making, or does it simply allow race to be considered as one of the factors in decisions? And if it allows a consideration of race, how much weight can be given to race? Does it require or allow that specific preferences be given to minority groups (and if so, how strong can those preferences be), or must all groups be treated equally?

As an example of the issues that can arise, let's consider the college admission program at the University of Texas. That program was changed after its affirmative action program, which gave specific preferences to blacks, was one of the programs that the courts struck down. (Its program giving specific preferences to football players in admissions was not struck down.) In response the University of Texas decided to allow automatic admission to the top 10 percent of all Texas high school students. Because many of the inner-city high schools in Texas are predominantly black and, on average, score low on standardized tests, whereas suburban high schools are predominantly white and, on average, score high on standardized tests, this new program gave blacks an advantage compared to their chances of admission if only test scores had been considered. Was this new program allowable under an affirmative action plan that used a "top 10 percent" standard, or did it represent a strategy to avoid the accusation that the schools were still giving preference to blacks? Even if it were allowable, is it desirable? (There were stories about some whites transferring into inner-city schools so that they would get admitted to the University of Texas.) The bigger question is, What is reasonable discretion in admissions (discretion similar to the allowable attempt of colleges to have a geographic diversity in their student body) and what is unreasonable discretion when it comes to race? Many such issues will have to be dealt with over the next decade.

Another example involved the University of Michigan, where applicants could be given 20 points for being black and 20 points for attending a predominantly minority high school, out of a total of 150 points. (SATs accounted for only 12 points.) Was this too much of a preference, and if so, what would not be too much? When thinking about an answer to this, consider also that "legacies" (children of alumni), who are generally white and well-off, were given 1 to 4 points for their alumni relationships. Was that too much, and if so, what would not be too much? In 2003 the U.S. Supreme Court, which has the ultimate power to make these decisions in the United States, decided that, at an undergraduate level, the points for black students were too much like affirmative action. However, it held that colleges could take race into account in their admission decisions, thereby legalizing affirmative action.

A field in which blacks have as yet made limited progress is business ownership or control. Though corporations are more willing than formerly to hire those who qualify for administrative positions, as yet blacks control comparatively few enterprises of any size. Principal exceptions are some insurance companies, banks, and publishing concerns that chiefly serve the black community. But even the larger black communities such as Harlem are served for the most part by concerns owned and operated by whites.

Eliminating the Vestiges of Discrimination.   When we consider the extent to which discrimination against blacks prevailed throughout this country from early colonial times to World War II, the progress toward equal treatment since that war has been substantial, even though it has fallen far short of the hopes and expectations of many. Segregation in the armed forces, formerly the unchallenged rule in all branches of the service, was completely abandoned as a policy by the mid-1950s. Discrimination against blacks in hotels, motels, restaurants, and other public places has been virtually eliminated, partly because of changes in public attitudes and partly because of laws forbidding it. To be sure, not all the subtler forms of discrimination have disappeared, but at least they are on the defensive.

Another area in which discrimination against blacks has been reduced is in the right to buy property. Formerly, the purchaser of a house might be required to sign a restrictive covenant in which he or she agreed not to rent or sell to members of specified racial or cultural groups. This covenant sometimes made it impossible for blacks to buy or rent housing except in overcrowded black neighborhoods that were often slums. But in 1948 the Supreme Court ruled that restrictive covenants are contrary to public policy and may not be enforced by the courts. Twenty years later, in 1968, Congress passed an Open Housing Act prohibiting racial discrimination in the sale or rental of about 80 percent of all housing, and in the same year the Supreme Court interpreted an 1866 federal law as banning racial discrimination in the sale or rental of any housing. Although these actions have not completely eliminated discrimination in the sale of housing, they have made it difficult, especially for real estate firms.

One place where social scientists have found significant discrimination against blacks is in entry-level jobs and low-skilled positions. Researchers had young high school graduates with similar job histories apply for the same jobs. Thirty-four percent of the white applicants were called back; 14 percent of the blacks were called back. In another experiment, social scientists had fictitious individuals apply for jobs on-line. Some had white-sounding names, such as Greg Kelly, and some had more African American names, such as Jamal Jackson. They found that the white-sounding names received many more callbacks and that the white-sounding name was worth approximately eight years of experience. Thus a person with a black-sounding name had to have eight years more experience to have the same callback rate as a similarly experienced white. The discrimination was even greater when both black and white applicants had criminal records; in the first experiment, a black with a criminal record had only a 5 percent chance of getting a callback, whereas a white with a criminal record had a 17 percent chance of getting a callback. Since nearly 17 percent of all black men have served some time, this presents a serious problem for integrating them back into the community.

Black–White Social Relations.   In his classic book *An American Dilemma,* Gunnar Myrdal observed that the area of strongest white prejudice against blacks had to do with intermarriage and other intimate social contacts. This seems still to be true. The great majority of whites believe that blacks should have equality of opportunity in employment, housing, education, health facilities, and legal rights, but many of them are still uneasy about intermarriage (just as many blacks are) and are often awkward in developing close social contacts.

Among some groups, especially in the younger generation, there is a trend toward breaking down the obstacles to social contacts between the races, including those to interracial marriages. After World War II, more than half of our states had laws prohibiting marriage between a white person and anyone defined legally as a Negro, but in 1967 the Supreme Court ruled that no state may ban interracial marriages. Still, today interracial couples constitute only about 3 percent of all couples, and only 6 percent of those are between blacks and whites. Opposition to these marriages, whether from blacks or whites, is diminishing, but it is still strong.

Discrimination occurs not only between blacks and whites but also among blacks, with darker-skinned blacks being called names and treated differently by lighter-skinned blacks. Moreover, the discrimination that does occur by whites seems to be more pronounced the darker the skin a person has. In a study of brothers from the same family who differed by skin color, it was found that the lighter-skinned brothers tended to have higher incomes and experience less discrimination.

Ultimately, we will know that the race problem has been solved if bringing home a black fiancée to a white family, or bringing home a white fiancée to a black family, raises no more eyebrows than bringing a blond fiancée home to a brunette's family, or a brunette fiancée to a blonde's family.

The Future of Black Americans.   In the early 1960s, some twenty years after he had completed *An American Dilemma,* Myrdal was asked if he foresaw any solution to our race problems. He replied, "Well, you can find solutions to technical problems; but in social problems, particularly those that are so intrinsically difficult and mixed up as the [black] problem, there is no solution in an absolute sense."

In his study, Myrdal called the race problem in the United States a white problem because the whites are the great majority and hold the bulk of wealth and power. He saw progress by blacks to be dependent on white cooperation, on a lifting of the bars of discrimination. But it is clear that even if all whites (and blacks) could quickly and completely rid themselves of racial prejudice, it would still take time for blacks as a group to overcome completely all the effects of generations of slavery followed by decades of extreme discrimination.

No group can give equality to another group except in the sense of treating its members fairly and sympathetically and helping to provide them with opportunities. Neither disadvantaged blacks nor disadvantaged whites will achieve equality with the average citizen merely by being given jobs for which they are not qualified or by being admitted to colleges whose academic standards they cannot meet. They can, however, be offered opportunities for job training and, if they have the will and ability, chances to make up academic deficiencies.

The debate over what to do about inequality has manifested itself in the debate about affirmative action programs. Advocates of affirmative action programs argue that they are necessary to offset past discrimination. Critics charge that such programs are unfair both to the minorities and to whites. They say that affirmative action programs place blacks in situations for which they are unqualified and that preference for blacks discriminates against needy whites.

As we stated earlier, in response to criticism some states such as Texas and California have started substituting need for race and gender as the determining factor for preferential treatment. For instance, in 1996 California passed a law designed "to abolish affirmative action." According to this law, "The state shall not discriminate against, or grant preferential treatment to, any individual or group on the basis of race, sex, color, ethnicity, or national origin in the operation of public employment, public education, or public contracting." This statement demonstrates neutrality, but it did abolish previous legislation that had favored preferential treatment for minorities and women. Some other states are considering similar legislation.

Eliminating affirmative action on the basis of race will not necessarily mean an end to giving preference to blacks; it will simply be preference not solely based on race, so a white child and a black child of upper-middle-class families will be treated equally. However, because many blacks are poor and come from backgrounds without a strong focus on education, they, along with whites from similar backgrounds, can be given preference in admissions and hiring because, to achieve what they did, they had to overcome greater obstacles than a person from a rich, pro-educational background.

It is doubtful whether racial prejudice and discrimination can be completely eliminated as long as blacks and whites constitute distinct racial and social groups in our society. Discrimination is inherent to some degree in most social relationships all over the world. It occurs in the contacts between individuals, between individuals and groups, and between groups of many types, including families. But to deny to an entire racial or cultural group equal civil rights and equal educational, political, and economic opportunities is a type of discrimination that all who really believe in justice and democracy should not tolerate.

If racial prejudice and discrimination in this country disappeared altogether, in a few generations blacks would disappear as a separate group. They would be biologically absorbed into the general population and in the process would somewhat change the average physical characteristics of what is now the white majority. In the long run, this is likely to happen, but few objective students of the race problem believe that such an outcome can be expected any time soon.

Hispanics

The largest minority group in the United States is **Hispanics,** or individuals of Spanish-speaking origin. These include **Latinos,** who have historical and cultural ties to Latin America, and **Chicanos,** who have historical and cultural ties to Mexico. From 1988 to 2000, the Hispanic population more than doubled. About 35 million U.S. citizens (more than 13 percent of the population) identified themselves as being of Spanish origin. Of the total number, about 66 percent gave Mexico as their country of origin, about 10 percent gave Puerto Rico, about 4 percent gave Cuba, and the remainder gave other Latin American countries. However, of all who considered themselves of Spanish origin, about 63 percent were actually born in the United States or in Puerto Rico, all of whose natives have U.S. citizenship. Immigration has been the key to Hispanic population growth. Over 13 million first-generation immigrants account for 40 percent of all Hispanics.

Chicanos.   The Chicanos are of special importance because they are the largest of all Hispanic minority groups. But they differ from other Americans of Spanish origin not only in their national origin but also in their racial background. "To be a Mexican," says Philip D. Ortega, "is to be a member of la raza, the race of Montezuma's children. More than two fifths of the Mexican population are pure-blooded Indians; more than half have some Indian blood in them. Yet, despite Indian resilience, the language of the conquerors dominated."

Except for the Native Americans, Mexicans, or Spaniards from Mexico, were the first settlers of what is now the southwestern part of the United States. All of this area was a part of Mexico before the United States annexed it in 1848 after the Mexican War. When the first settlers from the United States began moving into the Southwest, Mexicans were already there, and many of their descendants can be found there today, especially in Colorado and northern New Mexico, where a few villages are still composed almost entirely of descendants of Mexicans.

The modern influx of Mexican immigration came after 1900. It was not affected by the quota restrictions, passed by Congress in 1921 and 1924, that greatly reduced the inflow of immigrants from eastern and southern Europe, because these did not apply to the Western hemisphere. Most Mexicans came as common laborers. Many were employed as seasonal migratory workers in agriculture; others found jobs on road-building projects or as railroad workers. However, up until 1964 many of our Mexican migratory workers were not citizens or residents of the United States. Rather, they were braceros, Mexicans who were allowed to enter this country seasonally as contract workers in agriculture. The law permitting these contract workers was allowed to expire in 1964, but it was reinstated in 1986.

In addition to contract workers, a number of Mexicans are in the United States illegally. They come to the United States to find jobs offering wages and working conditions better than they can find in Mexico. Given the 2,000-mile-long border between Mexico and the United States, limiting the flow of illegal immigration from Mexico is very difficult.

In 1986 Congress passed a law that was meant to deal with this problem. Among other things, it allowed certain illegal aliens who had been in the United States for at least five years to receive amnesty and to apply for U.S. citizenship. The requirements of this law were quite strict, but many thousands of Mexican illegal aliens came forward to apply.

Today the Chicanos are one of our most rapidly growing groups. Because of their high birthrate, a large proportion of them are young. Four out of five Chicanos are con-

The proprietor lends a hand in the kitchen of his Mexican restaurant.

centrated in the Southwest. The great majority live in Texas and California, but substantial numbers are found in Arizona, New Mexico, and Colorado. They go where the work is, and the U.S. economy's high demand for workers in states such as Iowa, Kansas, and Georgia has meant that in the 1990s and early 2000s many are to be found in those states. Although some are of European descent, most are of mixed European and Indian ancestry. They tend to live in segregated residential areas, to retain their own customs, and to continue to speak Spanish. They often lack the level of education of their U.S. neighbors, and many do not speak English fluently. In states where they have previously been sparsely represented, they sometimes are discriminated against not only by the long-established population but also by Mexicans who have been in the country longer than the newest arrivals. All these factors contribute to slow their economic and social progress.

Though many Chicanos still live in the Southwest and are employed in agriculture, and a relatively small number of them are still migrants, the great majority—close to 85 percent—live in urban areas, where they sometimes form small colonies. In cities, Chicanos work in many job areas, but as yet relatively few are found in high-ranking occupations. As a group, their incomes are much lower than those of white Americans of European descent, and more than 21 percent live below the poverty level. But like the descendants of earlier immigrant groups, some are finding their way up the social and economic ladder, and today about 34 percent of them hold white-collar jobs.

Latinos.   A relatively new racial-culture group has appeared with its own set of problems. The largest subset of this group are Puerto Ricans who have come to the United States in the last fifty years. Though most Puerto Ricans are Caucasians, a substantial proportion of them are of black or mixed ancestry. There are now more than 3 million Puerto Ricans scattered throughout the United States, although most live in New York City.

Because Puerto Ricans are U.S. citizens, they have the same rights as all other citizens, but because of language difficulties, lack of skills, lack of education, and discrimination, those living in the United States often earn low wages and are forced to live in blighted areas where health conditions are poor and crime rates are high. Also, many social difficulties arise because their cultural patterns are so different from those they encounter in the United States. Some return home, disappointed. Others "commute," staying only long enough to earn whatever amount of money they need to sustain them for a while.

In addition to Puerto Ricans, other Latin groups have increased in significance. One large group has come from Cuba. Immediately after Fidel Castro came to power in Cuba in 1959, several hundred thousand refugees came to this country under special congressional legislation that created a Cuban refugee program. These first-wave Cubans have done well in the United States and make up a large percentage of the middle class in Miami, for example. From 1960 until 1980, the influx of refugees declined; in 1980 another large group of Cuban refugees was admitted into the country as political refugees.

Asians

In the early 2000s, over 12 million Asians lived in the United States. They have spread throughout the country, but most live in large cities. Despite prejudice against them, many of them have done well both financially and socially.

Chinese Immigrants. The Chinese first came to this country in large numbers when gold was discovered in California. In the single year of 1852, some twenty thousand were admitted. They worked as cooks and launderers and as laborers in the mines. When the gold rush was over, many of them were employed in building the western portion of the transcontinental railroad. They also spread out into occupations such as agriculture and fishing. But to the white settlers, they were strange and unwelcome. As their numbers grew, antagonism increased and they endured many types of discrimination. There were even riots in which they were chased through the streets and beaten or lynched. Part of this antagonism resulted from the competition for jobs. The Chinese were willing to live on very little and, if forced to do so, would work for extremely low wages. Finally, in 1882 Congress passed the Chinese Exclusion Act, which virtually suspended all Chinese immigration until 1943.

In 1965 a revision of immigration laws ended discrimination against the Chinese and the immigrants from all other countries by abolishing quotas based on national origin. Due in part to U.S. response to the upheavals in Southeast Asia that began at least as early as 1970, immigration laws have undergone several subsequent liberalizations, especially for highly trained individuals. Immigration law is complex, but at the present time we can say that it has permitted a significant increase in the number of Chinese and Southeast Asian immigrants to the United States.

Japanese Immigrants. After Congress passed the Chinese Exclusion Act, the Japanese began arriving on the West Coast in increasing numbers. Most of them settled in California, and before long they, like the Chinese before them, began to encounter prejudice and discrimination. As with the Chinese, the feeling against them was partly based on conflicting economic interests. Many Japanese became truck gardeners (growers of fresh vegetables), and because whole families were willing to work hard and live on very little, the native California truck gardeners complained that they could not meet Japanese competition. Also it was argued that the strong loyalty of the Japanese to their homeland made assimilation impossible.

During World War II, anti-Japanese feelings increased. The U.S. government forcibly moved 117,000 people of Japanese birth or ancestry away from the West Coast to relocation centers further inland. This move was explained as a security measure, but it is now generally recognized as an inexcusable injustice, for removal was not based on disloyalty but only on national origin, and it meant gross discrimination against thousands of loyal U.S.

The U.S. Gulag

On February 11, 1942, U.S. authorities began rounding up Japanese Americans and shipping them to internment camps simply because of their Japanese heritage. Fear that these Americans would support Japan in that country's war with the United States was the ostensible cause, but anger at the Japanese attack on Pearl Harbor in Hawaii on December 7, 1941, and racial prejudice were major unstated reasons. Just as angry people often strike out in vengeance without thinking, angry societies sometimes strike out in revenge and thoughtlessness.

citizens. In 1945 the evacuation order was rescinded, but many Japanese did not return to the West Coast, preferring to live in areas where prejudice against them was less marked.

In recent years, prejudice against the Japanese has disappeared or greatly diminished. In 1988 the U.S. government finally apologized to the surviving Japanese Americans who had been interned and agreed to pay each of them $20,000.

Other Asian Immigrants.   Over the years there have been varying numbers of other Asian immigrants. In the 1970s, hundreds of thousands of Vietnamese immigrants were allowed into the United States to escape political oppression in their native country. More recently, many highly trained Indians, Pakistanis, and other Southeast Asians have been allowed in because of a shortage of workers in high-tech fields. In a number of high-tech companies, foreign-born workers outnumber U.S.-born workers.

Asian American immigration has been highly self-selective. It has primarily consisted of highly educated individuals who have found it relatively easy to succeed in the United States. Often they have taken low-level jobs that were only loosely controlled as to minimum wage and hour requirements, and they have worked hard to advance. For example, many Indians worked in motels and then bought the motels, providing jobs for new Indian immigrants. Once they learned the business and saved enough money, the new immigrants went out and bought their own motels. Today, many local motels are owned by Indians. The same is true of doughnut shops; for example, most doughnut shops in California are owned by Indians.

The success of Asian Americans has lead to the stereotype of them as a "model minority." Thus, even though they are a minority, they are not seen as being discriminated against in work opportunities and education, and thus not in need of affirmative action. If anything, they are discriminated against in education because they attend school in greater numbers and often achieve better results than other groups, including whites. Thus, to maintain diversity some colleges, especially those located in areas with a large Asian population, discriminate against Asian Americans by making it more difficult for them to get accepted into those colleges. Not all Asian Americans are rich, educated, and successful, however. Asian Americans still have higher poverty rates than whites.

Arab Americans and Americans of Middle Eastern Descent.   The last minority we will discuss is Arab Americans, of whom there are roughly 3 million, 90 percent of whom live in urban areas. As a group, Arab Americans have done relatively well, and their incomes are 22 percent higher than the U.S. national average. Traditional multicultural efforts often overlook this ethnic group, though they face stereotyping and prejudice. The first wave of immigration of Arabs from the Middle East took place between 1875 through 1920. Most of these early Arab immigrants were from Lebanon and Syria; most were Christian and seeking economic opportunities. Immigration then slowed as the United States began imposing restrictions. The second wave began in the 1940s because of the Arab–Israeli conflict and civil wars; this group came from a much more diverse area, and many practiced Islam. But like the earlier group, most were more financially secure when they came, or became financially secure relatively soon after arriving.

The early 2000s have been particularly difficult for Arab Americans. Because the September 11th terrorists were of Middle Eastern descent, many Arab Americans have been subject to discrimination and prejudice, even though almost all of them strongly condemn the terrorists and consider themselves Americans. Although they may feel that U.S. policy in the Middle East is tilted in Israel's favor, that is a feeling shared with many other Americans, and with many individuals throughout the world, and is in no way unpatriotic. New Arab American immigrants are especially singled out. The U.S. government has implemented a mandatory registration for nonimmigrant aliens from the Arab and Muslim world. They are also profiled and subject to special surveillance by law enforcement. Thus, the "crackdown" on terrorism created discrimination toward Arab Americans in travel, housing, and educational and work opportunities. Whether that discrimination was a necessary side effect of the government's need to provide security, or was an unacceptable form of discrimination, is currently being debated.

Immigrants and Minorities

In the early 1900s, when immigration into the United States reached its peak, some one million persons were arriving every year, the great majority from Europe. Nationalities tended to group together. For a while they became isolated islands of culture, continuing among themselves to speak their own language and to perpetuate their own traditions. At first most immigrants took the unskilled jobs and occupied the lowest place in the class structure, consequently pushing into the upper classes a larger proportion of older immigrant residents than might otherwise have been found there. These older residents had the advantage of being on high ground earlier, as a result of which they not only knew the language and customs, but also in many cases had accumulated property.

In some ways, the situation of European immigrants was like that of a minority racial group, but the difference lay in the fact that although most second- and third-generation individuals from racial groups were still set apart and considered unassimilable no matter how Americanized they became, those from the Caucasian nationality groups had little trouble, in a generation or two, in identifying with the major group.

Restrictions on Immigration. Until 1890 most immigrants to the United States were from northwestern Europe. Then immigration from southern and eastern Europe began to exceed that from northwestern Europe, and Mexican immigration also increased. Many "old" Americans, and even some of the earlier immigrants, were strongly prejudiced against southern and eastern Europeans. Demands for restrictive legislation led to laws limiting immigration.

In 1921 the first **Immigration Quota Act,** designed to reduce immigration to certain annual quotas for each national group, was passed. The quota for each country was 3 percent of the number of people living in the United States in 1910 who were of that national origin. The effect of this legislation was to reduce sharply immigration from the countries of central, eastern, and southern Europe. Later the quotas were reduced, and in 1924 the maximum total number of immigrants to be admitted annually was cut to 150,000. The quota laws did not apply to countries in the Western hemisphere.

During the years following World War II, Congress passed various immigration acts to admit considerable numbers of immigrants over and above the quotas. Most of these were Europeans displaced from their homes by World War II or by the 1956 Hungarian rebellion against communist rule. Later, as we have already mentioned, Cuban and Asian refugees were admitted under special legislation.

But in 1965, under pressure from people who considered our immigration laws discriminatory, Congress passed an act that provided for the complete abandonment of national quotas by mid-1968. Under this act, admittance is based not on national origin

Illegal immigrants sometimes die during their attempts to sneak into the United States.

but on the U.S. need for the training or skills of a would-be immigrant. Various special immigration laws applying to groups such as Cubans, Southeast Asians, Irish, and political refugees have been passed since 1965. In addition, many classes of immigrants are exempt from any numerical limitations—such as immediate relatives of U.S. citizens. The change in the composition of immigration can be seen in Figure 12.1.

In 1989 the United States again changed the quotas, cutting the number of Asians allowed and increasing the number of Soviets. These actions created a political stir. In 1990, Congress overhauled the immigration laws, raising the quota of immigrants by nearly 50 percent and allowing entry for a larger percentage of immigrants who were not related to U.S. citizens. It also created 30,000 slots for wealthy foreigners of any origin who would guarantee that they would invest $1 million in the United States. This led to charges that the United States was selling U.S. citizenship.

In 1997 the Illegal Immigration Act went into effect. It substantially deliberalizes the conditions under which a U.S. citizen or legal resident can sponsor a would-be immigrant and makes permanent residence much harder to achieve than under the older laws. It also increases the requirements for various formal certificates, such as birth and marriage, that an immigrant has to meet. This legislation makes it harder for immigrants to comply with the formalities that the law directs employers to investigate before giving a job to an immigrant. In 2004, President George W. Bush proposed legislation to loosen restrictions on illegals and allow them to work and pay and receive Social Security. He proposed that this period of lenience last only three years, and it was unclear what the fate of this legislation would be.

The effectiveness of our immigration laws, especially when we consider that some seem to conflict with others, has been questioned. First, their application and enforcement have not been consistent: Leverage can and has been exerted for individuals or small groups. Second, the crucial task of controlling illegal entry along our long northern and southern borders and the approaches by sea (not to mention exotic tactics, such as parachuting) is a formidable one for the available authorities. Even legal admissions are difficult to enforce because there is insufficient monitoring of students and other visitors to see that they comply with the restrictions of their visas or do not outstay their permissions.

Dealing with Illegal Aliens. The **Immigration and Naturalization Service (INS)** estimates that about 6 million illegal aliens live in the United States, a number that increases by more then 200,000 each year. About 40 percent of illegal aliens have entered the country legally but outstay their visas. This 6 million does not include those immigrants folded into the population when in 1986 the United States passed legislation imposing more restrictions on new illegal immigration while at the same time making provisions for legitimizing the status of some of the 2.7 million aliens already illegally living and working in the United States. This law legalized a large group of formerly illegal aliens, but also made employers subject to penalties for employing illegal aliens. The resulting large jump in Mexican immigration can be seen in Figure 12.1.

The 1986 law was not highly successful. Some studies have suggested that this law reduced only 20 percent of the illegal immigration. The effect of the stricter 1997 law

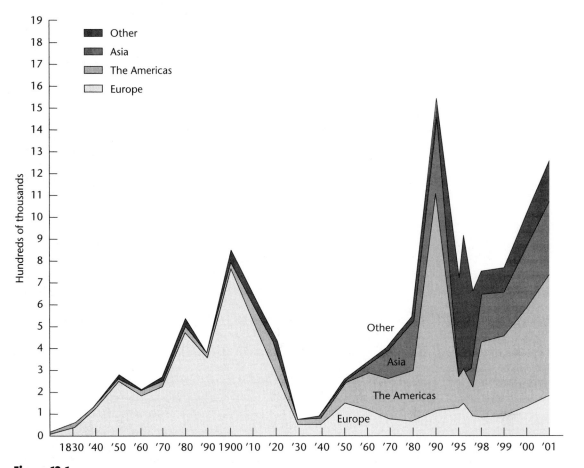

Figure 12.1

Immigrants by continent, 1820 to 2001. The large jump in 1990 is due to the legalization of many Mexican immigrants. (Source: U.S. Bureau of the Census, Statistical Abstract of the United States; BCIS, Yearbook of Immigration Statistics.)

remains to be seen. With respect to Mexican immigration, however, late in 1997 the Bi-national Study on Migration conducted jointly over a two-year period by the U.S. and Mexican governments concluded that previous estimates of the number of Mexican illegal immigrants were much too high. Recently there has been an increase in the number of immigrant visas for Mexicans because the United States, with its healthy economy, has a need for low-wage workers, a need that Mexicans are willing to meet. In 2000 the newly elected president of Mexico, Vicente Fox, paid an official visit to the United States. He had many ideas for the future of Mexican–U.S. relations. Some of these ideas dealt with immigration issues. He proposed that the number of Mexican workers allowed into the United States be increased until 2010, at which time all restrictions would be eliminated. The United States is unlikely to accept this suggestion. The question of immigration is likely to figure prominently in the news for many years.

After September 11, 2001, the debate on immigration shifted to the need to control borders as a measure of national security. The trend toward a more open border between Mexico and the United States, for now, is moving in reverse. When the Center for Immigration Studies learned that twenty-two of the forty-eight foreign-born al Qaeda-linked terrorists had violated immigration laws, the antiterrorism effort added strict enforcement of immigration laws to the strict border enforcement—and the United States' new Homeland Security attitude toward illegal aliens was formed.

Religious Minorities

A number of religious groups in this country espouse beliefs that lead them to follow ways of life somewhat different from the general pattern of U.S. culture. These include sects such as the Amish, the Seventh-Day Adventists, and the Jehovah's Witnesses. But their total number is small. At one time the Mormons could have been included, but after they officially abandoned polygamy they became, in their relation to U.S. culture, not very different from any other Christian sect.

The Jews, however, form an important minority group whose influence on our society is greater than their numbers alone would seem to indicate. We have already considered the nature of Judaism in Chapter 9, but we will take up here a brief discussion of anti-Semitism. Prejudice or severe discrimination against the Jews, called anti-Semitism, has existed for centuries and has been strong in certain countries at certain periods. Sometimes it has been tied to religion; sometimes it has been rationalized by dislike on the part of the majority of the population for certain cultural or "racial" characteristics, largely imaginary, attributed to the Jews as a group. In some parts of eastern Europe, anti-Semitism has at times been taken to such extremes that thousands of Jews were killed, as in the pogroms, or organized massacres, that occurred in czarist Russia. But it was in Nazi Germany that anti-Semitism reached its height, for Jews constituted the great majority of the estimated 7 million people who were murdered in Hitler's concentration camps.

Anti-Semitism continues to exist, although in the United States it has slowly diminished, perhaps in part because it was overshadowed by the greater problem of black–white relations. But in recent years, some Jews have felt that the level of prejudice was rising. Two factors may have contributed to this. First, when the new nation of Israel was established and conflict with the Arabs began, the majority of Jews were drawn together by a sense of pride, and many gave their full support to Israel. Often non-Jews do not share their sentiments. Second, as blacks have increased their demands for equality, some of them have tended to identify the Jewish merchant in the black ghetto as the symbol of white oppression.

In spite of such developments there is no clear evidence that in the country as a whole anti-Semitism is increasing. The long-run trend appears to be in the other direction. Inter-marriage seems to be more and more common, although according to polls taken in recent years, Jewish opposition to it has fluctuated. Whether the Jews in the United States will, after a few generations, lose their identity as a separate cultural group remains to be seen. But under modern conditions in our society, this may happen. At least there are no racial differences of the kind that make the complete assimilation of the blacks relatively difficult.

Another religious minority that has been experiencing discrimination is the Muslim population. Although we discussed discrimination against some Muslims earlier, it is important to remember that not all Arabs are Muslims and not all Muslims are Arabs. The U.S. Muslim population, estimated to be more than 5 million, is diverse, with only about 12.5 percent ethnically Arab. The large percentage of Muslims are also African Americans; they make up over 40 percent of all U.S. Muslims. The next largest percentage is South Asians at about 25 percent. Muslims can be found in every U.S. state, with the largest numbers in California and New York. Since 2001 many U.S. citizens have associated Islam (the religion of Muslims) with terrorism, even though almost all Muslims have condemned the terrorism. Despite their patriotism, in recent years Muslims have been discriminated against based on guilt by association.

Sexual Minorities

In today's society, the roles of men and women differ: Women are in some ways subordinated to men. Thus, although women make up a majority of the U.S. population, given this subordinate position they are still often referred to as a minority. Whether this subordinate position is acceptable is up to each one of us to decide, but in making that decision, we must be aware of the facts.

One fact is that our society has decided that discrimination is not legally allowed on the basis of sex, age, race, or national origin. Despite the law, there is discrimination against women. This discrimination takes many forms. Sometimes it is disguised as protection: Women are not allowed to do things because they are perceived as *the weaker sex;* the prohibition against women serving in combat in almost all of the armed forces is an example. Other times the discrimination is built into the way men treat women—as objects rather than as human beings; pornography is a good example. Still other times the discrimination is in women's access to jobs: The perception that firms have of women's abilities often differs from the reality. The list goes on. We cannot provide a comprehensive list of the various practices of discrimination, partly because our space is limited and partly because the perception of discrimination varies from individual to individual.

To deal with this complex, subtle discrimination, many people supported a constitutional amendment, the **Equal Rights Amendment (ERA)**, which stated simply: "Equality of rights under the laws shall not be denied or abridged . . . on account of sex." It needed ratification by two-thirds of the states, which it did not receive. Supporters point out that the state legislatures that defeated this amendment were all overwhelmingly staffed by males.

History of the Women's Movement. We can trace the women's movement, sometimes called feminism, at least as far back as the early nineteenth century. In the late 1800s and early 1900s, the suffragist movement continued its work. Women whose primary aim in the women's movement was to win the right to vote were called suffragettes. The women

Pornography treating women as objects.

did win this campaign in 1920. During World Wars I and II, women were called on to assume many of the tasks that had been assigned to men until the men were called into military service, and the women reaped many of the satisfactions. They found it difficult and, indeed, absurd to give up the freedoms they had won just because the wars ended and the men came home. But, as can be seen in the movie *Rosie the Riveter,* the government exerted strong pressure on women to resume their so-called proper role at home and to give up their jobs to men.

The principal permanent achievement marking women's contributions in World War I is the passage of the Nineteenth Amendment to the U.S. Constitution (1920) that gave them the right to vote. During World War II, women's performance in the civilian economy and their actual service in the armed forces gave them confidence to assert claims for greater equality. Their performance in the Persian Gulf War was superb, and following the war Congress passed a law authorizing women pilots to take part in combat. In the 2003 Iraq war, women served honorably in combat roles, and women were captured and held as prisoners of war. Still, the army is far from sex-neutral, and it maintains limited combat roles for women. Additionally, all men are required to sign up with the Selective Service System and thus may be drafted should the need arise. Women are not required to sign up and under present law cannot be drafted.

The fact that women were in the past and are now an actual majority of our people but yet have had a subordinate status similar to that of a minority makes their situation paradoxical. They are not a minority, but they are treated as one. In 1848, Lucretia Mott and Elizabeth Cady Stanton organized the first U.S. women's rights convention at Seneca Falls, New York. Then in 1869 Elizabeth Cady Stanton, together with Susan B. Anthony, founded the National Woman Suffrage Association, which became known as the suffragist movement. More recently, the push for women's equality has been known as women's liberation.

Women have made significant gains in many areas. There are now more women in better-paying jobs; more women in colleges and graduate schools, in government office, in corporate boardrooms, in the highest ranking positions of financial institutions; and more women in professions such as medicine, the law, and engineering. Yet when we examine the record more closely, in many areas these gains seem to have little overall effect on equality. For example, only 20 to 25 percent of state legislators are female. In 2003 only 59 out of the 435 members of the House of Representatives were women, and there were only 14 female senators. Thus, primarily men are both the lawmakers and the law enforcers.

The average earnings of a woman are still less than the average for a man, even where equal work is performed. At managerial levels, women usually rise only to middle management jobs, and they tend to stay there. Many women tend to be segregated into "pink-collar jobs" such as teaching, nursing, and library work, which pay less than white-collar jobs. To see how women's earnings compare with those of men, see Table 12.2.

Table 12.2

Earnings for Men and Women by Occupation 2003

MEDIAN EARNINGS FOR VARIOUS FULL-TIME WORKERS BY OCCUPATION IN 2003 (WEEKLY, IN DOLLARS)

Occupation	Male	Female
Managerial and professional	1058	786
Sales and office	645	503
Construction and extraction	605	408
Production	563	407
Service	477	366
Farming, fishing, and forestry	375	323

Source: Bureau of Labor Statistics.

In addition, as women have comparatively recently entered occupations such as construction work, fire fighting, and police forces, they tend to be the last hired and the first fired. None of these acts is necessarily discriminating on the individual or firm level. For example, many companies have established a seniority system that governs their hiring and firing. Thus they are required by the system to fire the last one hired, of which women constitute a larger percentage. With respect to the pink-collar jobs, the schools, hospitals, museums, and libraries that offer these positions say they merely hire from the pool of those who apply and that they are not directing women to take the jobs.

Much of the gender discrimination occurs too early and is too subtle and built into the system to attribute to specific individuals. If you take a poll in your class, you may find that the men have higher career aspirations than the women. Why?

It might be that in childhood the boys were pressured harder; it was made clear to them that they would be ultimately responsible for their own lives. When a girl had difficulty completing a project, she might have been treated leniently. Or it may have been a career counselor who guided girls in a different direction from boys. A woman who was, say, a brilliant mathematician and a straight A student may have been counseled into education courses rather than to professional schools of business, finance, or international relations. Frustrated with teaching, she may leave that occupation to marry and have children. The fact that she made that decision does not mean she is unhappy or that her life is any less fulfilling (it may be more), but it does show the process by which women are channeled into certain careers.

Reasons for Women Entering the Workforce. Former Congresswoman Patricia Schroeder pinpointed one of the most important reasons for women to enter the workforce when she argued that the primary reason they do so in such unprecedented numbers is that they have to maintain their families. Many family women work because they must work. For others, although families have become smaller, wants have become larger. Therefore, for these family women, work is not an actual necessity but it is a social need: It is the only way the family can meet its desires. However, for black and other minority females, work has been a necessity for much longer than for white females. Women in the workforce as a percentage of total women of working age rose from 32 percent in 1972 to 60 percent in 2003. According to the 2000 census, 64.5 percent of two-parent families with children under age eighteen had both parents working. (This percentage had risen from 33 percent in 1976.) Analysts who study such trends say that the percentage of working women with children is expected to continue to grow even though some very high-income women may choose to stop working and stay home with their children.

It is sometimes argued that for many women the decision to work is not as important as that for men because they work only to provide "extras," which are often listed as

One Woman's Struggle

Stratification is millions of personal stories. What breaks down stratification is individual fortitude and initiative. Here's one of those stories.

Burnita S. Matthews, who was born in 1894, was the first woman ever appointed as a judge to a U.S. federal court. She had to wait until she was sixty-four years old to get that judgeship.

Her father sent her brother to law school and Burnita to a music conservatory. On her own, she went to law school at night, graduating in 1919. She then applied to the U.S. Veterans Administration for a lawyer's job; the Veterans Administration told her they would never hire a woman. She sent her membership dues to the Bar Association; they returned her check. She opened her own law office anyway.

In 1949, President Harry S. Truman appointed her to the judgeship. All the other judges in her court were men, of course. One of them made a public announcement: "Mrs. Matthews would be a good judge, but there is one thing wrong—she's a woman." The other judges agreed among themselves to give her the most boring work the court had. She did the work and stuck to her job. In fact, she never officially retired. She heard her last district court case in 1983, when she was eighty-eight.

As the years went on after her appointment, things got better for women. Matthews eventually got important cases on which to work. For instance, she ruled that Black Muslims had a right to attend religious services of their choice even though they were in jail. She ruled that people who receive disability benefits from Social Security can't have the money suddenly cut off just because the government decides they aren't disabled anymore. The people are entitled to a hearing and a chance to show that the government is wrong, and they are allowed to keep their checks unless the government can justify stopping the money.

A federal judge has younger lawyers working for her (or him). Matthews always employed women lawyers. She said, "I always chose women because often when a lawyer does well, the authorities say that some man did the work. I wanted everyone to know that when one of my lawyers did well, the work was done by a woman."

Burnita Matthews died in 1988, her life a symbol of overcoming barriers of stratification.

a second car, a vacation home, restaurant meals—items that can be seen as frivolous or self-indulgent. If this is so, then women can be paid less because their earnings are not essential and their attachment to the labor force is intermittent. Opponents point out that this argument is wrong for two reasons. First, not all women are one-half of a couple, and approximately half of all families headed by women live below the poverty level. Their need for income is as great as, or greater than, a man's. But, more important, the argument is wrong because it is both immoral and illegal to pay one individual less than another individual for the same work.

The breakdown of the family has had its most telling impact on women. The outlook for women and their children who do not have their father living with them is not bright—many absent fathers make no child support payments, or do so at a level substantially lower than the amounts ordered by the court. In the last thirty years, laws have been passed to improve the situation. For example, in 1984 Congress allowed attachment of wages in certain cases, and in 1991 a federal law authorizing wage attachment for all absent parents who did not live up to their child support obligations was passed. Subsequent adjustments to federal law have mandated additional measures such as that employers must report newly hired employees to a national data bank to find out whether any of them owe child support payments. But it is still difficult for most single parents (generally women) to collect.

The situation for divorced women is also precarious. It has been said that for a woman the surest road to poverty is divorce. The majority of women who should receive alimony payments often do not, as many men who are supposed to make these payments default (some, in all fairness, cannot meet these financial demands). The tendency to give child custody to women still prevails, although more recently judges have been awarding custody either jointly or solely to the father. Because most women earn less than men, the financial burden of a divorced woman with children can be overwhelming.

We have been saying that women work for the same reasons men do: to make a living and provide for their families. But there are other reasons, which women share with men, for their desire to work: self-fulfillment and personal satisfaction. Apart from the basic satisfaction of seeing their work rewarded with money—the symbol of reward in our society, whatever opinion we may have of that symbol—women want to accept the challenges of competition and the acquisition and manipulation of new skills, to associate with peers, and to make contributions to the success of projects and enterprises.

Many men feel threatened or inconvenienced by the changes at home and at work caused by new attitudes and conditions. Men who were raised by traditional patriarchal fathers are baffled and confused by what has amounted to a kind of social revolution.

Yet the women's movement has affected men in several positive ways. Large numbers of men, either married or divorced, have become househusbands, taking on household and child care tasks and finding a new joy in being closer to their children. Although many women still end up with a larger share of the housework and the care of the children, men for the most part are beginning to appreciate the burdens and drudgery that women have long handled alone. Significant numbers of men have found themselves liberated from ancient stereotypes that barred them from kitchens and nurseries at home and nursing and clerical work in the workplace. Some men have begun to realize that to equalize duties is also to free males from the superman image of sole provider and family mainstay, reducing their tension.

Not all men are willing or able to take on the duties of child care. Good day care is hard to come by, and although some firms have established on-site day-care facilities, these companies represent a tiny minority. One solution has been the classic method of changing the problem instead of finding the answer: namely, to reduce the number of children. Especially among professional women earning high incomes and enjoying the exhilaration of the competitive business or professional world, childbearing has been postponed or even specifically declared to be completely outside their plans.

This tendency has been countered in recent years by a number of women finding that the desire to have at least one child is strong, resulting in an upsurge in the number of children born to mothers between the ages of 35 and 45. Such a development brings us full circle: Trying to work at a full-time job while simultaneously caring for a house and family, even if the family work is shared, is demanding, requiring almost a superwoman to achieve it. As one woman said in a *New York Times* inter-

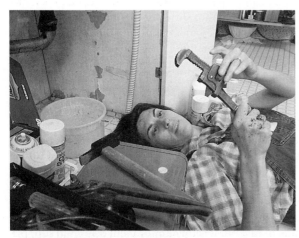

More and more women are doing "male" jobs.

view, "People say to me, 'You go to school, you have a great job, a wonderful child and a wonderful husband, and your house looks clean. Wow!' But what's interesting is that I'm not planning to do that anymore. I've done the superwoman thing. And now that I know that I can do it, my question is: Do I want to do it? Do I want to live like that? Do I want to set the alarm for two and study until four? And the answer is absolutely not!"

Despite the problems, the issue of women's rights will not disappear—their proportion of the total workforce and their need to work and earn a decent wage cannot be denied. Many men remain unconvinced that helping women surmount the obstacles still in their path will probably be good for men. It is, however, quite possible that both sexes can gain from a more equitable policy toward women and that both men and women can find, through their less traditional roles, a new sense of trust, mutual respect, and cooperation.

Discrimination Based on Sexual Preference.   Women are not the only sexual minority. Members of the Lesbian, Gay, Bisexual, and Transgendered coalition argue that they experience enormous discrimination, both in the way people think about them and in finding work. For example, the U.S. armed forces had a rule that all homosexuals must resign from the army. Some homosexuals who have been discharged from the armed services have gone to court to try to gain reinstatement. In 1991 there were signs from the secretary of defense that this discriminatory barrier would be reconsidered. In 1994 the Department of Defense agreed to a compromise policy allowing homosexuals to serve in the military—known as the "don't ask, don't tell, don't pursue rule," which effectively allows those who do not reveal their sexual preference to serve in the military.

Other instances in which people with same-sex sexual preferences have tried to overcome discrimination by going to court include the case of the Boy Scouts of America. The Boy Scouts refused to let a scoutmaster continue in that work when they found out he was gay. He sued on his own behalf and on behalf of other gays, but he lost in every court to which he appealed, including the U.S. Supreme Court, which in 2000 decided that the Boy Scouts had a right to exclude persons based on their sexual orientation.

To try to counteract that discrimination, gays have been pushing for explicit gay rights laws and hate-crime bills. Some of the proposed gay rights laws specifically prohibit discrimination on the basis of sexual orientation, and the proposed hate-crime bills make crimes that reflect underlying prejudice subject to stronger than normal penalties. Other such proposed laws would allow gay couples to marry. As of 2003, no state permitted gay marriage, but Vermont did allow "civil unions" that give the couples almost all of the benefits of marriage, and Massachusetts was considering allowing gay marriage.

Senior Citizens

A final characteristic that plays an important role in our society is age. Age stratification must be considered on a slightly different basis from the other characteristics we have been discussing. Whereas we are born either male or female, the characteristics of aging are universal for both sexes. Aging is inevitable, and Ponce de León's fountain of youth remains a legend.

Some stratification according to age is inevitable. As children, we are unable to care for ourselves and are thus separated from older age groups who productively contribute to society. As we grow old, our physical abilities decline and we are not able to do all that we once could, again creating a group separate from others. There is, however, no clear demarcation line as we move from youth to being middle-aged to being elderly. **Chronological age,** or age measured in years, often does not reflect a person's mental age or capacity to work and contribute to society.

Senior Citizens' Role in Society.   In primitive societies, few individuals live to an old age because of poor health care systems and their difficult lifestyle in general. The few who do live to old age are venerated as sources of information and wisdom. In modern industrial societies, because of advanced technology life expectancy has almost doubled since 1900, and the elderly are not a scarcity. Because in these societies great value is placed on physical achievement, grace, and agility, the normal physical slowdown that characterizes aging has been accompanied by decreased status for the elderly. Sometimes the output of senior workers has not been thought to be worth their wages. Even though it is against federal law for employers to discriminate against older workers, businesses have often been successful in finding ways around the law to get rid of these workers. Most of the elderly do live productive and active lives, but when they can no longer do so they have retreated to retirement communities if they can afford them, or, if they need a lot of care, they have had to enter nursing homes, some of which have been described as "waiting rooms for death."

As medical technology advances, the perception of what it is to be an older person, and what an older person can do, has changed. In the early 2000s, a significant number of older people are reaching their mideighties or older and doing so in good health. The proliferation of knowledge about DNA and gene function had fostered so much research that previously unheard-of increases in life expectancy have been predicted, although today the work is highly theoretical and practical results, if any, are probably decades in the future. But it is not outside the realm of possibility that in the coming decades life expectancy could increase by 20 or 30 percent should the "aging gene" be found and science discover how to modify it.

The Growth in the Proportion of Senior Citizens.   As you can see in Figure 12.2, the proportion of the elderly population has been growing. In 1900, less than 4 percent of the total population was sixty-five years of age or older. In 2000 they numbered about 35 million, about 13 percent of the total population. Projections are that their number will rise to about 70 million by the year 2030, or about 20 percent of the projected population. The growth is more substantial for those over eighty-five. In 1985 there were more than 2 million people over age eighty-five; in 2000 there were more than 4 million, and it is projected that by the year 2050 there will be about 19 million, or about 5 percent of the projected population.

This growth of the elderly population is beginning to present significant economic and social problems. For instance, the amount of Social Security benefits,

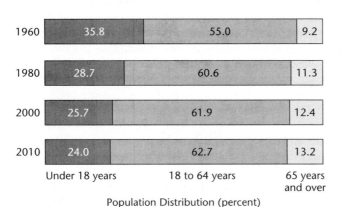

Figure 12.2

Resident population: age distribution. (Source: U.S. Bureau of the Census, *Statistical Abstract of the United States.*)

including medical insurance payments, for the elderly has placed a strain on the Social Security system, and as the proportion of mostly nonworking elderly grows in relation to the number of younger, working contributors, fewer and fewer workers will be supporting more and more elderly. This causes anxiety about the solvency of the fund and resentment on the part of younger workers.

In the early 2000s, over 35 percent of the federal budget was spent on the elderly, and federal spending is projected to be 42.8 percent of the 2010 budget, yet some studies show that the over-sixty-five group is financially better off than younger groups, partly because of relatively generous Social Security benefits and partly because of various tax advantages. Many younger workers believe that they themselves will find the Social Security fund empty when it is their turn to seek benefits as elderly persons; in the meantime, they are making high Social Security tax payments—in many cases higher than their income tax liability—and some are bitter about this mix. They ask why they should pay for all of these giveaways. Various proposals to change the financing of Social Security have been made—for instance, to allow people to privately invest money that would otherwise have been withheld as Social Security tax. President George W. Bush is in favor of that kind of modification, although he has not pushed it.

The problem of care for the elderly is increasing, along with the difficulty of providing older people with opportunities for a meaningful life. These problems have been worsened by changing family structures. With the decline of extended families, children often do not include their parents in social activities. These changing family structures are likely to continue for many years, and as they do the problems of finding a role for grandparents and great-grandparents in the family are likely to increase. To argue that a role for grandparents in the family is desirable does not mean that parents should be considered an appendage of their children's family. On the whole, the elderly prefer to live independently, yet at the same time contact with family and friends remains a vital part of their lives.

Senior activists march against age discrimination.

Age Discrimination.   In reaction to the problems facing older people, the gerontological set has turned to political and social activism, demanding their rights as individuals and as workers. They have formed groups such as the Gray Panthers, who play an active role in the political arena. These groups helped to win passage of the Age Discrimination Act of 1967, which prohibits discrimination against persons between the ages of forty and sixty-five. Moreover, in the Age Discrimination in Employment Act of 1978 the mandatory retirement age was raised from sixty-five to seventy, and in 1986 it was eliminated for most occupations. The elderly are an effective political force; when the American Association of Retired Persons (about 35 million members in 2003) speaks, lawmakers tend to listen. Because their numbers are expected to continue to grow at such an impressive rate, their influence can only increase over the next few decades.

The issues involved in age discrimination are not simple ones. For example, a sixty-year-old person differs from a twenty-five-year-old person; each relates to people in a different way. If a store believes customers prefer to have younger salespeople, should it be against the law if it "discriminates" on the basis of age? Under current laws, it is. Alternatively, some firms used the sixty-five retirement age to ease out employees who were unable to keep up, without having to state explicitly the reason for their release. Under the Age Discrimination in Employment Act, they cannot blame the change on a general rule and thus save face for both. Training older persons as new employees presents another problem. Many jobs require years of training, and in order to recoup an investment in a worker, a firm counts on that employee working for the firm for a sufficiently long period of time.

The argument can, of course, be reversed. Some firms have fired workers right before retirement in order to save pension payments. Others have merely fired older workers in order to have a better image, using "training" or "customers' perception" as an excuse. Age group conflicts are beginning to appear as the percentage of wage earners goes down and the number of pension recipients increases. The dilemma in many firms is in deciding whether to keep on older workers, who have had much experience, or to hire in their place a younger workforce with more energy and newer ideas. In the future we are certain to hear more about the employment issues of age, whether discussing a young workforce or an older workforce, because, as indicated here and earlier in the chapter, they are indicative of an ongoing change in the structure of our society.

Conclusion

At this point we end our discussion of stratification and the issues it raises, but not because we have exhausted the topics—we have only touched on many of them. We end it because of the pressure of space and the variety of other topics to be covered. Most of these other topics—social institutions, economics, and politics—deal with some of the same issues from a different perspective, and each perspective provides yet another insight into the problems of society and the workings of social scientists' minds.

Our discussion of stratification was designed to encourage you to draw your own conclusions. Obviously, merely in the way the chapters are written, certain biases became clear, although we worked hard to keep the analyses as objective as possible.

We can, however, conclude that stratification and discrimination do exist. Of that there is little doubt. It also seems fair to say that the issues are far more complicated than the advocates of either side generally present, and we must be careful not to focus too strongly on one side's argument. We raise the methodology issue at this point because most of us are involved in some type of discriminatory action—either discriminating or being discriminated against. It is at precisely such instances when our objectivity leaves us and we find the fairness or unfairness of the situation clear and beyond question. At this point, rational discourse breaks down. Whenever you seem to have such a strong belief, count to ten and try to "walk a mile in the other person's shoes."

Key Points

- Four reasons for racial prejudice are the influence of tradition, psychological needs, ego, and economic advantages.
- A minority group is a group of people singled out for unequal negative treatment, whereas a dominant group is singled out for positive treatment.
- Although the United States has made progress in dealing with the race problem, it still has a long way to go.

- Hispanics with historical and cultural ties to Latin America are called Latinos, whereas those with ties to Mexico are called Chicanos.
- Illegal Mexican immigration continues to be a problem despite several recent laws meant to deal with it.
- Anti-Semitism has been reduced, but it remains a potential problem.
- Anti-Islamic discrimination is on the rise in the United States.
- Women have made strides toward equality but still have a way to go before they achieve full equality.
- Senior citizens are likely to be a major political force in the twenty-first century.

Some Important Terms

affirmative action programs (262)
Chicanos (266)
chronological age (280)
de facto segregation (259)
de jure segregation (259)
discrimination (255)

dominant groups (256)
Equal Rights Amendment (ERA) (274)
ethnic group (252)
Hispanics (266)
Immigration and Naturalization Service (INS) (272)

Immigration Quota Act (270)
Latinos (266)
minority groups (256)
prejudice (255)
separate-but-equal doctrine (259)

Questions for Review and Discussion

1. Why are racial and ethnic differences largely independent of each other?
2. Has it been proved that some racial groups are superior to others in their capacity for mental development? Has it been proved that all racial groups are alike in their inborn capacities for mental and emotional development? Explain.
3. How would you explain the existence and the extent of racial prejudice in the world?
4. What is the relationship of prejudice to discrimination?
5. Why is the position of the black minority different from that of any other minority group?
6. What effect did the Supreme Court cases of *Plessy v. Ferguson* and *Brown v. Board of Education* have on legal segregation?
7. What are the obstacles to the elimination of de facto school segregation?
8. How does the economic position of blacks compare with that of whites? List the major factors that have brought economic gains to blacks.
9. What advances have been made in protecting the civil and political rights of black Americans? Which do you think have been most significant? Discuss what still needs to be accomplished.
10. Are blacks continuing to improve their social, political, and economic position? Defend your point of view.
11. What does Gunnar Myrdal mean when he says that no social problem as complex as the U.S. race problem is ever solved in an "absolute" sense?
12. Why are friendly relations between ethnic groups important to both the dominant and the minority groups?
13. What is the social and economic status of Latinos and Chicanos in U.S. society?
14. Discuss the history of Asian migration to the United States.
15. How do you account for the existence of anti-Semitism in both Europe and the United States?
16. Is discrimination against Muslims acceptable because of national security needs?
17. What might be some of the reasons the average earnings for a woman are lower than the average earnings for a man? Does this necessarily imply discrimination by individuals or firms?

18. What determined your career aspirations? Do those aspirations reflect institutional discrimination?
19. How is the growth in the proportion of people over age sixty-five in the population likely to affect our society?
20. What differentiates age discrimination from other types of discrimination?
21. If a store prefers to hire younger salespeople, should it be allowed to do so? Why or why not?

Internet Questions

1. What is the NLGLA, whose website is www.nlgla.org?
2. Go to www.eeoc.gov, the website of the U.S. Equal Employment Opportunity Commission. What is their latest news announcement?
3. Using the U.S. Navy site www.chinfo.navy.mil/navpalib/people/women/wintop.html, what are the latest numbers of women on active duty? What areas, or communities, are not open to women officers? What three ratings are not assigned to enlisted women?
4. The Arab American Institute identifies some famous Americans of Arab descent, www.aaiusa.org/famous_arab_americans.htm. List the names that are familiar to you, perhaps through sports or entertainment.
5. Based on http://hrw.org/doc/?t=usaac=us dom, what does the Human Rights Watch organization list as one of the issues involving the United States and human rights?

For Further Study

Blum, Deborah, *Sex on the Brain: The Biological Differences between Men and Women*, New York: Viking Press, 1997.

Carmichael, Cathie, *Ethnic Cleansing in the Balkans: Nationalism and the Destruction of Tradition*, London: Routledge, 2002.

Harris, Eddy L., *Still Life in Harlem*, New York: Holt, 1997.

Herrnstein, Richard, and Charles Murray, *The Bell Curve*, New York: Free Press, 1994.

Lewis, David Levering, *W. E. B. Du Bois: Biography of a Race*, New York: Henry Holt, 1994.

Lokko, Lesley Naa Nerle, ed., *White Papers, Black Marks*, Minneapolis: University of Minnesota Press, 2000.

Malcomson, Scott L., *One Drop of Blood: The American Misadventure of Race*, New York: Farrar, Straus & Giroux, 2000.

Murphy, Patrick T., *Unequal Protection: Women, Children and the Elderly in Court*, New York: Norton, 1991.

Myrdal, Gunnar, *An American Dilemma*, 2 vols., New York: Pantheon, 1975.

Nussbaum, Martha, *Women and Human Development: The Capabilities Approach*, New York: Cambridge University Press, 2000.

Pérez y González, María, *Puerto Ricans in the United States*, Westport, CT: Greenwood Press, 2000.

Rekdal, Paisley, *The Night My Mother Met Bruce Lee: Observations on Not Fitting In*, New York: Pantheon, 2000.

Rodriguez, Luis J., *Always Running, La Vida Loca: Gang Days in L. A.*, New York: Touchstone/Simon & Schuster, 1994.

Suárez-Orozco, Carola, and Marcelo M. Suárez-Orozco, *Children of Immigration*, Cambridge, MA: Harvard University Press, 2001.

Williams, Lena, *It's the Little Things: The Everyday Interactions That Get under the Skin of Blacks and Whites*, New York: Harcourt, 2000.

WWW   American Association for Retired Persons www.aarp.org

WWW   Anti-Defamation League   www.adl.org

WWW   Human Rights Watch   www.hrw.org

WWW   National Association for the Advancement of Colored People   www.naacp.org

WWW   National Organization for Women   www.now.org

WWW   U.S. Citizenship and Immigration   http://uscis.gov

WWW   U.S. Department of Justice   www.usdoj.gov

Yalle, Victor M., and Rodolfo D. Torres, *Latino Metropolis*, Minneapolis: University of Minnesota Press, 2000.

Young, Cathy, *Ceasefire! Why Women and Men Must Join Forces to Achieve True Equality*, New York: Free Press, 1999.

The Functions and Forms of Government

After reading this chapter, you should be able to:

- List five primary functions of government
- Identify three contrasting views of government
- Explain the liberal, conservative, radical, reactionary, and anarchist philosophies of government
- Distinguish a democracy from an autocracy
- List some distinguishing characteristics of a democracy
- Explain the democratic concept of the individual
- List the common justifications for an autocracy
- List four characteristics of an autocracy

Government after all is a very simple thing.

—**Warren G. Harding**

There never was a more pathetic misapprehension of responsibility than Harding's touching statement.

—**Felix Frankfurter**

Are governments necessary? To answer this question, all we have to do is look around the world to what happens when an effective government does not exist: to Iraq, where, after the U.S. victory, the country was left without an effective government, and anarchy and looting were widespread; and to Liberia, where in the early 2000s, because no effective government existed, competing factions fought for control, spreading devastation throughout the countryside—looting, raping, and murdering almost indiscriminately. The list could go on, but these two examples make the point: Effective government is necessary.

Government is the set of institutions by which a society is ruled. People often disagree violently about the role that government should play in society, which accounts for many of the political conflicts within a nation. Much of the controversy over the proper role of government in society arises from different conceptions of society and government, and any discussion of political and governmental concepts requires some common agreement on the meaning of these terms.

In the first part of this chapter we look at the various functions of government. Then in the second part we consider the various forms of government and how they operate. Finally, in the third section we examine various views of government.

As with all social institutions, there is a presumption that if an institution exists it serves some function. Government is no exception. At times, some social scientists have carried the functionalist approach to an extreme. The **functionalist approach** to government argues that what exists must exist as it is and not be tampered with because it serves a necessary function. That is too rigid a position for most social scientists. In this book we have emphasized change and how change modifies the role that institutions play in society. Thus we may find that institutions that once played a functional role may now play a quite different role, maybe functional, maybe dysfunctional. To decide that, we have to consider carefully the functions government serves in our society.

The Primary Functions of Government

In every society of any size, some form of organized government develops due to the need for an agency capable of exercising overall social control. The role of government can be better understood if we examine the specific functions most governments perform or claim to perform.

Maintaining Internal Order and External Security

Though the functions of government are many and varied, its basic job is to protect its citizens from internal and external enemies. The highest value in every political society is self-preservation, and the government is the one agency equipped to protect a nation. It alone possesses the power to enforce obedience to the rules of life that the society has established, and it alone has at its disposal all the military might that the nation can provide to repel aggression.

Government, as the guardian of internal social order, employs police, prisons, and courts in its attempts to protect persons, property, rights, and whatever society designates as worthy of preservation. None of our other social institutions could exist without the "domestic tranquility"—the peace and safety—that government provides. Wherever law and order break down, the government is unable to perform its other functions; the people become fearful, and all aspects of society begin to disintegrate. **Anarchy** is a society without government or law.

Anarchy is generally so injurious to society that, after a period of social confusion, people sometimes welcome as a blessing an absolute monarch or a modern dictator who can restore peace and order. Recognition of this fact led Thomas Hobbes, the seventeenth-century English philosopher, to conclude that government results from a contract among free men desirous of preserving life and of increasing its contentment—"that is to say, of getting themselves out from that miserable condition of war" that necessarily results from the absence of effective government.

Most advanced modern nations have eliminated internal warfare and reduced internal violence to such a low level that nearly all the conflicts that arise among their citizens are settled in an orderly and peaceful manner. When countries have not succeeded in doing this, bloodshed, destruction, and agony tear them apart, as we have seen clearly in places such as Bosnia, Somalia, Rwanda, the Republic of Congo, and others on a sad list.

Ensuring Justice

The belief in justice appears to be universal, and every modern government professes devotion to it. **Justice** is the maintenance or administration of what is just by law, by judicial or other proceedings. It is a concept that involves the relationships of individuals (and

*A*narchy in Iraq

After the 2003 Iraq War, Saddam Hussein's government was eliminated, which left Iraq without a government. The United States and Great Britain had armed forces there, but these forces were trained to win a war, not maintain the peace or govern. The result was anarchy—widespread looting and destruction of property. Hospitals, museums, power plants, banks—all were broken into and almost anything that could be moved was taken. Priceless historical treasures were taken from the National Museum of Iraq, and some hospitals were left with no beds or medicine. Shopkeepers didn't open for fear of robbery and even stayed in their locked shops twenty-four hours a day to protect them from break-ins. Neighborhoods organized vigilante groups and established patrols to protect their homes.

In short, the social and economic functions of the economy came to a complete halt as Iraqis attempted to provide the basic functions that governments provide to deal with anarchy. Eventually, the United States and British forces took a stronger role and established an interim authority that started to provide the functions of government, but for a short period in 2003, we saw firsthand the necessity of government and the effects of anarchy.

Looting in the Iraq War.

groups) both to society and to one another. Though justice means different things to different people and no one definition has been agreed on that describes its content, nearly every society considers it to mean "to everyone their due."

Not all governments strive for justice, although most generally profess to do so. All governments based on popular support aspire to convince the people that they are being treated justly. In fact, justices of the peace, sheriffs, judges, and courts exist in some form almost everywhere, and their main function is to administer justice.

People have confidence in their governments to the extent that they deal out rewards and punishment in accordance with the popular conception of justice. People willingly submit their private disputes for public settlement when they have faith that justice will be done. For example, a person whose home has been burglarized is generally willing to have the burglar prosecuted in a court of law, rather than attempting to secure personal revenge, as long as that person is convinced the courts will deal fairly with the matter. When government fails to perform this function adequately, or loses the ability to enforce its decisions, lawlessness begins to spread, and revolution may even result.

Safeguarding Individual Freedoms

Without some kind of government there can be no organized, stable society, and without a stable society there can be little real freedom for individuals. All governments profess to try to safeguard certain freedoms by maintaining law and order. But like the case of ensuring justice, not all governments actually do so. Democratic governments go further than nondemocratic governments; they have come to accept the defense of individual freedoms as a primary function. For example, the Constitution of the United States declares that a fundamental purpose of the union is to "secure the Blessings of Liberty to ourselves and our Posterity."

But in past times, when modern democracies were in the early stages of their development, government was often considered to be the enemy of freedom. Faith in government as the defender of individual freedoms has developed slowly over the years, until now in modern democracies there is a trend to look toward government for protection. Our federal government, for example, has taken action against monopolies, corrupt political practices, and discrimination against blacks, other ethnic minorities, and women.

There are, to be sure, two sides to this picture. Sometimes government regulations unjustly or needlessly restrict personal freedom, and there is always the danger that government may fall under the influence of special interests and fail to reflect the will of the majority. There is also likely to be debate about how much individual freedom should be infringed on to protect society. For example, after the 9/11 attacks, the United States passed the **Patriot Act,** which gave the government the right to detain people it felt might be terrorists or others who might support them. The act greatly broadened the circumstances under which surveillance was permitted, especially with on-line activities. It required financial institutions to provide information on client transactions and bookstores and libraries to provide information about what books individuals checked out or bought. Some felt this law went too far; others felt it didn't go far enough. These debates are healthy. The reality is that individual freedoms can be safe only when large numbers of individuals, and also organized groups, are dedicated to their defense. The preservation of these freedoms necessitates an active and responsible vigilance on the part of the people who enjoy them. Individual freedoms are responsibilities as well as rights, and as such, they must be defended to ensure their continued strength and legitimacy.

Regulating Individuals' Actions

In the growth of modern societies, many institutions and groups have developed to perform various functions. Some of these institutions and groups provide important social services, but often they also have selfish interests that are contrary to the welfare of society. Where this is true, government may find it necessary to regulate their activities. Our great public utility enterprises illustrate this well. Because of the nature of their business, they tend to be monopolies, and, in the past, when they were left to themselves they often charged excessive prices and gave poor service. Therefore, to protect the public the government established procedures for controlling them. Since the 1980s, both in the United

States and in other countries, many public utilities have been privatized—that is, sold by the government to private companies. Along with this has come some lessening of government regulation. However, some of the consequences of privatization and deregulation have been unexpected and undesirable. Examples include loose accounting regulations that played a role in the Enron and Worldcom accounting scandals, and electricity deregulation in California that led to an energy crisis there. In such areas, governments are reinstituting controls and regulation.

Promoting the General Welfare

Government as the agency for overall social control cannot escape the task of promoting the general welfare in a variety of ways that go beyond the functions we have discussed. The general welfare activities of government have multiplied many times in recent decades, but governments have always to some degree undertaken by positive means to promote the material well-being of their citizens. Even the governments of antiquity carried on some welfare activities. At times they gave aid to farmers, subsidized other private enterprises, and even controlled prices. The Bible relates how Joseph in Egypt supervised an extensive government program of buying and storing surplus grain to provide food in times of famine. The modern state extends and intensifies this ancient function of government.

Government provides the institutional structure within which economic and social interaction can take place. It regulates the economy; levies taxes; and prohibits, protects, and provides services in order to benefit individuals, groups, and the whole of society. Whether we think about it or not, every person every day is affected by the demands of government and by the benefits it provides. Whenever citizens leave home in a car, they drive on streets and roads provided by government; they can enjoy parks set aside by government; they can send their children to government-supported schools; they can travel abroad on government-issued passports, and in case of trouble can go to the consular or diplomatic agents of their government for aid; they can receive help from the government when they are unemployed or disabled; and if accused of breaking a law, they can be heard in a court established by government. These are only a few of the ways in which individuals are taxed, controlled, or benefited by government, all for the purpose of promoting the general welfare.

Welfare activities of government include health services, education, social security systems, and various other benefits. In the United States today there is debate about what kind of health insurance coverage the federal government should provide citizens, or about how to restructure the way it provides welfare services.

Governments furnish these benefits to meet public demands and to increase their own strength. Even dictatorships find it in their interest to provide workers with vacations and pensions on retirement. People who are deprived of their liberties are less likely to revolt against a government that appears to show consideration for their welfare. In democracies, where the political system makes public policy more directly responsive to public opinion, government has greatly broadened its welfare activities in response to the wishes of an enlarged electorate.

For centuries, students of politics have believed that if the masses were given the right to vote they would demand a redistribution of wealth and privileges. In modern democracies, wealth and income have been redistributed by such means as progressive income taxes, inheritance taxes, Social Security benefits, welfare payments, and public housing projects. This redistribution has happened to varying degrees. For example, in the 1960s the income tax was highly progressive, inheritance taxes were high, and there were numerous government programs to help the poor. In the past decade, however, that tendency toward redistribution has been reduced; the degree of progressiveness of the income tax has been reduced, the inheritance tax has been reduced, and programs to help the poor have been reduced. Many of these changes have been supported by the lower middle class. This support can be explained by a belief, held by many in the United States, that more effort should go into increasing total outputs—raising everyone's income—and less into redistribution of income.

*D*ebates about the Nature of Government

The preceding brief discussion summarized the various functions of government and debates about those functions. As you can see, although a government serves definite functions, there are spirited debates about these activities. In the evolution of the state over the centuries, the nature of government functions has in many ways remained the same. However, as other social institutions, such as the family and social mores, have evolved in response to technological change, the ways that governments carry out these functions have changed and so have the forms of government. Differences in culture have led different states down different paths and, therefore, to differing forms of government. We now turn to this issue.

Political Theory and Government

Government is by far the most powerful of all social institutions. It controls resources of extreme physical coercion, and it has taken over countless functions and responsibilities that once resided in the family, religion, and business enterprises, such as education and various social services. For example, in earlier times children took care of elderly parents; today, the government often does this through social programs such as Medicare. Although government today is in a position to regulate and control all other social institutions, it is in turn controlled by them. People's beliefs and attitudes and the ways they behave in the family, religion, and business enterprises determine the kind of government they develop, and often the expansion of government functions results from the failure of other institutions to meet social needs.

Politics is the means by which individuals affect government. Because of the importance of government and politics, an immense area of study, called political theory, has developed to study governments and politics. **Political theory** is that area of inquiry dealing with the nature of government and politics. Political theory has its origins in the writings of Aristotle, but our current systems of government are founded more on the writings of political theorists John Locke or Thomas Hobbes. Their alternative views of the relationships between the individual and the state form the basis of many modern **political ideologies,** deeply held beliefs in an idea—held so deeply and with such conviction that a person is willing to die for those beliefs. For example, **democracy**—the rule of the people—is the ideology of the United States, and it is rooted in the writings of John Locke. An alternative ideology, **fascism**—the belief in the rule of an elite whose members have special abilities—is the basis for what some countries think is the preferable form of government, and it is, to some degree, derived from the writings of David Hume.

When two political ideologies meet, there is often conflict. For example, World War II was in some ways a conflict between fascism and democracy. Ideologies are closely related to various views of the nature of government. If we believe that there is no role in society for government, we will likely have a significantly different ideological position than someone who believes that government has a positive role.

Three Views of the Nature of Government

To organize our thinking about these issues, it is helpful to differentiate the following three views of the nature of government: (1) government as a necessary evil; (2) government as a positive good; and (3) government as an unnecessary evil.

Government as a Necessary Evil.   Government follows us all through life, telling us what we can and cannot do. If we want to drive a car, we must first pass a government examination and buy a government license; then government forbids us to park in convenient places and fines us for exceeding the speed limit. It forces us to stay in school when we want to go to work. (We are told that we are too young to work.) Later it may take us out of school (when we want to remain) and compel us to enter military service. We can only become a lawyer or a doctor by securing a license from the government. If we earn any amount of money, government claims a share in taxes. If we are fortunate enough during our lifetime to accumulate enough wealth to leave to our children, government may impose an inheritance tax. Such activities as these make government the object of complaint and abuse and cause many people to feel that, at best, government is a necessary evil.

The very essence of government is to prohibit, to restrain, to regulate, to compel, and to coerce. For example, government possesses the authority to pass laws and the power to enforce them. Parents, therapists, and employers may cajole and condemn, but only government can legally imprison. It regulates the affairs of family and economic enterprise in accordance with its conception of public security, morality, and welfare. Of all institutions of social control, government is the most inclusive and the most powerful. Here, indeed, is a power so great that no one can safely ignore it.

Government as a Positive Good.   Another picture of government can also be painted. Many years ago, Supreme Court Justice Oliver Wendell Holmes was asked by a young law clerk, "Don't you hate to pay taxes?" Justice Holmes is reported to have answered, "No, young man, I like to pay taxes. With taxes I buy civilization."

Some years later, when taxes were much higher, Supreme Court Justice William O. Douglas made another classic statement about government. He wrote,

> Government is the most advanced art of human relations. It dispenses the various services that the complexities of civilization require or make desirable. It is designed to keep in balance the various competing forces present in any society and to satisfy the dominant, contemporary demands upon it. As a result it serves a high purpose; it is the cohesive quality in civilization.

People such as those we have quoted think of government as a positive good. They realize there is some truth in Thomas Paine's contention that government is necessary "to supply the defect of moral virtue," to force us to do right when our moral weakness would lead us to injure one another. For these people, government is more than a "punisher"; it is a promoter of the common good. It is the proper social instrument for positive action to bring the essentials of the good life to all the people.

Government as an Unnecessary Evil.   Writers of communist doctrine offered another picture of government. **Communism** is a theory of social organization based on the holding of all property in common, actual ownership being ascribed to the community or state. Marx, Lenin,[1] and Stalin,[2] for example, portrayed government as an instrument of oppression, "special machinery for the suppression of one class by another." All capitalist governments, so the argument runs, are tools of the rich used to enforce the exploitation of the poor. Capitalist democracy allows the people "once every few years, to decide which particular representatives of the oppressing class should be in parliament to represent and oppress them." In communist theory, the **bourgeoisie** is the class that, in contrast to the proletariat or wage-earning class, is primarily concerned with property values.

In this way of thinking, machinery for suppression will be necessary only until the internal and external enemies of communism are converted or destroyed. In general, communist theory pictures government, or at least the coercive powers of government, as an unnecessary evil of our day, to be abolished as soon as possible.

In this respect, communist theory resembles that of the anarchists. Communists have always considered government to be an unnecessary evil and have advocated the eventual abolition of all political authority and all instruments of coercion. It should be noted, however, that although Karl Marx, the early communist theoretician, wrote that there should be an end to the "coercive powers of government" and a "withering away" of the state, the former USSR and other communist nations found it difficult to follow their own ideology. Communist governments in the Soviet Union and a number of eastern European countries ended not because they withered away, but because they were removed by the very people whose interests, in theory, they were serving. Today there are very few purely communist governments. In China the Communist Party still rules, but it is reducing its pervasive role in the economy. The two countries that come the closest to having pure communist governments are Cuba and North Korea. In both, there are signs of change.

How Powerful Should Government Be?   Another way to classify people's views of government is by how strong a role they see government playing. Figure 13.1 represents various classifications of people's views, starting with those who see the least role for government and ending with those who see the strongest.

Individuals who believe in the least role for government, such as anarchists and libertarians, argue that government necessarily limits individual freedom in an unacceptable way. **Anarchists** are people who believe that the institutions of society, such as private property and the state, exploit and corrupt humans. If these authoritarian structures were removed, people would be free to realize their intrinsic goodness and establish the communal lifestyle instinctive to all human beings. **Libertarians** are people who advocate greater freedom for individuals. They dislike arbitrary authority and argue for active freedom and the free expression of the individual personality. Libertarians, such as the philosopher Robert Nozick, see a role for a minimal state. They disagree with the anarchists,

---

[1] V. I. Lenin, *State and Revolution.* A good edition in English is the revised edition, New York: International Publishers, 1932.

[2] Joseph Stalin, *Foundations of Leninism,* New York: International Publishers, 1939.

Figure 13.1

Views of the role of government.

arguing that we need the state to provide defense against other states, but that much of what modern states do is harmful.

Next in our classification system come reactionaries. **Reactionaries** are people who believe that more than a minimal government is necessary, but that the role government currently plays in society is much too large. They prefer turning back the clock and organizing under the smaller role they believe the government played in earlier times.

Anarchist, libertarian, and reactionary views are not widely held in the United States. Most individuals accept the need for government in a form similar to that which we now have. They differ primarily in degree and in the role they see government playing. The most commonly used terms, with their generally accepted descriptions, are the following: **Conservatives** are people who favor a smaller role for government than currently exists; **moderates** are those who favor about the same role for government as exists; and **liberals** are people who favor a broader role for government than exists. These views of government are the predominant ones in the United States.

By considering the three different views of the role of government, you can see that the distinction between liberals and conservatives is not as clear-cut as the listing in the previous paragraph implies. In actuality, liberals tend to see government as a necessary evil and thus they favor limiting government's role of infringing on individual rights, emphasizing concepts such as freedom of speech and freedom to worship as one wishes. When liberalism was founded, its focus was on limiting the role of government—the position we now call conservatism. But over time, liberalism became associated with government establishing a framework within which individuals' freedoms have real meaning, and thereby it became associated with increasing the size of government, even though liberalism maintained its view of government as a necessary evil.

When conservatism was founded, its focus was on a strong government because conservatives saw the government as a keeper of the public morals and, hence, as a potential public good. Therefore conservatives felt that it was proper for government to legislate morality and to tell people what was right and what was wrong. With the rise in the 1980s of the Christian Coalition political groups in the United States, we can see some of these conservative positions being taken up again. The conservative viewpoint in the United States is also associated with policies such as lower taxes; elimination or reduction of regulation, both of public and private activities; highly structured elementary and secondary education, with frequent tests to be sure students are learning the basics; and an emphasis on the family values of stable marriage and careful rearing of children by the parents.

To illustrate, it is the conservatives who generally support the government's right to legislate whether certain sexual activities such as sodomy are legal. Liberals generally oppose the government's right to control an individual's intimate life. In this example, liberals support less, not more, government. New Right conservatives generally support the government's right to control individual sexual practices, because these conservatives see the government as a positive good—as the keeper of the society's moral code. Therefore, on such issues conservatives favor a stronger government role whereas liberals favor a weaker government role. Over such issues the commonly accepted distinctions break down.

Not all groups fit this classification. For example, you may often hear the term *radical.* **Radicals** believe that the existing government must be changed from what it is to something else. They do not necessarily favor a larger or smaller role for government—just a change from the existing situation.

Elements of Truth in Each of the Views

All of these views of the role government plays in society contain elements of truth. Differences of opinion arise in part from differences in governments and in part from the different functions that every government performs. Governments have been oppressive and have exploited the masses; they have at times been almost exclusively concerned with restraining the unruly elements in human society; they have also been used by society to promote by positive means the common good. A rational evaluation of government must be based on many considerations, and important among these is an examination of the primary functions of government common to all modern societies.

Forms of Government

Of the many ways to divide governments, none is perfect. The first distinctions we draw are democratic, nondemocratic, and partially democratic countries.

Both the word and the concept of *democracy* come from the Greeks: *demos* means "people" and *kratos* means "rule." Thus democracy means rule of the people. Democracies are governments based on a popular vote; elections decide who will be in power.

The map on the opposite page shows how over 190 countries of the world could be divided in the early 2000s. About 30 percent were democracies, 25 percent were partial democracies, and 45 percent were autocracies. In later chapters, we discuss each in more detail. Here we simply present a basic overview.

Democracies

Democracy is a word that means different things to different people. To the ancient Greek philosopher Plato it meant mob rule, or anarchy. To some people today it means capitalism; to others it means socialism. Before the nineteenth century, few people in the world considered democracy desirable. But today comparatively few people will admit opposition to democracy. Now almost every important nation, including the republics of the former Soviet Union, claim to be democratic. In pre-1990 Soviet terminology, communism, in which individuals' rights to undertake actions within the economy were limited, was the only true form of democracy. Soviet and some U.S. scholars argued that in capitalist countries control is actually in the hands of a small group of people—sometimes called

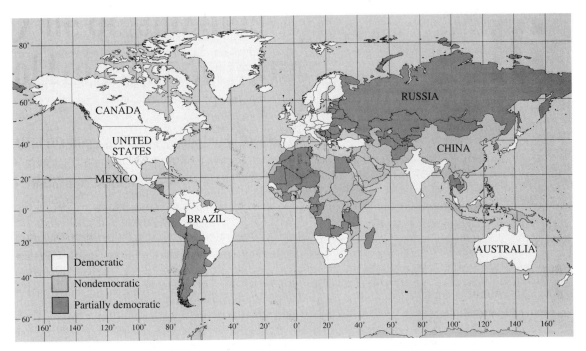

Democratic, partially democratic, and nondemocratic governments of the world. There is some ambiguity about how democratic a number of countries are, and this list reflects judgments of the author over the last decade. Countries can change quickly if there is a coup. Almost all countries call themselves democratic. For example, North Korea calls itself the Democratic Peoples Republic.

the power elite (the wealthy and the autocracy)—and that the so-called democratic states of the West are in reality states serving the interests of the power elite.

These arguments may have been correct, but they were discredited by the reality of most of these communist states. In these states, the Communist parties were not the protectors of the workers; often they were the exploiters. With their inefficient economic systems, to live well they had to exploit a lot, creating enormous animosity among the people. That's why most people in the Western democracies believed that the communist states were dictatorships. Some people in the West even went so far as to maintain that democracy and any form of extensive governmental interference in the economy, such as they had in the Soviet Union, are in the long run incompatible—that we have one or the other, but not both. That's debatable, but what happened in the communist countries has been an enormously positive advertisement for democracy. As is often said, "Democracy is the worst form of government, except for all others."

The facts indicate that scarcely any other word in current usage has more shades of meaning than are at times ascribed to the word *democracy*. Because democracy is good and noble, many people see their own system as democratic and noble and other systems as undemocratic and ignoble.

Characteristics of a Democracy.   Obviously, democracy cannot be defined in any precise way that satisfies everyone. However, we can clarify some of the concepts and opinions involved. For instance, we can distinguish between democracy as a form of government

A couple demonstrates their belief in popular sovereignty as they demand a complete vote count in the 2000 presidential election.

and democracy as a theory of economic and social relationships. We can describe the characteristics that the West includes under the term democracy and, having done this, we can distinguish between profession and practice and between democratic ideals and democratic realities.

In thinking about a democracy, the first thing that usually comes to mind is the concept of popular sovereignty. **Popular sovereignty** is the right of individuals to select their leaders by voting for them. A state that does not have popular sovereignty cannot be a democracy. We use the complicated term *popular sovereignty* rather than *voting* because the mere act of voting does not guarantee that the people decide who will be their leaders. In deciding whether a government is really democratic, we must consider whether popular sovereignty prevails, or whether the voting is simply a matter of form. Universal adult suffrage is not sufficient to make a political system democratic if the voters have no real choice among candidates.

The essential requisite for political democracy is that the people (not a king, an elite, or a class) are ultimately sovereign. Not only are the people the source of all political power, but also they are the masters of any government they establish to serve their interests. The "consent of the governed" means more than passive acquiescence; it means the power to control. In order for the people to control the government, there must be (1) freedom of speech, (2) effective legislative organs to represent the people, and (3) free elections in which the people may change the government by legal and hence peaceful methods.

Most modern democrats in the West consider freedom or liberty to be an essential element of democracy. But popular sovereignty means, in effect, majority rule, and there is always some tension or conflict between majority rule and the ideal of individual liberty. There is no way of completely resolving this conflict, but if the ruling majority is reasonably tolerant, it attempts to limit personal freedom only in situations in which such freedom would seriously interfere with the freedom and rights of others.

Key words that indicate important aspects of the democratic method are *free discussion, accommodation* or *compromise, moderation, tolerance,* and *reconciliation.* If these aspects exist to a sufficient degree, the definition of democracy as majority rule is perhaps acceptable. But democracy really means more than majority rule, for in the absence of these methods of resolving conflict, a majority can be just as tyrannical as any absolute monarch or modern dictator. It means that the majority will respect and guarantee the rights of the minorities, and that it will allow the minorities the right to try to become the majority. Democracy means that the end, no matter how noble, cannot justify the means. It holds that no goal, however desirable, is worth the price of sacrificing democratic methods.

Democratic Concept of the Individual.   Every philosophical, social, and political system is based on certain assumptions about the nature of human beings, and no political system can be understood without a knowledge of the assumptions it makes about humans and their relationship to society and government. Democratic assumptions are worlds apart from those made by dictatorships. Not all democratic assumptions can be scientifically demonstrated, but they are part of the democratic faith and the democratic ideal. In the absence of these assumptions, democracy could not operate successfully, for no other system of government puts so much faith in the average person or depends so much on the average person for its success. Democracy demands that the common people exercise sovereign authority over themselves, maintain freedom, and employ the judgment needed to secure the blessings of good government.

Rationality and the Democratic Way of Life.   Democratic theory assumes that people are capable of developing a culture in which individuals will have learned to listen to discussion and argument, and in which they will try to discover the truth by a rational weighing of the evidence. It assumes that a human society is possible in which the people will realize that they cannot get all they want from government, and that it is therefore in everyone's interest to make compromises. In a successful democracy, every important group must be willing to make such concessions to the interests of others as are necessary.

Equality.   Democratic theory holds that all humans should be regarded as equal, not in ability or in achievement, but in legal status and in their right to seek the good life. It does not insist that people are equal in beauty, brawn, and brains; in money and morals; or in power and prestige, but it does assert that all are equal before the law. It may even be said that the basic assumption underlying democratic government is that all—or at least most—citizens are potentially capable of reaching wise political decisions. It follows, therefore, that all should be given equal opportunities to participate in the political process: to vote, to hold office, to have opinions, and to strive to make their opinions prevail. No individual group is regarded as having a monopoly on political wisdom. Equality implies that public laws apply equally to all and that they will be impartially administered.

The democratic ideal of equality has developed considerably in the United States since the Declaration of Independence was written and has played an important role in eliminating slavery, in expanding educational opportunities, and in stimulating efforts to eliminate extreme poverty. Its work is still unfinished and necessarily always will be, but the widespread sharing of respect and power that democracy implies depends on a broad distribution of economic goods and the means of intellectual enlightenment. Further movements toward equality of opportunity will bring closer to full realization the ideal of popular control of government and should improve the quality of popular political decisions.

Primacy of the Individual.   Democratic philosophy and democratic government put primary emphasis on the dignity and worth of the individual. Government and society are considered to exist for the individual. The best organization of society—the best form of government—is regarded as the one that enhances the dignity of the individual and provides for the fullest and richest development of personality. The individual is considered to be the primary unit, one whose interests should be served by all social institutions. Individuals are not to be considered as means; they are the ends, for which all else exists.

The primary values of liberal democracy are freedom for and respect for the individual personality, and these values provide the basis for resolving the apparent contradictions between other democratic values. For example, freedom and equality are permitted and

*L*etting a Guilty Person Go Free

The primacy of the individual can be seen in various aspects of life in the United States. One example is Miranda Rights, which were established by a decision of the U.S. Supreme Court in 1966 (*Miranda v. Arizona*). In that case, Ernesto Miranda had been convicted of kidnapping and rape after appearing in a police lineup, being questioned, and signing a statement. The Supreme Court held that the courts cannot use statements obtained by the police while a suspect is in custody unless the suspect has been warned of the protection against self-incrimination provided by the First and Fifth Amendments to the Constitution. The Court laid out the points that must be covered. You may have heard them on television crime stories.

The Miranda Warning: *You have the right to remain silent. Anything you say can be used against you in a court of law. You have the right to the presence of an attorney. If you cannot afford an attorney, one will be appointed for you prior to the questioning if you so desire.*

If these individual rights are not read to the suspect, or are not understood by the suspect, the individual's statement cannot be used as evidence against him or her. Other examples of our concerns for the rights of the individual include limitations on how evidence is obtained: For instance, illegal wiretapping and unwarranted search may also be grounds for letting a person who may be guilty go free.

promoted insofar as they create the best environment for the development of individual personality. Freedom that disrupts social order is prohibited because order in society is necessary for the fullest exercise of the kind of freedom that promotes the development of wholesome personality. Individual or group freedoms that seriously limit the freedoms of either the majority or minorities are curtailed because the goal is as much freedom as possible for all, in order that all may lead full and satisfying lives. Complete social equality is not enforced, because such enforcement would destroy the individual freedom required for personality development. The line between freedom and order is a difficult one to draw, and inevitably there will be differences of opinion.

At times democracies may have exaggerated the value of individualism and failed to give full recognition to the value of social cooperation for the common good. In a world in which many nations glorify the state and tend to subordinate the individual completely, the democratic emphasis on the value, freedom, and dignity of the individual personality serves as a powerful bulwark to protect the social progress made in Western societies through centuries of struggle.

Where Democracy Works Best.   Democracy is a Western ideology, and we often think that it is the solution to all political problems. Unfortunately, it is not. For democracy to work, one needs the right environment. The right environment includes a tradition of respect for individual rights, a commitment to solving problems peacefully, a relatively homogeneous population (in which subgroups of the population are not antagonistic to one another), a commitment to minority rights, a commitment to democracy over other obligations such as religion, a generally acceptable distribution of income and wealth, an educated population, a free press, and a commitment to law. In many countries of the world, this environment does not exist, making the establishment of a well-functioning democracy difficult if not totally impossible.

Alternative Forms of Democracy.   The fundamental requirements of democracy are not to be confused with any precise type of governmental organization. Students of government agree that political democracy exists in many forms. It may be direct (as in a New England town meeting, which every citizen can attend) or representative (as it must be in all units with large populations). It may be presidential (as in the United States) or parliamentary (as in Britain, Canada, and Italy). It may be unitary (as in Britain and France) or federal (as in the United States). It may exist where there is either a written or an unwritten constitution, but there must be in some sense a constitution or fundamental law that the government respects. It may exist in a republic (as in the United States and France) or in a constitutional monarchy (as in Sweden and Britain).

Autocracy

In the preceding discussion, you saw that the term *democracy* was far more complicated than you might have thought. The same is true of the term **autocracy,** a government in which a single person or a small group of people has or claims unlimited power. Like democracies, autocracies come in many varieties. Antiquity had rulers in the clan, tribe, city-state, and empire. The names of some of the great Roman dictators are well known: Julius Caesar, Augustus Caesar, and Marcus Aurelius. The short-lived and limited democracy of the Greek city-states was replaced by autocracies under men such as Pisistratus, the Athenian tyrant.

The absolute monarchies that emerged from the disintegration of feudalism in the Middle Ages constituted the type of authoritarian rule commonly found before the emergence in the twentieth century of fascism and communism. Like many twentieth-century autocracies, these earlier absolute monarchies were marked by arbitrary rule, which at times tended to become irresponsible. Nevertheless, many of their rulers provided "popular" or "benevolent" government. Unlike most contemporary autocracies, the absolute monarchies were fairly stable because usually one hereditary ruler followed another without introducing any basic changes in society. In modern societies, we do not have absolute monarchies. Instead, we have limited monarchies in which the monarch plays a ceremonial role but has little to say in the governing of the country.

In the twentieth century, various types of autocracies developed in accordance with different conditions in different countries. The two basic types of autocracies that remain are the authoritarian and the totalitarian.

An **authoritarian autocracy** is one in which the society is ruled by a dictator or clique that forbids all activities that threaten its position. Although this group ruthlessly guards its power, it is generally indifferent to activities that do not threaten its rule. It wants to rule because it likes ruling or because it likes the benefits of ruling, such as the enormous potential income. The societies of the eighteenth-century empress Catherine the Great of Russia and, in the twentieth century, Francisco Franco of Spain, are examples of past authoritarian autocracies, and the military juntas in a number of countries of Africa are examples of current authoritarian autocracies.

A **totalitarian autocracy** is one that wants to control all aspects of an individual's life. A totalitarian ruler is different from an authoritarian ruler who does not care who teaches in a school as long as he or she takes no political stand and does not threaten the ruler's power. Put simply, "an authoritarian wants obedience; the totalitarian wants worship." The concept of totalitarianism was not formally introduced until the twentieth century.

A despot giving orders.

The reason is that overwhelming dominance of the political authority emanating from a totalitarian nation was not possible until twentieth-century technology succeeded in significantly increasing the scope of the state's control.

Most totalitarian autocracies are based on an ideology. With this ideology, they can justify their actions in terms of the goal of a better world. Nazism and Marxism are two examples of ideologies underlying totalitarian rule.

An authoritarian autocracy is not necessarily better or worse than a totalitarian autocracy. For example, authoritarian autocracies often plunder their countries' wealth, living in splendor while the people they rule may starve. Because totalitarian autocracies are generally based on ideology, totalitarian leaders are often far less interested in wealth for themselves and are more interested in seeing that individuals in their society share their own ideology. Thus, in a totalitarian autocracy people can be better off financially but have fewer personal freedoms.

Justifications Given for an Autocracy. Because most of the countries that we classify as autocracies claim to be democracies, to gain a better sense of an autocracy we must consider their arguments about why they do not allow free elections. Here we find continual debate about what is meant by *free*. For instance, some communists argue that when workers depend on businesses for jobs they are not free to express their own will—that their will is just an expression of the capitalists' and power elite's will. They argue that the control of a government by the Communist Party is a temporary expedient necessary to prevent the existing vested interests (the bourgeoisie) from thwarting the state's movement to a higher, freer stage. The theory is that only by accepting some limitation on freedom in the present can citizens under communism achieve true freedom in the future. Given the recent upheavals in most communist countries, this justification did not satisfy many of those who lived under communism.

In similar fashion, the autocracies of many underdeveloped countries claim that they are merely caretakers, that if they were not in charge, some other group far less benevolent and far less committed to democracy would take over and eliminate any possibility of the country ever becoming a democracy. They argue that because the environment of their country is not suitable for democracy, they must preserve order so that the environment can be made safe for democracy. They argue that they are not antidemocratic; on the contrary, they are protective of democracy. An example of a relatively beneficent caretaker autocracy is the African country of Uganda, where the president, Yoweri Museveni, has led Uganda back from chaos and created the stability needed for economic growth while at the same time maintaining a relatively uncorrupt government. He has tried to be inclusive in his government, but nonetheless has not allowed significant political opposition, arguing that with the ethnic hatreds that are so pervasive in Uganda, the country is not yet ready for democracy. This lesser-of-two-evils justification for autocracy goes back to the political philosophy of Thomas Hobbes, who justified monarchy in this fashion.

Each of these arguments has some validity. Democracy has its weaknesses. Modern democracies were developed to reflect Western cultural values and social institutions, and these may not flourish when transplanted. The will of the people is not well defined and so the concept can be manipulated. Moreover, democracies operate within certain legal frameworks that restrict individual liberties in certain areas. As recently as the 1950s here in the United States, during what is called the McCarthy era,[3] a congressional body, the Committee on Un-American Activities, summoned people suspected of being communists or of being "fellow travelers" (having friends who are communists). As a result of their testimony, or refusal to testify, some lost their jobs or could not find work in their professions, and some were even arrested and jailed. More recently, as part of the war on terrorism, individuals of Islamic beliefs or origin are being singled out as possible terrorist supporters. They can lose their jobs, even be arrested or jailed for having contact with suspected terrorists. Some believe that this treatment is a reasonable price to pay to root out terrorism. Others believe it has trampled on the rights of individuals that are supposed to be sacrosanct.

Similarly, developing countries do have problems making democracy work. In a country with two (or more) separate and opposing cultures, democracy is almost doomed to failure. Examples include Nigeria, with its many tribes and deep divisions between the Christians and Muslims; Iraq, with the Kurds, Shiites, and Sunnis; Afghanistan, with its many tribes; and the Republic of the Congo, with its many ethnic divisions.

Western countries have been frustrated with recent efforts to promote liberal democracy in Asia, Africa, and Latin America. However, the leaders in the West need to realize and accept that it is difficult to impose the typical Western model of democracy on non-Western societies, which possess distinct (and often contrary) cultural and sociopolitical characteristics. Therefore, classifying a country as an autocracy does not necessarily mean it is bad; it means it is not responsive to the will of the people in the way that Western democracies are.

Autocracy and Power.   As we stated earlier, an autocracy is a government that exists independently of, or beyond, the will of its citizens. It may or may not act in contradiction to the wishes of those it governs. It is important to note that in an autocracy the people have

---

[3]This era takes its name from a U.S. senator of the time, Joseph McCarthy, who conducted an infamous campaign against communists in government and in influential positions throughout U.S. society.

"Frankly, it's no better or worse than any other form of government."

limited means of calling the government to account. Its right to rule does not depend on majority support but, rather, derives from power that for authoritarian autocracies can be an end in itself. However, even in an autocracy, a leader who has lost the support of the people may find it difficult to stay in power.

A dramatic overthrow of an autocratic dictator occurred in Romania in 1989. Nicolae Ceauşescu had ruthlessly governed Romania during the cold war and was responsible for numerous human rights violations. When the tide of the pro-democracy movement engulfed eastern Europe in the late 1980s, Romania was the stage for a massive revolt against the incumbent dictatorship. On December 16, 1989, Ceauşescu declared a state of emergency after hundreds of protestors died during demonstrations in the city of Timisoara. The wave of protest spread rapidly throughout Romania and people openly marched into the capital, Bucharest, demanding Ceauşescu's dismissal. Army units joined the rebellion and on December 22, 1989, a group calling itself the Council of National Salvation announced that it had overthrown the government. A bloody conflict followed between security forces still loyal to the dictator and the new government. The Council of National Salvation gained control and Ceauşescu and his wife were captured. After a speedy trial, they were found guilty of genocide and were executed on December 25, 1989. On the same day, Ion Iliescu, the leader of the rebellion, was sworn in as the new president of Romania. In 1991 a new constitution set up a system by which the president and the legislature are elected by popular vote.

Whereas for authoritarian autocracies power is an end in itself (and possibly a tool for personal enrichment), and they need claim no other justification, for totalitarian autocracies the power is nearly always a means to a higher ideological end. There is generally some belief that the ruling elite possesses the "best brains," the "best blood," the "highest political insight," and the "capacity to rule."[4] Autocrats do not expect people to know what is good for them; they tell the people what is best and hope the people will believe it. If the people do not believe it, the autocrats can try to do what is good for them anyway. Of course, they can also listen to the people and carry out popular wishes, either because they believe that is the right thing to do or because they fear an uprising or a coup. Thus we can have autocracies that are responsive to the general will. They remain autocracies because the decision to be responsive rests with the ruler, not the people.

Characteristics of an Autocracy. The central characteristic of the totalitarian autocracies that came into power after World War I was their policy of controlling the total life of individuals and private groups. They employed whatever devices they could to make possible the effective control by the state of all social activity. The sphere of private freedom, which democracy attempts to maximize, is narrowly restricted by totalitarianism. Totalitarian government attempts to regulate all of life for state ends. Capital and labor, press and religion, family and fraternal organizations, work and play, individuals and society—all are subject to strict controls designed to promote the general welfare and to enhance the power and prestige of the state.

Loyalty to the Party and the State. Totalitarian autocracies demand complete loyalty and obedience to the party and the state. Fascist theory glorified and exalted the state. Some forms of communism exalt the social revolution and require of the individual complete dedication to the objectives of the Communist Party. But under both systems, the political party has direct control of the government and determines what government policy will be. Totalitarian communist states, for example, are the instrument for carrying out the policies of the Communist Party. Both fascism and totalitarian communism demand that individuals, where there is any conflict, subordinate their own interests to those of the party and the state.[5]

In the 1990s there were signals of a possible resurgence of fascism in Europe, with the relative success of extremist parties in France, Germany, Italy, and Russia. These movements exist, but at least by the early 2000s they have generally remained without effective power.

Rule by Leaders. Democracy emphasizes constitutionalism and rule by law; an autocracy is often characterized less by the rule of law and more by the rule of leaders. Until

---

[4]For example, the classic totalitarian autocrat, Adolf Hitler, wrote, "A philosophy of life which, by rejecting the democratic concept of the mass-man, endeavors to give this earth to the best nation, the highest type of human beings, must in turn, logically, obey the same aristocratic principle within that nation and must secure leadership and greatest influence for the best brains. It rests on the basis of personality, not on that of majority." Translated from *Mein Kampf,* Munich, 1938, p. 493 (earlier editions in 1925 and 1927).

[5]Benito Mussolini, the fascist leader of Italy between the two world wars, wrote: "For Fascism the State is an absolute before which individuals and groups are relative. . . . When one says Liberalism, one says the individual; when one says Fascism, one says the State. . . . The Liberal State does not direct the interplay and the material and spiritual development of the groups, but limits itself to registering the results; the Fascist state has a consciousness of its own, a will of its own." "The Doctrine of Fascism" quoted in William Ebenstein, *Great Political Thinkers: Plato to the Present,* New York: Holt, 1951, pp. 597, 598.

Hitler's Germany embodied fascist theory.

1515, England was a complete autocracy and no rule of law limited the ruler's power. In that year England adopted the **Magna Carta,** or "great charter," which forced King John to agree that free men had rights and liberties that could not be trampled on. After King John accepted the Magna Carta, his rights were limited, and England took a step from autocracy to democracy. As we have stated, autocracies differ from one another, and so do countries. However, where the power of the autocracy is strong and the ruler or ruling party unresponsive to the wishes of the citizens, the autocrat can change the political rules arbitrarily to meet the purposes of the moment; no law or established procedure is permitted to interfere with the continued existence and absolute rule of the power holders. Under such circumstances, life, liberty, and property are insecure, for a person may be found guilty on false charges without any genuine trial.

One-Party Monopoly.   Autocracy desires a monopoly on control; it generally tolerates no organized opposition, but it sometimes makes use of a political party. The one highly disciplined party that exists may have begun as a traditional political group struggling for parliamentary control. Once in power, however, it loses its private character and becomes an official control agency of the state. The purposes it serves are very different from those served by parties in a democracy. It offers the people no alternatives and it gives them no opportunity to participate in the formulation of public policy. Its purpose is to serve the organizational needs of the autocratic leaders and their followers. It provides for close contact between the rulers and the people, for the dissemination of the party line, and for the control and regimentation of the people in the interest of the rulers. It may, as in China, possess a legal monopoly on the power to nominate candidates. Regardless of its legal position, the state party carries out the will of the autocratic leaders and prevents the people from forming a legal opposition party to challenge the present rulers. Thus the party becomes in practice synonymous with the state; its personnel, policies, and programs become those of the state.

A Controlled Press.   If a leader is to maintain control without resorting to elections, she or he often finds it necessary to control the press and the other media to ensure popular support for the regime. **Propaganda** is the product of the state controlling the press and structuring the flow of information to the people in order to make the state look good. Totalitarian autocracies often employ an elaborate propaganda machine designed to secure mass support through intellectual conformity. The people are denied the privilege of hearing any other side of an issue. For these reasons, autocracies often have strong public support, but without a free press and freedom of expression for individuals, it is difficult to say whether that support would exist if people were offered a wider range of choices.

Communism, Fascism, and Autocracy.   When thinking of autocracy, we often think of communism and fascism because the terms *communism* and *fascist Nazism* have sometimes been used synonymously with *totalitarian autocracy.* This is somewhat misleading because communism and fascism are not really types of government. Rather, they are different systems of social, economic, and political theory that have produced totalitarian governments of a similar character. The differences between them are largely matters of detail and ideology, but as we stated at the beginning of the chapter, ideological differences are important.

Under communism the totalitarianism is meant to be temporary, and rule by the Communist Party is said to be a transition toward a higher stage of society in which "the State will wither away" because true equality and freedom have been achieved and totalitarian rule no longer has any function. Fascism, which was originally developed as an ideology to combat communism, does not see itself as a mere stage; it sees itself as a complete system capable of withstanding all assaults. (Adolf Hitler, the German founder of fascist Nazism, proclaimed that the Third Reich, which he established, would last a thousand years—it lasted less than twenty years.)

The development of fascism in reaction to communism shows the problem that ideologies present to society. The goals of communism (to each according to his needs; from each according to his abilities) sound noble, but when that ideology conflicts with a democratic ideology, one or the other must give. In the 1930s, communist ideologists argued that the democratic ideology must give. Once one group in a democracy no longer accepts the democratic ideology, it becomes more and more difficult for other groups to accept the limitations democratic ideology places on them. For example, if you're playing cards and the person you're playing with cheats, at some point you are likely either to cheat too or quit playing. In the 1920s and 1930s, fascists argued that because communists were not playing by the rules, fascists didn't have to play by the rules either. In Germany that argument carried the day, and Germany became a fascist state to "protect itself from the communists." The ultimate result was World War II.

Often fascism and communism are seen as opposite ends of the spectrum—communism on the left and fascism on the right. It is better to think of a circle, as depicted in Figure 13.2. At the top of the circle are autocracies without any ideological commitment. Traveling all the way around the left side of the circle to the bottom would bring us to

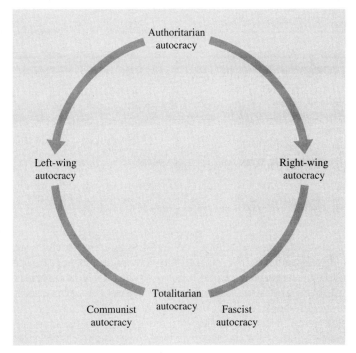

Figure 13.2

Continuum of autocracies.

communism, and tracing around the right side would end in fascism. Thus almost at the bottom, but not quite touching, are communists and fascists.

Governments Are Far from Simple

Having come to the end of this first chapter on political systems, we are in a better position to see why a former Supreme Court justice, Felix Frankfurter, attacked President Warren Harding's view that government, after all, is a very simple thing. Government is far from simple. Understanding the role of government is not like understanding mathematics or logic. There is an art to government, and although the goals of government may remain constant, the means of achieving those goals may vary with the temper of the times.

We could go on about the nature of governments, but you'll learn far more by considering examples. In the next chapter we take up the U.S. form of government, and in Chapter 15 we look at five other governments, some of which are autocracies and some of which are democracies.

Key Points

- Five primary functions of government are maintaining internal order and external security, ensuring justice, safeguarding individual freedoms, regulating individuals' actions, and promoting the general welfare.
- Three contrasting views of government are government as a necessary evil, government as a positive good, and government as an unnecessary evil.
- The liberal, conservative, reactionary, and anarchist philosophies of government differ in their view of how strong government should be.
- The two primary forms of government are democracy and autocracy.

- Three distinguishing characteristics of a democracy are freedom of speech, effective representation of the people, and free elections.
- The democratic concept of the individual is that he or she is rational, equal to all others, and primary.
- Common justifications for an autocracy include the repressiveness of markets, the need for a temporary caretaker, and the lack of the requirements for a democracy.
- Four characteristics of an autocracy include loyalty to the party and state, rule by leaders, one-party monopoly, and a controlled press.

Some Important Terms

anarchists (292)
anarchy (286)
authoritarian autocracy (299)
autocracy (299)
bourgeoisie (292)
communism (292)
conservatives (293)
democracy (290)
fascism (290)

functionalist approach (285)
government (285)
justice (286)
liberals (293)
libertarians (292)
Magna Carta (304)
moderates (293)
Patriot Act (288)
political ideologies (290)

political theory (290)
politics (290)
popular sovereignty (296)
propaganda (305)
radicals (294)
reactionaries (293)
totalitarian autocracy (299)

Questions for Review and Discussion

1. What are some of the functions of government that make it such a powerful institution?
2. Distinguish between anarchists and libertarians.
3. What three different attitudes toward government are predominant in the United States?
4. What are some of the reasons people disagree over the role government ought to play?
5. What does equality mean to you?

6. How do you think a government can administer the ideal of individual freedom without infringing on the freedom of other individuals?
7. Some forms of government advocate individual liberty; some others advocate individual control. Name one or two ideologies on each side and describe what you think each would mean for a citizen under such a government.

8. What are some of the differences between an authoritarian autocracy and a totalitarian autocracy? Name a state governed under each of these systems, and give reasons for your choices.

9. In what ways can communism be said to advocate liberty? In what ways can democracy be said to lead to repression?

10. What kind of government provides open elections but with only one candidate on the ballot? What kind might give voters a choice of candidates but have soldiers stationed at the polling place?

Internet Questions

1. Go to the Frontiers of Freedom website www.ff.org. What is their mission statement?
2. Using www.kentlaw.edu/ilhs/haymarket.htm, find out what the Haymarket Riot was.
3. Looking at the Homeland Security threat and protection information, www.dhs.gov/dhspublic/display?theme=29, what alert status are we in right now, and what does that mean?
4. Who was Idi Amin? (You can use www.multied.com/bio/people/amin.html.)
5. Take the "World's Smallest Political Quiz" on the Libertarian Party website, www.lp.org/quiz. How do you score?

For Further Study

Aristotle, *Politics* (trans. H. Rackham), Cambridge, MA: Harvard University Press, 1944.

Aycoberry, Pierre, *The Social History of the Third Reich* (trans. Janet Lloyd), New York: New Press, 2000.

Brinkley, Alan, *Liberalism and Its Discontents,* Cambridge, MA: Harvard University Press, 2000.

Dorfman, Ariel, *Exorcising Terror: The Incredible Unending Trial of General Augusto Pinochet,* New York: Seven Stories Press, 2002.

Ericson, Richard V., and Nico Stehr, eds., *Governing Modern Societies,* Toronto, Canada: University of Toronto Press, 2000.

Everdell, William R., *The End of Kings: A History of Republics and Republicans,* Chicago: University of Chicago Press, 2000.

Ferry, William E., ed., *Postcommunist States and Nations,* Newark, NJ: Harwood Academic Publishers/Gordon Bream, 2000.

Friedman, Thomas L., *Longitudes and Attitudes: Exploring the World after September 11th,* New York: Farrar, Straus & Giroux, 2002.

Hayek, Friedrich A., *The Constitution of Liberty,* Chicago: University of Chicago Press, 1960.

Hitler, Adolf, *Mein Kampf* (1927), Boston: Houghton Mifflin, 1962.

Hobbes, Thomas, *Leviathan* (1651), Baltimore: Penguin, 1982.

Locke, John, *Of Civil Government, Second Essay* (1690), Chicago: Henry Regnery, 1960.

Marx, Karl, and Friedrich Engels, *The Communist Manifesto* (1848), ed. Samuel H. Beer, New York: Appleton-Century-Crofts, 1955.

Rebhun, Joseph, *Leap to Life: Triumph over Nazi Evil,* New York: Arbor Scribendi, 2000.

Tocqueville, Alexis de, *Democracy in America* (1835), Garden City, NY: Doubleday, 1969.

WWW Advocates for Self Government www.self-gov.org/index.html

WWW American Civil Liberties Union www.aclu.org/

WWW The Christian Coalition www.cc.org

WWW Department of Homeland Security www.dhs.gov/dhspublic/

WWW Directory of U.S. Political Parties www.politics1.com/parties.htm

WWW Home of Liberalism www.turnleft.com/liberal.htm

Democratic Government in the United States

After reading this chapter, you should be able to:

- Give a brief account of the development of the U.S. government
- List the five key elements in the Declaration of Independence
- Outline the structure of the U.S. federal government
- Explain the distribution of powers as set out in the U.S. Constitution
- Describe the political process in the United States
- Summarize the role of the fourth estate, the political elite, the military-industrial complex, and PACs in the political process

An oppressive government is more to be feared than a tiger.
—**Confucius**

The ideas behind governments are one thing—how they work in practice is another. In this chapter, we consider the most important features and characteristics of U.S. democratic government, and in the next chapter we consider the operations of five other governments. As you will see, government, like all other aspects of life, is in a continual process of evolution.

Historical Development of U.S. Government

Because the United States started as a colonial possession of Great Britain, it is natural that our government reflects a British heritage. Initially the ties to Britain were strong, but when Britain tried to tighten up controls over colonial trade and to levy taxes on the colonists without obtaining the consent of the colonial legislatures, the colonies took action to end British rule and set up their own state. The most important event in the formation of the U.S. government took place when the Second Continental Congress met in 1776, issued the Declaration of Independence, and resolved to draw up a plan for the United States of America. (The Declaration of Independence can be found at www.usconstitution.net/declar.html if you want to read the full text.)

The Declaration of Independence declares that:

1. The people have the right to revolt against oppressive government.
2. Legitimate government must be based on the consent of the governed.

3. Both the ruler and the ruled are obligated to preserve a government that pursues legitimate purposes.

4. All men are created equal.

5. All men are endowed with certain inalienable rights, including life, liberty, and the pursuit of happiness.

These principles became the foundation of the U.S. form of government.

The Declaration of Independence formalized the war that had begun with the Battle of Bunker Hill in April 1775. It proclaimed the colonies "free and independent states." Having declared themselves independent, the states faced the problem of establishing a workable form of government. This was done in a Constitutional Convention held in Philadelphia in May 1787.

The Constitutional Convention succeeded because the delegates were willing to compromise. The decision to have a federal government was probably the biggest compromise. It satisfied both supporters of a **unitary government**—a government in which all the power is centralized in the national government, and the central government is absolutely supreme over all other government within such a nation—and supporters of a **federation,** a number of separate states, each of which retains control of its own internal affairs. The federal system of government had aspects of both. States retained control of some issues; the central government retained control over others.

Other important compromises included:

1. The differential representation in the House (by population) and Senate (two per state).

2. The establishment of an Electoral College to choose the president. The **Electoral College** is a body of electors chosen by the voters in each state to elect the president and the vice president. In the Electoral College, each state is allowed to have as many electors as it has representatives and senators in Congress, and each state can determine the method of choosing its electors.

3. The direct election by all the people of a particular state of its House members and the selection by the U.S. Congress of the two senators allowed each state.[1]

In addition to those just mentioned, compromises on many other issues were necessary because of the extensive conflict of interests and opinions. In short, the Constitution can be characterized as a bundle of compromises.

The U.S. Constitution—the foundation of the U.S. government and legal system—was signed on September 17, 1787, and forwarded to Congress with the recommendation that it be submitted to state conventions for ratification and that it become effective on acceptance by nine states, which it was after much struggle. (The U.S. Constitution can be found at www.usconstitution.net/const.html if you want to see the full text.)

Many of the states ratified the Constitution on the condition that amendments protecting private rights be adopted as soon as the new government was formed. The first ten amendments, adopted in 1791, accomplished this insofar as the national government was concerned. This **Bill of Rights**—a formal statement of the fundamental

---

[1]The election of senators by the people is one change that has taken place in the Constitution.

rights of the people of a nation—forbade the national government to invade basic private rights.

The Structure of U.S. Government

Because of the compromises in the Constitution, the United States has a federal government. It operates on three levels: national, state, and local. Over time the relative strengths of these various levels have changed. Specifically, the national government has been strengthened in part by wars, in part by advances in communication and transportation, and in part by the increasing complexity and nationwide scope of social problems. Nevertheless, state and local governments are still of great importance both to the individual and to our entire society.

Each of the fifty states, with its independent constitution, its own supreme court, and its own governmental agencies, exercises jurisdiction over most personal relationships, such as those of husband and wife, parent and child, and employer and employee, and also over property and business matters, including contracts, deeds, wills, corporations, and partnerships. Each state regulates commerce within its borders; establishes and controls local government; protects health, safety, and public order; conducts elections; and provides education.

Local governments are subdivisions of the state, are incorporated by the state, and possess varying degrees of autonomy. They include the county, city, town, township, village, borough, and school district and also include special agencies such as park districts, sanitary districts, and planning and zoning boards. Local governments are close to the individual, who can hardly escape noticing the services they provide. The sidewalks, lights, schools, public health service, police and fire protection, parks, beaches, and libraries are largely provided by local governments.

Structure of the National Government

Because the national government has become most important, we describe it in some detail. The national government of the United States as established by the Constitution is divided into three branches: the executive branch, the legislative branch, and the judicial branch. Figure 14.1 is worth careful study; it provides an outline of the structure of our national government.

The **executive branch,** the branch of government charged with the execution of laws and the administration of public affairs, is headed by the president, who is in charge of enforcing or executing the laws. Under the president, to whom all members of the executive branch are directly responsible, are the vice president, who would become president if the president were unable to serve, and the **cabinet,** the heads of the major administrative departments of government. These cabinet members, called secretaries, are appointed by the president, subject to approval by the Senate. Within the executive department there are also a number of agencies and commissions such as the Environmental Protection Agency. The extent to which these are responsible to the president is determined by law. The executive branch of the government is primarily concerned with enforcing the laws and with carrying on daily the many activities in which a modern government must engage. However, the president also plays an important role in determining governmental policies.

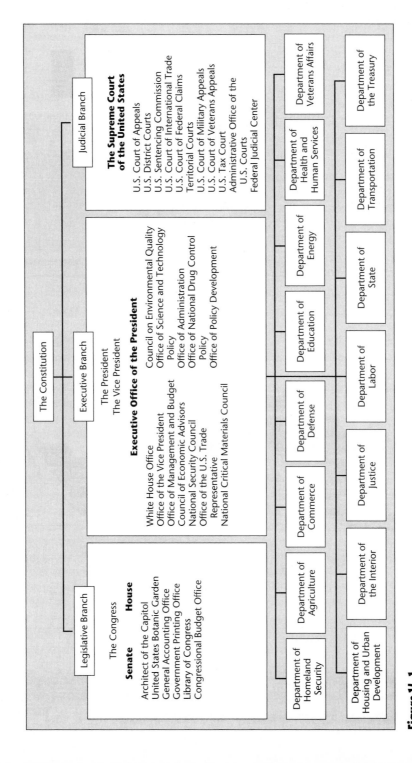

Figure 14.1

Diagram of the government of the United States as of 2004. The U.S. government is organized into three branches: the legislative, executive, and judicial. (Source: U.S. Bureau of the Census, Statistical Abstract of the United States.)

The **legislative branch** is the branch of the government vested with the power to enact and legislate the law. It consists of the two houses of Congress: the House of Representatives and the Senate. The legislative branch is chiefly the policymaking agency of government. It determines government policies by passing laws, or statutes. See Figure 14.2 and the box on page 320 for a better understanding of how a bill becomes a law.

The **judicial branch** is the branch of government that interprets the laws as they apply to particular cases that may arise. It consists of the Supreme Court and of the various lower and special federal courts. Once the meaning of a law has been decided in its application to a case, a precedent is said to have been established, and similar cases are likely to be decided in the same way. The federal courts interpret not only the laws passed by Congress but also the Constitution itself. For legal purposes, the Constitution of the United States means whatever the Supreme Court says it means. If the Court should obviously and persistently misinterpret the Constitution, the primary redress would be for the House of Representatives to impeach the justices responsible. Then the Senate would try them and, if they were convicted, remove them from office. In the more than two hundred years of its existence, this has never happened to the U.S. Supreme Court.

We now turn to the broad issues, clarifying our national government.

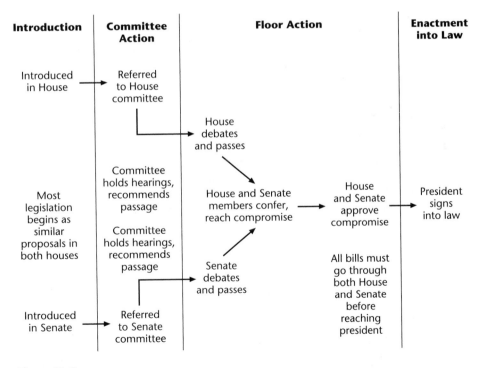

Figure 14.2

How a bill becomes law. This diagram illustrates the most typical way in which proposed legislation is enacted into law. There are more complicated, as well as simpler, routes. Most bills fall by the wayside and never become law.

The Nature of Our National Government

A short answer to the question, What kind of national government do we have? would contain as few as four words: democratic, republican, federal, and presidential. Our national government is democratic rather than dictatorial or oligarchical; it is republican rather than monarchical; it is federal, in contrast to most of the governments of the world, which are unitary; and it is presidential rather than parliamentary. It should be noted that the governments of all the fifty states have the same basic characteristics as the national government except that they are unitary rather than federal.

Why Our Government Is Both a Democracy and a Republic. There is an old but fruitless argument as to whether the United States is a democracy or a republic. Actually, the nation has the essential characteristics of both of these forms, and therefore it may be described as both democratic and republican. A **republic** is a form of government in which the head of the state, the president, does not inherit the office but is elected by those citizens who are qualified to vote. The United States is a republic according to this definition. Our Supreme Court has expressed the American concept of a republic as follows: "The distinguishing feature of the republican form of government is the right of the people to choose its own officers." This makes *republic* synonymous with *democracy,* which is the kind of government we have. Technically the United States has a **representative democracy,** a form of government in which the people make most governmental decisions not directly but through elected representatives, rather than a **pure democracy,** a political system under which all citizens vote directly on every piece of legislation. Pure democracy is possible only in very small communities.

The Meaning of Presidential Government. We have noted that the U.S. national government is presidential. In a **presidential form of government,** the chief executive (usually called the president) is elected for a definite period of years independent of the legislative or law-making body and has certain powers derived directly from the Constitution. In contrast, under the **parliamentary form of government** the executive branch is a committee, or cabinet, that represents the majority party in the legislative body and holds office only as long as it can command a majority in that body.

Great Britain presents a good example of parliamentary government. There the cabinet and its chief, the prime minister, are responsible to Parliament, and they can hold office only as long as Parliament supports their policies. The Parliament may withdraw its support for the prime minister by approving or introducing a vote of no confidence against the government. This system makes for close coordination of the executive and legislative departments. Under the presidential system, as exemplified in the United States, it is possible for the president and the majority in Congress to represent different parties and therefore fail to cooperate. On many issues, however, party lines are not sharply drawn.

In practice, the president usually takes the leadership in developing a legislative program, and insofar as this lead is effective, our system of government operates somewhat like the parliamentary system. Unfortunately, there are times when the president and the majority in Congress clash on major issues and are unable to resolve their differences. This may make it difficult for the president to take decisive and effective action to meet problems as they arise both at home and abroad.

Clashes were the rule in the 1990s as Congress was controlled by one party and the presidency by another. These clashes led to the impeachment of President Bill Clinton in

Bush supporters demonstrate in Florida.

1998. In 2000 there was an extraordinarily close election in which President George W. Bush narrowly won the election, while losing the popular vote. The election was heavily contested as only a few thousand votes separated Bush and Albert Gore, his opponent, in Florida, and all knew that whoever won Florida would win the election. After much legal wrangling, the Supreme Court issued a decision that essentially made Bush the winner. Many Gore supporters saw the election as unfair, but they accepted the outcome.

The president has two major functions: to take the lead in formulating policies and proposing legislation to Congress, and the administrative task of keeping the vast and unwieldy government organization operating smoothly and efficiently to perform its various normal duties. The latter includes many important responsibilities including acting as commander-in-chief of the nation's armed forces. Thus, when the United States went to war against Iraq, it was President Bush who ultimately was responsible for making the decision to do so.

Distribution of Powers by the Constitution.   A broad view of the national Constitution as originally devised and as it stands today reveals a wide distribution of political power. The founding fathers, though desiring a central government strong enough to govern, feared too great a concentration of power and therefore attempted to devise means for preventing the abuse of power. Broadly speaking, power is distributed in accordance with four constitutional principles:

1. **Federalism,** by which power is divided between the national government and the separate states.
2. **Separation of powers,** by which legislative, judicial, and executive powers are divided among three separate branches of the national government, each with its own duties and limitations of power.

3. **Checks and balances,** by which the decisions of one branch must be ratified by different branches of government. This system is designed so that no one branch of government can become too powerful.
4. **Limited government,** by which power is divided between the people and the government. This fourth principle includes the democratic doctrines of popular sovereignty, the inviolability of personal rights, and constitutionalism.

Division of Powers between the Nation and the States.   One of the great problems under federalism is how to divide powers between the central government and the states. In the United States, the national government theoretically possesses only the powers delegated to it, and all others belong to the states. Powers delegated to our federal government are of two kinds, enumerated and implied. The **enumerated powers** are those powers expressly delegated by the Constitution, which include the grant of legislative powers to Congress (Article I, Sections 1 and 8), executive powers to the president (Article II), and judicial powers to the Supreme Court and other federal courts (Article III). In general, the enumerated powers delegated to the national government are those dealing with all international affairs and those domestic affairs of a national, rather than merely state, concern. The **implied powers** are those that can only be inferred from the Constitution and for which no explicit provision exists. They have, however, provided the flexibility necessary for the national government to meet the new problems arising over the years from economic and social change. They have also, as some critics of expanding federal powers put it, enabled the central government to encroach on the rights and functions of the states. The implied powers are based on the so-called **elastic clause** (Article I, Section 8), which gives Congress the power "to make all laws which shall be necessary and proper for carrying into execution the foregoing powers, and all other powers vested by this Constitution in the government of the United States, or in any department or officer thereof."

The constitutional provisions for the division of powers also distinguish, though not very clearly, between exclusive and concurrent powers. **Exclusive powers** are those powers belonging only to the national government or only to the states. **Concurrent powers** are those powers belonging to both the national and state governments, such as the power to tax, borrow, and spend. Many government powers were not mentioned in the original Constitution, and the general understanding was that these belonged to the separate states. The Tenth Amendment made it plain that these reserved or residual powers "are reserved to the States respectively, or to the people."[2]

In the final analysis, however, it is clear that in spite of a careful attempt to separate powers, national supremacy has become a principle of the U.S. constitutional system. This principle grows out of the supreme-law-of-the-land clause, which states that the Constitution, laws of Congress in pursuance thereof, and treaties are the supreme law of the land, despite anything to the contrary in state constitutions and laws. In case of conflict, the states must make the necessary changes to conform to national law. Moreover, a branch of the national government, the Supreme Court, decides the issue when a conflict exists, so that in effect the national government judges its own case.

Separation of Powers of the Branches of Government.   As an additional safeguard against tyranny, the founding fathers divided governmental powers on a functional basis in accordance with the principle of separation of powers. James Madison wrote,

---

[2]In some federal systems (Canada, for example), the reserved powers belong to the national government.

𝒜 United States of Europe?

The European Union as of 2003.

In 1958 a few western European states formed to-gether into a common economic market. In 1967 they strengthened their mutual ties and forged the European Community, also establishing a European legislature called the Council of Europe. Over the years, the common market evolved into the European Economic Community (EEC), and after the historic Maastricht Treaty of 1992, it formed the European Union (EU), a confederation of sovereign member states. When formed, the EU contained approximately 350 million people from twelve member countries: Belgium, the Netherlands, Luxembourg, Italy, Germany, Greece, France, Spain, Portugal, Denmark, Ireland, and Great Britain. On May 4, 1994, the European Par-liament voted in favor of enlarging the EU's mem-bership to sixteen to include Austria, Finland, Norway, and Sweden, but the voters of Norway voted against joining. Thus in 2003 the EU had

fifteen members and approximately 371 mil-lion people. Malta, Cyprus, the Czech Repub-lic, Hungary, Poland, Slovakia, Slovenia, and the Baltic countries of Estonia, Latvia, and Lithuania, are in the process of joining the union. Others, such as Turkey, Bulgaria, and Romania, are also discussing entry.

The goals of the EU are virtually unprec-edented for any regional organization in the international community. The Maastricht Treaty established a tariff-free Europe; cre-ated a central bank to oversee banking in all member countries by 1997; and introduced a common currency, the euro, in some of the countries. In 2002, euro notes and coins went into circulation, with twelve of the member states adopting the currency. Further, the EU had two other long-range objectives: first, the formation of a European Political Union (EPU), which would harmonize the foreign policy interests of the member states and give the union a common voice in international relations, including matters of defense and se-curity; second, a joint action plan to regulate agri-culture, education, energy, the environment, public health, tourism, trade, and so on. Essentially it was a call for a far-reaching economic and political union that would eventually become the United States of Europe.

The treaty, however, has proven overly ambi-tious. Member countries have been too divided to commit to a revolutionary level of economic inte-gration. The formation of a central bank and the adoption of a single currency have been difficult, with a number of countries refusing to use them. The countries have been opposed to surrendering considerable sovereign power to a supranational federal authority based in Belgium. Considerable progress has been made, however, in the areas of eliminating tariffs and establishing passport-free travel among member countries.

No political truth is certainly of greater intrinsic value, or is stamped with the authority of more enlightened patrons of liberty, than that ... the accumulation of all powers, legislative, executive, and judiciary, in the same hands ... may justly be pronounced the very definition of tyranny.

The overconcentration of power in the colonial royal governors and the exalted position of the legislatures in the state governments of the Revolutionary War era had both proved unsatisfactory. The founding fathers feared tyranny by a majority of the electorate as well as by a strong executive. Most of the fathers were conservatives who wanted, among other things, to safeguard property against the "ill-humor" of popular majorities. They decided to place legislative, executive, and judicial powers in three different branches, each independent of the others. Each of the three branches of government was designed to be not only independent of the others but also directly dependent on different sources for office. The president was to be chosen by the electors in the Electoral College for four years; senators by state legislatures for six years; representatives directly by the people for two years; and judges by the president and Senate for life. As a consequence, it would be difficult for even the majority of citizens to "seize" complete control of the government and "tyrannize" over the minority, even though these constitutional mechanisms might not frustrate the will of the majority forever.

Checks and Balances. Supplementing and modifying the principle of separation of powers is that of checks and balances. Because of this principle there has never been in practice a complete separation of executive, legislative, and judicial powers. Broadly speaking, the separation of powers is part of the checks-and-balances system, for it fulfills Madison's dictum, "Ambition must be made to counteract ambition." Strictly speaking, however, checks and balances refer to restraints placed on each branch by requiring it to divide some of its powers with the others so that it cannot exercise independently the major functions allotted to it. Despite some popular opinion to the contrary, the authors of the Constitution never intended the three branches to be completely independent of each other. What they wanted to prevent was all legislative powers and all executive powers from falling into the same hands.

The Constitution clearly provides for interdependence between the three branches, which Madison also said was essential to free government.[3] Each branch of the government has some responsibility and power to influence the functions of the other two. Congress enacts laws, but they are subject to the president's veto, and that veto can be overridden by a two-thirds majority in each house. The Supreme Court can declare acts of Congress void, but Congress determines the appellate jurisdiction of the Court, and the president and the Senate appoint the judges. The president can make treaties, but only with the advice and consent of the Senate, and presidential appointments to government offices must receive Senate confirmation. The president and two-thirds of the Senate can make a treaty, but the House of Representatives must approve if any money is involved. The president administers the laws, but Congress must establish the departments and agencies and provide for their support. Many of the regulatory commissions (which are administrative agencies) created by Congress actually exercise executive, legislative, and judicial powers. Congress, by investigative committees and other means, attempts to secure the faithful administration of the laws. In a very real sense, all three branches participate in the making and the administration of public policy.

The extent of the power of the various branches is continually being tested. For example, the Constitution (in Article I, Section 8, paragraph 11) specifically gives Congress

---

[3]He wrote that "unless these departments be so far connected and blended as to give to each a constitutional control over the others, the degree of separation which the maxim requires, as essential to free government, can never in practice be duly maintained."

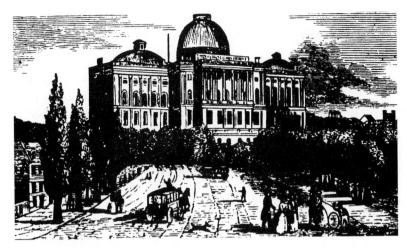

The Capitol building in the early 1850s.

the right to declare war, yet presidents have often entered government forces into battle without having Congress declare war. When they do this, presidents say it isn't really a war but a "police action." The Vietnam conflict is the most vivid example.

In response to the Vietnam police action, Congress passed the War Powers Act, which was meant to define clearly when the president must consult Congress about a warlike action, but it hasn't worked out that way, as you can see by considering the invasion of Granada, the actions of U.S. ships in the Persian Gulf off Iran in the war between Iraq and Iran, and the bombing of Kosovo in 1999, all of which were done without congressional approval. In the Persian Gulf War of 1991, President George Bush (the father of George W. Bush) maintained his right to commit forces to war unilaterally, as did President Clinton in Kosovo. However, usually presidents do try to get congressional approval before entering into war (as President George W. Bush did in the 2003 Iraq War), even though they argue that they don't need it.

An Independent Judiciary and Judicial Review.   U.S. tradition places great faith in an independent judiciary, one free of all pressure and all fear of political reprisal. Democratic theory has not demanded that the courts be directly subject to popular control. The U.S. Constitution provides for a Supreme Court relatively free of the executive and legislative branches, for once the judges are appointed, they can be removed only by impeachment. The function of the courts is to interpret the law and apply it in individual cases. For this task, independence is necessary in order to avoid decisions influenced by public sentiment or thoughts of job security and patronage.

The power to interpret the law is an enormous power. As you have seen throughout this book, concepts are often vague and somebody must give them specific meaning. Does "equal rights for all" require busing students to particular schools? Are segregated private clubs violating the rights of nonmembers? Do we have a constitutional right to doctor-assisted suicide? How much newly presented evidence, and what kind, is necessary to overturn a death sentence? Making these decisions and others like them is the main function of the courts.

Funny Things Happen to an Idea on Its Way to a Law

So that you can get a sense of how the national government functions, let's briefly follow a fictional idea through the various stages from conception to law. Let's say the idea begins with a social science professor who figures out that if the government establishes a new reform of the welfare system everyone will be better off. At a cocktail party, she meets a legislative assistant for one of the congresspeople (congresspeople have a number of assistants who analyze potential bills for them). The legislative assistant hears the idea, likes it, and decides to talk it over with some friends who work as assistants at the White House. If the White House staff like it, they may make it part of their proposals; if the White House doesn't like it, the congressperson or a senator may introduce it as a bill (a proposed law) on his or her own. If it is to get any further than that, other congresspeople or senators must be interested in it, and often, if they like it, several will become joint sponsors.

If possible, a similar bill will be introduced in the other legislative body. Then the bill will be sent to the appropriate committee, which will decide whether to consider the bill. The committee chair has significant flexibility in deciding which bills to consider. The bill might also be sent to subcommittees. By now, if the committee has chosen to, it will consider the bill for a formal vote and bring it up to the House or Senate with its recommendation (many bills die in committee). At this stage, it is important that the bill have other

backers. For example, if the bill is part of the president's program, the president can probably generate significant pressure to bring the bill to the floor—that is, to introduce the bill to the full House and Senate. Let's say one of the legislative bodies passes the bill. Then it is sent to the other legislative body. At each stage, the bill is subject to debate and can be amended. Thus, even if the bill passes both houses, it will probably be different from the originally proposed bill.

If both houses of Congress pass the bill in some form—say, simple majority vote—it is sent to a resolution committee that irons out the differences between the two versions (the one passed by the House of Representatives and the one passed by the Senate). Once that's done, the bill is sent to the president, who can either sign it, at which point it becomes law, or veto it. If the president vetoes it, Congress can override that veto with a two-thirds majority. But that is a rather hard thing to come by, and usually the politicians will try to compromise on a bill so that the president will agree to it in the first place.

Now the professor's idea is a law. But it's still subject to judicial review—an examination by the Supreme Court to determine whether the law is in accordance with the Constitution when a case relevant to that law is brought before it. If the Supreme Court holds that it is unconstitutional, that idea is no longer law.

This is a fairly succinct description of how an idea becomes a law. In reality the process is more complicated, but this summary should give you some idea of what happens to a bill on its way to becoming a law.

As the Supreme Court has evolved, it has become a protector of the rights of the people (as it interprets those rights). Every law passed in the United States is subject to judicial review by the Supreme Court of the nation or the supreme court of the state in which it was enacted. Under **judicial review,** the Supreme Court passes judgment on the constitutionality of a legislative or executive act. If the Court decides a law is unconstitutional, it is no longer a law. This independent judicial review, the third in our system of checks and balances, is a unique U.S. contribution to government and it has served us well. The national Constitution does not expressly grant or deny the Supreme Court the power of judicial review, but the Court has exercised it since 1803, when Chief Justice John Marshall concluded in the case of *Marbury v. Madison* that the Court must do so to fulfill its expressed duty of exercising jurisdiction over all cases arising under the Constitution.

Whether the founding fathers intended it to be so is uncertain, but our system of government required that this function be performed by some agency, and the Court was the logical choice. Marshall's opinion may have been partially political, but it was logical and has proved expedient. His basic assumption, which democratic theory endorses, is that the Constitution is superior to ordinary law.

The necessity for judicial review arises from federalism, the separation of powers, and the inviolability of private rights. The Court decides whether the national government has encroached on the powers reserved to the states, whether the states have exceeded their constitutional powers, whether the president or Congress have encroached on the rightful sphere of the other, and whether the national or state governments have violated constitutionally guaranteed private rights. This, of course, provides no safeguards against encroachment by the Court on the allotted spheres of the other agencies, including the states.

The aspect of judicial review that has provoked the greatest opposition is the voiding of acts of Congress. To nullify acts of Congress is to frustrate the will of the people expressed by democratically elected representatives, or so the critics have argued. There is truth in this accusation, but most Americans prefer having the majority will occasionally frustrated to having a system of government in which the majority is free of constitutional restraints. If a measure really has powerful public support, the people can always resort to a constitutional amendment or new legislation, adjusted to meet the Court's objections.

Over the years, the Supreme Court has gained great prestige by the manner in which it has protected the constitutional rights of national and state governments, Congress, the president, and individuals. However, its prestige has fluctuated greatly from time to time, and its decisions have never, of course, pleased everyone. In the 1960s, the Court was regarded as liberal. It found legal justification for giving the federal government greater power to deal with national problems, to expand its real or alleged welfare activities, and to protect individual rights when the states fail to do so. Then in the 1970s and 1980s, through the appointments made by Presidents Nixon, Ford, Reagan, and George Bush, the Court became more and more conservative and tended to limit federal governmental powers and follow a more "New Right" conservative view of the role of government. In the early 1990s, the movement of the Court to the right increased with the appointment of conservative justices such as Clarence Thomas. Many felt that his appointment would ensure a conservative majority in the courts for decades. President Clinton attempted to redress this perceived imbalance with his nominations to the Supreme Court: Ruth Bader Ginsburg in 1993 and Stephen Breyer in 1994. If President George W. Bush wins reelection in 2004, the court will likely turn more conservative should any moderate or liberal judge leave office during his presidency.

Federal judges, however, do not sit in an ivory tower rendering their decisions completely apart from public opinion. When the Court reverses a previous decision, this almost invariably reflects a basic change in public opinion. In 1954 the Supreme Court rendered a long-awaited decision on the constitutionality of "separate-but-equal" public school facilities. It reversed a fifty-six-year-old decision and found segregation in public schools to be a denial of "equal protection of the laws." Some people of the South accused the Court of playing politics, but in this case the justices were making a reasonable interpretation of the Constitution that agreed with the contemporary evaluation of majority opinion in the United States.

Limited Government.   Our national government under the Constitution has limited power. First, it shares power with the states. Second, at fairly frequent intervals, the voters, at free elections, may reject those in office or extend their tenure. Third, every citizen has certain inalienable rights recognized by our Constitution. These include freedom of speech, assembly, and religion, and they also include the right not to be tried, convicted, and punished for crimes without due process of law—that is, without being given the benefit of certain procedures and privileges that the law provides for an accused person in order to assure a fair trial.

Two characteristics of U.S. government, both of which are closely related to the subject of judicial review, require special comment at this point. One is the recognition by our laws and Constitution that every citizen has certain inalienable rights. The second is the fact that, though our federal Constitution is difficult to amend, the meanings ascribed to many of its clauses change gradually, as new situations arise, through the process of reinterpretation by the courts. For this reason it has sometimes been called a living constitution.

Individuals' Inalienable Rights.   The Preamble of our Constitution contains the declaration that one of the great purposes of government is "to secure the blessings of liberty to ourselves and our posterity." The U.S. concept of limited, constitutional government is based on the proposition that the people reserve to themselves certain areas of freedom that government may not invade, that people have inherent rights no political authority may either give or take away, "and among these are life, liberty, and the pursuit of happiness." Democratic government assumes that the majority will rule but also that the minority has the right to dissent. In the United States, as in any democracy, the majority rules legitimately only so long as it respects minority rights.

The founding fathers considered government to be largely an enemy of freedom rather than a friend. As stated earlier, the original Constitution and its Bill of Rights provided safeguards against the national government, and the Fourteenth Amendment extended most of these to the states.[4] We have learned through experience that government can be both the enemy and the friend of freedom. Most of us do not regret that our government was forbidden the right to invade a wide sphere of private rights, though we may no longer believe that government is a necessary evil. We know that liberty and security are inseparable and that without the security provided by stable, effective government, there would be few freedoms to enjoy. Thus the trend for more than a hundred years has been toward popular dependence on government to promote basic human rights.

Rights versus Duties.   Rights are never absolute. Furthermore, rights involve duties. The right to freedoms involves the duty of respecting the freedoms of others, whether these concern their choices of religion, political party, economic philosophy, or place of residence. Our freedoms are guaranteed only so long as we exercise them responsibly and refrain from using them as a cloak for obscenity, slander and libel, murder, public nuisances, incitement to riot and insurrection, and other unlawful acts. It is always the

---

[4]All responsible U.S. citizens would do well to acquaint themselves with the Bill of Rights and its significance for their welfare. These rights include (1) substantive rights, such as freedom of religion, of the person, of speech and the press, and of peaceable assembly; and (2) procedural rights, such as due process of law, just compensation for property taken for public use, specific warrant for arrest or search, writ of habeas corpus, speedy and fair trial by jury, and freedom from excessive bail, unusual punishment, bills of attainder, double jeopardy, compulsory self-incrimination, and ex post facto laws.

Symbol of a dream, Abraham Lincoln, the president who freed the slaves, was present symbolically as participants in the 1963 March on Washington massed at the Lincoln Memorial to hear Rev. Martin Luther King, Jr.

duty of the courts to draw a line between the legitimate and the illegitimate exercise of freedom, between controls essential for the welfare and safety of society and controls that unnecessarily invade the area of protected personal freedoms. No duty of government is more important or more difficult than this one.

There is no simple way of drawing a hard and fast line between the inalienable rights and freedoms of the individual and the controls that are required to protect the rights and freedoms of others. Many people, including a number of respected lawyers and judges, feel that in recent years the Supreme Court, in its efforts to guard the civil rights of individuals, has shown more concern for the rights of those accused of crime than for the rights of their alleged victims. Other critics, equally respected, defend the Court's decisions on the ground that protection of accused persons who may be innocent requires strict adherence to correct legal procedures. Since 1985, however, the Supreme Court has begun to crack down on criminals by giving the police more rights. That push has been strengthened by new laws, such as the Crime Act of 1994, which imposed mandatory life imprisonment for three-time convicted felons. The 9/11 terrorist attacks on the United States led to the passage of the Patriot Act, which gives the government significant power to detain individuals suspected of terrorist motives. Under this law, it is possible to keep these detainees for an indefinite period without charging them with a specific crime nor allowing them to speak with a lawyer. The reviews on the Patriot Act are mixed. Some see it as undermining the basic rights of individuals; others see it as a necessary deterrent to terrorism.

Figure 14.3 shows the basic rights that, under our U.S. system of government, are designed to protect an accused person against an unfair trial. One great protection is the right to trial by jury. In criminal cases, conviction requires a unanimous decision. (Some states do not require unanimity for deciding civil cases.)

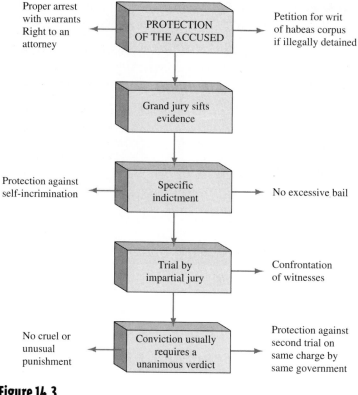

Figure 14.3

Civil liberties: An American heritage.

Growth of the Living Constitution.   U.S. government is constitutional government, and we Americans are proud of our written Constitution. In Great Britain, democratic government and the fundamental principles on which it is based developed slowly, so that no need was felt for a formal written document expressing these principles. But in the United States, a new nation had to be suddenly created out of thirteen independent colonies or states, and the only solution for this problem was to draw up in writing a formal agreement describing the structure and powers of the new government and also expressing the principles on which it was based. Because of our long and successful experience with this written Constitution, we have perhaps come to feel that fundamental political principles cannot be trusted to provide a framework for government unless they have been formally agreed on and duly recorded.

A written constitution is, however, rigid in that it cannot be easily amended. The amendment procedure stated in Article V of the U.S. Constitution provides for two methods of proposing and two methods of ratifying amendments. They may be proposed by two-thirds of both houses of Congress (the only method ever used to date) or by a constitutional convention called on the petition of two-thirds of the states. A number of states have made a call for such a constitutional convention, although most observers do not believe as many as two-thirds of the states would agree to petition Congress to call such a convention. Once proposed, amendments may be ratified by legislatures in three-fourths of the states (the method used all but once) or by conventions in three-fourths of the states (the method used to ratify the Twenty-first Amendment). The procedure was set up to ensure that the integrity of the document will not be violated by frequent revisions prompted by transient shifts in public and governmental opinion.

In spite of the difficulty in amending it, the Constitution has been a flexible instrument for meeting new situations. It has changed, not so much through amendment as through re-interpretation by the courts, to meet new practices and new situations that those who drew up the Constitution could not have foreseen. It has thus become a living constitution in the sense that it has been able to adjust in many ways to the changing beliefs and needs of the people. Through custom the undemocratic elements of the Electoral College were largely eliminated. Originally, the people elected leading citizens to the college and these then selected the president. But the practice soon evolved for candidates to the Electoral College to pledge themselves to a presidential candidate in advance, so that for all practical purposes when a citizen voted for an elector, the vote was for a certain person for president.

The rise of national political parties has also brought considerable unity to our national government in spite of the separation of powers provided for in the Constitution. Also, the growth of nationalism, the need for giving the executive great powers in times of crisis, and other influences have resulted in the emergence of the president as a strong unifying element in government. Much expansion of government functions has also been made possible by new interpretations of the Constitution. When the people wanted the government to play a more vigorous role in the regulation of business activity, they and their Supreme Court found the necessary authority implied in the enumerated powers of the Constitution. When new social problems arose and the people demanded more government services, the needed authority was again found to exist, by implication, in the original document.

If you look again at Figure 14.1 and note the major agencies of the executive branch of the federal government, you will have some idea of the vast expansion in government functions that has taken place over the years. Whether that expansion should continue or whether it should be reduced is a major issue that must be faced in the coming years.

The Political Process

Earlier we described democracy as it works in theory. We also touched on some examples of its workings in practice. We would be remiss in stopping there because, as with just about everything else, practice is different from theory. In our large country, decisions cannot be made by the institutions of democracy alone. Instead, they are made by a political process that includes numerous influences, some of which have no lofty goals—only the goal of establishing and using a power base. Others play a more beneficent role, but it is a role that was not foreseen by the early proponents of democracy. Political pressure groups and elites that have direct influence on governmental decisions are prime examples of practices deviating from theory.

Individuals influence government in our democracy through the political process. This political process includes numerous factors that determine policy formation, including public opinion, political pressure groups, the military-industrial complex, political parties, nominations and elections, and, finally, legislation. We can't give a complete discussion of each of these, but we can mention the most important.

President George W. Bush.

Political Parties

Although political parties in the modern sense did not begin to develop until the middle or later part of the eighteenth century, today they are universal in democracies. George Washington advised the new American nation to avoid dividing into parties, and they are not mentioned in the U.S. Constitution. But as democratic government developed, political parties came into existence because they fulfilled two important functions: interest aggregation and policymaking. They are not the result of theory but of practical experience, and they are necessities in representative democracies.

Compromising Conflicting Interests.   Probably the most important role of political parties is in compromising conflicting interests. In a dynamic society, many conflicting interest groups compete for control of the government and for favorable legislation. The majority of these sincerely believe that their programs represent justice, progress, and the general welfare, but they cannot all have their way. No government can provide at the same time for prohibition of and the right to manufacture, sell, and consume marijuana; for outlawing strikes and the freedom to strike; for the complete separation of church and state and publicly supported church schools. If all the conflicting groups that arise from differences in race, nationality, social class, creed, economic interest, and geographic location refused to accept any compromises, a unified national policy would be impossible. In the United States and other countries with two-party systems, most of the necessary compromises are brought about within each political party.

The political party, especially in the two-party system, acts as a mediator and cushion between, on the one hand, the individuals and groups that belong to it and, on the other hand, the government. Individuals and interest groups can bring pressure to bear on the party to adopt policies they favor. The organized party then seeks to reach compromise agreements and to convert them into legislation.

The Two-Party System.   Although the number of parties is not determined in the Constitution, the United States has generally operated on a two-party system. Most observers believe that this provides a more workable system than the alternative multiparty system. However, because of the necessary compromise on issues, a two-party system seldom shows sharp and clear-cut differences in program or principle, and often differences that appear to exist before an election tend to disappear once a party gets into power. The need of each of the two major parties to appeal to a large segment of the population contributes to the development of relatively moderate philosophic orientations. Moreover, in their attempt to attract people from all interest groups, the two parties tend to promise everything to everybody. Voters who want to influence some particular policy (such as extension of civil liberties, more public housing, gradual elimination of farm price supports, or a planned reduction of foreign aid) often feel frustrated because they cannot make their voices heard in the party. Periodically, there have been attempts to establish a third party. The Reform Party's candidate won significant votes in the 1992 presidential election and Ralph Nader, the Green Party candidate, won about 3 percent of the votes in the 2000 election. Although these votes were far from the number needed to win those elections, they were sufficient to influence the outcome, and some Gore supporters argued that Nader was responsible for Bush's victory.

The argument in favor of two parties is that in a nation as large and diverse as the United States, unity is essential, and each of our major parties performs the valuable function of bringing together under one umbrella a number of groups whose interests vary considerably. If a portion of the population is not happy with the policy alternatives presented by the two major parties, however, it is at liberty to create a third party, or more. This potential for the development of a third party helps keep the two major parties responsive to the needs and demands of the people.

An important trend in party affiliation that has been increasingly evident is the decline in the number of people who identify themselves with one or the other major party. Today more than one-third of the voters in the United States described themselves as independents. Some of the reasons for this are (1) people do not need to rely as much on favors being extended to them by their party as they did fifty or seventy-five years ago, when formal support systems were less common; (2) they wish to split their votes among candidates of different parties; (3) they are disillusioned with the party system or with some kinds of government activities; and (4) they have so many social and professional interests that they no longer see a political party as a kind of club. Relaxation of party ties does not mean, however, that people have given up the privilege of voting and of voting within the choices offered by the two-party system.

Elections

Democratic government implies the wide extension of the **franchise**—the right to vote. Citizens of modern dictatorships also enjoy this privilege, though for them it is a privilege stripped of power. The right to elect government officials and to vote on public policies has been achieved by centuries of effort. We have already noted how suffrage was restricted in early America by property and religious qualifications. Because of such requirements, in 1790 only about 15 percent of adult white males, and no women, could vote. Thus women were not included in the suffrage at all.

Over time the United States has done away with property, religious, racial, and gender qualifications. The gradual trend throughout the world has been to extend the franchise and make it universal for all responsible citizens. In the United States, black males won the right to vote in national elections in 1870, when the ballot was awarded them by the Fifteenth Amendment to the Constitution. It was not until 1920, when the Nineteenth Amendment to the Constitution was ratified, that women won the right to vote in U.S. national elections, although some individual states had granted them local rights much earlier. The most recent such movement in the United States was to reduce the voting age from twenty-one to eighteen, which was accomplished by the ratification of the Twenty-sixth Amendment to the Constitution in 1971.

As we discussed earlier, one of the important compromises of the original Constitutional Convention was the establishment of the Electoral College. The people elect members of the Electoral College, which then elects the president. In a number of elections, the most recent being in 2000, the popular vote and the Electoral College vote differ. This led to calls for the elimination of the Electoral College, but we are unlikely to see any such change because constitutional change comes very slowly, and small states, who would lose power, are likely to block any effort to abolish the Electoral College.

Obstacles to Effective Popular Control.   The right to vote is not equivalent to the power to control the government. The electorates in democracies throughout the world have had their ballot power weakened in many ways, including the following:

1. Overburdening voters with a long ballot
2. Permitting voters to participate only in indirect elections
3. Forcing voters to declare their choices publicly
4. Providing inadequate voting facilities
5. Allowing nominations to be controlled by the privileged few
6. Limiting categories of those who can hold office
7. Conducting corrupt elections
8. Denying elected officials the right to vote
9. Placing on the ballot only candidates sponsored by the official government party

Some of these limitations have existed and still exist in the United States and other democracies. In the early 1990s, some electorates, such as those of Colorado and California, limited their own power by voting to limit the number of terms their elected representatives could serve. They did this because they disliked the idea that the representatives, once elected, tended to get reelected indefinitely. However, the voters were also preventing themselves from constantly reelecting individuals if they liked them well enough. The debate over whether term limits should be repealed or whether more electorates should adopt them is likely to be discussed well into the present century.

The Nonvoter.   In the United States, perhaps 60 percent of the civilian population of voting age exercise their franchise in presidential elections; in the off-year congressional elections, only about 40 percent participate; and in local elections, a mere 15 percent is not uncommon. In Britain and the other democracies, the percentage is considerably higher (it is over 75 percent in Britain). Why do Americans fail to vote? The many reasons include the long ballot, the belief that politics are irrelevant to contemporary concerns, lack of interest, or feelings that one vote can't matter.

Probably the most important reason is indifference produced by lack of political education and experience. People simply feel no compulsion to participate in the electoral process. Many of them come from homes with a long tradition of nonparticipation in political affairs. Such people are often considered selfish and unpatriotic, but in many cases ignorance of issues and candidates is the main reason for not voting. Only increased education can improve the percentages of voters.

One of the reasons people don't vote is the belief that their vote cannot make a difference. Generally, they are right—one vote does not swing an election, but in the 2000 elections numerous votes were extremely close, and a few votes either way could have changed the result in various House and Senate races. In the U.S. presidency race, the election came down to who would get Florida's twenty-five electoral votes. After initial recounts of the votes, only about 900 out of 6 million votes separated the candidates, and there was much legal wrangling about which votes could be counted. The number of partially punched ballots in those counties that had punch card ballots far exceeded the 900 vote difference, so the presidential election hinged on decisions made about these ballots. Ultimately, George W. Bush was declared the winner, but only after a Supreme Court decision. Had a few more Gore supporters voted, or even had they been more careful when they voted,

Gerrymandering and the U.S. House of Lords

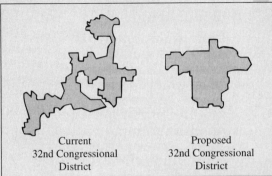

Current
32nd Congressional
District

Proposed
32nd Congressional
District

Gerrymandering.

The U.S. democracy doesn't work perfectly. Incumbents use their powers—PAC money,* free use of the postal service, perks of office, the large support budgets they are given to pay for staff—to vest themselves in office. These powers are sufficiently great that in the last forty years, 80 percent of all members of the House of Representatives who have run for reelection have indeed been reelected. In 1986, 98 percent of such members were reelected; in 1988, 99 percent were reelected, leading the *Wall Street Journal* to call this body "The House of Lords." In 2000 and 2002, the benefits of incumbency were less clear, but the large majority of incumbents who decided to run did retain their seats.

One of the ways incumbents win reelection is to have the districts from which they are elected gerrymandered, or drawn up in such a way that it is difficult for them to lose. For example, consider the strange shape of the Thirty-second District of California, shown on the left side of the drawing. Why does it have that shape? Why isn't it shaped like the proposed district on the right side of the drawing? Answer: Because demographic characteristics make the odd-shaped district a safe district for the incumbent; the "reformed" district wouldn't be safe.

Shaw v. Reno (1993) illustrated some of the problems that plague democracy in the United States. In that case, white voters claimed that a long, skinny North Carolina district was unconstitutional because it was drawn to include blacks and exclude whites. The Supreme Court sent the case back to the lower court for a review of the issues: the meaning of the constitutional "right" to vote and the propriety of racially motivated state legislation designed to benefit members of historically disadvantaged racial minority groups. The lower court then said that the district was constitutional because it helped remedy past discrimination and that its odd shape alone was not enough to void the legislation. The white voters appealed the decision by going back to the Supreme Court in 1995, this time in a case called *Shaw v. Hunt.*

When the Supreme Court decided *Shaw v. Hunt* in 1996, it said that the legislation was indeed unconstitutional because North Carolina had not overcome the presumption that the use of race as the "predominant factor" in drawing district lines is unconstitutional. In response, North Carolina wrote a new version of the statute, and the case again worked its way up to the Supreme Court, where it appeared in 1999 as *Hunt v. Cromartie.* This time the Court said that to think that states must absolutely eliminate the use of race in drawing up their electoral districts was to misinterpret the 1996 decision. Instead, the Court said, a state might have other reasons, besides focusing on black voters, for drawing a district that happened to have large numbers of black voters, and that anyone challenging such a law must be prepared to prove that the state's main motive was to isolate or favor black voters. Boiled down, the Court meant: "Case not proved." North Carolina was left to ponder yet again the reasons for the shape of the district. In 2001, the case was ultimately decided, and the Supreme Court ruled that race could be used in redistricting, as long as it was not the predominant factor. With the significant redistricting that came with the 2000 census, this issue will remain contentious. Just how contentious can be seen in Texas, where a large number of democratic representatives hid out of state so that their legislature could not achieve the quorum necessary to vote on redistricting.

*For a further discussion of PACs (political action committees), see p. 343.

In the 2000 presidential election, every vote counted.

Al Gore might have won. So individual votes do matter.

Referendums, Recall Elections, and Direct Democracy. In the United States, most elections are indirect—we elect a governor and a legislature and they then determine the laws. Decisions can, however, be more directly related to the voting public if a referendum is held and the people decide directly what the law will be. These referendums avoid the governmental structure and allow direct voter input into a law.

The direct approach is used most in California, which allows voter initiatives on a large number of issues, and these voter initiatives often play an important role in the laws that are passed. For example, property taxes are limited due to a referendum, and in 2003 Governor Gray Davis was recalled and actor Arnold Schwarzenegger was elected.

The California experience demonstrates both the benefits and the problems with direct democracy. To pass an issue by referendum requires large spending on advertising and organization, and this means that some special interest is usually behind those referendums that pass. So, whether these referendums lead to better government or simply to another means through which special interest can achieve their desires, is much in debate.

The Fourth Estate

Most politicians now acknowledge that the **fourth estate**—the journalistic profession or its members, including the press and television—is equal in importance to the president, Congress, and the judicial system. *Public opinion* is a general term that everyone talks about, but no one is quite sure what it is or what determines it. Nonetheless it is extremely important, and political leaders keep a close watch on the mood of the public by listening to feedback from their local representatives and through opinion polls. Politicians try to shape public opinion by giving speeches, selectively granting interviews, and allowing information leaks. As they do this, they must listen to the press and television because these institutions control the information that flows to the general population. The ease of publicizing one's individual opinions by means of the Internet can also affect public opinion, but unlike print or television the Internet is not a good medium for political control because it can't organize concentrated action.

Inherent in our Constitution is the guarantee of freedom of the press, but the press is not free from influence by private pressure groups and businesses. The press and television are important because they play such central roles in influencing public opinion. For example, consider our earlier discussion of the process by which a bill becomes a law. If the social scientist who had the idea has good contacts with the press and can get it to write stories on how wonderful the idea is, she will probably be much more effective in getting her idea considered by the political process. Similarly, if the press doesn't like the idea, the idea will probably disappear quickly.

Despite the time, energy, and skill they devote to obtaining favorable press and television coverage, politicians are often not pleased with the results. For example, Presidents Nixon, Carter, and Clinton felt hounded by the press. Both Nixon and Carter believed it to have played an important role in their political defeats. On the other hand, President Reagan, whose career until well into middle age was based in radio announcing and film and television acting, was called "the Teflon president" because press and television criticism would not stick to him. His personality and experience served him well in politics, where he was also called "the great communicator" because he could get his points across to the American people so effectively.

In recent years there has been a disturbing trend in the role played by the fourth estate: The media has become increasingly involved in scrutinizing the private lives of politicians. The late 1990s were filled with stories about President Clinton's personal affairs and his attempts to cover them up. Most political analysts agree that such stories detract from the credibility and impartiality of the media, but they argue that because the stories involve potentially impeachable actions, it is the duty of the press to report them.

The Political Elite

A basic assumption in the United States is that all individuals are created equal, but it would be a mistake to assume that practice follows that ideal. In practice, there is an elite in the United States whose feelings, aspirations, and influence carry more weight than those of other groups, either because they can use money or power to influence events or because they have direct access to those in power. If they don't like what is going on, they get on the phone and call a high-ranking U.S. official to let him or her know their concerns.

Who are the political and economic elite in the United States? Any list would have to include the president, U.S. senators and representatives, governors, state senators, state representatives, and high executives in government, which, using U.S. civil service rankings, would be Grade Service Level 15 and above. To these we would need to add approximately 15,000 to 20,000 executives who hold most of the power afforded by the top manufacturing corporations and e-commerce enterprises; the executives of the top financial organizations, law firms, universities, and religious bodies; judges; and independent professionals such as writers, doctors, and scientists. Roughly estimated, we would arrive at about 100,000 people who would have to be considered the political and economic elite of our society.

Does the political elite rule our country and thwart democracy? That's debatable. For example, consider the two presidential candidates in the 2000 election—one was the son of a former famous senator; the other was the son of a former president. That suggests that the elite tend to pass on their control to their children. The authors' view of the elite is that it certainly doesn't rule our country directly, but indirectly it holds a considerable degree of power. All agree, however, that there are limits to that power.

The Military-Industrial Complex and Pressure Groups

In a living democracy, the division among the various groups is often not as clear-cut as it seems. A good example of this is what is often called the **military-industrial complex,** the nexus between the armed forces, the Pentagon, and defense industries. The term was originated in 1961 by President Dwight D. Eisenhower, who had just ended his term of office. In his farewell radio and television address, he said,

This conjunction of an immense military establishment and a large arms industry is new in the American experience. The total influence—economic, political, even spiritual—is felt in every city, every statehouse, every office of the federal government. We recognize the imperative need for this development. Yet we must not fail to comprehend its grave implications. Our toil, resources, and livelihood are all involved; so is the very structure of our society.

In the councils of government, we must guard against the acquisition of unwarranted influence, whether sought or unsought, by the military-industrial complex. The potential for the disastrous rise of misplaced power exists and will persist.

We must never let the weight of this combination endanger our liberties or democratic processes. We should take nothing for granted. Only an alert and knowledgeable citizenry can compel the proper meshing of the huge industrial and military machinery of defense with our peaceful methods and goals, so that security and liberty may prosper together.

Eisenhower's warning is no less relevant today than it was in 1961. The simple reality is that there is money to be made in defense (in 2003, defense spending totaled well over $400 billion), and when there is, firms and individuals will try to make money by expanding their particular areas, using whatever political means they can to ensure political support. This has continued to be true in the early 2000s even though most observers believe that the enormous changes in the former Soviet Union have significantly reduced the need for defensive arms. Thus it is possible to have weapons systems that serve little purpose other than to make profits for defense firms, jobs for their workers, and votes for congresspeople. This means that once the building of such a weapons system is begun, it is extremely hard to stop.

Of course, it is not only industry and the military that combine to create pressure groups for continuation of their programs. Advocates of other kinds of programs also form pressure groups. But the potential damage from weapons systems is so great that the military-industrial complex deserves special mention.

Another way in which groups interact is by means of **pressure groups,** groups that have organized to influence the political process. Pressure groups play an important role in trying to shape public opinion. In addition to exerting this type of influence, they often try to influence legislators directly. Thus pressure groups fill a gap in a two-party system, enabling people with common interests to petition government for redress of grievances and to make their will known on many specific issues. Through the use of lobbyists, they keep national and state legislators and executives informed about what the people they represent really want from government. They also present a threat to well-functioning democracies in that certain special interests may become so powerful that, unless the public is alert, they frustrate the will of the majority and thus obstruct government by and for the many.

Fortunately, one powerful interest group (such as organized labor) is often balanced by another powerful interest group (such as business). However, certain interest groups that lack effective organization, such as hired farm labor and consumers, tend to suffer from pressure-group government. But to say that consumers are likely to suffer from the activities of pressure groups is only one way of saying that the public interest is likely to suffer, for everybody is a consumer.

Political Action Committees.   The problems presented by special-interest pressure groups have surfaced in a new way with the advent of political action committees (PACs). PACs are essentially campaign committees established by individuals to raise money for particular political purposes. They sprang up as a result of the revised 1974 federal election laws that limited the amount of money individuals were allowed to contribute to a candidate. Under the law, an individual contributor could give only $1,000 to a candidate's primary and general election campaigns, whereas a PAC can give $5,000 to each.

In 1992 campaign finance reform became a major issue for Bill Clinton during his presidential race. After his election, however, little reform occurred because the Republicans and Democrats could not agree on the nature of the reform. The issue was again important in the 2000 election. However, the politician who made campaign finance reform one of the cornerstones of his appeal, Republican Senator John McCain, was not nominated by his party. All politicians need lots of money if they want to win elections, and therefore it will probably be impossible to achieve significant reform in this area unless there is some basic, universal change in the way elections are run.

Some change has been made. In 2002, President George W. Bush signed the Bipartisan Campaign Reform Act, which regulated soft money for issue ads, contribution limits, uses of campaign funds, and reporting. The Reform Act, however, is in the federal courts, with various plaintiffs arguing that several of the provisions are unconstitutional. Many reformers take the other position; they not only agree with the provisions of the act, but they also believe that further legislation will be necessary once individuals and groups learn to evade these new limits and requirements.

One important element of campaign finance is **soft money,** that is, money contributed to political parties rather than to individual candidates. In 2000 some candidates claimed that they would agree to reject soft money if their opponents would do the same, but such mutual agreements could not be reached. Under existing laws, no limits are placed on such contributions, allowing large amounts of money to be given to support the "general philosophy" of a party, not to specific candidates. The line between the two is a fine one.

A second big campaign finance issue was illegal contributions by foreign countries, such as China, to the political parties. These issues are clouded by ambiguous records and the unwillingness of participants to detail their actions. Therefore campaign financing remains a hot political issue that both sides talk about, but neither seems willing to actually undertake serious reform.

Some writers maintain that the most effective defense against special-interest groups is the organization of still other groups to check and balance those that now exist. The weakness of this theory is that if great numbers of people cannot organize effectively to protect themselves, the general interests of the public—which may constitute the most vital interests of every group—are often neglected.

Evaluation of the Democratic Political Process

The political process in the United States is complex and confusing but nevertheless challenging. To win election to a major office takes time, work, money, and patience; from an idea to the enactment of a law is often a long journey. To reach such goals, mountains of obstacles must be scaled and arid deserts of electoral inertia must be crossed. Compromises are necessary, and concessions must be made by many conflicting interest groups, each of which has a somewhat different destination in mind. Ignorance and other human limitations must be taken into account all along the route. Fraud and favoritism are constant dangers. But democracy offers ordinary people the challenge of the opportunity to rule themselves.

In the United States, the democratic way of life has become so firmly embedded in our culture and has brought us so many personal and social advantages that few of us can really conceive of living under any other social system. No other system can give us such a high degree of personal liberty or protect our individual rights so well. If at times we complain about the faults of democracy and its failure to achieve perfection, we are only being human. When we consider the alternatives, most of us believe that our U.S. brand of democracy is providing us with benefits that can be matched in few other countries, and we believe that if we meet our responsibilities, democracy will provide these benefits in greater measure in the future. Most Americans believe that, on balance, our government is and will continue to be a government of the people, by the people, and for the people.

Key Points

- The United States revolted from Britain in 1776 and became a new nation in 1781.
- The Declaration of Independence declared that the right to revolt is reserved by the people, consent to be governed is necessary, governmental action is limited, and all people are created equal and are endowed with certain inalienable rights.
- The national government of the United States as established by the Constitution is divided into three branches: the executive, the legislative, and the judicial.
- The Constitution provides for federalism, separation of powers, checks and balances, and limited government.
- The political process in the United States is a mess that works.
- The fourth estate, the political elite, the military-industrial complex, and PACs all play an important role in the political process.

Some Important Terms

Bill of Rights (310)
cabinet (311)
checks and balances (315)
concurrent powers (315)
elastic clause (315)
Electoral College (310)
enumerated powers (315)
exclusive powers (315)
executive branch (311)
federalism (315)
federation (310)
fourth estate (330)

franchise (327)
implied powers (315)
judicial branch (313)
judicial review (320)
legislative branch (313)
limited government (315)
military-industrial complex (331)
PACs (332)
parliamentary form of government (314)

presidential form of government (314)
pressure groups (332)
pure democracy (314)
representative democracy (314)
republic (314)
separation of powers (315)
soft money (333)
unitary government (310)

Questions for Review and Discussion

1. Is the United States a democratic society? Explain your answer.

2. In what positive ways did British politics and government influence the U.S. Constitution?

3. What important decisions were made by the Constitutional Convention?

4. What major compromises were made at the Philadelphia convention?

5. Compare federal government with unitary government.

6. What are the three levels of government in the United States, and how are they related to one another?

7. What are the three branches of our national government, and what is the function of each?

8. What are the four basic characteristics of the U.S. system of government?

9. Compare presidential government with parliamentary government.

10. In what ways does the Constitution distribute power?

11. How does the principle of checks and balances modify that of separation of powers?

12. What is the meaning and significance of judicial review?

13. How is the "living constitution" related to the written one, and how does it keep pace with changing conditions and new problems?

14. What role do political parties play in a democratic system?

15. What are the primary reasons people do not vote?

16. What is the "fourth estate"? How does it influence our government?

17. What is the military-industrial complex? How does it influence our government?

18. What role do PACs play in shaping legislation? Is it a positive or negative role?

Internet Questions

1. Go to the Federal Election Commission website, www.fec.gov/pages/ecmenu2.htm. Which states have more than twenty electoral votes? Which states have fewer votes now than in 1990?

2. Who are your present senators and in what year were they first elected? Check www.congress.org.

3. Use www.supremecourthistory.org to find out: Who are the nine justices on the Supreme Court today?

4. What is the Preamble to the United States Constitution? See www.house.gov/Constitution/Constitution.html.

5. Using www.whitehouse.gov/government/cabinet.html, who is in the president's advisory cabinet?

For Further Study

Evans, Harold, with Gail Buckland, *The American Century*, New York: Knopf, 1999.

Farnsworth, Stephen J., and S. Robert Lichter, *Nightly News Nightmare: Network Television's Coverage of U.S. Presidential Elections, 1988–2000*, Lanham, U.K.: Rowman & Littlefield, 2003.

Foner, Eric, *The Story of American Freedom*, New York: Norton, 1998.

Johnson, Paul, *A History of the American People*, New York: HarperCollins, 1998.

Ketchum, Richard M., *Saratoga: Turning Point of America's Revolutionary War*, New York: Henry Holt, 1998.

Kobrak, Peter, *Cozy Politics: Political Parties, Campaign Finance, and Compromised Governance*, Boulder, CO: Lynn Rienner Publishers, 2002.

Kryssar, Theodore, *The Right to Vote: The Contested History of Democracy in the United States*, New York: Basic Books, 2000.

Lieberman, Jethro K., *The Enduring Constitution: An Exploration of the First Two Hundred Years*, New York: Harper & Row, 1987.

Moynihan, Daniel Patrick, *Scorpion Tongues: Gossip, Celebrity, and American Politics*, New Haven, CT: Yale University Press, 1998.

Silk, Leonard, et al., *Making Capitalism Work,* New York: Twentieth Century Fund/New York University, 1997.

United States Government Organization Manual, Office of the Federal Register, National Archives and Records Service, Washington, DC: Government Printing Office, issued annually.

WWW   Official Search for the U.S. Government   www. firstgov.gov

WWW   Reform Party   www.reformparty.org

WWW   The U.S. Constitution   www.usconstitution.net

WWW   The U.S. House of Representatives   www.house. gov

WWW   The U.S. Senate   www.senate.gov

WWW   The U.S. Supreme Court   www.supremecourt us.gov/

WWW   The White House   www.whitehouse.gov

Governments of the World

chapter 5

After reading this chapter, you should be able to:

- Give a history and describe the key features of the French government
- Give a history and describe the key features of the Mexican government
- Give a history and describe the key features of the Japanese government
- Give a history and describe the key features of the Russian government
- Give a history and describe the key features of the Saudi Arabian government

If the gods should hand down to mortals, as mortals now are, a perfect system, it would be all banged up and skewed twistways inside of ten years.

—**Don Marquis**

A knowledge of the U.S. system of government is only a start in understanding how governments work. To gain perspective on how the U.S. government operates and on how various governments achieve their ends, we consider the governments of five other countries: France, Mexico, Japan, Russia, and Saudi Arabia. All governments have certain ends they must achieve, but as you will see, these ends may be different and governments may pursue different ways to achieve them. We observe how the historical context within which each country developed has shaped its specific form of government and how much variance there is among autocracies and among democracies.

French Government

France, the country where democracy was reborn, is a good country with which to begin our consideration of governments besides our own. The current system of French government developed in reaction to the absolute monarchy that had become non-responsive to the changing social conditions—specifically the emerging middle class. **Bastille Day** is the equivalent of our Fourth of July and commemorates the storming of the Bastille prison in Paris. The French celebrate it every year on the fourteenth of July.

The storming of the Bastille in 1789 marked an uprising of the people, the **French Revolution**—the revolt in France against the monarchy and aristocracy, lasting from 1789 to 1799—and led to a decade of chaos and terror, with the revolutionaries tearing down the political structure and other social institutions of the country but not replacing them. This chaos ended when a dictator, Napoleon Bonaparte, took control. Although Napoleon reversed the process of democratization and returned France to an autocracy, after his reign there was a gradual evolution away from autocracy and toward a liberal parliamentary system that characterizes the French government today. In 1871, after France was defeated in a short war with Germany, the Franco-Prussian War, all vestiges of autocracy were ended, and the democratic French republic was established.

Although the republics of France have always had a written constitution, the French constitution has never been as firmly established as the U.S. Constitution. In fact, there have been sixteen constitutions since the revolution of 1789. There is some continuity, however, and their present constitution refers to the Declaration of the Rights of Man, part of the preamble to the original constitution written in 1789.

The lack of a stable constitution has made the French people regard laws differently than they are regarded in the United States, where for many people the law is the law; the law is right. For the French people, laws are simply technical rules under which they live. The difference is not so much in what actually happens in each country—in both some people break the law. In the United States, if you break the law (for example, by evading taxes) you probably feel guilty about it. In France, people are often proud of having broken what they regard as mere rules made by people who made different ones last week and will make still different ones next month.

The French Parliamentary System

France is now organized under what is called the Fifth Republic. Each of its republics has had a different constitution. Ever since the Third Republic, established in 1871, France has had a modified parliamentary system, modeled after the British parliamentary system. Perhaps the most distinctive aspect of French government and politics has been their instability. During the seventy years of the Third Republic (1871–1940), France had more than a hundred prime ministers, each one holding office less than eight months. This occurred because of the many political parties and the unwillingness of the members of the legislature to compromise. The Fourth Republic, established in 1946 after World War II, was even worse than the Third Republic. In response, on September 28, 1958, with the country on the brink of civil war, the Fifth Republic was instituted. In the Fifth Republic, it is much more difficult for the parliament to vote on a **censure motion,** a motion that, if successful, means the prime minister does not get a vote of confidence and must resign or call for a new election. A **vote of confidence** is a formal and constitutionally binding expression of preference in favor of the prime minister by the parliament.

The legislative branch of French government is elected every five years and consists of two houses: the National Assembly, whose members are elected directly by all citizens over age eighteen, and the Senate, which is chosen by an electoral college and provides stronger representation for rural areas than does the other house. When there is disagreement between the two houses, the National Assembly takes precedence. Compared with the U.S. Congress, however, neither of these legislative bodies has significant power. Once having elected executive officers, the executive branch can in many cases both legislate and carry out the laws. The strength of the executive branch was a change made in the Fifth Republic and accepted because the previous governments had been so unstable.

France

Population: 60 million (2002)

Area: 211,209 square miles (547,030 square km)

Distribution: 74 percent urban; 26 percent rural

Capital city: Paris

National anthem: "La Marseillaise"

Government leaders: President Jacques Chirac
   (since 1995) Prime Minister Jean-Pierre Raffarin
   (since 2002)

Ethnic divisions: Celtic and Latin with Teutonic,
   Slavic, North African, Indochinese, and Basque
   minorities

Literacy rate: 99 percent

Religion: 88 percent Roman Catholic; others
   include Protestant, Jewish, and Muslim

GDP: $1.54 trillion; per capita: $25,700 (2002)

Currency unit: Euro

Monetary conversion rate: 1 euro = $1.18 (June
   2003) $1 = .85 euro

Internet users: 16.97 million (2002)

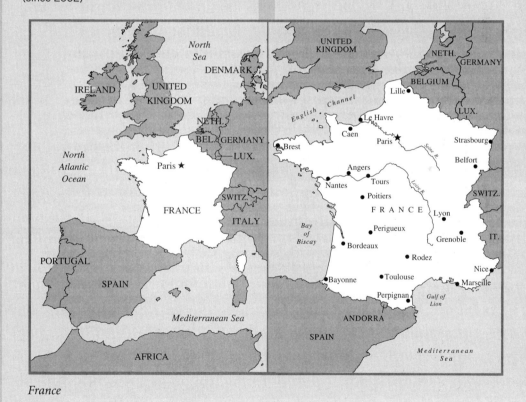

France

The French Executive Branch

The executive branch of the French government has two leaders: a prime minister and a
president. Unlike many parliamentary systems, in France both leaders wield considerable

Declaration of the Rights of Man and of the Citizen

Adopted by the National Assembly during the French Revolution on August 26, 1789, and affirmed by the constitution of 1958.

Preamble

The representatives of the French people, formed into a National Assembly, considering ignorance, forgetfulness or contempt of the rights of man to be the only causes of public misfortunes and the corruption of Governments, have resolved to set forth, in a solemn Declaration, the natural, unalienable and sacred rights of man, to the end that this Declaration, constantly present to all members of the body politic, may remind them unceasingly of their rights and their duties; to the end that the acts of the legislative power and those of the executive power, since they may be continually compared with the aim of every political institution, may thereby be the more respected; to the end that the demands of the citizens, founded henceforth on simple and uncontestable principles, may always be directed toward the maintenance of the Constitution and the happiness of all.

In consequence whereof, the National Assembly recognizes and declares, in the presence and under the auspices of the Supreme Being, the following Rights of Man and of the Citizen.

Article 1—Men are born and remain free and equal in rights. Social distinctions may be based only on considerations of the common good.

Article 2—The aim of every political association is the preservation of the natural and imprescriptible rights of man. These rights are Liberty, Property, Safety, and Resistance to Oppression.

Article 3—The source of all sovereignty lies essentially in the Nation. No corporate body, no individual may exercise any authority that does not expressly emanate from it.

Article 4—Liberty consists in being able to do anything that does not harm others; thus, the exercise of the natural rights of every man has no bounds other than those that ensure to the other members of society the enjoyment of these same rights. These bounds may be determined only by Law.

Article 5—The Law has the right to forbid only those actions that are injurious to society. Nothing that is not forbidden by Law may be hindered, and no one may be compelled to do what the Law does not ordain.

Article 6—The Law is the expression of the general will. All citizens have the right to take part, personally or through their representatives, in its making. It must be the same for all, whether it protects or punishes. All citizens, being equal in its eyes, shall be equally eligible to all high offices, public positions and employments, according to their ability, and without other distinction than that of their virtues and talents.

Article 7—No man may be accused, arrested or detained except in the cases determined by the Law, and following the procedure that it has prescribed. Those who solicit, expedite, carry out, or cause to be carried out arbitrary orders must be punished; but any citizen summoned or apprehended by virtue of the Law, must give instant obedience; resistance makes him guilty.

Article 8—The Law must prescribe only the punishments that are strictly and evidently necessary; and no one may be punished except by virtue of a Law drawn up and promulgated before the offense is committed, and legally applied.

Article 9—As every man is presumed innocent until he has been declared guilty, if it should be considered necessary to arrest him, any undue harshness that is not required to secure his person must be severely curbed by Law.

Article 10—No one may be disturbed on account of his opinions, even religious ones, as long as the manifestation of such opinions does not interfere with the established Law and Order.

Article 11—The free communication of ideas and of opinions is one of the most precious rights of man. Any citizen may therefore speak, write and publish freely, except what is tantamount to the abuse of this liberty in the cases determined by Law.

Article 12—To guarantee the Rights of Man and of the Citizen a public force is necessary; this force is therefore established for the benefit of all, and not for the particular use of those to whom it is entrusted.

Article 13—For the maintenance of the public force, and for administrative expenses, a general tax is indispensable; it must be equally distributed among all citizens, in proportion to their ability to pay.

Article 14—All citizens have the right to ascertain, by themselves, or through their representatives, the need for a public tax, to consent to it freely, to watch over its use, and to determine its proportion, basis, collection and duration.

Article 15—Society has the right to ask a public official for an accounting of his administration.

Article 16—Any society in which no provision is made for guaranteeing rights or for the separation of powers, has no Constitution.

Article 17—Since the right to Property is inviolable and sacred, no one may be deprived thereof, unless public necessity, legally ascertained, obviously requires it, and just and prior indemnity has been paid.

power. The president is the head of state and the executive head of government. He or she is elected every seven years by direct popular vote. The president appoints the prime minister and together they choose the cabinet.

In the 1990s, no single party managed to secure a firm hold on executive power in France. After two terms in office, President François Mitterand of the Socialist Party

The Difference between a Parliamentary and a Presidential System

Democracy has many forms. To hold meetings where everyone in the country can come and be heard is impossible when countries have millions of people. Therefore, every democracy must establish systems of representation. The United States has a presidential system, but most democratic countries in the world use a parliamentary system. The difference is found in who elects the leader of the country. In a presidential system, the people elect the leader, called the president, by direct election or indirectly through an electoral college. In a parliamentary system, people elect the members of the legislature and the legislators elect the executive leader, generally called a prime minister. Thus, in a presidential system, the legislature and the executive can be of opposing parties (as happened in the United States in the 1990s

when Bill Clinton, a Democrat, was president but Congress was controlled by the Republicans). In a parliamentary system, the majority in the legislature and the executive are of the same party or collection of parties. If the prime minister loses the support of the parliament, the government is said to fall and the prime minister must call for a new election or resign.

Parliamentary systems also often have presidents, whether elected by the legislature or by popular vote. The job of a president in such a system is usually to be a functionary—that is, to attend receptions and play a largely ceremonial role. In Great Britain, the king or queen serves the function that a president serves in other parliamentary systems. France presents an exception to both the parliamentary and the presidential system. In France the president is elected by popular vote and then appoints the prime minister from the party or coalition of parties that rules the legislature.

stepped down in May 1995, following the election to the presidency of Jacques Chirac of the neo-Gaullist Rally for the Republic (RPR) Party. Chirac had defeated Edouard Balladur, the conservative prime minister, in a hotly contested election. Chirac and his prime minister, Alain Juppé, drew legislative support from the conservative coalition, an alliance between the RPR and the center-right Union for French Democracy (UDF), led by Mitterand's predecessor Valéry Giscard d'Estaing. The UDF maintained an 80 percent majority in the National Assembly. Chirac was forced to concentrate on belt-tightening as France struggled to meet the financial criteria for joining the European Monetary Union. Chirac succeeded in leading France to replace its historic currency, the franc, with the euro. This step led to significant labor unrest.

In April 1997, Chirac called early parliamentary elections in advance of the hard policy decisions that would have to be made to meet the European single currency criteria. This backfired on Chirac as the Left, led by Lionel Jospin of the Socialist Party, won an unexpected solid majority. Soon Jospin replaced Juppé as prime minister. By 2000, Jospin, who hoped to succeed Chirac as president in 2002, was losing popular support, especially from the public sector and from business. In the public sector, the unions were upset over issues of the government retirement plan and what they saw as a retreat from his socialist position. Business, although financially sound, was upset over high taxes, the high level of spending on welfare, and the slow pace of the privatization of state-owned industry.

In the 2002 election, voters were fed up with the "cohabitation" of the right-wing Chirac and the left-wing parliament and government. With over one-third of the voters staying home, Jean-Marie Penn, who ran on an anti-immigration platform, beat out socialist Jospin in the first round, giving Chirac, whose platform focused on crime, tax cuts, labor laws, and state pensions, a landslide victory in the second round over the far-right leader. Chirac's center-right allies also did well in the elections and have a majority in both the National Assembly and the Senate.

Mexican Government

The government of Mexico is particularly interesting for two reasons: It reveals the blurred line between democratic and autocratic governments, and it demonstrates that governmental systems are still in the process of change.

Mexico is ostensibly a democracy—it has multiple parties and popular elections—but until 1988 the nature of those elections left no doubt as to who would be the chosen leader, and Mexico was ruled as an autocracy. But in 1988 this changed, and in 2000 Vicente Fox, a non-PRI candidate, won the general election for president.

To understand the current political situation in Mexico, we need to consider its history. Mexico won independence from Spain in 1821 and initially set itself up as a monarchy, but the monarchy was quickly overthrown and replaced with a republic marked by political and social confusion. In 1848, Mexico lost the Mexican–American War to the United States, and with that loss went about half its territory, including Texas, New Mexico, and parts of what are now eight other states. The loss of that war led to a civil war in Mexico and ultimately to the country's annexation by Napoleon III of France. In 1867, Mexico again won its independence, and under Porfirio Díaz a liberal dictatorship known as the Porfiriato began. It was conducted under the general ideas of the constitu-

President Vicente Fox of Mexico.

tion established by the liberals who had won the civil war: the rule of law, a strong federalist government, and the separation of church and state. These ideas are reflected in Mexico's current constitution as well.

What the 1867 constitution did not provide was equity, and the growth of the Mexican economy at that time was marked by a major transfer of land from the peasantry to a group of rich landowners and by a labor force with few rights. This transfer resulted in significant social unrest, characterized by strikes and revolts that were suppressed by the government.

Although Mexico called itself a democracy during this time, while Díaz was in power no one ever ran against him. However, the repressive measures of the early 1900s resulted in the growth of an opposition party that looked as though it had a chance of winning until the opposition leader was thrown in jail. The jailing of this leader led to a revolution, the establishment of the modern Mexican state, and a new constitution in 1917. This new constitution reflected the social problems of the previous period.

Specifically, the new constitution followed the old in maintaining a federal republic, but it took strong, definite social steps. For example, private ownership of land was no longer a right—it was a privilege that could be revoked by the state at will when land ownership did not serve a positive social function. Labor was given the right to strike, an eight-hour working day, and a minimum wage. Compared to the U.S. Constitution, this Mexican constitution was much more specific and dealt more extensively with social and economic concerns.

Politically the constitution created an extremely powerful president who comes close to choosing his or her successor. The legislative body consists of a Chamber of Deputies and a Senate, both of which are elected by popular vote. The president can serve only one (six-year) term.

To end the political turmoil that existed under the former constitution, the 1917 constitution gave the president enormous power. The president has the **line-item veto,** which means the power to veto any part of a bill, leaving the rest of it intact. This line-item veto makes legislative compromises difficult because the president has the power to accept part of the compromise and reject another part of it. The president also has the power to declare a state of siege, which gives him enormous police power, and he can appoint a cabinet without consulting the legislative body.

Although the constitution guarantees a strong president, the actual bureaucracy and institutions have given the president almost dictatorial authority. With the government controlling so many economic rights, individuals are indebted to the president for their jobs. For example, to pick through garbage you must belong to a union, the leader of which is appointed by the president. The union leader's job is to deliver the members' votes to the government.

As we stated earlier, the constitution gives individuals significant social and economic rights and gives the government—and hence the president—power to implement these rights. The result is a large, bureaucratic government structure with deep involvement in most aspects of economic and social life. The members of this bureaucratic structure are appointed by the government, to which they owe their allegiance.

Mexico

Population: 103 million (2002)

Area: 761,605 square miles (1,972,547 square km)

Distribution: 71 percent urban; 29 percent rural

Capital city: Mexico City

National anthem: "Mexicanos, al grito de Guerra" ("Mexicans, to the Cry of War")

Government leader: President Vicente Fox (since 2000)

Ethnic divisions: 60 percent Mestizo (Indian-Spanish); 30 percent Amerindian or predominantly Amerindian; 9 percent white or predominantly white; 1 percent other

Literacy rate: 88 percent

Religion: 89 percent nominally Roman Catholic; 6 percent Protestant

GDP: $920 billion; per capita: $4,000 (2002)

Currency unit: Peso

Monetary conversion rate: 1 peso = $.09 (June 2003) $1 = 10.54 pesos

Internet users: 3.5 million (2002)

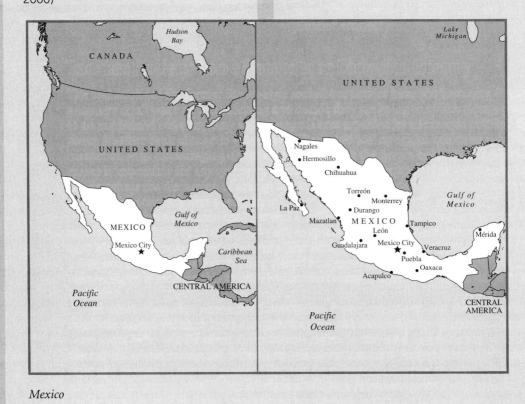

Mexico

After the revolution, the **Institutional Revolutionary Party** (**PRI**), the political party that was by far the most important, took control of the bureaucratic apparatus and used it to stay in power. The PRI remained the ruling party for more than seventy years. It instituted **land reform**—the redistribution of land from the large landholders to the middle-sized farmers and the peasantry—that was carried out under Lázaro Cárdenas, one of the most famous presidents of Mexico. He redistributed almost fifty million acres of land from rich landlords to peasants, but instead of giving ownership of the land directly to the peasants, he gave it to a communal *ejido,* or cooperative, the leader of which got much of his power from the government. The *ejido* leader delivered the votes and could maintain his or her little fiefdom. Similar fiefdoms existed in most industries, and there are about two hundred decentralized joint government/private agencies such as Pemex, the agency that controls Mexico's oil industry.

The PRI's control of politics in Mexico started to break down in the 1988 election as the PRI candidate, Carlos Salinas, just barely won. That breakdown created much tension within the PRI, and the end of Salinas's presidency in 1994 was marked by charges of corruption, the murder of a PRI candidate, and drug scandals in government. Nonetheless, the PRI's presidential candidate Ernesto Zedillo, an economist trained in the United States, won the 1994 election. But with that election, most observers felt that Mexican politics had entered a different phase.

In 1995 the Mexican economy went into a severe recession following the financial crisis triggered by a loss of confidence in the peso. A $40 billion international financial package and the adoption of tough financial measures helped stabilize the economy. In addition to grave economic woes, the Zedillo administration faced serious problems including widespread poverty, corruption, drug trafficking, and an armed peasant uprising in the state of Chiapas.

In trying to deal with these problems, Zedillo and the PRI had to make political concessions. These included developing a greater role for the Congress and a reduced role for the presidency. The government actively pursued electoral reforms that strengthened the authority and independence of electoral institutions. Judicial reforms were also initiated, in part to allow the judiciary to be an effective counterbalance to the executive and the legislature. The Zedillo administration also gave additional discretion to state and local governments in areas such as health and education administration.

These reforms have changed the nature of government in Mexico. The congressional elections in July 1997 brought an end to the seven decades of PRI monopoly in the Congress, as opposition parties won control of the majority in Congress and also won the mayoral race in Mexico City. In 2000 the PRI candidate lost his bid for reelection and Vicente Fox, the candidate of the **National Action Party (PAN)**, won the election. Fox, a former Coca-Cola executive, was not significantly different in background and view from the PRI candidate, but the very fact that he was not a PRI candidate meant major changes in the bureaucratic structure of government.

After his election, Fox proposed a number of new initiatives, one of which involved persuading the United States to open its borders to many more Mexican immigrants. He favored free trade and proposed that the North American Free Trade Agreement (NAFTA) be expanded until it creates a network similar to the European Union. He hoped to increase enforcement of the laws against the illegal drug trade. He also proposed to the United States that it drastically increase economic aid to Mexico.

The United States welcomed the increased vigilance over illegal drugs, but U.S. reaction to some of Fox's other initiatives was cool. In February 2001, Fox and the newly elected U.S. president, George W. Bush, held a press conference in Mexico where the two presidents expressed friendship and mentioned a number of issues on which they hoped to cooperate. One dealt with terminolgy: They wanted to apply the term *migrants,* rather than *immigrants,* to Mexican citizens crossing the border into the United States. Another was more substantive: They expressed a hope that energy resources such as electricity, oil, and natural gas could be treated as what Bush called a "hemispheric" issue—developed and used cooperatively, perhaps with Canada also a partner. Whether these changes ultimately will be made remains to be seen. These initiatives and the focus on Mexico never got off the ground as the United States became focused on the war on terrorism and problems geographically distant from Mexico.

Japanese Government

Japan was ruled by **shoguns,** or emperors, for much of its early history, and well into the nineteenth century it remained a feudal society in which religion and state were combined. In 1853 the United States forcibly opened Japan to foreign influence by sending a fleet of ships into Tokyo Bay, an event that led to the establishment of the Meiji government, whose goal was to modernize the country. Forsaking its previous closed-door policy, Japan under the Meiji government sent students abroad to study. As they returned to Japan, Western ideas became integrated into Japanese institutions.

One of these Western ideas resulted in the Meiji constitution, adopted in 1889. Based on the Prussian (German) constitution, the Meiji constitution stated that the emperor was supreme, but it simultaneously made provision for a bicameral legislature with restricted powers known as the National Diet. The Meiji constitution differed from the U.S. Constitution in that it was seen as a gift from the emperor to his people, a gift that could be taken back if the people abused their powers. The U.S. Constitution is "of the people, by the people, and for the people." The emperor retained his position not only as a political leader, but also, under Japanese religious belief, as a god.

Although the constitution gave the emperor almost unlimited power, in fact he passed on that authority and power to a variety of civil officials. Thus in practice, under the Meiji constitution Japan was run by a collective of officials. In the late 1800s and the first half of the 1900s, military leaders played a greater and greater role in that collective. By the 1930s, the military had gained almost total dominance over the other elements of the governing coalition, and in 1931 Japan attacked Manchuria, a province of China. The civilian leadership had no choice but to acquiesce.

In 1941, Japan successfully attacked the United States at Pearl Harbor in Hawaii. By this act, Japan entered World War II against the United States. Under the generalship of Douglas MacArthur, the United States defeated Japan in 1945. MacArthur then administered Japan's reconstruction and return to national independence. He saw to it that Japan's postwar constitution, ratified in 1947, was an amalgam of U.S. and British institutions and practice. This constitution remains in force in Japan today.

One borrowing from the British system is that the Japanese emperor is maintained as a symbol of state, but he has no political power. Also, he is no longer officially considered a god. The constitution contains significant differences from the U.S. and British documents as well, the most important of which is that the constitution renounces war and guarantees that the Japanese will not maintain an army. Although this has now been interpreted as outlawing only offensive weapons and military establishments, the provision has held down Japanese military expenditures, much to the benefit of the Japanese people.

Japan

Population: 127 million (2002)

Area: 145,879 square miles (377,836 square km)

Distribution: 76.7 percent urban; 23.3 percent rural

Capital city: Tokyo

National anthem: "Kimi ga yo" ("The Reign of Our Emperor")

Government leaders: Emperor Akihito (since January 1989); Prime Minister Junichiro Koizumi (2001)

Ethnic divisions: 99.0 percent Japanese; 1.0 percent other (mostly Korean)

Literacy rate: 99 percent

Religion: 84 percent Shintoism and Buddhism; about 16 percent belong to other faiths

GDP: $3.55 trillion; per capita: $28,000 (2002)

Currency unit: Yen

Monetary conversion rate: 1 yen = $.01 (June 2003) $1 = 117.17 yen

Internet users: 56 million (2002)

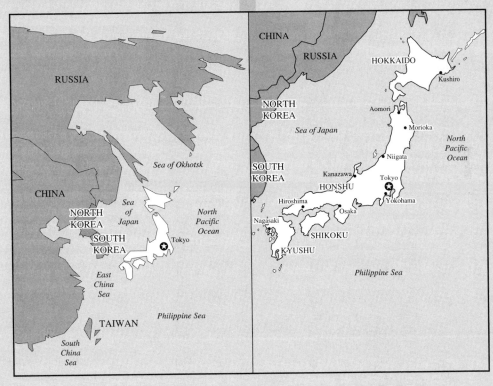

Japan

Prime Minister Junichiro Koizumi of Japan.

The constitution established a bicameral legislature, which, like its predecessor, is called the Diet. It consists of an upper chamber, called the House of Councillors, with 250 members who are popularly elected and serve staggered, six-year terms. Some of the councillors are elected from specific districts, and the rest are elected at large.

The other chamber, the House of Representatives, has 511 members serving four-year terms, except that their terms may prove to be shorter if the government is dissolved by the prime minister, which he can do to win a mandate from the people, or which can be forced on him if the legislature pronounces a vote of no confidence. In practice, this House of Representatives has the most power and acts in much the same manner as the British Parliament. It chooses the prime minister, who in turn selects his cabinet, all of whom must be members of the Diet. Once selected, the prime minister has significant powers as long as he maintains the support of his party.

Although modern Japan has, in large part, been controlled by the Liberal Democratic Party (LDP), that party itself is a splintered party of twelve or thirteen factions. In 1993 the thirty-eight-year reign of the LDP was broken when the splintered parties forced a vote of no confidence for the LDP prime minister. After a series of short-term prime ministers, a coalition of parties headed by the Social Democratic Party of Japan (SJDP), but which included the LDP, elected the first socialist prime minister, who instituted policies of relative protectionism and isolationism.

The socialist coalition lost in January 1996, and Ryutaro Hashimoto of the LDP became prime minister. Hashimoto presided over the LDP–socialist coalition that had been established by a predecessor. In the 1990s, Japan experienced a recession and that recession led to Hashimoto's resignation in 1998. He was replaced by Keizo Obuchi, but after a short time in office Obuchi suffered a massive stroke and died. Yoshiro Mori, a long-time politician, became prime minister. Mori had the reputation of being a careful, conservative man but he did not have a lot of political support in Japan. Thus, in 2001 he lost the election.

The voters elected reform-minded Junichiro Koizumi, a popular politician with an 85 percent approval rating. He took office with a promise to sweep away collusion between business, politicians, and bureaucrats; put in place new economic reforms; and rein in government spending. The Japanese economy, in a financial crisis of a decade-long recession, was further dragged down by the banks' inability to deal with billions in bad loans. Koizumi's economic reform plans were widely criticized and they failed to get international or domestic support. His claim to depart from traditional LDP tactics was seen as mainly gesturing that led to few achievements. Koizumi's government was racked with scandals of top politicians and bureaucrats involved in rigged overseas construction bids, kickbacks, tax evasion, and embezzlement. In 2003 his tenure in office was questionable, but the big threat to his government was not from the Democratic Party but from the conservative LDP faction led by Ryutaro Hashimoto.

Russian Government

In 1991 the Union of Soviet Socialist Republics ended and the republics each became independent states, connected by history and a loose commonwealth. To understand the recent momentous events in Russia, we need to consider the history of the former Soviet government, which began in 1917. Before that time, the Soviet Union, then known as the Russian Empire, was a centralized autocracy ruled by czars. World War I created severe economic difficulties for the Russian Empire and led to political confusion and civil war. In 1917 the **Bolsheviks,** members of the more radical majority of the Russian Social Democratic party, under the leadership of Vladimir Lenin took over the Russian government and, after winning the civil war, established their control over the country. In 1922, Lenin designed a federal type of constitution that incorporated republics surrounding Russia, republics that had previously been part of the Russian Empire. The constitution marked the beginning of the USSR (Union of Soviet Socialist Republics). Although the constitution was revised in 1936 and again in 1977, this constitution was, in many of its parts, the same one in force until the 1991 breakup of the Soviet Union.

A key element of that constitution and the government of the Soviet Union was the relationship between the government and the Communist Party. Article 6 of the earlier Soviet constitution stated: "The Communist party of the Soviet Union is the leading and guiding force of the Soviet society and the nucleus of its political system and of all state and public organizations."

Given that control of government by the Communist Party, there was much debate about what to call the government. Until 1959 the Soviet government was described by the Soviets as a "dictatorship of the proletariat," a definition that was changed to an "all people's state" in 1959.

Because of the domination of the Soviet government by the Communist Party, the actual government was, in large part, simply a rubber stamp and administrative institution for carrying out policies made by the party. All that changed in the early 1990s. Initially, Soviet leader Mikhail Gorbachev introduced a number of liberalizing reforms. These reforms reduced the power of the party and unleashed a wave of nationalistic and economic upheaval that undermined the central authority of the Soviet government. The various republics declared themselves independent and set up their own governments.

The chaos preceding the breakup of the union upset a number of communist leaders, and in 1991 a group of them attempted a **coup d'état**—an extraconstitutional takeover of a country. That coup failed because the military and a majority of the people in the former Soviet Union resisted, and leaders such as Boris Yeltsin, the head of the Russian republic, refused to accept the coup and began a struggle against it. The coup leaders were arrested and the Soviet Union ceased to exist. Each of the republics claimed its independence. The early 1990s saw an attempt at a commonwealth, but most observers believed there was little chance of such a loose federation succeeding.

Russia

Population (approximate): 144,979,000 (2003)

Area: 6,592,800 square miles (17,075,400 square km)

Distribution: 73.3 percent urban; 26.7 percent rural

Capital city: Moscow

National anthem: "Hymn of the Russian Federation" (formerly "The Patriotic Song" and "God Save the Tsar")

Government leaders: President Vladimir Putin (1999); Prime Minister Mikhail Kasyanov (2002)

Former Soviet Union: Russia is the largest republic of the former Soviet Union. The other new republics are Armenia, Azerbaijan, Belarus, Estonia, Georgia, Kazakhstan, Kirghizia, Latvia, Lithuania, Moldova, Tadzhikistan, Turkmenistan, Ukraine, and Uzbekistan.

Ethnic divisions: 81 percent Russian; 4 percent Tatar; 3 percent Ukrainian; 12 percent other

Literacy rate: 99 percent

Religion: 70 percent atheist; 18 percent Russian Orthodox; 9 percent Muslim; 3 percent Jewish, Roman Catholic, Protestant, or Georgian Orthodox

GDP: $1.27 trillion; per capita: $8,800 (2002)

Currency unit: Ruble

Monetary conversion rate: 1 ruble = $.03 (June 2003) $1 = 30.61 rubles

Internet users: 18 million (2002)

Russia

Chaos reigned in the early 1990s in all the countries that made up the former Soviet Union. After the aborted coup, the Soviet Union broke apart. The legislative branch of the government, the Congress of People's Deputies, dissolved itself, and the republics declared themselves independent. Russia, the largest of the republics, took control of most of the former Soviet government.

Russia created a governmental system comprised of a president and a legislative branch, again called the Congress of People's Deputies. The two shared roughly equal powers. The result was gridlock because the presidency was controlled by Boris Yeltsin, who favored fast movement toward a market economy, and the Congress, which favored a much slower movement. The stalemate between Yeltsin and the Congress was resolved in a referendum on a new constitution in December 1993. That new constitution created a strong presidency, but it also maintained a Federal Assembly composed of an upper Chamber of the Federation and a lower State Duma with some checks on presidential power. In elections for that Assembly, Communists and ultra-nationalists won, keeping the presidency and the legislature at odds. With the power

*T*he Russian Federation

The Constitution

The current Constitution of the Russian Federation came into force in December 1993, following its approval by a majority of participants in a nation-wide plebiscite. It replaced the Constitution (Fundamental Law) originally passed on April 12, 1978, but amended many times after 1990.

The Principles of the Constitutional System

The Russian Federation (Russia) is a democratic federative, law-based state with a republican form of government. Its multiethnic people bear its sovereignty and are the sole source of authority. State power in the Russian Federation is divided between the legislative, executive, and judicial branches, which are independent from one another. Ideological pluralism and a multiparty political system are recognized. The Russian Federation is a secular state and all religious associations are equal before the law. All laws are made public and in accordance with universally acknowledged principles and with international law.

Human and Civil Rights and Freedoms

The basic human rights and freedoms of the Russian citizen are guaranteed regardless of sex, race, nationality, or religion. The Constitution declares the right to life and to freedom and personal inviolability. The principles of freedom of movement, freedom of expression, and freedom of conscience are upheld. Censorship is prohibited. Citizens are guaranteed the right to vote and stand for election in state and local elections and to participate in referendums.

The Organization of the Federation

There are eighty-nine members (federal territorial units) of the Russian Federation. Russian is declared the state language, but all peoples of the Russian Federation are guaranteed the right to preserve their native tongue.

The President of the Russian Federation

The president is elected to office for a term of four years by universal, direct suffrage. The same individual may be elected to the office of President for no more than two consecutive terms. The president may appoint the Chairman of the Government of the Russian Federation, with the approval of the State Duma, and may dismiss the Deputy Chairmen and the federal ministers from office.

Source: Eastern Europe and the Commonwealth of Independent States, London: Europa Publications, 1994.

President Vladimir Putin of Russia.

given him by the new constitution, however, Yeltsin remained the dominant figure in Russian politics.

In 1996 Yeltsin retained the presidency following a close victory over Gennadiy Zyuganov of the Communist Party, but because of his shaky health and often erratic behavior, he did not instill confidence in the Russian government.

In 1999 Vladimir Putin was elected president, and he provided more strength and stability than Yeltsin had. He began dealing with the widespread corruption and the lack of tax institutions to finance government. He used a strong hand in asserting internal power, but at the same time he reached out to the West. He joined the West in the war on terrorism, while disagreeing strongly with the United States' war on Iraq. After that war, however, Russia joined with other countries in authorizing U.S. and British plans for postwar Iraq. In 2003 his party won an overwhelming victory in the elections.

Saudi Arabian Government

Unlike the other four countries we have considered, all of which are, to varying degrees, democracies, Saudi Arabia makes no such claim. It is a monarchy, and it provides us with an example of an authoritarian autocracy.

The Saudi Arabian government is relatively modern; the present kingdom was established in 1932. Before that time, what is now Saudi Arabia, like the other countries in the Arabian peninsula, was a collection of tribes generally following Islamic religious traditions. Life in the individual tribes and among the various tribes was governed by those traditions and by the **Koran,** the primary Islamic religious body of writings. Until the twentieth century, no one, long-term leader emerged from this collection of tribes.

That changed in the early 1900s when Ibn Saʿūd conquered most of the tribes in central Arabia and became the political and spiritual leader of the Bedouin tribe. He extended his authority during the first third of the twentieth century and created the kingdom of Saudi Arabia in 1932.

The kingdom has no written constitution, relying instead on historical precedent, the Koran, and royal decrees as its guides. There are no legislative bodies and no political parties. It is in a very real sense an absolute monarchy. But even absolute monarchies have their limits. Although the Saudi state has no constitution and no laws that restrict the king's powers, the Koran and historical custom limit what the king does, and over time a quasi-constitutional system has developed. The ruler is chosen by members of the royal family from among its members, subject to the approval of a group of Muslim leaders (the ulema). The ulema can remove the ruler, and he is also dependent for support on tribal leaders and, more recently, on important businessmen. Notice that there is no question of female rule in Saudi Arabia, because Islam's view of women precludes them from taking any such role.

Saudi Arabia

Population (approximate): 23,513,300 (2002)

Area: 830,000 square miles (2,150,000 square km)

Distribution: 73 percent urban; 27 percent rural

Capital city: Riyadh

National anthem: "As-salaam al-malaki as-Saud" ("Royal Salute of Saud")

Government leader: Prime Minister Crown Prince Abdullah, acting for King Fahd (since 1995)

Ethnic divisions: 90 percent Arab; 10 percent Afro-Asian

Literacy rate: 78 percent

Religion: 100 percent Muslim

GDP: $241 billion; per capita: $10,600 (2002)

Currency unit: Riyal

Monetary conversion rate: 1 riyal = $0.27 (June 2003) $1 = 3.75 riyal (fixed since 1994)

Internet users: 570,000 (2002)

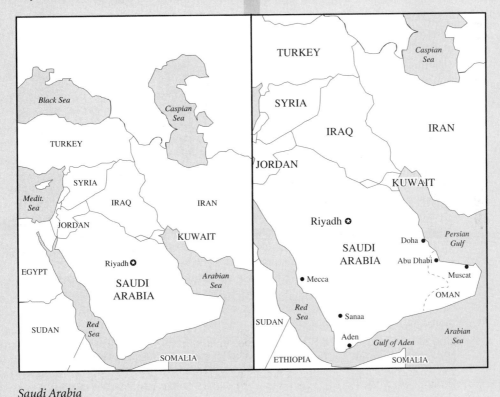

Saudi Arabia

    Running a government is too much for any one person, and in 1953 King Sa'ūd created a Council of Ministers to assist him, with a prime minister playing a significant role partially independent of the king. The prime minister appoints the Council, along with other advisory councils who assist him in both legislative and executive matters. This

Crown Prince Abdullah of Saudi Arabia.

dual power base created a tension between the king and the prime minister that was temporarily resolved when the prime minister, Prince Faisal, became king in 1964. King Faisal was assassinated in 1975 and the tension returned. King Faisal's successor was King Khālid, who died in 1982. Khālid was followed by the present king, Fahd, who solved the tension by naming himself as prime minister. When King Fahd's health became frail, Crown Prince Abdullah was named prime minister.

As is the case with many governments, especially those established in the twentieth century, the Saudi system of government is still evolving. In 1980 a committee was established to define a basic system of rule based entirely on Islamic principles. In 1992 the committee reported to King Fahd, who set up a sixty-one-member *Majlis al-Shura,* or Consultative Council. This council could make recommendations to the king and prime minister but would have no ability to make law (the king retained that right). He also reorganized provincial administrations and formalized the existing system of government, keeping the throne in the al-Sa'ūd family in perpetuity.

Although King Fahd announced that the political system would be directed by *Sharia* (Islamic Law), he recognized that the public expects the *Majlis* to be more than another rubberstamping institution with the sole purpose of legitimizing the regime. Fahd and the Crown Prince Abdullah have declared that they would like to see the *Majlis* and the thirteen regional councils (composed of 210 appointed ministers) play a more influential role in policymaking in the future. However, it is still uncertain how responsive the royal family will be to the advice of these ministers.

People tolerate strong autocracies in which they have little or no power for numerous reasons including military force wielded by the government, historical precedent, fear of the chaos that a change would bring, or satisfaction with the existing state of affairs. In the Saudi case, despite the enormous income taken by the Saudi monarchy, the Saudi people are relatively satisfied. The reason is the huge amount of oil income received by the government that allows it to undertake numerous social projects for the people. For example, all Saudis are entitled to free medical care. These projects are financed without significant taxation, even while providing lavish lifestyles for the Saudi royal family.

Since the Persian Gulf War of 1991, the ability of the monarchy-led government to "buy its legitimacy" has eroded. Low oil prices squeezed the government budget and led to severe austerity measures in the mid-1990s. Although those measures were somewhat relaxed by 1997, agitation against the absolute monarchy of the al-Sa'ūd family has continued to increase. King Fahd is still nominally the king, but because of frail health the kingdom is run on his behalf by the prime minister, Crown Prince Abdullah. Abdullah has continued modernizing and is in negotiation for membership in the World Trade Organization (WTO) and is trying to liberalize Saudi Arabia's policy toward foreign investment. The country's oil revenues constitute more than 75 percent of its annual budget, and therefore its economic health goes up and down with oil prices. Abdullah's budget strategies can no longer ignore external economic developments. Although in 2003 revenues soared beyond estimates due to unexpectedly high oil prices, expenditures also rose drastically because of security spending due to the war in Iraq.

The Saudi government finds itself in a difficult middle position. On the one hand, it is under pressure by the ultrareligious Sunni Muslims, who advocate a return to a more strict Islamic tradition. On the other hand, it faces intense criticism by women's groups and Western-oriented Saudis, who advocate democracy and equal treatment for women under the law. The westernization of Saudi Arabia, and especially Saudi Arabia's decision to allow U.S. troops to remain on Saudi soil, infuriated a number of Saudis, especially a rich businessman named Osama bin Laden. Bin Laden moved to Afghanistan, where he created a terrorist organization to attack the West and thereby force the United States out of Islamic holy lands. It was his group that directed the 9/11 attacks, and a majority of the highjackers were Saudi citizens. When the United States went to war in Iraq in 2003, the Saudis gave limited support, because anti-American feeling among the Saudi population was strong. The Saudi government found itself walking a fine line trying not to alienate its Sunni religious population or the West. The U.S. victory in Iraq presented Saudi rulers with another problem: If Iraq is made into a democracy, the pressure on Saudi Arabia to become a democracy will be greater. In short, the future is likely to bring significant political change to Saudi Arabia. Abdullah is in his late seventies, and his probable successor, Prince Soltan, is almost as old. It is certain, therefore, that power will be exercised in the near future by a younger generation.

Some Lessons about Governments

This survey of governments of the world should give you a sense of the variety and diversity of governments—both democratic and autocratic. From it you can see that there are many types of democracy and autocracy and that it is difficult to compare one with the other.

A number of general points about governments can be made:

1. Governments reflect their history (for example, after 1947 the Japanese government reflected the U.S. desire to keep it fractious, and the strong French government reflects its unstable history).

2. Governments are evolving. France, Japan, and Saudi Arabia do not have the same governmental structure they had fifty or sixty years ago, and the Soviet Union no longer exists. These countries are unlikely to have the same governmental structure fifty years from now as they have today. The rate of change depends on the historical tradition as current government practices become embodied in society and place limitations on change.

3. Autocracies are more likely to change than long-standing democracies. The reason is that the process of change is easier. When the former Soviet Union decided to change governmental form, it could do so relatively easily compared with the United States. Saudi Arabia would be able to do so even more rapidly.

4. Changes in autocracies occur from within as much as from without. The changes in the Mexican and former Soviet governments are examples. Often the process of liberalization brings about opposition that otherwise would have been silent or suppressed.

More rules and insights are embodied in the examples, but we leave them for you to draw out.

Future Changes in Governments

What does the future hold for these and other governments? As usual, it is unclear. We are likely to see significant changes in the structure of government of the republics of the former Soviet Union and some Middle Eastern autocracies such as Kuwait and Saudi Arabia, as well as many eastern European countries. If the coming years hold prosperity and countries manage to avoid all-out war, the present forms of most other governments are likely to continue. If the economic and social conditions worsen, however, more changes can be expected. And if there is a major nuclear war, who knows what will remain of government, culture, or society? Obviously, we hope such major changes will not occur because of war, but current troublesome social and economic conditions could dash those hopes.

Some of these social and economic conditions are high unemployment rates in many countries, including much of industrialized Europe; the proliferation of destructive weapons systems in areas of the world where social, political, economic, and religious quarrels are already disrupting ordinary life; repression and denial of opportunity to large populations in some countries; widespread financial hardship in some countries burdened with heavy debt they owe to more prosperous nations; and environmental pollution that threatens to change whole areas of the world. Fortunately not all of these conditions exist in any one country, and it is always possible that diplomacy and, ultimately, good sense exercised by governments will enable the compromises and adjustments necessary for peacekeeping to prevail.

Key Points

- The French government is a parliamentary democracy with both a president and a prime minister.
- The Mexican government has been a partial autocracy ruled by the PRI, but it is moving toward a competitive democracy.
- The Japanese government is a constitutional democracy.
- The governments of republics of the former Soviet Union are in a state of major transition.
- The Saudi government is an autocracy based largely on Islamic principles.
- Some lessons about governments that can be drawn from these examples include the following: governments reflect their history, governments are changing, autocracies can change quickly, and autocracies often change from within.

Some Important Terms

Bastille Day (337)
Bolshevik (349)
censure motion (338)
coup d'état (349)
French Revolution (337)
Koran (352)

land reform (345)
line-item veto (343)
National Action Party
  (PAN) (345)
PRI (Institutional
  Revolutionary Party) (344)

shogun (346)
vote of confidence (338)

Questions for Review and Discussion

1. What is the relationship between the Declaration of the Rights of Man and the French constitution?
2. How can the French prime minister be removed from office?
3. Is Mexico a democracy or an autocracy?
4. What are some differences between the Mexican constitution and the U.S. Constitution?
5. What is a line-item veto?
6. Explain how *ejidos* in Mexico worked to maintain the power of the PRI.
7. Did the Japanese emperor have unlimited power under the Meiji constitution?
8. Why did an American play an important role in designing the current Japanese constitution?
9. What was the relationship between the Communist Party and the former Soviet government?
10. How does the new Russian Federation differ from the former Soviet Republic?
11. What are some concerns about Russia's ability to deal with its problems? What are some causes of optimism?
12. Does the Saudi autocratic government have unlimited power?
13. Why do the Saudi people tolerate the Saudi autocracy?
14. State five lessons about government that can be derived from this chapter.
15. What do you believe would be the ideal system of government?

Internet Questions

1. Look at the composition of the French government on the embassy site www.info-france-usa.org/atoz/gouv.asp. What are the fourteen minister posts under the prime minister?
2. Go to http://jin.jcic.or.jp/navi/category_2.html; what are the seven Japanese political parties listed?
3. According to www.saudia-online.com/saudi_arabia.htm#gov, what does the legislative branch of Saudi Arabia's government consist of?
4. What was Russia's Prime Minister Kasyanov's career path, www.nupi.no/cgi-win/Russland/personer.exe?1148?
5. Using the CIA World Fact Book, www.odci.gov/cia/publications/factbook/geos/mx.html, what are the administrative divisions of Mexico?

For Further Study

Ajami, Fouad, *The Dream Palace of the Arabs: A Generation's Odyssey,* New York: Pantheon, 1998.

Anderson, N., *The Kingdom of Saudi Arabia,* rev. ed., London: Stacey International, 1986.

Apter, Emily S., *Continental Drift: From National Character to Virtual Subjects,* Chicago: University of Chicago Press, 1999.

Ash, Timothy Garton, *In Europe's Name: Germany and the Divided Continent,* New York: Random House, 1994.

Brady, Rose, *Kapitalism: Russia's Struggle to Free Its Economy,* New Haven, CT: Yale University Press, 1999.

Braginski, S. V., *Incentives and Institutions: The Transition to a Market Economy in Russia,* Princeton, NJ: Princeton University Press, 2000.

Camp, Roderick A., *Politics in Mexico: The Decline of Authoritarianism,* New York: Oxford University Press, 1999.

Chaudhry, Kiren Aziz, *The Price of Wealth: Economics and Institutions in the Middle East,* Ithaca, NY: Cornell University Press, 1997.

Curtis, Gerald L., *The Logic to Japanese Politics,* New York: Columbia University Press, 2000.

Hellman, Judith Adler, *Mexican Lives,* New York: New Press, 1994.

Langewiesche, William, *Sahara Unveiled: A Journey across the Desert,* New York: Pantheon, 1996.

Le Hir, Marie-Pierre, and Dana Strand, eds., *French Cultural Studies: Criticism at the Crossroads,* Albany: State University of New York, 2000.

Levy, Daniel C., Kathleen Bruhn, and Emilio Zebadúa, *Mexico: The Struggle for Democratic Development,* Berkeley: University of California Press, 2001.

Lippman, Thomas W., *Understanding Islam: An Introduction to the Muslim World,* New York: Penguin Putnam, 2002.

Lustig, Nora, *Mexico: The Remaking of an Economy,* Washington, DC: Brookings Institution, 1998.

Miller, Judith, *God Has Ninety-Nine Names: Reporting from a Militant Middle East,* New York: Simon & Schuster, 1996.

Ruett, Riordan, ed., *Mexico's Private Sector: Recent History, Future Challenges,* Boulder, CO: Lynne Rienner, 1998.

Santos, John Phillip, *Places Left Unfinished at the Time of the Creation,* New York: Viking Press, 2000.

Vanden Heuvel, William J., *The Future of Freedom in Russia,* Radnor, PA: Templeton Foundation Press, 2000.

Wallach, Janet, *Desert Queen: The Extraordinary Life of Gertrude Bell: Adventurer, Adviser to Kings, Ally of Lawrence of Arabia,* New York: Nan A Talese/Doubleday, 1996.

WWW The French Prime Minister www.premier-ministre.gouv.fr/en

WWW The Government of the Russian Federation www.gov.ru/main/page8.html

WWW Japan Foundation www.jpf.go.jp

WWW Mexico Online www.mexonline.com

WWW The Organization of Japanese Central Government www.kantei.go.jp/foreign/index-e.html

WWW Partido Acción Nacional (National Action Party) www.pan.org.mx

WWW The Royal Embassy of Saudi Arabia www.saudiembassy.net

The Organization of Economic Activities

chapter 6

After reading this chapter, you should be able to:

- State what the great economic problem is
- Distinguish between a planned and an unplanned economy
- Discuss the evolution of our economy from feudalism, to mercantilism, to a market economy, to a mixed economy
- Explain the terms *supply* and *demand* and use them to explain how a market economy works
- Discuss the changing roles of agriculture in the U.S. economy
- Summarize the historical development of socialist thought
- Give reasons why Soviet-style socialism was abandoned

The ideas of economists and political philosophers, both when they are right and when they are wrong, are more powerful than is commonly understood. Indeed, the world is ruled by little else.

—John Maynard Keynes

Economics is a branch of social science that is concerned with the ways in which people provide themselves with material goods and services. Defined more precisely, it is the study of the social organization through which people satisfy their wants for scarce goods, including services. In the process of satisfying these wants, economic institutions develop that govern individuals' economic interactions in the same way that social institutions govern individuals' social interactions. These economic institutions include government organizations, business firms, unions, and the laws that facilitate the production, distribution, and consumption of goods. To understand how an economy operates, we must be well acquainted with these institutions. In this chapter, we consider how economies are organized.

The Nature of an Economy

In modern industrial societies, economic relationships are complex. Almost nothing can be produced and made available to the final buyer without the help of a variety of economic institutions and the conscious or unconscious cooperation of great numbers of workers. This is true of almost every commodity, whether it be a shirt, a computer, a ballpoint pen, or frozen yogurt. Our ability to satisfy our daily economic wants depends on the existence of many highly systematized social arrangements. Without these organizations, our economic efforts would be largely futile, and most of us, especially in the cities, would soon starve to death.

Taken together, all the complex social arrangements by which we satisfy economic wants constitute an economic system, or an economy. An **economy** may be defined as the social organization by means of which the people of a given society produce and distribute economic goods.

Functions of an Economy

An economy must perform at least four basic functions, and ideally it should perform them in such a way as to confer maximum benefits on the community. It must determine:

1. The kinds of goods to be produced
2. The amount of each good to be produced
3. The resources that are to be allocated to a good's output
4. The ultimate division of the goods among those who are to enjoy them.

In addition, an economy should provide a favorable environment for economic progress.

Economics and the Social Sciences

Before we consider these issues, we need to consider how economic issues fit in with other issues in social science. Some social scientists believe that economic issues are at the center of all social science issues. Although as economists we would strongly argue that economic issues are important, we would not argue that they are the central elements of our lives. Often economic goods are wanted for only social and cultural reasons (if you have enough money to buy that sports car, that cute girl or guy will go out with you; otherwise, she or he won't give you the time of day). Ultimately it is not money or economic goods that we desire—it is happiness.

Although economic wants are not the *most* important, they are important. If you're hungry or lack adequate clothing or shelter, you're probably not happy; and if all your friends have new cars, you probably aren't happy unless you have a new car, too. Thus it is important to study economic needs and wants, and how societies fulfill them.

Economic Wants and Economic Goods

Economic wants are desires for things that can be obtained by labor or through exchange and on which, in a modern society, a money value can be placed. Not all wants are economic. People want love and affection, respect, health, happiness, and many other things that cannot be measured in money. These things may be affected by the economic circumstances of the individual, but they are not primarily economic. A certain amount of money and the things that money can buy are necessary to sustain life and to make it worth living, but beyond that the relationship between money and happiness is not so clear.

Economic goods are the things that money can buy and that are the objects of our economic wants. If we possess such goods, we can obtain money or other valuable things in exchange for them. If we wish to acquire them, we can do so by offering enough money to pay the price demanded. In some cases we can produce them for ourselves if we are willing to invest the necessary labor.

Economic goods have monetary value because they are desirable and because they are scarce. By scarce, we mean that if the goods were free, the amount that individuals want would exceed the supply, the amount available. Because the whole supply is owned or controlled by people, if we want more of such goods than we already have, we must either produce them for ourselves or offer something valuable in exchange to induce others to part with them.

Economic goods are not necessarily material. They may consist of services such as those of a housekeeper or a doctor, and, more and more, services are becoming the most important economic goods in the United States. Anything that offers benefits in exchange for a definite sum of money is an economic good. Economic goods in the form of services can be obtained from things as well as from people. If people want to enjoy the benefit of a house, they usually have a choice: They may buy the services of one in return for a monthly payment called rent, or they may buy one outright, thereby obtaining all the benefits the house is capable of yielding until it wears out or falls down. But when we wish to enjoy the benefits of a housekeeper or a doctor, we do not have this choice, because slavery is illegal.

Wealth is what we call the material economic goods—the kind we can see, feel, and accumulate. All economic goods take the form of either wealth or services.

The Economic Aspects of Culture

We have already emphasized many of the economic aspects of culture in earlier chapters. People's problems in adjusting to their physical environment are largely economic. The solutions require producing the kinds of goods that the environment demands; for example, in a cold climate, warm clothing, fuel, and well-insulated housing are necessary goods. Our attempts to improve our economic situation motivate technological progress.

Economic factors also play an important role in shaping the mores and the institutions of every society. Many of our most firmly held beliefs of what is right and wrong have to do with property and property rights, as illustrated by our strong condemnation of theft, robbery, cheating, and embezzlement. Most of our social institutions, even those that are not usually regarded as primarily economic, have economic aspects of major importance. The family is an excellent example. When a man and woman marry, they not only signify their intention of living together and establishing a family, but they also undertake important economic obligations to care for each other and, if they have them, their children.

The Great Economic Problem

Producing economic goods to satisfy human wants requires resources. **Factors of production** are all the human and nonhuman resources that go into the production of material goods. These resources are of three principal types: first, **labor,** or the efforts of human beings; second, **natural resources,** resources such as land, raw materials, and so on that are the basis of all the material products that humans make; and, third, **capital,** or productive equipment, which includes tools, machines, factory buildings, and all the things that human beings have made to help them produce more easily and efficiently the kinds of goods they ultimately require to satisfy personal wants. Goods in the form of capital do not *directly* satisfy human wants. Their importance is that they ultimately enable us to produce a much greater quantity and variety of consumer goods than would otherwise be possible, and often goods of a more desirable kind or quality.

However, all productive resources—labor, natural resources, and capital—are limited in quantity, whereas in modern societies human wants seem to be practically unlimited. Our own society may be affluent in comparison with others, and a very small minority of its members may have few wants of consequence that remain unsatisfied, but the vast majority find it difficult to stretch their incomes enough to provide all the things they desire. The great economic problem facing every modern society is how to make scarce resources satisfy as fully as possible the ever-expanding wants of its members. But, as we have noted in earlier chapters, we cannot continue indefinitely to satisfy greater and greater economic wants for an ever-increasing population without encountering shortages of resources and more and more polluting of the environment. In the 1970s, the trend in thinking was that economic growth is undesirable and that "small is beautiful." By the 1980s and continuing into the twenty-first century, most people were seeking ways to have increasingly higher levels of economic growth without diminishing efforts to master pollution and conserve and extend resources.

Economizing—making the best possible use of the resources that we employ at any time, regardless of what we think of growth—is one of the most important functions of an economic system. Determining the best mechanism for economizing, or allocating resources, is the fundamental task of economic policy.

Planned and Unplanned Economies

Some societies, such as the United States, are called market or **unplanned economies**— economies that rely primarily on the market to control economic decisions. Because they rely on private capital markets to raise money for building production facilities such as factories, and because any profits or losses from production accrue to the owners of those facilities, these societies are also sometimes called *private enterprise* or *capitalist* economies. In an unplanned or market economy, individuals have significant freedom to own and operate productive enterprises, to produce economic goods, and to develop specialized institutions such as banks and insurance companies to fulfill their needs.

Other societies, such as North Korea and, until recently, the former Soviet Union, have Soviet-style socialistic or **planned economies,** which rely primarily on a government-controlled production and distribution system. In such societies, the money for building the production facilities comes from government, and any profits or losses from production accrue to government. If the economy incorporates certain additional political and ideological goals, these economies are called communist. In a totally planned economy, some central governmental authority has the power to plan, own, and operate directly all productive activities.

An important lesson of the political economy aspect of social science is understanding the distinction between planned and unplanned economies and how that distinction relates to autocracies and democracies. To understand the difference, consider what happens when a person graduates from school. In a planned economy, graduates are told where and at what jobs they will work; they do not have to worry about being unemployed. In an unplanned economy, they have freedom of choice about what jobs to take, but they might not find jobs. Alternatively, consider the top person at a company. In a planned economy, the top person receives a plan from the government, and he or she must fulfill that plan, which dictates what product to produce, what to make it out of, and what to sell it for. In an unplanned economy, the top person at a company decides what to produce and sells it for whatever price he or she sets, depending only on what top management believes will earn the most profit. We consider these issues in more detail later.

In the 1990s, the major planned economies either switched to market economies or are in the process of introducing significant elements of markets into their economies. These include China, Russia, countries of the former Soviet Union, and the countries of eastern Europe. To gain some perspective on this most recent change, it is helpful to consider the history of economic systems.

The Evolution of Economic Systems

Throughout the Middle Ages, markets grew as trade among diverse areas expanded. Governments were not well developed in those times, and for the market to exist it was necessary to work out agreements with leaders of the various towns. As the Western political system evolved, first controlled by local lords or nobility and then by monarchs, all individuals who wanted to undertake economic activities were required to get permission from the noble or the royal head of state. Those who did not have permission were not allowed to undertake such economic activities.

From Feudalism to Mercantilism

As we discussed in Chapter 3, early on the economic system of the Western world was **feudalism,** in which tradition ruled and most people were peasants tied to the land and their feudal lord. A few individuals escaped this pattern; these included the workers who built the great medieval cathedrals of Europe (and who gave the term *Freemason* to our vocabulary) and traders who traveled in caravans they set up as temporary markets in or near feudal estates. These traveling workers and traders played a pivotal role in spreading culture and ideas from one estate to another and in establishing the political geography that evolved into our modern states. For example, many of the temporary markets became permanent and formed the centers around which towns and cities grew. Traders brought ideas as well as goods, providing peasants with a view of the wider world. As trade progressed, people began living in towns and producing goods full time for the market.

As people moved into the city, the economic system evolved into the **mercantilist system,** in which manufacturing or processing was favored above agriculture, and governments determined who could do what. The important aspect of the mercantilist system was that permission to engage in economic activity had to be obtained from local

Open-air trading continues today, as this scene of a person selling fish in New York City's Chinatown demonstrates.

authorities, and as increasing trade fostered the development of the nation-state, traders soon found that they had to obtain permission from the evolving governments.

From Mercantilism to a Market Economy

Beginning in the eighteenth century, the Industrial Revolution brought about a change from artisan production to machine production, which required a large number of individuals to work at specific manufacturing tasks in a common place (instead of scattered around in small enterprises). The Industrial Revolution was characterized by specialization of individuals in their work tasks. It unleashed an engine for material growth through growth in technology that transformed not only the economy and economic institutions, but also the social institutions of society.

The Industrial Revolution placed an economic strain on the mercantilist system, which had incorporated so many limitations on individual enterprise that many who might have been very good at some economic activity were simply not allowed to undertake that activity; this created tension and opposition to the existing social structure. By the mid-eighteenth century, opposition to the limitations of the mercantilist system had grown important, and in 1776 Adam Smith, a moral philosopher, wrote a book called *The Wealth of Nations,* in which he expressed the underlying economic ideas that became central to the development of modern Western economic institutions.

Smith argued that for the government to prevent individuals who were good at something from doing it was not beneficial to society. Individuals, he held, should be free to do what they want, and he argued that such freedom would not lead to chaos. Instead the **invisible hand**—the rise and fall of prices that guide individuals' actions in a market—of the market would guide individuals' choices, so that each individual pursuing his or her own self-interest would simultaneously help society and create the greatest wealth for the greatest number of people in that society. For example, Smith argued that bakers will supply bread to people when they can make a profit, and this bread will satisfy people's hunger. If the baker charges too high a price, as long as there is competition others will enter and drive the price down to its cost of production. Alternatively, say there is too little bread. The price of bread will rise, and as it does, as long as individuals are free to become bakers, more people will become bakers, more bread will be produced, and there will no longer be too little bread. Then the price of bread will fall. People's needs are met by the market not because people are nice or concerned about others' welfare, but because people are selfish and pursue profit. But the market, through changes in prices, guides individuals' choices like an invisible hand, so that what helps them personally also helps society.

Laissez-faire is a policy that allows the market to operate with a minimum of government regulation. The policy of laissez-faire was quite different from the mercantilist economic system in which the government played an important role in determining who could and could not produce certain goods. The debate that began between mercantilism and laissez-faire has continued. On a global scale, it is tied to the debate between planned and unplanned economies. Within the United States, we see it surfacing currently in the debates about how much government involvement in and regulation of the market should exist. Laissez-faire advocates argue that the government should stay out of economic activities except to provide the framework within which individuals can themselves carry out those activities.

Opponents argue that such a policy can cause people enormous pain. They point out that in the 1930s laissez-faire led to a depression in which unemployment rose to 25 percent, and that such economic calamities can be prevented only if government takes a much larger role in organizing and coordinating individuals' decisions. A second argument against laissez-faire is that it permits the market, rather than society, to distribute the goods of the society, and the market may well distribute goods unfairly, making some people rich while others starve. Such concerns about laissez-faire led the United States to impose a variety of laws and regulations, such as the Pure Food and Drug Act (1906) and the Sherman Anti-Trust Act (1890), that limited market decisions and made the U.S. economy a more regulated market economy.

From a Market Economy to a Mixed Economy

Because of these changes in their structure, most Western economies that we today call capitalist economies are better described by the term **mixed economy,** in which both the market and the government determine how goods are produced and distributed. If some laissez-faire advocates from the 1920s were to rise from their graves and come to the United States, they would probably view our economy as socialist. In the 150 years since the writings of Karl Marx, the nature of capitalist economies has changed in response to the tendencies that caused Marx to condemn **capitalism,** which we now formally define as an economic system based on private property, markets, entrepreneurial initiative, and the ownership of the means of production by capitalists. Over the last fifty or so years, the role of government in the economy has dramatically increased.

Today in most advanced industrial countries, the tax burden for the maintenance of all government activities absorbs from 29 to over 54 percent of the entire national income. Korea devotes about 29 percent, whereas in Sweden about 54 percent of the total gross domestic product (GDP) is taken in taxes. In the United States, the figure is about 30 percent, far more than any advocate of capitalism would have believed possible only sixty years ago. The changes will continue, causing textbook writers, and hence students, problems in deciding how to define various systems.

We come back to a discussion of a mixed economy later, but first we need to consider more carefully how both planned and unplanned economies work. We begin with a discussion of how the invisible hand of the market operates.

Market Economies

A **market economy** is an economic system that relies on the initiative of private citizens for the production of economic goods. In such a system, those who organize and control production must have incentives, and in a market economy the chief incentive is the possibility of making profits. Subject to the law of the land, anyone who chooses to is free to undertake the establishment of almost any kind of business enterprise. Businesspeople can choose both the products to be produced and the methods to be employed in their production; can buy materials, labor, and managerial services; and can sell their products wherever people will buy them and at any price that customers are willing to pay. The chief problem in getting started is likely to be finding sufficient capital. If the new business is to be small, the owner's capital plus personal credit or borrowing power may be sufficient.

But if the business is to be larger, the owner must interest other people and induce them to contribute capital as partners or, if a corporation is formed, as stockholders.

There is no such thing as a pure or absolute **free enterprise economy**—an economy in which the government plays no part at all—because freedom itself is always relative. When we describe our own economy as a free enterprise system, we do not mean that anybody can establish just any kind of business without meeting obstacles. We mean that in most cases it is quite feasible for people who can obtain capital, and who have the necessary personal qualities, to organize and operate new business enterprises, and that they have a wide range of freedom in making the decisions involved. But in some industries, certain obstacles are difficult to overcome. In the automobile industry, for example, the capital required to establish a new company is huge, and the risk of failure is great, and in the public utility industries, local monopolies are sometimes supported by law because this is believed to be in the public interest. Free enterprise, however, means more than the right to start a business. Fully as important is the right of those who already own business enterprises to operate and control them—to determine policies—subject only to laws and restrictions deemed necessary and reasonable by government.

The government must provide the legal and economic framework and the general rules within which private enterprises operate. Although government participation in economic affairs may be great or small, no government follows a complete policy of laissez-faire with respect to the economic activities of private individuals.

Figure 16.1 provides an example of the interrelationships within a market economy. In it we see that producers (firms) and consumers relate through the market. Workers earn income from firms and, in turn, spend their income on goods that the firms produce. What the workers don't spend they save in financial institutions that, in their turn, lend money to firms. The government enters the picture in two ways. It establishes the laws and regulations that govern the interaction of individuals and producers, and it collects taxes and provides services for firms and consumers.

How a Market Economy Works

In a free enterprise system, markets and prices play a dominant role in organizing and controlling economic activities. Any commodity that cannot be sold in the market at a profitable price will not be produced, at least not for long, whereas any commodity that can be sold at a profit is probably going to be produced by someone sooner or later.

When prices are not regulated and when markets are highly competitive, price changes keep adjusting production to consumption and consumption to production. For simplicity, let us assume that by a competitive market we mean one in which there are many small independent sellers of the same product and many independent buyers. Under these conditions, if people wish to increase their purchases of a commodity, the resulting increase in demand will cause the price to rise and production to be stimulated. Simultaneously, the rise in price will restrict the increase of market demand.

On the other hand, if people decide to decrease their purchases, the price will fall and this will discourage production, but the lower price will tend to limit the decline in sales and consumption. As long as more of the commodity is still being produced and offered for sale than people are willing to buy, the price will continue to drop. In competitive markets, the price always tends to rise or fall until the amount of a commodity that is being

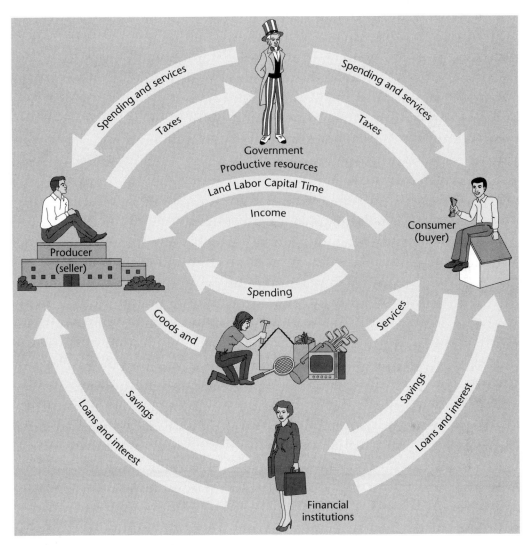

Spending and services

Taxes

Spending and services

Taxes

Government

Productive resources

Land Labor Capital Time

Income

Producer
(seller)

Consumer
(buyer)

Spending

Goods and

Services

Savings

Loans and interest

Savings

Loans and interest

Financial
institutions

Figure 16.1

Model of a market economy.

produced and offered for sale is equal, at the market price, to the amount that consumers are willing to buy. This determines the **equilibrium price,** or the price at which demand exactly equals supply.

Figure 16.2 is far too simple to take into account all the conditions in a real market, but it does illustrate the tendency under competition for the price of a commodity to rise or fall until **demand,** the amount of a product that people are willing to buy at a given price and time, equals **supply,** the amount that others are willing to sell. The vertical *y*-axis measures the price of potatoes per bushel; the horizontal *x*-axis measures the number of

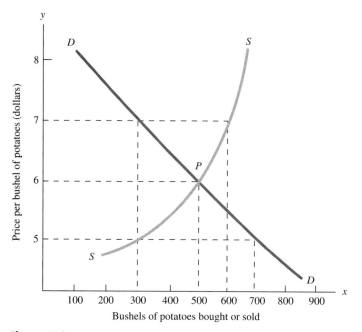

Figure 16.2

Determination of equilibrium price.

bushels. The **demand curve,** *DD,* shows the amount of a good buyers would be willing to purchase at different prices in the market on a certain day. The **supply curve,** *SS,* shows the amount of a good sellers would be willing to offer at different prices on the same day.

The point of intersection, *P,* shows that under the assumptions made in constructing these curves, the market price would tend to be $6. The price could not, for example, stay at $7, for then buyers would take only 300 bushels, whereas sellers would offer 600 bushels. Because there are many competing sellers, some would soon reduce their prices as they saw sales lagging. Likewise, the price could not stay at $5, for in that case buyers would want 700 bushels, but sellers would offer only 300. As soon as buyers sensed that there were not enough potatoes to go around, some would raise their offers. Only at the equilibrium price of $6 would the forces of supply and demand be in balance, for at that price, buyers would be willing to purchase 500 bushels, just the amount that sellers would offer.

To see the way markets work, it is useful to consider two important historical events: an oil "crisis" and the computer revolution. Four times in the last fifty years there has been a sudden dramatic decrease in the supply of oil. In each case, the market's reaction has been a rise in the price of oil. The resulting price rise hurt consumers, and it made them change their consumption habits. For instance, smaller, more energy-efficient cars were developed. The result was a decrease in the quantity of oil demanded, induced by the higher price. The higher price acted like a stick, leading people to decrease the quantity of oil they used. Simultaneously, the higher price acted like a carrot, encouraging oil-producing firms to produce more and explore for more oil.

The floor of the New York Stock Exchange.

Now let's consider the computer revolution, which represents a more pleasant side of the market for consumers. Major technological breakthroughs in the development of computers increased supply, quality, and capacity. In response, prices of computers fell, and individuals, firms, and schools developed new ways to use computers, increasing the quantity demanded. This revolution is continuing and will be an important phenomenon well into the twenty-first century. An increase in supply causes prices to fall, giving individuals more for less. Thus, not only does the market act as a stick as individuals are forced to change their ways because of higher prices, but it also acts as a carrot, causing individuals to find new uses for goods and services whose prices have fallen.

The Role of Government in Market Economies

Although governments under the free enterprise system produce relatively few goods or services for sale, they regulate private business in many ways. The extent of government regulation of business in market economies provides a legal and institutional setting within which the market can operate, and the amount of regulation tends to increase as the economy becomes more complex and as business units become larger. This is only natural.

The expansion of the economic activities of government is not necessarily either good or bad. Some of it is necessary and desirable. For example, as we stated before, in the 1930s when the private enterprise system was caught in a depression in which unemployment rates reached 25 percent and stayed there, most individuals accepted the proposition that the government has a role to play in maintaining high employment through the management of the government budget (fiscal policy) and the money supply (monetary policy).

This belief, and the economic analysis associated with it, was developed by John Maynard Keynes and is often called Keynesian macroeconomics. **Macroeconomics** focuses on the aggregate economy, in contrast to **microeconomics,** which focuses on economic decisions facing the individual. Recently, as we see later, there has been a movement away from Keynesian macroeconomics, raising important questions about the proper role of government in the economy.

The Changing Nature of the U.S. Economy

One of the advantages of markets is that they allow enormous changes to occur—changes that evolving technology requires. Consider the U.S economy. When this country was founded, U.S. business was primarily agricultural, and in the 1700s approximately 97 percent of the population was engaged in farming. In the 1990s, less than 3 percent of the workforce was devoted to farming, and the number of family farms continues to decrease as corporations take over farms and merge them into large commercial operations. So it is obvious that over the years the nature of business organizations in the United States has changed and continues to change, especially as experiments with Internet business go forward. In the 1800s, this change was from farming to manufacturing as the technology for mass production of goods developed, making the economy more interrelated and more complex. As mass production developed, the size of the typical business enterprise increased, and business organizations played increasingly important roles.

A business operated by one person with two or three employees presents simple organizational problems, but when a business employs 50,000 workers and manufactures a complicated product, problems of organization become difficult, and their satisfactory solutions become absolutely essential to carrying on production. Large numbers of individuals and quantities of machines and materials produce nothing unless they are organized, and whether they produce a small output at high cost or a large output at low cost depends for the most part on how efficiently they are organized. The organizational needs of manufacturing were for large plants and large firms. Thus from 1870 until about 1970, we saw manufacturing businesses become larger and larger.

In the late 1970s, the structure of the U.S. economy started changing. Service and distribution grew in importance and manufacturing declined. Biotechnology, computers, and related software technology became leading industries and the engine for U.S. growth. By the 1990s, these two technologies had grown enormously, and the U.S. economy entered into the longest expansion it had ever experienced. The inflation that had accompanied many previous expansions did not occur because productivity gains held costs down and wages stayed down due to international competition.

Why did these technologies grow in the United States much more than elsewhere? Part of the reason was luck and part was U.S. government support. (The Internet developed in part because of Department of Defense subsidies to scientists.) Still another part was U.S. market institutions that encouraged entrepreneurial activity and venture capital markets in which loans to new industries are made.

Because of the noninflationary expansion of the late 1990s and early 2000s, many people talked about a "new economy" that would continually grow without inflation. However, that talk ended abruptly when the value of new economy stocks (especially dot-com stocks) fell drastically and the economy entered into a recession, or slow growth period. Then the talk turned to **deflation**—the steady and continual fall in the price level—and a possible worldwide serious recession.

The Upheaval in the Formerly Socialist Economies

Having briefly considered the nature of the market economy, we now take a look at an alternative system: Soviet-style socialism, or a planned economy. The ideas of socialism discussed here were spawned in the mid-1800s when laissez-faire capitalism was at its peak. Capitalism then had many of the advantages described earlier, but it also had many negative side effects. Wages were low, living conditions were poor, and people thrown out of work were starving. Whereas individuals under feudalism had a society with built-in supports to fall back on, they had none under capitalism. Industrialists wanted it that way: The fear of starvation kept wages low and profits high.

Historical Development of Socialist Thought

In response to these conditions there were numerous calls for reform. These included the writings of utopian socialists such as Charles Fourier and Robert Owen, who favored establishing new communities where all members would contribute to the output of the community and use whatever community resources they needed. There, the decision of the community rather than the decision of the market would be the determinant of the allocation and distribution of goods. Utopian socialists believed that the market system was flawed, but they did not see a need for revolution against the system, nor did they see the development of an inevitable class struggle between workers and the owners of the means of production.

More radical reformers did see such needs and developments. These radical social reformers, such as Karl Marx and Friedrich Engels, saw the market system as inherently flawed. They argued that as the capitalists, or the owners of the means of production, exploited the workers, the workers would unite and establish a new form of economic organization called *communism,* under which each person would work according to his or her ability and each would consume according to his or her needs. Thus communism would evolve into somewhat the same type of economic system as that envisioned by the utopian socialists, but the path by which society would reach its destination was different. Under socialism the path would be peaceful, with everyone joining in for the good of society; under communism the path would be one of revolution against the existing social structure.

Socialism and Communism

The terms *socialism* and *communism* are not easy to define; they developed slowly over time, and the nature of the concepts themselves has changed and is continuing to change. From the 1930s until about the late 1980s, both were associated with what we now call **Soviet-style socialism**—an economic system in which the government, rather than the market, makes decisions about the allocation and distribution of goods. Communism was a type of

Soviet-style socialism in which the Communist Party played a key role in the economy. In the 1990s, as the former Soviet-style socialist countries underwent tremendous upheavals, some socialists were suggesting different definitions under which socialism was compatible with the use of markets to distribute goods. Most people, however, still used the definition that associated socialism with government decisions about the allocation and distribution of goods. But a change in that definition would not be surprising; the definition of socialism has continually changed.

In the mid-1800s, for example, the French writer and reformer Louis Blanc, one of the originators of socialism, argued that all individuals had an inherent right to a decent job. Capitalism failed to achieve that goal and, therefore, violated individuals' rights. Initially, the right to a job was a central tenet of socialism.

Having a right to a job means that somehow jobs must become available, and quickly the principle expanded to include not only the right but also the means by which government would supply jobs to all—through government ownership of the means of production. As this happened, government ownership of the means of production became a key element in the definition of socialism. The focus on jobs also switched to a focus on equality of income, and the advocacy of equality of income became another key element of socialist thought. Thus programs designed to equalize income in a country are often called socialistic.

Given this evolution, there is no unambiguous description of socialism. Because we need some definition, however, we define **socialism** in the traditional way, as an economic system under which society as a whole takes the primary responsibility for producing and distributing economic goods. Using this broad definition, Soviet-style socialism is a particular type of socialism. Although there is no inherent political system associated with socialism, the focus on society as a whole as the producer and distributor of economic goods quickly linked the theory of socialism to a comprehensive plan of government and hence, autocracy, although the relationship is subject to debate.

In practice, socialism has taken on a variety of forms, and elements of socialist thought have influenced the evolution of capitalist societies. For example, the establishment of social security systems was originally a socialist goal, as were many of the social welfare programs that we now regard as part of our capitalist economic system.

We formally define **communism** as a type of autocratic or state socialism in which the Communist Party is the small group of people—not subject to elections—that determines society's goals. But communism also includes specific political elements and thus must be differentiated from socialism. Communism includes a set of beliefs following from communist writers such as Karl Marx and Vladimir Lenin. As we stated earlier, Marx's criticisms of capitalism were more widely focused than those of the socialist writers; he saw capitalism as being doomed by the laws of history. He argued that history progressed in stages and that each stage had two opposing elements—thesis and antithesis. Each stage played a role in history, but once the role was played, society would progress to the next stage.

In capitalism Marx saw one of the opposing forces as the bourgeoisie—the capitalists who brought about growth by exploiting the workers. This exploitation, he argued, played an important role in causing the economy to grow, but once that growth had brought society enough income, he believed that the workers would unite to overthrow the capitalists, who were no longer needed. Then the workers would constitute a communist form of economic organization, with the following creed: From each according to his ability; to each according to his need.

Marx had little to say about how a communist economy would operate. In practice it involved the same key points as socialism—a stated belief in the equality of income and a centralized system of distribution and production. Marx also argued that under communism the state would wither away, which might be interpreted to mean not the complete disappearance of an administrative mechanism but the complete disappearance of any need for controlling people by force. Presumably, after the state had withered away, production would be carried on by cooperative groups of workers in complete harmony and without any need for coercion. But in no country that we called communist has the state withered away.

The following list summarizes the reasons why Soviet-style socialism was abandoned:

1. Soviet-style economies weren't delivering goods.
2. Communist Party members were using their position to obtain desired goods and favorable treatment.
3. Socialist economies were significantly lagging behind capitalist economies.
4. New technological developments made it more difficult for the government to repress information and ideas that were contrary to the interest of the ruling parties.
5. Long-standing ethnic and cultural differences undermined the ability of the societies to form a national consensus.

In response to these upheavals, socialism and communism underwent enormous changes. Most Soviet-style socialist countries dumped Soviet-style socialism completely; others, such as China, attempted to integrate the market into their socialist institutions, freeing up certain areas of the economy while keeping others under government control. Still others talked about following some as yet undefined third way—an alternative path that was neither socialist nor capitalist. As this occurred, the repressive nature of the Communist Party was made clear to all, and most pretense to maintaining a higher moral ground was lost. The Communist Party was not the protector of the working people; it was simply another group vying for political control.

How Planned and Unplanned Economies Work

To understand the difference between a Soviet-style socialist, or planned, economy and a market, or unplanned, economy, and to put these recent momentous events into perspective, it is useful to consider how planned and unplanned economies work.

Let's start by considering how bread is produced in a planned economy. Wheat is raised on government-owned farms. The central planners decide on a set of production goals for a five-year period and determine what they will need in the way of equipment, seed, money, and other efforts to meet those goals. Once those decisions are made, the farms and central planners are responsible for meeting the goals. The farms do not calculate profit or loss (although the central planners do consider such issues), nor is there any necessary relationship between the costs of production and the price of the wheat. Production goals are set in terms of quantities, not economic value.

After the wheat is produced, the flour is sent to a bakery, which has also negotiated with central planners about its own five-year plan. Wheat is one of the "inputs" for which the bakery planned. Thus the bakery's goal might have been to produce 5 million loaves of bread with 4.5 thousand tons of wheat. Having baked the bread, the bakery sends it to a government-owned retail store, which sells it to the consumer at whatever price the government tells the retailer to charge. In the Soviet planned economy in the 1980s, the price set for bread was far lower than the price of a loaf of bread in the United States because the Soviet government wanted to make this essential food widely available.

There is one other element, or input, in the production that we should mention, and that is labor. Each of the government production facilities needs a certain number of workers. Once the planning commission has determined the labor requirements of the firm, the government assigns individuals to various jobs in that facility. Thus, in the pre-1990 Soviet economy, when a Soviet citizen graduated from school, she or he was assigned to a job. However, students in the top 2 percent of their class were allowed to choose their jobs. The government also set the wages that workers received.

In the market economy of the United States, no production quotas are assigned. Farmers, bakers, and retail stores individually decide how much they want to produce on the basis of expected prices and costs of input. If they make a mistake, they—not the government—are responsible for the loss, and if they make a profit, they—not the government—receive that profit. Workers are not assigned to jobs; they seek their own.

Problems with Central Planning

Clearly, such a brief description is insufficient to allow you to judge the two systems, but it should give you some idea of how the systems work and allow you to use your imagination to figure out some of the problems that are likely to come up in each system. We have seen many of the problems of the market economy in the United States in the 1980s, 1990s, and early 2000s. Farmers suffered enormous losses and many were losing their farms. In the planned economy there might be losses, but they would not be suffered by the farmer, and the farm operation would continue uninterrupted. In the United States, some people graduating (or dropping out) from school cannot find a job, and they join the ranks of the unemployed. In the planned economy, all graduates have jobs.

The planned economy has its problems, too. Farmers try to negotiate a low production goal with high costs. If they don't get a tractor they need, they are less likely than U.S. farmers to find ways to manage without it, and they are apt to use the lack of a new tractor as an excuse for not meeting the production goal. Similarly, workers are often assigned a job they don't want, and they simply don't show up for work, or, if they do, they don't put their hearts into the job, doing only what they are told to do and no more. These and related problems led to the breakup of the Soviet Union and the movement away from their planned economy, socialism, and communism.

Why Central Planning Did Not Meet Its Goals

The goals of socialist or communist economies are admirable. In the ideal society envisioned by communist theorists, citizens would be completely free of coercion by the state and would be happy enough to accept all their social responsibilities. Social classes would disappear. Everyone would work, the entire product of the economy would go to labor, and all workers would have equal rights to share it. They would share, however, not equally but according to need. If money were used as a medium of exchange, presumably wages

Selling live eels at a street market in China. As a result of economic reforms that began in the 1980s, markets in China have flourished.

would be paid to workers according to their needs. In any case, certain basic essential goods would be provided free to all citizens.

To some degree, communist countries achieved their goals. Basic necessities were relatively much cheaper in the former Soviet Union and China than they are in market economies; however, luxuries were much more expensive. For example, in 1986 an average two-room apartment in the former Soviet Union cost approximately $24 per month, and all workers were guaranteed a one-month holiday. Similarly, medical care and education were free. In China the communist government made the provision of health care a top priority. It instituted a "barefoot doctor" program that sent doctors out to teach paramedics the basics of sanitation, hygiene, preventative medicine, and birth control. It similarly embarked on an educational program for all their people.

Despite these impressive showings, both the Chinese and the Soviet systems often fell short. The $24-a-month apartments often required a ten-year wait, and consumer goods were generally rationed or impossible to get except on the black market, where they were enormously expensive. The medical care was inept. There were serious shortages of goods of all kinds. Productivity—the amount of output per worker—lagged and economic growth slowed. New technologies were not developed because no one had an incentive to develop them.

Planned economies were characterized by significant food shortages, causing people to line up to buy scarce goods.

One goal they did not meet was equity and fairness. The shortages did not fall on all people equally. Through special commissaries, government leaders and Communist Party members easily got the goods that were in short supply, while other people had to wait in long lines. By the 1980s, the general view of most social scientists and of many citizens in communist countries was that the planned economy was not delivering the goods. The people were becoming dissatisfied.

In response, China introduced major modifications in its economic system, allowing the development of private markets while maintaining overall political control. The former Soviet Union and a number of the countries of eastern Europe took much more drastic measures. They essentially abandoned the socialist planned economy.

Transition Problems from a Planned to an Unplanned Economy

The transitions of the former Soviet-style socialist countries have not been easy. People of a country don't wake up one morning and decide they are going to switch from a planned to an unplanned economy. Any such change is accompanied by enormous political fights about whether such change is warranted. These political struggles can delay any implementation with discouraging uncertainty about what the future holds. Such uncertainty makes it impossible for any system to operate. That's what happened in the former Soviet Union, where the discussion of change to a market system undercut the planning process and sent the economy into a tailspin.

The transition in China has followed a different route. There, the Communist Party maintained political control but gave either its implicit or its explicit blessing to significant amounts of private market activity. The result was an enormous growth spurt in the 1990s and early 2000s, a growth that placed strains on the political control of the Communist Party. How long this political–economic compromise will remain viable is open to debate.

In other countries where the Communist Party lost power but there remained a relatively united political front for transforming the economy, the problems of reform were huge. Who will be given the property rights to the land and business? What will the nature of ownership be? What laws will govern market transactions? How quickly does one change to market prices? Who will be allowed to borrow money? Who will be allowed to import goods? What foreigners will be allowed to invest in the country, and under what terms? In some transitional economies such as Poland, Hungary, and the Czech Republic, they are well on their way to answering these questions. In others, such as Romania, Bulgaria, and the Ukraine, they have a long way to go. In the meantime, their economies continue to face high unemployment, lack of investment, and political and social unrest.

$\mathcal{T}$he Continuing Evolution of Economies

In the 1980s and 1990s, not only formerly socialist countries but also a number of Western market economies moved more toward the market. To understand why this change was occurring, it is important to recognize that in the 1940s, 1950s, and 1960s the movement was the other way: Market economies were becoming more socialized.

In Great Britain, for example, the British Labour party moved to partial socialization of the economy in the late 1940s, when several basic industries such as railroads, coal mines, steel, and power were taken over by the government. When the Conservative Party came to power in the 1970s, the socialization program was halted and, to a limited extent, reversed. The steel industry was returned to private ownership, and some of the commodity exchanges were reopened in order to reestablish private trading at competitive prices. However, many of the economic changes made by the Labour government were retained, and the British economy is best described as a mixed economy.

Probably the most dramatic socialization of all the Western mixed economies has occurred in Sweden, the pioneer of the welfare state. There, individuals have a practically risk-free society, with tax rates to pay for it. Taxes are so high that a quarter of Sweden's working population chooses to work only part time. By the 1990s, the task of providing individuals with incentives while simultaneously providing an equitable society was growing difficult, and Sweden was talking about moving back toward the market by eliminating some of its welfare programs.

As you can see from the discussion of the evolution of economic systems, most economies have a mixture of different institutions, some of which use the market and some of which don't. The collapse of many Soviet-style socialist planned economies has led some observers to say that the market is definitely preferable to other ways of organizing economies. The market certainly does have its advantages, but it is also important to remember that most Western countries do not use pure market systems. They use a mixed economic system.

Think of the United States. We have government-sponsored unemployment insurance, government-regulated retirement programs (Social Security), government-owned schools, and an enormous number of government regulations that limit our actions in the market. We have a mixed economy rather than a pure market economy.

The largest and fastest growing movement toward governmental responsibility for regulating the economy in the United States occurred after the Great Depression of the 1930s. Bad economic times make people desire a different form of economy, no matter what the existing form is. If they make it through the transition period, most formerly socialist countries will become mixed economies with economic institutions that reflect their history and culture.

One can already see a trend away from the almost total commitment to move as quickly as possible to a market economy in many of these transitional economies. For example, in Poland the former socialist government was reelected on its promise to slow down reforms. One can expect much more of such wavering.

In short, there is no perfect economic system. Organizing the economic affairs of millions of persons is a difficult process and will be continually marked by problems. As new problems are faced, it is likely that the economies will continually evolve, perhaps into types we have not yet classified. Economic systems, like culture and human beings, adapt to changes and evolve, as new ways of coordinating behavior are tried and as those new ways create new problems.

Key Points

- The great economic problem that faces every modern society is to make the scarce resources available satisfy as fully as possible the ever-expanding wants of its members.
- Unplanned economies rely on markets to control economic decisions; planned economies rely on government.
- Our economy has evolved from feudalism to mercantilism to a market economy and finally to a mixed economy.
- Markets create carrots and sticks when supply differs from demand, leading the invisible hand to get people to do what is in society's interest.

- Socialist thought developed in reaction to the problems caused by a nonregulated market economy.
- Soviet-style socialism was abandoned because its economies weren't delivering the goods, many of the goods were distributed unfairly, economic growth lagged behind that of capitalist countries, technology in communications promoted dissent, and ethnic and cultural differences undermined national unity.

Some Important Terms

capital (361)
capitalism (365)
communism (372)
deflation (371)
demand (367)
demand curve (368)
economic goods (360)
economics (359)
economic wants (360)
economizing (362)
economy (360)

equilibrium price (367)
factors of production (361)
feudalism (363)
free enterprise economy (366)
invisible hand (364)
labor (361)
laissez-faire (364)
macroeconomics (370)
market economy (365)
mercantilist system (363)
microeconomics (370)

mixed economy (365)
natural resources (361)
planned economies (362)
socialism (372)
Soviet-style socialism (371)
supply (367)
supply curve (368)
unplanned economies (362)
wealth (361)

Questions for Review and Discussion

1. Economics studies the social organization through which people satisfy their wants for scarce goods, including services. Give some examples of economic wants.
2. What four important functions must every economy perform?
3. What are economic goods? What are economic needs? What are economic wants?
4. What economic aspects does the family have?
5. What three factors of production are necessary to produce economic goods?
6. What is the great economic problem facing every society?
7. In a planned or socialist economy, who is responsible for building the factories and distributing the goods?

8. What economic changes took place when Western societies turned from agriculturally based economies to urban-based economies?

9. How did the Industrial Revolution contribute to economic growth?

10. In 1776 Adam Smith published a book titled *The Wealth of Nations.* How did he believe a nation could become wealthy?

11. In an unplanned or market economy, who raises the money and builds the factories? Who gets the profits or suffers the losses?

12. What enabled the U.S. economy to grow at the same time that the percentage of people engaged in agriculture shrank?

13. Why has the role of large manufacturing business become somewhat less important since the 1970s?

14. If the price of Coca-Cola went up to $2 a can, what would you expect to happen to the quantity of Coca-Cola demanded?

15. What two methods does a government use to control unemployment?

16. Do you believe that everyone has a right to a job? If so, whose responsibility is it to provide that many jobs?

17. If the government controls the means of production, what is produced, and how the goods are distributed, what are the advantages? What are the disadvantages?

18. Give an example of how a socialist idea has been adopted in a market economy.

19. Give an example of how a capitalist idea has been adopted in a socialist economy.

20. In a planned economy, if weather and plant disease caused an agricultural disaster, would farms go out of production? Why or why not?

21. What are some of the reasons that some consumer goods are scarce and of poor quality in a socialist economy?

22. In market economies, such as the United States and Sweden, taxes are quite high. How does this blur the distinction between the terms *capitalist* and *socialist*?

*I*nternet Questions

1. To construct a market economy, R. Vernon, at www.cipe.org/publications/fs/ert/e20/ver_E20.htm, states three lessons to learn from history. What are they?

2. Using information found at www.auburn.edu/~johnspm/gloss/index.html, what is the definition of a black market?

3. Go to www.res.org.uk/society/mediabriefings/pdfs/1996/november/agell.asp and read about the welfare state. What lesson can be learned from Sweden's experience?

4. Using http://news.nationalgeographic.com/news/2002/10/1002_021002_indiabirds.html, what are the seven practices determined to be reasons for the large black market in exotic birds in India?

5. What is the mission statement of the New York Stock Exchange, www.nyse.com/home.html?

6. While reading about the economic causes of the war for independence at www.gbt.org/wilkins/causes_of_the_war_of_independenc.htm, find out what bullionism is.

*F*or Further Study

Aoki, Masahiko, *Information, Corporate Governance, and Institutional Diversity: Competitiveness in Japan, the USA, and the Transitional Economies,* New York: Oxford University Press, 2000.

Bernstein, Peter, *The Power of Gold: The History of an Obsession,* New York: Wiley, 2000.

Boeri, Tito, *Structural Change, Welfare Systems, and Labour Reallocation Lessons from the Transition of*

Formerly Planned Economies, New York: Oxford University Press, 2000.

Bowles, Samuel, *Understanding Capitalism: Competition, Command, and Change in the U.S. Economy,* New York: HarperCollins, 1993.

Chernov, Ron, *Titan: The Life of John D. Rockefeller,* New York: Random House, 1999.

Friedman, Milton, *Capitalism and Freedom,* Chicago: University of Chicago Press, 1962.

Galbraith, John Kenneth, *Economics and the Public Purpose,* Boston: Houghton Mifflin, 1973.

Gilder, George, *Wealth and Poverty,* New York: Basic Books, 1981.

Hayek, Friedrich, *The Road to Serfdom,* Chicago: University of Chicago Press, 1944.

Kaplan, Robert D., *An Empire Wilderness: Travels into America's Future,* New York: Random House, 1999.

MacDonald, Heather, *The Burden of Bad Ideas,* Chicago: Ivan R. Dee/Romlan & Littlefield, 2000.

Olson, Mancur, *Power and Prosperity: Outgrowing Communist and Capitalist Dictatorships,* New York: Basic Books, 2000.

Sassoon, Donald, *One Hundred Years of Socialism: The West European Left in the Twentieth Century,* New York: New Press, 1997.

Schumpeter, Joseph A., *Capitalism, Socialism and Democracy,* New York: Harper & Row, 1962.

Shane, Scott, *How Information Ended the Soviet Union,* Baltimore: Dee, 1994.

Strouse, Jean, *Morgan: American Financier,* New York: Random House, 1999.

Ulam, Adam B., *The Communists: The Story of Power and Lost Illusions: 1948–1991,* New York: Charles Scribner's Sons, 1994.

Weber, Max, *The Protestant Ethic and the Spirit of Capitalism* (1904), New York: Scribner, 1958.

WWW Capitalism.org www.capitalism.org

WWW The Economist www.economist.com

WWW The Freedom network www.free-market.net

WWW Informal Communist Discussion www.communism.com

WWW Max Planck Institute for Research into Economic Systems www.mpiew-jena.mpg.de

WWW Organization for Economic Cooperation and Development www.OECD.org

WWW The Socialism Organization http://socialism.org

Government and the Economy

After reading this chapter, you should be able to:

- Explain how the U.S. economy changed from a pure market economy to a welfare capitalist economy
- Explain why the Social Security system is not an insurance program
- State the Keynesian explanation for the Great Depression
- Define the term *multiplier* and state why it is important
- Discuss the role of fiscal and monetary policy
- Explain the political difficulties of using fiscal policies and the government's bias toward deficits and debts

The business of government is to keep the government out of business—that is, unless business needs government aid.

—Will Rogers

In all economies, the government plays a central role. In this chapter, we describe and discuss the role that the government plays in the economy. That role is both direct—through its expenditure and taxation policy—and indirect—through its control of the laws that specify what individuals and businesses can and cannot do, and how they can and cannot interact.

Government's Direct Role in the Economy

Government's direct role in the economy involves its expenditures and its taxes, which it needs to finance those expenditures. Each year the federal government spends about $2 trillion to finance its own activities. Each year state governments spend over $1.3 trillion to finance their activities. Figure 17.1a shows the division of federal government expenditures; Figure 17.1b shows the division of state government expenditures. As you can see, the federal government spends the largest percentage of its tax revenue on income security programs. By contrast, after administration, state governments spend most of their money on education and income support. In addition to federal and state governmental activities, there are also local government activities. Local governments spend most of their budgets on education and roads.

These activities must be financed either by taxes or by government borrowing, and each year the governments combined collect over $3 trillion in taxes. Figures 17.2a and b show the divisions of tax revenues for the federal and state governments. As you can see, for

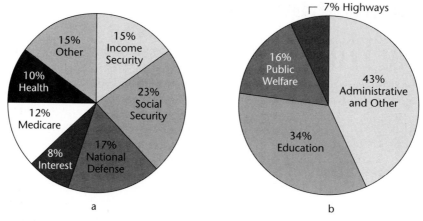

Figure 17.1

(a) Federal outlays by use, 2002. (b) State outlays by use, 2000. (Source: U.S. Department of Commerce, U.S. Department of Treasury.)

the federal government the money comes primarily from Social Security taxes, individual income taxes, and corporate income taxes. For state and local governments, most of the money comes from a combination of two sources—sales taxes and revenue from the federal government. Local governments get most of their income from property taxes.

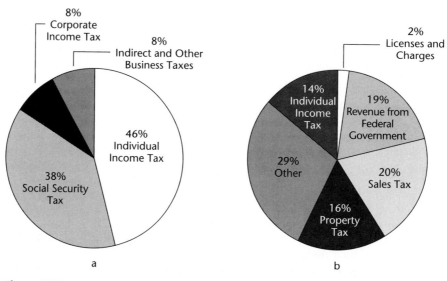

Figure 17.2

(a) Federal revenue by source, 2002. (b) State revenue by source, 2000. (Source: U.S. Department of Commerce, U.S. Department of Treasury.)

Government-Supplied Goods

Why do all societies spend money on government? (1) Because we need someone to officiate—to determine what the laws are; that's government's indirect role; (2) because some things are better done collectively than individually; that's government's direct role. Let's consider one example of something best done collectively: defense. If each of us provided for our own defense, our country would likely be taken over by another country—each individual in our country couldn't afford to provide even one plane or one battleship. These collective consumption goods, sometimes called public goods, are more efficiently supplied by government than by individuals.

If government is to supply a good, it has to pay for it. The two main options for paying are voluntary contribution and taxes. All governments use the latter option—taxes. To have a government is to have taxes. Why not pay for those goods through voluntary contributions? The reason is that people have a natural tendency to avoid contributing toward public goods, even when they are receiving the benefits. Therefore, all governments have the power to tax—to force people to pay for the goods that government supplies.

Once a government exists, the political process can decide which goods the government should provide, which goods should be supplied privately through the market, and what other roles the government should have. Many different arrangements are possible. Consider education. It could be supplied privately with individuals paying for the education they want, in the same way they pay for their cars. But this is not the way most societies provide education. Most societies provide education for all students by paying for it with money collected by taxes. Why? Because they feel education benefits the society as a whole as well as the individuals getting the education. In the United States, tax-paid public education ends with the completion of high school, although most states have colleges and universities that receive part of their budgets from tax money.

Currently there is a debate about whether public schools are doing an adequate job of providing a quality education. Some reformers are advocating a hybrid system—public funding but private provision—through vouchers given to parents, allowing them to choose which school to send their children to and to pay for at least part of the school cost with the government vouchers.

Education is not the only good that can be paid for and supplied either by government or by private firms. For instance, health care and prescription drugs are goods that could be paid for and supplied privately but are paid for in part by the government, although supply remains private. Some reformers are advocating a much larger role for government in paying for and supplying these goods.

Income Redistribution through Government. Perhaps government's most controversial responsibility is to redistribute income. Redistribution of income involves policies through which government uses its taxing power to impose high taxes on people who have high incomes to use that tax money to provide additional income to people whose income would otherwise be much lower. There are three ways this is done in the United States:

1. We have a progressive income tax system—people who earn high incomes are taxed at a high rate so that the government can use tax money to provide programs for lower-income people. Although our income tax is progressive, it is far less progressive than it has been in the past. During World War II and for a short while thereafter, the top federal tax rate on high-income individuals was over 90 percent. Today top

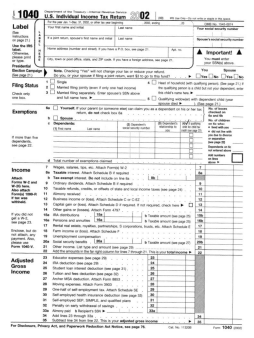

A U.S. individual income tax return.

federal tax rates on earned income such as wages are about 35 percent. Some other income, such as increases in the value of stock and stock dividends, is taxed at a lower rate. Even at these lower rates, however, there is still some redistribution of income.

2. We have low-income tax credits. Low-income people are given a tax credit, so instead of paying taxes, they receive a direct payment from the government.

3. We have entitlement programs that favor the poor. The majority of income support our government provides is through entitlement programs such as Social Security, Medicare, and Medicaid, which are designed to favor the poor somewhat. For example, the federal government pays the Medicare (health insurance) premiums for many low-income people.

Each of these programs is complicated, and we could write a book about each one just trying to explain their intricacies; we won't do that here. We focus our discussion on one example, the Social Security program, the largest government expenditure program, and only briefly touch on the other programs.

The U.S. Social Security System

The first comprehensive government-administered social insurance system was enacted by imperial Germany in 1889, sponsored by the famous German chancellor Otto von Bismarck, who apparently conceived of it as a plan for allaying social unrest. Over the next three decades, similar plans were adopted by most other major industrial nations. It was not until the Great Depression of the 1930s that the United States passed the Social Security Act of 1935, providing a broad program of social insurance. Under pressure from President Franklin D. Roosevelt, Congress enacted the **Federal Insurance Contributions Act (FICA)**, a plan providing a broad program of social insurance funded by a tax levied half on employers and half on employees. The plan was a compromise between liberals who wanted a much larger guarantee of government income support and conservatives who opposed any such plan.

Social Security Is Not Insurance.   Because of the debate surrounding it, Social Security was described to the public as a type of contributory insurance plan, even though it really did not meet that definition. A true insurance plan would collect money, invest it, and out of the proceeds pay people who found themselves in the circumstances against which they were insuring themselves. As it developed, the Social Security system paid out the money almost as soon as it took it in. Thus it was not funded like an insurance plan but was a system in which there was only a small reserve; benefits were paid from current contribu-

Government's Macroeconomic Role

One of the major economic debates over the last fifty years has concerned the government's macroeconomic role. Because this role is quite confusing to beginning students, we will consider it more closely.

The **macroeconomic** role of government is to institute policies that concern only general welfare as a whole. Specifically, it considers policies that affect inflation, unemployment, and growth. Government's **microeconomic** role is protecting and increasing society's welfare based on the consideration of individuals' welfare. Thus macroeconomics begins with the aggregate society—that is, with society as a group—and microeconomics begins with the individual. Both categories consider the welfare of society, but they approach it differently.

Over the past hundred years there has been significant fluctuation in unemployment, inflation, and output. These fluctuations in aggregate output are called **business cycles.** A typical business cycle is shown in Figure 17.3; it has a boom period and a recession period.

Up until the 1930s, most economists thought such business cycles were inevitable. Society should put up with them just as one endures minor aches and pains in one's body. They are inevitable parts of life. That view changed in the 1930s when the economy fell into a deep depression.

A **depression** is a period of drastic decline in an economy, characterized by decreasing business activity, falling prices, and unemployment. Most Americans, judged by today's standards of income and consumption, were relatively poor in the middle and late 1920s, but we must be cautious in judging the past by the present, for in comparison with anything they had known before, people were enjoying a period of unprecedented prosperity. True, some groups, including farmers, did not share in this prosperity, but most Americans had achieved higher incomes than ever before. Furthermore, a great speculative rise in the prices of real estate and stocks had helped to create a general feeling of optimism.

This feeling was soon dissipated by rude shocks. In October 1929 there was a spectacular break in the stock market, and this was only the first of a series of developments that, by 1932, brought the country to the greatest depths of depression in its entire history. From 1929 to 1932, industrial production and national income dropped by about half, and unemployment rose from about 3 million to between 12 and 15 million, or about a

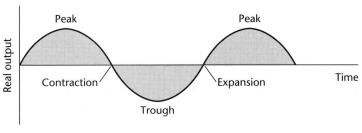

Figure 17.3

Idealized business cycle.

quarter of the nation's labor force. These developments brought losses, discouragement, and great hardship to millions of people.

In response to that depression, in the 1930s the government instituted many of its income security programs. It also took a much greater role in maintaining the level of employment in the economy. This change was closely tied to what has become known as the **Keynesian revolution**—the concept that government can and should play a stabilizing role in the economy—in economic theory, which created the field of macroeconomics as distinct from that of microeconomics. It is named after John Maynard Keynes, the English economist who led the change to this approach.

The primary macroeconomic policies advocated by Keynesians are fiscal and monetary policy. **Fiscal policy** is a policy of using the government budget surplus or deficit to control the level of spending in the economy. Using Keynesian policy, if total spending in the economy is too low, the government runs a budget deficit; this deficit adds income to the total flow of income and has a multiplied effect on the total level of spending. If total spending is too high, the government runs a budget surplus; this surplus subtracts income from the total flow of income and has a multiplied downward effect on the total level of spending. In Keynesian economics, some government budget deficits can be useful in stimulating the economy out of a recession. Therefore, if the U.S. economy falls into a recession, we are likely to hear calls for increases in government spending or decreases in taxes in order to stimulate the economy. That is precisely what we heard in 2003 as the U.S. economy was sluggish and President Bush wanted to get it going again by cutting taxes. However, in early 2001, when the economy was doing well, he also wanted to cut taxes, so it seemed to some observers that he wanted to cut taxes no matter what the situation.

Government budget issues have some similarity to an individual's budget issues. They concern how to get income and what uses the income should be put to. Like an individual, government can get money by borrowing, but unlike an individual, government can also get money by collecting taxes. Government's spending issues are different from an individual's spending issues. Government has significant pressure to spend and significant pressure to hold down taxes. If it doesn't collect as much in taxes as it spends, it runs a deficit. If it collects more in taxes than it spends, it runs a surplus.

From World War II until the late 1990s, the United States ran continuous deficits, as you can see in Figure 17.4. Then, in the late 1990s, the federal government agreed on a spending limitation law that required it to meet certain deficit-reduction targets. Until the targets were met, whenever spending on one category was increased, spending in some other category had to be cut or taxes had to be raised. This was called an offset. This offset requirement made it politically more difficult for the federal government to spend and run deficits.

This institutional change, combined with the unprecedented growth in the economy during this period, led to the government running surpluses. Most state governments and many local governments also benefited from the nation's expansive growth and had budget surpluses.

Why do surpluses often occur when the U.S. economy does well? When the U.S. economy does well, tax revenue rises. If government spending doesn't increase, the budget goes into surplus. Over the years, the U.S. government had accumulated over $6 trillion in debt. With the surplus, the government was in a position to decide whether to increase services, cut taxes, or do some combination of the two.

When economic growth slowed in 2002, the surpluses for both the federal government and the state and local governments evaporated and turned into deficits. The deficits were made even worse by the expiration of the offset requirement in 2002. In response,

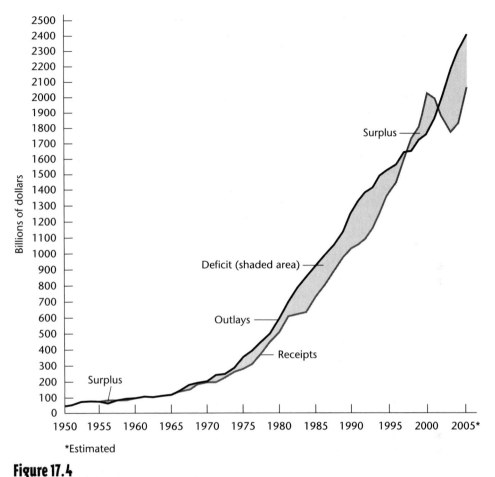

Figure 17.4

Federal budget receipts and outlays, 1950 to 2005. (Source: Economic Report of the President.)

state and local governments, most of which are legally obligated to maintain balanced budgets, cut expenditures and tried balancing their budgets with accounting gimmicks; a few raised taxes. Mostly they hoped that the slow growth would end and their revenues would increase. The federal government is not obligated to run a balanced budget, and it cut taxes, making the deficit larger. It was hoped that the increased incomes of individuals would lead to increased spending and growth, and eventually to increased government revenues, but in 2003 and 2004 the U.S. ran the largest deficits in history.

Influencing the level of income in the economy by changes in taxes and spending is called fiscal policy. Another tool to control the economy is monetary policy. **Monetary policy** is a policy in which the Central Bank (in the United States, the Federal Reserve) varies the level of money and credit in the economy to affect the level of income. Credit and the financial sector are important because a lack of coordination in the financial sector means that savings are not translated into investment, and this is one of the major causes of instability in the economy. Figure 17.5 demonstrates the way in which credit affects the economy.

A simple definition of the **money supply** is the amount of cash and deposit accounts (savings and checking accounts in banks) in the economy. The way in which monetary policy works is relatively simple: When there is more money in the economy, people have more money to spend and invest; as they spend more, the economy expands. When there is less money in the economy, people have less money to spend and invest; as they spend less, the economy contracts. When the Fed increases the money supply, it is called expansionary monetary policy; when the Fed decreases the money supply, it is called contractionary monetary policy.

Notice that the Fed, not the government, controls the money supply. The Fed is a semiautonomous agency that is only indirectly responsible to Congress and the president. It is run by a board of governors appointed by the president.

The **Fed (the Federal Reserve Bank)** is a type of central bank or bankers' bank. It issues IOUs (also called notes) that serve as the basis of our money supply. (If you look on a dollar bill, you will see that it is a Federal Reserve note.) Whereas at one time gold backed

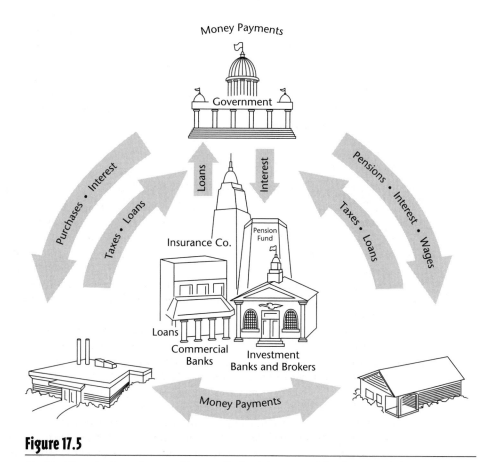

Figure 17.5

Credit affects the flow of money. (Source: Federal Reserve Bank of New York.)

the dollar, presently only trust in the fact that others will accept this dollar backs it. What gives money its value is that the Fed issues only a limited quantity of its notes, or IOUs.

The discussion of the technical operation of these Fed tools is best left to economics courses. What you should know now is that monetary policy does not affect the level of income directly; rather, it affects the interest rate by making it easier or harder for individuals and firms to borrow. Expansionary monetary policy makes credit easier to get and lowers interest rates; as interest rates fall, investment increases, which in turn has a multiplied effect (upward) on the level of income. Contractionary monetary policy makes credit harder to get and raises interest rates. As interest rates rise, investment decreases, which in turn has a multiplied effect (downward) on the level of income.

Government's Indirect Role in the Economy

The government's indirect role in the economy is to provide a legal and institutional setting for the workings of the market by establishing and enforcing laws that regulate actions of individuals and businesses. Currently many such laws on the books have significant influence on how people spend their money and conduct economic activities. For example, if people want to own a car they are required in most states to have car insurance. You must wait until you are a certain age to begin to work and when you do work, you must keep certain records and file tax returns. Firms must abide by certain nondiscriminatory practices when hiring. Goods-producing firms are required to meet certain regulations that limit the type of goods they produce and affect the costs of those goods. Just as sports teams do not always agree with officials, neither do market participants always agree with government's "officiating."

The Problem of Regulating the Economy

All individuals agree that some regulation is needed, but many in the United States feel that the U.S. economy is overregulated and that Congress considers only the benefits of regulation and not the costs. One type of regulation that has come under specific attack is **unfunded mandates,** or regulations that impose significant costs on individuals and states but do not provide the funds to pay those costs. One example is the mandate to make all public buildings in the United States accessible to all individuals, including people with physical and mental disabilities. Passing the law was easy and seemed right to many Americans. But the law imposed serious costs on many businesses, and that law does not provide those businesses with a way to pay for them.

The debate over regulation will continue. Supporters will argue that regulations serve the important purpose of protecting individuals and of ensuring that economic activities are carried out in a way that the legal system considers fair. Opponents will cite examples such as the following, which appeared in the *Wall Street Journal.* An upstate New York nursing home had been cited by state officials as "a shining example" of what such an establishment ought to be. However, not long afterward the owner of this home closed it down with the following explanation: "It was just impossible. There were eighteen state and federal agencies putting forms, questions, and statistical requests across my desk. Medical reports . . . census figures . . . Social Security . . . unemployment insurance . . . workers' compensation . . . withholding taxes . . . daily time sheets . . . work plans. . . . It was just one thing after another."

According to the owner, she sometimes spent eighteen hours a day just handling the government paperwork required for only twenty patients and fourteen employees.

The weight of the regulatory burden can be comprehended more easily when you consider Figure 17.6. Such excessive regulations have brought about a reemergence of the doctrine of laissez-faire, the theory that government should interfere with business as little as possible, and the emergence of the new classical school of economics that supports a laissez-faire policy.

There are huge differences of opinion about how much and what kind of regulation is desirable. It is clear that many government controls have served the public interest, but it seems equally clear that some that were intended to do so have not. As the U.S. economy has become increasingly complex, government has necessarily played a more and more direct role in economic life.

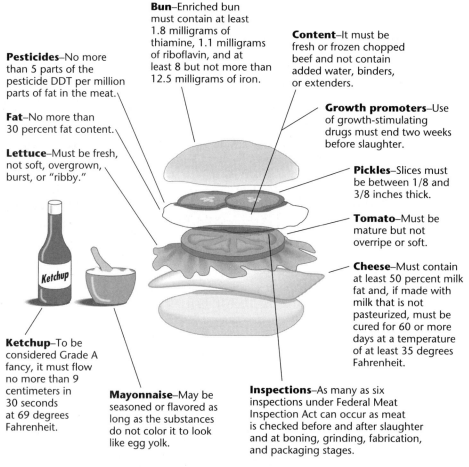

Bun–Enriched bun must contain at least 1.8 milligrams of thiamine, 1.1 milligrams of riboflavin, and at least 8 but not more than 12.5 milligrams of iron.

Content–It must be fresh or frozen chopped beef and not contain added water, binders, or extenders.

Pesticides–No more than 5 parts of the pesticide DDT per million parts of fat in the meat.

Fat–No more than 30 percent fat content.

Lettuce–Must be fresh, not soft, overgrown, burst, or "ribby."

Growth promoters–Use of growth-stimulating drugs must end two weeks before slaughter.

Pickles–Slices must be between 1/8 and 3/8 inches thick.

Tomato–Must be mature but not overripe or soft.

Cheese–Must contain at least 50 percent milk fat and, if made with milk that is not pasteurized, must be cured for 60 or more days at a temperature of at least 35 degrees Fahrenheit.

Ketchup–To be considered Grade A fancy, it must flow no more than 9 centimeters in 30 seconds at 69 degrees Fahrenheit.

Mayonnaise–May be seasoned or flavored as long as the substances do not color it to look like egg yolk.

Inspections–As many as six inspections under Federal Meat Inspection Act can occur as meat is checked before and after slaughter and at boning, grinding, fabrication, and packaging stages.

Figure 17.6

Your hamburger: More than 41,000 regulations.

U.S. attitudes toward this increased role of government have fluctuated. In the 1960s and early 1970s, regulation was seen as a necessary limit to private powers. About the mid-1970s and well into the 1980s, the pendulum of public opinion shifted, and many believed that the U.S. economy was suffering from overregulation and that the solution to our economic problems was deregulation or the removal of those excessive regulations. Whether deregulation is responsible for the renewed growth our economy experienced in the 1990s and early 2000s is unclear, but in the early 2000s regulations are increasing as the problems with deregulation, seen in the accounting scandals in 2002, become more obvious.

One example of this increased regulation can be seen in the U.S. government's prosecution of Microsoft for **antitrust violations**—violations of statutes concerning how businesses may and may not compete in the marketplace. The government argued that the Microsoft company competed unfairly—that it used its monopoly in computer operating systems to gain control over aspects of the software and Internet browser market. Microsoft argued that its methods were not unfair, claiming that it was only trying to give its customers the best possible value. In a trial, Microsoft was found guilty. The company quickly appealed. The verdict was reduced, and in the end Microsoft came away from the trial almost as powerful as it was before the trial.

Government Inefficiency and Waste

The debate about what role government should play in the economy generally includes some discussion of government bureaucracy, waste, and inefficiency. To some degree, the problem is inevitable. All large organizations, not just government, involve waste and inefficiency. Moreover, because the staffers of the government programs work under political appointees who can change every four years, or even more frequently, the staff is always struggling to do what the new director wants. What the new director wants may often be exactly the opposite of what the old director wanted. Given such difficult circumstances, many believe that the government bureaucracy does a credible job in administering the various programs that society, through the political process, has decided it wants.

Whether specific government programs make sense or not is another issue. Democracy does not always ensure that only reasonable programs are undertaken. The cost to an individual of any one government expenditure is likely to be negligible, and thus no one pays attention to it. This is a case of what should be everybody's business becoming nobody's business, and the relevant question is whether there are sufficient safeguards in the system to ensure that government's role in the economy is generally positive.

*C*onclusion —————————————————————————————

As you have read from Chapters 13 through 17, it should be obvious that government can take many forms and that those forms are forever changing. The U.S. government and the role it plays in economics are no exceptions. Its activist role that we have described in this chapter has largely resulted from the experience of the Great Depression in the 1930s. Although the sizes of government expenditures and programs to stabilize the economy have for the most part grown since then, large deficits in the late 1980s and early 1990s placed limitations on this role of government.

However, in 2002, as the focus of government shifted to the war on terrorism, the offset requirement in government spending and taxes was ended. The government increased its concentration on the spending side, while at the same time decreasing its concentration on the taxing side, and the deficits became substantial. Eventually, these deficits will lead to a reconsideration of the government's direct role in the economy, and either taxes will increase or government spending will decrease. Thus, the government's direct role in the economy fluctuates with the times. The government's indirect role has also fluctuated with society's mores and the political climate, at times increasing regulation and at other times reducing regulation of economic activities.

Key Points

- For a government to operate, it must raise money, principally by taxing and borrowing, and choose what is fair and necessary to spend that money on.
- An important federal government expenditure is the Social Security program, and financing the program may present problems in the future.
- Rising health care costs, especially for prescription drugs, present a challenge to government budgeting.
- The government must try to choose policies that benefit the general welfare by providing services to individuals and business, keeping its expenditures within reason, and being as evenhanded as it can be.
- The government directly manages the country by fiscal policy—using the government budget surplus or deficit to control the level of spending in the economy—and indirectly by monetary policy—allowing the Federal Reserve Bank to control the level of money and credit in the economy.
- Vital government functions include providing a legal and institutional environment and enforcing the law.
- To manage the country, the government must be flexible and adaptable.

Some Important Terms

antitrust violation (393)
business cycles (387)
depression (387)
Fed (Federal Reserve Bank) (390)

Federal Insurance Contributions Act (FICA) (384)
fiscal policy (388)
Keynesian revolution (388)
macroeconomic (387)

microeconomic (387)
monetary policy (389)
money supply (390)
unfunded mandates (391)

Questions for Review and Discussion

1. About how much does the federal government spend each year to finance its activities?
2. On what major category do state governments spend the most money per year?
3. Individuals must decide how to earn money and what to spend the money on. How does the government get money, and what are some of the factors it must consider when deciding how to spend the money?
4. What problems is the government likely to face in paying Social Security benefits in the future?
5. Besides Social Security, what are some of the biggest expenditures that the federal govern-

ment must make? Use information from the text of the chapter and also add one or two that you know about from your own experience.

6. Should the federal government spend more money on health and education? Why or why not?

7. Briefly describe a government surplus and explain how a government surplus arose in the United States.

8. What is fiscal policy and what entity conducts it?

9. What is monetary policy and what entity conducts it?

10. What is the Keynesian revolution?

11. Some of the things the government could do with the government surplus are spend more of it on Social Security, use it to reduce taxes, buy more military weapons, or use it to pay off government debt. If it were up to you, which of these things would you spend it on and which would you not spend it on? Give your reasons for each of your decisions.

12. Is the U.S. government inefficient and wasteful? Explain your answer.

13. List two activities government undertakes but that you wish it would stop doing. Explain why you wish it would stop, and what you would substitute for those activities.

ᒿnternet Questions

1. The website of the Federation of Tax Administrators, www.taxadmin.org, has listed state tax revenue by source. Using the latest figures, what is the percentage breakdown for your state? What is the breakdown for the aggregate?

2. Log on to the Internal Revenue Service's site, www.irs.gov/individuals/index.html. What is the Earned Income Tax Credit? What are the two types of educational credits available under the Tax Relief Act of 1997?

3. Go to www.publicdebt.treas.gov, the site of the Bureau of the Public Debt. What is the

current amount of the national debt? What is the interest expense for the latest month? For the last complete fiscal year?

4. Using a quick calculator, www.ssa.gov/planners/calculators.html, estimate what your Social Security benefits, in future dollars, may be with the information you have now.

5. According to the Federal Reserve, www.federalreserve.gov/faq.htm, what are its responsibilities?

ᒿor Further Study

Aronowitz, Stanley, *From the Ashes of the Old: American Labor and America's Future*, Boston: Houghton Mifflin, 1998.

Friedman, Milton, and Walter H. Heller, *Monetary versus Fiscal Policy*, New York: Norton, 1969.

Jansson, Bruce S., *The Sixteen-Trillion-Dollar Mistake: How the U.S. Bungled Its National Priorities from the New Deal to the Present*, New York: Columbia University Press, 2001.

Lindner, Marc, and Ingrid Nygaard, *Void Where Prohibited: Rest Breaks and the Right to Urinate on Company Time*, Ithaca, NY: Cornell University Press, 1998.

Peterson, Peter G., *Will America Grow Up before It Grows Old? How the Coming Social Security Crisis Threatens You, Your Family, and Your Country*, New York: Random House, 1996.

Polakow, Valerie, *Lives on the Edge: Single Mothers and Their Children in the Other America*, Chicago: University of Chicago Press, 1993.

Shorris, Earl, *New American Blues: A Journey through Poverty to Democracy*, New York: Norton, 1997.

Simon, Julian L., and Herman Kahn, eds., *The Resourceful Earth*, New York: Basil Blackwell, 1984.

Smith, Mark A., *American Business and Political Power: Public Opinion, Elections, and Democracy*, Chicago: University of Chicago Press, 2000.

Starr, Douglass, *Blood: An Epic History of Medicine and Commerce*, New York: Knopf, 1998.

White, Joseph, *False Alarm: Why the Greatest Threat to Social Security and Medicare is the Campaign to "Save" Them*, Baltimore: Johns Hopkins University Press, 2001.

WWW   Antitrust Division of the Department of Justice www.usdoj.gov/atr/overview.html

WWW   Federal Reserve   www.federalreserve.gov

WWW   Internal Revenue Service   www.irs.ustreas.gov

WWW   Medicare   www.medicare.gov

WWW   Office of Budget Management   www.access.gpo.gov/usbudget

WWW   Social Security Administration   www.ssa.gov

WWW   U.S. Treasury   www.treas.gov

International Political Relations

After reading this chapter, you should be able to:

- Explain the role of the state in international relations
- Define power and explain why nothing is more basic to an understanding of international relations
- Define foreign policy and discuss five issues that policy-makers must heed when forming foreign policy
- List the three ideologies that have been prevalent since World War II
- Summarize the role of Congress and the president in conducting foreign policy

We are trying to make a society instead of a set of barbarians out of the governments of the world.
—**Woodrow Wilson**

With the development of modern means of travel, the world has shrunk. Whereas only a hundred years ago our community meant our town, today it is the entire world. To understand this community, with its component states and their objectives, its problems and their possible solutions, its history, its economy, its wars, and its processes of order and stability—all this is the task of those who aspire to understand contemporary international relations. Real as this world community is, you should be warned that it differs greatly from communities of individual persons because its units—states—are so different from the men and women who inhabit towns, cities, and nations.

The State in International Relations

The term *state* has a number of different meanings. In this country it is most commonly used to refer to any one of the fifty members of our national union. But as the word is used in discussing international relations, and as we are using it in this chapter, a **state** is a body politic organized for civil rule and government. It is an independent political unit that can carry on negotiations or make agreements with other such units. In this sense, the United States qualifies as a state, but political entities such as Alabama, California, and Michigan do not.

Consider the map of the world on pages 398–399, on which you can count a total of about 190 states. Not all of these states are completely sovereign or independent, nor are

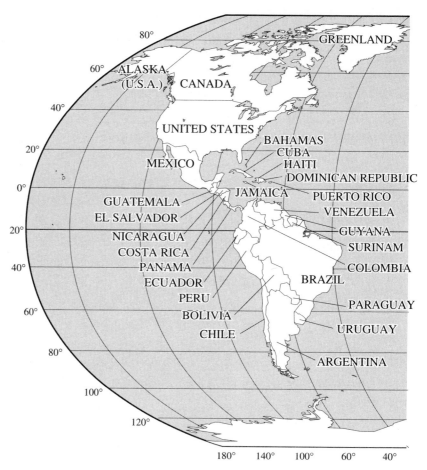

Nations of the world. A few of the smaller countries have been left out. See how many of them you can name.

they fully comparable. There are extreme variations among them in both physical characteristics and in cultural matters such as religion, education, ethnic background, industry, standards of living, and government.

For instance, in area they range from Russia, with an area of 6.6 million square miles, down to Monaco, with less than 1 square mile, and tiny Vatican City, with a mere 106 acres of land; only eight states possess more than a million square miles of territory. In population the largest states are China (over 1.3 billion people) and India (over 1 billion); the smallest are Andorra (68,000) and Vatican City (under 1,000). Some states are overwhelmingly Roman Catholic in faith (such as Spain and France); some are almost entirely Protestant (Denmark and Sweden); others are both Catholic and Protestant (Germany); some accommodate a wide variety of faiths (the United States). There are also states in which other religions prevail, including Islam, Buddhism, Judaism, and Hinduism. Per capita incomes range all the way from about $36,000 in the early 2000s in the United States to estimates of less than $300 in some countries in Africa and eastern Asia.

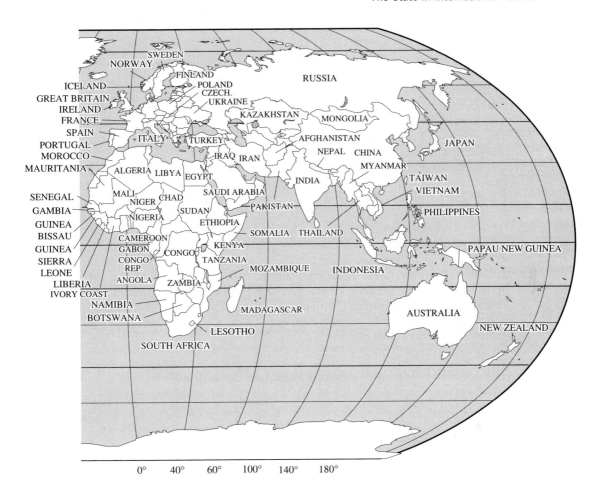

The Nation-State

In this chapter, we are using the terms *state* and *nation* more or less as synonyms. Strictly, however, they carry different meanings, and in the precise language of international law and diplomacy only "state" is employed; this is true, for instance, in the Charter of the United Nations, in the Statute of the International Court of Justice, and in treaties generally. The characteristics of a **state,** according to the Charter of the Organization of American States (1948) are (1) a permanent population, (2) a clearly defined territory, (3) a government, and (4) sovereignty that requires a capacity for international relations. The term **nation** was originally applied to groups of people with the same ethnic background, such as the Germans or the French, each of whom could point to a common language and a common cultural heritage.

The explanation of the modern popular practice of using state and nation as synonyms lies in the fact that for some centuries now the **nation-state**—a state that has tended to include substantially the same people as the ethnic nation—has been one of the most prominent forms of state in existence. The French state, for instance, is for the most part made up of a French-speaking people with a common historical and cultural background. There are some nation-states, however—including Switzerland, India, Russia, and Canada—that do not have a common language or cultural background. These differences in language and in cultural and ethnic background can cause problems, as we have seen in recent years in Canada, Belgium, Sri Lanka, India, the emerging African states, the republics of the former Soviet Union, and Bosnia.

As we saw in Chapter 3, the structure of the modern nation-state was constructed on the ruins of feudalism in western Europe. In the conflict of feudal lords with one other, a certain lord within an area would emerge as victor, and eventually large areas where the people spoke similar dialects were brought together under a ruler who called himself king.

England was one of the first nation-states, and by the latter part of the twelfth century the authority of the king, then Henry II, extended over almost all of the country, as well as over parts of what is now France. Most of France was unified a little later, and by the middle of the fifteenth century English authority had been forced off the continent; by the end of the reign of the French king Louis XI (1461–1483), France could claim to be a new nation-state. Other nation-states gradually emerged, so that in time the map of Europe showed a substantial group of them—England, France, Spain, Denmark, Hungary, Russia, Poland, Norway, and Sweden. The Treaty of Westphalia (1648) put its stamp of approval on the new system by recognizing that the political authority of the pope and of the old Holy Roman Empire was dead.

The Establishment and Disappearance of Nation-States

Since 1648 many new nation-states have sprung into being, and from time to time old ones have died out. For example, during the nineteenth century, Turkish authority was expelled from most of Europe, and new states took its place on the Balkan peninsula: Greece, Bulgaria, Serbia, Romania, Albania, and Montenegro (later included in Yugoslavia). By the mid-1990s, several of these nation-states were again in political turmoil. Yugoslavia broke apart, and how that area is to stabilize is still unclear.

Change occurred in the western hemisphere in the 1800s. For example, approximately twenty new states were formed from the old holdings of Spain and Portugal in the New World. About the middle of the nineteenth century, China and Japan, ancient countries of the Far East, opened their doors to Western trade. They, too, were admitted into the community of nation-states, in 1842 and 1854, respectively.

World War I tore down the old multinational state of Austria-Hungary and built up several new states: Poland, Czechoslovakia, Austria, Hungary, Latvia, Lithuania, and Estonia. It also added to the territory of already existing states such as Romania. World War II snuffed out Latvia, Lithuania, and Estonia, but it led directly to the establishment of Israel and the divisions of Korea and Germany into new political units.

After World War II, a surge of nationalism took place in the colonial areas of Africa, and in the 1960s a number of African and Asian states emerged from the British and French empires. These countries combined different ethnic groups and experienced turmoil in the 1990s, not all of which has subsided. Their structure may yet change. (Significant areas of turmoil included Nigeria, Somalia, and Rwanda and its neighbors.)

As you can see, we should not consider states as unchanging. Often, the historical creation of states has combined numerous social and cultural groups while breaking up other groups. In the 1990s, social, ethnic, and cultural pressures broke down many of these historical creations in states besides the former Soviet Union. For example, East and West Germany reunified, forming a single Germany; and Kuwait was invaded by Iraq, which claimed that Kuwait was a part of Iraq that had been inappropriately separated in political maneuvering after World War II. After Iraq lost the war over Kuwait, instead of expanding, it has found itself under pressure to hold itself together. The Kurds in the north attempted to break away and form their own independent state. Saddam Hussein brutally repressed the Shiite revolt but was forced out of the Kurdish territory, which meant that the Kurds, although without a formal state, were semiautonomous. This left Iraq's neighbors, Turkey and Iran, with a difficult problem. Although these neighbors opposed the Iraqi government, they had been hesitant to support the Kurds because Turkey and Iran, too, have significant Kurdish populations, and they are concerned about pressure from all Kurds for a new state, Kurdistan, to be formed. When the 2003 Iraq War led to the ousting of Saddam Hussein and his regime, the United States, together with its British allies, set up an interim authority to oversee Iraq and create a new government.

All states are legally sovereign, which means they are not legally subordinate to any other state. In practice, however, their sovereignty is limited by economic and political realities. For example, many Latin American countries rely on aid from the International Monetary Fund and the United States. Therefore they generally consider carefully the probable reaction of the United States and the Western "alliance" in determining their international position.

Similarly, after the 9/11 attacks on the United States, and President Bush's war on terrorism policy of preemption—in which the United States will attack a country if it is believed to be harboring, aiding, or abetting terrorists—countries such as Pakistan, Syria, and Iran needed to carefully consider the United States' views before undertaking any policy. With the strongest military power in the world threatening you, it is hard to consider yourself fully sovereign and independent.

Power in the World Community

Nothing is more basic to an understanding of international relations than an appreciation of the role of **power**—the capacity to compel another party to commit an action contrary to its explicitly stated will. Countries have national goals, and to achieve those goals they need power. Current expressions such as "power politics," "the great powers," the "small powers," and the "balance of power" all attest to the importance of that role. Power has many dimensions: military, economic, moral, geographic, and political, and in the next sections we discuss some of them.

The Nature and Sources of National Power

In the final analysis, the power of a state consists of the means it possesses for promoting its vital interests by influencing or controlling the behavior of other states. Although military force is the most obvious type of power, it is not the only one. The principal forms of pressure available to states in their dealings with each other are military power, power over opinion at home and abroad, economic power, and geographic power. Possession of any of these attributes tends to augment the power of an individual nation and thus increase its ability to realize its political, social, economic, and military goals.

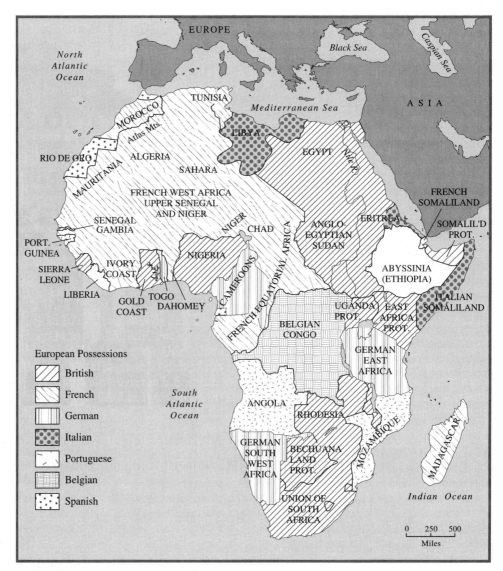

Africa before World War II.

Of all the sources of power, military power is the most important. The parallel to individual relationships is clear: If you can beat up everyone on the block, you are free to do pretty much what you want. There are, of course, limits if you want to maintain friendly, rather than fearful, relations with others, but a nation with clear military superiority can generally boast control of its destiny. It is seldom the case, however, that one country emerges as indisputably superior militarily. Instead, competing spheres of military power develop, leading to a standoff.

In historical terms, the beginning of the twenty-first century was unusual in terms of military power. The United States was a **hegemon,** a country with almost indisputable su-

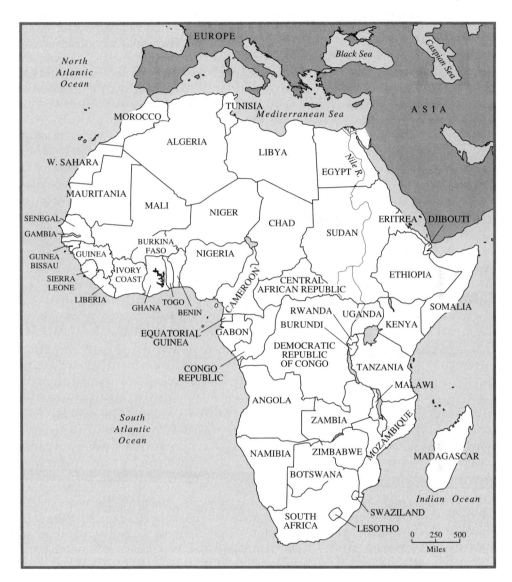

Africa today.

perior military power. That military might gave it enormous power, and its desires became much more important than that of other sovereign countries. It had the power to say: If you don't like it, tough, we're going to do what we want. Thus, when the United States wanted to use military force to rid Iraq of its **weapons of mass destruction** (its biological, chemical and nuclear weapons), it did so even though a majority of the world's countries felt that military force was not yet called for.

There was no overwhelming cry for the United States to apply its mandate equally—Israel had significant weapons of mass destruction, but when Arab countries tried to raise

Power has almost inevitably been based on military might, as this monument to El Cid memorializes.

that issue, they were ignored by the United States. In fact, the very definition of weapons of mass destruction was itself a reflection of the U.S. point of view. Cruise missiles and Big Brother bombs, which the United States used against Saddam Hussein, were not classified as weapons of mass destruction, but chemical and biological agents, which the United States accused Iraq of developing, were.

Another example of the strength of U.S hegemony was when the United States attacked Iraq and found no conclusive evidence of these weapons, and no state condemned the United States for an inappropriate preemptive war. Instead, the United Nations Security Council officially recognized the United States and Great Britain as legitimate occupying powers. Such is the power of a military hegemonic state.

Military power depends on far more than weapons. It also depends on the will to use that military power and the will to accept the losses that the use of military action entails. For example, the United States has the most advanced and the greatest number of military weapons in the world. Yet in the 1991 conflict with Iraq, it did not convince Iraq that it would use its military power to achieve its objective of forcing Iraq to withdraw from Kuwait. One of the important reasons was that, compared with Iraq, the United States was far less willing to accept losses of its soldiers. This knowledge—that the United States would not accept large losses—and the belief that the U.S. public would not long sustain the will to fight were probably central factors in Iraq's decision not to bow to the United States and the world community's insistence that it withdraw from occupied Kuwait. Only the actual use of military power enforced that withdrawal.

President George W. Bush's willingness to use overwhelming military force in Afghanistan and Iraq in the early 2000s convinced more nations of U.S. resolve, and thereby strengthened its perceived military power. However, the difficulties the United States faced in maintaining the peace in Iraq after the war reduced that perceived power because it made many think that the United States will be hesitant to undertake a similar war.

Military power is also limited by social and cultural conventions. In the 1991 U.S. war with Iraq, the United States could have used nuclear weapons to achieve its objective much more quickly, but it was prevented from doing so by cultural, social, and political pressures. The belief that Iraq was not going to be limited by those pressures played a role in the U.S. decision to go to war against Iraq. The United States wanted to eliminate Iraqi weapons of mass destruction. If Iraq did have such weapons, however, it did not use them during the war.

After the Iraq War, the United States searched for evidence of chemical and biological weapons in Iraq but found little evidence of them. (They did find some trailers that may have been designed to manufacture chemical weapons.) Despite the absence of such weapons, few criticized the United States, because it had won the war quickly and decisively. In international politics, a country's military power limits criticism by others. By showing that the United States was willing to use its military might on grounds that it determined, and that it would not accept outside limitations on its power, including UN limitations, the United States changed the international political landscape. Thereafter, all

U.S. soldiers wearing chemical warfare masks in Iraq.

countries were a bit more careful about how they talked about the United States and in criticizing it. Thus the war extended the power of the United States, even as it undermined much of the world's view about its commitment to fairness.

A second example is Haiti. In September 1991, the popularly elected President of Haiti, Jean-Bertrand Aristide, was ousted in a military coup. Under intense pressure by the United Nations and the United States, the leaders of the military coup agreed in July 1993 to step down and allow President Aristide to return. They reneged on that promise; to force it to comply, the United States, with a UN mandate, imposed economic sanctions in 1993 and threatened to invade. In mid-1994 the United States got approval for an invasion from the United Nations, but in last-minute negotiations the leader of the military coup agreed to give up power, and U.S. troops entered Haiti peacefully. Haiti remains troubled, and President Aristide won a second term in 2000 and took office in early 2001.

These limiting factors mean that the structure of government plays a role in determining the military power of a country. In Western liberal democracies, in which the press and individuals enjoy extensive freedoms, public opinion plays a significant role in determining governmental policy. Public opinion plays less of a role in the policies of autocratic governments. Such governments can partially shape public opinion through tight control of the media. If, in spite of such control, dissent develops, they can use secret police or other repressive organizations to ferret out and kill or imprison its leaders and, in some cases, whole groups of dissenters. Saddam Hussein used this power ruthlessly. Just how strong the control of the press was in Iraq is shown by the briefings of the Iraqi Ministry of Information during the final days of the war. As U.S. tanks were driving through the city of Baghdad, the minister of information was briefing reporters on how Iraq was winning the war and driving back the Americans.

We should point out that while democracies have less control over public opinion, they can still influence it, and during times of war they directly control the flow of news that reaches reporters. An example is the Persian Gulf War, in which the United States

Anti–Iraq War protesters in England.

carefully filtered the information that was available to reporters working with the armed forces. Because reporters got news from other sources, the control was not complete, but it was there.

In the 2003 Iraq War, the members of the press were "embedded" within military units, giving them a much closer look at the war. Critics pointed out that embedding was a way of shaping the reporter's view, because it is difficult to criticize individuals who are protecting you. The difference in control of the press in an autocracy and in a democracy is one of degree. In an autocracy, the control over the press is often direct; in a democracy, it is generally indirect, with the government relying on creating an appropriate "spin" on the reporting.

Although the government of an autocratic state may be able to shape public opinion at home, it has no direct control over foreign opinion. In their attempts to influence opinion abroad, both autocratic and democratic governments are likely to resort to propaganda, and though there are no very dependable ways of measuring its results, it is safe to assume that the large-scale propaganda campaigns conducted by all strong nations would not be undertaken unless they were thought to be effective, either in strengthening home morale and winning support abroad or else in undermining the morale of potential enemies.

Following World War II, the United States enjoyed the confidence and respect of most other Western nations. This confidence reflected not so much propaganda and military might (although the United States had much of the latter) but the appreciation of most countries for the U.S. role in the war. That confidence gradually eroded through the 1980s. This erosion reflected the impact of issues such as our role in Vietnam and dissension at home. With the downfall of the Soviet Union, and the economic boom in the United States in the late 1990s, respect for U.S. military power returned, but the confidence that the United States would use that military might for the benefit of the world, and not for itself, did not. The 2003 Iraq War reinforced that view.

Other Sources of Power

The usefulness of economic power in international relations has been demonstrated often. During the struggle against Napoleon Bonaparte in the early 1800s, it enabled Great Britain not only to expand its own military forces but also to provide money and supplies for its allies. More than a century later, it enabled the United States to do likewise in both world wars; and after World War II it enabled us to make an important contribution to rebuilding the economies and the military forces of the countries of western Europe that had been overrun by the Nazis and that later felt threatened by the expanded military power of the former Soviet Union.

Though the sources of a nation's power are varied, some of them are more basic than others. For a state to generate great national strength, it helps to be large, both in area and population. Size is an advantage enjoyed by both Russia and the United States, and that size helps explain their importance. On the other hand, Japan is geographically small, but it is a major economic power. Industrial might is another vital source of power, for in its factories a country must produce the equipment for modern warfare, including tanks, ships, planes, missiles, and nuclear bombs. The high industrial output of the United States is a great asset in the power game, and Japan's industrial output is what its strength is based on. It must also be noted, however, that Japan's power is limited by its dependence on foreign oil. Japan's industrial needs require that it maintain friendly relations with the United States and the Organization of Petroleum Exporting Countries (OPEC), and its power is partly conditional on the hold other countries have over its fuel supply.

Another major source of economic power is dependable access to adequate supplies of raw materials because without these no nation can develop and maintain a large and efficient industrial complex. Yet another condition that is still a factor in national power is geographic location. This can, among other things, affect both access to raw materials and the degree to which a nation is vulnerable to a military attack. Geographic location is one element of U.S. strength. We are separated by oceans from any other major power, and though these can be crossed in a few minutes by nuclear missiles, there are, as we have pointed out, strong deterrents to the use of such weapons. Meanwhile, the oceans still protect us against attack by great armies using conventional weapons.

However, given size, a well-developed industry, and dependable access to adequate raw materials, probably the most important source of a nation's power is the characteristics of its people. Among the people there should be a substantial number of able scientists, artists, educators, businesspeople, military leaders, and politicians, and also a great many highly skilled workers of all types. In a democracy, perhaps the characteristic of a people that, if they have it, contributes most to the power of the nation in dealing with others is a strong sense of patriotism and loyalty that makes them willing to support their government in any policy they consider reasonable. But in dealing with foreign countries, the governments of democracies can face difficult problems at home. Negotiations cannot be carried on by all the people; they must be conducted by those who represent them in government.

This creates no great problem if those who represent the country are following policies with which the vast majority of the people agree. Frequently, however, there are large dissenting minorities, or there may even be an almost equal division of public opinion on the wisdom of government policies. When such differences of opinion concern questions about which people have strong emotions, the power of a government to formulate clear foreign policies and to make satisfactory agreements with other countries is likely to be impaired.

Maintaining Security

In a world community of sovereign nation-states, there are several ways in which a given state could conceivably attempt to achieve security from attack without war and at the same time gain some of its other international objectives.

If it is a large state, such as the United States, with adequate resources and industrial development, it might attempt to make a **unilateral**—independent or one-sided—buildup of its military power to such a degree that no other state or probable combination of states would dare to challenge it. In the contemporary world, this would be a difficult achievement for any nation. First, it would mean diverting to military uses vast amounts of resources badly needed to improve the living conditions of its people and also needed to meet various other social problems. Second, other nations, fearful for their safety and their power to control their own affairs, might form alliances to protect their interests. Thus, after the 2003 Iraq War, a war that a majority of U.S. allies strongly opposed, a number of European nations began reconsidering their alliance with the United States and began exploring the creation of a separate European defense organization that would operate independently of the United States.

Another conceivable approach to the problem of security, one that a group of cooperating states could attempt to implement, would be to organize all the states of the world into a system of world government. To have much chance of success, such a system or organization would have to include most of the states of the world, especially the more powerful ones. It would have to be a kind of federation or superstate, with courts for settling disputes between nations and with a military establishment capable of forcing a recalcitrant nation to accept court decisions. The chances of establishing such a system in the foreseeable future are small because most power is in the hands of several very large countries, many of whose interests appear to be in opposition.

Furthermore, few nations seem willing to give up much of their sovereignty or their right to adopt any foreign policies they please. The United Nations, which we discuss in Chapter 21, may be regarded as a first step toward a system of world government, but actually it has very little power to protect its members or to prevent war. It does, however, perform many useful international services.

The most common way of preventing or at least indefinitely delaying a disastrous war between the world's most powerful nations is to develop and, if possible, maintain a stable balance of power. The term **balance of power** means an equilibrium or adjustment of power that for the time being no nation is willing to disturb. The power of one nation prevents the other nation from using its power. During the century that followed the Congress of Vienna (1815), a fairly effective power balance was maintained, for though that era did witness some adjustments of power and even several sizable wars, until World War I no state attempted to radically challenge the existing balance. After World War I, the United States became a major power, and its power significantly increased during and right after World War II. After World War II, the balance of power was between the Western bloc (the United States, western Europe, Japan, and their allies) and the Eastern bloc (the Soviet Union, eastern Europe, and their allies). This balance was structurally indicated by their membership in the formal alliance organizations.

In the 1990s, that balance of power became unbalanced. The United States was the world's strongest military power, much stronger than any other country. Given that reality, there was talk of a **new world order**—an international order in which the United States would follow the dictum of right rather than might in its conduct of external and internal affairs—replacing the balance of power.

As social scientists discussed the emergence of a new world order, a political theory emerged to fit the changing order. It is called the **theory of complex interdependence,** in which the largest nation's powers are limited by a variety of interdependencies. This new theory is in contrast to the **realist theory,** a theory in which a balance of power with two competing nations was necessary to maintain the peace. As the world gradually moved toward a unipolar system, with the United States as the primary superpower, without an offsetting balancing force, the theory of complex interdependencies has gained acceptance. The question political scientists were asking was what interdependencies were limiting the United States' use of power.

The emerging international new realities are bringing into question the purpose of some international organizations. One example is the **North Atlantic Treaty Organization (NATO),** the organization that was responsible for the collective defense and protection of the West. Members of NATO included Belgium, Britain, Canada, Czech Republic, Denmark, France, Germany, Greece, Hungary, Iceland, Italy, Luxembourg, the Netherlands, Norway, Poland, Portugal, Spain, Turkey, and the United States (see Figure 18.1). In the 1990s, NATO lost much of its former purpose. But, like many organizations that have lost their purpose, it continued in existence, searching for a new purpose. As it searched, it expanded, adding some states that it had previously been established to counterbalance, such as Poland, Hungary, and the Czech Republic in 1997. Other states were also asking for membership, and NATO even worked out a cooperative agreement with Russia. By 2006, NATO will likely have up to nine new members.

After the 2003 war in Iraq, a war that many large NATO countries opposed, NATO scaled back its mission and began refashioning itself as an "all-purpose military and

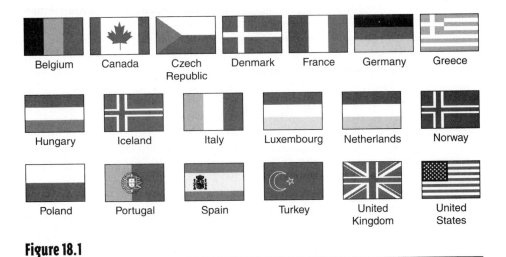

Belgium Canada Czech Republic Denmark France Germany Greece

Hungary Iceland Italy Luxembourg Netherlands Norway

Poland Portugal Spain Turkey United Kingdom United States

Figure 18.1

The members of NATO (as of 2003).

political toolbox that can be tapped at short-notice by ad hoc clusters of NATO countries." The difference would be that NATO could commit its NATO forces to peacekeeping activities even if all NATO countries don't agree. Whether that redefining will work, or whether NATO will be given up, remains to be seen.

Whereas with a balance of power each country limits its actions for fear of upsetting that balance, in the new world order it is foreseen that each country will limit its actions according to "what is right." How is "what is right" determined? It is determined by the major power who, for the new world order to work, must interpret "what is right" in a way that seems right to most people regardless of what is in the countries' individual interests. Making the new world order work is a tall order, an issue that we discuss further in Chapter 21.

Foreign Policies

Relationships between states that affect the national security or general welfare of each are the core of international relations. The **foreign policies** of a nation are the courses of action a nation uses to achieve its international objectives. As a rule, the nation's primary purposes are to increase its own security and its own general economic welfare. Sometimes, however, a foreign policy may further the interests of some politically powerful pressure group rather than those of the nation as a whole. When this is so, those who support it usually attempt to convince the majority that it benefits the entire nation.

Generally speaking, the foreign policies of a state are designed to serve the national interests as these are conceived by the public or by those in direct control. Security and prosperity are always major objectives; other objectives may include the spread of an ideology such as the expansion of national power and prestige. Unfortunately, there is no simple formula guaranteeing that the right foreign policy decisions will always be made. Debate is, therefore, inevitable.

An example of the problems of foreign policy is the first Persian Gulf War of 1991. Here, Iraq, which the United States had supported in the Iran–Iraq war, invaded Kuwait, which was also a U.S. ally. In response the United States aligned itself with Syria, which had been one of its major enemies, and kept its close ally, Israel, a country that was hated by Kuwait and Syria, out of the war while the United States simultaneously tried to establish closer ties with Iran. And who knows what secret agreements were made between the countries? The intrigue of soap operas pales in comparison with the intrigue of foreign policy.

Geography and Foreign Policy

Conspicuous among the facts and forces that act as determinants of foreign policy is, as we have pointed out, the geographic position of a nation. For the promotion of the country's security and prosperity, policymakers must give heed to matters such as the following:

1. The defensibility of the state's boundaries
2. The effects of distance on its powers of offense and defense by means of long-range missiles
3. The availability of ports for useful trade and for naval bases
4. The attitudes of neighboring states and their size and power
5. The state's own size and natural resources

If a state is satisfied with its geographic lot in life, it can direct its efforts toward protecting what it has; if it is dissatisfied, it will, if possible, maneuver its policies toward the elimination of its alleged handicaps, asserting itself dynamically, perhaps even aggressively, in order to get from others what it believes it needs.

The term **geopolitics** refers to the relation between geography and security that foreign policymakers attempt to take into account. According to Nicholas Spykman, geopolitics is "the planning of the security policy of a country in terms of its geographic factors." No nation pursued the subject as seriously as prewar Germany, which under the Nazis embraced the theories of earlier geopoliticians, and through General Karl Haushofer worked out a "scientific" policy of expansion calculated to secure Germany's position as a master power for an indefinite future, all at the expense of "decadent" neighbors.

Without constructing a complicated theory of geopolitics comparable to that of the Nazis, most states nevertheless have exhibited their geographic aspirations in their foreign policies. Russia for centuries has sought good warm-water ports; it has wanted control over the Dardanelles, and it has tried to get buffer territory on its western frontier to make up for its lack of defensible boundaries there. Its activities in Iran and Afghanistan in the 1970s and 1980s reflected that desire. France long felt that its geographic position required it to seek a frontier on the Rhine River and to undermine the strength of its dangerous neighbor, Germany, which had several times invaded France's territory. In the Far East, Japan attempted before World War II to add to the security of its position by absorbing Korea, Manchuria, Taiwan, and many islands of the Pacific and by controlling China. Iraq's 1990 invasion of Kuwait was in part an attempt by Iraq to gain control of two of Kuwait's islands, which would give it better control of the shipping lanes out of the Iraqi port of Basra, and the 2003 Iraq war was seen by some observers as an attempt by the United States to gain a strong military presence in the Middle East so that it could protect its oil interests and provide better protection for Israel.

Values, Ideologies, and Foreign Policy

After World War I, foreign policies were strongly impregnated with ideologies. This resulted from the contest of various social doctrines, especially fascism, communism, and democracy, for the control of people's minds and for dominance in world affairs. We all have, and should have, strong feelings about political issues and forms of government. However, we must be extraordinarily careful about letting our emotions affect our considerations of those issues so that we do not become **ideologues**—individuals who are so fixated on certain ideologies that they cannot reasonably examine opposing arguments.

Fascist Ideology.   Since World War I, the three ideologies that have been prevalent are the communist ideology, the democratic capitalist ideology, and the fascist ideology. **Fascist ideology** argued that a natural leader must arise in a country and tell the people what the people want. Under fascist ideology, the leader will make the people, the nation, and their culture great. With the defeat of Hitler in Germany and Mussolini in Italy in World War II, fascism declined as an ideology, but you can still hear fascist rantings in the small Nazi Party in the United States and in some countries where there is significant social turmoil.

In the 1990s there was a resurgence of fascism across Europe. In Italy, after general elections in April 1994, the neofascist party—the Italian Social Movement (MSI)—became a crucial component of the government. And in the 1990s in Russia the ultranationalist (and by many accounts fascist) Vladimir Zhirinovsky's Liberal Democratic Party garnered over 30 percent of the popular vote.

The Author's Ideological Positions. Although social scientists must always be careful about making categorical statements, this social scientist will categorically state that, given his values—a strong belief in democracy and equality—the extinction of fascism would be a good thing. If an ideology considers one group of people or one nation better than any other group or nation, that ideology can justify almost any action. War and destruction become unavoidable unless all other peoples and nations capitulate to those who are asserting such exclusive superiority. Thus even a person who believes in freedom can, in the name of a higher freedom, ultimately justify restricting individuals' rights to advocate certain ideologies. However, taking that line is dangerous, and it is far better to use reason and convincing arguments against such ideologies. (That is why the American Civil Liberties Union supports the rights of the U.S. Nazi Party.)

If you agree with these value judgments and arguments about foreign policy, this means that a country should have a policy condemning fascism and should do what it can, within the confines of international law, to combat and restrict it.

Another value I hold is that human life is sacred and individuals have certain rights. Often when I hear of what occurs in other countries, my immediate reaction is one of abhorrence, and I wish our country would "do something." There have been numerous examples: the restriction of Soviet Jews' right to emigrate from the former Soviet Union; the practice of Idi Amin, former ruler of Uganda, of arbitrarily killing opponents (probably by the thousands); South Africa's apartheid policy; Latin American right-wing death squads; the systematic killing of millions in Cambodia; and more recently the mass genocide and ethnic cleansing in Bosnia and the terrible atrocities in Rwanda.

When should a country use its power, and what powers should it use, to stop or prevent such activities? Unfortunately, there is no easy answer. Not all cultures have the same regard for human rights as we do, and I also believe that we generally do not have the right to impose our personal values on others. In all cases, it is proper to use diplomatic channels and public channels to do what can be done to support human rights, but in doing so a country must apply the same criteria to friendly countries as to unfriendly countries, recognizing differences in social values. For instance, if a country has a mandatory military draft, that draft may violate the concept some have of human rights, but it would be wrong to assume that such opposition is a universally agreed-on human right.

More difficult choices than one about a military draft confront us when issues such as forced labor camps for large minorities within a population, involuntary abortion, infanticide, and apartheid surface. There comes a point when the offenses against human rights become too great to sit back and accept (again, this is based on my particular value judgments, which are not universally shared). Examples include the annihilation of the Jews in Germany in the 1930s and 1940s (to which the United States initially responded by restricting immigration visas for Jews) and Pol Pot's massacre of millions of his fellow citizens in Cambodia in the 1970s (which the United States ignored, at least officially). The U.S. position in regard to Iraq shows the difficult choices. When Iraq used chemical weapons against Iran and the Kurds in the 1980s, Iraq was a U.S. ally and the United States said nothing; in fact, it shipped Iraq more weapons. However, in 2003 it used Iraq's previous use of chemical weapons as one of the reasons it should "liberate" Iraq from Saddam Hussein.

Communist Ideology.   Communism as an ideology is far more problematic to make a value decision about. First, it is unclear what the communist ideology is. When Karl Marx wrote *Das Kapital* and *The Communist Manifesto,* he spent almost no time discussing how a communist society would be implemented or would operate. It was only through the experience of the Soviet Union under its communist government after World War I and in the writings of the Soviet leader and practical theorist Lenin that the nature of what we now call communist countries became clear.

Because, according to Marx, communism involves the eventual withering away of the state, even so-called communist countries would agree that they are currently still in a transition stage. It is not communism that goes against my values; it is the transition stage. I also condemn the Stalin era, during which large numbers of Soviet people were liquidated. Stalinist justification for that policy—that the end justifies the means—was, and is, personally unacceptable to me. Nothing justifies such wholesale killing. Similarly unacceptable was the expansionist component of their ideology that was devoted to the spread of communism by whatever means possible.

The 1980s and 1990s saw an enormous change in communism. Many states, including the formerly communist eastern European states such as East Germany and Poland and many of the republics of the former Soviet Union, have simply abandoned it, and in others, such as China, communism has evolved both economically and politically. This evolution, to some, suggests a victory of capitalist and democratic ideology, and in many ways it is. People in both China and the former Soviet Union focused their demands for reforms on achieving markets and democratic elections. Clearly, the totalitarian nature of communism and the favoritism these countries showed to Communist Party members were opposed by the majority of people in these countries.

But other observers point out that the Communist Party itself should also have been opposed by true communists. The party was meant to protect the rights of the working class, not to become the class of people with special privileges that it became. These other observers argue that communism failed because it abandoned communist ideals.

Most social scientists accept the argument that communism abandoned its ideals. They differ, however, on the question of whether that abandonment was inherent in the structure of communism—no society can ever give that much power to any group—or whether the communists simply didn't try hard enough to preserve their ideals. Whatever the answer is to that question, the reality is that communism is not yet dead. For example, in 1998 communist parties still controlled the governments of China, North Korea, and Cuba. The Communist Party has, however, lost any claim to a higher moral ground that it once made. Whether it can be revived or whether it belongs on the scrap heap of history remains to be seen. As long as the Communist Party accepts that it is one of many parties and will abide by the democratic decisions of the people, democratic ideology holds that it must be free to try to convince people of its ideas and goals.

The United States in the World Community

The separation-of-powers doctrine, modified by a system of checks and balances, was embodied in the U.S. Constitution of 1787 to prevent tyranny, and it applies to the field of foreign affairs as well as to domestic politics. Although the judiciary has no hand in policy-making and is confined in its work to the interpretation and application of treaties and statutes, the other two branches of the government—the president and Congress (especially the Senate)—are both equipped with far-reaching authority to determine foreign policy.

The President and Foreign Policy

The president derives great power in foreign affairs from the right to appoint diplomats (with the consent of the Senate) and to receive the diplomats of other countries, and has ultimate responsibility for the diplomatic messages our government transmits abroad and for the operations of the Department of State generally. Presidential control of diplomacy gives the president a strong initiative in foreign affairs, for diplomatic correspondence can be a vehicle of policy, as in 1899 when Secretary of State John Hay originated the Open Door policy in China by messages to selected governments. The president's prerogative in diplomacy confers, too, the right to deny or to extend recognition to a new government or state, for it is usually by establishing diplomatic relationships that recognition is accorded. President Carter demonstrated that policy when he established formal relations with the People's Republic of China as the appropriate representative of the Chinese people and cut relations with Taiwan.

The president has the initiative in treaty making, too, but here these actions require the approval of two-thirds of the senators present when a vote is taken. This arrangement, indeed, is a good example of the system of checks and balances that pervades all of government in the United States. Much criticism has been aimed at the Senate for its obstructive tactics in its consideration of treaties—notably the Treaty of Versailles (1919)—and several proposals have been submitted to amend the Constitution to substitute a majority of both houses of Congress in place of two-thirds of the Senate in treaty making, but such proposals have never had much support. Some of the problems that can develop from this dual responsibility can be seen in the Law of the Sea Treaty negotiated between 1974 and 1980 under UN auspices. This treaty was signed by President Carter but was never approved by the Senate. When President Reagan was elected, he specifically disavowed the treaty, leaving the United States in an ambiguous position.

President George W. Bush took a strong position against U.S. involvement in international treaties, opposing multilateral cooperation, in which countries attempt to negotiate their differences through international treaties and organizations, and favoring unilateralism, in which each country goes it alone. Soon after being elected, he withdrew from or rejected numerous international treaties and organizations, including the Biological Weapons Convention, the Kyoto Protocol, the Anti-Ballistic Missile Treaty, and the International Criminal Court. These actions convinced many that under George W. Bush the United States saw itself as above the international community and was willing to rely on its military power to achieve its ends.

The president's authority in foreign affairs is augmented by some more general powers. As commander-in-chief of the armed forces, the president can dispatch the army, navy, marines, or air force to any part of the world to carry out a policy, and can conclude executive agreements by which bases abroad are placed at the disposal of the services. This gives the president enormous power, in effect, to enter into war without Senate approval. For example, during President Kennedy's administration, the U.S. government supported the Bay of Pigs invasion of Cuba with no Senate approval. Similarly, in 1964 President Johnson began the direct U.S. military role in Vietnam by ordering attacks on North Vietnamese military targets following attacks on U.S. warships in the Gulf of Tonkin.

A scene from the Vietnam War, which challenged U.S. beliefs about the United States' role in the world.

In response to the latter incident, Congress passed a series of laws that placed stricter limits on presidential actions. Because the Constitution explicitly gives Congress the powers to declare war and control military and naval expenditures, it was argued that the president's discretionary powers as commander-in-chief had become too broad. These laws removed the president's power to "wage war, sell arms, conduct covert operations, or enter into executive agreements with foreign governments." According to these laws, a president can deploy troops to protect our interest only for a limited time without the consent of Congress.

In 1986 the president's National Security Council sold arms to Iran without informing Congress and used the proceeds to fund the Nicaraguan contras, thereby violating these laws and creating a scandal for the Reagan administration. In the 1980s, when President Reagan considered increasing the U.S. military presence in trouble spots in Latin America, the Senate played an active role. The reduced power of the presidency has led some to suggest that the president no longer wields any power at all.[1]

Such suggestions were exaggerations, as was made clear by the first President George Bush's actions in the 1991 Persian Gulf War, President Clinton's actions in the bombing of Yugoslavia, and President George W. Bush's decision to go to war against Iraq. In each case, some members of Congress argued that the president had to get congressional approval before actually starting a war, but the presidents denied that they were required to do so. The issues became academic when Congress, faced with widespread public approval of the president's actions, authorized the president to use force. Thus this question of war powers remains unanswered.

---

[1] Such complaints are not totally new. Harry Truman, who normally said what he thought, described the problem as follows: "People think I sit here and push buttons and get things accomplished. Well, I spent today kissing behinds."

With such ambiguous divided powers between the presidency and Congress, co-operation between the two branches of the government is essential to avoid paralyzing deadlocks. On occasion cooperation has not been forthcoming and the nation has found itself seriously embarrassed. The president has signed treaties that the Senate would not approve, and the president has dispatched troops overseas and then taken a broadside of criticism from Congress. Such conflicts are likely to continue, however, owing to the fundamental structure of the U.S. democratic system.

U.S. Foreign Policies

Throughout much of the nineteenth century, the United States was deeply committed to a policy of isolation. **Isolationism,** a policy according to which the United States made no alliances abroad and kept as free as possible from the political embroilments of Europe, reigned supreme. Even after the Spanish-American War (1898), the nation remained aloof, though the acquisition of scattered dependencies such as Hawaii as a result of the war had widened U.S. interests a great deal. Isolationism broke down when the United States in 1917 became a belligerent in World War I, but it was revived in 1919–20, when the Senate rejected membership in the new League of Nations. Although under attack in the 1920s and 1930s, isolationism continued to have strong support, as shown by U.S. neutrality legislation (1935 and later) and by the efforts from 1939 to 1941 to keep the United States from becoming involved in World War II.

But the Japanese attack on Pearl Harbor in 1941 changed all this and moved us from a period of isolationism to internationalism. **Internationalism** refers to the belief that world peace can be realized by the friendly association of all nations. As a result, the United States quickly became enmeshed in world politics and has continued to be deeply involved ever since.

Since World War II, the United States has made or affirmed a number of alliances and maintained troops or military outposts in various parts of the world, especially in Europe and the Far East. The United States has committed large military forces to the fighting of three local undeclared wars: Korea, Vietnam, and Iraq.

Much of our foreign policy in the postwar era has been dedicated to the protection of capitalism and "liberal" democracy. For example, our foreign policy immediately following World War II revolved around the Truman Doctrine of 1947. Essentially, the **Truman Doctrine** stated that if any country threatened by communist aggression was willing to resist that threat and asked for help, the United States would come to its aid. This was often referred to as a policy of containing communism and was part of what was called the **cold war,** the tension between communist countries, such as the former Soviet Union, and the United States and its allies following World War II until the 1990s. During the cold war, the United States believed that if it did not take the lead in resisting the aggressive moves of the Soviet Union and the other communist nations, there would probably be no effective opposition, and a domino effect would occur, with one country after another falling to the communists.

The basis of the peace in the cold war was a **nuclear standoff**—a position of stalemate brought about by the recognition that if attacked, the other party possesses sufficient ability to launch a devastating nuclear counterattack. In a nuclear standoff, because each country has the ability to destroy the other ten or fifteen times over, the concept of military superiority becomes difficult to define. This was especially apparent in the 1980s when the United States and the former USSR negotiated a reduction of the

An Outline of U.S. Foreign Policy*

1789–1897: Isolationism/unilateralism, with the following examples showing how we followed this policy:

> 1796—Washington's Farewell Address: "Beware of entangling alliances" (balance of power entanglements in today's words).
> 1834—Monroe Doctrine. U.S. promises not to interfere in European affairs and demands that Europe not interfere in Latin America.

1898–1918: Interventionism.

> 1898—Spanish-American War: events leading to it and results/fruits of this interventionism.
> 1917—U.S. intervention into World War I.

1919–1941: Return to isolationism/unilateralism as the nation sees the result of interventionism.

> 1919—U.S. Senate rejects joining the League of Nations.
> 1930s—Neutrality Acts of 1935, 1937, and 1939 as we see Europe heading toward war.

1941–1945: No special change in policy necessary; United States simply responds to attack. Any nation follows a similar policy of defending itself.

1945–Present: Internationalism. Actually starts with the Truman Doctrine (1947), even though we join UN in 1945.

> 1949—NATO.
> 1950—Korean conflict (even though UN sponsored).
> 1961–1973—Involvement in Vietnam (really following tenets of the Truman Doctrine).
> 1972—Nixon Doctrine (so called, although it should rightfully be called a corollary to the Truman Doctrine).
> 1991—Persian Gulf War; beginning of new world order, or at least Western control.
> 1993—U.S. tries to enforce its will with UN backing in a variety of states such as Haiti, Somalia, Bosnia, North Korea. The results are questionable.
> 1990—Foreign policy directed at working with rather than against Russia.

2000—Unilateralism and preemption
> 2001—9/11 attacks on United States and beginning of war on terrorism.
> 2003—Bush Doctrine of Preemption: President Bush declares the United States has the right to wage preemptive war against countries that allow terrorists on their soil.

*We are grateful to Prof. W. K. Callam for supplying an initial draft of this outline.

arms buildup. Both sides claimed that the other had military superiority; which side actually did was unclear.

The containment approach to U.S. foreign policy lost favor following our involvement in Vietnam in the 1960s and early 1970s, and a period of **détente**—an easing or relaxation of strained relations and political tensions between countries—replaced the cold war. Under détente the U.S. involvement in world political affairs decreased, and the United States reduced its expenditures on defense as a percentage of GDP. That changed in September 2001, when terrorists attacked the United States and the United States declared a war on terrorism.

That war on terrorism pitted the United States not against a particular country, but against an ambiguous enemy who could be anywhere. A new Homeland Security Department was established in the United States, and military expenditures increased substantially. But exactly how this war on terrorism was to be fought remained open. Does the United States have the right to fight terrorism anywhere? Are preemptive wars truly possible? What limitations on individual rights are acceptable trade-offs for increased security?

Does the United States have the right to eliminate governments who it feels are harboring terrorists and developing weapons of mass destruction? What proof does it need to carry on such preemptive wars? And, finally, will fighting such a war do more harm than good, creating hatred for the United States that will lead to more terrorism?

Key Points

- The state is the institution empowered to conduct international relations for its citizens.
- Power is the capacity to compel another party to commit an action contrary to its explicitly stated will. Ultimately, power determines whether a foreign policy will be successful.
- Governments use foreign policy to achieve their international objectives, but they must take geography and other nations' strengths into consideration when they make policy.

- Since World War II, the three most prevalent ideologies have been the communist ideology, the democratic capitalist ideology, and the fascist ideology.
- The president is responsible for foreign policy and is commander-in-chief of the armed forces, but only Congress can declare war.
- In the early 2000s the United States adopted a policy of unilateralism and preemption.

Some Important Terms

balance of power (408)
cold war (416)
détente (417)
fascist ideology (411)
foreign policies (410)
geopolitics (411)
hegemon (402)
ideologues (411)
internationalism (416)

isolationism (416)
nation (399)
nation-state (399)
new world order (409)
North Atlantic Treaty
   Organization (NATO) (409)
nuclear standoff (416)
power (400)
realist theory (409)

state (399)
theory of complex inter-
   dependence (409)
Truman Doctrine (416)
unilateral (408)
weapons of mass destruction
   (403)

Questions for Review and Discussion

1. In what sense do the nation-states of the world form a community?
2. List the more important differences between nations and states.
3. As the term is used in this chapter, which of the following are states: Alaska, Luxembourg, Scotland, Bavaria, Australia, Michigan, Hong Kong? On what basis did you make your selection?
4. Historically, how did nation-states develop?

5. The effectiveness of a nation's military power in supporting its foreign policies depends on what factors in addition to the size, training, and equipment of its armed forces?
6. Why are democratic governments more restricted in their actions by public opinion than are totalitarian governments?
7. What is a hegemon?
8. What factors make up a nation's economic power?

9. What are three possible approaches to the problem of achieving some degree of national security? Explain each.
10. Explain how the theory of complex interdependence is becoming a substitute for the balance of power in maintaining the peace in today's world.
11. How may foreign policies be influenced by (a) geography and (b) an ideology?
12. What powers does the president of the United States have in foreign affairs? What powers are held by Congress? Point out the advantages and disadvantages of this division of responsibility.
13. Do you believe that the president of the United States should have more power or less power to determine and carry out foreign policies? Defend your answer.
14. Was the Iraq War justified?
15. What is the U.S. policy of preemption, and is it justified?
16. Explain the shift of U.S. foreign policy away from an attitude of aloofness to one of active participation in world affairs.

Internet Questions

1. Go to www.embpage.org, and click on embassy. What is the latest transnational issue listed?
2. See www.house.gov/Constitution/Constitution.html. What does Article II, Section 2, clauses 1 and 2 of the United States Constitution state?
3. Read M. Walker, http://worldpolicy.org/walker.html. What is the Nye Report, and what is its suggestion about Asian security?
4. Using the website of the American Foreign Policy Council, www.afpc.org, what is one of their latest news stories about?
5. Using the NATO site, www.nato.int, what is the Euro-Atlantic Partnership Council, and how many members are there?

For Further Study

Andrews, Peter, *Border Games: Policing the U.S.–Mexico Divide*, Ithaca, NY: Cornell University Press, 2000.

Kissinger, Henry, *Years of Renewal,* New York: Simon & Schuster, 1999.

Nicholson, Philip Yale, *Who Do We Think We Are? Race and Nation in the Modern World,* Armonk, NY: Sharpe, 2000.

Reynolds, David, *One World Divisible: A Global History since 1945,* New York: Norton, 2000.

Sloan, Stanley R., *NATO and Transatlantic Relations in the 21st Century: Crisis, Continuity or Change?,* New York: Foreign Policy Association, 2002.

WWW Council on Foreign Relations www.foreignpolicy2000.org/home/home.cfm

WWW The Electronic Embassy www.embassy.org
WWW Foreign Policy Association www.fpa.org
WWW Geopolitics www.balkan-archive.org.ya/kosta/geopolitics
WWW International Information Programs http://usinfo.state.gov/homepage.htm
WWW League of Nations Archives www.unog.ch/library/archives/archives.htm
WWW NATO www.nato.int

Zunes, Stephen, *Tinderbox: U.S. Foreign Policy and the Roots of Terrorism,* Monroe, ME: Common Courage Press, 2003.

International Economic Relations

chapter 9

After reading this chapter, you should be able to:

- Differentiate between the balance of payments and the balance of trade
- Compare the advantages and disadvantages of international trade
- State the arguments in favor of and against protective tariffs
- Distinguish between a fixed and a flexible exchange rate
- State whether the United States is a debtor or a creditor nation and explain what that means

One of the purest fallacies is that trade follows the flag. Trade follows the lowest price current. If a dealer in any colony wished to buy Union Jacks, he would order them from Britain's worst foe if he could save a sixpence.

—Andrew Carnegie

Can we be frank? Once we cut through many of the high-sounding moral positions nations (and individuals) take, often there is a crass materialistic or economic motive underlying those positions. Therefore, to understand international relations, we must understand international economics, which includes the study of international trade, determination of foreign exchange rates, and foreign investment.

In Chapter 3, we discussed the rise and importance of international trade in the development of society and the evolution of cultures. As nations developed, trade transferred culture and made merchants rich, which helped break up the feudal system and led to the modern nation-state. The modern role of international trade is no less important, but without the perspective of history we are less likely to see it.

In the 1930s, the United States followed an isolationist policy toward trade. Since that time, the importance of international trade for the United States has grown significantly over the last few decades, and now accounts for well over 10 percent of our total GDP. But even this percentage underestimates its importance. It fails to take into account the fact that once export industries become established, people employed in them furnish a part of the market for industries producing products for domestic consumption. Hence, if exports decline, production and employment, in accordance with the multiplier principle, also fall off in other industries.

That figure also does not take into account the importance of imports to us. A number of our imports are necessary or desirable commodities that we cannot produce ourselves, or cannot produce as much of as we would like, such as coffee, bananas, natural rubber, nickel, tin, and oil. The crisis and shortages in the U.S. economy as a result of the Arab oil embargo in the 1970s demonstrate the importance of international trade. Similarly, the fear that an unfriendly government would control a large portion of the world oil supply was a significant factor in the quick reaction of the United States to the invasion of Kuwait by Iraq in 1990, and its continued strong role in the Middle East. International trade is fundamentally important to the U.S. economy.

The Terminology of Trade

The expanding importance of international trade has led to the introduction of new terms and growth of the importance of others. For example, many corporations have become **global corporations** (also called multinational corporations), which have production and distribution facilities in a variety of countries. Another term that has become important is **cartel,** an organization of countries that produce a specific good and that agree to limit production of that good in order to increase the price the countries in the organization get. Probably the most well known of these cartels is the Organization of Petroleum Exporting Countries (OPEC), which played a significant role in international trade in the 1970s and 1980s and again in the early 2000s.

The Balance of Trade and the Balance of Payments

In discussing international trade, two terms are used frequently: the balance of trade and the balance of payments. The term **balance of trade** refers to the relation of our total exports to our total imports. It tells us the dollar difference between exports and imports. Figure 19.1 shows that the U.S. balance of trade significantly worsened in the mid-1980s as the country ran large deficits. The deficits improved somewhat in the early 1990s, but worsened again in the late 1990s and early 2000s.

The term **balance of payments** refers to the relation of total payments made abroad to total payments received from abroad. It includes not only traded goods and services but also currency flows, such as loans and investments, among countries. Even though the balance of trade has been in deficit recently, the balance of payments has not, because the trade imbalance is being offset by large foreign capital inflows into the United States.

The difference between the balance of payments and the balance of trade can be seen by considering the U.S. position in the early 2000s when it was running a significant balance-of-trade deficit of over $400 billion a year. However, at that same time foreigners were investing heavily in the United States, largely in the form of bonds. Therefore, because the balance of payments includes flows of investment, even though the balance of trade was in deficit, the balance of payments was not.

That does not mean we don't have to worry about the international trade deficit. When foreign money is invested in the United States, foreigners acquire U.S. assets and will take profits from them and have control over them in the future. They also can decide to no longer hold their assets in the United States, in which case the value of the dollar can fall substantially, as it did in mid-2003.

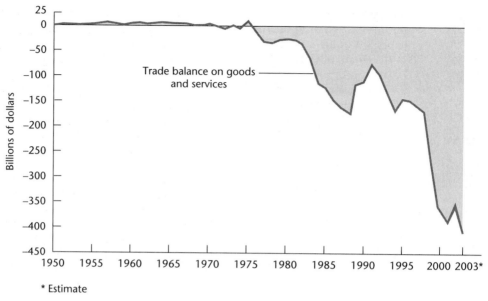

Figure 19.1

U.S. trade balance (including services), 1950–2003. (Source: Bureau of Economic Analysis.)

Visible and Invisible Trade

Many people, when they think of imports and exports, have in mind only the **visible items of trade**—material goods such as wheat, pianos, or machinery. But to think of foreign trade as consisting of these alone is misleading, because the so-called invisible items may be just as important.

Invisible items of trade consist of services of all sorts for which the people of one country pay those of another. For example, in normal years we pay British citizens and other foreigners large amounts in freight charges for carrying U.S. goods on their ships and planes. U.S. tourists also pay British citizens, French citizens, Italians, and others large sums to buy hotel accommodations and transportation in their countries. Such items represent purchases abroad just as truly as do imports of coffee or shoes. Another important invisible item of trade is the interest Americans receive from foreign investments. This is payment for permitting foreigners to use our capital, something that is just as truly a service as their permitting us to use their hotel rooms.

As far as the visible items of trade are concerned, before World War II we normally exported much more than we imported. But in respect to the invisible items, the reverse was true. Therefore, for the most part imports equaled exports, so that our money payments to other countries were offset by their payments to us. However, this balance was upset by World War II. From then until the 1960s, the United States ran a substantial balance-of-trade surplus that was offset by foreign aid and loans that the United States made to other countries. Since the end of the 1960s, the flow has been reversed, and the United States has been running large balance-of-trade deficits that we have paid for by our previously accumulated reserves. In the 1980s, the deficit became so large that the United States became a net debtor

The Changing Nature of International Trade

In the 1960s, 1970s, and 1980s, international trade expanded in the developing countries, mainly in the area of manufacturing. One after another the manufacturing plants moved abroad to take advantage of cheaper labor, and today the majority of goods you consume are manufactured abroad. The 1990s marked a new dimension in the expansion of international trade. Companies began dividing up their production processes into components and looking for ways to shift the various subcomponents of production abroad. Each aspect of production was separated—such as bookkeeping service, maintenance service, and advertising—and ways to achieve lower costs by outsourcing—contracting out for others to provide that activity for the firm rather than having someone in the firm do it—were explored.

Beginning in the 1990s, services began moving abroad. For example, accounting for some firms is done in India, where labor costs one-tenth what it does in the United States. Likewise with telephone service: When you actually reach a service representative, it might well be a person in India, Pakistan, or Bangladesh who has been trained to speak "American" and who receives a wage that is a fraction of what a U.S. citizen would get. Such movement overseas of subcomponents of production is likely to continue and even increase in the coming years.

nation (a country that owes more than it is owed). The deficits continued in the early 2000s, and the United States now owes trillions of dollars more than it is owed.

Advantages and Disadvantages of International Trade

Trade is the lifeblood of a modern economy, and the benefits of international trade are so great that it is inconceivable that a modern nation should adopt a policy of complete economic isolation. The full utilization of power machinery, with its attendant specialization, requires mass production, and mass production calls for extensive trade in very wide markets. To limit the market of an industry to one country would often mean reduced efficiency and higher costs. Also, modern society requires a great variety of goods, both for consumption and as raw materials for its industries, including tea, coffee, cotton, rubber, petroleum, iron, manganese, aluminum, nickel, coal—a complete list would be long indeed. No country has or can produce all of these products. The missing ones can be obtained only through trade. When trade flows freely between countries, the world tends to become more prosperous. When trade languishes, production lags, unemployment increases, and the world's income shrinks.

Three Advantages of Trade

There are three primary advantages of international trade. The first is that it enables a country to obtain products that cannot be produced at home at all or that cannot be produced in adequate quantities and at acceptable costs. Sometimes the inability of a country to produce certain things is a matter of climate, such as the difficulty in growing tea and coffee in the United States. In other cases it is a lack of certain natural resources. Italy, for example, has no good coal deposits, and Britain does not have enough good farmland to meet its demands for food.

U.S. exports being loaded onto a Panamanian-registered South Korean ship.

The second advantage of international trade is that it often enables a country to get a better product than can be produced at home. This may be due to differences in climate and soil or to differences in natural resources. Sometimes, however, it is owing to the fact that the people of some foreign countries have, over a long period of time, acquired certain techniques that are not easily transferred. English factories for years produced finer woolens than most U.S. factories because they had specialized in fine woolens for generations.

A third advantage of international trade is that it often makes products available at a lower price than would be possible if they were produced at home. This raises standards of living by increasing consumer purchasing power. Consider a country that, like Great Britain, produces only about half of its needed food supply. Conceivably, Britain might be able to raise enough food within its own borders to feed its people. However, any attempt to do this would mean inadequate amounts of many foods and the absence of commodities such as oranges, tea, and coffee. It would also mean high prices for the foods that could be produced. Britain has a large population relative to the amount of land available for cultivation. To raise all of its food, it would have to cultivate its good land more intensively, in spite of the tendency toward diminishing returns; it would also have to resort to inferior land not really suitable for agriculture. Both methods are expensive and result in high prices. In the long run, Britain can provide its people with better standards of living by selling industrial goods and buying a substantial portion of its food supply abroad.

Disadvantages of Trade

If international trade had only advantages, there would be free trade among nations and little debate over what to do about international trade. There is significant debate, however, so obviously there must be some disadvantages to international trade. To see these disadvantages, let's consider some examples. Say, for instance, that China began building automobiles that would sell in the United States for $4,000. This would benefit the Chinese who make the automobiles and U.S. consumers of automobiles, but it would hurt one group of producers—U.S. automobile companies—and one group of workers—U.S. automobile workers—a lot.

Other examples abound. Importing potatoes helps U.S. consumers but hurts Maine and Idaho potato producers; importing textiles from Bangladesh helps U.S. consumers but hurts textile firms here in the United States. When we look at both groups together, we see that the benefits of international trade almost always outweigh the costs, but the benefits are spread over a large group of people, whereas the costs are imposed on a few. Those few who are hurt express their opposition to international competition loudly, and so in the United States, as in most countries, there is often a tendency to encourage exports and discourage imports. The complainers argue something like the following: Just as it seems plain that selling goods abroad gives profits and wages to U.S. producers, so it seems equally plain that buying goods abroad robs U.S. producers of the profits and wages they might have received had these goods been purchased at home.

The notion that U.S. producers as a group are injured by foreign purchases is a fallacy. As we show shortly, if trade is on a business basis, in the long run the United States can sell goods to other countries only if it also buys goods from them. If we reduce our imports, we reduce our exports. Though we may gain home markets for the products of some U.S. workers, we do this only at the expense of losing foreign markets for the products of other U.S. workers. For the country as a whole, these two things cancel each other out, and the net result is that U.S. consumers pay higher prices or receive inferior goods.

On the other hand, if we increase our imports, in the long run our exports will also increase. Any decline in the home market for U.S. goods will be offset by an increase in the foreign market. If we buy British textiles because they are cheaper or better than domestic textiles, and if the British buy U.S. refrigerators because they are cheaper or better than those made in Britain, the consumers of both countries gain. Further, there is no loss in employment. In the United States, the smaller demand for labor in the textile industry is offset by the larger demand for labor in the refrigerator industry. In England the smaller proportion of refrigerator workers is offset by the larger proportion of textile workers.

Why You Can't Get the Advantages without the Disadvantages

Why is it that we can sell goods to other countries only if we also buy goods from them? Briefly, the reason is that, in the long run, foreign countries can pay for what they buy only with the goods they sell. Let us explain as simply as possible how imports pay for exports, and vice versa. For simplicity, we first assume that trade takes place only between Britain and the United States.

Suppose that at a certain time a British importer wishes to buy $1 million worth of U.S. machinery. The U.S. firms that have this machinery for sale are unlikely to want British money, or pounds sterling. Rather, they want dollars. Therefore, in order to buy the machinery, the British importer must find some way to change British money into dollars—that is, to find someone who has dollars and who is willing to sell them in exchange for pounds.

Who will have dollars and be willing to exchange them for pounds? For the most part, they can be found in two groups: (1) Americans who want pounds in order to buy goods or services from Britain, and (2) British exporters who have accepted checks or drafts in dollars for British goods that they have sold to Americans. In either case, the source of the dollars available to the British to buy American goods is the payments Americans have made, or plan to make, for British goods.

If for any reason U.S. imports of British goods should decline, the British would be forced to curtail their purchases of U.S. goods because they could no longer obtain sufficient dollars to buy in the previous volume.

The preceding explanation disregards certain complicating factors. Actually, British importers do not go directly to British exporters to obtain U.S. money. The banks act as middlemen. If British exporters accept in payment dollar-value checks drawn on U.S. banks, they do so because they can take them to their own banks and there exchange them for pounds sterling and deposit them to their own accounts. Their banks can then deposit these checks in New York banks and sell dollar drafts to British importers who need them in order to pay for U.S. goods.

Another factor that our explanation disregards is that trade does not take place just between Britain and the United States. Other countries come into the picture. For example, British exporters might receive dollars for textiles sold in the United States, and British importers might in turn use these dollars to buy beef in Argentina. The dollars would then be available to Argentine importers to buy machinery in the United States. In this case, the dollars we spent for British textiles made it possible for Argentines to buy our machinery.

A final qualification is the time dimension. In the long run, any country's imports must equal its exports. In the short run, however, this statement must be qualified. Over considerable periods of time, one country may be able to buy substantially more from another country than it sells, or vice versa. This can happen for two reasons: (1) Countries may have stocks of gold, other reserve currencies, or financial assets that they are willing to send us in payment for their purchases, and (2) countries may be willing to sell goods on credit. However, a country's monetary reserves and its financial assets are limited, and credit must some day be repaid.

Restrictions on International Trade

We have seen that there are significant advantages to international trade, and in most cases nations would derive the greatest economic advantage from international trade if they allowed free trade. This, however, is not the usual practice; instead, numerous controls are applied. These controls include subsidies on exports, tariffs, quotas, exchange controls, and bilateral barter agreements. In the past, tariffs have been the principal device for regulating trade, but in recent years other methods of control, especially quotas, have assumed greatly increased importance.

The reason for these controls has to do with how economics relates to politics. The benefits of trade are spread widely among consumers, who simply take these benefits for granted. The costs fall on a relatively small group and often affect them rather severely, causing firms that can't compete to go out of business and workers to lose their jobs. Even though the total costs are less than the total benefits, the politicians will listen to, and make laws to protect, the few who are hurt. Therefore there is continual pressure for trade restrictions. We now consider some of these.

Tariffs on Imports

A **tariff** is a tax, or duty, usually on an imported commodity. When tariff duties are levied as a fixed charge per barrel or yard, they are said to be *specific*. When they are levied as a percentage of the value of a commodity, they are said to be *ad valorem* (value-added). A tariff generally has one of two purposes: either to raise revenue or to protect the market of a domestic industry by keeping out the products of foreign competitors. To a degree these two purposes are incompatible because a tariff that would keep the foreign product out entirely would raise no revenue at all. In practice, however, protective tariffs are seldom high enough to exclude imports completely and hence do raise some revenue. But if the chief purpose of a tariff is to raise revenue, it should not be high enough to discourage most imports. Further, instead of being levied on a commodity produced both at home and abroad, it should, if possible, be levied on one that cannot be produced at home. This eliminates the possibility that imports and revenues may fall off because buyers turn to home producers.

Although tariffs for revenue interfere with trade to some extent, that is not their purpose, and such interference is usually kept at a minimum. Their use is in no sense incompatible with a policy of free trade. Whether they represent a desirable kind of tax is another question, and we might point out that, unless they are levied chiefly on luxuries, they have the same drawback as a sales tax—namely, their burden falls more heavily on people of low income than on the well-to-do. On the other hand, the only justification for a protective tariff is a belief that it is in the public interest to keep people from buying goods abroad and to force them to buy at home.

Most economists oppose the levying of protective tariffs and the setting up of other trade barriers designed to limit competition and maintain or raise prices. Studies of congressional hearings and debates indicate that protective tariffs are nearly always enacted as a result of political pressure from business and labor groups interested in the production of a certain product, and who expect to benefit from a reduction of foreign competition.

The Case against Protective Tariffs.   The basic argument against protective tariffs is that, by restricting international trade, they rob us of part of its benefits. Further, we emphasize again that free admission of imports is one of the most effective ways of expanding the foreign markets of home industries because it is payments for our imports that furnish foreigners with most of the funds with which to buy our exports.

When one country institutes tariffs, it is likely that other countries will follow. The result will be a contracting spiral of trade, making all countries worse off. That is precisely what happened in the Great Depression of 1929 to 1933 (see Figure 19.2). As one country after another instituted tariffs to protect jobs at home—the United States instituted the infamous Smoot-Hawley tariff—trade declined, and the entire world fell into a serious economic depression.

The Arguments in Favor of Protective Tariffs.   The advocates of protective tariffs support their point of view with a number of plausible arguments: the home-market argument, the high-wages argument, the infant-industry argument, and the self-sufficiency argument.

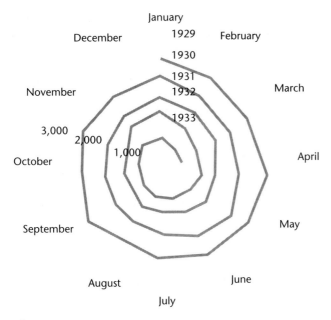

Figure 19.2

The contracting spiral of world trade, 1929 to 1933. Total imports of 75 countries (monthly values in terms of old U.S. gold dollars in millions). (Source: Original diagram by League of Nations.)

Home-Market Argument. One of the most effective of the claims made by the protectionists is the home-market argument. According to this reasoning, a tariff that keeps out foreign goods increases the market for U.S. goods and thereby increases home profits and employment. Undoubtedly there is some truth in this contention if we consider only short periods of time, but, as we have already pointed out, the final result is that a home market is created for some goods at the expense of losing a foreign market for others. This loss of the foreign market comes all the faster because, when we raise our tariffs on their goods, other countries retaliate by raising their tariffs on our goods. Meanwhile, as we have seen, U.S. consumers pay higher prices or receive inferior products.

High-Wages Argument. A second claim that protectionists make is expressed by the high-wages argument. They assert that the tariff maintains the U.S. wage level and the U.S. standard of living by protecting our workers from having to compete with cheap foreign labor. This argument is also plausible, but a little analysis and observation robs it of most of its force. In the first place, if a tariff makes possible higher wages, it does so only by enabling producers to sell their products at a higher price. This may benefit one group of employers and workers, but it reduces the purchasing power and standard of living of all others who must buy the product. If this kind of price raising were applied to a great many products, the general reduction in standards of living might be serious.

Infant-Industry Argument. A third defense of the protective tariff is the infant-industry argument. Those who advance it often disclaim any wish to give permanent tariff protection to an industry not able to survive without it. But, they say, a small new industry in the United States cannot hope to produce at as low a cost as an old, established industry abroad. Let us give it protection until it can get established and grow. Eventually it may become more efficient than its foreign competitors. If so, it can provide consumers with goods at reduced prices, and it will no longer need tariff protection.

The infant-industry argument has been advanced in the United States at one time or another in support of tariffs to protect various industries, including steel and dyes. In theory it is sound, but it is difficult to find any clear case in which it has been successfully applied—that is, where an industry has been established as a result of tariff protection and then has continued successfully without such protection.

Self-Sufficiency Argument.   A final argument for protective tariffs is that they make a country more self-sufficient and thus less dependent on foreign countries for essential commodities in time of war. This argument is sound in theory, but the situations to which it can usefully be applied in practice are probably rather limited. Though our experience in World War II emphasized the importance of having dependable supplies of vital raw materials, to keep such products out of the country by tariffs would not always result in building up home production. Moreover, many products once deemed essential are less so today because of greatly improved substitutes. Familiar examples are wool, tin, and natural rubber.

When there is real danger of a shortage of strategic materials in time of war, the best solution is probably to build up stockpiles. The U.S. government has followed this policy with a number of minerals and with oil, but many students of the problem believe that much of this stockpiling has been unjustified and is a waste of the taxpayers' money.

Import Quotas

Another device for protecting home industries is the import quota. An **import quota** limits the quantity or the value of a commodity that can be brought into a country in a given period of time. For example, the government may decide to limit sugar imports to 2 million tons a year, and it may decide to assign definite parts of this quota to specified foreign countries. Usually, import quotas, like protective tariffs, are imposed to keep out foreign goods for the benefit of domestic producers, but sometimes they are imposed chiefly to limit payments to foreign countries in order to conserve limited supplies of foreign currency.

Anti-Japanese sentiment being actively expressed by U.S. lawmakers.

Many advocates of freer trade consider quotas more objectionable than tariffs. For one thing, though quotas restrict trade, they bring no revenue to the government of the importing country as a tariff would. But for those who wish to restrict imports, quotas have certain advantages over tariffs. Often they do not require special legislation but instead may be imposed or changed by administrative decrees. Moreover, a quota can be fixed to admit a definite amount of a commodity, whereas if a protective tariff is levied, there is no way of knowing just how much of it will enter.

Beginning in the late 1970s there was great concern in the United States about competition from Japanese producers, especially in the auto industry. In response, Japan and the United States negotiated a quota limiting the number of automobiles exported to the United States. Similar quotas were instituted on South Korean shoes. These trade restrictions helped the U.S. automobile and shoe industries, but they hurt average U.S. consumers by raising the price of these goods. Economists generally believe that international competition is a necessary force, holding down wages and prices in the United States. If the

U.S. industries cannot stand up to international competition, then they must lower their wages, become more efficient, or both.

Over time, more and more U.S. industries sought the protection of tariffs, quotas, and other devices because the United States found that it was importing many more goods than it was exporting. Wages in foreign countries such as Taiwan were so low that many foreign goods could sell much more cheaply in the United States than could similar goods made in the United States. As this kind of trade made the foreign country, say Taiwan, more prosperous, its wage level rose. Then another foreign country, such as China, whose wages were even lower than those in Taiwan, began to supplant not only goods made in the United States but also goods made in Taiwan for export to the United States. In this way, some advantages and disadvantages of exporting and importing get passed around, as in a game of musical chairs.

Removing Trade Restrictions

Most economists believe that if trade could flow freely and securely through the world, there would be a great expansion of its total volume and that in the long run all nations would be more prosperous. There would be less talk of have-not countries and less need for foreign aid because every country would have free access to the markets and raw materials of the world. The average price of consumer goods would be lower everywhere. Nothing would contribute more to the expansion of world trade than removal of the great mass of restrictions that have been placed on it by government action. But as we saw earlier, decreasing these restrictions will be a slow and tortuous process.

Some steps have already been taken. The Reciprocal Trade Agreements Act of 1934 empowered the president to make reciprocal trade agreements and to reduce tariff duties by as much as 50 percent in return for trade concessions by other countries. This act was extended in 1947 through the **General Agreement on Trade and Tariffs (GATT)**, an agreement in which most Western nations agreed to a mutual effort to reduce trade barriers. Countries met every so often under GATT in order to reduce trade restrictions. In the mid-1990s, GATT was replaced by the **World Trade Organization (WTO)**, an international organization designed to foster trade among countries.

Every two years a ministerial conference is held in which all the WTO member countries, close to 150, make decisions on all matters of trade agreements. This includes launching negotiations for new agreements, which begin when members see limits to their existing rules. Member countries negotiate, during a certain period of time, on many trade issues simultaneously; this period of negotiation is called a "trade round." The ninth round, the Doha Development Round, was started during the fourth WTO conference, held in Qatar in 2001. This round is specifically meant to help poor countries; for the first time, development issues are at the core of a round. Negotiations in this round have been contentious and the successful completion of it was in doubt in early 2004.

The slow going in decreasing world trade restrictions was accompanied by the creation of a number of free trade areas, the most prominent of which are the **European Union (EU)**—the economic customs union of a number of European states (see box, p. 432)—and the North American Free Trade Agreement involving the United States, Canada, and Mexico. These agreements eliminate trade barriers among member countries and establish common barriers against nonmember nations. Economists, who generally favor free trade, are of two minds about these associations. They favor associations because they reduce barriers among countries, but they fear that the associations make it harder to achieve a worldwide reduction in barriers.

Globalization and Trade Restrictions

The late 1990s and early 2000s were marked by significant demonstrations against **globalization**—the integration of various world economies in terms of production, distribution, and finances. In a fully globalized world, global firms can move across national borders with ease. We are a long way from this, but global firms have played a major role in expanding international trade, and in doing so they have significantly changed the international economic environment. When workers in one country demand wages that are too high, these firms are in a position simply to transfer production to another country where workers are willing to work for lower wages. For instance, IBM recently announced that it would close some of its production facilities in the United States and move them to Asia where labor costs are significantly lower. Many other companies have done the same, and manufacturing in the United States has languished. Even with an economic recovery in 2003, few jobs were being created in the United States. In the early 2000s, it was not only manufacturing industries that were transferring jobs abroad, but it was also service industries. When you phone a company for technical assistance or to buy something, you are likely to speak to an operator in the Phillipines or India.

Global corporations affect the trading environment in another way. Say, for instance, that the United States were to establish unilateral quotas for Japanese cars. By becoming a global company and establishing production or assembly plants in the United States, a Japanese company could avoid the quotas and sell as many cars in the United States as it wished. That is exactly what happened in the 1980s when a number of foreign-car producers established assembly plants in the United States. In the late 1990s and early 2000s, it was U.S.-based global firms that were establishing production facilities elsewhere. This upset some U.S. workers who felt they were losing their jobs and others who felt that the firms were being imperialistic and paying unacceptably low wages to their foreign workers. These beliefs led to demonstrations against globalization.

*F*oreign Exchange

When the balance of payments is in imbalance, actual transfers of wealth from one country to another can usually be made only in the form of goods or an **international reserve currency**—a currency that all countries are willing to accept as final payment for obligations owed to it—such as the U.S. dollar. If for any reason a country cannot export enough goods to pay for its imports, it must settle the balance with a reserve currency or by borrowing abroad. When a country cannot meet its international obligations, it will be forced to depreciate its currency, which means it must lower the foreign exchange price of its currency. In the 1990s, the dollar was the only reserve currency, but in the early 2000s the euro was becoming an alternative reserve currency.

The Meaning of Foreign Exchange

Foreign exchange refers to the process of exchanging the money of one country for that of another and to the monies themselves. Thus the Japanese yen is called foreign exchange

The European Union

Countries in the EU, including new members.

The land mass known as Europe contains numerous countries, and usually the little group of islands off the western coast of France known as Great Britain is also included when we use the term *Europe*. These countries have joined together economically, and to a limited degree politically, to form the European Union (EU).

The EU began in 1958 when several governments of Europe, to expand their markets and increase competition, decided to form a common economic market, or customs union, in which the members agreed to allow free trade among themselves. The EU began with only six countries, but by 1998 had expanded to include fifteen countries—France, Germany, Italy, Great Britain, Ireland, Denmark, Belgium, the Netherlands, Luxembourg, Greece, Spain, Portugal, Austria, Finland, and Sweden.

In 1994 the European Parliament voted to include Norway in the EU, but Norwegian voters elected not to join. Ten more countries—Slovakia, Estonia, Poland, Cyprus, Latvia, Lithuania, Malta, Slovenia, Hungary, and the Czech Republic—will join soon, and eight more have applied to join. The inclusion of such a diversity of countries will present many problems, and the solution to all of those problems is by no means assured.

During the 1990s, the EU moved slowly toward the development of close economic and political ties among its member nations. In the late 1990s, it established a single currency, the euro, that was designed to replace the existing currencies. By 2002, twelve countries had adopted the euro as their currency. Other EU countries, such as Britain, continue to debate whether they want to adopt the euro or keep their current currency.

in the United States. Goods are generally paid for in terms of money, but in international trade the buyer uses one kind of money and the seller another, so the price that one pays and the other receives depends in part on the rate at which their two currencies exchange. For example, in 1980, when the price of a British pound in terms of dollars was $2.20, a setting of chinaware selling for 10 pounds in London would have cost a U.S. tourist $22. In 1985, when the pound had depreciated to $1.20, the same setting of chinaware would have cost a U.S. tourist only $12. In 2003 a pound cost about $1.68, so the chinaware would cost that tourist about $16.80.

In studying foreign exchange, we are concerned first of all with exchange rates and how they are determined. It is desirable for exchange rates between two countries to be at a level that will encourage trade. They should also be reasonably stable. Erratic fluctuations in exchange rates are a handicap to trade because they increase the uncertainty and risk involved in transactions that require time for their completion.

Fixed and Flexible Exchange Rate Systems

For many years before World War I, the principal trading countries of the world maintained monetary systems based on **fixed exchange rates,** exchange rates in which the relative values of the various currencies are established by agreement. (Under **flexible exchange rates,** in contrast, the government allows the market forces of supply and demand to fix the exchange rate of that country.) A fixed exchange rate system was achieved during this time by using the **gold standard,** a fixed exchange rate system in which the prices of the various currencies are set in relation to the price of gold. During the war, this standard broke down in most countries, and though it was revived for a time after the war, it suffered a second general breakdown with the coming of the Great Depression in the early 1930s.

When two or more countries are on the gold standard, only very small fluctuations can take place in the exchange rates between their currencies. Under the traditional gold standard, each country will exchange its paper money freely for a fixed amount of gold. When paper money and gold are freely interchangeable in each of two countries, the relative values of their currencies depend almost entirely on the relative amounts of gold they represent.

Let us suppose that the French franc once represented 4 grains of gold and the U.S. dollar 20 grains of gold.[1] Then a dollar would always exchange for approximately 5 francs. Slight variations in the exchange rate could still occur because of the cost of shipping gold. For example, though under the gold standard Americans could always exchange dollars in this country for a fixed amount of gold, in order to use this gold to obtain francs in Paris they would first have to pay the cost of shipping it to France.

The weakness of the gold standard was that, in order to maintain it, a government had to keep on hand enough gold to meet all demands for redeeming its currency. The advantage of this standard was that, as long as there was a determination to maintain it, it was an effective check on inflation. It forced a government to limit the expansion of bank deposits and the issue of paper money. Otherwise, demands for conversion of paper into gold would soon reach such a level that the government would be forced to stop redemption, thus automatically placing its money on a paper, or fiat, standard.

Paper Standards and the Gold Exchange Standard.   A **paper standard** is a system under which the basic monetary unit of a country is represented by engraved pieces of paper. These have value only because they are limited in quantity and, in the country of issue, are legal tender and acceptable in trade.

After World War II, the Western world initially went on a modified gold standard, under which countries were allowed to adjust their exchange rate (devalue) slightly (by no more than 10 percent), but no major devaluations were allowed without approval from other countries. The approval came from the **International Monetary Fund (IMF),** an international organization set up just after World War II, both to aid in the adjustment and stabilization of exchange rates and to bring about the development of free exchange markets. The IMF could help its members meet temporary exchange difficulties by lending them limited amounts of gold or redeemable foreign currency.

---

[1] Under the gold standard as it existed before World War I, U.S. gold coins actually contained 23.22 grains of pure gold per dollar, and French gold coins contained slightly less than one-fifth of this amount per franc. (A grain is equal to 1/7,000 of a pound.)

Though the IMF has not entirely lived up to the hopes of its founders, it has helped stabilize foreign exchange markets. The system worked well until 1958, when the United States stopped running a balance-of-payments surplus and began running a balance-of-payments deficit. This led to runs on the dollar in which foreign holders of dollars wanted gold for them.

From a Fixed System to Our Current System: The Dirty Float. In 1971 the foreign demand for gold was so great that the United States stopped convertibility, and our international exchange mechanism moved from a fixed exchange rate and a gold standard to flexible exchange rates. Under the new system, our reserves are no longer held only in gold, but are instead held in reserve currencies and a type of paper gold, or special drawing rights. These special drawing rights can now be used, within limits, for meeting international obligations, and they can be lent by the IMF to countries whose other reserves are being rapidly reduced by an adverse balance of payments.

Other countries can no longer get gold for dollars from the United States, but they can exchange dollars for U.S. goods. As the supply and demand for U.S. goods fluctuates, the supply and demand for U.S. currency fluctuates also, changing its relative price. Thus one month you might be able to buy an English pound for $1.60, and the next month it might cost $1.70. If that happens, we say the exchange rate of dollars for pounds has fallen from 1.6/1 to 1.7/1. In a perfectly flexible exchange rate system, the balance of payments must always be in equilibrium. Put another way, the supply of currency must always equal the demand for that currency. This follows from the definition of balance of payments as the relation of total payments made abroad to total payments received from abroad.

Actually, although the U.S. exchange rate system is generally a flexible rate system, it is not perfectly flexible. Every so often the United States and other countries enter into the foreign exchange markets to attempt to raise or lower the value of the dollar. This makes our exchange rate system a **dirty float**—a partially flexible exchange rate system through which every so often the government enters into the foreign exchange market to affect the exchange rate.

Problems of Flexible Exchange Rates. One of the problems facing the international flexible exchange rate system is the pressure of what can be called *hot money.* In the past, long-term investment has predominated, and capital flows among countries tended to be rather stable. With the continued development of computer technology for transfer of funds, however, in the last ten years short-term investments have become far more important. These short-term investments—sometimes called hot money—will flow in or out of a country at the slightest change in relative interest rates. On an average day, more than $200 billion may be traded in this way.

The last part of 1997 provides us with a vivid example of the problems hot money can present to countries. At that time, investors lost confidence in a number of Pacific Rim countries, such as Thailand and Korea, and moved their money out of those countries. This created a currency crisis for these countries. Emergency loans were arranged to prevent their exchange rates from falling precipitously, but these loans came with conditions that slowed growth in these countries for the remainder of the twentieth century. In 2003 the hot money was leaving the United States, increasing the demand for foreign currencies and decreasing the demand for dollars. The result was a significant fall in the value of the dollar.

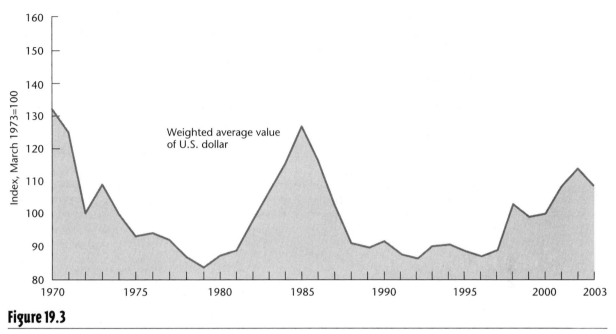

Figure 19.3

Fluctuations in the value of the dollar. (Source: Federal Reserve System.)

Fluctuations in the value of the dollar can be seen in Figure 19.3. You can see that the value of the dollar has recently been on a roller coaster track. Such fluctuations cause serious problems for U.S. companies, so how long the system of flexible exchange rates will continue to work is subject to debate, and you are likely to hear more of international financial problems in the future.

Conclusion

As you can see, there is much to be learned about international economic relations, and we have only touched the surface. The international economy is complicated and operates on faith and goodwill among nations. If countries each try to go their own way, instituting protective tariffs and other forms of protectionism, the entire world will likely suffer. Therefore, cooperation is as essential in the international economy as it is in the domestic economy.

What makes international economic issues all the more important is their close relationship to international political relations. Countries that trade together generally do not fight wars. Thus international economic and political relations will probably determine the direction the world takes in moving toward peace or moving toward war.

Key Points

- Balance of trade refers to the relation of our total exports to our total imports. Balance of payments refers to the relation of total payments made abroad to total payments received from abroad.
- Trade enables a country to obtain better products cheaper, but trade can hurt the domestic producers of those products.
- Protective tariffs restrict international trade and rob us of part of its benefits. This argument is countered by the home-market argu-

ment, the high-wages argument, the infant-industry argument, and the self-sufficiency argument.
- In a fixed exchange rate system, the relative values of currencies are set by agreement; in a flexible exchange rate system, the relative values of currencies are set by the market.
- The United States is the largest debtor nation in the world; we owe trillions of dollars more to foreigners than foreigners owe to us.

Some Important Terms

balance of payments (421)
balance of trade (421)
cartel (421)
dirty float (434)
European Union (EU) (430)
fixed exchange rate (433)
flexible exchange rate (433)
foreign exchange (431)

General Agreement on Trade and Tariffs (GATT) (430)
global corporation (421)
globalization (431)
gold standard (433)
import quota (429)
International Monetary Fund (IMF) (433)

international reserve currency (431)
invisible items of trade (422)
paper standard (433)
tariff (427)
visible items of trade (422)
World Trade Organization (WTO) (430)

Questions for Review and Discussion

1. What are the three main advantages of international trade? What are some disadvantages?
2. Exports depend on imports, and vice versa. Why is this true?
3. Is it more desirable for a country to build up its visible or its invisible trade? Explain.
4. Is a favorable balance of trade possible? Is it desirable? Explain.
5. State and evaluate the principal arguments for protective tariffs.
6. The use of quotas to limit imports has been spreading recently. Are import quotas less damaging to consumers than tariffs? Why or why not?

7. Explain the impact of the formation of OPEC on the international economy.
8. In what ways can a country meet an excess of foreign payments over foreign receipts? Can it meet such an excess indefinitely? Explain.
9. Besides the example of Japanese car assembly given in the text, can you think of some examples of foreign investment in the United States?
10. What is the nature and purpose of the European Union?
11. Why were foreign exchange rates stable under the gold standard?
12. What is the purpose of the International Monetary Fund?

𝓘nternet Questions

1. Look up the exchange rate at www.economagic. com/fedstl.htm for U.S. dollars to the euro for the latest date and then for a year before. How did the rate change?
2. From U.S. census statistics, found at www. census.gov/foreign-trade/www/statistics.html, go to Country Data, then Trade Balance by Country, and pick one. What is the current trade balance of that country? What was it in 1995?
3. Using http://dataweb.usitc.gov/scripts/tariff 2000.asp, the U.S. International Trade Commission's database, find out what the tariff is per liter of beer. What preferential tariff program is applicable to beer?
4. Using www.worldbank.org/data/countrydata/ countrydata.html, pick a country under Profile Tables. What is its trade in goods as a percentage of GDP for the latest year? What is the trend for the last three years? Compare it to another country.
5. Go to www.jobsabroad.com/search.cfm and search India for a job listing for a customer service trainer. What is the job description and for whom is the position?

𝓕or Further Study

Cameron, Maxwell A., and Brian W. Tomlin, *The Making of NAFTA: How the Deal Was Done,* Ithaca, NY: Cornell University Press, 2000.

DeSoto, Hernando, *The Mystery of Capital: Why Capitalism Triumphs in the West and Fails Everywhere Else,* New York: Basic Books, 2000.

Evans, David, and Richard Schmalensee, *Paying with Plastic: The Digital Revolution in Buying and Borrowing,* Cambridge, MA: MIT Press, 2000.

Garten, Jeffrey E., *The Big Ten: The Big Emerging Markets and How They Will Change Our Lives,* New York: Basic Books, 1997.

International Bank for Reconciliation and Development, annual reports, Washington, DC.

Milner, Chris, and Robert Read, *Trade Liberalisation, Competition, and the WTO,* Cheltenham, UK; Edward Elgar, 2002.

Pomeranz, Kenneth, and Stephen Topik, *The World That Trade Created: Society, Culture, and the World Economy, 1400–the Present,* Armonk, NY: Sharpe, 2000.

Steger, Manfred B., *Globalism: The New Market Ideology,* Lanham, MD: Rowman & Littlefield, 2002.

United Nations: Various agencies of the UN from time to time publish reports and statistics on world economic conditions in particular nations. Write to United Nations Office of Public Information, New York, NY 10017.

WWW   Bureau of Economic Analysis   www.bea.doc. gov/bea/glance.htm

WWW   The European Union   www.eurunion.org

WWW   The International Monetary Fund   www.imf.org

WWW   Universal Exchange Rate Converter   www.xe. com/ucc

WWW   USA Trade Online   www.census.gov/foreign-trade/www

WWW   U.S. International Trade Commission   www. usitc.gov

WWW   The World Trade Organization   www.wto.org

Yergin, Daniel, and Joseph Stanislaw, *The Commanding Heights: The Battle between Government and the Marketplace That Is Remaking the Modern World,* New York: Simon & Schuster, 1998.

Zachary, Pascal, *Global Me: Comparative Edge and the New Cosmopolitans,* New York: Public Affairs, 2000.

*T*he Political Economies of Developing Countries

After reading this chapter, you should be able to:

- List six problems facing all developing countries
- Explain why each of those problems is so difficult to solve
- List three suggestions you might give to a potential leader of a developing country
- List and discuss the various policy options of developing countries
- Discuss developing countries' problems with specific reference to the cases of China, Mexico, and Uganda

A poor country is poor because it is poor.

—Ragnar Nurske

A country becomes rich because it is already rich.

—P. Chaunu

There are over 190 countries in the world; of these, about 56 might be considered developed. Others are called **developing countries**—countries that are still in various stages of economic and political development. Developing countries are called developing because they have far lower incomes than developed countries. As a group, they make up about 80 percent of the world's population but consume only about 25 percent of the world's output. Table 20.1 shows some other dimensions of the schism between developed and developing countries. As you can see, people in developing countries live shorter lives and earn less money.

Developing countries can be divided into a variety of groupings. The position of many Latin American countries, such as Mexico, Brazil, and Argentina, which have developed to some degree, is better than that of some others. A second group of developing countries, primarily those in the Pacific Rim, have managed to maintain rather rapid economic growth. These include South Korea, Taiwan, Singapore, and Hong Kong, which have had high growth rates (over 7 percent) over the last thirty years. The growth rate in Pacific Rim countries slowed appreciably in the late 1990s as these countries experienced financial crises. Despite these crises, their economies are still considered relatively strong. A number of these Pacific Rim countries have grown sufficiently fast so that they are sometimes considered to have left the developing country classification and entered the "newly industrialized country" classification. The worst performers in terms of economic growth have been the countries of Africa, which for the most part have not grown. Some have even seen their total output per capita decline. To differentiate these less developed

Table 20.1

The Schism between Developed and Developing Countries in the Early 2000s

	HIGHER-INCOME DEVELOPED COUNTRIES	LOWER-INCOME DEVELOPING COUNTRIES
Population	1 billion	4 to 5 billion
Per capita GDP	$25,000	$2,500
Life expectancy	79 years	64 years
Literacy rate	99%	60%

Source: Projections and estimates based on World Bank data.

countries in the early 2000s, the UN created a new category, least developed country, with per capita GDPs of under $900. The forty-nine countries listed below fall into this category. For a country profile, go to http://r0.unctad.org/en/pub/poiteiiad3.en.htm.

Afghanistan
Angola
Bangladesh
Benin
Bhutan
Burkina Faso
Burundi
Cambodia
Cape Verde
Central African
    Republic
Chad
Comoros
Democratic
    Republic of
    Congo
Djibouti
Equatorial
    Guinea
Eritrea
Ethiopia
Gambia
Guinea
Guinea Bissau
Haiti
Kiribati
Lao People's
    Democratic
    Republic
Lesotho
Liberia
Madagascar
Malawi
Maldives
Mali
Mauritania
Mozambique
Myanmar
Nepal
Niger
Rwanda
Samoa
Sao Tome and
    Principe
Senegal
Sierra Leone
Solomon Islands
Somalia
Sudan
Togo
Tuvalu
Uganda
United Republic
    of Tanzania
Vanuatu
Yemen
Zambia

The different performance of these various groups is a result, in part, of their contrasting policies. East Asian countries have generally adopted policies to promote exports and have worked hard to maintain competitive exchange rates. Many of the African countries have not. Another difference concerns the government and political structure. Asian governments have been strong and stable; African governments have been weak and unstable; Latin American governments' stability has generally fallen between the two. Stable governments are a requirement of economic growth.

The economic growth of developing countries has varied. Figure 20.1 shows the growth rates of developing countries compared with those of industrialized countries. Since 1965 developing countries have grown at a faster rate than industrial countries, but, in absolute income, they have fallen more and more behind.

Dead Rwandans washed up on the shores of Lake Victoria—victims of internal political strife.

Developing countries were once called backward, but, on belated recognition of the value judgment inherent in that term, we began to call them underdeveloped, and, on belated recognition of the value judgment inherent in that term, we now call them developing. Although developing is preferable to backward, even the current term embodies a value judgment and suggests that some day developing nations will turn into, or that they want to turn into, developed nations. That is not necessarily the case; it is possible that some countries may not want to develop. One of the reasons is that the term *developing* refers primarily to economies, not cultures. So-called developing countries can have highly refined cultures that are inconsistent with modern economies. It would be ethnocentric of us to think that their cultures are any less refined than ours, or that they should want to become like us.

What is less developed are their economies and their systems of government. Those developing countries that do not develop do not have the stable governments and social systems

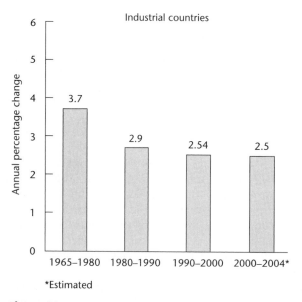

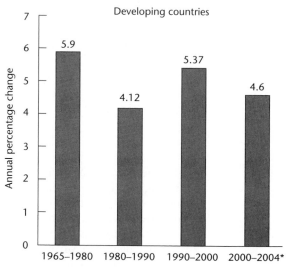

Figure 20.1

Economic growth rate among regions of the world. (Source: International Monetary Fund.)

that hold a country together. In another world, that would not necessarily present a problem, but in today's world, without stable governments it is unlikely that they will be able to maintain their culture or their society as they currently exist. They will simply be overrun by our culture. That is not good or bad; that's just the way it is. Thus developing countries find themselves at a point of choice.

Problems of Developing Countries

To summarize and review much of what we have previously written on politics, economics, and their interrelationship, in this chapter we consider some of the problems facing developing countries, both in terms of their choice of social, economic, and political systems and of their attempts to maintain whatever such systems they have chosen. Although these problems are not unique to developing countries—many of the same problems are faced by developed countries—the severity of the problem in developing countries makes them worth emphasizing.

In looking at their choices, we would like to consider the full range of possibilities open to them. Given that there are over 190 countries in the world, it would seem they have a wide range to choose from existing societies, but that is not the case. The various societies have not developed separately; they have been influenced by the other societies. Thus we now have two main economic systems, capitalism and socialism, and two main systems of government, democracy and autocracy. These systems do not necessarily span the range of possibilities, and probably many forms of society have not been tried. So we must keep an open mind about new possibilities.

The Political Consensus Problem

The central problem facing nonindustrial nations is what might be called the political consensus problem. **Political consensus** means sufficient political order and government efficacy so that the leaders of the state are able to rule. The political consensus problem is the following: Any state that is to operate as a nation-state must have a political consensus. The ability to rule can be derived from military might, force of personality, or cultural and social mores, but it must exist if the country is to develop.

In the United States, we have information availability, an educated public, cultural unity, and a long tradition of democracy. That tradition limits individuals' actions and holds our society together. For example, when a political party loses an election, it does not declare the election null and void; it accepts the election results. Developing countries seldom have all of these qualities, and they often do not have any of them. In those countries, it is unlikely that the democratic model will serve them well in the present, although it may provide a goal for the future. Generally the developing state evolves into, at best, a partial democracy, or an autocracy.

When the ability of autocracy to rule is based on military might, the military has a final say on what is and is not to be done. Haiti is an example. The regime of President François Duvalier lasted for twenty-five years, and when he died in 1986 he was followed by his nineteen-year-old son, J. C. Duvalier, who called himself "President for life" but was overthrown by the army within a year. The military tolerated a temporary government until 1988, when a new president was chosen, who was overthrown the same year.

From then until 2000, Haiti had nine presidencies, including three-time Jean Bertrand Aristide, who won a disputed election that was boycotted by the opposition. Aristide supporters regularly clash in the streets with antigovernment demonstrators. Almost all of the presidents were members of the military or initially chosen through strong military influence, and were overthrown by the military when the army found them unsatisfactory. Aristide is a civilian, but it has been through significant military influence that he was chosen, overthrown, replaced, and returned.

Both autocracy and democracy present problems for developing countries. Democracies often lead to continual changes of government, and the general population's will is not always what is best for a country. Autocracies often lead to arbitrary and capricious rule. The old saying that power corrupts is not without merit. However, when leaders are not strong, power bases often develop outside the state framework. These power bases have their own means of enforcement; they might require payment for protection and make their own rules. Drug dealers in Colombia are an example. In 1985, when the Colombian Supreme Court cracked down on drug dealers, the head of the Supreme Court in that nation was killed. Then one of the many terrorist groups in Colombia invaded the Hall of Justice, and in a shoot-out with the military, twelve more justices were killed. The violence has continued. Americas Watch, a U.S.-based human rights group, has reported that over the past few years, there have been more than 24,000 murders in Colombia, of which almost 4,000 were committed by terrorist groups formed by drug dealers. These included assassinations of senators and a finance minister.

The Corruption Problem

Closely associated with the lack of an established government, one that has inherent legitimacy, is the problem of corruption. Corruption is a way of life in developing countries. For example, in Mexico City, when you park your car a police officer might ask you for a protection payment. If you want to import an item, you often must bribe the appropriate authorities to obtain permission. No bribe, no importing. In the Philippines, President Marcos amassed a fortune estimated at $5 billion to $10 billion, although his presidential salary was only about $6,000 per year. Either he was an awfully shrewd investor or he was heavily involved in skimming money from the Philippine economy and government. Marcos was forced to leave the country in 1986, but the corruption problems continued. The Philippines then went through three short administrations, with the thirteenth president, Joseph Estrada, being impeached because of kickbacks and corruption. This led to the 2000 election of then Vice President Gloria Arroyo (the daughter of Dosdado P. Macapagal, the president before Marcos) with the hope that the corruption problems would end. However, in 2003, with her administration embroiled in graft and corruption scandals, Arroyo announced that she would not run for reelection in 2004.

The examples of the corruption problem are wide ranging and are not tied to any particular country or party within that country. What we call corruption here may be simply accepted practice there. We see no easy answer to the problem of corruption, or even a complicated answer.

No system clearly offers a way around corruption. Only a deep-seated conviction built into the social mores offers some help, a conviction that regardless of the temptations, the leader will not take advantage of the situation to amass power and wealth. This is a bit like sitting you in a room of a hundred beautiful people of the opposite sex and telling you not to talk to any of them.

In Cambodia in the late 1970s, the Khmer Rouge government killed millions of people as it attempted to force resettlement to bring about economic and social change.

The Economic Problem

When income is below the starvation level, some form of economic development seems necessary. At that point the question is not, Should a country develop? but, how? The answer is unclear. To develop, a country requires savings and investment, but when you don't have enough to eat, how can you save or invest? Therefore, at below a certain level of income, societies find themselves in a vicious cycle from which there is no easy escape—and sometimes no escape at all. They must try, somehow, to pull themselves up by their own bootstraps to reach a point where they begin to grow.

To achieve takeoff into economic growth, a country needs to raise the level of investment to a certain minimum proportion of the national income. What is also essential, and what must develop along with any substantial increase of savings and investment, is an understanding on the part of the people of how a successful industrial society operates. The citizens must then be able and willing to develop the attitudes, the patterns of behavior, and the initiative that are required for vigorous economic growth. Simply pouring in capital is not enough.

Sometimes because of lack of understanding, or to satisfy the pride of politicians, countries striving for economic growth spend their available capital on the wrong things. They may, for example, produce impressive government projects such as national airlines or power dams, when what would help most, initially, might be greater production of food. Economic growth will proceed faster if it is balanced, if a foundation is gradually laid for a broad expansion of output. Before too many new airlines are founded or power plants are built, increased provision should be made for certain types of education and training; basic transportation, communication, and banking facilities should be provided; and efforts should be made to raise standards of living in order to increase both the welfare and productivity of workers and also to make possible a significant amount of saving and investment.

As is always the case, social, political, and economic factors interact. For example, many companies simply will not invest in certain foreign countries because of the unstable governments there, and they are unwilling to pay the bribes necessary to carry on business in such countries. Here we can see the clash of two different cultures. U.S. firms would be breaking U.S. law if they were to pay bribes to foreign government officials, yet without paying bribes they could not operate in some countries.

Foreign Aid and Trade Barriers.   When countries cannot pull themselves up by their own bootstraps by developing internal savings and investment, they have another option. They can seek foreign infusion of investment, which can come in the form of private foreign investment or governmental **foreign aid,** which consists of financial and practical assistance given by one country to another, especially by a technologically advanced country to a less developed one. In recent years, both public and private aid have decreased.

The World Bank

Various international institutions have been developed to assist developing countries. One of these is the World Bank. The **World Bank** is an international organization whose goal is to help in world development through making loans and giving out economic advice. It receives funds primarily from developed countries, and makes loans primarily to developing countries. The World Bank was formed in 1944, and since that time it has provided low-interest loans to many developing countries. It has a staff of about 11,000.

The World Bank's initial loans focused on large projects such as dams and power plants. The World Bank received strong criticism in the early 1990s for the nature of its loans. Critics said that the loans were too heavily focused on large projects that hurt the environment. In 1994,

when the bank celebrated its fiftieth anniversary, it responded to the criticisms by saying that it would change its lending practices. It reiterated its basic goal of promoting broad-based economic growth that benefits the poor, but it said that to achieve that goal it would increase its investment in human, as opposed to physical, resources. Specifically, it would increase its support of educational, nutritional, and family planning programs. It also stated that it would concentrate on environmentally sound physical investments, and that it would help fund programs that built on and expanded the role of women in development. Since that time it has changed its lending practices, but it has continued to be the target of criticism because of its association with free trade and because protestors feel it is still not doing enough.

The decrease in aid has caused developing countries to call for increases in aid in the future. But more aid is unlikely to be forthcoming from governments. Over the last sixty years, in response to the developing world's need for development, the United States has given foreign aid at the rate of about one-half of 1 percent of our total output. The results

Anti-WTO protests provide an example of how social, political, and economic factors interact.

of that aid have been mixed. Much of it has not gone for humanitarian purposes; rather, it has had political and military purposes.

The biggest recipient of U.S. foreign aid is Israel, and that aid has been provided out of blatantly political motives. Even aid that was given for humanitarian purposes has undergone strong criticism. Much of that aid was eaten up in bureaucracy and skimmed by foreign politicians; thus it never reached its intended recipients. In response to these criticisms, more and more aid is flowing to *nongovernmental agencies*—so much so that they have acquired the acronym **NGA.**

Foreign aid and investment are only part of the answer. An equally, or even more important, part of the economics answer is removing developed countries' trade barriers. The reality is that developed countries are not very open to exports from developing countries. For example, the EU provides enormous subsidies to its farmers who then export subsidized farm products to countries that could have produced them expensively. In addition, the EU maintains tariffs against many farm imports. This combination of policies makes it difficult for developing countries to develop or expand their farm exports, countering much of the benefit of EU foreign aid. The United States is not as bad as the EU in this regard, but it still has significant trade barriers built into its farm policy. Combining all policies that help or hurt developing countries, the Centre for Global Development ranked twenty-one rich countries in a "Commitment to Development Index." The United States came in next to last.

The Historical Legacy of Colonialism.   When Western governments' budgets are tight, the amount of foreign aid they give often comes under attack. Opponents of aid argue that the developed countries owe nothing to the developing countries. Supporters of aid, on the other hand, point to history in providing justification not only for giving aid, but also for giving even more than we do. The historical argument goes as follows: Western countries colonized the developing countries, creating artificial political entities that brought together incompatible ethnic groups, and extracted what they could from those countries. These developing countries were not allowed to develop in their own way. In following these policies, the West created the problems that developing countries face today. Given the West's role in creating many of the problems that developing countries face, supporters of foreign aid argue that the West has a moral obligation to assist them.

The Debt Problem

The reliance on private investment, including loans from U.S. and other banks, has created a new problem for many developing countries: the debt problem. Private investment and loans must be serviced, which means that interest must be paid.

In the 1980s, the problem of the **international debt**—the amount of outstanding loans among different nations—grew in importance. The large borrowings of the developing countries throughout the 1970s, together with high interest rates, made it almost impossible for a number of developing countries to meet their debt obligations.

In the 1990s that debt problem was greatly reduced by **debt restructuring**—allowing repayment of debt over extended periods of time—and a fall in the world interest rate. In 2001 the IMF granted debt relief for twenty-two countries, continuing the trend of debt restructuring. Still, particular developing countries had large debt overhangs, and paying off that debt will remain a problem through the first decade of the 2000s.

The Population Problem

Even if they begin to grow, developing countries will not necessarily escape the vicious cycle we have discussed, because they face another large problem. Put simply, as long as population continues to grow at current rates, these countries are going to have enormous, perhaps insurmountable, difficulties in increasing their **per capita output,** the total output divided by the country's population. The vicious cycle that Thomas Malthus[1] wrote about is very real to developing countries. All developing countries face a serious problem of population. Although with sufficient technological development there is no limit to the amount of production one can get from land, one must overcome the initial investment hurdle, which will provide them with the means to make that technological progress.

The Brain Drain Problem

As bad as the preceding problems are, they do not leave developing countries without hope. The emergence of nation-states and their development show that the transition to developed states is possible. But before we say, We grew, why don't you? we should consider that the nation-states of Western society enjoyed significant advantages over currently developing countries.

In the 1700s, when Western economies developed, travel was limited and individuals tended to stay home and to consider their life in relation to their society. The bright, dynamic individuals modified their society, but because their lives were in their society, their modifications were generally small and consistent with that society's culture. That is often not the way it happens in developing countries today. Developing countries have a **brain drain,** a process in which the individuals who could make a country develop leave that country.

Having attended school in Great Britain and Germany, one of the authors came to know a number of the brightest and best students of a variety of developing countries. They were sent away to school because they were so outstanding. They often do well, but in doing so they become immersed in the developed culture.

When they finish their studies, these students are often presented with a choice between two totally different economies and cultures. One offers enormous amounts of material goods, intellectual challenge for which their training has prepared them, and excitement. The other offers traditional values from which their foreign education has taught them to escape, material shortages, and enormous intellectual challenges for which they have no preparation. Faced with such choices, many decide to remain in the developed country or to join an international agency that pays as well as a good job in the United States. The result is the brain drain.

Consider the brain drain problem from the perspective of an outside observer. Doctors trained in India, where doctors are in short supply, are constantly immigrating to the United States, where there are many more doctors per capita; the same with engineers. The United States benefits enormously from this immigration. Immigrants constitute up to 20 percent of all U.S. medical doctors and 23 percent of all Ph.D.s, and account for 26

---

[1]See Chapter 5 for a discussion of Thomas Malthus and his theories.

percent of all patents issued. Removing the best and the brightest from a society makes it that much harder for the society to develop.

Mission Impossible: Advice to a Potential Leader

What, then, should a developing country do?

Neither we nor any other social scientist knows what to do. Advice has ranged over the gamut of possibilities. The results have been so bad that we are going to deviate from standard textbook policy: We do not tell you what the experts think should be done. Instead, we are asking you what you think should be done. So, we hereby appoint you as social advisor to Hopelandia. (If you have foreign students in your class, you might find that the exercise is not so far-fetched. Many of them are the future leaders of their countries.)

Your task, should you decide to accept, is to prepare a development plan and de-termine what set of policies a developing country should follow to solve the problems mentioned earlier. To make the assignment easier, we begin by providing you with some general advice that we would give a potential leader, a set of policy options to help for-mulate your thinking about the problems, and some initial background information on three developing countries.

Keep an Open Mind.   The first piece of advice to an advisor to a developing country is don't rule out options arbitrarily and do use all available knowledge of the interrelation-ships of various aspects of social science. Don't try to emulate any specific developed country. Do what is right for your country, because what works for one country might not work for another. For example, in Uganda there are enormous tribal differences, and individuals' allegiance is to their tribe rather than to the larger society or to their country. Voting almost invariably means voting for whichever candidate is from one's tribe. Within such a situation, democracy is unstable. For democracy to succeed, the allegiance must be to the entire country, not to an individual subsection of that country.

Recognize the Difficulties.   The second piece of advice is to set goals and priorities with full recognition of the difficulties that the development plan will encounter. Should a country grow economically, or should it instead set different goals, such as maintaining its tradition and furthering its religion? In the Middle East, the Shiite Muslims tend to be fundamentalists who believe that economic growth means the infusion of Western values into their society and a worsening, not an improvement, of the society. Therefore the goals they choose have little to do with economics other than as a means to the end of preserving their religion and their way of life. In other countries, economic growth is weighted more heavily, and although maintaining tradition always plays some role, when faced with the inevitable trade-off, these countries, such as South Korea, will make choices based on economic development.

Maintain Your Idealism.   A final and most important piece of advice is to maintain your idealism. Unless you love your country and are willing to use whatever power you have for the good of the country as well as you understand that good, and not for your own gain or that of your friends, then forget about being a leader and give your support to an individual who will.

O ptions of Developing Countries

Developing countries have a variety of options to deal with their almost impossible problems. Let's briefly consider their options.

Political Options

Political options include democracy, autocracy, and various shades in between the two. Somehow the system chosen must be one that combines the various ethnic and regional groupings into a complete whole and makes them feel that they belong together, rather than that they are blood rivals who must be continuously fighting with each other. The policies you suggest to meet this necessity will determine the type of policies you can advocate in regard to the economic problem.

Economic Options

The range of economic options goes from (1) a type of unfettered capitalism, in which the government enters into the economy as little as possible; to (2) socialism, in which individuals can operate in certain areas, but the government plays a much stronger role in guiding the choice of each individual decision; to (3) communism, in which the government plays an extremely important role in all areas of the economy and owns both the land and the means of production; to (4) some new kind of economic organization that you think of. The choices are interrelated.

Foreign Policy Options

As these countries develop, they aren't developing in a vacuum. Other countries are playing roles, at times stabilizing a regime, at other times destabilizing a regime, depending on whether the individuals guiding these regimes are following their own stated goals, and on whether the particular major power can live with the operation of the regime to which it has lent support. Therefore, you have to choose a foreign policy.

During the cold war, developing countries could play the former Soviet Union against the United States. With the breakup of the Soviet Union, this strategy has become less of an option. The United States and its allies are about all there is left to flirt with. That's why in the early 2000s most development plans are democratic, market-oriented plans.

Population Options

You need to ask yourself some questions about population. First, do you have a population problem? Facing this issue is one of the most difficult tasks confronting human beings, whether on a personal level, a national level, an international level, or—now that space colonization is not just a wild, science-fiction dream—a cosmic level. Second, if you have an overpopulation problem (and in the countries we are talking about here, let us hint that you may likely have overpopulation problems), then do you go in and direct people not to have children, or at least to limit the number to one or two? How would you do this? Third, having made the decision which way to go, and how to go that way, what consequences can you foresee will have to be dealt with when the results of your policy begin to show up in the census figures?

The Brain Drain Option

Should you encourage your top students to go abroad? If you do, how can you be sure they'll come home again to use their new skills in the country that sent them to be educated? Suppose you decide the other way, that is, to keep your most promising youth at home. In that case, how will you foster new ideas, youthful enthusiasm, and the importation of valuable ideas and methods that have already been developed in other countries (you don't want to reinvent the wheel)?

Who Will Be the Next Leader?

What qualities do you want and what qualities does your country need in a leader? Should there be a committee or coalition of some kind, rather than a single leader? In either case, how will leadership qualities be developed? How will leadership qualities be recognized? What will the leader, or leaders, do once in power? How should the leadership be controlled, if it should be controlled? How can you search for and pick out the leaders in your country? Perhaps that search won't be fruitful, or not as fruitful as you expect. Should you look for imported talent? Where should you look for it, if this is your choice? Ask the same questions about the imported talent that you asked about possible homegrown leaders.

You could, of course, ask many other questions, but these few should start you on the way.

Case Studies

To really get a sense of the problems facing developing countries and their options, we need to look at specific experiences of real-world countries. Thus we conclude this chapter with three case studies.

China

Of all the case studies to consider, China is a must. It is the largest and most populous developing country in the world, and it has approximately as large an area as the United States. Its main language is Mandarin Chinese, although there are eight separate dialects. Ostensibly it is a federal republic with twenty-three provinces, five autonomous regions, and, since July 1997, Hong Kong. Its political regime rules a socialist state, with the Communist Party of China specifying the state ideology.

In 1989 strong student pressures for democracy were crushed, and political control by the Communist Party has held firm into the early 2000s. The box on page 452 gives an overview of the statistics relevant to China.

Beginning in the late 1980s, China has undergone an enormous economic liberalization with the introduction of markets and market incentives to try to encourage

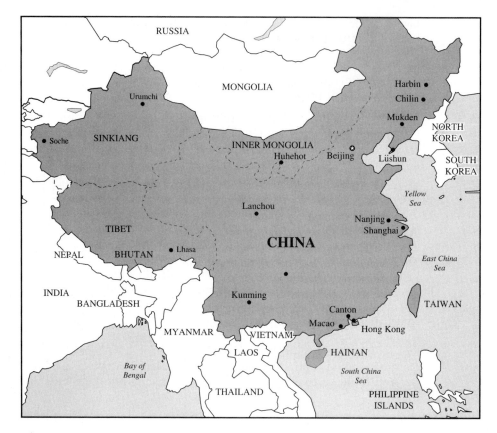

China.

individual production without generating what China believes are the negative side effects of markets. It has moved away from central planning, although in what it considers key goods, government production still rules.

The freeing of the market in many sectors has led to China's becoming the world's fastest growing economy at the turn of the century, creating a substantial middle class and many "newly rich" people. This income growth has been highly skewed, and the large majority of Chinese remain poor.

The key to China's future will be the manner in which the Communist leadership reconciles political reform and liberalization with economic progress. If China can sustain its economic performance, it will become a vital player in the international system: Given the present trajectories, it seems set to join the United States as a genuine international superpower in the twenty-first century.

Background of China.   China is surrounded by a variety of natural barriers: the sea to the east, mountains and desert to the southwest and north. There are three natural regions: the west, which is an area of high plateaus and desert; the north, an area of fertile plains; and the south, mostly hills and valleys. The two main rivers, the Yangtze and the Yellow, are both of extreme economic importance. Most of the population of China belongs to the Mongolian race, and 95 percent are Chinese speaking, although there are many dialects and a variety of other languages.

Though now officially atheist, the main religion is Taoism, a form of Buddhism that was introduced in the third century A.D. Even before that, Confucianism, based on patriarchal dominance, had established extraordinarily strong family and social ties based on male supremacy. As one result of the communist takeover in the 1940s and the establishment of communes, many of these ties have been replaced by loyalty to the commune and state. As that occurred, the status of women in Chinese society improved greatly.

Although China remains principally an agriculturally based nation, with 72 percent of its population living in the countryside, the total population is so large that it supports a number of large cities, such as Beijing and Shanghai, each of which has a population of over ten million.

The key to recent Chinese economic history is the communist takeover of the government in 1945 and its attempt to introduce socialism into the Chinese system and culture. Then, in 1978, a change in leadership gradually introduced market-oriented reforms and decentralized economic decision making.

China's Population Problem.   Population growth remains the government's biggest problem, and it has introduced a variety of rather strong policies to limit that growth. Birth control has been a national priority in China since 1971, when the government instituted a new program, an edict pronouncing as a norm the two-child family. Because of improved health and longer life spans, even this was projected to result in an enormous increase in population. In 1979 the two-child limit was cut to a one-child limit, and the system is backed by a variety of economic rewards for those who comply and penalties for those who do not. Families having more than one child lose rights, lose income, and are counseled by most of the members of the commune that they are not doing the right thing.

The initial results were significant. By 1982 the majority of newly formed families in the cities were having only one child. This was not the case, however, in the countryside, where the desire to have several children and, above all, to have boys, meant that families ignored the limit or, in some cases, killed newborn female babies. Recognizing the difficulty of policing these vast rural areas, in the late 1980s the authorities relaxed their one-child policy for those areas.

In the largest cities, such as Shanghai and Beijing, the one-child policy prevails, but by the early 2000s economic conditions in parts of China had become so favorable that many families wanting to have more than one child simply do so and willingly risk having to pay a large fine. In some localities, government officials, eager to have the income from such fines, even propose that families have a second or third child. This trend is thought to be sufficiently offset by the vast numbers of families sticking to the one-child limit or opting to have no children at all. In the early 2000s, China's population was about 1.3 billion, which is higher than an earlier goal of only 1.2 billion by 2000, but which is much lower than what its population would have been without the programs.

Even though it is the third largest food producer in the world, because of its enormous population China still produces barely enough to feed its own people. All available land is already under cultivation. One bright side of the Chinese economy is that it has relatively rich mineral resources, and in recent years, with its introduction of a market economy, it has expanded production enormously.

China: Selected Statistics

Population: 1.3 billion (early 2003)
   Urban: 28%
   Rural: 72%
   Sex distribution
      Male: 51%
      Female: 49%
   Age distribution
      Under 15: 24%
      15–64: 68%
      Over 64: 7%
Household size
   Rural: 4.6
   Urban: 3.4
Birthrate per year per 1,000 population: 16
Death rate per year per 1,000 population: 6.8
(world average: 9.3)
Infant mortality: 27.3 per 1,000
Life expectancy at birth
   Male: 70
   Female: 74
Marriage rate per year per 1,000 population: 7.0
Divorce rate per year per 1,000 population: 1.0
Hospital Beds: 1 per 424 persons

Religions
   Nonreligious: 59.2%
   Chinese folk: 20.1%
   Atheist: 12.0%
   Buddhist: 6.0%
   Muslim: 2.4%
   Christian: 0.2%
   Other: 0.1%
Educational attainment among those aged 25 and older
   No schooling: 29.3%
   Incomplete primary: 34.3%
   Completed primary school: 34.4%
   Postsecondary: 2.0%
Literacy rate among those aged 15 and older: 82%
GDP per year: $6 trillion (2002)
   GDP per capita: $4,600
Number of radios: 195 per 1,000
Number of television sets: 400 million
Number of telephones: 135 million
Cellular telephones: 65 million
Personal computers: 19 per 1,000
Internet users: 45.8 million
Website: www.china-embassy.org

China's Political Problems. Politically, China remains controlled by the Communist Party, although it is moving more and more toward a market economy. The way to its present state has been a zigzag path. From 1966 until 1976, China was governed by a radical faction that attempted a **Cultural Revolution,** a youth-led movement that tried to purge the economy and society of excesses and external influences that it felt had adverse consequences for China. Universities were torn apart and strong attempts were made to break down the vested ruling interests. It is estimated by some that millions of people were killed in this revolution. In 1976, after the death of Mao Ze-dong, the group that brought the Cultural Revolution to China was thrown out of power, and moderates, headed by Deng Xiaoping, took over. They started developing economic incentives and economic modernization.

After Deng retired in 1986, Zhao Ziyang and Li Peng shared China's leadership. They cautiously continued Deng's economic modernization policies, while maintaining communist control. Economic modernization led to demands for political liberalization as well, and in 1989 the world saw millions of students and ordinary citizens clashing with China's government. The uprising was repressed, and Zhao lost his post while Li retained leadership. In the late 1990s, President Jiang Zemin emerged as the leader of China. He has continued the economic reform process and has been quick to suppress political dissension.

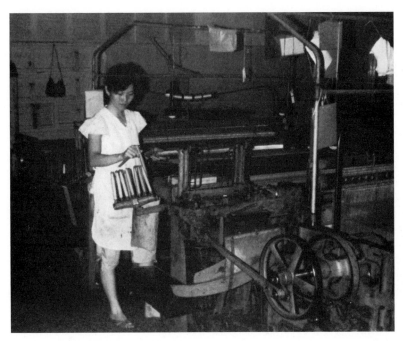

Low-tech silk production in China.

Uneven economic growth has widened the gap between the rich minority and the millions of poor workers and peasants. Some observers believe it is likely that growing resentment among the poor will have substantial repercussions in the near future. Official corruption has rapidly grown to become one of China's major problems. In 1997, Hong Kong was returned to China as a Special Administrative Region after almost one hundred years of British colonial rule.

China's relationship with Taiwan was complicated, and its one-China policy may cause conflict in the early 2000s. In summary, China is emerging as a full-fledged super-power in the early 2000s, but it remains to be seen whether China's "market socialism" ideology—involving concurrent political repression and economic liberalization—will be viable over the long haul.

Mexico

Mexico is the third largest country in Latin America. It is bounded on the north by the United States and on the south by Guatemala and Belize. About 75 percent of Mexico is a central plateau with low hills, basins, and mountains that are bounded by the Sierra Madre Occidental and Sierra Madre Oriente. The southern edge has many volcanoes, and the region is subject to earthquakes. Much of southern Mexico is laced with swamps and lagoons, and northern Mexico is arid and has few rivers.

Mexico's population is about 103.5 million in an area of 761,605 square miles, for a population density of almost 139 people to a square mile. The language is primarily

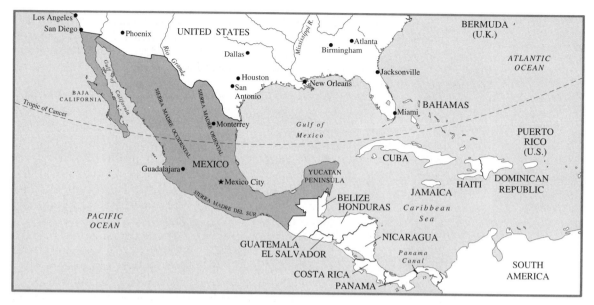

Mexico.

Spanish, although there are some Indian languages. The religion is mainly Roman Catholic. Population has been increasing rapidly, and 74 percent of the population lives in towns and cities. About 60 percent of Mexicans are Mestizos (of mixed Indian and European ancestry), 30 percent are pure Indian, and 9 percent are Caucasian. About 10 percent of the population is illiterate.

The Mexican economy has expanded significantly since World War II, and it has changed from an agricultural to an industrial and service economy.

The present system of government in Mexico was established by the revolution of 1910, in which most large estates were expropriated and land was redistributed among peasants organized into landholding communities.

A federal republic was created in 1924, and the Madera Revolution of 1910 had already established the political forces that are there currently. The central party, the National Revolutionary Party, was formed from all major political groups in 1929. It was later renamed the Institutional Revolutionary Party (PRI) and goes under that name today.

In recent times, Mexico has had a stable government. From 1924 through the 1990s, the PRI was in control, and that long period of power, along with its strong government control of industry, meant that it established a powerful, entrenched bureaucracy that fostered corruption and bribery.

In 1988, Carlos Salinas, a U.S.-trained economist, took office for six years and started the country on the road to democratic reform and economic liberalization. He sold some government-owned monopolies, entered into a free trade pact with the United States, reduced the amount of corruption in government-controlled businesses, and significantly reduced the role of government in the economy.

His program dramatically accelerated Mexico's economic modernization and integration into the North American economy. That integration was furthered by the creation of the North American Free Trade Agreement (NAFTA), in which Mexico, Canada, and the United States agreed to reduce and eventually eliminate tariffs and other trade restrictions between the countries.

In 1994, another PRI candidate, Ernesto Zedillo, was elected, but he did not have a majority of the vote. Soon after Zedillo's inauguration, protests by armed rebels and the arrest of Salinas's brother for assassinating a PRI candidate shook the confidence of foreign investors in Mexico. The previously fixed peso began a tumultuous decline, bringing Mexico to a financial crisis. Mexico faced capital outflow, high inflation, and a possible prolonged contraction. Zedillo attempted to restore confidence in democratic and economic reforms by negotiating an acceleration in electoral reforms and adopting austerity economic measures, and the United States, along with international lending institutions, provided loan guarantees to support the peso.

The congressional elections in July 1997 brought an end to the long-time stranglehold on Congress. Voters, disgusted with the PRI autocracy and its inability to deal with issues of crime, corruption, and poverty, voted in large numbers for opposition parties such as the Party of Democratic Revolution and the National Action Party. Then in 2000 they elected their first non-PRI candidate, Vicente Fox, as president. Fox, an extremely popular personality with the Mexican people, has lacked the ability to get things done politically. Well into his presidency, few of his major initiatives have made it out of opposition-controlled Congress at a time when economic reforms are desperately

*M*exico: Selected Statistics

Population: 103 million (early 2002)
  Urban: 74%
  Rural: 26%
  Sex distribution
    Male: 49%
    Female: 51%
  Age distribution
    Under 15: 33%
    15–64: 63%
    Over 64: 4.5%
Household size
  Average household size: 5
Birthrate per year per 1,000 population: 22
Death rate per year per 1,000 population: 5.0
Life expectancy
  Male: 69
  Female: 75
Marriage rate per 1,000 population: 7.7
Divorce rate per 1,000 population: 0.4

Religions
  Roman Catholic: 89%
  Protestant: 6%
  Other: 5%
Educational attainment among those aged 15 and older
  No primary school: 14.1%
  Some primary school: 22.3%
  Completed primary school: 20.7%
  Some secondary school: 10.4%
  Completed secondary school: 24.2%
  Some postsecondary school: 8.3%
Literacy rate among those aged 15 and older: 90%
GDP: $920 billion (2001)
  GDP per capita: $9,000
Number of radios: 329 per 1,000
Number of television sets: 25.6 million
Number of telephones: 12.3 million
Cellular telephones: 2 million
Personal computers: 33.5 per 1,000
Internet users: 3.6 million
Website: www.inegi.gob.mx

needed. The PRI is expected to do well at the midterm elections, strengthening its control of the Congress.

Uganda

Uganda has an area of 93,070 square miles and a population of about 25 million. A variety of languages are spoken, including Bantu, Swahili, and English. Its religions are Christian, Muslim, and a variety of tribal sects. Uganda lies on the equator and has an average elevation of 4,000 feet above sea level. The fertile plateau is bounded by the Great Rift Valley. Annual rainfall is about 40 inches, and temperatures generally remain between 60°F and 85°F.

Uganda's biggest problem is political coherence; it comprises a dozen major tribes, of which the Bantu-speaking groups form the majority. Ugandans, in the south, are now the most numerous and have given their tribal name to the whole country. Most people depend on agriculture for a living, although some of the northern tribes are also wandering herders. Illiteracy is extremely high. Most agriculture consists of subsistence and livestock farming, although Uganda remains one of the world's largest producers of coffee, which accounts for almost all of its export earnings.

Uganda developed, in its current form, as a British protectorate in 1894, and was extended to its present boundaries in 1914. It became independent in 1962, and in 1971 Idi Amin deposed President Milton Obote in a military coup. In 1972, Amin expelled Uganda's Asian population and launched a rule of terror.

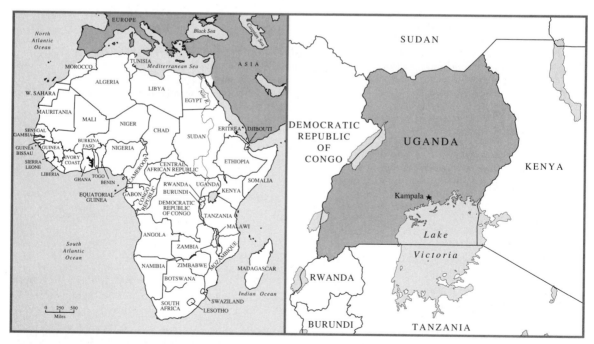

Africa (left); Uganda (right).

Uganda: Selected Statistics

Population: 25 million (early 2002)
   Urban: 16%
   Rural: 84%
   Sex distribution
      Male: 50%
      Female: 50%
   Age distribution
      Under 15: 51%
      15–64: 47%
      65 and over: 2%
Household size: 5 people
Birthrate per year per 1,000 population: 47
Death rate per year per 1,000 population: 17.5
Infant mortality: 89 per 1,000
Life expectancy
   Male: 43
   Female: 44

Religions
   Roman Catholic: 33%
   Protestant: 33%
   Muslim: 16%
   Other: 18%
Educational attainment: Percentage of population age 25 and over having
   No formal schooling or less than one year: 46.9%
   Primary school: 42.1%
   Secondary school: 10.5%
   Higher: 0.5%
Literacy rate among those 15 and higher: 63%
GDP: $29 billion (2001)
   GDP per capita: $1,260
Number of radios: 5 million
Number of television sets: 500,000
Number of telephones: 80,000
Cellular telephones: 9,000
Personal computers: 5.1 per 1,000
Internet users: 60,000
Website: www.ubos.org

In 1979, Uganda was invaded by Tanzania, and Amin fled. (In 2000 he died in exile in Saudi Arabia.) With Amin's exile, the ex-president, Obote, returned to rule the nation. Obote ruled for five years but favored his own tribe, the Langi, and in mid-1985 was again deposed, being replaced by a military man, Tito Okello, a member of the Acholi tribe.

In 1986, Okello was replaced by Yoweri Museveni, who turned what seemed to be a hopeless situation—a country that existed more in name than in reality, a country that earlier editions of this book described as a basket case—into a more politically stable country that since 1987 has continued to grow impressively.

How did he do this? First, he kept his idealism; he did not appropriate large amounts of the country's wealth to himself and his followers. Second, he opened his government to other tribes and built a political alliance among tribes that, although tenuous, allowed the fighting to stop. Third, he reduced major corruption in government while leaving minor corruption in place to maintain the support of the government workers. Fourth, he established a sufficiently stable system of laws that allowed international and domestic investment to occur. Fifth, although he is a socialist, he established free markets and reduced the number of government monopolies and government-controlled businesses. And finally, he maintained a strong army under his control.

President Yoweri Museveni of Uganda.

It should be noted that the commendable economic performance in Uganda has not led to political reform. In the elections of 1989, the ruling party, the NRM, was the only party. Museveni has maintained that while multiparty democracies suit Western societies, which divide horizontally by class, they only deepen divisions within African societies, which are vertically split along ethnic or regional lines. This arrangement of severely restricted, though not banned, political parties is known as the "Movement" system. Ten years after he came to power following the 1986 coup, Museveni was elected to a five-year term as president in 1996 amid complaints that he was virtually assured of victory because of the resources and apparatus of the Ugandan government backing him. Museveni argued that, given the ethnic problems Uganda faces, Western-style democracy is not appropriate for Uganda or most other African nations, and that Western countries should consider the results of his rule and not worry about whether it has a Western-style democracy. In 2001, Museveni, though faced by a major challenger calling for political pluralism, won the presidential election. In 2003, Museveni indicated support for a multiparty system in the name of peace building, calling for a countrywide referendum. He also called for the Movement to remain, not as a political party but rather as an organization. Therefore, although Uganda's economic future seems optimistic, it still has a long way to go before it can achieve competitive liberal democracy.

Conclusion

In considering the choices a developing country must make, you will see the game of society played in its entirety. The individuals who succeed in making the right choices launch their countries into prosperity and political stability.

The preceding descriptions have been necessarily brief. You can find more information in the library, and you'll need a lot more information before you can make reasonable choices. Even if you don't take that step-for-social-science into the library, keep your eyes and ears open for stories about these and other countries in the newspapers; in newsmagazines such as *Time, Newsweek,* and *U.S. News & World Report;* and on television and the Internet—because these countries will be in the news. The issues of social science surround you and will continue to surround you all your life.

Key Points

- Six problems facing all developing countries are the political consensus problem, the corruption problem, the economic problem, the debt problem, the population problem, and the brain drain problem.
- Each of these problems is interrelated with the others and is deeply ingrained in the culture of the society.
- Reasonable suggestions for a potential leader of a developing country include keeping an open mind, recognizing the difficulties, and maintaining your idealism.
- Policy options for developing countries include political options, economic options, foreign policy options, population options, and brain drain options.
- To truly understand the problems of developing countries, we must do case studies of specific countries.

Some Important Terms

brain drain (446)
Cultural Revolution (452)
debt restructuring (445)
developing countries (438)

foreign aid (443)
international debt (445)
NGA (445)
per capita output (446)

political consensus (441)
World Bank (444)

Questions for Review and Discussion

1. What is the chief characteristic that identifies a country as developing?
2. Name three groups of developing countries, and state briefly what distinguishes one group from another.
3. If a developing country cannot find a way to hold itself together, what is likely to happen to it?
4. Why might democracy not be the best choice of political system for a developing country?
5. Are there any good things to be said for autocratic government? If so, what are some of them?
6. What are some of the abuses a corrupt government indulges in?
7. A poor country might solve its problems by becoming richer. How can a poor country save and invest?
8. Aid to developing countries from the governments of developed countries has been decreasing. Give some of the reasons.

9. Some developing countries have borrowed so much money from foreign banks that they are having great difficulty paying it back. What is likely to happen in such countries?
10. What problems does rapid population growth present to a developing country? Are there any advantages to rapid population growth in developing countries?
11. How can a developing country acquire the human skills, training, and valuable ideas it needs in order to compete in modern industrial society?
12. Are there guaranteed solutions to the problems of developing countries? If so, describe some of the solutions.
13. How did you come out on your proposals for the development of the country of Hopelandia?

Internet Questions

1. What countries does the World Bank, http://web.worldbank.org/WBSITE/EXTERNAL/COUNTRIES/0,,pagePK:180619~theSitePK:136917,00.html, identify as developing in the South Asia region?
2. Look at the International Fund for Agricultural Development's approved projects for Bangladesh, www.ifad.org/operations/projects/regions/PI/BD_all.htm. Choose an ongoing project. What is the project cost and what are its main objectives?
3. According to the World Bank, http://web.worldbank.org/WBSITE/EXTERNAL/COUNTRIES/

0,,pagePK:180619~theSitePK:136917,00.html, what are three of Jamaica's economic problems?
4. What is the United Nations Conference on Trade and Development's special program for least developed countries? Use www.unctad.org/Templates/StartPage.asp?intItemID=2068.
5. Go to the International Monetary Fund page, www.imf.org/external/np/exr/glossary/index.asp. What is the HIPC Initiative?

For Further Study

Marquardt, Michael J., and Nancy O. Berger, *Global Leaders for the Twenty-First Century,* Albany: State University of New York Press, 2000.

Michalopoulos, Constantine, *Developing Countries in the WTO,* New York: Palgrave, 2002.

Naipaul, V. S., *Beyond Belief: Islamic Excursions among the Converted Peoples,* New York: Random House, 1998.

Shleifer, Andrei, and Daniel Treisman, *Without a Map: Political Tactics and Economic Reform in Russia,* Cambridge, MA: MIT Press, 2000.

Soyinka, Wole, *The Open Sore of a Continent: A Personal Narrative of the Nigerian Crisis,* New York and London: Oxford University Press, 1996.

Stiglitz, Joseph E., *Globalization and Its Discontents,* New York: W.W. Norton, 2002.

WWW   The Chinese Embassy   www.china-embassy.org

WWW   Economy and Environment Program for Southeast Asia   www.eepsea.org

WWW   International Monetary Fund   www.imf.org

WWW   Mexico Online   www.mexonline.com

WWW   NAFTA   www.mac.doc.gov/nafta

WWW   Uganda   www.government.go.ug

WWW   United States Agency for International Development   www.usaid.gov

WWW   The World Bank Group   www.worldbank.org

International Institutions and the Search for Peace

After reading this chapter, you should be able to:

- Explain the statement, "War is merely a continuation of politics by other means"
- Define the Bush policy of preemption and explain its implications for international harmony
- Describe the usefulness and limitations of international law
- List the five principal organs of the UN
- Summarize the United States' position on the UN
- Summarize the current outlook for peace
- Give a history of the Arab–Israeli conflict

Nothing is more important than the war on war.

—Pope Leo XIII

September 11, 2001, changed the way the United States relates to the rest of the world. After some 3,000 people were killed by the **al Qaeda**-highjacked airliners that crashed into the New York World Trade Center and the Pentagon, the United States declared a war on terrorism. This war was different from previous wars in that it was not a war against specific countries, but against an ambiguous foe—terrorists. Soon after, the nature of that war was determined. President Bush decided that the United States would follow a **policy of preemption**—a policy in which the United States would attack terrorists wherever they were before they commit terrorists acts. This policy of preemption became known as the Bush Doctrine. Two aspects of this change were highly controversial—the first was that the United States declared that it had the right to go into any sovereign country and fight terrorists, and that if the country harbored terrorists, that country itself would be considered a terrorist country and thus subject to U.S. attack. Second, those attacks could be based on suspicions and clandestinely gathered information, which would be hard for any other country to verify.

President Bush singled out four countries as an Axis of Evil—Iraq, Iran, Syria, and North Korea—and implied that if these countries did not change their ways, they would be made to do so. In 2003 he implemented that policy by attacking Iraq (assisted by what he called the Coalition of the Willing, the most important country of the coalition being Great Britain) and deposing Saddam Hussein, even after the United Nations refused to directly sanction the attack. The war ended in a month, but that left the United States with the problem of establishing a government in Iraq that would be friendly to the United States but not be seen as a "puppet" government of the United States by the Iraqi people and the world.

These recent events came about in part because of a significant change in the world order that occurred with the breakup of the former Soviet Union. That breakup left the United States as the dominant superpower and changed political scientists' vision of equilibrium in the world from a *realist,* balance-of-power conception to a *complex interdependency* conception. With this new conception, one superpower—in this instance the United States—would be held in check either by its own goodwill and ethical behaviors, in which case one has a new order of harmony and peace, or by a variety of cultural, social, and military constraints on action, in which case one has a precarious balance with the superpower on one side and a complex collection of constraints on the other. Political scientists had hoped for the former. After 9/11 and the Bush Doctrine, it was clear that the latter was the case, and that the interrelationships among countries would be contentious.

In this chapter, we consider these issues in specific relation to the international institutions that have developed to help maintain international relations and to alleviate the primary trouble spots of the world, and consider how the change in U.S. foreign policy challenges those institutions.

The main purpose of these institutions is to prevent war and maintain the peace. Therefore, before we consider the role of these international institutions, let's consider the problem of war.

The Problem of War

Besides the thousands of lives and billions of dollars that are lost, war brings about enormous social and cultural changes. World War I paved the way for the success of communism in the former USSR, it helped to bring on the Great Depression of the 1930s, and it unleashed forces that produced fascism in Italy and national socialism (Nazism) in Germany. Similarly, World War II changed the nature of the world, bringing an end to the colonial empire system. The Persian Gulf War of 1991 changed the nature of the Middle East political alignments in ways that were not anticipated when hostilities began, and the full effects of the 2003 Iraq War won't be known for years to come.

The Causes of War

Few things are certain about war, but it seems that inevitably it is the other side who started it and that the stated cause of the war will mask other underlying causes. Analyzing the causes of war is not a task about which a person can afford to be dogmatic. We can point to many forces at work and can reason as to how the forces work, but we cannot with exactitude draft any formula that will fully explain, evaluate, and relate the many pressures, conditions, emotions, ambitions, and practices behind international discord. Carl von Clausewitz, an influential German general and military strategist of the nineteenth century, argued that "war is merely a continuation of politics by other means."

When peaceful methods don't accomplish their objectives, countries consider force. Generally speaking, identifying forces that tend to bring about war is easier than explaining or evaluating them. Factors that may contribute to bringing on war include the desire

Soldiers in action during the 2003 Iraq War.

of a nation for power, economic rivalries, religious and political divisions (such as those in Northern Ireland or India), social unrest, the ambitions of political and military leaders, fanatical devotion to revolutionary ideologies (as in some Middle Eastern countries), intense ethnic rivalry among various groups, the desire for security or territory (as in Israel), the need to protect a country's national honor, or simply mistaken ideas about another country's intentions.

Because states are the work of human beings, inquiry into the causes of war goes back to the nature of human beings. Although psychologists and biologists admit that war may seem to reflect the impulses and emotions of humans—anger, fear, suspicion, and frustration—the general opinion is that people are not so made that they require war for the satisfaction of their basic drives. Their war making is believed to depend more on acquired attitudes, beliefs, and points of view than on their inherent nature.

The nation-state, as typified by public opinion and by its leaders, may be sensitive, quick to take offense, and hasty to retaliate. In the Falkland Islands War of 1982, negotiations were almost impossible once Argentina actually invaded the islands. It was only a matter of time before Great Britain, even though it does not have a recent militaristic tradition, rallied its forces in order to recover those islands, although their economic and political significance to Great Britain was minor. National honor and reputation and Great Britain's responsibility to British subjects on the islands seem to have required intervention. Likewise with The Persian Gulf War and the Iraq War: The initial positions of the countries involved became entrenched, and both sides continued merely to restate their original positions until the war broke out. In the 2003 Iraq War, once the United States had decided that Saddam Hussein was harboring "weapons of mass destruction," negotiations proved fruitless.

Within states or within the community of states as a whole, certain conditions often add to the chances of war at any given time. Poverty in a nation may produce a restlessness that breeds civil strife, and this in turn may result in international war or lead to dictatorships that foster warlike conditions. Dissension or economic depression within a state may cause governments to welcome war in order to establish national unity or to create a diversion from internal problems incapable of solution. When a spirit of militarism has been developed within a nation, as it was in the Germany of the 1930s, touching off a war is relatively simple. That same spirit of militarism exists, although to a lesser extent, in the Middle East today, which is one of the reasons that area has been the site of numerous wars and is also why it is likely to be the site of more trouble in the future.

Among conditions in the international community that are conducive to war is a sharp ideological split, like the one that, up until the early 1990s, existed between the former Soviet Union and its allies on the one hand and the United States and its allies on the other. The existence of a power vacuum of sizable proportions is another hazardous condition in the world community, and it is frequently found when an empire has just been demolished or an alliance has broken down. Thus the Soviet turmoil, while reducing the ideological friction between the former Soviet Union and the United States, produced numerous tinderboxes in eastern Europe and in the former Soviet Union itself. It also changed international political dynamics, and there was no effective counterbalance to the United States, allowing the United States to enter into small wars without any expectation of serious reprisals.

Approaches to the Problem of War

Throughout history most people have probably desired peace, though in some tribal societies war, in combination with customs such as war dances, head hunting, and scalp collection, became an integral part of the group culture. War helped to give life meaning by providing danger, excitement, and opportunities for winning prestige. Nevertheless, the quest for peace goes back at least to the biblical prophet Isaiah's long look ahead to the time when "nation shall not lift up sword against nation, neither shall they learn war anymore."

Ever since nation-states began to develop in the late Middle Ages, various poets, philosophers, and politicians have presented plans for maintaining peace. These peacemakers include Dante, King Henry IV of France, William Penn, and Immanuel Kant. But none of the plans were practical, nor did they reach the masses or receive serious consideration from governments.

Diplomacy. Disputes are, or at least seem to be, inevitable among people, bullies and ninety-pound weaklings alike. The alternative to a slugfest is reasonable discussion, which on the international level is called diplomacy. The problems of states are first of all handled by diplomats, usually with success. Occasionally, however, diplomacy fails, and then a dispute has arisen the settlement of which may be important not only to the countries involved but also to the entire world. Because a serious dispute that gets out of hand can result in war, states that are genuinely anxious to stay at peace will keep their diplomats at work as long as there is any hope of a solution. Throughout the history of the nation-state, diplomacy has done much to avoid war.

The contributions of diplomacy to peace include the efforts of third states as well as the parties to disputes. A disinterested state may try to get disputants together for further negotiations when they reach a deadlock and when unfortunate developments appear imminent; or, injecting itself a little further into a controversy, a third state may attempt **mediation,** a procedure that calls on the mediating government to make suggestions for solutions, thus concerning itself with the merits of the issues involved. Diplomacy and mediation may by used to terminate a war as well as to prevent one; the United States, for example, has played a major mediation role in the enmity that has stricken Arabs and Israelis in Israel and its neighboring countries for more than fifty years. Various U.S. presidents have attempted to mediate the dispute, and Camp David, the U.S. presidential retreat, has been known as a place where Palestinians and Israelis have met to try to work out their differences. The latest U.S. attempt to mediate the dispute is with President Bush's **Roadmap to Peace,** which was designed to achieve peace and Palestinian statehood in 2005.

A number of countries and the United Nations have ongoing mediation activities in countries such as East Timor, Sierra Leone, Kyrgyzstan, and Serbia. The **United Nations (UN)** is an organization of independent states that debate, and sometimes do something about, international problems. When mediation breaks down, the mediators must choose whether to become actively involved by providing peacekeeping forces or military force to achieve what they consider to be a fair resolution to the problems, or, less frequently and very reluctantly, to give up, admitting that some situations are, at least for a time, immune to outside influence.

International Government.   As we have seen, governments, for all their problems, generally maintain order within their boundaries by providing alternative mechanisms for settling disputes. Thus it is only natural that some of the proposals for preventing war between nation-states have involved an international government, or at least some option other than war, for settling disputes on an international level. These include the international courts and the UN, which together compose the rudimentary beginnings of world government, although when nations don't like the decisions, they often disregard them. Thus, when the United Nations failed to officially sanction war against Iraq, the United States attacked anyway, with some U.S. government officials declaring the UN irrelevant.

International Law and International Courts.   For centuries the ideal of a world ordered by a unified system of law has persisted. The ancient Greek city-states applied among themselves an elemental body of rules relating to matters such as diplomacy, treaties, and war. In Rome there was a *jus gentium,* or forum, to regulate the relations of the diverse peoples within the empire. As soon as the system of nation-states got under way centuries ago, it began constructing for itself a body of law. Hugo Grotius, a Dutchman, is usually referred to as the founder of modern **international law**—the system of rules on rights and duties of states in their mutual relations—because of his systematic organization and discussion of the law of his day in his famous book entitled *The Law of War and Peace* (1625). Often, however, emphasis was put on what nations ought to do rather than on their customary behavior.

By the nineteenth century, the actual practices of states in their relations to one another began to be stressed more and more in discussions of international law, and less attention was paid to what they ought to do from the point of view of abstract justice. Today, established procedures in the form of custom, treaties, conventions, and formal agreements are the chief basis of international law. Its subject matter is extensive, embracing items such as the recognition of new states and governments, diplomatic privileges and immunities, the acquisition of territory, nationality, extradition, the treatment of aliens, commerce, the jurisdiction of states, the responsibility of states, the beginning of war, the conduct of war, and the effect of war on treaties.

The Usefulness and the Limitations of International Law. The usefulness of international law in the maintenance of order and peace among nations has always been limited. No system of criminal law and prosecution has been established to date, although the war crimes trials of Nazi leaders at Nuremberg after World War II were a step in that direction, and later the International Law Commission of the United Nations considered the project of an international criminal court. Without criminal processes and courts, the community of nations lacks an important instrument of order. Then, too, the community has no real legislature, and consequently new laws must be made through treaties or by the slow development of fixed custom. In these processes of lawmaking, no sovereign state can be bound by a new rule without signifying its assent in one way or another; consequently, international lawmaking is slow, and the confusing situation may arise in which the law for one state may be quite different from the law applying to another.

Submission to an international court's justice is voluntary, and there are no effective means available to the community of states for the enforcement of the law. A violator may be threatened by the injured party, it may be the object of retaliatory measures, and in the last analysis it may be challenged in war. But these are not orderly procedures comparable to the methods possessed by a state for enforcing laws internally. For example, in the mid-1980s, when the United States was found to be in violation of international law with its policy in Central America, and especially in Nicaragua, it simply ignored the ruling. However, in the 1990s and early 2000s, the United States argued that Iraq was violating international law and should be punished for its violations. When in 2003 the UN punishment was insufficient from the U.S. point of view, it declared that it could attack Iraq on its own. A country's view of international law depends on which side of the law it finds itself.

Despite these deficiencies of the community of states, the usefulness of international law should not be underestimated. Nations may be able to violate the law and get away with it, but they much prefer not to do so, for they do not like to be regarded as lawbreakers. A bad reputation can be harmful to a state, even a powerful one such as the United States. The fact that nations constantly appeal to the standard of the law in their communications and negotiations with each other, both in claiming rights and in meeting their obligations, is evidence that they at least like to appear law abiding.

In recent history, many states discovered the high costs of having a bad reputation (due to a consistent violation of international law). Many states have experienced dramatic backlashes. For example, South Africa finally ended over four decades of apartheid in response to significant pressure that included economic sanctions and condemnations. Similarly, in 1999 Indonesia let one of its components, East Timor, declare independence after significant pressure from the international community. Serbia faced strong pressure in the early 2000s to remove its president, Slobodan Milosevic, who was declared a war criminal because of his role in the Kosovo conflict. He was defeated in Serbia's 2000 election and arrested by Kosovo police in 2001.

The real issue recently has been how the United States will be seen by the world due to its disregard for the views of other countries in its conduct of foreign policy. To some degree, the successful use of military power generates its own support—countries recognize that they must live with the power realities. But the United States' recent use of military power to achieve its objectives, regardless of the views of other countries, has left a wake of hostility against the United States throughout the world, not only among countries regarded as somewhat hostile to the United States, such as many of the Muslim countries, but also among states generally considered allies, such as Germany and France. Whether that hostility will ultimately cause more harm to the United States, and to the cause of world peace, than the gain achieved through military action remains to be seen.

The United Nations

The United Nations is the closest institution we have to a world government. The UN was formed in reaction to a surge of enthusiasm after World War II for a world organization able to keep the peace. On August 4, 1941, Prime Minister Winston Churchill of Great Britain and President Franklin Roosevelt announced in the famous Atlantic Charter the need for a "permanent system of general security." On January 1, 1942, soon after the United States entered the war, a United Nations Declaration was signed confirming the objectives of the Atlantic Charter. This declaration gave the United Nations, which was established on October 24, 1945, its name. The primary purpose of the United Nations, according to Article 1 of the Charter, is maintaining "international peace and security."

The UN is not the first attempt at a worldwide organization that would keep the peace. The first comprehensive approach to the problem of war by a group of states was written into the Covenant of the League of Nations in 1919 following World War I. This organization failed, however, to receive the international support necessary to make it a viable world organization. Although the United States was cooperative, it never became a member, and in 1939, after numerous ineffective attempts to use the League as an arbitration tool, it folded.

The most important organs of the UN are the Security Council, the General Assembly, and the Secretariat. The **Security Council**—the legislative body of the UN that has "primary responsibility for the maintenance of international peace and security"—is

The Security Council of the United Nations adopting a resolution.

the most powerful organ of the United Nations. The council deals with international disputes and decides when aggression is taking place or when there is a threat to the peace. It is composed of fifteen nations, of which five—the People's Republic of China, France, Russia (which took over the seat of the former Soviet Union), the United Kingdom, and the United States—are permanent members. The other ten members are nonpermanent and are elected by the General Assembly for terms of two years, with the elections being staggered so that five new countries come into office each year.

The Security Council must have the affirmative vote of nine of its members. When an issue is procedural in nature, any nine suffice, but in all other matters, the nine must include all five permanent members of the council. On major questions, each of the five permanent members has, therefore, a **veto,** a vote that forbids or blocks the making of a decision. This veto has been used relatively often, reducing the Security Council's ability to make decisions on controversial issues.

The **General Assembly** is a legislative body of the UN that includes representatives of all the member states. It meets annually and concerns itself "with any questions or matters within the scope of the present charter or relating to the powers and functions of any organs provided for in the present charter." It has no legislative power, but it discusses a wide variety of international problems. When it arrives at a decision, it is in the form of a recommendation, either to states or to other organs.

The **Secretariat** is the executive arm of the UN. It is headed by the secretary-general, who is elected by the General Assembly and traditionally holds the post for a period of five years. The Secretariat carries out a variety of organizational, research, publication, and communication functions, and the secretary-general plays an important role in diplomacy among states.

Is the UN Worth It?

When the UN began, there was great hope for it as a vehicle for resolving disputes among nations without resort to violence and for discussion that could prevent war in the future. Initially the UN was dominated by the United States and its allies, with the former USSR as the odd country out, and the Soviet Union used its veto to stop a wide variety of activities. As the UN expanded from its initial 55 members to its approximately 191 members today, the general tenor of the organization changed. The new states tended to disagree with the United States, and in the 1970s and 1980s the UN was, instead, often at odds with U.S. policy.

This change was reflected in U.S. voting in the Security Council. Whereas in the early years of the UN the United States never used its veto, in the 1970s and 1980s the United States used its veto power relatively often to prevent action by the UN. In the late 1980s, the nature of the UN changed from what it was in the 1970s and early to mid-1980s. Changes in the former Soviet Union and China made agreement in the Security Council more likely, and the UN more often reflected U.S. desires. This agreement within the UN with regard to U.S. desires gave more legitimacy to U.S. actions in maintaining the peace and achieving its international goals. More recently, the UN has not been so supportive of U.S. positions, and when the UN has been unlikely to support its position, the U.S. reaction has been to withdraw, if not in fact at least in principle, and look to other means of handling international disputes. That's precisely what it did in 2003. When it was clear that the UN would not sanction war against Iraq to eliminate weapons of mass destruction, but instead wanted to give UN weapons inspectors more time to determine whether Iraq had such weapons, the United States simply went to war on its own with the Coalition of the Willing.

Similarly, the United States had no compunctions about undertaking activities in Nicaragua that were condemned by the UN or in not signing the Law of the Sea treaty that was developed by the UN. It also withdrew from the United Nations Educational, Scientific, and Cultural Organization (UNESCO) in 1984, claiming extraneous politicization and "an endemic hostility toward the institutions of free society, particularly those that protect the free press, free markets, and, above all, individual human rights." An assistant secretary of state said, "When UNESCO returns to its original principles, the United States would be in a position to return to UNESCO." Since that time, UNESCO has reformed some of its practices, and the United States rejoined UNESCO in 2003. However, the funding for its membership remained politically contentious.

Because the U.S. contribution is almost one-fourth of the UN's budget (see Figure 21.1), the UN was forced to take notice of the U.S. position, and over the past twenty years, the UN has modified its organization in order to be more in accordance with U.S. desires. In 1997 the United States recognized these changes and agreed to pay its past assessments over the next three years under the condition that the UN continue to cut its staff. Some in Congress weren't satisfied with that condition, and demanded a cut in the U.S. contribution. In December 2000, the United States' share of the UN's operating budget was cut from 25 percent to 22 percent and Congress voted to pay it, subject to certain conditions. Debate continued on the United States' peacekeeping contributions, which the UN computes separately from its operating budget. The 1994 U.S. legislation capping U.S. assessed contributions to UN peacekeeping at 25 percent caused the United States to accrue arrears. In 2000 the UN agreed to cut the U.S. share from its 30 percent to 25 percent. In 2003, legislation was discussed to lift the cap temporarily in order to meet the obligation of outstanding arrears. Of course, this figure is in dispute.

The reality is that U.S. support for the UN depends on how supportive the UN is of U.S. positions. Some in the United States argue that we should pull out of the UN. They

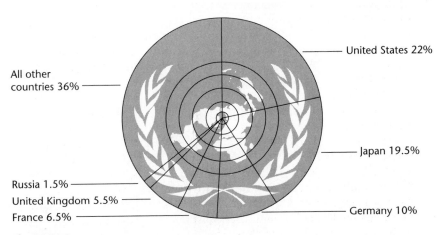

All other countries 36%

United States 22%

Japan 19.5%

Germany 10%

Russia 1.5%
United Kingdom 5.5%
France 6.5%

Figure 21.1

Approximate assessments for paying for the UN, 2003.

argue that the UN is superfluous; economic and military power, not the UN, will determine international world events. According to these opponents, the UN has become an enormous bureaucracy that does little more than provide good incomes and pleasant jobs for its employees.

The UN's Role in Keeping the Peace

Supporters of the UN point out that for all its problems, the UN is still the only world force for peace that we have, and therefore it is worthwhile considering how it has kept peace and how it can continue to do so.

In the event that there is a "threat to the peace, breach of the peace, or act of aggression," the Security Council may invoke **sanctions**—diplomatic, economic, or military punitive actions undertaken through a collective security system—against the state that is to blame. The charter lists three types of coercive measures:

1. Severance of diplomatic relations
2. The complete or partial interruption of economic relations with the dissident state
3. The use of armed forces

The amount of pressure that diplomatic sanctions produce would ordinarily be limited. The more powerful economic sanctions are seldom tried, although in 1990 economic sanctions were imposed against Iraq after its invasion of Kuwait. All countries were forbidden to trade with Iraq, and the use of force was condoned. Because Iraq did not comply with the terms of the peace treaty, these sanctions continued until after the 2003 Iraq War, when the United States began establishing an alternative government. These sanctions had caused considerable hardship for the Iraqi people but were not successful in leading to the end of Saddam Hussein's rule, as some had hoped they would be.

Bombed-out U.N. Headquarters in Iraq.

In 1992 similar but more limited sanctions were proposed by the United States and Britain and accepted by the UN against Libya because of its failure to turn over suspected terrorists. Libya eventually turned over two men for trial and one of those suspects was found guilty by a special court set up in Scotland. Because both men seemed to have connections with the Libyan government, the United States argued for a continuation of the sanctions. In the early 2000s Libya offered $2.7 billion in compensation to the families of the plane victims and declared itself willing to end all of its weapons of mass destruction programs for a lifting of sanctions. The UN trade sanctions were suspended in response to this move, but as of early 2004 U.S. trade sanctions were continued.

The military sanction is supposed to be the final recourse of the UN in its peacemaking efforts. To make the system function more smoothly, the charter imposes on each member of the organization the duty of contributing to the UN military force, with the Security Council responsible for defining each member's contribution to the joint effort should an occasion for military sanctions arise.

Impressive as the charter provisions regarding military sanctions may appear at first glance, in fact they have been of limited value. When the North Koreans attacked South Korea on June 25, 1950, the Security Council had no force on which it could draw because no agreements had been reached about what members were expected to provide. The failure to make those agreements had resulted from the inability of the Military Staff Committee to specify the general principles that such agreements should embody; no nation had yet undertaken a definite obligation with respect to any possible joint military action.

When the report came that South Korea had been invaded, a meeting of the Security Council was immediately called to deal with the problem. The council urgently asked for a cessation of hostilities and a withdrawal of the invading troops. Because two days later the ceasefire order had not been respected, the Security Council set to work to apply military sanctions against North Korea. This action would undoubtedly have been vetoed by the former Soviet Union had its delegates been present, but months earlier they had withdrawn from the UN meetings in anger because Taiwan, rather than China, had been given the Chinese seat in the organization. Because the Soviet delegate was not present at the ensuing Security Council meeting, the council was able to call for a ceasefire and authorize a UN-led military action—the Korean War, which lasted from 1950 to 1953.

After the Korean War, the next important conflict with which the UN had to deal involved the Suez Canal in 1956. The first uniformed peacekeeping unit of the UN was used during this period to sustain a ceasefire between the Israelis and the Egyptians. British and French troops, who had entered the area in order to ensure free shipping through the canal, were forced to withdraw. The success of the UN in this incident is still considered one of its highest achievements. In the late 1980s, the UN had two additional successes: It arranged a ceasefire in the Iran–Iraq war, and it helped arbitrate an end to the internal conflict in Angola.

However, it was not so successful in 1990 in its diplomatic attempt to keep the peace in the Middle East. When Iraq invaded Kuwait, the UN imposed economic sanctions against Iraq and authorized military force to achieve Iraq's withdrawal from Kuwait. These authorizations occurred in the Security Council and were supported by the former USSR and accepted by China (both of whom had veto power). The UN hoped the economic sanctions and the threat of war would bring about a diplomatic solution. No diplomatic solution was found, and in 1991 the UN authorized the use of force to achieve the directives. However, instead of establishing a UN military force, the UN simply authorized the United States to lead a coalition in a war against Iraq. The U.S.-led forces quickly won the

An anti–Iraq War protest in Los Angeles.

war, and the UN played a key role in establishing the framework under which Iraq surrendered. It also played an important role in assisting the refugees from the war and in undertaking weapons inspections.

The UN did not maintain those weapons inspections, and in the early 2000s, Iraq expelled the UN inspectors, leading to intense diplomatic negotiations. In fall 2002, the United States pushed the UN to give Saddam Hussein an ultimatum, and in spring 2003, Hussein let the weapons inspectors back in to Iraq. Despite this concession, the United States was not satisfied with the progress made in finding weapons of mass destruction. The United States pushed the UN to declare Iraq in material breach of the earlier peace accord agreements and to allow the use of military force to assure compliance.

When it became clear that the Security Council was not going to authorize force at this time, the United States, together with Great Britain, declared that a UN mandate was unnecessary and attacked Saddam Hussein to "eliminate weapons of mass destruction" and thereby help protect the world from terrorism. Initially, there were significant antiwar activities, especially in Europe, where a large majority of the population opposed the U.S. unilateral action. But the war was quickly won, and the antiwar pressure stopped.

Once in control, the United States found little in the way of weapons of mass destruction—the given reason for the war. Despite this, because the war was won, and because Saddam Hussein was deposed, even many who opposed the war felt the outcome was a good thing, because Hussein had been a brutal dictator. After the war was won, a large majority of the U.S. population supported it—the "it dussint matter why we dundit as long as we wunnit" approach to war.

After winning the war without UN approval, the United States took major control of the establishment of a new government in Iraq, freezing the UN out of much of the process. Essentially, it told the UN, "We will do what we want; if you condone it, we will let you play a role; if you don't, we will do what we want anyway."

That U.S. attitude did not sit well with the rest of the world, and there were significant anti-U.S. feelings outside the United States. But there was also an acceptance of the "realpolitik"—the United States has unsurpassed military power—and thus there was little that other countries could do if the United States decided to use that power. In many people's eyes, the UN had lost any effective role in providing for peace and security in the world. The United States had usurped it. However, as the difficulties of maintaining the peace become enormous for the United States, it came back to the UN, asking for its help and conveying a willingness to consider giving up some control.

Another area in which the United Nations has been generally unsuccessful has been in stopping fighting and ethnic violence within a country. In the early 1990s, its numerous attempts to bring about an end to the fighting between Serbs and Muslims in the former Yugoslavia failed. Similarly, such attempts failed in Somalia and Rwanda. The success of ongoing peacekeeping forces in Kosovo, East Timor, and Sierra Leone is still up in the air. Put simply, the UN has neither the international mandate nor the power to end strife within a country.

The failure of many UN peacekeeping attempts has led to a UN report calling for a permanent UN-controlled army so that the UN will have "the tools" to address any conflict situation. Because countries are reluctant to give up autonomy to the UN, there may be some increase in and modernization of the UN peacekeeping department, but the troops will likely remain "on loan" from individual nations. The problem is one of control. The UN does not have the high-level military structure to successfully direct the operations even if it gets the troops. Therefore control generally falls to one country. And, if a peacekeeping state becomes unhappy with the action, it can simply recall its troops, as India did with its troops in Sierra Leone in 2000.

In considering the UN, a key point to remember is that the UN is not a superstate. It cannot force individuals or states to accept its decisions, and oftentimes it simply lacks the ability to impose its will on the member states. All it can do is impose sanctions, which are methods of exerting pressure on recalcitrant states. In imposing sanctions, two basic handicaps limit its effectiveness: (1) its member states retain their sovereignty, and (2) much of the power of the world is concentrated in a few powerful states, and unless these states concur, and choose to use the UN as a vehicle to achieve their ends, the UN will not be effective.

Other UN Approaches

Some of the other approaches the UN has tried include the following:

- Registration of treaties in order to avoid obstructive secret treaties
- Further development of international law
- Promotion of education through the programs of UNESCO
- Encouragement of regional arrangements devoted to the preservation of peace
- International control of nuclear energy
- Regulation of national armaments, including missiles and nuclear weapons

The practice of having treaties registered and published by the Secretariat has become firmly established, and although it does not guarantee that secret agreements will be eliminated, it does reduce the chances of their existence. An International Law Commission has tried to promote the progressive development of international law, and it has made headway slowly. The programs of UNESCO have aimed at the furtherance of fundamental education, technical and vocational education, the exchange of books between nations, the exchange of students, and many other objectives, all designed to produce a better international outlook on the part of people everywhere. However, these methods for advancing the cause of peace are necessarily slow and their results somewhat uncertain.

Efforts to establish international control of nuclear energy and national armaments began in 1963 under the direction of President Kennedy, and they were formalized in 1968 with the Treaty on Nonproliferation of Nuclear Weapons (NPT), which provided for non-nuclear nations to forgo nuclear bomb development in exchange for aid in building peaceful nuclear power programs. Nations with the bomb were ordered to reduce armaments. Despite UN efforts, about fifty nations failed to sign the agreement. The UN's International Atomic Energy Agency (IAEA) has supervisory power over this treaty, but its authority and capabilities are limited. Thus, in 2003, when North Korea decided to develop a nuclear bomb, it simply expelled the UN observers who had been there expressly to ensure this did not happen.

Given its limited sanctions and tools, the UN has not been especially successful in stopping even small wars, and it certainly has not been capable of coercing the largest and most powerful members of the international community. Even when dealing with small conflicts among member nations, the UN currently has no facility to force anyone to follow its policy. Thus, in the Iran–Iraq war in the mid-1980s, the UN was unable to enforce a ceasefire for years simply because the countries refused to obey the order. Only in 1988, when both countries chose to have a ceasefire, could the UN "enforce" its policy. In the Kosovo conflict in the late 1990s, it was not the UN that organized the air campaign against Serbia. Instead, that task was undertaken by the **North Atlantic Treaty Organization (NATO)**. NATO is an alliance of Western nations, one of whose purposes is joint military and economic cooperation. Finally, in the 2003 Iraq War, the United States went to war without UN authorization.

Loyal supporters of the UN still hope that in time it will develop into an organization capable of maintaining international law, order, and justice. As the world grows smaller and smaller and as the range and deadliness of weapons increase, the need for such an organization becomes ever greater. However, with the current U.S. attitude toward the UN one of disdain and neglect, few observers see its role increasing any time soon.

The Outlook for Peace

The beginning of the new millennium was marked by the end of the cold war and the beginning of a period of U.S. domination in the world militarily and politically. This changes the nature of the outlook for peace. The fears associated with the cold war and the "communist threat" that filled the United States in the 1950s and 1960s are gone. Today the communist threat seems a long way behind us, and it is hard to believe that in the 1950s and early 1960s, U.S. schools conducted air raid drills in which students practiced what to do in case of a Russian attack and U.S. families built and stocked air raid shelters. For the United States, at least, such imminent threats are gone, but other threats have replaced it. Ironically, the decline of fear of a global nuclear disaster has increased the likelihood of regional conflicts and the possibility that those regional conflicts could be nuclear. Why? Because a decreased fear that any regional conflict will pit two superpowers against each other in unreconcilable positions frees nations from automatically expecting a small war to lead to a large war. But simply because the expectation of a large war is reduced, it is not necessarily the case that the actual probability of a large war is reduced, and regional conflicts might, in fact, lead to such unreconcilable positions and the possibility of World War III. Just as fights between siblings can erupt at any time, so too can disagreements among supposedly friendly nations.

The rise of U.S. dominance has also provoked an anti-U.S. backlash and the development of terrorists cells throughout the world whose goal is to inflict harm on the United States and make it pay for its "bullying ways." This is particularly true among Arab and Islamic individuals who feel that the United States has been biased in its support of Israel in the Israeli–Palestinian war. The power of these groups was seen in the 9/11 attacks on the Pentagon and the World Trade Center and in the terrorist bombing of the United States and U.S.-ally institutions around the world. To fight such threats, the United States has established a war on terrorism, an ongoing war in which the United States claims the right to attack terrorists with preemptive strikes. Unfortunately, each of these strikes convinces others of the United States bullying ways and leads more to join the terrorist cause, or at least to implicitly or explicitly support them. What the right mix of strength and understanding is for the United States to follow is still much in debate.

Those countries that have been accused of harboring terrorists and of being part of President Bush's Axis of Evil fear attacks by the United States, which leads them to aggressive policies that might prevent attack. In the case of North Korea, this meant trying to increase its nuclear bomb capabilities, under the assumption that such a capability, and a willingness to use it, would prevent a U.S. attack.

The breakup of the Soviet Union has been marked by substantial ethnic unrest, and significant political shifts are still possible. For example, in early 1993 an ethnic region in Russia, Chechnya, declared its independence, and in 1995 a long-lasting war between Chechnyan independence supporters and the Russian army created havoc not only in Chechnya but also in Russia, where many opposed the Russian army's use of force to subdue the independence movement. That use of force also created tension between the United States and Russia. Still, in the early 2000s, the United States and Russia see eye to eye on many issues, and both are committed to peaceful coexistence. It is, however, an uneasy alliance, and it is possible that a fight between Russia and some of its ethnic regions, or between Russia and some of the former republics of the Soviet Union, could break down that alliance or create tension between the United States and a former republic. A republic could have significant nuclear power, and the United States could find itself in a position in which it felt compelled to stop the republic's leader. The result could be a war. Therefore it is vital to be vigilant in keeping the peace.

Whatever happens, it is important to recognize that "right" is almost inevitably a gray area, and each side will often do what is politically and economically in its own interest. We can expect that any government with the power to do so will attempt to impose its will on its people and on the world. It is a maxim of politics that power corrupts and absolute power corrupts absolutely. The only way peace will have a chance is if those possessing power do not interpret to their advantage what is "right" in the large number of gray areas. Unfortunately, there haven't been many examples of such objective interpretation of what is "right" in history. Instead, history has contained many more examples of the view that "might makes right."

At the end of the 1990s there was much talk of a **new world order,** a relationship among the nations of the world governed by what all countries believe is right and enforced primarily by the military superiority of the United States. If this new world order was to succeed, it depended on the United States being seen as an objective and fair arbiter. Without that perception of fairness, the new world order is doomed. Given the history of the United States, this is not the way it has worked out, and the United States is currently seen as a country willing to unilaterally impose its will on other countries. There is a new world order, but not the one that optimists had hoped for.

Trouble Spots of the World

The events of the last decade have changed the way the United States thinks of trouble spots and of war. The war on terrorism has less of a geographic component than did previous wars. Terrorists could be anywhere—they could be living right next door to you. Similarly, the damage from terrorism is not limited to some far-off country. It could be right here in the United States. Still, terrorism often has its roots in conflicts in particular geographic areas; thus, a consideration of these conflicts is important to any consideration of the search for peace.

African Stability. During the postwar period, many African countries won their independence from European colonial nations, but that independence has been marked by bloody internal strife, coups d'état, and disputes over borders with neighboring countries.

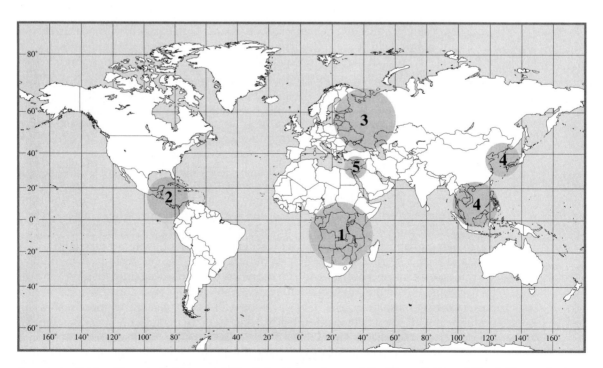

Some potential trouble spots. 1: African stability. 2: Latin American and Caribbean Basin stability. 3: Former Soviet Republics and eastern Europe stability. 4: Far East stability. 5: Middle East stability.

Few of the countries have the underlying social infrastructure necessary for a democratic government, so the governments have generally been autocracies, and the fights have been over which and what type of autocracy will rule.

With the transfer of power to blacks in South Africa, most African nations are controlled by blacks, but because of the historically imposed boundaries that combine competing ethnic groups, there will likely be continuing internal wars and fights throughout the early 2000s. Examples include Somalia, where fighting between competing groups has led to famine; Rwanda, where fighting between the Tutsi and Hutus has torn the country's social fabric apart; and in Congo, the Democratic Republic of Congo, and Sierra Leone, where competing groups have been vying for power.

Although in the late 1990s, with the end of apartheid, South Africa has begun to show a glimmer of hope, many observers are worried about the future. South Africa has too few resources to achieve the economic ends many of the poor South African blacks had hoped for.

Latin American Stability.   The problems of Africa are mirrored in Latin America, where some cynics have claimed that governments change almost as frequently as the seasons. In Latin America, racial issues play a less important role than they do in Africa, but economic and ideological issues still create enormous tensions that can flare up at any moment.

Up until the 1990s, the cold war played a significant role in the disputes in the area. For example, the early 1980s saw bloody civil wars in Nicaragua and El Salvador as both the United States and the former Soviet Union jockeyed for position, supporting a variety of leaders. During this time, Cuba remained tied to the USSR and worked hard to export its ideological views.

Latin America is no longer the troubled region it was for most of the past twenty or thirty years. With the end of the cold war, the region ceased to be a location for a proxy war between the competing superpowers. Significant problems remained, however. Some of these problems were simply leftover antagonisms from the earlier conflicts. Others resulted from the large disparities in income within countries, the weak democratic traditions in many of them, and the powerful drug cartels.

Venezuela, for example, is faced with serious internal problems: an embattled president who had to push back a coup attempt in 2002, a divided military, an overdependence on the petroleum industry, and irresponsible mining practices that endanger both the rain forest and indigenous people. Venezuela also faces a major problem at its border with Colombia, an area of cross-border violence, kidnapping, smuggling, and drug trafficking. Colombia has constant internal violence with the drug cartels, an anti-insurgent army of paramilitaries, and the terrorist group FARC, which grew from the military wing of Colombia's Communist Party into an army for bombing, murdering, and kidnapping political and economic targets.

Another example of the type of problem faced in Latin America is found in Peru, where the election of President Fujimori was disputed, causing him to resign in 2001, and in mid-2002, the new president had to declare a state of emergency because of the violence of protesters in the south over the privatization of electric companies. By mid-2003, the president declared martial law because of widespread strikes throughout the entire country. Still, despite the internal instability, there is little threat of war among countries of Latin America.

One place where we can expect change in the early 2000s is Cuba, the one communist country remaining in the western hemisphere. The breakup of its friend the Soviet Union in 1991 deprived Cuba of support from that source, and the trade boycott imposed by the United States on Cuba made the island nation more isolated and hurt its economy. When its aging leader, Fidel Castro, leaves office, there will likely be a struggle for power and a rearrangement of Cuba's international political alignment.

Stability in the Former Soviet Republics and Eastern Europe. The early 2000s remain a time of potential instability for a number of the countries of eastern Europe. Although in the 1990s explicit fighting between Croats, Muslims, and Serbs ended in Bosnia and Kosovo, ethnic hatreds remained high. Albania remains unstable and its economy floundering. The situation in Russia and the republics of the former Soviet Union remained tenuous as they struggled with transformation problems; the Chechnyan war is just one example there. Before the U.S. war on terrorism, the United States had strongly opposed Russian military action in Chechnya. After the war on terrorism began, Russia pointed out that the Chechnyans were allied with terrorists, and U.S. opposition to Russian military action then decreased.

Of special concern for the rest of the world is the question, What will happen to the nuclear arsenal and nuclear weapons experts of the former Soviet Union? If even a small part of that arsenal is dispersed to countries with disputes, and if those nuclear weapons experts hire themselves out to the highest-bidding country, the probability of nuclear war or nuclear terrorism may have turned out to increase with the breakup of the Soviet Union and the end of the cold war.

Stability in the Far East and Indochina. In the early 2000s, the border between North and South Korea still remains a trouble spot. President Bush declared North Korea a member of the Axis of Evil, which led to great fear among North Koreans that the United States would launch a preemptive war against them. To try to prevent such a war, North Korea tried to increase the number of nuclear bombs it had, creating difficulties for the détente approach that South Korea has been following. Because most observers believed North Korea had and was willing to use nuclear weapons, they also believed that a preemptive war by the United States would lead North Korea to retaliate with an attack on Seoul, the capital of South Korea, killing hundreds of thousands of people. Unlike its approach to Iraq in 2002 and 2003, the United States has so far used diplomacy to achieve its ends. Since the United States has thousands of U.S. troops stationed in Korea, the Korean peninsula will likely remain a trouble spot.

The status of China is also of some concern. In China there are significant pressures for political reform, which are kept under control by repressive actions of the government. The United States opposes those repressive measures, but wants to stay friendly with whatever Chinese government is in power.

Politically China remains a communist state, but economically it is turning more and more to the market. Significant concern exists in the United States about political repression of groups such as the Fulong Gong. The Fulong Gong claims to be an "exercise club," but the Chinese government claims that it is a subversive group and has outlawed it and jailed some of its members. Whether the political repression and liberal economic activity can both continue remains to be seen. Once the war on terrorism began, the concern about China diminished because the United States saw its main threat as being from small countries with weak governments where terrorists could operate. Because China opposed terrorists, the United States found itself closer to China after the war on terrorism began than before the war.

The relationship between China and Taiwan is still a hot international issue. The United States has accepted a one-China policy, which states that Taiwan is part of China, not a separate country. At times China has suggested that it might try to forcibly take control of Taiwan. If that happened, the United States would probably extend aid to Taiwan because the Taiwanese have close ties with the United States despite the one-China policy. Most believe the issue will eventually be settled peacefully.

Stability in the Middle East.   Despite the problems and potential instability in other areas of the world, they are not considered the major trouble spots of the world. This dubious honor goes to the Middle East.

Practically since the beginning of history, the Middle East has been a virtual hotbed of warring peoples. The countries of the area, such as Libya, Syria, Iraq, Israel, and Iran, have periodically fallen under the influence of rulers from many different nations. During World War I, the area was occupied by French and British troops, and between 1922 and 1939 the Jewish population in Palestine (now Israel) rose from 84,000 to 445,000. The land they bought and occupied had been previously owned by absentee landlords, and the displaced Arabs who had previously rented the land remained hostile to the new settlers. The land became disputed territory.

As the Jewish population increased, so did **Zionist**—individuals who support the establishment of a Jewish homeland—activities. During World War II, Zionist forces fought on the side of the Allies, but continually reminded the Allied forces that their own central motive was to seek independence for a Jewish nation. The area in which the nation was proposed was a British protectorate, and in 1942 Britain passed the Biltmore Resolution, which called for the first steps to be taken to secure Palestine for the Jews. It provided for

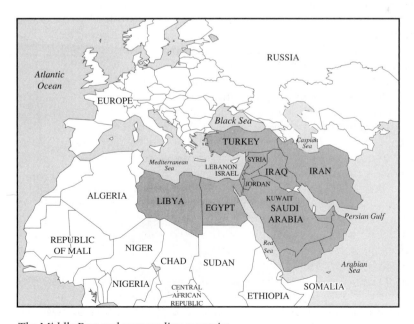

The Middle East and surrounding countries.

unrestricted Jewish immigration into Palestine and eventual establishment of a Jewish commonwealth.

The Palestinian Arabs, meanwhile, did not put up a united resistance to the Zionists. Therefore, at the end of World War II, the Palestinian Arabs had only the League of Arab States (Egypt, Syria, Lebanon, Transjordan, Iraq, Saudi Arabia, and Yemen) to turn to. They voiced opposition to the Biltmore Resolution. Britain, undecided about how the situation should be handled, called for the establishment of a binational state in Palestine, and refused to admit some 100,000 European Jewish refugees to the area. Another outbreak of violence caused the UN to intervene. On September 1, 1947, the UN commission of inquiry called for the division of the territory into two states—one Arab and one Jewish.

The Arabs, who constituted a majority in both the "states" the UN had created, refused the order and thus the Palestinian War began. The well-organized Zionist forces overcame the Arabs, and by May 1948 they had obtained control of not only the Jewish share of Palestine but the Arab share as well. On May 14 the state of Israel was proclaimed. Since that time there has been continual strife between Israel and its surrounding Arab neighbors. The first outbreak of violence was the Suez War in 1956, when Israel staged a surprise attack on Egypt in the Sinai area. In 1967 the tensions broke into war again, and in what is called the Six-Day War, Israel made large territorial gains, taking land from Egypt and Jordan. Israel continued to occupy the territory it won in the war, citing the need for national security. In 1973 Arab forces attacked Israel in an attempt to regain their land, and sporadic fighting continued until mid-1974 when both sides agreed to a ceasefire.

In 1974 the UN General Assembly passed what has come to be known as **Resolution 242,** which called for the return of land and property taken by Israel during the wars and recognized the Palestine Liberation Organization (PLO), giving it permanent observer status in the UN. Israel rejected this, citing security reasons and arguing that it could not give land back to a group committed to the annihilation of Israel. In response, Israel began to settle the occupied land.

Palestinian demonstrators throw stones at Israeli soldiers during clashes in the West Bank.

Some hope of accord existed in 1979 as Egypt and Israel agreed to a peace treaty calling for Israel's withdrawal from the Sinai Peninsula, but the more difficult Palestinian question was skirted. That question eventually led to continued fighting and war as Israel invaded Lebanon in 1982 in an attempt to eliminate the PLO. As a result of this fighting, much of Beirut, the capital of Lebanon, fell into ruins as Israel, the PLO, and Syria struggled for political power in the area. In Lebanon the many internal groups are differentiated by intense religious, political, and economic rivalries, and they fight bitterly with each other while at the same time outside interests, such as those of Syria and Israel, attempt to enforce their own versions of order on the country. In the early 1990s, a Syrian-backed faction took control, and it looked as though the long ordeal in Lebanon was finally coming to an end. Conflict still existed, however, in south Lebanon, where Lebanese troops attempted to regain land occupied by fighting PLO guerrillas and Israelis. The Golan Heights, which was once part of Syria but was annexed by Israel in 1984 and settled by Israeli citizens, remained in dispute.

In August 1993, Israeli Prime Minister Yitzhak Rabin and the chairman of the PLO, Yasser Arafat, signed a historic peace accord to bring to a conclusion almost five decades of incessant turmoil and conflict. Israel agreed to turn over specific regions of the West Bank and Gaza Strip to the Palestinian Arabs, who would administer them as autonomous divisions. The negotiations leading toward final settlement continued but with enormous fights and complaints on both sides. In 1996 a militant Israeli who was against peace assassinated Rabin because of his role in the peace process, and a conservative critic of the peace process was elected in his place. That critic, in turn, was defeated by Ehud Barak in 1999.

Barak unilaterally withdrew Israeli troops from Lebanon and reentered negotiations with Yasser Arafat. Some accords were agreed to, but significant disagreements about the status of Jerusalem remained. The situation deteriorated as both sides clashed over who would control parts of Jerusalem after the creation of a Palestinian state. Each leader felt politically constrained to offer concessions to the other side because the anger between the two groups over past events ran so deep. The failure to arrive at a peace accord and the increased fighting led to Barak's defeat by Ariel Sharon in 2001. Sharon stated that he would not be bound by any previous agreements, and any movement toward peace seemed far in the future.

Sharon took a hard-line stance against the Palestinians, and in retaliation for suicide bombings, sent the army in and occupied much of the West Bank and Gaza, destroying and laying siege to PLO headquarters and houses of suspected terrorists and their relatives. In 2003 the United States and other Western countries established a Roadmap to Peace,

*T*he Most Elusive Gift of All

If you
asked
most sane
and temperate
men and women
throughout
the world
what they
wanted most
for the
holidays,
their first choice
wouldn't come
in a magnificent
box
with a fancy
ribbon.
They couldn't
find it on
a colorful page
of a fat
Christmas catalog.
They wouldn't
see it
glistening out
at them from
a window
of a smart boutique.
Because it's
the most
precious
and elusive
gift of all . . .
peace on earth.

United Technologies advertisement.

World Trade Center attacks, September 11, 2001.

which required both Palestinians and Israelis to move simultaneously toward peace, with the Palestinian police force stopping the militant Palestinians from attacking Israelis and the Israeli forces withdrawing from Palestine and stopping settlements. Few believed that the Roadmap would work, but all believed that it was best to try.

Other Mideast areas also remain unstable. Islamic militants oppose the Saudi Arabian monarchy, and after the 2003 Iraq War, in which the Sunni leader Saddam Hussein was removed from Iraq, the Saudi monarchy worried that its Shiite majority would revolt against the monarchy. Two other countries in the area, Iran and Syria, were classified by President Bush as part of the Axis of Evil and, soon after the 2003 Iraq War ended, the United States started claiming that Iran was harboring terrorists and developing nuclear weapons. Most observers believed that Iran was not harboring major terrorists, but they also believed that Iran learned the North Korean lesson—that the United States would not attack a country that has nuclear weapons and would use them. So Iran could very well be trying to develop such weapons in a preemptive attempt to stop a U.S. preemptive war. Because of its multiple hot areas, the Mideast remains the most likely place a new war might emerge.

The War on Global Terrorism

As stated at the beginning of this section, the United States is currently engaged in a war on terrorism, and for U.S. citizens, this terrorism is very likely to disrupt aspects of their lives. The question is what to do about it. What drives people to be willing to commit terrorist acts, and what will stop them? Is it possible for a country to be so strong and forceful that it can prevent terrorist attacks, or does such force simply create more terrorists? Views differ enormously on these questions, but as the United States embarks on a policy based on the Bush Doctrine of preemption, we are going to find out. Unfortunately, the cost of being wrong can be very high.

Key Points

- If countries don't get what they want, and they have the power to do so, they often go to war to get what they want.
- International law is a good idea, but it lacks any way of enforcing its decisions.
- Three principal organs of the UN are the General Assembly, the Security Council, and the Secretariat.
- The United States doesn't pay its dues for UNESCO for the same reason that Billy takes his ball away if he doesn't like the way the game is going.

- The new world order is order to be determined collectively by the major powers, primarily the United States. The U.S. policy of preemption makes it the ultimate arbiter of right and wrong in the world.

- The Arab–Israeli conflict has many dimensions and affects the area like a cancer that has metastasized.

Some Important Terms

al Qaeda (461)
General Assembly (468)
international law (465)
mediation (464)
new world order (475)
North Atlantic Treaty
   Organization (NATO) (474)

policy of preemption (461)
Roadmap to Peace (465)
Resolution 242 (480)
sanctions (470)
Secretariat (468)

Security Council (467)
United Nations (UN) (465)
veto (468)
Zionist (479)

Questions for Review and Discussion

1. How do you explain the prevalence of wars throughout human history?
2. Is the threat of war over with the end of the cold war? Explain your position.
3. Give what you think are some of the causes of war.
4. Explain the statement that war is "merely a continuation of politics by other means."
5. Explain how diplomacy is used to prevent war.
6. What are some of the reasons that international government cannot prevent all wars?
7. What are the three most important organs through which the UN acts?
8. What is the difference between the UN General Assembly and the UN Security Council?
9. How does the veto power of the Security Council hinder the search for peace? Are there any ways the veto power helps the search for peace?
10. Discuss some of the accomplishments of the UN.
11. What are some of the worst trouble spots in the world today? Can you think of ways to deal with any of these problems?
12. Give a history of the Arab–Israeli conflict.
13. What is the new world order? Do you think there is going to be more or less stability in the world under this order?
14. What is the most significant problem the world faces?
15. How would we know if the war on terrorism is justified?
16. If Mexico established a policy of preemption, how would the United States likely respond?
17. If the amount of money now spent on weapons systems could be used for something else, what do you think the money should be spent on?

Internet Questions

1. Go to www.un.org/Depts/dpko/dpko/ops.htm. What are the current United Nations peacekeeping operations?

2. What is the mission statement of the International Committee of the Red Cross? Consult its website, www.icrc.org.

3. According to Graça Machel, the UN expert on the impact of war on children (see www.unicef. org/graca), why are children particularly vulnerable to land mines?

4. According to Women Building Peace, www. international-alert.org/women, what are some of the activities women can perform in order to work toward constructing peace?

5. Using the International Peace Bureau site, www. ipb.org/web/index.php, what is the Hague Appeal for Peace program?

For Further Study

Boot, Max, *The Savage Wars of Peace: Small Wars and the Rise of American Power*, New York: Basic Books, 2002.

Brzezinski, Zbigniew, *The Grand Chessboard: American Primacy and Its Geostrategic Imperatives*, New York: Basic Books, 1997.

Carr, Caleb, *The Lessons of Terror: A History of Warfare against Civilians: Why It Has Always Failed and Why It Will Fail Again*, New York: Random House, 2002.

Clemens, Walter C., *America and the World, 1898–2023: Achievements, Failures, Alternative Futures*, New York: Palgrave/St. Martin's Press, 2000.

Cortwright, David, and Gregory A. Lopez, *The Sanctions Decade: Assessing UN Strategies in the 1990s*, Boulder, CO: Lynne Rienner, 2000.

Diamond, Jared, *Guns, Germs, and Steel: The Fates of Human Societies*, New York: Norton, 1997.

Goldman, Alvin L., *Knowledge in a Social World*, New York: Oxford University Press, 2000.

Hechter, Michael, *Containing Nationalism*, New York: Oxford University Press, 2000.

Hobsbawm, Eric, et al., *On the Edge of the New Century*, trans. Allan Cameron, New York: New Press, 2000.

Lovett, William, *U.S. Trade Policy: History, Theory, and the WTO*, Armonk, NY: Sharpe, 2000.

Rawls, John, *The Law of Peoples*, New York: Oxford University Press, 2000.

Requiem, by the Photographers Who Died in Vietnam and Indochina, eds., Horst Faas and Tim Page, New York: Random House, 1998.

Scanlon, T. M., *What We Owe to Each Other*, Cambridge, MA: Belknap/Harvard University Press, 1999.

Shawcross, William, *Deliver Us from Evil: Peacekeepers, Warlords, and a World of Endless Conflict*, New York: Simon & Schuster, 2000.

WWW   Center for War/Peace Studies   www.cwps.org

WWW   The International Court of Justice   www.icj-cij.org

WWW   Organization for Economic Co-Operation and Development   www.oecd.org

WWW   The United Nations   www.un.org/english

WWW   United Nations Educational, Scientific and Cultural Organization   www.unesco.org

WWW   Women's Federation of Peace International   www.wfwp.org/home.html

WWW   The World Health Organization   www.who.int/en

Index

Abdullah, Crown Prince of Saudi Arabia, 353, 354
Abortion, 183, 184, 205
Absolute monarchy, and arbitrary government, 299
Academic freedom, attacks on, 41
Accountability, and performance of U.S. schools, 222–225, 230
Adjustment, and social concerns, 168
Administration, state government expenditures, 381–382
Affirmative action, and African Americans, 262, 265
Africa
    and authoritarian rule, 299
    and poverty, 241
    and stage of development, 438–439
    and world peace, 476–477
African Americans
    and Jews, 273
    number of, in U.S., 257
    origins of, 257–258
    and ownership, 263
    and the professions, 262
Africanus ramidus, and human evolution, 45, 46
Age
    and the family, 170–171, 175
    and stratification, 233, 251
Aging, and social problems, 280–281
Agnostic, 13
Agriculture
    and declining participants, 172
    and human development, 54
    in the Middle Ages, 63, 64
    in planned and unplanned economies, 374
    and its share of the economy, 370
Akihito, Emperor of Japan, 347
Alleles, and genetic characteristics, 33–34
al Qaeda
    and September 11, 2001, 461

and terrorism in United States, 273
Amish, 273
Anarchists, defined, 292
Anarchy, and disintegration of government, 286
Anthropology
    and religious history, 187
    summarized, 6
Anti-Ballistic Missile Treaty, and U.S. position, 414
Anti-Semitism
    roots of, 194, 196–197
    in United States, 273–274
Apartheid
    and caste system, 235
    and international law, 466
Arab Americans, and stratification, 269–270
Arafat, Yasser, 481
Archaeology, and religious history, 187
Argentina, as developing country, 438
Aristide, Jean-Bertrand, 405, 442
Aristotle, 27, 32, 58, 263, 290
Armed forces
    and homosexuals, 279
    in Japan, 346
    and segregation, 263
    in Uganda, 457
Art, and Islam, 205
Asian refugees, and U.S. immigration, 270, 271
Asians, and stratification, 268
Assimilation
    and Native Americans, 257
    of U.S. immigrants, 270
Astrology, and scientific method, 13
Astronomy, separated from physics, 28
Australopithecus, and human evolution, 42
Autocracy
    characteristics of, 303

and communism, 305–306, 372
    and control, 300–303
    defined, 299–303
    in developing countries, 441–442, 448
    and fascism, 305–306
    in France, 338
    and military might, 441–442
    and Nazism, 305
    overthrow of, 302
    and planned economies, 363–364
    and power, 301–303
    and public opinion, 405, 406
    and Saudi Arabia, 352
    and Soviet Union, 349
    in underdeveloped countries, 301
Autocratic government, 294
Axis of Evil, 461, 475, 478, 482

Baby boom
    and school enrollment, 212
    and Social Security, 385
Balance of payments
    and how to deal with imbalance, 431
    and international trade, 421–423, 434
Balance of power, and breakup of former Soviet Union, 462
Balance of trade, and international trade, 421–423
Barter, and international trade, 426
Bay of Pigs, and Cuba, 414
Behaviorists, and psychology, 13
Beliefs, surveying, 21
Bias, 221–222, 255
Big Bang theory, and creation of the universe, 41n
Bill of Rights, and U.S. Constitution, 310–311, 322
Biological Weapons Convention, and U.S. withdrawal from, 414
Birthrates, and population control, 170, 175, 279

Black market, and planned economies, 375
Blacks (*see* African Americans)
Bonaparte, Napoleon, 194, 338, 407
Bonds, issued by government, 386
Borrowing, by government, 381, 386
Bourgeoisie, defined, 372
Boy Scouts of America, and homosexuals, 279
Brain drain, and developing countries, 446, 449
Brazil, as developing country, 438
Buddhism, 190, 192–193, 205
Bulgaria, and transition to unplanned economy, 375
Bureaucracy
    and government inefficiency, 393
    in Mexico, 343, 344
Bureau of the Census
    definition of poverty, 243–244
    and racial/ethnic classification, 252
Bush, George H., 321
Bush, George W., 225, 281, 315, 319, 321, 328, 330, 333, 345–346, 388, 404, 414, 465, 475, 482
Business
    and choice of enterprise, 365, 366
    and the economy, 359
    and types of organization, 370
Business cycles, 387

Calendar, and roots in language of ancient Rome, 62
Capital
    and business operation, 365–366
    and distribution of income, 244
    and production, 361–362
Capitalism
    and democracy, 294–295
    in developing countries, 441, 448
    early phase of, 70
    and negative effects, 371
    protection of, by U.S. foreign policy, 416
    and Protestant religions, 204
Capitalist economy, its composition, 365
Capitalist society, and Karl Marx, 248
Cartel, definition of, 421
Carter, Jimmy, 331, 414

Case method, and social science, 18–19
Caste
    and apartheid, 235
    as hierarchical class, 234–235
    in Hinduism, 191
    and India, 234–235
    and Native Americans, 235
Castro, Fidel, 267, 478
Caucasoid, 252
Celera Genomics, and genetic mapping, 35
Cenogamy, and the family, 164, 182
Ceylon, and Buddhism, 193
Charisma, and social science, 15
Charter schools, and educational funding, 218–219
Checks and balances
    in U.S. campaign financing, 333
    in U.S. government, 318–321
Chemical analysis, and debate about human evolution, 42
Chemistry, separated from physics, 28
Chicanos, as division of Hispanics, 266
Child care, expense of, 172–175, 278–279
Child custody, and women's prevalence, 278
Children
    decision to have, 177
    as economic assets, 168
    family function of, 172
    the only child and upward mobility, 245–246
    and parental custody, 180
    and relationship to marriage, 176
    and responsibilities of rearing, 169, 172
    and unmarried parents, 175
Child support payments, unreliability of, 277
Chimpanzees, and their divergence from human beings, 43, 44
China
    and Buddhism, 193
    and communism, 450, 452
    and market economy, 364
    as potential trouble spot, 478–479
    and poverty, 241
    and private markets, 375

problems of, as a developing country, 449–453
    profile of, 450–452
    and socialism, 373
Chirac, Jacques, President of France, 339, 342
Christian Coalition, role in government, 293
Christianity
    and ancient Rome, 61
    development of, 200–203
    and events reported in the Gospels, 201–202
    and fundamentalism, 188–189
    influence of, on Islam, 198
    in the Middle Ages, 6, 64–65, 66
    and number of adherents, 193
    organization of, 202
    and patriarchy, 166
    principle tenets, 201, 202, 204
    and religious wars, 187
    and split between West and East, 202–203
    spread of, 202, 203
Cities
    and anonymity, 173
    basic political institution, 55
    and beginning of settlement, 54
    development of, in ancient Greece, 58
    organization of, 54–55
    rise of, in the Middle Ages, 64
    and Roman civilization, 61, 62
Citizenship, and social science, 21
Civil Rights Acts, and discrimination against African Americans, 259–260
Civil union (*see* Gay marriage)
Class system, development of, in the Middle Ages, 63–64, 65
Clinton, Bill, 314–315, 319, 321, 331, 333, 415
Cloning, and genetic engineering, 35, 36
Code of Hammurabi, early collection of laws, 56
Cognitive science, 3
Cold war
    and détente, 417
    and disputes in Latin America, 477
    end of, 474

Colleges (*see* Universities)

Colonial America, and mandatory education, 210

Colonial system, end of, 462

Colonization, in ancient Greece, 58

Columbia, and rule by drug dealers, 442

Committee on Un-American Activities, in United States, 301

Common Era, 200

Common sense, in social science, 20

Communication, rapidity of, 23

Communism
  and anarchy, 292
  and arbitrary rule, 299, 300, 303
  and autocracy, 305–306
  and China, 450
  containment of, 416
  defined, 292, 371–373
  and democracy in former Soviet Union, 294–295
  in developing countries, 448
  goals of, 374–375
  ideology of, 413
  increase of, after World War I, 462
  and Karl Marx, 248
  and threat to United States, 474
  and U.S. Committee on Un-American Activities, 301
  and Utopian society, 371
  and world dominance, 411

Communist economies, 363

Communist government, and stratification, 256

Communist Party, in China, 292, 349

Community colleges, 215–216

Comparative method, and social science, 19

Comparative psychologists, and imagination, 9

Competition
  among theories, 13
  from foreign countries, 424–425, 426, 429–430
  and stratification, 233

Compromise
  and democracy, 297, 298
  and U.S. political parties, 326

Computers
  and advances in social science, 11

and data management, 21

and effect on the family, 183

and grammar issues, 217

and international flow of money, 434

and library use, 217

and market economy, 368–369

the supercomputer, 20

Conflict, between religious learning and rationalist learning, 28

Conflict theory, 13, 17, 18

Confucianism, 190

Congress, United States
  and amendment of the U.S. Constitution, 324–325
  appointive power of, 318
  legislative power of, 316, 318
  and the media, 330
  and nullification of its laws, 321
  and the party system, 314–315

Conservatives, defined, 293, 294

Constitution (*see also* Constitution of the United States)
  of former Soviet Union, 349
  of Great Britain, 324
  of Japan, 346, 348
  Mexican, 342–343
  quasi-constitutional system in Saudi Arabia, 352
  of Russia, 351–352

Constitution of the United States
  amendments to, 298, 322, 324–325, 414
  and derivation of government powers, 314
  and distribution of power, 315–321
  and division of power, 315, 316, 318
  as "living constitution," 324–325
  principal provisions of, 310–311
  and protection, 288
  and U.S. Supreme Court, 319

Constitutions, of individual states in United States, 311

Consumers
  and market economies, 366–369
  and pressure groups in the United States, 332

Contractionary monetary policy, 390, 391

Control
  and autocracy, 300–303
  in the family, 166
  and international relations, 401–408
  and methods of reckoning family descent, 170
  of a population, 373
  and power in democracy, 296
  of the press, 298, 305
  of social action, 23
  and totalitarianism, 299–300
  in U.S. government, 314–315

Controversy, and development of knowledge, 13

Cooperation, and international economic relations, 435

Copernicus, 20

Corporations
  global (or multinational), 421
  and raising capital, 366

Corruption, and developing countries, 442, 453, 457

Covenant marriages, 180

Creation, and the Bible version, 40–42

Credentializing, and education, 208–209

Credit
  effect of, on the family, 172
  and foreign trade, 426

Crime, as social science problem, 21, 23

Critical thinking, and education, 209

Cro-Magnons, and human evolution, 49, 50

Cross-cultural method, and social science, 19

Crusade, Islamic, 201

Crusades
  effect of, on modern civilization, 65, 69
  and Magna Carta, 70, 304
  and progress, 9, 69
  and religious war, 187, 205
  and spread of knowledge, 27

Cuba
  and the Bay of Pigs, 414
  and communism, 292
  as potential trouble spot, 477–478
  and U.S. immigration, 267

Cuban refugees, and U.S. immigration, 267, 270, 271
Cultural change, and war, 462
Cultural diffusion, and its necessity, 170
Culture
  and dating (social), 173–175
  and stratification, 251
  transmission of, 208, 209
Curiosity, and scientific method, 9
Curricula, and education, 225–227
Czech Republic, and transition to unplanned economy, 375

Darwin, Charles, 32, 38
Data, the raw numbers describing a phenomenon, 22
Dating (numerical systems), 200
Dating (social), and family characteristics, 173–175
Debt
  in developing countries, 445
  and war, 72–73
Declaration of Independence,The, 309–301
  and emphasis on equality, 297
  and faith in equality, 211, 249
Defense
  and expenditures, 417
  and federal budget, 385–386
  and government, 383
  spending in the United States, 332
Deficit, international, 422, 423, 434
Deflation, and recession, 371
Demand, for goods and services, 366–369
Democracy (see also Democratic government in the United States)
  characteristics of, 295–296
  in developing countries, 441–442, 448
  and failure, 301
  and its forms of organization, 299
  and majority opinion, 23
  measuring, 14, 239
  and Mexico, 342
  and military industrial complex in the United States, 331–332
  and origins in France, 337–338

and the political elite in the United States, 331
  and the rule of law, 303–304
  U.S. ideology, 290, 291
  and unplanned economies, 363–364
  what it needs to work, 298–299
  and world dominance, 411
Democratic government, 294, 295–299, 309–336
Democratic government in the United States
  comprehensive features of, 314
  and Constitutional Convention of 1787, 310
  and Declaration of Independence, 309–310
  development of, 309–311
  and the Electoral College, 316, 325, 327
  expansion of, 322
  and federal form of government, 310, 311
  and limitations on its power, 322
  organization of, 311–313
  presidential form of, 314–315
  and system of checks and balances, 318–320
Democrats, and campaign finance in the United States, 333
Demography
  of Asians in the United States, 268
  of Hispanics in the United States, 266–267
  of Japanese in the United States, 268
  and social classes, 237
  and stratification, 233
Department of Defense, United States, and the Internet, 370
Depression (see also Great Depression)
  in the United States, 365, 366, 384, 387–388
Descent, and family composition, 166–167, 170
Descent of Man, The (Darwin), 32
Determinism, versus free will, 38
Devaluation, of a currency, 433
Developed countries, 438, 439
Developing countries, 438, 458
  and brain drain, 446, 449

and corruption, 442, 453, 457
  economic problems of, 443
  and the European Union, 445
  and foreign aid, 443–445
  and foreign policy, 448
  and leadership, 449
  and moral obligations of the West, 445
  and policy options, 447–449
  and population growth, 446, 448–449, 451
  social systems of, 441
  and trade barriers, 445
Dictators, limits of their power, 23
Diderot, Denis, 30
Diplomacy
  and the United Nations, 470–471, 472
  in war and peace, 464–465, 472
Direct election, 330
Dirty float, and foreign exchange rates, 434
Discrimination
  and African Americans, 258–260, 264
  and assimilation, 255–256
  in education, 227–228
  and ethnic cleansing, 254
  and federal law against age discrimination, 281–282
  and gay marriage, 182
  and government protection, 288
  legally barred in the United States, 274
  and sexual preference, 279
Disease, sexually transmitted, 175, 176
Diversity, 21, 23
  and change in social patterns, 176
  and community colleges, 216
  and education, 210
  in the social sciences, 30
  and stratification, 233
Divorce
  legal grounds of, 180
  problems of, 180–181
  rate of, 178, 179, 180
  reasons for, 178–179, 180
  and women's poverty, 278
DNA (deoxyribonucleic acid)
  and aging, 280
  and chemical analysis, 42

and divergence of humans from
    apes, 43
mitochondrial, 44
role in genetics, 35
Dollar
    fall in value of, 434–435
    as international reserve currency,
        431
Dominant group, defined, 256
Dot.com phenomenon, 240
Dropouts
    problems and solutions, 220–221
    and unemployment, 374
Drug dealers, and terrorism, 442
Duties, of U.S. residents, 322–323

Earnings
    by level of education, 240
    and poverty, 241–242
    and women, 275–277
East, The, and contributions to
        Western culture, 59, 64
Eastern Europe
    and market economy, 364
    and political stability, 478
Econometric models, and economic
        prediction, 13
Economic decisions, and transition
        from planned to unplanned
        economy, 375
Economic elite, in the United States,
        331
Economic goods, and money, 360–361
Economic institutions, and
        economic organization, 359
Economic interest, and what is right,
        475
Economic policy, and allocation of
        resources, 362
Economic power
    and international relations, 401,
        407
    and resources, 407
Economic psychology, 4
Economics (*see also* International
        economics)
    and Adam Smith, 364
    and ancient Greeks, 27
    and children, 168
    defined, 12, 359
    of developing countries, 441

development of, in the Middle
        Ages, 64
    and its relation to policy, 426
    and religious sacrifice, 191
    and retirement, 178
    and rights, 166
    and selection of mates, 169
    and social class system, 235–236
    and social mobility, 240
    and social science, 360
    and stratification, 233
    wants of, and their satisfaction, 360
    and war, 462–464
Economic systems
    and inefficiency, 295
    and the market economy, 365–370
Economic theory
    and democracy, 296
    and judgments about what is
        right, 386
Economic welfare, and foreign
        policy, 410
Economies, organization of, 359–380
    Japanese, 348
    Mexican, 343
    regulation of, 391–393
    and Saudi Arabia, 354
    United States, and importance of
        international trade, 420–421
    ways of viewing throughout
        Western history, 68–69
Education
    and African Americans, 260, 262,
        265, 269
    and charter schools, 218–219
    compulsory, 217
    conservative position, 293
    and democracy, 209–210, 298
    development of, 4
    and dropouts, 220–221
    and earnings level, 240
    and funding, 209, 210, 211, 215,
        217–218, 381–382, 389
    and government, 209, 217–218,
        289, 290
    and Hispanics, 267
    history of, 7
    and home schooling, 217–218
    and interaction of social sciences,
        229–230
    and Native Americans, 257

and No Child Left Behind, 225
    and opportunities, 210
    optimal levels of, 228–229
    and private schools, 209, 217–218,
        230
    its prominence in life, 208
    quality of, 224–225
    quantity of, 209
    and rights, 166
    and social class, 236
    and socially desirable expense, 245
    and social mobility, 240
    and textbooks, 220
    and training, 216, 228–229
    and the United Nations, 469, 473,
        474
    and vouchers, 11
    and who supplies it, 383
    and women, 275
Egypt
    and beginning of recorded history,
        54–57
    and divinity of kings, 204
    productive society of, 57
Einstein, Albert, 1, 3, 5, 12, 24, 187
Eisenhower, Dwight D., 331–332
Elections
    and campaign finance from
        foreign countries, 333
    and campaign finance in the
        United States, 333
    direct and indirect, 330
    and political process in the United
        States, 333–334
    recall, 330
    referendum, 330
    and soft money in the United
        States, 333
    and term limits, 328
Electoral College, in U.S.
        government, 316, 325, 327
Emancipation Proclamation, and
        African Americans, 258
Empire, as concept developed in
        ancient Rome, 61, 62
Employment
    and Native Americans, 257
    of U.S. immigrants, 270
    and women, 275–277, 279
Enclosure, of land and its
        consequences, 70

Endogamy, and marriage, 174
Engels, Friedrich, 371
Engineering, and influence of
    ancient Rome, 62
Enlightenment, as feature of
    Buddhism, 192–193
Enlightenment, The, and rational
    organization of knowledge,
    28–30
Enrollment, in schools, 212, 216,
    217, 218
Epistemology, defined, 28
Equalitarian families, 166
Equality, and democracy,
    297–299
Equilibrium, between supply
    and demand, 367–369
Equal Rights Amendment (ERA),
    its fate, 274
Equity, as goal of planned
    economies, 375
Estate, as hierarchical class, 234
Ethics, code of, 187
Ethnicity
    and stratification, 251
    and war, 462–463, 473, 475
Euro
    as common currency, 342
    as international reserve currency,
        431
European Monetary Union, and
    France, 342
European Union (EU)
    and competition from developing
        countries, 445
    and free trade, 430–431
    history and members of, 317
Evaluation, of schools, 218
Evolution
    and Charles Darwin, 32, 38
    human, 42–50
    of humans' ancestors, 32
    of knowledge, 6
    of social science, 27–30
Evolutionary social psychology, as
    new field of psychology, 38
Excellence, in U.S. schools, 224–225
Exchange rates (*see also* Foreign
    exchange, Foreign exchange
    rates)
    and East Asia, 439

fixed, 433
flexible, 433
Exchange theory, approach to social
    science, 17, 18
Executive branch, of U.S.
    government, 311–313
Exogamy, and marriage, 174
Expansionary monetary policy, 390,
    391
Expenditures
    on education, 208, 209, 210, 211,
        215, 217–218, 381–382, 389
    and government, 381–382, 383,
        389
Experimental method, function of,
    10–11
Experiments, controlled, 14–15

Facts, and classification, 14
Fahd, King of Saudi Arabia, 353, 354
Falkland Islands War of 1982, 463
Family
    adaptations of, 173
    breakdown of, 277–278
    conservative position, 293
    constant association within, 31
    defined, 19, 163–164
    dominance in ancient Rome, 62
    as economic institution, 361
    future of, 183–184
    and gay marriage, 279
    and government, 290
    and group living, 166
    and incomes, 21
    legal forms of, 164
    and marital breakups, 173
    and seniors, 281
    and similarities between humans
        and apes, 44–45
    size of, 177–178
    and social classes, 235–236,
        237–239
    and technology, 183
    and the working woman, 276–277,
        278
Family planning, 172
Family tree, how to reckon and
    design, 166–167
Fascism
    and arbitrary rule, 299, 300
    and autocracy, 305–306

and rule by political elite, 290, 291
    and world dominance, 411–412
Federal form of government, in the
    United States, 310, 311
Federal Reserve Bank (Fed), 390–391
Feminism, and the Women's
    Movement, 274–276
Feudalism, 63, 64–65, 68–70
    disintegration of, 299
    as an economic system, 364
    in Japan, 346
    in the Middle Ages, 63, 64, 65
    and the nation-state, 399–400
Fiscal policy
    and level of spending in the
        economy, 388
    and unemployment management,
        368–370
Fixed exchange rates
    and the balance of payments, 434
    and computer transfer of funds,
        434
    defined, 433
    and the gold standard, 434
Ford, Gerald, 321
Foreign aid, and developing
    countries, 443–445
Foreign exchange
    defined, 431–432
    and international trade, 426
Foreign exchange rates (*see also*
        Exchange rates, Foreign
        exchange)
    determination of, 432
    and international relations, 420
Foreign investment, and
    international relations, 420
Foreign policy
    and developing countries, 448
    as tool of international relations,
        410
    in the United States, 416–418
Foreign trade, and offsets, 425
Fossils
    and evolutionary split between
        humans and apes, 42–43
    of humanlike species, 32–40, 45,
        46
    and punctuated equilibrium, 38, 39
Fourth Estate, in the United States,
    330

Fox, Vicente, 273, 342, 344, 455–456
France
    and geographic aspirations, 411
    government of, 337–342
    and organization of government, 338, 341
    profile of, 339
Franco, Francisco, 299
Freedom
    from censorship, 209
    and choice in marriage, 165–166
    and economics, 363
    as essential element of democracy, 296–299, 304, 305
    and government, 288, 304
    individual, 405
    of press in the United States, 330–331
    protection of, in the United States, 334
    rights in the United States, 322
    and the sexual revolution, 173, 174
    under an autocracy, 300–301, 304
Free enterprise system, and limitations on, 366
Free thinking (see Rational thinking)
Free trade
    and expansion of trade, 430–431
    and foreign exchange rates, 432
    and globalization, 431
    restrictions of, 426–431
    and the World Bank, 444
Free will, 2, 38
French Revolution, and rights of Jews, 194
Freudians, and psychology, 13
Functionalist approach
    described, 285–286
    to social science, 17–18
Functionalists, and psychology, 13
Fundamentalism
    and Christianity, 188–189
    and Islam, 188–189, 199–201, 205
Funding
    of education, 209, 210, 211–215, 218–219, 227, 228
    and government bonds, 386
    of Social Security in the United States, 384–385
Future, the, and education, 217

Gallup poll, 21, 176
Gay marriage, 279
    and the family, 164
    and legalization, 182
Gay rights, and religion, 205
Gays, and discrimination, 279
Gender
    and stratification, 233, 251
    and upward mobility, 245–246
Gender Equity in Education Act, and gender bias, 222
General Agreement on Trade and Tariffs (GATT), and international trade, 430
General Assembly, of the United Nations, 467–468
General Equivalency Diploma (GED), and dropouts, 221
Generalization, in social science, 14
Genes
    and aging, 280
    and splicing, 35
Genetics
    and duplication, 35
    and evolutionary process, 33
    and how living beings change, 33
    Human Genome Project, 35–36
    and patriarchal family, 170
    and propagation of one's genes, 169
    role of DNA, 35
    and social/ethical dilemmas, 36
Genetic theory, 4
Geographic power, and foreign policy, 401, 407, 410–411
Geography, and society, 9, 31–32
Geopolitics, defined, 411
Gerrymandering, and U.S. elections, 329
Globalization, and free trade, 431
God
    and his place in Judaism, 194
    and Jesus' relation to, 201
    and religious belief, 188
Gold
    and foreign trade, 426
    and national finance, 70
Gold standard, and fixed exchange rates, 433, 434
Goods
    and international trade, 423–424

    and paying for international trade, 431, 434
    public, 383
    supplied by government, 383
Gore, Albert, 315, 328, 330
Government (see also Democratic government in the United States)
    basic job of, 286
    benefits of, 289
    and changes in the future, 356
    and direct role in an economy, 381, 391–394
    and economic interaction, 289
    and economic regulation, 364
    and the economy, 359
    and education, 289, 290
    and the family, 290
    and foreign countries, 337
    and freedom, 288, 293, 304, 305
    French, 337–342
    and functionalist approach, 285–286
    and general principles, 355
    goals of, 306
    and health services, 289, 290
    and indirect role in the economy, 391–393
    and individual freedom, 288, 304, 305
    and inefficiency, 393
    institutions by which society is ruled, 285
    in Japan, 346–349
    and justice, 286–288
    in Mexico, 342–346, 454–456
    as necessary evil, 291
    organization in former Soviet Union, 349
    parliamentary system, 341
    as positive good, 291–292
    and its power, 286, 292–294, 301–302
    presidential system, 341
    and private enterprise, 366
    and property rights, 286
    and public well-being, 289–290
    and redistribution of income, 383–384
    and regulation of business, 369–370

Government (*continued*)
and religion, 290
role of, in society, 294
in Russia, 349–352
of Saudi Arabia, 352–353, 354, 355
and social security, 289
and social services, 290
and stability in developing
countries, 440–441
and system of world government,
408
as unnecessary evil, 292
and why we need it, 383
Governmental systems, blurring of,
342
Governments, types of, 294, 295
Granada, and U.S. invasion, 319
Great Britain, and evolution of
market economy, 377
Great Depression (*see also*
Depression)
and aftermath of war, 462
and the gold standard, 433
and government's activist role, 393
and protective tariffs, 427–428
Greece
and dictatorship, 299
and the Persian empire, 60
and the Renaissance, 60
revival of its culture in the Middle
Ages, 65, 66, 67
and roots of Western civilization,
58
Green Party, 326–327
Group living, and the family, 166
Growth
in China, 452
and developing countries, 443
and exploitation of workers, 372
in Mexico, 454
and recession, 370–371
in U.S. economy, 370–371
Growth rates, of developed and
industrial countries, 439–441

Haiti, and military might in
government, 405, 441–442
Happiness
and economics, 360
and social science, 21
Harding, Warren G., 285

Hare Krishna, and Hinduism in the
West, 192
Harris poll, 21
Hawaii, U.S. acquisition of, 416
Head Start, preschool education
program, 215
Health, and income, 21
Health care
and economic inequality, 244, 245
and government payment, 383
and government spending, 386
Health insurance, and social
experiment, 11
Hierarchy, and stratification,
233–249
High wages argument, for tariffs,
427, 428
Hinduism, 190, 191–192
and caste system, 234–235
multiple kinds of, 191–192
principal tenets of, 191
Hirohito, Emperor of Japan, 190
Hispanics, and stratification,
266–267
Historical method, and social
science, 18
History
documentation versus theory, 28
of Mexican political situation,
342–343
of nations carved in art, 205
as social science, 9
thesis and antithesis of, 372
Hitler, Adolph, 273, 303n, 305, 411
Homeless persons, and social
problems, 241
Home market argument, for tariffs,
427, 428
Home schools, prevalence of, 217
Hominidae, and human evolution, 42
Homo antecessor, and human
evolution, 46
Homo erectus, and human evolution,
42, 45–46
Homo habilis, and human evolution,
42, 45–46
Homo sapiens, and human evolution,
42, 46, 47, 49
Honor, and war, 462–463
Hot money, and flexible exchange
rates, 434

Hourly earnings, and their
variations, 242, 243
Human beings
concern with selves, 31
evolution in tropical regions, 34, 35
knowledge of, 1
modern people's distinctions,
49–50
Human evolution
basic outline, 42
Hominidae and, 42
Homo antecessor and, 46
Homo erectus and, 42, 45–46
Homo habilis and, 42, 45–46
Homo sapiens and, 42, 46, 47, 49
Human Genome Project, and
mapping of human genes,
35–36
Humanities, 3, 28, 204–205
Human rights
and the Communist Party, 413
and Magna Carta, 70, 394
and statement of in French
Revolution, 73
and use of national power, 412
Humans, and divergence from apes,
42–45
Human species, its origination, 32
Hungarian Rebellion of 1956, and
U.S. immigration, 270
Hungary, and transition to
unplanned economy, 375
Hussein, Saddam, 199, 401, 405, 412,
461, 463, 470, 472, 482

Illegal aliens (*see* Immigration)
Imagination, as supplement to
thinking, 10
Immigration, 270–273
of Arab Americans to the United
States, 269
of Chinese to the United States,
268
and illegal aliens in the United
States, 272–273
and Mexico, 266, 345
and a society's continuation, 168
and talent from developing
countries, 446–447
of Vietnamese to the United
States, 268

Immigration law, effectiveness of, 267, 268, 271–273

Immigration legislation in the United States, 270–273

Impeachment, and U.S. government, 314–315

Imports
and how we pay for them, 425–426, 427
and international trade, 420–421, 422–423

Incentives, for economic progress, 244–245

Income
and African Americans, 260–261
of Arab Americans, 269
of Chicanos, 267
distribution of, 242–243, 244–245, 383–384
expenditure of, 366, 367
and social class, 235–236, 237, 238, 239–240, 241
sources of, 241–242
and stratification, 233
and U.S. standard of living, 246–247

Income distribution, and democracy, 298

Income security
government expenditures on, 381–382
and U.S. depression, 388

Incomes, surveying, 21, 22

Income support
and amount of Social Security benefits, 385
and state government expenditures, 381–382

Income tax
and distribution of income, 245
progressive, 383–384

Independence, of former Soviet Union republics, 349, 351

India
and Buddhism, 192
and caste system, 234–235
and Hinduism, 191
and poverty, 241
and religious art, 205

Indirect election, 330

Individualism, and education, 209

Industrialization, and upward mobility, 246

Industrial Revolution, The, 71–74
and effects of pollution, 33
and transformation of social institutions, 364

Inefficiency, in government, 393

Inequality, and money income, 241

Infant industry argument, for tariffs, 427, 428

Infertility, and technology, 183

Inflation, in the United States 370–371

Institutional Revolutionary Party (PRI), 344–345, 454. 455–456

Intelligent design, as theory of creation, 41–42

Interdisciplinary approach, and social problems, 21, 23

Interest, as government expense, 386

International affairs, and U.S. scandals, 415

International Atomic Energy Agency (IAEA), and the United Nations, 474

International Criminal Court, U.S. attitude toward, 414

International economics, and international relations, 420–435

International law
and peace, 465–467
successes of, 466
and the United Nations, 473–474

International Monetary Fund (IMF), and exchange rates, 433–434

International political relations, and international economic issues, 435

International relations
and international economics, 420–435
and the state, 397–398

International reserve currency, and imbalance of payments, 431

International trade
and foreign exchange, 431–432
and international relations, 420
and international reserve currency, 431, 434

Internet
business, 370
and effect on the family, 183
and increasing association, 31
and political control in the United States, 330
and rapid communication, 23
and upward mobility, 247

Internment, of Japanese in the United States, 268–269

Investment
requirement for developing country, 443, 457
and savings, 389–390

IQ tests, as stratification device, 253

Iran
and nuclear weapons, 482
religious and political authority, 199
and War on Terrorism, 461

Iraq (*see also* Mesopotamia)
and failure of government, 285, 286
and geographic aspirations, 411
and Islamic sects, 199
and U.S. power, 403–404, 405, 406
and War on Terrorism, 461

Iraq War of 1991 (*see* Persian Gulf War)

Iraq War of 2003, 386, 406, 461–462, 468–469, 471–472
and democratic government, 199
effects of, 462, 463
and European reaction, 408
and interim authority in Iraq, 401
and North Atlantic Treaty Organization (NATO), 409–410
and President George W. Bush, 319
and Russia, 352
and Saudi Arabia, 355, 482
and the United Nations, 474

Irish, immigration to the United States, 271

Islam, 190, 197–200
and its art, 205
its basis, 197
and fundamentalism, 188–189, 199–201
and 9/11, 475

Islam *(continued)*
    and number of adherents, 193, 195
    and Saudi Arabia, 352, 482
    sects of, 198–199
    spread of, in the world, 198
    and Western countries, 205
Islamic law, 354
Isolationism
    and international trade, 420, 423
    and U.S. foreign policy, 416
Israel
    and Middle East Arabs in the
        United States, 269–270
    and U.S. foreign aid, 445
    and U.S. support, 475
Israeli-Egyptian conflict, 471
Israeli-Palestinian conflict, 465,
    479–482

Jail, number of inmates in, 21
Japan
    and Buddhism, 193
    and divinity of emperor, 204
    and education, 209
    and geographic aspirations, 411
    profile of the country, 347
    and U.S. immigration, 268
Jehovah's Witnesses, 273
Jesus of Nazareth, 200–201
Jews
    and discrimination in the United
        States, 273
    and Palestinians, 197
    and race, 195
    and race/ethnicity problem, 252
    in the United States, and Israel,
        273
Jobs
    created in the Industrial
        Revolution, 72
    U.S., and globalization, 431
Johnson, Lyndon B., 414
Judaism, 190, 193–197
    divisions of, 194–195
    influence of, on Islam, 198
    and number of adherents, 193
    and persecution, 194
    precursor of Christianity, 200
    principle tenets of, 194, 195–196
Judicial branch, of U.S. government,
    311–313

Judicial system, U.S., and its
    organization, 318
Judiciary, its independence in the
    United States, 319–322
Justice, administered by government,
    286–288
Juvenile delinquency, and reasons
    for, 21

Kennedy, John F., 414, 474
Keynes, John Maynard, 359, 370, 388
Keynesian revolution, and
    government's stabilizing role
    in the economy, 388
Kindergarten, and school structure,
    215
Kingdoms, and the organization of
    society, 55–57
Kingship, and its origin in the
    Middle Ages, 65
Knowledge, 1
Koizumi, Junichiro, 347, 348
Koran, The, and the revelation of
    God's will, 197
Korea, and Buddhism, 193
Korean War, 471
Kyoto Protocol, and U.S. rejection
    of, 414

Labor
    and influence of organized labor
        in U.S. politics, 332
    and planned economy, 374
    and production, 361–362
Laboring class, of peasants, 55–56
Labor movement, and class
    distinctions, 248
Laissez faire
    as economic policy, 364–365
    and government regulation, 392
Language
    development of, in India, 205
    and expressions of social science,
        24–25
    and influence of Latin, 61–62
    native, 2
    Native American, 257
    and Neanderthals, 47
    of U.S. immigrants, 270
Latin America, and world peace,
    477–478

Latinos, as division of Hispanics, 266
Law *(see also* Rules)
    in a democracy, 298, 303–304
    and the economy, 359
    and the power to interpret, 319–321
    and private enterprise, 366
    and Roman origins, 62
    and rule of social science, 14
    in the United States, 313
    in Uganda, 457
Lawmakers, and women, 275
Leadership, in developing countries,
    449
League of Nations
    and U.S. Senate rejection, 416
    and world government, 467
Least developed countries, 438–439
Legislation, in the United States, 314,
    320
Legislative branch, of U.S.
    government, 311–313
Lenin, Vladimir, 292
Lesbians, and discrimination, 279
Liberal Democratic Party (LDP), in
    Japan, 348
Liberals, defined, 293, 294
Liberia, and failure of government,
    285
Libertarians, defined, 292–293
Libraries, and computers, 217
Lincoln, Abraham, 258
Linnaeus, Carolus, and organization
    of species, 32, 37
Literacy, and education, 210
Living together, prevalence of, 182
Lobbyists, and influence in U.S.
    government, 332
Local government, in the United
    States, 311
Loyalty, and its power in a
    democracy, 407
Luck, as fact of life, 246
Luther, Martin, 67, 203

Macedonia *(see* Greece)
Macroeconomics
    and the aggregate economy, 370
    and role of government, 387
Madison, James, 316–317, 318
Magna Carta, as statement of human
    rights, 70, 304

Majority rule, and democratic government, 296
Making a difference, and voting in the United States, 328–330
Malthus, Thomas, 446
Mandatory registration in the United States, for certain Arabs and Muslims, 270
Manufacturing, the decline of, 370
Mao Ze-dong, 452
Market economy
    and class struggle, 371
    evolution of, 377
    and how it works, 365
    in Russia, 351
    in the United States, 374
Market incentives, in China, 449–450, 451
Markets
    and change, 370–371
    and the computer revolution, 368–369
    laissez-faire policy, 364
    and the Middle Ages, 364
    and the oil crisis, 368–369
    regulated by law, 391
    in Uganda, 457
Marriage
    and age of the parties, 170–171
    as a contract, 176
    and divorce, 178–181
    and gays, 164, 182
    and how it is formed, 169–170, 171, 180
    and living together, 182
    and the middle class, 176–177
    rate of, 179
    and singles, 181
Marx, Karl, 248, 292, 365, 371, 372–373, 413
Mass production
    and its development, 370
    and international trade, 423
Mates, selection of, 164–165, 174–175
Matriarchy, and the family, 166
Media, and influence on U.S. government, 330, 331
Mediation, and peace, 465
Medicaid, and government income support, 384

Medicare
    and alleviation of poverty, 244–245
    and government income support, 290, 384
    and government spending, 290, 386
Medicine, and stratification, 233
Men
    and their liberation, 172
    and positive effects of women's movement, 278, 279
Mendel, Gregor, 33
Mercantilism, as an economic system, 70, 364–365
Merchants, their development in ancient Greece, 58
Mesopotamia
    and beginning of recorded history, 54–57
    and the Persian empire, 58, 59, 60
Messiah, The, as deliverer of the Jews, 200–201
Methodology
    limitations of, 13
    of social science, 11–14
Methods, in social science, 14–17
Mexico
    and culture of work, 19
    as developing country, 438
    government of, 342–346
    and illegal aliens, 273
    and individual economic decision, 370
    and North American Free Trade Agreement (NAFTA), 345
    profile of, 344, 453–456
    and role of government, 387
    and U.S. immigration, 270, 345
Microsoft, Inc., and anti-trust violations, 393
Middle Ages, 63–66
    and arbitrary rule, 299
    and Christianity, 202–203
    and cultural influence of Christianity, 204
    and influence of religion, 28
    and Judaism, 194
    and markets, 364
    and religious war, 187
    and tradition, 9

Middle class
    and the French Revolution, 337
    growth of, 73
    and ideal family, 177–178
    in the United States, 236
Middle East
    and international friction, 196–197
    as potential trouble spot, 479–482
Military aristocracy, formation of, 55–56
Military-industrial complex, and influence in the United States, 331–332
Military power
    and government, 286, 472
    in international relations, 401–406, 407
    limitations of, 404, 405
    and undeclared wars, 416
    and unilateral buildup, 408
    and U.S. indifference to international community, 414, 472–473
Military service
    and stratification, 233, 234
    and women, 275
Minorities
    and their opinions in international relations, 407–408
    in the United States, 256–282
Minority group, defined, 256
Miranda rights, in U.S. legal system, 298
Missionary movement, and Christianity, 203
Mixed economy
    and Great Britain, 377
    and prevalence in West, 365
Mohammed, founder of Islam, 197–198
Molecular biology, and debate about human evolution, 42, 44
Monarchy, absolute, French government system, 337
Monetary policy
    and level of income in the economy, 389–391
    and unemployment management, 368–370

Money
   and community colleges, 216
   and control of private schools,
      209, 218–219
   and economic goals, 360
   and the euro, 342
   and international trade, 431–432
   as a method of payment, 69–70, 71
   paper, as a standard, 433–434
   and political influence, 331
   and power of U.S. House of
      Representatives, 318
Money supply, defined, 390
Mongoloids, racial classification, 252
Monogamy, and the family, 164, 168,
   169
Monopolies, and government
   control, 288–289
Monopoly
   of one political party, 304–305
   in public utilities, 366
Moore's law, 20
Moral standards, and social values, 24
Mormons (Church of Jesus Christ of
   Latter Day Saints), 273
Multiculturalism, in education, 221
Museveni, Yoweri, 301
Muslims (see also Islam)
   discrimination against in the
      United States, 274
   dominance of, in the Middle Ages,
      63
   and religious wars, 187
   and spread of their culture, 63, 66
Mussolini, Benito, 411
Mutations, and evolution, 33–35
Myanmar, and Buddhism, 193
Myth, and religion, 187

Nader, Ralph, 326–327
Names, acquisition of, 167
National Action Party (PAN),
   Mexican political party, 345
Nationalism, origin of, in the Middle
   Ages, 65
Nation-state (see also State)
   appearance and disappearance
      of, 400–401
   defined, 397–400
   and formation of boundaries, 73
   and political consensus, 441

rise and organization of, 71, 73
   and security, 408–410
   and trade, 71, 365
   and war, 462–463
Native Americans
   as a caste, 235
   rights of, as U.S. citizens, 257
   as U.S. minority, 256–257
Natural selection, and human
   evolution, 32, 33, 50
Nature, of human beings, 296–297
Nazi Germany, and anti-Semitism,
   273
Nazi Party, and American Civil
   Liberties Union, 412
Nazis
   and geographic aspirations, 411
   and international law, 466
Nazism, and autocracy, 305
Neanderthals, and human evolution,
   46–47, 49, 50
Negroids, 252
New economy, and continual growth,
   370–371
New Right, and control of sexual
   practices, 294
New Testament, source of Jesus'
   teaching, 201
New world order, and its
   enforcement, 475–476
9/11 (see September 11, 2001)
Nirvana, goal of Buddhism, 192
No Child Left Behind, educational
   program, 225
Nondemocratic government, 294
Nongovernmental agencies (NGA),
   in developing countries, 445
North American Free Trade
   Agreement (NAFTA)
   and free trade, 430–431
   and Mexico, 345, 455
North Atlantic Treaty Organization
   (NATO), 409, 410, 474
North Korea
   and communism, 292
   and War on Terrorism, 461
Nuclear arsenal, and potential use,
   478
Nuclear energy, and international
   control, 473, 474, 475
Nuclear weapons, and Iran, 482

Numerology, and scientific method,
   13

Objectivity, and scientific method, 9
Occupation, and social class, 236,
   237, 238–239
Oil crisis, and market economy,
   368–369
Oil supply, and international
   relations, 407, 421
On-line association, compared with
   physical association, 31
Open Housing Act, and African
   Americans, 263
Operation Far Cry, dropout
   program, 221
Opportunity, and economic
   inequality, 244, 245
Organization of Petroleum Exporting
   Countries (OPEC), and
   international trade, 421
Origin
   of Hispanics in U.S., 266
   of U.S. immigrants, 270, 272
Origin of Species, The (Darwin), 32
Osama bin Laden, and war against
   the West, 200–201, 355
Oxford, as educational institution, 5

PACs (Political Action Committees),
   and their political influence,
   329, 332–333, 343
Pakistan, exemplar of Eastern
   culture, 64
Palestinians, and Jews, 197
Parapsychology, and information
   transmission, 13
Parliamentary government,
   exemplified, 314, 338
Parliamentary system, of
   government, 338, 341
Partially democratic governments,
   294
Partnerships, and raising capital,
   366
Patriarch
   and the family, 166
   and women's role today, 278
Patriot Act, 288, 325
Patriotism, and its power in a
   democracy, 407

Pattern, as social science tool, 21
Peace
    and diplomacy, 464–465, 472
    and the future, 356
    and human goals, 464
    and international trade, 435
    and Iraq War of 2003, 461–462
    and Islamic debates, 201
    and mediation, 465
    and a new world order, 475–476
    and the nuclear standoff, 416–417,
        475, 482
    and its possibilities, 474–476
    and preemption, 482
    and the United Nations, 470–474
    and U.S. commitment to, 475
Pearl Harbor, and World War II, 346,
    416
Peasants, their life in the Middle
    Ages, 63
Persian empire, 58, 59, 60
Persian Gulf War, 319, 462–463
    and freedom of the press,
        405–406
    and presidential power, 415
    and United Nations authorization,
        471–472
Personality, development of, in a
    democracy, 297
Philosophy, and social values, 24
Physics, development of, 27, 28
Plague, effect of "Black Death" in the
    Middle Ages, 65
Planned economy
    how it works, 373–376
    problems of, 374
    Soviet-style, 371
    and transition to unplanned
        economy, 375
Plato, 2, 27, 294
Poland, and evolution of market
    economy, 375, 377
Policies, and their adoption, 386
Policymaking, and government, 387
Policy options, for developing
    countries, 447–449
Political administration
    development of, in the Middle
        Ages, 63, 64
    and influence of ancient Rome,
        61, 62

Political consensus, and developing
    countries, 441–442
Political division, and war, 462–463
Political economy, 45, 439
Political elite, in the United States,
    331
Political interest, and what is right,
    475
Political parties, in the United States,
    326–327
Political process, in the United States,
    325–334
Political rights, and control, 166
Political science
    and ancient Greeks, 27, 58, 294
    summarized, 12
Political systems, of developing
    countries, 441
Political theories, 292–294
Political uprising, in China, 452
Politics
    relevance of, in the United States,
        328, 330
    and stratification, 233
    in Uganda, 458
    as way to affect government, 290
Pollution, and economics, 362
Polyandry, and the family, 164
Polygamy
    and the family, 164, 182
    and the Mormons, 273
Polygyny, and the family, 164
Popular sovereignty (*see also* Voting)
    and democracy, 296
Population
    of Arab Americans in the United
        States, 269
    of Asians in the United States, 268
    decreases in the Middle Ages, 65
    of Hispanics in the United States,
        266
    and number of seniors in the
        United States, 280–281
    and reproduction, 170
    and social science, 21
Population control
    and family planning, 172
    and technology, 183
Population growth
    in developing countries, 446,
        448–449, 451

    in early settlements, 54
Poverty
    defined, 241, 242–243
    and divorce, 278
    elimination of, 243–245
    and Jews, 196
    as social science problem, 23
    and women, 277
Power
    and African Americans, 262
    balance of, and world peace,
        408–409
    and bases outside state framework,
        442
    derivation of in the United States,
        314
    distribution of, in U.S.
        government, 315–321
    in French government system, 338,
        339, 341–342
    and government, 286, 290, 292–
        294, 301–303
    of human beings, 29–30
    and industrial might, 407
    and international relations,
        401–408
    and interpretation of law in the
        United States, 319–322
    limitation of, in U.S. government,
        322
    limits of, 23, 301–302
    and marriage, 165
    in Mexican government, 343,
        344–345
    a nation's most important source
        of, 407
    and political influence, 331
    and the power elite, 294–295
    in Saudi Arabia, 352, 354
    and size of a nation-state, 407, 408
    and stratification, 233
    to tax, 383
    and theory of complex
        interdependence, 409
    of U.S. government and individual
        states, 315, 316
    of U.S. presidency, 414–416
    use of, 475
    and war, 462–463
Powers, separation of, in U.S.
    government, 315, 316–319

Power vacuum, and war, 464
Precedent, in Saudi Arabia, 352
Preemption
    and North Korea, 478
    U.S. attack policy, 461, 475
    and world peace, 482
Pregnancy, teenage, 175
Prenuptial agreements, and
        marriage, 176
Prescription drugs
    and government payment, 383
    and government spending, 386
Presidency of the United States, power
        of, in foreign affairs, 414–416
President, United States
    as commander of the armed
        forces, 414–415, 416
    powers and obligations, 311, 315,
        318–319
Presidential system of government, 341
Press, freedom of, 405, 406
Pressure groups
    and foreign policy, 410
    in the United States, 325, 330, 332
Price
    in communist countries, 375
    and fall in, 371
    and international trade, 424
    and role in market economy,
        366–369
Price control, of prescription drugs,
        386
Priesthood, formation of, 55–56
Primates, and human evolution, 42
Private enterprise
    and government framework, 366
    and religion, 204
Private schools
    Accelerated Christian Education,
        Inc., 217–219
    and enrollment figures, 217
    and government money, 209
    and nursery school, 215
Privatization, of certain government
        activities, 288–289
Privatizing, of education, 219
Problems, and their approaches,
        17–18
Production
    and business organization, 370
    and economics, 360, 361–362

    and government ownership of
        means of production, 372
    in planned economy, 373–375
    and types of economies, 364–365
    and U.S. depression, 387–388
Profit, and the market economy,
        364–367
Propaganda
    defined, 305
    and social science, 15
Property
    and divorce, 180
    and economics, 361
    and marriage, 165
    in the Middle Ages, 63
    and poverty, 241–242
    rights protected by government,
        286, 343
Property ownership, and African
        Americans, 263
Property rights, 286, 343
Protestant Reformation
    and progress, 10
    and revolt against Catholicism,
        202–203
    and the rise of critical thinking,
        67, 68
Protestants, and division into many
        sects, 203
Protomics, and genome project, 36
Psychological economics, 4
Psychological needs, and the family,
        169
Psychology, 13
Public interest, and tariffs, 476
Public policy, and social scientists, 23
Public schools
    commitment to, 210–212
    enrollment figures, 212
    functions of, 209–210
    and vouchers, 383
Public welfare, and level of spending
        in France, 342
Puerto Ricans, and U.S. citizenship,
        267
Punctuated equilibrium, and
        evolution through stable
        periods, 38–40
Pure Food and Drug Act, and
        government regulation, 365
Puritan ethic, precepts of, 172

Puritans, 203
Putin, Vladimir, 350, 352

Quakers, 203
Quotas
    and globalization, 431
    and international trade, 426,
        429–430

Race
    and stratification, 233, 251–255
    and upward mobility, 245–246
Racial discrimination, as social
        science problem, 23
Radicals, defined, 294
Rationality, and democracy, 297
Rational theory
    and independence from theology,
        27
    and logical connection, 28
Rational thinking, its rise and
        influence, 67
Reactionaries, defined, 293
Reagan, Ronald, 321, 331, 414, 415
Recall, in U.S. elections, 330
Recession
    in Mexico, 345
    and slow economic growth,
        370–371
Referendum, in U.S. elections, 330
Reform Party, 326–327
Reformation, and progress, 10
Regulation
    and Congressional Acts to affect
        market economy, 365
    conservative position, 293, 364–365
    of the economy, 391–393
    by the government of business,
        369–370
Reincarnation (see Transmigration)
Religion
    and acceptance based on faith, 28
    in ancient Rome, 61, 62, 63
    and caste system, 234–235
    in China, 452
    civil, 188, 199, 205
    conflict between Catholics and
        Protestants, 29
    and conflict with law, 188
    and decreasing secular influence,
        67, 68

defined, 189
and democracy, 298
and government, 290
and growth of science, 9
and the humanities, 204–205
in India, 191
internal conflicts of, 67
in Japan, 347
and mandatory education,
      210–211
membership numbers, 190
in Mexico, 344
in the Middle Ages, 28, 63, 64–65,
      66
negative roles of, 205
origins of, 187, 189
pagan institutions, 55
in primitive times, 203–204
promises of, 187
and religious schools, 217, 218–219
rites of, 188
in Russia, 350
in Saudi Arabia, 353
and small sects, 273
and social values, 24
and stratification, 251
and theories of creation, 41–42
in Uganda, 457
and war, 462–463
and what it means, 188–189
Renaissance, 66–68
and comprehensive knowledge, 6
and ideas from ancient Greece, 60
and progress, 9
and reform of Christianity, 202–203
and spread of knowledge, 27, 28
Renaissance man, and ability to
      know everything, 27–28
Reproduction
and the family, 167–168
and population control, 170
Republicans, and campaign finance
      in the United States, 333
Research institutions, and role in
      education, 208
Reserve currency, and international
      trade, 431, 434
Resources
and economics, 360
and military power, 408, 473
and production, 361–362

Retirement, and adjustment to, 178
Revenue, government, 381–382, 389
Revolution, sexual, effects of, 173,
      175–176
Rights
and economics, 361
and French Declaration of the
      Rights of Man, 340–341
and their protection in the United
      States, 334
in the United States, 252–260,
      310–311, 322–324
and U.S. Supreme Court, 320–321,
      323
Right to vote, in the United States, 327
Robots, and the home, 183
Roman civilization, 61–62
Roman Empire
and Church of Rome, 202
and the classical world, 29
and dictatorship, 299
duration of, 61, 62
the fall of, 62–63, 64
positive and negative
      accomplishments of, 62
Romania, and transition to
      unplanned economy, 375
Roosevelt, Franklin D., 384, 467
Rousseau, Jean-Jacques, 188, 199, 205
Rules (*see also* Law)
codification into laws, 56
enforced by government, 286
and eligibility for marriage,
      164–165
as organizational tool, 6, 8, 65–66
and Roman codification of law, 61
Russia
and anti-Semitism, 273
and fascism, 411–412
and geographic aspirations, 411
and history of former Soviet
      Union, 349
and market economy, 364
profile of, 350
Russian Social Democratic Party, 349

Sacrifice, as religious rite, 191
Salvation, Christian, 210
Sanitation, and population growth,
      54
Sanskrit, and modern languages, 205

Satisfaction, measuring, 14
SAT scoring, changes in, 223
Saudi Arabia
and Iraq War of 2003, 355, 482
and Islamic militants, 482
profile of, 353
and tribal government, 352
Savings, requirement for developing
      country, 443
Scarcity, and economics, 362
Schism, in Christianity, 202–203
School choice, and educational value,
      218
School prayer, 184
Schools
evaluation of, 218
function of, in child care, 172–173
and religious foundation, 204
and sex education, 184
Schwarzenegger, Arnold, and
      California elections, 330
Science, 3, 4
Science, natural, 3, 28
Scientific creationism, versus
      evolution, 40–41
attacks on, 41
and continual testing, 34
explained, 9–11
Scopes, John, and evolution debate,
      40
Secretariat, of the United Nations,
      467–468
Security
and foreign policy, 410
and the nation-state, 408–410
and war, 462–463
Security Council, of the United
      Nations, 467–468, 470, 471,
      472
Segregation
and African Americans, 263
and U.S. Supreme Court, 321
Self-sufficiency argument, for tariffs,
      427, 429
Semites, and Mesopotamian culture,
      56–57
Seniors
and age stratification, 279–282
and fate of the family, 171
and the federal budget, 281
role of, in society, 280

Separation of powers,
  and foreign affairs, 413
  in U.S. government, 315, 316–319, 325
September 11, 2001, 1
  and border control, 273
  and defense spending, 386
  and government action, 288
  and Islam, 475
  and Middle East Arabs, 269–270
  and Patriot Act, 323
  and Saudi Arabia, 355
  and U.S. international influence, 401
  and U.S. relation to world, 461–462
  and War on Terrorism, 417
Services, as economic goods, 361, 370
Seventh Day Adventists, 273
Sexual activity, and government's legislation, 294
Sexual codes, types of, 175–176
Sexual preference, and stratification, 251
Sharon, Ariel, 481
Sherman Anti-Trust Act, and government regulation, 365
Shiites, 199, 200
Shintoism, 190
Singapore
  as developing country, 438
  and population control, 170
Single parents, and child support payments, 277
Singles, opportunities of, 181
Skepticism, and scientific method, 9
Skills, and education, 208
Slave trade, and African Americans, 257–258
Smith, Adam, 364
Social change
  and upward mobility, 246
  and war, 462
Social class
  defined, 235, 236–239
  distinguishing membership, 236–237
  and stratification, 233, 235–239
  under communism, 248
Social conflict, and religion, 204

Social Democratic Party of Japan (SJDP), 348
Social groups, organized, 31
Social institutions, pressure of, 169
Socialism
  defined, 371–373
  and democracy, 294
  in developing countries, 441, 448, 457
  failures of, 373
  goals of, 374–375
  influence of, 372
  Soviet-style, 371–372
Socialization, and education, 209
Social order, components of, 286
Social organization
  development of, in the Middle Ages, 63
  and influence of Roman civilization, 61
Social problems
  in Japan, 348–349
  in Mexico, 343–346
  and religion, 28–30
  in Saudi Arabia, 354
Social progress, measuring, 14
Social relationships, and democracy, 296
Social science
  breakup of, 3
  cognitive, 3, 4
  components of, 3
  different perspectives, 4–5
  and difficulty of experimenting, 11–12
  and economics, 360, 361–362
  history of, 226
  and methodology, 11–14
  new fields, 4
  purpose of, 2
  roots of, 27–30
  sociobiology, 3, 37–38
  and testability, 28–29
  and unified theory, 5 (see also Unified theory)
Social Security, United States
  and aging population, 280–281
  and government income support, 384
  and privatization, 281

Social Security Administration, determination of poverty, 242
Social Security payments, and alleviation of poverty, 244–245
Social Security program, 384–385
Social Security systems, and socialism, 372
Social stability, and selection of mates, 169
Social status, and relative unimportance in the United States, 277–278
Social values, makeup of, 24
Sociobiology, 3, 37–38
Sociology, and social classification, 248
Sociopolitical anthropology, 4
Soft money, and campaign finance in the United States, 333
Sole proprietorship, and organizational problems, 370
Southeast Asia, and Buddhism, 193
Southeast Asians, and the American economy, 269
South Korea
  as developing country, 438
  and Korean War, 471
Sovereignty, of nation-states, 399–400
Soviet Union
  breakup of, 374, 462. 475
  economic transitions, 375
  and evolution of market economy, 377
Spanish-American War, 416
Special drawing rights, and reserve currency, 434
Special interests
  and government, 288, 328–330
  and organized labor in the United States, 332
  and political pressure in the United States, 332
Specialists, and their incentives, 24
Specialization, 8
  and education, 208
  and the Industrial Revolution, 364
  necessity of, 6

and proliferation of knowledge, 27–28
Species, and categorizing, 32, 37
Sri Lanka, and Buddhism, 193
Stability, in Uganda, 457
Stalin, Joseph, 256, 292, 413
State (*see also* Nation-state)
    defined as nation-state, 399
    as one of the fifty United States, 397
States of the United States, and their constitutions, 311
States' rights, in the United States, 321
Statistics, and measurement in social science, 21
Stockholders, and raising capital, 366
Stock market, role in U.S. depression, 387–388
Stone Age, and technological development, 50, 53–54
Stratification
    and belief in superiority, 252–253
    in European societies, 247
    in former Soviet Union, 256
    gender-based, 274–279
    groups of, enumerated, 233
    and Muslims, 254, 256
    types of, 251, 255–256
    and the United States as melting pot, 255–256
    in the United States, 247
Structure
    of European school systems, 213, 214
    of U.S. school system, 213–216, 229–230
Subsidies, and exports, 426
Suburbs, proliferation of, 172
Suffrage (*see* Voting)
Sumerians (*see* Mesopotamia)
Sunnis
    Islamic sect, 199–200
    in Saudi Arabia, 354–355
Superpower
    and China, 453
    the United States, 73, 462
Supplemental Security Income, and alleviation of poverty, 244–245

Supply, of goods and services, 366–369
Supply and demand, and exchange rates, 433
Supreme Court, United States
    and Acts of Congress, 318
    authorization of, in U.S. Constitution, 319
    and Boy Scouts of America, 279
    and civil rights, 323
    and conflicts with presidents, 321
    and definition of U.S. government, 314
    and funding education, 227, 259
    and legal rights, 298
    and presidential election, 328
    and protection of rights, 320–321
    and rights of African Americans, 259, 263, 264
    role in presidential election, 315
    and segregation, 321
Surplus, 393
    in government budget, 388–391
Surveys, as social science tool, 21, 22
Survival of the fittest, and evolution, 33
Sweden, and move to market economy, 377
Symbolic interaction theory, approach to social science, 17, 18
Symbols, and abstract reasoning, 47
Syria, and War on Terrorism, 461

Taiwan, as developing country, 438
Taoism, 190
Tariffs
    and developing countries, 445
    and the Great Depression, 427–428
    and international trade, 426, 427, 430
    and theory, 11
Tax burden, in industrial economies, 365
Tax credits, and education, 230
Taxes
    conservative position, 293
    and government financing, 383
    and role of government, 381–382

Technology
    and advances in social science, 11
    and aging, 280
    and agriculture, 54
    and change, 370–371
    and developing countries, 446
    development of, in the Middle Ages, 63
    and economics, 361
    and the family, 172, 183
    and fire, 46
    and the Industrial Revolution, 71–72, 364
    and market economy, 368–369
    and the need for labor, 70
    in planned economies, 375
    rejection by Islam, 201
    and religion, 189
    and shaping education, 217
    and social/ethical dilemmas, 36–37
    and social instability, 170
    and upward mobility, 247
    and warfare, 54
Terror, in the French Revolution, 337–338
Terrorism (*see also* War on Terrorism)
    and Arab Americans, 269–270
    goals of, 475
    and religious war, 187
Terrorists, and religion, 205
Testing, in education, 222–224, 225
Tests
    of scientific method, 34
    of theories, 13–14
    theories that are not testable, 28–29
Textbooks
    and controversial content, 41–42
    and high prices, 386
    level of content, 220
Thailand, and Buddhism, 193
Theory as explanation of scientific law, 10
Theory of complex interdependence, and limitation of national power, 409
Tibet, and Buddhism, 193

Tools
and beginning of human history, 45
development by humanlike creatures, 34
and human power, 48
and Neanderthals, 47
Tocqueville, de, Alexis, 211–212
Totalitarianism, 299–301
Trade
in ancient Greece, 58
development of, in the Middle Ages, 64–65
and the emergence of nation states, 71
modern beginnings of, 68–69
Trade barriers, and developing countries, 445
Trade-offs, and upward mobility, 245–246
Trade restrictions, alleviation of, 430–431
Tradition
and feudalism, 63, 64–65, 68–70
and loss of influence, 73
as obstacle to scientific method, 9
and religion, 68, 188, 204
and scientific method, 9
Transcendental meditation, and Buddhism, 193
Transfer payments, and poverty, 241–242, 245
Transgendered people, and discrimination, 279
Transmigration, of the soul, 192, 234–235
Transportation, and the automobile, 172
Treaties,
and international law, 466
and separation-of-powers, 414, 416
and the United Nations, 473, 474
and U.S. government, 318
Truman, Harry, 415n
Truman Doctrine, The, and the cold war, 416, 417
Tyrants, role of, in civilization, 58

Uganda
as developing country, 456–458

profile of, 457
Ukraine, and transition to unplanned economy, 375
Underdeveloped countries, and autocracy, 301
Unemployment
and African Americans, 260–264
defining, 19
and dropouts, 221, 223
and international trade, 423
and U.S. depression, 365, 369, 387–388
in the United States, 374
Unemployment insurance, and alleviation of poverty, 244–245
Unified social science, need for, 21
Unified theory, 5, 6, 8
Unions
and discrimination against African Americans, 261–262
and the economy, 359
United Nations (UN)
funding of, 469
and Haitian turmoil, 405
and Iraq war, 403
and Israeli-Palestinian conflict, 480–481
limitations of, 473, 474
and military sanction, 471–472, 473
and nuclear energy control, 473, 474
and peace, 465, 466, 470–474
structure of, 467–468
successes of, 471
value of, 468–470
and world government, 408, 465–474
United States
and Buddhism, 193
and evolution of market economy, 377
and geographic aspirations, 411
hostility toward, 466–467, 472–473
and international law, 466–467
and a new world order, 475–476
and political consensus, 441
support of the United Nations, 469–470

transition from rural to urban, 172
Universities
and community colleges, 215–216
curricula of, 225–227
enrollment figures, 212, 216, 226–227
and highly specialized education, 208
and religious foundation, 204
University admission, and affirmative action, 262–263
Unplanned economies, 362–365
how they work, 373–376
Upward mobility
and components of achievement, 245–246
and the estate system, 234
and social change, 246
and social classes, 239–240
Urbanization, and the Industrial Revolution, 364
Utopian societies, 371

Values, and education, 208
Venture capital, 370
Veto, and U.S. president's power, 318
Vietnam, and U.S. military role, 319, 406, 414–415
Villages (*see* Cities)
Vocational training, 216, 228–229
Vote, the right to, 211
Voting (*see also* Popular sovereignty)
and African Americans, 258
and the nonvoter, 328, 330
and obstacles to, 328–330
and redistribution of income, 289–290
in the United States, 314
and U.S. elections, 327–330
and women's rights, 274–275
Vouchers, and educational value, 218
Voyages of discovery, and progress, 9

War
causes of, 462–464
and change, 462
and consequences for religion, 29
cost of (monetary), 462
and debt, 72–73
and effective government, 286

and ethnic cleansing, 254
and formation of nation-states,
    400–401
Franco-Prussian, 338
and freedom, 412
goals of, 65
and international trade, 435
and Kosovo, 319
Mexican-American, 342
and nation states, 71, 73
Persian Gulf, and Saudi Arabia,
    354
Persian Gulf War of 1991, 319,
    410, 462–463
potential for, in the Middle East,
    479–482
and potential trouble spots,
    476–482
and religion, 187, 203, 205
and Rome's military undertakings,
    61, 62
as social science problem, 23
United States and Japan, 346
and U.S. invasion of Granada, 319
U.S. power to declare, 318–319
Vietnam police action, 319
World War II, 268–269, 291, 406,
    407, 416
War on Iraq (*see* Iraq War of 2003)
War on Terror, and individual liberty,
    205, 256
War on Terrorism, 461, 475
    and defense spending, 386

global aspects of, 482
and individual Islamic beliefs, 301
and right to wage preemptive
    wars, 417–418
and Russia, 352, 478
and U.S.-China relations, 478
and U.S.-Mexican relations, 346
Washington, George, 326
Wealth
    and democracy, 298
    as an economic good, 361
    and the family, 164, 165
    as social class characteristic, 238,
        239
Wealth of Nations, The (Smith), 364
Weapons of mass destruction
    (WMD), 403, 404, 463, 472
Welfare, and social science, 21
Welfare, public
    and alleviation of poverty,
        244–245
    payments and social inequality,
        241, 245
Well-being, and government,
    289–290
Western democracy, and attempts
    to impose on other cultures,
    301
Women
    control of, in the family, 166, 172
    dependence of, on men, 172
    heir rights in ancient Rome, 62
    and Islam, 352, 355

in military service, 275
as a minority, 274
and poverty, 180
and the right to vote, 274–275
Women's liberation movement, 275
Work
    and Hispanics, 267
    and religion, 204
    value of, 229
Work at home, and the computer,
    183
Workforce, and women, 275,
    276–278
World Bank, and help for developing
    countries, 444
World government, and peace, 465
World Trade Organization, (WTO)
    and international trade, 430
    and Saudi Arabia, 354
World War II
    and efforts to escape U.S.
        involvement, 416
    and ideologies, 291
    and Japanese in the United States,
        268–269
    and U.S. role, 406, 407
Writing, its development, 54, 58

Zinjanthropus, and human
    evolution, 45
Zionists, and independence of Jewish
    nation, 479–482

Credits